Accounting for Investments

Volume I

Equities, Futures and Options

Accounting for Investments

Volume I

Equities, Futures and Options

R. Venkata Subramani

WILEY

John Wiley & Sons, (Asia) Pte Ltd

Published in 2009 by John Wiley & Sons (Asia) Pte. Ltd.
2 Clementi Loop, #02-01, Singapore 129809

Other Wiley Editorial Offices

John Wiley & Sons, Inc., 111 River Street, Hoboken, NJ 07030, USA
John Wiley & Sons, Ltd., The Atrium, Southern Gate, Chichester, West Sussex P019 8SQ, UK
John Wiley & Sons (Canada), Ltd., 5353 Dundas Street West, Suite 400, Toronto, Ontario M9B 6H8, Canada
JohnWiley & Sons Australia Ltd., 42 McDougall Street, Milton, Queensland 4064, Australia
Wiley-VCH, Boschstrasse 12, D-69469 Weinheim, Germany

Library of Congress Cataloging-in-Publication Data

ISBN-13 978-0470-82431-3

Typeset in 10.5/13pt Minion by Macmillan Publishing Solutions, Chennai, India.

Printed in Singapore by International Press Softcom Limited
10 9 8 7 6 5 4 3 2 1

Dedicated to my respected parents,
my wife and my daughter.

Contents

Foreword

Accounting for Investments is a complex exercise in view of the varied kinds of instruments that have emerged in the market recently. The flow of funds across the borders in the form of financial instruments is ever increasing in the global scenario. Equities, futures and options have trade life cycles, and accounting treatments on those life cycles from the front office and back office perspectives call for detailed elucidation. There are hardly any books that provide guidance in these matters. This book is a commendable effort to fill the knowledge gap that exists in the accounting of financial instruments.

International Financial Reporting Standards (IFRS), encompassing IAS 32, IAS 39, and IFRS 7, deal with the principles involved in recognition, measurement, disclosure, and presentation of financial instruments. The Institute of Chartered Accountants of India (ICAI) has come out with corresponding Accounting Standards (AS): AS 30 on "Financial Instruments—Recognition and Measurement," AS 31 on "Financial Instruments—Presentation," and AS 32 on "Financial Instruments—Disclosures."

In sum and substance, the Indian Accounting Standards are the same as the corresponding IFRS. This book deals with the principles laid down in the IFRS as well as the similarities and differences between U.S. generally accepted accounting principles (GAAP) and IFRS. In that sense, one can say without fear of contradiction that this book is a comprehensive treatise of the subject.

Mr. R. Venkata Subramani is a learned person, having immense knowledge and expertise in the matters discussed in this book. The benefit of his hands-on experience and in-depth practical knowledge is reflected in the illustrations given in the various chapters. In view of the tremendous growth recently witnessed in the investment banking institutions, hedge funds, and other financial institutions, this book will become handy for understanding and capturing the entire trading process of the financial instruments. Mr. Subramani is also known as a technology wizard. Consequently, the lucid exposition that he has adopted will help in automating the system of proper accounting of the entire trade cycle of each of the financial instruments.

Investment bankers, financial institutions, dealers, brokers, professionals, and other investors will find this book immensely useful in their day-to-day operations, as Mr. Subramani explains various concepts unique to the financial instruments, besides laying down the accounting treatment in a detailed manner. This book is a useful addition to any library, serving as a source of knowledge and information with reference to various financial products dealt with in the market. Mr. Subramani has done a splendid job in authoring this book in order to share his wealth of information and knowledge on the subject.

Mr. T. N. Manoharan
Former President
Institute of Chartered Accountants of India

Preface

Accounting for Investments attempts to give an exhaustive treatment of various accounting entries that should be recorded by any entity holding any financial asset. Over the past two decades, there have been several innovative financial instruments from the Street that call for special treatment from the accounting, legal, and regulatory perspectives. The accounting requirements are constantly being monitored and enhanced by the regulators and standard setters to provide more transparency in recording and reporting these financial products.

This book is written from the practical angle and is meant to cater to the needs of accountants as a handbook. The first volume covers equities, futures, and options. It also covers the hedge accounting treatment for equity options, depositary receipts (ADR/GDR), contract for difference (CFD), short selling, and boxed position accounting.

This book assumes that the reader already has basic accounting knowledge. Those who are entirely new to the field of accounting should refer to some basic accounting book before attempting to use this book. However, Appendix A gives an overview of the basic accounting principles and concepts.

The entire trade life cycle of each of the afore-mentioned financial assets is covered in detail with the accounting entries that should be recorded. For each illustration, the journal entries, general ledger accounts, trial balance, income statement, and balance sheet are presented to give a complete understanding of the accounting treatment. Also, for all calculated numbers, the details of such calculations are given. The notes on accounts and presentation and disclosure requirements for derivative products are covered in a separate chapter and not included for each and every illustration. Appendix C gives the complete financial statements for a sample fund with all the necessary notes on accounts and disclosures as required by International Financial Reporting Standards (IFRS).

Even though the investment banking institutions have suffered a serious setback due to the financial crisis that began in 2008, banks, hedge funds, and several other financial institutions do trade and invest in several financial instruments covered in this volume. The need for comprehensively understanding these financial instruments, including the accounting aspects involved, assumes great importance. Even before the beginning of a trading day, the front office should know the positions of the various financial instruments held by the entity and have the flexibility to obtain a detailed breakdown of cost and so on. Technology has made all this possible today at the touch of a button, and technology experts are much sought after to do the needful for these financial institutions. However, in spite of having the domain knowledge in financial products, the technology experts sometimes feel the need to have an in-depth understanding of the entire trade life cycle with the accounting treatment that accompanies it. This book proposes to fill the knowledge gap of these aspiring technology wizards and aspiring finance and accounting professionals who want to jump into the banking and financial domain.

An overview of the trade life cycle for each financial instrument is given. However, the reader is advised to refer other resources for a detailed treatment of the trade life cycle from the front office and middle office perspective. The trade life cycle insofar as it relates to the back office—that is, the accounting aspects—is covered in detail with appropriate reference to generally accepted accounting principles (GAAP) requirements. For each financial instrument, the relevant accounting standards that are applicable are given and a comparative chart showing the similarities and differences between the U.S. GAAP and IFRS is given. While the first volume covers broadly equities, equity options, and equity futures, subsequent volumes will cover the other financial instruments.

CHAPTER ARRANGEMENT

Chapter 1—Financial Instruments

The first chapter covers the accounting standards for financial instruments and discusses the definition of *financial instruments*, *financial assets*, and *financial liabilities*. The various categories of financial instruments covered by the accounting standards are discussed along with the fair value measurement concepts. Recognition and derecognition of financial instruments is covered in brief.

The different types of investments an investor can make are outlined, even though this volume covers only investments in equity, equity futures, and equity options. The primary difference between investment and speculation is given.

The two major accounting standards—U.S. GAAP and IFRS—are discussed, giving the hierarchy of both and the measures taken towards the convergence of these standards.

Chapter 2—Accounting for Equity Investments: Trading

Chapter 2 covers accounting for equity shares held for trading purposes. After defining equity investment as per the accounting standards, the different types of investments—passive investments and investments commanding significant influence as well as controlling interest—are discussed. The broad classifications of trading and available-for-sale are given. The distinction between exchange-traded securities and over-the-counter (OTC) securities is briefly analyzed. The trade life cycle for equity shares held as trading securities is given with the accounting entries to be passed at the various stages. A comprehensive illustration of investment in long equity shares held as trading securities is covered, giving the journal entries, general ledger, income statement, and balance sheet for the illustration.

The distinction between foreign exchange (FX) revaluation and FX translation is given in great detail along with an explanation of functional currency, presentation currency, trade currency, and the requirements of accounting standards in this regard. Another illustration covers equity shares in trade currency of JPY with the functional currency of US$, explaining the FX revaluation and FX translation processes.

The differences between trade date accounting and settlement date accounting are explained, giving the behavior of held-for-trading and available-for-sale securities on trade date, reporting date, and settlement date for various parameters like the financial asset and the liability, as well as the changes in the fair value of the financial asset.

The distinction between capital gains and currency gains and the treatment and presentation of such gains for equity shares is given in detail.

Chapter 3—Accounting for Equity Investments: Available-for-sale

This chapter covers the accounting steps required for equity shares that are held as available-for-sale. The trade life cycle for equity shares classified as available-for-sale securities is given with the accounting entries to be passed at the various stages. A worked-out illustration covers equity shares in the functional currency of US$ held as available-for-sale. One more illustration is given on trade currency with FX translation into the functional currency of US$.

Chapter 4—Transfer of Categories

This chapter covers the transfers from trading securities to available-for-sale securities and vice versa. It also discusses the presentation in the income statement when there is an impairment of securities as well as realized and unrealized gains or losses. When a category change happens, it also impacts the deferred tax on unrealized gain/loss, and this is explained with an illustration.

Chapter 5—Equity Derivatives: Theory

Chapter 5 explains derivatives in a financial security and lists various types of derivative contracts with the corresponding underlying variable. The definition of *derivatives* according to accounting standards is covered, and the differences between U.S. GAAP and IFRS in respect of derivative accounting are given. This chapter covers the distinction between a forward contract and a futures contract and outlines the essential components of a futures contract. The subtle differences between hedging, speculation, and arbitrage are discussed, as well as the limitations of forward markets and the advantages of futures contracts.

Open interest in derivatives contracts, the method of computing the same, and the implications of a change in open interest are discussed. Pricing of a futures contract and the cost of carry are analyzed. Stock futures and index futures and the concept of systematic and unsystematic risks are also covered in this chapter.

Chapter 6—Accounting for Equity Index Futures

This chapter covers the accounting requirements for equity index futures contracts. The salient features of a stock index and index futures are discussed with special reference to systematic and unsystematic risks. The trade life cycle for equity index futures is given with the accounting entries to be passed at the various stages.

A worked-out illustration exhaustively covers equity index futures, both in trade currency other than US$ and in the functional currency of US$.

Chapter 7—Accounting for Equity Stock Futures

This chapter covers the accounting requirements for equity stock futures contracts. The trade life cycle for equity stock futures is given with the accounting entries necessary at the various stages.

The worked-out illustration covers exhaustively equity stock futures, both in trade currency other than US$ and in the functional currency of US$.

Chapter 8—Accounting for Equity Call Options

Chapter 8 covers the accounting requirements for exchange-traded equity call options. The trade life cycle for equity long call options is given with the accounting entries necessary at the various stages. This chapter covers only the case of a call option held as a speculative position and not as a hedge against the underlying shares. The worked-out illustration thoroughly demonstrates equity long call options, both in trade currency other than US$ and in the functional currency of US$.

The trade life cycle for equity short call options is also covered in this chapter with the accounting entries necessary at the various stages. The worked-out illustration covers exhaustively the treatment of equity short call options in US$.

Chapter 9—Accounting for Equity Put Options

This chapter covers the accounting requirements for exchange-traded equity put options. The trade life cycle for equity long put options is given with the accounting entries necessary at the various stages. This chapter covers only cases where the put option is held as a speculative position and not as a hedge against the underlying shares. The illustration used demonstrates equity long put options both in trade currency other than US$ and in the functional currency of US$.

The trade life cycle for equity short put options is also covered in this chapter, with the accounting entries to be passed at the various stages. The worked-out illustration outlines the treatment of equity short put options in US$.

Chapter 10—Equity Options: Hedge Accounting

Chapter 10 lays out the accounting for equity options that are held as a hedge against an underlying share. The definitions of *derivative, financial asset,* and *financial liability* as per the accounting standards are discussed. The similarities and differences between the U.S. GAAP and IFRS insofar as they relate to derivatives and hedge accounting are discussed in various aspects like definition, initial measurement, subsequent measurement, changes in the fair value of derivative instrument, and hedge accounting criteria. The salient features of the accounting standards are covered in detail.

Specific features of the accounting standards are covered insofar as they relate to options as hedge, the rationale of hedge accounting for written options and covered calls, exception to single fair value measure rule, as well as the question of whether hedge accounting is possible for a delta-neutral hedging strategy. A table illustrates when hedge accounting is permissible as far as options are concerned.

The trade life cycle for long equity options is covered in this chapter with the accounting entries necessary at the various stages. The worked-out illustration covers exhaustively the treatment of equity put options in US$ that are purchased as a hedging instrument against an underlying share.

Chapter 11—Accounting for Contract for Difference

This chapter covers the accounting requirements for contract for difference (CFD) contracts. Definition and product features of CFDs are covered including the concepts of margin, funding cost, interest on clear margin, and so on. The advantages and disadvantages of CFDs as an investment instrument are analyzed. The method of terminating CFDs and its effects are also discussed.

The trade life cycle for CFD contracts is given with the accounting entries necessary at the various stages. A worked-out illustration covers exhaustively a contract for difference, both in a trade currency other than US$ and in the functional currency of US$.

Chapter 12—Accounting for Short Equity Investments

This chapter covers the accounting requirements for short-selling, including the requirements for a box position where both the long and short positions are maintained by the investor. Typically, hedge funds are the entities that resort to this practice. Since there are some regulatory issues regarding short-selling, the investor will do well to comply with the laws of the land whenever short positions are taken. The custodian also makes sure to maintain the long and short positions separately for the investor to facilitate position reconciliation and accounting. The stock lending that is intertwined with the short position trading is also dealt with in this chapter, especially the requirements and accounting treatment of cash collateral deposited with the broker as well as the stock lending fee payments and the interest receipts relating to the cash collaterals with the broker.

Chapter 13—Accounting for ADR/GDR Investments

International depositary receipts are becoming increasingly popular, and this chapter covers the accounting treatment of American depositary receipts (ADRs). The investor usually holds positions in the same stock in both the local exchange as well as in ADRs. The stock is sold at a convenient time in the local stock exchange and to that extent the ADRs are converted into the local equity shares, incurring conversion charges. This chapter illustrates how the cost of such conversion is arrived at and how the profit on liquidation is computed and accounted.

Chapter 14—Presentation and Disclosures

Accounting standards require specific presentation and disclosure norms for financial instruments. The similarities and differences between U.S. GAAP and IFRS insofar as they relate to equity investments are given in tabular form under various topics like definition, recognition, valuation, impairment, reclassification, and so on. The disclosure requirements of both these accounting standards are given at the end of the chapter.

Appendix A—Basics of Accounting Theory

This appendix gives an overview of the basics of accounting theory, covering the basic assumptions underlying the accounting framework. It also discusses the basic accounting concepts and the basic principles of accounting. The accounting model and the elements of basic reporting are also discussed with reference to the concept statement number 6 of U.S. GAAP.

Appendix B—Accounting Standards for Financial Instruments

Appendix B gives an overview of the various accounting standards for financial instruments. It covers IAS 39—Recognition and Measurement of Financial Instruments; IAS 32—Presentation of Financial Instruments; and IFRS 7—Disclosure of Financial Instruments.

Appendix C—Financial Statements of Sample Fund

This appendix gives the financial statements of a sample fund to illustrate the concepts of presentation and disclosure requirements of the various accounting standards for financial instruments in the context of IFRS as it stands today.

Appendix D—Glossary of Technical Terms

The final appendix gives a quick reference of various technical terms that are used in the context of accounting for investments. These terms are elaborated in detail elsewhere in this book.

KEY FEATURES AND APPROACH

This book proposes to cover the domain knowledge as well as the accounting treatment for the various financial products. It should be a good addition to the library of books that deal exclusively with the treatment of all financial products handled by financial institutions, banks, hedge funds, and so on, covering the domain knowledge about the respective financial products and the accounting treatment of the same with special reference to the regulatory requirements. A one-point source of information has been needed by the financial services industry for a long time. This book proposes to fulfill that need, as part of a series of books aimed at providing that one-point reference.

Throughout this book, the approach is to give illustrations and show detailed workings of the same. Wherever there is a computed number, the details of such calculations are given even at the cost of being somewhat repetitive for some advanced readers.

INTENDED AUDIENCE

This book is intended for all those who are directly involved in different capacities and roles in the financial sector, which today is one of the largest emerging sectors in the global economy. Since this book deals with the domain knowledge of many of the exotic products that have evolved over the past two decades, it will be of interest to accountants and non-accountants alike who wish to know about the trade life cycle of these products.

For an advanced user, the book is expected to provide depth, while for a novice this book starts with the fundamentals. It starts from the basics for any financial product—defining the product, the way it is structured, its advantages and disadvantages, the different events in the trade cycle—and then discusses accounting journal entries that are passed for the same. Additionally, this book shows how the entries get reflected in the general ledger accounts, so as to a give a macro-level picture for the reader to understand the basics of the effect of such accounting. Last but not the least in importance is the presentation of the results in the final accounts; the income statement and balance sheet are also well covered in this book. Thus this book is expected to be extremely useful to an expert as well as a novice, not to mention the ever increasing number of tech consultants who are in great need of such a book.

Acknowledgments

I would like to thank Nick Wallwork, Publisher, John Wiley & Sons (Asia) Pte Ltd. for agreeing to publish this book. I would like to thank Fiona Wong, Janis Soo, Joyce Poh and the entire production team at John Wiley. Without their persevering efforts and help, this book might have never seen the light of the day. I want to acknowledge Missy Garnett of Cape Cod Compositors, Inc. for her wonderful copyediting of my text.

I am thankful to Variman Capital Markets Services Private Limited, where I was able to get rich experience in accounting for various types of investments. I am very grateful to my colleagues at Variman who painstakingly verified the workings for the illustrations spending several weekends on this assignment. I want to particularly thank my father Ramachandran who took very active interest in correcting the manuscript of this text. I would like to express my deepest gratitude to my mother Parimala who motivated me to complete the book amidst my other commitments. Last but not the least, my heartfelt gratitude goes out to my loving wife Dr. Rama and my affectionate daughter Ramya who encouraged and motivated me constantly to pursue my cherished goal of completing this first volume.

R. Venkata Subramani

CHAPTER 1

Financial Instruments

LEARNING OBJECTIVES

After studying this chapter, you should have a grasp of the following concepts:

- Accounting standards for financial instruments.
- Definition of financial instruments.
- Financial assets and financial liabilities.
- Categories of financial instruments.
- Fair value measurement concepts.
- Recognition and derecognition of financial instruments.
- Types of investments.
- Difference between investment and speculation.
- Two major accounting standards: U.S. GAAP and IFRS.
- Hierarchy of U.S. GAAP and IFRS.

ACCOUNTING STANDARDS FOR FINANCIAL INSTRUMENTS

The topic of accounting standards for financial instruments covers the following aspects:

- Definition of *financial instrument, financial asset, financial liability,* and *equity instrument.*
- Definition of a *derivative instrument.*
- Different types of contracts that are covered within the scope of the accounting standards for financial instruments.
- Four categories of financial instruments.
- Fair value and fair value determination.
- Accounting treatment of different categories of financial instruments.
- Recognition and derecognition of financial instruments.
- Initial measurement and subsequent measurement of financial instruments.
- Effect of changes in fair value.
- Reclassification and its impact.
- Impairment and its treatment for different categories.
- Hedge accounting concepts.

The synopsis of the accounting standards under the International Financial Reporting Standards (IFRS), IAS 39, is given in Appendix B.

Relevant Accounting Standards	
U.S. GAAP	**IFRS**
FAS 52—Foreign Currency Translation	IFRS 7—Financial Instruments: Disclosure
FAS 94—Consolidation of All Majority-owned Subsidiaries	IAS 21—The Effects of Changes in Foreign Exchange Rates
FAS 109—Accounting for Income Taxes	IAS 32—Financial Instruments: Presentation
FAS 115—Accounting for Certain Investments in Debt and Equity Securities	IAS 36—Impairment of Assets
FAS 130—Reporting Comprehensive Income	IAS 39—Financial Instruments: Recognition and Measurement
FAS 157—Fair Value Measurements	
FAS 159—The Fair Value Option for Financial Assets and Financial Liabilities	

DEFINITION OF FINANCIAL INSTRUMENTS

A *financial instrument* is any contract that gives rise to a financial asset of one entity and a financial liability or equity instrument of another entity. Investments in equity shares are a form of financial instrument.

Financial Assets and Financial Liabilities

A *financial asset* is defined as one of the following types of assets, according to the accounting standards:

- Cash.
- An equity instrument of another entity.
- A contractual right:
  - To receive cash or another financial asset from another entity.
  - To exchange financial assets or financial liabilities with another entity under conditions, potentially favorable to the entity.
- A contract that will or may be settled in the entity's own equity instruments and is:
  - A non-derivative resulting in receiving a variable number of the entity's own equity instruments.
  - A derivative that will or may be settled other than by the exchange of a fixed amount of cash or other financial asset for a fixed number of the entity's own equity instruments.

A *financial liability* is defined as one of the following types of liabilities, according to the accounting standards:

- A contractual obligation:
  - To deliver cash or another financial asset to another entity.

    - To exchange financial assets or financial liabilities with another entity under conditions, potentially unfavorable to the entity.
- A contract that will or may be settled in the entity's own equity instruments and is:
    - A non-derivative resulting in delivering a variable number of the entity's own equity instruments.
    - A derivative that will or may be settled other than by the exchange of a fixed amount of cash or another financial asset for a fixed number of the entity's own equity instruments.

Equity Instrument

An equity instrument is any contract that evidences a residual interest in the assets of an entity after deducting all of its liabilities.

Derivative

A derivative is a financial instrument or other contract with all three of the following characteristics:

1. Its value changes in response to the change in an *underlying*.
2. It requires no initial net investment or an initial net investment that is smaller than would be required for other types of contracts.
3. It is settled at a future date.

CATEGORIES OF FINANCIAL INSTRUMENTS

The four basic categories of financial instruments are:

1. Fair value through profit and loss (FVPL).
2. Held-to-maturity (HTM).
3. Available-for-sale (AFS).
4. Loans and receivables (LAR).

Investments in equity shares, futures, and equity options are classified as either fair value through profit and loss or as available-for-sale securities only. Investments in equity shares cannot be classified as held-to-maturity as there is no maturity period for equity shares. Redeemable preference shares can be classified as loans and receivables. Loans and receivables are not defined under the U.S. GAAP as a separate category, even though IAS 39 under IFRS has this category.

Fair Value through Profit and Loss (FVPL)

A financial asset or financial liability at fair value through profit or loss is one that meets either of the following two conditions:

1. It is classified as held for trading—in other words, one of the following statements is true:
    - It is acquired or incurred principally for the purpose of selling or repurchasing it in the near term.

    - It is part of a portfolio of identified financial instruments that are managed together and for which there is evidence of a recent actual pattern of short-term profit-taking.
    - It is a derivative other than a financial guarantee contract or for hedging purposes.
2. Upon initial recognition, it is designated by the entity as at fair value through profit or loss.

Note: Investments in equity instruments that do not have a quoted market price in an active market, and whose fair value cannot be reliably measured, should not be designated as at fair value through profit or loss.

Available-for-sale

Available-for-sale financial assets are those non-derivative financial assets that are designated as available for sale or are not classified as one of the other types of assets mentioned already, namely:

- Loans and receivables.
- Held-to-maturity investments.
- Financial assets at fair value through profit or loss.

FAIR VALUE MEASUREMENT CONCEPTS

The fair value of a financial asset or liability is the amount for which the financial asset could be exchanged, or the financial liability settled, between knowledgeable, willing parties in an arm's length transaction. The presumption is that an entity is a going concern without any intention or need to liquidate or curtail materially the scale of its operations or to undertake a transaction on adverse terms.

Hierarchy

When determining the fair value of a financial instrument, the accounting standards set out a hierarchy to be applied to the valuation. If quoted prices or rates exist in an active market for the instrument, they must be used to determine the fair value. The appropriate quoted market price for an asset held is the *bid* price, and for a liability held is the *offer* price.

Valuation Methodology

Where there is no active market available from which to draw quoted prices, a valuation technique should be used. Valuation techniques include:

- Recent market prices or rates where available, adjusted for relevant subsequent events.
- Reference to the current fair value of another instrument that is substantially the same.
- Discounted cash flow analysis.
- Option pricing models.
- A standard industry valuation technique that has been demonstrated to provide reliable estimates of prices obtained in actual market transactions.

Credit Quality

Fair value should reflect the credit quality of the instrument. For those items traded in an open market, this is likely to be incorporated in the price.

For over-the-counter derivatives, the standard approach is to value the derivative using the AA-rated curve in the valuation model. For others, the market quoted rates used in the valuation model should be adjusted for credit risk.

Any changes in the credit quality will need to be considered when remeasuring fair value.

RECOGNITION AND DERECOGNITION OF FINANCIAL INSTRUMENTS

An entity should recognize a financial asset on its balance sheet when, and only when, the entity becomes a party to the contractual provisions of the instrument.

Derecognition of a financial asset or a portion of a financial asset occurs under the current standards when, and only when, the entity loses control of the contractual rights that comprise the financial asset.

An entity loses control if it realizes the rights to benefits specified in the contract; if those rights expire; or if the entity surrenders those rights.

TYPES OF INVESTMENTS

Investment can be in any of the following types of assets:

- *Physical assets.* Examples are real estate, commercial real estate, or machinery. In a real estate investment, property is purchased with the purpose of holding or leasing it for income. Commercial real estate is the owning of a building or warehouse that is rented out for business purposes.
- *Intangible assets.* These are patents, software, goodwill, and so on, and these are usually generated over a period of time. Sometimes, these assets are also purchased from another entity.
- *Financial assets.* These are often marketable securities such as investment in shares of a company or fixed-income securities like bonds. Financial assets also include investments in financial derivatives like futures and options.

In this book we explore accounting concepts involved in investment in financial assets. In particular, this volume covers investments in equities, equity futures, and equity options.

DIFFERENCE BETWEEN INVESTMENT AND SPECULATION

Speculation is the assumption of the risk of loss, in return for the uncertain possibility of a reward. If a particular position involves no risk, then such a position represents an investment.

Financial speculation involves either the buying, holding, selling, or short-selling of stocks, bonds, commodities, currencies, collectibles, real estate, derivatives, or any other financial instrument to profit from short-term fluctuations in its price, whereas buying the same asset for use or for generating a constant source of income, like dividends or interest, is regarded as an investment.

TWO MAJOR STANDARDS: U.S. GAAP AND IFRS

The United States generally accepted accounting principles (U.S. GAAP) literature is rule-based while that of the International Financial Reporting Standards (IFRS) is principle-based. Due to its rule-based nature, and also because it has been around for a longer period of time, U.S. GAAP literature is more voluminous than IFRS literature. The International Accounting Standards Commission (IASC) reorganized itself in April 2001 to form the new International Accounting Standards Board (IASB) in line with its U.S. counterpart, the Financial Accounting Standards Board (FASB), mainly with a view to get out of the International Federation of Accountants (IFA) and to interact with the leading standard setters around the globe to work on the convergence of national standards. Today, the IASB has gained a reputation as a global standard setter, with the European Union and a number of countries agreeing to adopt IFRS from 2005 onwards. The IASB has since then consistently attempted to reduce the number of options in the standards and include more guidance.

Being rule-based, the U.S. GAAP is based on conservatism and has attracted criticism that such an approach can distort the economic substance of financial statements. By contrast, IFRS, being principle-based, relies on fair value measurement principles for assets and liabilities, requiring a higher level of professional judgment.

Hierarchy of U.S. GAAP

Financial Accounting Standards (FAS) 162 came into effect in May 2008, with *The Hierarchy of Generally Accepted Accounting Principles*. By this standard, the hierarchy is being moved from auditing literature to become part of the accounting literature. The American Institute of Certified Public Accountants' (AICPA) Statement on Accounting Standards (SAS) 69, which dealt with GAAP hierarchy before FAS 162 came into existence, was criticized because it was directed to the auditor rather than the enterprise and also because it was complex. As per FAS 162, the hierarchy given is as follows:

Level	U.S. GAAP Literature
Level A	1. FASB standards and interpretations 2. FAS 133 Implementation Issues 3. FASB Staff Positions 4. AICPA Accounting Research Bulletins 5. Accounting Principles Board Opinions that are not superseded by actions of the FASB
Level B	1. FASB Technical Bulletins that are cleared by the FASB 2. AICPA Industry Audit and Accounting Guides and Statements of Position
Level C	1. AICPA Accounting Standards Executive Committee Practice Bulletins that have been cleared by the FASB 2. Consensus positions of the FASB Emerging Issues Task Force (EITF) issues 3. Topics discussed in Appendix D of EITF Abstracts
Level D	1. FASB Implementation Guides 2. AICPA Industry Audit and Accounting Guides and Statements of Position not cleared by the FASB 3. Practices that are widely recognized and prevalent either generally or in the industry

Hierarchy of IFRS

The following is the hierarchy, in decreasing authority of guidance within IFRS that is followed in developing and applying an accounting policy for any transaction.

When a standard or an interpretation specifically applies to a transaction or other event or condition, the accounting policy or policies applied to that item shall be determined by applying the standard or interpretation and considering any relevant implementation guidance issued by the IASB for the standard or interpretation.

In the absence of a standard or an interpretation that specifically applies to a transaction or other event or condition, management shall use its judgment in developing and applying an accounting policy that results in information that is:

- Relevant to the economic decision-making needs of users.
- Reliable, in that the financial statements:
  - Represent faithfully the financial position, financial performance, and cash flows of the entity.
  - Reflect the economic substance of transactions or other events and conditions, and not merely the legal form.
  - Are neutral (i.e., free from bias).
  - Are prudent.
  - Are complete in all material respects.

In making such judgment, the management shall refer to, and consider the applicability of, the following two sources in descending order:

1. The requirements and guidance in standards and interpretations dealing with similar and related issues.
2. The definitions, recognition criteria, and measurement concepts for assets, liabilities, income, and expenses in the framework.

In making the judgment, management may also consider the most recent pronouncements of other standard-setting bodies that use a similar conceptual framework to develop accounting standards, as well as other accounting literature, and accepted industry practices.

Convergence of U.S. GAAP and IFRS

The IASB and the U.S. FASB have been committed to converging IFRS and U.S. GAAP since the Norwalk Accord of 2002. In order to simplify financial reporting and also to reduce the compliance issues for listed companies, the regulators and preparers of the standards have called for convergence of these two major standards.

Even the Securities and Exchange Commission (SEC), in a bid to remove the U.S. GAAP reconciliation requirement for foreign private issuers using IFRS, has called for the continuing convergence of IFRS and U.S. GAAP. It is pertinent to note that the European Commission has also been supporting the convergence as it does help protect European investors who invest in non-European companies.

The growing acceptance of IFRS as a basis for U.S. financial reporting represents a fundamental change for the U.S. accounting profession. According to the AICPA website (www.ifrs.com), as of November 2008, "nearly 100 countries require or allow the use of IFRS for the preparation of financial statements by publicly held companies.

In the United States, the Securities and Exchange Commission (SEC) is considering taking steps to set a date to allow U.S. public companies to use IFRS, and perhaps make its adoption mandatory."

More than 12,000 companies in these 100 countries adopt IFRS as of now. Australia, New Zealand, and Israel have essentially adopted IFRS as their national standards. Canada, which previously planned convergence with U.S. GAAP, now plans to require IFRS for publicly accountable entities in 2011. The Accounting Standards Board of Japan (ASBJ) and the IASB plan convergence by 2011.

SUMMARY

- A financial instrument is any contract that gives rise to a financial asset of one entity and a financial liability or equity instrument of another entity. Investments in equity shares are a form of financial asset.
- An equity instrument is any contract that evidences a residual interest in the assets of an entity after deducting all of its liabilities.
- A derivative is a financial instrument or other contract with all three of the following characteristics:
  - Its value changes in response to the change in an underlying.
  - It requires no initial net investment or an initial net investment that is smaller than would be required for other types of contracts.
  - It is settled at a future date.
- Financial instruments are categorized into the following four types: fair value through profit and loss (FVPL), held-to-maturity (HTM), available-for-sale (AFS), and loans and receivables (LAR).
- Investments in equity shares, futures, and equity options are classified only as either fair value through profit and loss or as available-for-sale securities.
- The fair value of a financial asset or liability is the amount for which the financial asset could be exchanged, or the financial liability settled, between knowledgeable, willing parties in an arm's-length transaction.
- When determining the fair value of a financial instrument, the accounting standards set out a hierarchy to be applied to the valuation.
- An entity should recognize a financial asset on its balance sheet when, and only when, the entity becomes a party to the contractual provisions of the instrument.
- Derecognition of a financial asset or a portion of a financial asset occurs under the current standards when, and only when, the entity loses control of the contractual rights that comprise the financial asset.
- Investments can be in any of three types: physical assets, intangible assets, or financial assets. This book covers accounting concepts involved in investments in financial assets comprising equities, equity futures, and equity options.
- Speculation is the assumption of the risk of loss, in return for the uncertain possibility of a reward. If a particular position involves no risk, the position represents an investment.
- Two major accounting standards are U.S. GAAP and IFRS.
- The United States' generally accepted accounting principles (U.S. GAAP) literature is rule-based.

- The International Financial Reporting Standards (IFRS) are principle-based.
- As U.S. GAAP is rule-based and has been around for a longer period than IFRS, U.S. GAAP literature is more voluminous than IFRS literature.
- The International Accounting Standards Board (IASB) and the U.S. Financial Accounting Standards Board (FASB) have been committed to converging IFRS and U.S. GAAP since the Norwalk Accord of 2002.
- According to the American Institute of Certified Public Accountants' (AICPA) website (www.ifrs.com), as of November 2008, nearly 100 countries require or allow the use of IFRS for the preparation of financial statements by publicly held companies.
- In the United States, the Securities and Exchange Commission (SEC) is considering taking steps to set a date to allow U.S. public companies to use IFRS, and perhaps make its adoption mandatory.

EXERCISES

Theory Questions

1. What are financial assets and financial liabilities?
2. What are the different categories of financial instruments?
3. What are the various types of investments?
4. Define two major standards: U.S. GAAP and IFRS.
5. What is meant by convergence of U.S. GAAP and IFRS?

Objective Questions

1. A derivative is a financial instrument or contract that settles at a
   a. Current date
   b. Trade date
   c. Future date
   d. None of the above
2. An equity instrument is a contract that evidences
   a. Bank interest
   b. Fixed interest
   c. Residual interest
   d. Money market interest
3. Investments in equity shares, futures, and equity options are classified as
   a. Either held-to-maturity or available-for-sale securities
   b. Either available-for-sale securities or loans and receivables
   c. Either loans and receivables or held-to-maturity
   d. Either fair value through profit and loss or as available-for-sale securities

4. An entity should recognize a financial asset on its balance sheet when, and only when,
   a. The financial liability becomes the contractual provision of the instrument
   b. The entity becomes a party to the residual provisions of the instrument
   c. The entity becomes a party to the contractual provisions of the instrument
   d. The financial liability becomes the residual provision of the instrument
5. Speculation is the assumption of
   a. Risk of profit, return for the certain possibility of a reward
   b. Risk of loss, return for the certain possibility of a reward
   c. Risk of loss, return for the uncertain possibility of a reward
   d. None of the above

CHAPTER 2

Accounting for Equity Investments: Trading

LEARNING OBJECTIVES

After studying this chapter, you should have a grasp of the following:

- Accounting standards for equity investments.
- Definition of *equity securities* and the different types of investment that an investor can make.
- Definition according to U.S. GAAP and exclusions from this definition.
- Definition according to IFRS.
- Distinction between passive investments, significant influence, and controlling interest in an investment.
- Classification of investments from the intention perspective: trading and available-for-sale.
- Exchange-traded securities versus over-the-counter (OTC) securities.
- Trade life cycle of equity investments held for trading purposes.
- Journal entries to be recorded during the different phases of the trade life cycle.
- Illustration of investments in long equity shares held for trading.
- Preparation of general ledger accounts, income statement, and balance sheet, after the equity investments are made.
- Foreign exchange (FX) revaluation and FX translation process.
- Consummated FX translation entries versus transient FX translation entries.
- Trade date accounting versus settlement date accounting.
- Functional currency and presentation currency.
- Distinction between capital gains and currency gains in unrealized gains.
- Illustration of investments in long equity shares in foreign currency.

ACCOUNTING STANDARDS FOR EQUITY INVESTMENTS

This chapter covers the accounting requirements for equity investments. At the highest level, the appropriate accounting for long-term investments in equity shares depends upon the percentage of shares acquired in the investee company, management's intention regarding the holding period, and the extent of marketability of these investments.

Investments in marketable equity securities are referred to as *passive investments* or nominal investments if the investor holds less than 20 percent interest of outstanding voting stock in the company in which the investments are made. These small investments in marketable equity securities are classified into two categories: trading securities and available-for-sale securities. The accounting treatment under the U.S. generally accepted accounting principles (GAAP) for both these categories is covered by the Financial Accounting Standard (FAS) 115. Under the International Financial Reporting Standards (IFRS), International Accounting Standard (IAS) 39 deals with this. A brief introduction to the accounting standards—U.S. GAAP as well as IFRS—is given elsewhere in this chapter.

Relevant Accounting Standards	
U.S. GAAP	**IFRS**
FAS 52—Foreign Currency Translation	IFRS 7—Financial Instruments: Disclosure
FAS 94—Consolidation of All Majority-owned Subsidiaries	IAS 21—The Effects of Changes in Foreign Exchange Rates
FAS 109—Accounting for Income Taxes	IAS 32—Financial Instruments: Presentation
FAS 115—Accounting for Certain Investments in Debt and Equity Securities	IAS 36–Impairment of Assets
FAS 130—Reporting Comprehensive Income	IAS 39—Financial Instruments: Recognition and Measurement
FAS 157—Fair Value Measurements	
FAS 159—The Fair Value Option for Financial Assets and Financial Liabilities	

DEFINITION OF EQUITY SECURITIES

Equity securities are represented by ownership shares as common stock or preferred stock, as well as rights to acquire ownership shares such as stock warrants, rights, or call options. Ownership of equity securities also includes rights to dispose of ownership in shares by way of put options. It should be noted that equity securities do not include preferred stock shares that are redeemable at the option of the investor or stock that is redeemed by the issuer. Shares of its own stock purchased by the company are often known as *treasury stock* and *convertible bonds*. However, this chapter examines the accounting requirements of equity securities that are represented by ownership shares by way of common stock or preferred stock. The other forms of equity securities are dealt with elsewhere in this book.

Note, however, that call options and put options that meet the definition of derivatives are outside the scope of the definition of equity securities for the purpose of accounting as equity securities.

Definition according to FAS 115 (U.S. GAAP)

Equity security is defined in FAS 115 as any security representing an ownership interest in an enterprise (for example, common, preferred, or other capital stock) or the right to acquire (for example, warrants, rights, and call options) or dispose of (for example, put options) an ownership interest in an enterprise at fixed or determinable prices. However, the term does not include convertible debt, nor does it include preferred stock that either must be redeemed by the issuing enterprise or is redeemable at the option of the investor. In other words, the definition includes preferred stock but does not include redeemable preference stock.

Exclusions from This Definition

This accounting standard does not apply to investments in equity securities accounted for under the equity method or to investments in consolidated subsidiaries. It is also not applicable for those entities that apply specialized accounting practices like accounting for investments in debt and equity securities at market value or fair value, with changes in value recognized in earnings or in the change in net assets.

Thus, brokers and dealers in securities, defined benefit pension plans, and investment companies are outside the purview of FAS 115. This statement also does not apply to not-for-profit organizations.

Note: Preference shares with fixed or determinable payments are classified as loans and receivables rather than as equity investments. It should be noted that such preference shares would be recorded as liabilities by the issuer, according to the accounting standard, if they have fixed or determinable payments and are not quoted in an active market.

Definition According to IAS 32 (IFRS)

An equity instrument is any contract that evidences a residual interest in the assets of an entity after deducting all of its liabilities. A financial asset is defined, among other things, as an equity instrument of another entity.

PASSIVE INVESTMENTS: LESS THAN 20 PERCENT

Investments in equity securities that are purchased and held for the short term, principally for the purpose of generating gains on resale, are classified as *trading securities* and reported at fair value with unrealized gains and losses included in the earnings.

Investments in equity securities that are not trading securities are classified as *available-for-sale* (AFS) securities and reported at fair value with unrealized gains and losses excluded from earnings and reported in a separate component of shareholders' equity. These are typically short-term investments made by the investor. It is generally presumed that if the investor holds less than 20 percent of the voting rights of the investee company then no significant influence can be exercised on the investee company unless there is evidence to prove otherwise. The *cost method* is adopted for investments of this nature.

Investments in equity securities are recorded at cost, including the brokerage fees, securities transaction taxes, and any other cost associated with the procurement of the securities. Both trading and available-for-sale types of investments are carried in the books of accounts at the fair value by a process known as *mark-to-market.* For marketable equity securities that are listed on recognized stock exchanges, fair value is determined based on the market quotes at the end of the day. For other equity securities, the rates are obtained from the over-the-counter (OTC) market. Investments that are considered to be non-tradable are carried at cost except for any permanent impairment in value of the investment. Even tradable securities that do not have any determinable market value are also carried at cost in the books of accounts.

What Is Readily Determinable Fair Value?

According to FAS 115, paragraph 3, the fair value is determinable if any of the following three conditions is fulfilled:

1. The fair value of an equity security is readily determinable if sales prices or bid-and-ask quotations are currently available on a securities exchange registered with the Securities and Exchange Commission (SEC) or in the over-the-counter market, provided that those prices or quotations for the over-the-counter market are publicly reported by the National Association of Securities Dealers Automated Quotations systems or by the National Quotation Bureau. Restricted stock does not meet that definition.
2. The fair value of an equity security traded only in a foreign market is readily determinable if that foreign market is of a breadth and scope comparable to one of the U.S. markets referred to above.
3. The fair value of an investment in a mutual fund is readily determinable if the fair value per share (unit) is determined and published and is the basis for current transactions.

Trading Securities

The categorization from the accounting standards perspective is *fair value through profit and loss*, commonly referred to as FVPL. As mentioned in the previous chapter, securities meant for trading are categorized as FVPL.

Trading securities are normally held by banks and other financial institutions that engage in active buying and selling of securities with a view to make gains on trading. The mark-to-market process values the securities at market rates, recording the unrealized gains/loss on such securities. The realized and unrealized gains/loss on those securities classified as trading securities is included in the income of the investor. However, when realized gains or losses have been previously reported as unrealized, only changes in the current period are reported as realized in the period during which the equity security is sold. Dividends on such equity securities are recognized as income when declared by the company. If the dividends received by the investor exceed the cumulative earnings by way of dividends since the acquisition of the shares, then the excess dividends received are accounted for as liquidating dividend.

A financial asset should be classified as held for trading if it is part of a portfolio of identified financial instruments that are managed together and for which there is evidence of a recent actual pattern of short-term profit taking. Even though the term *portfolio* is not explicitly defined in the accounting standards, the context in which it is used suggests that a portfolio is a group of financial assets that are managed as part of that group, and if there is evidence of a recent actual pattern of short-term profit taking on financial instruments included in such a portfolio, those financial instruments qualify as held for trading even though an individual financial instrument may in fact be held for a longer period of time.

Available-for-sale (AFS) Securities

When the investor invests in equity securities just to utilize idle cash without any intention to hold it for a long period or without any intention to generate gains on current resale, then such investments in equity securities are classified as available-for-sale securities.

From the accounting standards perspective, available-for-sale securities are designated as such during the recognition of the financial asset or an item of non-derivative financial asset that is not categorized as any of the following:

- Loans and receivables.
- Held-to-maturity investments.
- Financial assets at fair value through profit or loss.

Equity investments classified as available-for-sale are also subject to the same mark-to-market process as mentioned earlier, resulting in unrealized gains/loss on such investments. However, such unrealized gains/loss are not included in the income of the period, but are reported as *other comprehensive income* (OCI). Other comprehensive income is included in the stockholders' equity on the balance sheet and is not reported as income in the income statement of the current period.

If the securities classified as available-for-sale are sold, then the realized gains/loss on such sale is taken to the current period income statement. Simultaneously, the OCI is reduced by that amount.

This is covered in detail in the next chapter.

SIGNIFICANT INFLUENCE: 20–50 PERCENT

Where the investor owns between 20 and 50 percent of the equity of the investee company, the investor is presumed to have a significant influence in the operating and financial decisions of the investee company. It should be noted that the 20 percent threshold is not a fixed limit and it is just a guide as per the accounting standards interpretation. There could be instances where the investor may not have a significant influence in spite of holding close to 50 percent of the equity of the investee company. Where the investor commands significant influence, the *equity method* of accounting is adopted.

CONTROLLING INTEREST: MORE THAN 50 PERCENT

When the investor acquires more than 50 percent of the outstanding voting stock of the investee company, the investor has controlling interest because of its majority ownership of the voting stock. Investments of this nature will necessitate the preparation of consolidated financial statements.

The preparation of consolidated financial statements is statutory for presentation of the final accounts to the outside world. However, internally, the investor may use either the cost method or the equity method to account for its investments. There is no requirement to consolidate if the ownership is temporary or if the ownership is not directly held by the investor, but instead through a trustee. Consolidation of accounts is necessary for domestic, foreign, similar, or dissimilar subsidiaries. Consolidation is necessary even if the subsidiary has a different accounting year. Where the difference between the accounting years of the two companies is less than three months, the investor should consolidate the accounts of the subsidiary, taking into account any material events occurring during the intervening period that impact the accounting statements. For the investor having a significant influence or having a controlling interest, there is no election-option to value the investments at fair value.

EXCHANGE-TRADED SECURITIES VERSUS OVER-THE-COUNTER SECURITIES

Equity investments are also divided into two types: (1) equity shares of publicly traded shares in recognized stock exchanges and (2) private equity investments. Even though the accounting requirements for both are more or less the same, there are subtle differences.

Equity shares are bought and sold through share brokers who are registered with the stock exchange concerned. In the case of equity shares traded in stock exchanges, usually the principle of *novation* is applicable. This means that the stock exchange acts as the counterparty in the strictest sense for any transaction made through the exchange. For example, if you buy some equity share through the exchange, it is the responsibility of the exchange to ensure that you get the equity share concerned. Equally, the exchange will ensure that the counterparty gets paid on time at the contracted rate.

In the case of private equity investments, the trade is executed *over-the-counter*, or simply OTC. Here, the broker becomes the actual counterparty and is responsible for the fulfillment of his part of the obligation. If the counterparty fails to perform his obligation under the contract, there are no means to enforce the specific performance other than to approach the appropriate court of law.

THE TRADE LIFE CYCLE FOR EQUITY TRADING SECURITIES

- Buy the share.
- Pay brokerage/commission on the buy transaction.
- Pay the contracted amount for the share.
- Ascertain the fair value at the end of reporting period.
- Reversal of mark to market.
- Dividend declaration by the company.
- Receipt of dividend and tax withholding on dividend.
- Sell the share.
- Pay brokerage/commission on the sell transaction.
- Receive the consideration.
- Ascertain the profit/loss on the sale.
- FX revaluation entries.
- FX translation entries.

Buy the Share

For exchange-traded shares, the buy order is placed with the broker registered with the stock exchange concerned. The stock exchange usually takes the responsibility for specific performance of the contract, ensuring that both the legs of the contract are fulfilled by the respective parties. When the investor places the buy order and when the broker executes the same, it becomes a binding contract between the investor and the stock exchange. Usually the trade date is referred to as "T + 0" or simply *trade date*. At this stage, the asset being the equity shares and the liability being the amount payable to the broker concerned are recognized in the books of accounts. (See trade date accounting versus settlement date accounting discussed elsewhere in this chapter.)

When the net holding of any share is positive, it is usually referred to as *long* position, and if the net holding is negative—that is, the shares sold are greater than the shares bought of the same security—it is referred to as a *short* position.

For example, Alan Kimberly Inc. acquires 1,000 equity shares of Gold Crest at $490 per share from the stock exchange through the broker Silver Man on October 3. The accounting entry recorded in the books of accounts is as follows:

Journal Entry

Date	Particulars	Debit (US$)	Credit (US$)
3-Oct-X1	Equity Shares, Gold Crest—Trading Account	490,000.00	
	To Silver Man Account		490,000.00
	(Being the Gold Crest shares bought at $490 per share through the broker Silver Man)		

Brokerage/Commission on the Transaction

The broker of the stock exchange charges a commission for the services rendered. This is usually settled along with the purchase value of the shares. Accounting standards require that this be treated as part of the cost of the shares procured. Hence, this is usually built into the cost of purchase of the shares.

On the 1,000 Gold Crest shares purchased through Silver Man, the brokerage payable per share is $3. The accounting entry that is recorded in the books of accounts is as follows:

Journal Entry

Date	Particulars	Debit (US$)	Credit (US$)
3-Oct-X1	Equity Shares, Gold Crest—Trading Account	3,000.00	
	To Silver Man Account		3,000.00
	(Being the brokerage payable to Silver Man at $3 per share on 1,000 Gold Crest shares bought through them)		

Pay the Contracted Amount for the Share

The next event in the trade life cycle is the payment of the contracted amount for the shares bought. Usually the receipt of the shares and the payment for them happens two days after the date of the trade, referred to as "T + 2." However, this varies from exchange to exchange. The shares are usually delivered electronically by the seller and the payment is made by the buyer on the same date. During this stage, the actual asset comes into the physical possession of the buyer and the liability created earlier is settled. For exchange-traded securities, the settlement automatically takes place on the settlement date through the clearing system of

> **Payment and Delivery**
>
> For exchange-traded securities, the delivery of the securities in either physical or electronic form takes place immediately after the payment is received by the stock exchange. In this case, due to the principle of novation, both the parties avoid counterparty risk altogether. For OTC trades, neither party wants to take any risk of not being able to get the securities after making payment. Hence the counterparties resort to a system known as *delivery versus payment* (DvP). In this case, simultaneous exchange of securities and cash takes place between the counterparties, namely, the buyer and seller, either directly or through their respective custodians. When DvP is agreed upon by both parties, the buyer need not pay for the shares until they are delivered by the seller, and the seller need not deliver the shares so long as the buyer has not paid for them. In this case both parties avoid what is known as the counterparty risk.

the exchange concerned. For OTC trades, both parties resort to their own accepted method of settlement to ensure that they effectively avoid each other's counterparty risk.

Assuming that the broker is paid on T + 2, the accounting entry that is recorded in the books of accounts is as follows:

Journal Entry

Date	Particulars	Debit (US$)	Credit (US$)
5-Oct-X1	Silver Man Account	493,000.00	
	To Bank Account		493,000.00
	(Being the amount paid to Silver Man on purchase of 1,000 Gold Crest shares together with the brokerage)		

Ascertain the Fair Value at the End of the Reporting Period

At the end of every reporting period, the fair value of the shares is ascertained and the shares are marked-to-market. This process is known as *portfolio valuation*, when the market rate at the end of the period is determined from the primary stock exchange where the shares are traded. If there is an increase in the market rate over and above the purchase rate, then such increase is recognized as a gain on the one hand, and the corresponding amount is reflected as an increase in the value of such shares. This accounting entry is reversed on the next day or the next valuation date, when a fresh entry for the then value is recorded in the books of accounts. Alternatively, the accounting entry can also be recorded only for the incremental value. If the investor follows this incremental value method, there is no need to reverse the entry for mark-to-market recorded earlier.

Assuming that the market rate of Gold Crest on October 31 (which is the next valuation date) is $497, the accounting entry that is recorded in the books of accounts is as follows:

Journal Entry

Date	Particulars	Debit (US$)	Credit (US$)
31-Oct-X1	Equity Shares, Gold Crest—Trading Account	4,000.00	
	To Unrealized Capital Gains/Loss—Equity Shares Account		4,000.00
	(Being the mark-to-market entry for 1,000 long position in Gold Crest Shares at $497 less the cost of acquisition viz., $490 plus $3 per share, amounting to $4,000)		

Reversal of Mark-to-market Entry

The accounting entry for mark-to-market is reversed on the next day or the next valuation date, when a fresh entry for the then value is recorded in the books of accounts. However, as mentioned earlier, if the investor follows this incremental value method, there is no need to reverse the entry for mark-to-market recorded earlier.

The accounting entry that is recorded in the books of accounts is shown below:

Journal Entry

Date	Particulars	Debit (US$)	Credit (US$)
1-Nov-X1	Unrealized Capital Gains/Loss—Equity Shares Account	4,000.00	
	To Equity Shares, Gold Crest—Trading Account		4,000.00
	(Being the reversal of mark-to-market entry for 1,000 long position in Gold Crest shares)		

Corporate Action

Corporate action is, as the name implies, an action taken by the issuing company that impacts the investments or earnings from such investments. Typical examples of corporate actions include cash dividend declaration by the company, stock dividends, stock splits, reverse splits, mergers and acquisitions by the company that result in change of the name or number of shares held by the investor, and so on. The nature of the corporate actions and the accounting entries that are to be recorded on such announcements of corporate actions by the company are given here.

Dividend Declaration by the Company

One of the key activities during the trade life cycle is the corporate action in the form of cash dividend. The company will announce the rate of dividend and the date on which it becomes ex-dividend. In other words, from the ex-dividend date, the shares purchased from the exchange are not entitled for the dividend announced by the company. Technically, the shares would be quoted lower by the amount of the dividend declared by the company on the ex-dividend date. The dividend income should be recognized by the holder of the shares on the date on which it becomes ex-dividend.

There are two types of dividends a company can issue: cash dividends and stock dividends. While generally only one or the other is issued at a specific period of time—either quarterly, biannually, or yearly—both may occur simultaneously. A cash dividend is straightforward in the sense that for each share owned, a certain amount of money is distributed to each shareholder. Thus, if an investor owns 100 shares and the cash dividend is $0.50 per share, the shareholder will receive $50 as dividends.

A stock dividend also comes from distributable equity but in the form of stock instead of cash. A stock dividend of 10 percent, for example, means that for every 10 shares owned, the shareholder receives one additional share. If the company has 1,000,000 of common stock outstanding, such a stock dividend would increase the company's outstanding shares to a total of 1,100,000. The increase in shares outstanding, however, has the effect of diluting the earnings per share and hence the stock price would decrease.

The following accounting entry that is recorded in the books of accounts assumes that Gold Crest announces a dividend of $7 per share and the ex-dividend date is October 17.

Journal Entry

Date	Particulars	Debit (US$)	Credit (US$)
17-Oct-X1	Equity Dividend Receivable Account	7,000.00	
	To Dividend Income Account		7,000.00
	(Being the dividend receivable on the 1,000 shares of long position in Gold Crest amounting to $7,000)		

Stock Split

A stock split is also referred to as *declaration of bonus shares*, even though technically there is a subtle difference between the two. Typically the term *stock split* is applicable for corporate entities having no par value shares, while bonus shares are declared by corporate entities having shares with par value. From the company perspective, certain accounting entries are required to be recorded when bonus shares are issued, as this will have the effect of reducing the reserves and increasing the share capital of the company.

A stock split divides each of the outstanding shares of a company in the ratio of the split announced by the company, thereby lowering the price per share, as the market will adjust the price on the day the stock split is implemented. A stock split, however, is a non-event, meaning that it does not affect a company's equity or its market capitalization, as only the number of shares outstanding changes. A stock split does not directly change the value or net assets of a company.

A company announcing a two-for-one (2:1) stock split, for example, will distribute an additional share for every one outstanding share, so the total shares outstanding will double. If the company had 50 shares outstanding, it will have 100 after the stock split. At the same time, because the value of the company and its shares did not change, the price per share will drop by half. So if the presplit price was $100 per share, the new price will be $50 per share.

The only journal entry needed for a stock split is a memo entry to note that the number of shares changed and that the par value per share has changed (if the stock has a par value.) However, a typical journal entry with debits and credits is not needed since the total dollar amounts for the par value and other components of paid-in capital and stockholders' equity do not change.

For example, if a corporation has 100,000 shares of $1.00 par value stock and it declares a two-for-one stock split, the corporation will have 200,000 shares with a par value of $0.50 per share. Before and after the stock split, the total par value is $100,000. Other account balances within stockholders' equity also remain the same.

However, in the case of receipt of bonus shares, the investor will have to adjust the existing cost of investments in proportion to the quantity of shares received as bonus shares and accordingly calculate the realized gains on every sale made thenceforth.

Reverse Split

A reverse split is implemented by a corporate entity that would like to increase the price of its shares. If a $1 stock had a reverse split of 1 for 10 (1:10), shareholders would have to exchange 10 of their old shares for one new one, but the paid-up value of the stock would increase from $1 to $10 per share. Sometimes a company decides to use a reverse split to shed its status as a *penny stock company.*

Receipt of Dividend and Withholding Tax

The actual receipt of the cash itself may take from one week to six weeks depending upon the regulatory requirement of the exchange on which the stock is listed.

Tax authorities in many countries require that tax be deducted on the dividend disbursed by a company. Withheld tax is claimed as such during the submission of income tax returns by the taxpayer. Until then, it is kept as an asset in the books of the buyer. In several countries, the tax is deducted only if the amount exceeds a specified amount; otherwise no tax is deducted. Assuming that the actual cash is received by the investor on October 25, and that $1 per share is deducted as withholding tax, the accounting entry that is recorded in the books of accounts is as follows:

Journal Entry

Date	Particulars	Debit (US$)	Credit (US$)
25-Oct-X1	Bank Account	6,000.00	
	Withholding Tax Account	1,000.00	
	To Equity Dividend Receivable Account		7,000.00
	(Being cash dividend received on the 1,000 shares of long position in Gold Crest amounting to $7,000 and entry for withholding tax amounting to $1,000)		

Sell the Share

Ultimately when the shares are sold through a broker of the exchange, an accounting entry is recorded for the contracted amount to be received on such sale.

Assuming that the entire quantity of 1,000 shares of Gold Crest is sold on November 6 for a consideration of $520 each, and assuming the brokerage fee per share amounts to $4, then the accounting entry that is recorded in the books of accounts is shown as follows:

Journal Entry

Date	Particulars	Debit (US$)	Credit (US$)
6-Nov-X1	Silver Man Account	520,000.00	
	To Equity Shares, Gold Crest—Trading Account		520,000.00
	(Being the 1,000 Gold Crest shares sold at $520 per share through the broker Silver Man)		

Brokerage/Commission on the Sell Transaction

The brokerage is paid while the shares are sold and only the net proceeds are taken into account. The accounting entry that is recorded in the books of accounts is shown as follows:

Journal Entry

Date	Particulars	Debit (US$)	Credit (US$)
6-Nov-X1	Equity Shares, Gold Crest—Trading Account	4,000.00	
	To Silver Man Account		4,000.00
	(Being the brokerage payable to Silver Man at $4 per share on 1,000 Gold Crest shares sold through them)		

Receive the Consideration

The consideration is received on T + 2 or based on the exchange concerned. The consideration is received net of brokerage. The accounting entry that is recorded in the books of accounts is shown as follows:

Journal Entry

Date	Particulars	Debit (US$)	Credit (US$)
8-Nov-X1	Bank Account	516,000.00	
	To Silver Man Account		516,000.00
	(Being the net consideration of $516 per share received from the broker Silver Man on sale of 1,000 Gold Crest shares)		

Ascertain the Profit/Loss on the Sale

The profit or loss on liquidation of the shares is ascertained by deducting the cost of sales from the net sale consideration. Cost of sales is arrived at by following the first in first out (FIFO), last in first out (LIFO), or weighted-average method.

In this case 1,000 shares of Gold Crest were bought at the rate of $490 and $3 was paid per share towards brokerage fees, resulting in the cost of acquisition of Gold Crest shares being $493 per share. These were subsequently sold for a consideration of $520 per share, and a brokerage fee of $4 per share was incurred, resulting in the net realization of $516 per share. Hence the profit on each share is $23 and the total profit for the entire lot amounts to $23,000. The profit or loss realized is always recognized on the date of liquidation and not on the date on which the net proceeds are received from the broker.

The accounting entry that is recorded in the books of accounts is as follows:

Journal Entry

Date	Particulars	Debit (US$)	Credit (US$)
6-Nov-X1	Equity Shares, Gold Crest—Trading Account	23,000.00	
	To Realized Capital Gains/Loss—Equity Account		23,000.00
	(Being the realized gains on the sale of 1,000 Gold Crest shares)		

Illustration: Long Equity Shares—Trading

Assume that Alan Kimberly Inc. trades in Microsoft shares in a U.S. stock exchange through Silver Man brokers, and the details are as follow:

Trade Details

Date	Product	Qty	Rate	B/S	Brokerage
5-Jan-X1	Microsoft	1,000	$34.00	B	$250
15-Jan-X1	Microsoft	2,000	$39.00	B	$650
5-Feb-X1	Microsoft	1,500	$39.00	S	$400

Other Details

- Settlement date T + 2
- Purchases on January 5 are settled on January 9 due to intervening holidays.
- A dividend of $0.45/share is declared by Microsoft on January 28, $0.05 being the withholding tax.
- The dividend is paid by Microsoft on February 4.

Liquidation Method

Weighted average

Market Rate

January 31: 36.00
February 28: 32.00
March 31: 40.00

Prepare

Journal entries, general ledgers, trial balance, income statement, and balance sheet for Alan Kimberly Inc., for the period January 1 to March 31.

Solution

T-1 On Purchase of Equity Shares and Brokerage

Journal Entry

Date	Particulars	Debit (US$)	Credit (US$)
5-Jan-X1	Investments—Equity Shares—Trading Account	34,000.00	
	To Silver Man Account		34,000.00
	(Being the equity shares bought through the broker Silver Man)		
5-Jan-X1	Investments—Equity Shares—Trading Account	250.00	
	To Silver Man Account		250.00
	(Being brokerage payable to the broker on purchase of equity shares)		

T-2 On Payment of Contracted Sum

Journal Entry

Date	Particulars	Debit (US$)	Credit (US$)
9-Jan-X1	Silver Man Account	34,250.00	
	To Bank Account		34,250.00
	(Being the payment made to the broker on purchase of shares together with the brokerage)		

T-3 On Purchase of Equity Shares and Brokerage

Journal Entry

Date	Particulars	Debit (US$)	Credit (US$)
15-Jan-X1	Investments—Equity Shares—Trading Account	78,000.00	
	To Silver Man Account		78,000.00
	(Being the equity shares bought through the broker Silver Man)		
15-Jan-X1	Investments—Equity Shares—Trading Account	650.00	
	To Silver Man Account		650.00
	(Being brokerage payable to the broker on purchase of equity shares)		

T-4 On Payment of Contracted Sum

Journal Entry

Date	Particulars	Debit (US$)	Credit (US$)
17-Jan-X1	Silver Man Account	78,650.00	
	To Bank Account		78,650.00
	(Being the payment made to the broker on purchase of shares together with the brokerage)		

T-5 Mark-to-market at End of Reporting Period

The total long position adds up to 3,000 shares and the market value of the shares is compared with the original cost of acquisition including brokerage to arrive at the mark-to-market. Since the market rate at the end of reporting period is lower than the cost of acquisition, this results in mark-to-market loss, which is reflected as a decrease in the value of investments. Since the shares are held in the *trading* category, the losses are taken to the profit and loss account.

Mark-to-market at end of reporting period: 31 Jan X1	**US$**
(a) Cost of acquisition of 1,000 shares @ US$34 including brokerage	34,250.00
(b) Cost of acquisition of 2,000 shares @ US$39 including brokerage	78,650.00
(c) Total cost of acquisition	112,900.00
(d) Market value at the end of reporting period	108,000.00
(e) Unrealized loss (d) − (c)	(4,900.00)

Journal Entry

Date	Particulars	Debit (US$)	Credit (US$)
31-Jan-X1	Unrealized Capital Gains/Loss—Equity Shares—Trading Account	4,900.00	
	To Investments—Equity Shares—Trading Account		4,900.00
	(Being the unrealized loss on purchase of equity shares)		

T-6 Reversal of Mark-to-market Entry

Journal Entry

Date	Particulars	Debit (US$)	Credit (US$)
1-Feb-X1	Investments—Equity Shares—Trading Account	4,900.00	
	To Unrealized Capital Gains/Loss—Equity Shares—Trading Account		4,900.00
	(Being the reversal of mark-to-market on equity shares)		

T-7 On Declaration of Dividend

Journal Entry

Date	Particulars	Debit (US$)	Credit (US$)
28-Jan-X1	Dividend Receivable Account	1,350.00	
	To Dividend Income Account		1,350.00
	(Being the dividend receivable on 3,000 equity shares of Microsoft)		

T-8 On Receipt of Dividend

Journal Entry

Date	Particulars	Debit (US$)	Credit (US$)
4-Feb-X1	Bank Account	1,200.00	
	To Dividend Receivable Account		1,200.00
	(Being the dividend received on 3,000 equity shares of Microsoft after withholding tax of $150)		

T-9 Withholding Tax on Dividend

Journal Entry

Date	Particulars	Debit (US$)	Credit (US$)
4-Feb-X1	Withholding tax on dividend receipts account	150.00	
	To Dividend Receivable Account		150.00
	(Being the withholding tax paid on 3,000 equity shares of Microsoft)		

T-10 On Sale of Shares and Brokerage

Journal Entry

Date	Particulars	Debit (US$)	Credit (US$)
5-Feb-X1	Silver Man Account	58,500.00	
	To Investments—Equity Shares—Trading Account		58,500.00
	(Being the shares sold at $39 per share through the broker Silver Man)		
5-Feb-X1	Investments—Equity Shares—Trading Account	400.00	
	To Silver Man Account		400.00
	(Being the brokerage payable to the broker Silver Man on sale of shares)		

T-11 On Recording Profit/Loss on Sale of Shares

The liquidation methodology is the weighted average method. Hence the weighted average cost of acquisition of 1,500 shares is first arrived at and compared with the net sales realization to arrive at the realized gains on liquidation.

Calculation of capital gains:		**US$**
(a) Sale value of 1,500 shares @ US$39 less brokerage		58,100.00
Cost of acquisition:		
1,000 shares @ US$34 including brokerage	34,250.00	
2,000 shares @ US$38 including brokerage	78,650.00	
Total	**112,900.00**	
(b) Weighted average cost of 1,500 shares [(112,900 × 1,500) / 3,000]		56,450.00
Realized gains = (a) − (b)		**1,650.00**

Journal Entry

Date	Particulars	Debit (US$)	Credit (US$)
5-Feb-X1	Investments—Equity Shares—Trading Account	1,650.00	
	To Realized Capital Gains/Loss Equity—Trading Account		1,650.00
	(Being the profit on the sale of shares)		

T-12 On Receipt of the Contracted Sum

Journal Entry

Date	Particulars	Debit (US$)	Credit (US$)
7-Feb-X1	Bank Account	58,100.00	
	To Silver Man Account		58,100.00
	(Being the net consideration received from the broker on sale of 1,500 Microsoft shares)		

T-13 Mark-to-market at End of Reporting Period

Mark-to-market at end of reporting period: 28-Feb-X1	**US$**
(a) Market value of 1,500 shares @ US$32	48,000.00
(b) Weighted average cost of acquisition of 1,500 shares	56,450.00
(c) Unrealized loss = (a) − (b)	8,450.00

Journal Entry

Date	Particulars	Debit (US$)	Credit (US$)
28-Feb-X1	Unrealized Capital Gains/Loss—Equity Shares—Trading Account	8,450.00	
	To Investments—Equity Shares—Trading Account		8,450.00
	(Being the unrealized loss on 1,500 equity shares of Microsoft)		

T-14 Reversal of Mark-to-market Entry

Journal Entry

Date	Particulars	Debit (US$)	Credit (US$)
1-Mar-X1	Investments—Equity Shares—Trading Account	8,450.00	
	To Unrealized Capital Gains/Loss—Equity Shares—Trading Account		8,450.00
	(Being the reversal of mark-to-market entry on equity shares)		

T-15 Mark-to-market at End of Reporting Period

Mark-to-market at end of reporting period: 31-Mar-X1	**US$**
(a) Market value of 1,500 shares @ US$40	60,000.00
(b) Weighted average cost of acquisition of 1,500 shares	56,450.00
(c) Unrealized gains US$ = (a) − (b)	3,550.00

Journal Entry

Date	Particulars	Debit (US$)	Credit (US$)
31-Mar-X1	Investments—Equity Shares—Trading Account	3,550.00	
	To Unrealized Capital Gains/Loss—Equity Shares—Trading Account		3,550.00
	(Being the unrealized gains on 1,500 equity shares of Microsoft)		

General Ledger Accounts

Investments—Equity Shares—Trading Account

Date	Particulars	Debit (US$)	Date	Particulars	Credit (US$)
5-Jan-X1	To Silver Man Account	34,000.00			
5-Jan-X1	To Silver Man Account	250.00			
15-Jan-X1	To Silver Man Account	78,000.00			
15-Jan-X1	To Silver Man Account	650.00			
			31-Jan-X1	By Unrealized Capital Gains/ Loss—Equity Shares—Trading Account	4,900.00
1-Feb-X1	To Unrealized Capital Gains/ Loss—Equity Shares—Trading Account	4,900.00			
			5-Feb-X1	By Silver Man Account	58,500.00
5-Feb-X1	To Silver Man Account	400.00			
5-Feb-X1	To Realized Capital Gains/ Loss Equity—Trading Account	1,650.00			
			28-Feb-X1	By Unrealized Capital Gains/ Loss—Equity Shares—Trading Account	8,450.00
1-Mar-X1	To Unrealized Capital Gains/ Loss—Equity Shares—Trading Account	8,450.00			
31-Mar-X1	To Unrealized Capital Gains/ Loss—Equity Shares—Trading Account	3,550.00			
			31-Mar-X1	By Balance	60,000.00
31-Mar-X1	Total	**131,850.00**	31-Mar-X1	Total	**131,850.00**
31-Mar-X1	To Balance	60,000.00			

Dividend Income Account

Date	Particulars	Debit (US$)	Date	Particulars	Credit (US$)
			28-Jan-X1	By Dividend Receivable Account	1,350.00
31-Mar-X1	To Balance	1,350.00			
31-Mar-X1	Total	**1,350.00**	31-Mar-X1	Total	**1,350.00**
			31-Mar-X1	By Balance	1,350.00
28-Jan-X1	To Dividend Income Account	1,350.00			
			4-Feb-X1	By Bank Account	1,200.00
			4-Feb-X1	By Withholding Tax on Dividend Receipts Account	150.00
31-Mar-X1	Total	**1,350.00**	31-Mar-X1	Total	**1,350.00**

Realized Capital Gains/Loss Equity—Trading Account

Date	Particulars	Debit (US$)	Date	Particulars	Credit (US$)
			5-Feb-X1	By Investments—Equity Shares—Trading Account	1,650.00
31-Mar-X1	To Balance	1,650.00			
31-Mar-X1	Total	**1,650.00**	31-Mar-X1	Total	**1,650.00**
			31-Mar-X1	By Balance	1,650.00

Unrealized Capital Gains/Loss—Equity Shares—Trading Account

Date	Particulars	Debit (US$)	Date	Particulars	Credit (US$)
31-Jan-X1	To Investments—Equity Shares—Trading Account	4,900.00			
			1-Feb-X1	By Investments—Equity Shares—Trading Account	4,900.00
28-Feb-X1	To Investments—Equity Shares—Trading Account	8,450.00			
			1-Mar-X1	By Investments—Equity Shares—Trading Account	8,450.00
			31-Mar-X1	By Investments—Equity Shares—Trading Account	3,550.00
31-Mar-X1	To Balance	3,550.00			
31-Mar-X1	Total	**16,900.00**	31-Mar-X1	Total	**16,900.00**
			31-Mar-X1	By Balance	3,550.00

Withholding Tax on Dividend Receipts Account

Date	Particulars	Debit (US$)	Date	Particulars	Credit (US$)
4-Feb-X1	To Dividend Receivable Account	150.00			
			31-Mar-X1	By Balance	150.00
31-Mar-X1	Total	**150.00**	31-Mar-X1	Total	**150.00**
31-Mar-X1	To Balance	150.00			

Silver Man Account

Date	Particulars	Debit (US$)	Date	Particulars	Credit (US$)
			5-Jan-X1	By Investments—Equity Shares—Trading Account	34,000.00
			5-Jan-X1	By Investments—Equity Shares—Trading Account	250.00
9-Jan-X1	To Bank Account	34,250.00			
			15-Jan-X1	By Investments—Equity Shares—Trading Account	78,000.00
			15-Jan-X1	By Investments—Equity Shares—Trading Account	650.00
17-Jan-X1	To Bank Account	78,650.00			
5-Feb-X1	To Investments—Equity Shares—Trading Account	58,500.00			
			5-Feb-X1	By Investments—Equity Shares—Trading Account	400.00
			7-Feb-X1	By Bank Account	58,100.00
31-Mar-X1	Total	**171,400.00**	31-Mar-X1	Total	**171,400.00**

Bank Account

Date	Particulars	Debit (US$)	Date	Particulars	Credit (US$)
			9-Jan-X1	By Silver Man Account	34,250.00
			17-Jan-X1	By Silver Man Account	78,650.00
4-Feb-X1	To Dividend Receivable Account	1,200.00			
7-Feb-X1	To Silver Man Account	58,100.00			
31-Mar-X1	To Balance	53,600.00			
31-Mar-X1	Total	**112,900.00**	31-Mar-X1	Total	**112,900.00**
			31-Mar-X1	By Balance	53,600.00

Trial Balance

As of 31-Mar-X1 (US$)

Particulars	Debit	Credit
Current Liabilities		
Bank Account		53,600.00
Investments		
Investments—Equity Shares—Trading Account	60,000.00	
Current Assets		
Withholding Tax on Dividend Receipts Account	150.00	
Income		
Dividend Income Account		1,350.00
Realized Capital Gains/Loss Equity—Trading Account		1,650.00
Unrealized Capital Gains/Loss—Equity Shares—Trading Account		3,550.00
Total	**60,150.00**	**60,150.00**

Income Statement

For the period ending 31-Mar-X1

Expenses	US$	Income	US$
		Direct Income	
		Dividend Income Account	1,350.00
		Realized Capital Gains/Loss Equity—Trading Account	1,650.00
Net Profit Carryover	6,550.00	Unrealized Capital Gains/Loss Equity—Trading Account	3,550.00
Total	**6,550.00**	Total	**6,550.00**

Balance Sheet

As of 31-Mar-X1

Liabilities	**US$**	**Assets**	**US$**
Capital Account	Nil	**Investments**	
Current Liabilities		Investments—Equity Shares—Trading Account	60,000.00
Bank Account	53,600.00	**Current Assets**	
Profit and Loss Account		Withholding Tax on Dividend Receipts Account	150.00
Opening Balance	Nil		
Current Period	6,550.00		
Total	**60,150.00**	Total	**60,150.00**

FX REVALUATION AND FX TRANSLATION PROCESS

Functional Currency and Presentation Currency

The currency of the primary economic environment in which the investor operates is the *functional currency*. The financial accounting records should be maintained in the functional currency and the investor is not free to choose otherwise. The investor's investment activities and the currency in which the fund raises money from investors predominantly determine the functional currency. *Presentation currency* is the currency in which the financial statements are presented to the investors.

Accounting standard FAS 52 provides general guidance on the indicators of facts to be considered in identifying the functional currency. When the indicators are mixed and the functional currency is not obvious, the standard mentions that the management's judgment will be required to determine the functional currency that most faithfully portrays the economic results of the entity's operations and thereby best achieves the objectives of foreign currency translation. The salient economic factors that are enumerated as indicators are cash flow indicators, sales price indicators, sales market indicators, expense indicators, financing indicators, and intercompany transactions and arrangements indicators.

A foreign currency transaction is a transaction that is denominated in a currency other than the investor's functional currency. According to the accounting standard FAS 52, *denominated* means that the balance is fixed in terms of the number of units of a foreign currency regardless of changes in the exchange rate. For example, when a U.S. company buys equity shares of a company listed on the Singapore stock exchange in Singapore dollars (S$), then on purchase of the equity shares, the number of units of S$ that is payable for such purchase is fixed and it stays the same regardless of the foreign exchange rates between the US$ and S$. Hence, until the liability is settled, the U.S. company assumes the foreign exchange risk on account of the purchase of the shares. Upon payment of the liability, based on the exchange rate at that point of time, the amount in US$ terms is crystallized, resulting in realized currency gains/loss.

Translation of Foreign Currency Statements

Under the relevant accounting standards (IAS 21), foreign currency monetary items are treated differently than foreign currency non-monetary items. The essential feature of a monetary item is the right to receive or an obligation to deliver a fixed or determinable amount of units of currency. A non-monetary item does not have this right.

Examples of monetary items include the following:

- Trade receivables and payables.
- Cash dividends recognized as a liability.
- Investments in debt securities.
- Deferred taxes.
- Pension and other employee benefits to be paid in cash.
- Provisions that are to be settled in cash.

Examples of non-monetary items include:

- Prepaid amounts for goods or services.
- Deferred income.
- Investments in equity instruments.
- Inventories and other fixed assets.
- Goodwill, patents, trademarks, and other intangible assets.

It should be noted that investments in equity instruments are regarded as non-monetary items.

For assets and liabilities, the exchange rate at the balance sheet date is used to translate foreign currency statements into the functional currency. For revenues, expenses, gains, and losses, the exchange rate at the dates on which such revenue or expense is recognized is used. The accounting standard allows weighted average exchange rate to be used for translating revenues, expenses, gains, and losses where the transactions are numerous and it is found impractical to translate on a daily basis.

If an entity's functional currency is a foreign currency, there would be translation adjustments occurring as a result of the translation process that converts the financial statements into the reporting currency. Such translation adjustments should not be included in determining the net income but should be reported separately and accumulated in a separate component of equity. It is only upon the sale or upon the substantial liquidation of such investment in foreign currency that the amount accumulated in the translation adjustment component of equity should be removed from the separate component of equity and should be reported as part of the gain or loss on liquidation of the investment for the period during which the sale or liquidation takes place. However, see the accounting treatment permitted for investment companies by SOP 93-4 later in this chapter.

FX Revaluation Process

If the reporting currency is different from the trading currency, then every journal entry recorded in the previous illustration is first revalued in the reporting currency, based on the market quote available for the trade currency. This process is known as *FX revaluation*. FX revaluation is performed on all the accounting entries recorded by the investor. FX revaluation of revenues, expenses, gains, and losses at the currency exchange rate freezes the amounts in the functional currency and they do not undergo any change due to fluctuation in the FX rates at the reporting period.

FX Translation Process

The income statement and balance sheet of the investor should be prepared in the functional currency, also known as the reporting currency. Hence, on the reporting date, all the assets and liabilities of the investor that are designated in foreign currency should be converted into the functional currency based on the official FX conversion rates on the reporting date. This is achieved by the FX revaluation process. However, apart from the revaluation process, another process known as *FX translation* is required to be performed by the investor to adjust the FX rate differential between the transaction date and the reporting date with respect to all assets and liabilities. Thus, the value of assets and liabilities is adjusted for fluctuations in the exchange rate between the date on which the asset or liability is recorded in the books of account and the reporting date. For profit and loss items, the actual amount gets crystallized on the date on which the income is realized or the expense is incurred and hence does not need any further treatment.

The FX translation process is applied on all the accounts that represent an asset or a liability. The variation in the value of the asset or liability on account of fluctuation in the exchange rate is recognized as a gain or loss, and such a gain or loss is recognized as a separate component of equity, on the one hand, and on the other, the value of the asset or liability would be restated based on the exchange rate on the reporting date. However, upon realization, the same would be taken to the income statement and the actual effect of such gains would be represented in the respective cash account.

FX Revaluation Entries

All the entries recorded heretofore are initially entered in the respective trade currencies. If the functional currency is different from the trade currency, then each and every entry recorded in the trade currency should be entered again in the functional currency by converting the entries at the respective day's FX rates. In other words, for each trade currency that the investor deals with, there will be a complete set of books representing that trade currency. This includes journal entries, general ledger postings, trial balance, income statement, and balance sheet. After revaluing each and every journal entry of all the trade currencies into the functional currency, a separate set of books is prepared, again comprising all the elements previously mentioned: journal entries, general ledger postings, trial balance, income statement, and balance sheet. It should be noted that the ultimate financial reports would be prepared and presented to all the stakeholders based on the financial statements prepared in the functional currency only, as this will encompass all the transactions of the investor in all trade currencies dabbled with.

Some accountants follow the method of revaluing the income and expense entries in functional currency based on the average rate for the month under review, meaning all the entries would be consolidated and one entry passed for each item of income or expense at the end of the month. Whatever method is adopted, it should be followed consistently.

However, in this book all illustrations are worked out on the basis of revaluing every single journal entry recorded in currencies other than the functional currency at the foreign exchange rate applicable on the day of the transaction.

Let us assume, for the sake of illustration (only for this paragraph), the functional currency of Alan Kimberly, Inc., is pounds sterling and the FX rate on November 6 for US$/GBP is 0.525.

The accounting entry in the books of accounts to record the profit or loss on sale of shares is shown as follows:

Journal Entry

Date	Particulars	Debit (GBP)	Credit (GBP)
6-Nov-X1	Equity Shares, Gold Crest—Trading Account	12,075.00	
	To Realized Capital Gains/Loss—Equity Account		12,075.00
	(Being the realized gains on the sale of 1,000 Gold Crest shares)		

FX Translation Entries

After revaluing all the entries in the functional currency at the respective FX rates for the day concerned, another entry needs to be passed in the books of the functional currency. This is mainly to adjust the currency gains or losses due to the fluctuations in FX rates between the reporting date and the date of recording the original entries. FX translation entries are recorded only for the asset and liability accounts. For income and expense accounts, the amount gets crystallized on the date of passing the FX revaluation entries in the books of the functional currency.

There are fundamentally two types of FX translation entries that are recorded in the books of the functional currency. The first type represents accounting for currency gains or losses that are realized or consummated. An example of this type is the currency gains realized on the amounts payable to the broker versus the amount actually paid to the broker as recorded in the functional currency. The difference between the amount payable and the actual amount paid recorded in the functional currency represents the realized currency gains or losses. Let us call this *consummated FX translation entries.*

The second type represents accounting for currency gains or losses that are seen on the continuing assets or liabilities of the investor. An example of this type is the currency gains on the market value of the equity shares as recorded in the functional currency. This type of gain or loss is temporary in nature and will be either reversed the next day or passed on an incremental basis, meaning that it is subject to change on a daily basis depending upon the FX rates prevailing on that day. Let us call this *transient FX translation entries.*

Consummated FX Translation Entry

Let us assume the following facts: Ram acquires 1,000 shares of ACC Ltd. at INR 650 (Indian rupees) each on January 5 when the US$/INR FX rate is 42.25, through the broker Peter & Co. Let us assume there is no brokerage fee involved here. The settlement for the purchases through the National Stock Exchange, India, is made on January 7 when the US$/INR FX rate is 41.90. Functional currency for Ram is US$. Let us find out the amount for which a consummated FX translation entry needs to be passed.

The following entries will be passed by Ram in trade currency, which is INR, on acquiring the shares and for making the payment to the broker.

T-1 On Purchase of Equity Shares

Journal Entry

Date	Particulars	Debit (INR)	Credit (INR)
5-Jan-X1	Equity Shares, ACC—Trading Account	650,000.00	
	To Peter & Co. Account		650,000.00
	(Being the ACC shares bought @ INR 650 per share through the broker Peter & Co.)		

T-2 On Payment of Contracted Sum

Journal Entry

Date	Particulars	Debit (INR)	Credit (INR)
7-Jan-X1	Peter & Co. Account	650,000.00	
	To Bank Account		650,000.00
	(Being the amount paid to Peter & Co. on purchase of 1,000 ACC shares)		

The following are the revaluation entries for this exchange in functional currency, which is US$.

F-1 On Purchase of Equity Shares (T-1 @ FX Rate: 42.25)

Journal Entry

Date	Particulars	Debit (US$)	Credit (US$)
5-Jan-X1	Equity Shares, ACC—Trading Account	15,384.62	
	To Peter & Co. Account		15,384.62
	(Being the ACC shares bought @ INR 650 per share through the broker Peter & Co.)		

F-2 On Payment of Contracted Sum (T-2 @ FX Rate: 41.90)

Journal Entry

Date	Particulars	Debit (US$)	Credit (US$)
7-Jan-X1	Peter & Co. Account	15,513.13	
	To Bank Account		15,513.13
	(Being the amount paid to Peter & Co. on purchase of 1,000 ACC shares)		

Consummated FX translation entry: While the broker Peter & Co. is settled in full in trade currency, the same when recorded in functional currency looks as if Peter & Co. is paid $128.51 more than what is actually due to him. But this is due to the fluctuation in

FX rate between the date of trade and date of settlement. Hence, this amount represents realized currency loss and the consummated FX translation entry would be as follows:

F-3 Consummated FX Translation Entry to Record the Realized Currency Gains/Loss on Settlement Date

Journal Entry

Date	Particulars	Debit (US$)	Credit (US$)
7-Jan-X1	Realized Currency Gains/Loss Account	128.51	
	To Peter & Co. Account		128.51
	(Being the consummated FX translation entry passed to record the realized currency gains on settlement of the broker Peter & Co.)		

Transient FX Translation Entries

Let us assume the following facts: Ram acquires 1,000 shares of ACC Ltd. at INR 650 each on January 5 when the US$/INR FX rate is 42.25. Assume that the US$/INR FX rate on January 31, the reporting date, is 41.50, and for the sake of this example the market rate of ACC Ltd. is the same at INR 650 per share. Functional currency for Ram is US$. The following entries will be passed by Ram in trade currency, which is INR, on acquiring the shares.

T-1 On Purchase of Equity Shares

Journal Entry

Date	Particulars	Debit (INR)	Credit (INR)
5-Jan-X1	Equity Shares, ACC—Trading Account	650,000.00	
	To Peter & Co. Account		650,000.00
	(Being the ACC shares bought @ INR 650 per share through the broker Peter & Co.)		

T-2 On Valuation of Shares Based on the Market Rate

No entry is required as there is no change in the value of the shares held. It is the same as the cost of acquisition of the shares.

The following are the revaluation entries for the preceding example in functional currency, which is US$.

F-1 On Purchase of Equity Shares (T-1 @ FX Rate: 42.25)

Journal Entry

Date	Particulars	Debit (US$)	Credit (US$)
5-Jan-X1	Equity Shares, ACC—Trading Account	15,384.62	
	To Peter & Co. Account		15,384.62
	(Being the ACC shares bought @ INR 650 per share through the broker Peter & Co.)		

F-2 On Valuation of Shares Based on the Market Rate (T-2 @ FX Rate: 41.50)

No entry is required as there is no change in the value of the shares held. It is the same as the cost of acquisition of the shares. There is no FX revaluation entry passed as there is no original entry in trade currency for mark-to-market valuation. However, in the functional currency, there is a change in the market value for which FX translation entry is passed, which is illustrated next.

Transient FX translation entry: While the market value of the shares bought on January 5 is the same as the cost of acquisition, in dollar terms the value is different and hence a transient FX translation entry should be recorded on January 31. This is called *transient entry* as either the entry will be reversed the next day or, on a subsequent day, when such an entry is passed, it will be done on an incremental basis.

The market value of the shares in functional currency is INR 650,000/41.50 = $15,662.65. Hence, the difference between this market value and the cost of acquisition in US$ terms, namely 15,384.62, is $278.04 and will be recorded as unrealized FX gains. The accounting entry is as follows:

F-3 Transient FX Translation Entry to Record the Unrealized Currency Gains or Losses on Valuation Date

Journal Entry

Date	Particulars	Debit (US$)	Credit (US$)
31-Jan-X1	Equity Shares, ACC—Trading Account	278.04	
	To Unrealized Currency Gains/Loss—Equity Account		278.04
	(Being the transient FX translation entry passed to record the unrealized currency gains on valuation date)		

TRADE DATE ACCOUNTING VERSUS SETTLEMENT DATE ACCOUNTING

Under the trade date accounting method, both the asset and the liability for the asset purchased are recognized on the date of trade, and the payable is derecognized once the payment is made. Under the settlement date accounting method, the entire transaction is recognized only on the date of settlement. While FAS 115 is silent regarding the date on which the transaction should be recorded, the other levels of U.S. GAAP literature require trade date accounting to be followed for regular-way securities contracts, especially for broker-dealers and investment companies. For regular-way contracts, the

International Accounting Standards Board (IASB) gives the option to follow either trade date accounting or settlement date accounting, provided that one is followed consistently for purchases and sales of financial assets in the same category. However, the changes in the fair value of the asset should be treated properly depending upon the classification of the asset acquired.

Trade Date Accounting

When an asset is purchased, in trade date accounting, the asset is recognized and brought into the books of account on the date of trade and a corresponding liability is established. The liability is knocked off when the settlement of the liability happens.

When the asset purchased is in a foreign currency, it leads to a little more complication. The asset is recognized in the functional currency in which the reporting is made, on the basis of the foreign exchange rate that prevails on the date of trade. The corresponding liability is also created equivalent to the asset purchased. However, when the settlement is done after a few days, the foreign exchange rate is likely to be different from the rate at which the asset was converted. Hence, when recording the settlement event in the functional currency, the liability would appear to be either overpaid or underpaid. This is dealt with by passing an appropriate FX translation entry known as *consummated FX translation entry*, previously discussed in this chapter.

Trade Date Accounting

Date	Account Details	Held for Trading	Available for Sale
Trade date	Financial asset	Recorded at historical cost	Recorded at historical cost
	Liability—payable for acquiring the asset	Recorded at historical cost	Recorded at historical cost
Reporting date	Financial asset	Recorded at the fair value (market value)	Recorded at the fair value (market value)
	Liability—payable for acquiring the asset	Recorded at historical cost	Recorded at historical cost
	Changes in the fair value to the financial asset	Taken to the retained earnings through profit and loss account	Taken to the equity through the other comprehensive income
Settlement date	Financial asset	Recorded at the fair value (market value)	Recorded at the fair value (market value)
	Liability—payable for acquiring the asset	Derecognized and does not appear since liability is settled	Derecognized and does not appear since liability is settled
	Changes in the fair value to the financial asset	Taken to the retained earnings through profit and loss account	Taken to the equity through the other comprehensive income

Settlement Date Accounting

Following settlement date accounting, the asset as well as the liability are recognized on the settlement date. Here the asset gets recorded only at the value at which it is actually settled. The difference between the actual cost of acquisition for the investment and the value at which it is recorded in the books of accounts is taken as realized gains on the date of acquisition itself. If the asset is held for trading, then it is taken to the profit and loss account directly, whereas if it is an available-for-sale asset, then it is taken directly to the equity account as other comprehensive income.

Even if the asset happens to be in foreign currency, since the asset is recorded only on the date of settlement, the revaluation entry in the functional currency is recorded only at the rate at which it actually gets settled and hence there is no necessity to record any FX translation entries in this case.

Settlement Date Accounting

Date	Account Details	Held for Trading	Available for Sale
Trade date	Financial asset	No entry—asset not recognized	No entry—asset not recognized
	Liability—payable for acquiring the asset	No entry—liability also not recognized	No entry—liability also not recognized
Reporting date	Financial asset	No entry—asset not recognized	No entry—asset not recognized
	Liability—payable for acquiring the asset	No entry—liability also not recognized	No entry—liability also not recognized
	Changes in the fair value to the financial asset	Taken to the retained earnings through profit and loss account	Taken to the equity through the other comprehensive income
Settlement date	Financial asset	Recorded at the fair value (market value)	Recorded at the fair value (market value)
	Liability—payable for acquiring the asset	Historical contracted amount paid on settlement date—no balance due on any date	Historical contracted amount paid on settlement date—no balance due on any date
	Changes in the fair value to the financial asset	Taken to the retained earnings through profit and loss account	Taken to the equity through the other comprehensive income

Broker-dealers that use the trade date basis of record keeping are in compliance with the AICPA Guide for Audits of Brokers and Dealers in Securities, while broker-dealers that use the settlement date basis of recordkeeping are in compliance with the Guide only if the difference between trade date and settlement date accounting is not material.

A broker-dealer must have a consistent policy of reflecting all transactions either on a trade date or a settlement date basis and must compute its net capital on the same basis as it uses in recording its transactions.

However, if settlement date accounting is used, and there is a "material difference" between trade date accounting, the net capital computation must reflect the trade date position for proprietary positions, and if there is a material difference on more than an occasional basis (i.e., twice in a six-month period), trade date accounting should probably be used on a consistent basis.

SEC Letter to AICPA, April 23, 1986

DISTINCTION BETWEEN CAPITAL GAINS AND CURRENCY GAINS

When the trade currency is different from the functional currency, then the total unrealized gains or loss consists of two components: capital gains and currency gains. The U.S. GAAP Statement of Position for investment companies pertaining to the disclosure and treatment of these two components in relation to investment companies is given in the accompanying box, with a suitable illustration.

U.S. GAAP Statement of Position (SOP 93-4) for Investment Companies

The change in value of an investment in respect of an asset denominated in a foreign currency on the valuation date from the original value at which it is recorded in the books of account in functional currency has two components, namely the capital gains/loss due to change in the market rate of the asset, and currency gains/loss due to change in the foreign exchange rate. Investment companies can either choose to combine these two elements for investment transactions or disclose the currency gains/loss due to change in the FX rate separately. According to the SOP, it is not mandatory to show them separately, even though it indicates that such separate reporting would provide valuable information to the users of the financial statements.

A. Net unrealized gains in functional currency:
(Market value in foreign currency × Valuation date spot rate)
− (Cost in foreign currency × Transaction date spot rate)

B. Unrealized capital gains in functional currency:
(Market value in foreign currency − Cost in foreign currency)
× (Valuation date spot rate)

C. Unrealized currency gains in functional currency:
(Cost in foreign currency × Valuation date spot rate)
− (Cost in foreign currency × Transaction date spot rate)

A should be equal to B + C.

Example

New Century Indian Fund acquired 1,000 shares of Bajaj Auto at INR 2,700 per share when the US$/INR was 45. The market rate of Bajaj Auto on valuation date was INR 3,000 and the exchange rate was 41. Find out the capital and currency gains on reporting date.

A. Net unrealized gains in functional currency:
(Market value in foreign currency × Valuation date spot rate)
− (Cost in foreign currency × Transaction date spot rate)
= [3,000,000 × (100/45)] − [2,700,000 × (100/41)] − [2,700,000 × (100/45)]
= \$66,666.67 − 65,853.67 = \$813 (Gain)

B. Unrealized capital gains in functional currency:
(Market value in foreign currency − Cost in foreign currency)
× (Valuation date spot rate)
= [(3,000,000 − 2,700,000) × (100/41)]
= $7,317.07 (Gain)

C. Unrealized currency gains in functional currency:
(Cost in foreign currency × Valuation date spot rate)
− (Cost in foreign currency × Transaction date spot rate)
= [3,000,000 × (100/41)] − [3,000,000 × (100/45)]
= $73,170.73 − 66,666.67 = $6,504.06 (Loss)

A should be equal to B + C.

Here the capital gains amounting to $7,317.07 is reduced by adverse currency movement amounting to $6,504.06, resulting in net unrealized gains of just $813.

Illustration: Long Equity, Trade Currency JPY

Japan Opportunities Fund traded in DoCoMo shares on the Tokyo Stock Exchange through Yoshio & Co. brokers and the details are as follows:

Trade Details

Date	Product	Quantity	Rate (JPY)	B/S	Brokerage (JPY)
5-Jan-X1	DoCoMo	1,000	5,600	B	16,800
15-Jan-X1	DoCoMo	1,000	5,000	B	16,800
5-Feb-X1	DoCoMo	1,700	5,200	S	20,920

Other Details

Settlement: T + 3

Liquidation Method

First in first out (FIFO)

Market Rate of DoCoMo Shares in JPY

January 31: 5,500
February 28: 5,800
March 31: 5,000

FX Rate, US$/JPY

January 5: 116.00
January 8: 114.00
January 15: 118.00
January 18: 120.00
January 31:119.00
February 5: 115.00
February 8: 111.00
February 28:116.00
March 31: 118.00

Functional Currency

US$

Prepare

Journal entries, general ledgers, trial balance, income statement, and balance sheet.

Solution—Long Equity Shares, Trade Currency JPY

T-1 On Purchase of Equity Shares and Brokerage

Journal Entry

Date	Particulars	Debit (JPY)	Credit (JPY)
5-Jan-X1	Investments—Equity Shares—Trading Account	5,600,000	
	To Yoshio & Co. Account		5,600,000
	(Being 1,000 shares bought @ 5,600 per share through the broker, Yoshio & Co.)		
5-Jan-X1	Investments—Equity Shares—Trading Account	16,800	
	To Yoshio & Co. Account		16,800
	(Being the brokerage fee payable to Yoshio & Co. on purchase of 1,000 shares)		

T-2 On Payment of Contracted Sum

Journal Entry

Date	Particulars	Debit (JPY)	Credit (JPY)
8-Jan-X1	Yoshio & Co. Account	5,616,800	
	To Bank Account		5,616,800
	(Being the amount paid to the broker on purchase of 1,000 shares together with the brokerage fee)		

T-3 On Purchase of Equity Shares and Brokerage

Journal Entry

Date	Particulars	Debit (JPY)	Credit (JPY)
15-Jan-X1	Investments—Equity Shares—Trading Account	5,000,000	
	To Yoshio & Co. Account		5,000,000
	(Being 1,000 shares bought @ 5,000 per share through the broker, Yoshio & Co.)		
15-Jan-X1	Investments—Equity Shares—Trading Account	16,800	
	To Yoshio & Co. Account		16,800
	(Being the brokerage fee payable to Yoshio & Co. on purchase of 1,000 shares)		

T-4 On Payment of Contracted Sum

Journal Entry

Date	Particulars	Debit (JPY)	Credit (JPY)
18-Jan-X1	Yoshio & Co. Account	5,016,800	
	To Bank Account		5,016,800
	(Being the amount paid to the broker on purchase of 1,000 shares and the brokerage fee)		

T-5 Mark-to-market End of Reporting Period

The total long position adds up to 2,000 shares and the market value of the shares is compared with the original cost of acquisition including brokerage to arrive at the mark-to-market. The market rate at the end of the reporting period is more than the cost of acquisition, resulting in mark-to-market gains, which is reflected as an increase in the value of the investments. Since the shares are held in the *trading* category, the gains are taken to the profit and loss account.

Mark-to-market at end of reporting period: 31 Jan X1	JPY
(a) Cost of acquisition of 1,000 shares @ JPY 5,600 including brokerage	5,616,800
(b) Cost of acquisition of 1,000 shares @ JPY 5,000 including brokerage	5,016,800
(c) Total cost of acquisition	10,633,600
(d) Market value at the end of reporting period	11,000,000
(e) Unrealized gains (d) − (c)	366,400

Journal Entry

Date	Particulars	Debit (JPY)	Credit (JPY)
31-Jan-X1	Investments—Equity Shares—Trading Account	366,400	
	To Unrealized Capital Gains/Loss—Equity Shares—Trading Account		366,400
	(Being unrealized gains on purchase of equity shares)		

T-6 Reversal of Mark-to-market Entry

Journal Entry

Date	Particulars	Debit (JPY)	Credit (JPY)
1-Feb-X1	Unrealized Capital Gains/Loss—Equity Shares—Trading Account	366,400	
	To Investments—Equity Shares—Trading Account		366,400
	(Being the reversal of mark-to-market on equity shares)		

T-7 On Sale of Shares and Brokerage

Journal Entry

Date	Particulars	Debit (JPY)	Credit (JPY)
5-Feb-X1	Yoshio & Co. Account	8,840,000	
	To Investments—Equity Shares—Trading Account		8,840,000
	(Being 1,700 shares sold @ JPY 5,200 per share through the broker, Yoshio & Co.)		
5-Feb-X1	Investments—Equity Shares—Trading Account	20,920	
	To Yoshio & Co. Account		20,920
	(Being the brokerage payable to Yoshio & Co. on sale of 1,700 shares)		

T-8 Recording the Profit/Loss on Sale of Shares

The liquidation methodology is first in, first out (FIFO); hence, the cost of acquisition of 1,700 shares is first arrived at and compared with the net sales realization to arrive at the realized gains on liquidation.

Calculation of capital gains	**JPY**
(a) Net sale consideration of 1,700 shares after brokerage	8,819,080
(b) Cost of acquisition of 1,000 shares including brokerage	5,616,800
(c) Proportionate cost of acquisition of 700 shares [(5,016,800 × 700) / 1,000]	3,511,760
(d) Total cost of acquisition of 1,700 shares	9,128,560
(e) Realized loss = (a) − (d)	**(309,480)**

Journal Entry

Date	Particulars	Debit (JPY)	Credit (JPY)
5-Feb-X1	Realized Capital Gains/Loss Equity—Trading Account	309,480	
	To Investments—Equity Shares—Trading Account		309,480
	(Being the loss on the sale of 1,700 shares)		

T-9 On Receipt of Contracted Sum

Journal Entry

Date	Particulars	Debit (JPY)	Credit (JPY)
8-Feb-X1	Bank Account	8,819,080	
	To Yoshio & Co. Account		8,819,080
	(Being the receipt of funds on sale of 1,500 shares)		

T-10 Mark-to-market at End of Reporting Period

Mark-to-market at end of reporting period: 28-Feb-X1	**JPY**
(a) Market value of 300 shares @ 5,800 on 28-Feb-X1	1,740,000
(b) Cost of acquisition of 300 shares @ 5,016.80 on 15-Jan-X1	1,505,040
(c) Unrealized gains = (a) – (b)	234,960

Journal Entry

Date	Particulars	Debit (JPY)	Credit (JPY)
28-Feb-X1	Investments—Equity Shares—Trading Account	234,960	
	To Unrealized Capital Gains/Loss—Equity Shares—Trading Account		234,960
	(Being unrealized gains on 300 equity shares)		

T-11 Reversal of Mark-to-market Entry

Journal Entry

Date	Particulars	Debit (JPY)	Credit (JPY)
1-Mar -X1	Unrealized Capital Gains/Loss—Equity Shares—Trading Account	234,960	
	To Investments—Equity Shares—Trading Account		234,960
	(Being the reversal of mark-to-market entry on equity shares)		

T-12 Mark-to-market at End of Reporting Period

Mark-to-market at end of reporting period: 31-Mar-X1	**JPY**
(a) Market value of 300 shares @ 5,000 on 31-Mar-X1	1,500,000
(b) Cost of acquisition of 300 shares @ 5,016.80 on 15-Jan-X1	1,505,040
(c) Unrealized loss = (a) – (b)	(5,040)

Journal Entry

Date	Particulars	Debit (JPY)	Credit (JPY)
31-Mar-X1	Unrealized Capital Gains/Loss—Equity Shares—Trading Account	5,040	
	To Investments—Equity Shares—Trading Account		5,040
	(Being unrealized gains on 300 equity shares)		

General Ledger Accounts

Investments—Equity Shares—Trading Account

Date	Particulars	Debit (JPY)	Date	Particulars	Credit (JPY)
5-Jan-X1	To Yoshio & Co. Account	5,600,000			
5-Jan-X1	To Yoshio & Co. Account	16,800			
15-Jan-X1	To Yoshio & Co. Account	5,000,000			
15-Jan-X1	To Yoshio & Co. Account	16,800			
31-Jan-X1	To Unrealized Capital Gains/ Loss—Equity Shares—Trading Account	366,400			
			1-Feb-X1	By Unrealized Capital Gains/ Loss—Equity Shares—Trading Account	366,400
			5-Feb-X1	By Realized Capital Gains/ Loss—Equity—Trading Account	309,480
			5-Feb-X1	By Yoshio & Co. Account	8,840,000
5-Feb-X1	To Yoshio & Co. Account	20,920			
28-Feb-X1	To Unrealized Capital Gains/ Loss—Equity Shares—Trading Account	234,960			
			1-Mar-X1	By Unrealized Capital Gains/ Loss—Equity Shares—Trading Account	234,960
			31-Mar-X1	By Unrealized Capital Gains/ Loss—Equity Shares—Trading Account	5,040
			31-Mar-X1	By Balance	1,500,000
31-Mar-X1	Total	**11,255,880**	31-Mar-X1	Total	**11,255,880**
31-Mar-X1	To Balance	1,500,000			

Realized Capital Gains/Loss Equity—Trading Account

Date	Particulars	Debit (JPY)	Date	Particulars	Credit (JPY)
5-Feb-X1	To Investments—Equity Shares—Trading Account	309,480			
			31-Mar-X1	By Balance	309,480
31-Mar-X1	Total	**309,480**	31-Mar-X1	Total	**309,480**
31-Mar-X1	To Balance	309,480			

Unrealized Capital Gains/Loss—Equity Shares—Trading Account

Date	Particulars	Debit (JPY)	Date	Particulars	Credit (JPY)
			31-Jan-X1	By Investments—Equity Shares—Trading Account	366,400
1-Feb-X1	To Investments—Equity Shares—Trading Account	366,400			
			28-Feb-X1	By Investments—Equity Shares—Trading Account	234,960
1-Mar-X1	To Investments—Equity Shares—Trading Account	234,960			
31-Mar-X1	To Investments—Equity Shares—Trading Account	5,040			
			31-Mar-X1	By Balance	5,040
31-Mar-X1	Total	**606,400**	31-Mar-X1	Total	**606,400**
31-Mar-X1	To Balance	5,040			

Yoshio & Co. Account

Date	Particulars	Debit (JPY)	Date	Particulars	Credit (JPY)
			5-Jan-X1	By Investments—Equity Shares—Trading Account	5,600,000
			5-Jan-X1	By Investments—Equity Shares—Trading Account	16,800
8-Jan-X1	To Bank Account	5,616,800			
			15-Jan-X1	By Investments—Equity Shares—Trading Account	5,000,000
			15-Jan-X1	By Investments—Equity Shares—Trading Account	16,800
18-Jan-X1	To Bank Account	5,016,800			

Yoshio & Co. Account (*Cont'd*)

Date	Particulars	Debit (JPY)	Date	Particulars	Credit (JPY)
			5-Feb-X1	By Investments—Equity Shares—Trading Account	20,920
5-Feb-X1	To Investments—Equity Shares—Trading Account	8,840,000			
			8-Feb-X1	By Bank	8,819,080
31-Mar-X1	Total	**19,473,600**	31-Mar-X1	Total	**19,473,600**

Bank Account

Date	Particulars	Debit (JPY)	Date	Particulars	Credit (JPY)
			8-Jan-X1	By Yoshio & Co. Account	5,616,800
			18-Jan-X1	By Yoshio & Co. Account	5,016,800
8-Feb-X1	To Yoshio & Co. Account	8,819,080			
31-Mar-X1	To Balance	1,814,520			
31-Mar-X1	Total	**10,633,600**	31-Mar-X1	Total	**10,633,600**
			31-Mar-X1	By Balance	1,814,520

Trial Balance

As of 31-Mar-X1 (JPY)

Particulars	Debit	Credit
Current Assets		
Bank Account		1,814,520
Investments		
Investments—Equity Shares—Trading Account	1,500,000	
Direct Income		
Realized Capital Gains/Loss Equity—Trading Account	309,480	
Unrealized Capital Gains/Loss—Equity Shares—Trading Account	5,040	
Total	**1,814,520**	**1,814,520**

Income Statement

For the period ending 31-Mar-X1

Expenses	JPY	Income	JPY
Direct Expenses			
Realized Capital Gains/Loss Equity Shares—Trading Account	309,480		
Unrealized Capital Gains/Loss—Equity Shares—Trading Account	5,040	Net Loss Carryover	314,520
Total	**314,520**	Total	**314,520**

Balance Sheet

As of 31-Mar-X1

Liabilities	JPY	Assets	JPY
Capital Account	Nil	**Investments**	
Current Liabilities		Investments—Equity Shares—Trading Account	1,500,000
Bank Account	1,814,520	**Current Assets**	Nil
		Profit & Loss Account	
		Opening Balance	Nil
		Current Period	314,520
Total	**1,814,520**	Total	**1,814,520**

Long Equity Shares, Functional Currency US$

The following are the FX revaluation entries in the functional currency converted at the respective FX rate, which is given within parenthesis. FX translation entries are clearly specified, indicating whether each is a consummated FX translation entry or a transient FX translation entry.

F-1 On Purchase of Equity Shares and Brokerage (T-1 @ FX Rate: 116.00)

Journal Entry

Date	Particulars	Debit (US$)	Credit (US$)
5-Jan-X1	Investments—Equity Shares—Trading Account	48,275.86	
	To Yoshio & Co. Account		48,275.86
	(Being 1,000 shares bought @ JPY 5,600 per share through the broker—Yoshio & Co.)		
5-Jan-X1	Investments—Equity Shares—Trading	144.83	
	To Yoshio & Co. Account		144.83
	(Being the brokerage payable to Yoshio & Co. on purchase of 1,000 shares)		

F-2 On Payment of Contracted Sum (T-2 @ FX Rate: 114.00)

Journal Entry

Date	Particulars	Debit (US$)	Credit (US$)
8-Jan-X1	Yoshio & Co. Account	49,270.18	
	To Bank Account		49,270.18
	(Being amount paid to the broker on purchase of 1,000 shares together with the brokerage)		

F-3 Recording the Currency Gains/Loss on Settlement of Broker (Consummated FX Translation Entry)

The settlement amount when converted into US$ based on the FX rate on the date of settlement results in a different amount than the contracted amount in US$ terms. This represents the currency gains or loss and is taken directly to the profit and loss account. If this FX translation entry is not passed, then the liability account of the broker will continue to have a balance even though the broker is settled in full in the respective local currency.

Currency gains/loss on settlement date: 08-Jan-X1	**US$**
(a) Purchase price including brokerage as of 05-Jan-X1	48,420.69
(b) Settlement amount in US$ terms on 8-Jan-X1	49,270.18
(c) Realized currency loss on settlement = (a) − (b)	**(849.49)**

Journal Entry

Date	Particulars	Debit (US$)	Credit (US$)
8-Jan-X1	Realized Currency Gains/Loss Equity—Trading Account	849.49	
	To Yoshio & Co. Account		849.49
	(Being the realized currency loss on settlement)		

F-4 On Purchase of Equity Shares and Brokerage (T-3 @ FX Rate: 118.00)

Journal Entry

Date	Particulars	Debit (US$)	Credit (US$)
15-Jan-X1	Investments—Equity Shares—Trading Account	42,372.88	
	To Yoshio & Co. Account		42,372.88
	(Being 1,000 shares bought @ 5,000 per share through the broker—Yoshio & Co.)		
15-Jan-X1	Investments—Equity Shares—Trading Account	142.37	
	To Yoshio & Co. Account		142.37
	(Being the brokerage payable to Yoshio & Co. on purchase of 1,000 shares)		

F-5 Payment of Contracted Sum (T-4 @ FX Rate: 120.00)

Journal Entry

Date	Particulars	Debit (US$)	Credit (US$)
18-Jan-X1	Yoshio & Co. Account	41,806.67	
	To Bank Account		41,806.67
	(Being the payment made to the broker on purchase of 1,000 shares together with the brokerage)		

F-6 On Recording Currency Gains/Loss on Settlement to Broker (Consummated FX Translation Entry)

The settlement amount when converted into US$ based on the FX rate on the date of settlement results in a different amount than the contracted amount in US$ terms. This represents the currency gains or loss and is taken directly to the profit and loss account. If this FX translation entry is not passed, then the liability account of the broker will continue to have a balance even though the broker is settled in full in the respective local currency.

Currency gains/loss on settlement date: 18-Jan-X1	US$
(a) Purchase price including brokerage as of 15-Jan-X1	42,515.25
(b) Settlement amount to the broker in US$ terms on 18-Jan-X1	41,806.67
(c) Realized currency gains on settlement = (a) − (b)	**708.58**

Journal Entry

Date	Particulars	Debit (US$)	Credit (US$)
18-Jan-X1	Yoshio & Co. Account	708.58	
	To Realized Currency Gains/Loss Account		708.58
	(Being the realized currency gains on settlement)		

F-7 Mark-to-market at End of Reporting Period (T-5 @ FX Rate: 119.00)

Mark-to-market at end of reporting period: 31-Jan-X1	JPY	US$
(a) Market value of 2,000 shares @ 5,500	11,000,000	92,436.97
(b) Cost of acquisition of 2,000 shares	10,633,600	89,357.98
(c) Mark-to-market = (a) − (b)		3,078.99

Journal Entry

Date	Particulars	Debit (US$)	Credit (US$)
31-Jan-X1	Investments—Equity Shares—Trading Account	3,078.99	
	To Unrealized Capital Gains/Loss—Equity Shares—Trading Account		3,078.99
	(Being the unrealized loss on purchase of equity shares)		

F-8 Reversal of Mark-to-market Entry (T-6 @ FX Rate: 119.00)

Journal Entry

Date	Particulars	Debit (US$)	Credit (US$)
1-Feb-X1	Unrealized Capital Gains/Loss—Equity Shares—Trading Account	3,078.99	
	To Investments—Equity Shares—Trading Account		3,078.99
	(Being the reversal of mark-to-market on equity shares)		

F-9 Currency Gains/Loss—FX (Transient FX Translation Entry)

Currency gains/loss on valuation date: 31-Jan-X1	US$
(a) Market value in US$ (11,000,000 JPY @ 119.00)	92,436.97
(b) Cost of acquisition of 1,000 shares including brokerage ($48,275.86 + $144.83)	48,420.69
(c) Cost of acquisition of 1,000 shares including brokerage ($42,372.88 + $142.37)	42,515.25
(d) Mark-to-market in US$ = (a) − (b + c)	1,501.03
(e) Mark-to-market as of 31-Jan-X1 in US$	3,078.99
(f) Currency loss = (d) − (e)	**(1,577.96)**

Journal Entry

Date	Particulars	Debit (US$)	Credit (US$)
31-Jan-X1	Unrealized Currency Gains/Loss Equity—Trading Account	1,577.96	
	To Investments—Equity Shares—Trading Account		1,577.96
	(Being the unrealized currency gains/loss)		

F-10 Reversal of Mark-to-market Entry

Journal Entry

Date	Particulars	Debit (US$)	Credit (US$)
1-Feb-X1	Investments—Equity Shares—Trading Account	1,577.96	
	To Unrealized Currency Gains/Loss Equity—Trading Account		1,577.96
	(Being the unrealized currency gains/loss)		

F-11 Currency Gains/Loss—Bank FX (Transient FX translation entry)

Date	Particulars	JPY	FX Rate	US$
08-Jan-X1	Purchase price including brokerage as of 5-Jan-X1	(5,616,800.00)	114	(49,270.18)
18-Jan-X1	Purchase price including brokerage as of 15-Jan-X1	(5,016,800.00)	120	(41,806.67)
31-Jan-X1	Net balance	(10,633,600.00)		(91,076.85)
	Net balance at current FX rate	(10,633,600.00)	119	(89,357.98)
	FX translation on Bank account			**1,718.87**

Journal Entry

Date	Particulars	Debit (US$)	Credit (US$)
31-Jan-X1	Bank Account	1,718.87	
	To Unrealized Currency Gain/Loss – Bank Account		1,718.87
	(Being the unrealized currency gains/loss on Bank)		

F-12 On Sale of Shares and Brokerage (T-7 @ FX Rate: 115.00)

Journal Entry

Date	Particulars	Debit (US$)	Credit (US$)
5-Feb-X1	Yoshio & Co. Account	76,869.56	
	To Investments—Equity Shares—Trading Account		76,869.56
	(Being 1,700 shares sold @ 5,200 per share through the broker Yoshio & Co.)		
5-Feb-X1	Investments—Equity Shares—Trading Account	181.91	
	To Yoshio & Co. Account		181.91
	(Being the brokerage payable to Yoshio & Co. on sale of 1,700 shares)		

F-13 On Recording the Profit/Loss on Sale of Shares (T-8 @ FX Rate: 115.00)

Realized loss on sale	JPY	US$
(a) Net realization of 1,700 shares after brokerage	8,819,080	76,687.65
(b) Cost of acquisition of 1,700 shares	9,128,560	79,378.78
(c) Realized loss in US$ = (a) – (b)	**(309,480)**	**(2,691.13)**

Journal Entry

Date	Particulars	Debit (US$)	Credit (US$)
5-Feb-X1	Realized Capital Gains/Loss Equity—Trading Account	2,691.13	
	To Investments—Equity Shares—Trading Account		2,691.13
	(Being the loss on the sale of 1,700 shares)		

F-14 On Recording Realized Currency Gains/Loss on Liquidation (Consummated FX Translation Entry)

The total realized loss in US$ terms on this liquidation amounts to $1,493.72. Even though we are able to arrive at this number directly by subtracting the cost of sales from the net sale proceeds, there is no direct journal entry passed for this amount. Instead, the capital loss amounting to US$2,691.13 is accounted for and, due to favorable FX movement, the realized currency gain is accounted for separately, amounting to US$1,197.41. Adding these together results in a net realized loss of $1,493.72.

Currency gains/loss on liquidation	JPY	US$
(a) Cost of sales in US$ based on FX rate on date of sale @ 115	9,128,560.00	79,378.78
(b) Cost of sales in US$ based on FX rate on date of purchase ($48,420.69 + $29,760.68)		78,181.37
(c) Realized currency gains on liquidation = (a) − (b)		**1,197.41**

This calculation can also be counter-checked with the following table where the total capital loss is first arrived at, and from that the realized capital loss component is subtracted.

Currency gains/loss on liquidation	US$
(a) Sale proceeds in US$ of 1,700 shares	76,687.65
(b) Cost of sales in US$ of 1,700 shares ($48,420.69 + $29,760.68)	78,181.37
(c) Total loss in US$ = (a) − (b) (capital loss + currency gains)	(1,493.72)
(d) Realized capital loss in JPY converted to US$	(2,691.13)
(e) Realized currency gains on liquidation = (c) − (d)	**1,197.41**

Journal Entry

Date	Particulars	Debit (US$)	Credit (US$)
5-Feb-X1	Investments—Equity Shares—Trading Account	1,197.41	
	To Realized Currency Gains/Loss Account		1,197.41
	(Being the realized currency gains on liquidation)		

F-15 On Receipt of the Contracted Sum (T-9 @ FX Rate: 111.00)

Journal Entry

Date	Particulars	Debit (US$)	Credit (US$)
8-Feb-X1	Bank Account	79,451.17	
	To Yoshio & Co. Account		79,451.17
	(Being the receipt of funds on sale of 1,500 shares)		

F-16 Currency Gains/Loss on Settlement from Broker (Consummated FX Translation Entry)

Currency gains/loss on settlement date: 08-Feb-X1	US$
(a) Sale price after brokerage as of 5-Feb-X1	76,687.65
(b) Amount received from broker in US$ terms on 8-Feb-X1	79,451.17
(c) Currency gains on settlement = (b) − (a)	**2,763.52**

Journal Entry

Date	Particulars	Debit (US$)	Credit (US$)
8-Feb-X1	Yoshio & Co. Account	2,763.52	
	To Realized Currency Gains/Loss Account		2,763.52
	(Being the realized currency gains on settlement)		

F-17 Mark-to-market at End of Reporting Period (T-10 @ FX Rate: 116.00)

Mark-to-market at end of reporting period: 28-Feb-X1	JPY	US$
(a) Market value of 300 shares on 28-Feb-X1	1,740,000.00	15,000.00
(b) Cost of acquisition of 300 shares	1,505,040.00	12,974.48
(c) Mark-to-market = (a) − (b)	**234,960.00**	**2,025.52**

Journal Entry

Date	Particulars	Debit (US$)	Credit (US$)
28-Feb-X1	Investments—Equity Shares—Trading Account	2,025.52	
	To Unrealized Capital Gains/Loss—Equity Shares—Trading Account		2,025.52
	(Being the unrealized gains on 300 equity shares)		

F-18 Reversal of Mark-to-market Entry (T-11 @ FX Rate: 116.00)

Journal Entry

Date	Particulars	Debit (US$)	Credit (US$)
1-Mar-X1	Unrealized Capital Gains/Loss—Equity Shares—Trading Account	2,025.52	
	To Investments—Equity Shares—Trading Account		2,025.52
	(Being the reversal of mark-to-market on equity shares)		

F-19 Currency Gains/Loss—FX (Transient FX Translation Entry)

Currency gains/loss on 28-Feb-X1	US$
(a) Market value in US$ (JPY 1,740,000 @ 116.00)	15,000.00
(b) Cost of acquisition of 300 shares in US$ terms	12,754.58
(c) Mark-to-market gains in US$ = (a) − (b)	2,245.42
(d) Mark-to-market as of 28-Feb-X1 in US$	2,025.52
(e) Unrealized currency gains = (c) − (d)	219.90

Journal Entry

Date	Particulars	Debit (US$)	Credit (US$)
28-Feb-X1	Investments—Equity Shares—Trading Account	219.90	
	To Unrealized Currency Gains/Loss Equity—Trading Account		219.90
	(Being the unrealized currency gains/loss)		

F-20 Reversal of Mark-to-market Entry

Journal Entry

Date	Particulars	Debit (US$)	Credit (US$)
1-Mar-X1	Unrealized Currency Gains/Loss Equity—Trading Account	219.90	
	To Investments—Equity Shares—Trading Account		219.90
	(Being the reversal of unrealized currency gains/loss on equity shares)		

F-21 Currency Gains/Loss—Bank FX (Transient FX translation entry)

Date	Particulars	JPY	FX Rate	US$
	Opening Balance	(10,633,600.00)		(89,357.98)
8-Feb-X1	Sell price including brokerage as of 5-Feb-X1	8,819,080.00	111.00	79,451.17
28-Feb-X1	Net balance	(1,814,520.00)		(9,906.81)
	Net balance at current FX rate	(1,814,520.00)	116.00	(15,642.41)
	FX translation on Bank account			**5,735.60**

Journal Entry

Date	Particulars	Debit (US$)	Credit (US$)
28-Feb-X1	Unrealized Currency Gain/Loss—Bank Account	5,735.60	
	To Bank Account		5,735.60
	(Being the unrealized currency gains/loss on Bank)		

F-22 Mark-to-market at End of Reporting Period (T-12 @ FX Rate: 118.00)

Mark-to-market at end of reporting period: 31-Mar-X1	**US$**
(a) Market value of 300 shares on 31-Mar-X1	12,711.86
(b) Cost of acquisition of 300 shares	12,754.58
(c) Mark-to-market loss = (a) − (b)	**(42.71)**

Journal Entry

Date	Particulars	Debit (US$)	Credit (US$)
31-Mar-X1	Unrealized Capital Gains/Loss—Equity Shares—Trading Account	42.71	
	To Investments—Equity Shares—Trading Account		42.71
	(Being the unrealized loss on 300 equity shares)		

F-23 Currency Gains/Loss—Bank FX (Transient FX translation entry)

Date	Particulars	JPY	FX Rate	US$
	Opening Balance	(1,814,520.00)		(15,642.41)
31-Mar-X1	Net balance	(1,814,520.00)		(15,642.41)
	Net balance at current FX rate	(1,814,520.00)	118.00	(15,377.29)
	FX translation on Bank account			**265.12**

Journal Entry

Date	Particulars	Debit (US$)	Credit (US$)
31-Mar-X1	Bank Account	265.12	
	To Unrealized Currency Gain/Loss—Bank Account		265.12
	(Being the unrealized currency gains/loss on Bank)		

General Ledger Accounts

Investments—Equity Shares—Trading Account

Date	Particulars	Debit (US$)	Date	Particulars	Credit (US$)
5-Jan-X1	To Yoshio & Co. Account	48,275.86			
5-Jan-X1	To Yoshio & Co. Account	144.83			
15-Jan-X1	To Yoshio & Co. Account	42,372.88			
15-Jan-X1	To Yoshio & Co. Account	142.37			
31-Jan-X1	To Unrealized Capital Gains/Loss—Equity Shares—Trading Account	3,078.99			
			31-Jan-X1	By Unrealized Currency Gains/Loss—Equity Shares—Trading Account	1,577.96
			1-Feb-X1	By Unrealized Capital Gains/Loss—Equity Shares—Trading Account	3,078.99

Investments—Equity Shares—Trading Account (*Cont'd*)

Date	Particulars	Debit (US$)	Date	Particulars	Credit (US$)
1-Feb-X1	To Unrealized Currency Gains/ Loss—Equity Shares—Trading Account	1,577.96	5-Feb-X1	By Yoshio & Co. Account	76,869.56
5-Feb-X1	To Yoshio & Co. Account	181.91			
			5-Feb-X1	By Realized Capital Gains/Loss—Equity—Trading Account	2,691.13
5-Feb-X1	To Realized Currency Gains/ Loss Equity—Trading Account	1,197.41			
28-Feb-X1	To Unrealized Capital Gains/ Loss—Equity Shares—Trading Account	2,025.52			
			1-Mar-X1	By Unrealized Capital Gains/ Loss—Equity Shares—Trading Account	2,025.52
28-Feb-X1	To Unrealized Currency Gains/Loss Equity—Trading Account	219.90	1-Mar-X1	By Unrealized Currency Gains/ Loss Equity—Trading Account	219.90
			31-Mar-X1	By Unrealized Capital Gains/ Loss—Equity Shares—Trading Account	42.71
			31-Mar-X1	By Balance	12,711.86
31-Mar-X1	Total	**99,217.63**	31-Mar-X1	Total	**99,217.63**
31-Mar-X1	To Balance	12,711.86			

Realized Capital Gains/Loss Equity—Trading Account

Date	Particulars	Debit (US$)	Date	Particulars	Credit (US$)
5-Feb-X1	To Investments—Equity Shares—Trading Account	2,691.13			
			31-Mar-X1	By Balance	2,691.13
31-Mar-X1	Total	**2,691.13**	31-Mar-X1	Total	**2,691.13**
31-Mar-X1	To Balance	2,691.13			

Realized Currency Gains/Loss Equity—Trading Account

Date	Particulars	Debit (US$)	Date	Particulars	Credit (US$)
8-Jan-X1	To Yoshio & Co. Account	849.49			
			18-Jan-X1	By Yoshio & Co. Account	708.58
			5-Feb-X1	By Investments—Equity Shares—Trading Account	1,197.41
			8-Feb-X1	By Yoshio & Co. Account	2,763.52
31-Mar-X1	To Balance	3,820.02			
31-Mar-X1	Total	**4,669.51**	31-Mar-X1	Total	**4,669.51**
			31-Mar-X1	By Balance	3,820.02

Unrealized Capital Gains/Loss—Equity Shares—Trading Account

Date	Particulars	Debit (US$)	Date	Particulars	Credit (US$)
			31-Jan-X1	By Investments—Equity Shares—Trading Account	3,078.99
1-Feb-X1	To Investments—Equity Shares—Trading Account	3,078.99			
			28-Feb-X1	By Investments—Equity Shares—Trading Account	2,025.52
1-Mar-X1	To Investments—Equity Shares—Trading Account	2,025.52			
31-Mar-X1	To Investments—Equity Shares—Trading Account	42.71			
			31-Mar-X1	By Balance	42.71
31-Mar-X1	Total	**5,147.22**	31-Mar-X1	Total	**5,147.22**
31-Mar-X1	To Balance	42.71			

Unrealized Currency Gains/Loss Equity—Trading Account

Date	Particulars	Debit (US$)	Date	Particulars	Credit (US$)
31-Jan-X1	To Investments—Equity Shares—Trading Account	1,577.96			
1-Mar-X1	To Investments—Equity Shares—Trading Account	219.90	28-Feb-X1	By Investments—Equity Shares—Trading Account	219.90
			28-Feb-X1	By Investments—Equity Shares—Trading Account	1,577.96
31-Mar-X1	Total	**1,797.86**	31-Mar-X1	Total	**1,797.86**

Unrealized Currency Gain/Loss—Bank Account

Date	Particulars	Debit (US$)	Date	Particulars	Credit (US$)
			31-Jan-X1	By Bank Account	1,718.87
28-Feb-X1	To Bank Account	5,735.60			
			31-Mar-X1	By Bank Account	265.12
			31-Mar-X1	By Balance	3,751.61
31-Mar-X1	Total	**5,735.60**	31-Mar-X1	Total	**5,735.60**
31-Mar-X1	To Balance	3,751.61			

Yoshio & Co. Account

Date	Particulars	Debit (US$)	Date	Particulars	Credit (US$)
			5-Jan-X1	By Investments—Equity Shares—Trading Account	48,275.86
			5-Jan-X1	By Investments—Equity Shares—Trading Account	144.83
8-Jan-X1	To Bank Account	49,270.18			
			8-Jan-X1	By Realized Currency Gains/Loss Equity—Trading Account	849.49
			15-Jan-X1	By Investments—Equity Shares—Trading Account	42,372.88
			15-Jan-X1	By Investments—Equity Shares—Trading Account	142.37
18-Jan-X1	To Bank Account	41,806.67			
18-Jan-X1	To Realized Currency Gains/Loss Equity—Trading Account	708.58			

Yoshio & Co. Account (*Cont'd*)

Date	Particulars	Debit (US$)	Date	Particulars	Credit (US$)
5-Feb-X1	To Investments—Equity Shares—Trading Account	76,869.56			
			5-Feb-X1	By Investments—Equity Shares—Trading Account	181.91
			8-Feb-X1	By Bank Account	79,451.17
8-Feb-X1	To Realized Currency Gains/Loss Equity—Trading Account	2,763.52			
31-Mar-X1	Total	**171,418.51**	31-Mar-X1	Total	**171,418.51**

Bank Account

Date	Particulars	Debit (US$)	Date	Particulars	Credit (US$)
			8-Jan-X1	By Yoshio & Co. Account	49,270.18
			18-Jan-X1	By Yoshio & Co. Account	41,806.67
31-Jan-X1	To Unrealized Currency Gain/Loss—Bank-Account	1,718.86			
8-Feb-X1	To Yoshio & Co. Account	79,451.17			
			28-Feb-X1	By Bank Account	5,735.60
31-Mar-X1	To Bank Account	265.13			
31-Mar-X1	To Balance	15,377.29			
31-Mar-X1	Total	**96,812.45**	31-Mar-X1	Total	**96,812.45**
			31-Mar-X1	By Balance	15,377.29

Trial Balance

As on 31-Mar-X1 (US$)

Particulars	Debit	Credit
Current Assets		
Bank Account		15,377.29
Investments		
Investments—Equity Shares—Trading Account	12,711.86	
Direct Income		
Realized Capital Gains/Loss Equity—Trading Account	2,691.13	
Realized Currency Gains/Loss Equity—Trading Account		3,820.02
Unrealized Currency Gain/Loss—Bank Account	3,751.61	
Unrealized Capital Gains/Loss—Equity Shares—Trading Account	42.71	
Total	**19,197.31**	**19,197.31**

Income Statement

For the period ending 31-Mar-X1

Expenses	US$	Income	US$
Direct Expenses		**Direct Income**	
Realized Capital Loss Equity—Trading Account	2,691.13	Realized Currency Gains/Loss—Trading Account	3,820.02
Unrealized Capital Loss—Equity Shares—Trading Account	42.71		
Unrealized Currency Gain/Loss—Bank Account	3,751.61		
		Net Profit Carryover	2,665.43
Total	**6,485.45**	Total	**6,485.45**

Balance Sheet

As of 31-Mar-X1

Liabilities	US$	Assets	US$
Capital Account	Nil	**Investments**	
Current Liabilities		Investments—Equity Shares—Trading Account	12,711.86
Bank Account	15,377.29		
		Current Assets	Nil
		Profit & Loss Account	
		Opening Balance	Nil
		Current Period	2,665.43
Total	**15,377.29**	Total	**15,377.29**

SUMMARY

- Equity securities are represented by ownership shares as common stock or preferred stock, rights to acquire ownership shares such as stock warrants or rights, or call options. The category also includes rights to dispose of ownership in shares by way of put options.
- Equity security is defined in FAS 115 as any security representing an ownership interest in an enterprise (for example, common, preferred, or other capital stock) or the right to acquire (for example, warrants, rights, and call options) or dispose of (for example, put options) an ownership interest in an enterprise at fixed or determinable prices. However, the term does not include convertible debt or preferred stock that by its terms either must be redeemed by the issuing enterprise or is redeemable at the option of the investor. The definition does not include redeemable preference shares.

- Under the trade date accounting method, both the asset and the liability for the asset purchased are recognized on the date of trade and the payable is derecognized once the payment is made.
- Under the settlement date accounting method, the entire transaction is recognized only on the date of settlement. While FAS 115 is silent as to the date on which the transaction should be recorded, the other levels of U.S. GAAP literature require trade date accounting to be followed for regular-way securities contracts, especially for broker-dealers and investment companies.
- For regular-way contracts, the IASB gives the option to follow either trade date accounting or settlement date accounting, provided that one is followed consistently for purchases and sales of financial assets in the same category. However, the changes in the fair value of the asset should be treated properly depending upon the classification of the asset acquired.
- Investments in equity securities that are purchased and held principally for the purpose of generating gains on resale are classified as trading securities. Investments in equity securities that are not trading securities are classified as available-for-sale (AFS) securities.
- Trading securities are normally held by banks and other financial institutions that engage in active buying and selling of securities with a view to make gains on trading. The mark-to-market process values the securities at market rates, recording the unrealized gains/loss on such securities.
- When the investor invests in equity securities just to utilize the idle cash, without any intention to hold it for a long period or without any intention to generate gains on current resale, then such investments in equity securities are classified as available-for-sale securities.
- Where the investor owns between 20 and 50 percent of the equity of the investee company, then the investor is presumed to have a significant influence in the operating and financial decisions of the investee company.
- When the investor acquires more than 50 percent of the outstanding voting stock of the investee company, then the investor has controlling interest because of its majority ownership of the voting stock. Investments of this nature will necessitate the preparation of consolidated financial statements.
- The currency of the primary economic environment in which the investor operates is the *functional currency.* The financial accounting records should be maintained in the functional currency and the investor is not free to choose the same. The investor's investment activities and the currency in which the fund raises money from investors predominantly determine the functional currency. *Presentation currency* is the currency in which the financial statements are presented to the investors.
- For assets and liabilities, the exchange rate at the balance sheet date is used to translate foreign currency statements into the functional currency.
- For revenues, expenses, gains, and losses, the exchange rate at the dates on which such revenue or expense is recognized is used.
- If the reporting currency is different from the trading currency, then every journal entry recorded is first revalued in the reporting currency, based on the market quote available for the trade currency.

- On the reporting date, all the assets and liabilities of the investor that are designated in foreign currency should be converted into the functional currency based on the official FX conversion rates on the reporting date. This is achieved by the FX revaluation process.
- As per the U.S. GAAP Statement of Position (SOP) 93-4, it is not mandatory to show the capital gains/loss due to change in the market rate of the asset and currency gains/loss due to change in the foreign exchange rate separately, even though the SOP indicates that such separate reporting would provide valuable information to the users of the financial statements.

EXERCISES

Theory Questions

1. Define equity shares as per the accounting standard FAS 115.
2. How are passive investments classified for accounting purposes?
3. What is readily determinable fair value as per FAS 115?
4. What is the fundamental difference between the *trading* and *available-for-sale* classifications of equity investments?
5. When is an investor supposed to have significant influence on the investee company, and what is the method of accounting for such investments?
6. Controlling interest is acquired if an investor holds more than 50 percent—is this statement true? Discuss your answer with examples.
7. What are the main differences between exchange-traded securities and over-the-counter securities?
8. Explain in brief the functions and functioning of stock exchanges.
9. List the various events during the trade life cycle for equity shares that are held as trading, along with the accounting entries to be recorded.
10. What are corporate actions and what is their impact with regards to accounting?
11. Commissions and other expenses for acquiring the shares are treated as part of the cost of the equity—is this true, and if so, what are the exceptions?
12. What are the differences between trade date accounting and settlement date accounting?
13. What is the reversal journal entry for mark-to-market?
14. Explain the process of FX revaluation and FX translation. What are the differences between the two?
15. What is meant by *functional currency* and how it is determined?
16. How do you distinguish between capital gains and currency gains due to fluctuation in foreign exchange rate? Is it mandatory to divulge the two gains separately?

Objective Questions

1. The equity method of accounting is adopted in:
   a. Controlling interest
   b. Significant influence
   c. Passive investments
   d. None of the above

2. In trade date accounting, a liability payable for acquiring the asset will be recorded on:
   a. The trade date
   b. The reporting date
   c. The settlement date
   d. All of the above
3. A broker-dealer who records the transactions on settlement date basis should compute the net capital on:
   a. The trade date
   b. The reporting date
   c. The settlement date
   d. Any of the above
4. The definition of *equity security* as per FAS 115 does not apply to:
   a. Investment companies
   b. Nonprofit organizations
   c. Brokers and dealers in securities
   d. All of the above
5. The shareholder will recognize the dividend income:
   a. On the date of dividend declaration
   b. On the ex-dividend date
   c. At the end of accounting period
   d. None of the above
6. A shareholder is said to have controlling interest in the company if he holds:
   a. Less than 20 percent shares of the investee company
   b. From 20 to 50 percent shares of the investee company
   c. More than 50 percent shares of the investee company
   d. None of the above
7. Unrealized gains or loss computed for available-for-sale (AFS) securities will be reported as:
   a. Income/loss on the income statement
   b. Other comprehensive income
   c. Dividend income
   d. None of the above
8. For private equity investment, the responsibility of fulfillment of the obligation is vested with:
   a. The stock exchange
   b. The broker
   c. The seller
   d. All of the above

9. If the net holding of any share is negative, then it is referred to as:
   a. Available-for-sale (AFS)
   b. A long position
   c. A short position
   d. Trading securities
10. Under the incremental value method, mark-to-market entry is reversed:
    a. On T + 2
    b. At the end of the accounting period
    c. On the next valuation date
    d. None of the above
11. The fair value of securities that are listed and traded through stock exchanges is determined based on:
    a. The highest bid price quoted on the exchange for each day
    b. Market quotes at the end of each day
    c. Market quotes at the opening of each day
    d. The forecasted price received from stock broker
    e. The average price of the high and low recorded in the exchange
12. In private equity investments where the trade is executed over-the-counter, who among the following will be the actual counterparty?
    a. The stock exchange in which the stock is listed
    b. The buyer
    c. The seller
    d. The custodian bank
    e. The broker
13. When the net holding of any given share is shown in negative value, it refers to:
    a. Quantity of short position
    b. Loss from long position
    c. Unrealized loss from short position
    d. Quantity of long position
    e. Dividend receivable
14. For exchange-traded securities, the delivery of the securities either in physical or in electronic form takes place:
    a. When the trade is booked
    b. When the broker confirms the receipt of payment
    c. Immediately after the payment is received by the stock exchange
    d. On T + 1
    e. At a predetermined future date

15. When a company announces a dividend, who is entitled to receive it?
    a. An investor listed as holder of stock as of the dividend declaration date
    b. An investor listed as holder of stock as of the ex-dividend date
    c. An investor listed as holder of stock as of the day before ex-dividend date
    d. An investor listed as holder of stock as of the record date
    e. An investor listed as holder of stock as of the dividend payment date
16. If an investor buys 1,000 shares at $50 and the initial margin is 60 percent and the maintenance margin is 30 percent, he will receive the first marginal call when the stock price falls below:
    a. $14.00
    b. $21.00
    c. $28.57
    d. $49.99

Journal Questions

Journalize the following transactions.

1. Michael James bought 8,500 shares of NovoSotia on April 15 for $12 per share. On the same day, the closing price of NovoSotia was $11.45 per share. Calculate the unrealized gains/loss at end of day and pass the journal entry.
2. On April 24, he sold 4,000 shares of NovoSotia at $14 per share. Pass necessary journal entries to record the sale of these shares and also the subsequent realized/unrealized gain or loss as of that date. The closing rate of NovoSotia shares on April 24 is $13.60.
3. On May 31, NovoSotia declared a dividend of $1 per share with record date of April 20. On June 10, the payment was made. Calculate the dividend amount received by Michael James and also pass entries for dividend declaration and actual receipt of such dividend.
4. On June 25, Mr. James bought an additional 2,000 shares of NovoSotia at $16 per share. On July 28, he sold another 4,000 shares at $14.65 per share. Mr. James follows the last in, first out (LIFO) method and the shares were held for trading purposes. Calculate the realized gains or loss and pass entry to give the effect for the same.
5. Prepare realized/unrealized gains and loss account (ledger account) giving effect to the preceding transactions.

Trading Securities: Foreign Currency—HKD

For the following scenario, prepare journal entries, general ledgers, trial balances, income statements, and balance sheets.

James Trading Inc. traded in Avichina Industry shares in a Hong Kong stock exchange through Nomura Securities brokers, and the details are as follows:

Trade Details

Date	Product	Quantity	Rate (HKD)	B/S	Brokerage (HKD)
8-Jan-X1	Avichina Industry	35,000	1.33	B	155
12-Jan-X1	Avichina Industry	20,000	1.39	B	120
15-Feb-X1	Avichina Industry	50,500	1.25	S	195

Other Details

Settlement: T + 3

Liquidation Method

FIFO

Market Rate of Avichina Industry Shares in HKD

January 31: 1.28.
February 28: 1.42.
March 31: 1.55.

FX Rate: US$/HKD

January 8: 7.72
January 11: 7.79
January 12: 7.69
January 15: 7.90
January 31: 7.83
February 15: 7.75
February 18: 7.81
February 28: 7.76
March 31: 7.99

Functional Currency

US$

Trading Securities: Foreign Currency—IDR

For the following scenario, prepare journal entries, general ledgers, trial balance, income statement, and balance sheet.

Jakarta Trading Fund traded in PT. Perusahaan Gas shares in a Hong Kong stock exchange through Vickers & Co. brokers, and the details are as follows:

Trade Details

Date	Product	Quantity	Rate (IDR)	B/S	Brokerage (IDR)
5-Jan-X1	PT. Perusahaan	16,000	10,071.39	B	161,150,080
15-Jan-X1	PT. Perusahaan	18,000	10,329.90	B	171,200,000
5-Feb-X1	PT. Perusahaan	30,500	10,700.00	S	271,200,000

Other Details

Settlement: T + 3

Liquidation Method

FIFO

Market Rate of PT. Perusahaan Shares in IDR

January 31: 10,101.10
February 28: 10,800.42
March 31: 10,255.15

FX Rate: US$/IDR

January 5: 9,013
January 8: 9,040
January 15: 9,115
January 18: 9,102
January 31: 9,100
February 5: 9,070
February 8: 9,109
February 28: 9,120
March 31: 9,125

Functional Currency

US$

Trading Securities: Foreign Currency—PKR

For the following scenario, prepare journal entries, general ledgers, trial balance, income statement, and balance sheet.

Karachi Overseas Fund traded in Adamjee Insurance shares in the Pakistan stock exchange through Auerbach & Co. brokers, and the details are as follows:

Trade Details

Date	Product	Quantity	Rate(PKR)	B/S	Brokerage(PKR)
15-Feb-X1	Adamjee	2,000	189	B	378
15-Mar-X1	Adamjee	1,600	198	S	316

Other Details

Settlement: T + 3

Liquidation Method

FIFO

Market Rate of Adamjee Insurance Shares in PKR

February 28: 190
March 31: 185
April 30: 205

FX Rate: US$/PKR

February 15: 60.81
February 18: 60.68
February 28: 60.71
March 15: 60.75
March 18: 60.72
March 31: 60.73
April 30: 60.78

Functional Currency

US$

Trading Securities: Foreign Currency—JPY

For the following scenario, prepare journal entries, general ledgers, trial balance, income statement, and balance sheet.

Itochu Capital Japan Fund traded in Nissan shares in the Nikkei through Akita Mori brokers, and the details are as follows:

Trade Details

Date	Product	Quantity	Rate (JPY)	B/S	Brokerage (JPY)
11-Feb-X1	Nissan	4,000	1,450	B	1,200
20-Mar-X1	Nissan	2,200	1,750	S	660

Other Details

Settlement: T + 3

Liquidation Method

FIFO

Market Rate of Nissan Shares in JPY

February 28: 1,620
March 31: 1,800
April 30: 1,760

FX Rate: US$/JPY

February 11: 104.50
February 14: 104.75
February 28: 104.85
March 20: 105.25
March 23: 105.35
March 31: 105.00
April 30: 105.50

Functional Currency

US$

CHAPTER 3

Accounting for Equity Investments: Available-for-Sale

LEARNING OBJECTIVES

After studying this chapter, you should have a grasp of the following:

- Accounting standards for equity investments held as available-for-sale (AFS).
- Basic understanding of available-for-sale securities.
- Trade life cycle for equity investments held as available-for-sale.
- Journal entries to be recorded during the different phases of the trade life cycle.
- FX translation on available-for-sale securities.
- Impairment of AFS securities.
- Illustration of investments in equity shares held as available-for-sale.
- Preparation of journal entries and general ledger accounts.
- Preparation of income statement and balance sheet after the equity investments are made.
- Illustration of available-for-sale investments in foreign currency.

ACCOUNTING STANDARDS FOR EQUITY INVESTMENTS: AVAILABLE-FOR-SALE

According to the accounting standards, available-for-sale financial assets are those non-derivative financial assets that are designated as available-for-sale or are not classified as one of the following:

- Loans and receivables.
- Held-to-maturity investments.
- Financial assets at fair value through profit or loss.

Thus, equity instruments that are not designated as financial assets at fair value through profit or loss are categorized as available-for-sale instruments. Additionally, investments in equity instruments that do not have a quoted market price in an active market, and whose fair value cannot be reliably measured, should not be designated as at fair value through profit or loss, and such instruments are designated as available-for-sale securities.

Relevant Accounting Standards	
U.S. GAAP	**IFRS**
FAS 52—Foreign Currency Translation	IFRS 7—Financial Instruments: Disclosure
FAS 94—Consolidation of All Majority-owned Subsidiaries	IAS 21—The Effects of Changes in Foreign Exchange Rates
FAS 109—Accounting for Income Taxes	IAS 32—Financial Instruments: Presentation
FAS 115—Accounting for Certain Investments in Debt and Equity Securities	IAS 36—Impairment of Assets
FAS 130—Reporting Comprehensive Income	IAS 39—Financial Instruments: Recognition and Measurement
FAS 157—Fair Value Measurements	
FAS 159—The Fair Value Option for Financial Assets and Financial Liabilities	

BASIC UNDERSTANDING OF AFS

Available-for-sale securities are debt or equity investments that are held for an indefinite period of time without any intention to resell for profit. They are not trading assets as in the case of short-term assets held for speculation, nor are they acquired with an intention to hold till maturity. In the case of equity securities, there is no concept of holding till maturity. Hence, whatever investments in equity are acquired without any intention to resell for profit are classified as available-for-sale (AFS) securities. Thus, AFS securities are a hybrid. While AFS securities are recorded at fair value or market value, the unrealized gains/losses on them are excluded from current earnings (P&L) and are instead recorded as an adjustment to equity on the balance sheet.

The AFS category includes all equity securities except those classified as fair value through profit or loss (FPVL). Available-for-sale financial assets are carried at fair value subsequent to initial recognition. Usually the fair value can be readily determined for most financial assets through an active market or by a reasonable estimation process. The exception to this rule is equity securities that are not actively traded and hence do not have a quoted market price for arriving at a reliable fair value. Such instruments, however, are measured at cost instead of fair value.

For available-for-sale financial assets, unrealized gains and losses are deferred until they are realized or impairment occurs. The unrealized gains on such financial assets are shown as other comprehensive income and adjusted directly in the equity without being routed through the income statement. Only interest income and dividend income, impairment losses, and certain foreign currency gains and losses are recognized in profit or loss.

THE TRADE LIFE CYCLE FOR AVAILABLE-FOR-SALE EQUITY

The trade life cycle for investment in equity securities that are designated as available-for-sale is identical to that given in Chapter 2 for trading securities, except that at the time of ascertaining the fair value at the end of the reporting period, the accounting entry that is recorded in the books of account is different. Also, when the equity securities classified as available-for-sale are sold, the realized gains/loss on such sale is transferred from the other comprehensive income (OCI) to the income statement and an entry is recorded to that effect. Thus, the two events in the trade life cycle which call for a different treatment than the ones given for trading securities are as follows:

1. Ascertain the fair value at the end of reporting period.
2. Ascertain the profit/loss on the sale and adjust OCI.

Overview of the Trade Life Cycle

Ascertain the Fair Value at the End of the Reporting Period

At the end of the reporting period, the fair value of the shares is ascertained and the shares are marked-to-market. The mark-to-market process adopted here is the same as the one followed for trading securities. However, if the market rate rises above the purchase rate, then such increase is recorded as part of the other comprehensive income and is not recognized as income in the current period. The other comprehensive income is shown as part of the shareholders' equity in the balance sheet.

This accounting entry is reversed on the next valuation date when a fresh entry for the then value is recorded in the books of accounts. Alternatively, the accounting entry can also be recorded only for the incremental value. If the investor follows this incremental value method, there is no need to reverse any entry for mark-to-market recorded earlier.

The exception to this general rule is when there is a permanent impairment to the value of the securities held as available-for-sale. Such permanent impairment should be recognized in the income and as such should be part of the income statement. If the perceived permanent impairment is later recovered, such increase in the value of the investments need not be recorded in the books until the liquidation of such securities.

Assuming that the market rate of Gold Crest, which is held by the investor as available-for-sale investments, is valued at $497 as of December 31, the accounting entry that is recorded in the books of accounts is shown in the following journal entry.

Journal Entry

Date	Particulars	Debit (US$)	Credit (US$)
31-Dec-X1	Equity Shares—Gold Crest—AFS Account	4,000.00	
	To Unrealized Capital Gains/Loss—Equity Shares Account (Other Comprehensive Income)		4,000.00
	(Being the mark-to-market entry for 1,000 long position in Gold Crest shares @ $497 less the cost of acquisition viz., $490 plus $3 per share amounting to $4,000)		

Ascertain the Profit/Loss on the Sale and Adjust OCI

The profit or loss on liquidation of the shares is ascertained by deducting the cost of sales from the net sale consideration. Cost of sales is arrived at by following first in first out (FIFO), last in first out (LIFO), or the weighted average method. For available-for-sale securities the increase or decrease in the value of the investment is not reported as income until the same is liquidated. Hence, on liquidation, when the profit/loss on the liquidation is ascertained, the same is transferred from other comprehensive income to the income account.

Assume that the Gold Crest shares are sold on November 6 for a consideration of $520 and a brokerage of $4 is incurred for the same, resulting in the net realization of $516 per share. Assume further that the Gold Crest shares were valued on October 31 at $510. Hence the profit on each share is $23 and the total profit for the entire lot amounts to $23,000. However, $13,000 would have been already credited to the OCI on October 31, being the previous valuation date. The profit/loss realized that is recognized on the date of liquidation should be taken to the income account, and the amount that was credited earlier to the OCI income account should be reversed.

The accounting entries that are recorded in the books of accounts are shown as follows:

Journal Entry

Date	Particulars	Debit (US$)	Credit (US$)
6-Nov-X1	Equity Shares—Gold Crest—AFS Account	10,000.00	
	To Realized Capital Gains/Loss—Equity Shares Account		10,000.00
	(Being the net profit realized on the sale of 1,000 Gold Crest shares)		
6-Nov-X1	Other Comprehensive Income Account	13,000.00	
	To Realized Capital Gains/Loss—Equity Shares Account		13,000.00
	(Being the net profit realized on the sale of 1,000 Gold Crest shares)		

Income Statement

For the period ending 31-Mar-X1

Expenses	US$	Income	US$
		By Unrealized Capital Gains/Loss—Equity Shares Account	2,825.00
To Profit—Transferred to Capital	5,500.00	By Realized Capital Gains/Loss—Equity Shares Account	2,225.00
		By Dividend Income	450.00
	5,500.00		**5,500.00**

Balance Sheet

As at 31-Mar-X1

Liabilities	US$	Assets	US$
Capital		***Investments***	
Profit transferred	5,500.00	Equity Shares Account	20,100.00
Current Liabilities		***Current Assets***	
Bank Account	14,650.00	Tax Withholding Account	50.00
	20,150.00		**20,150.00**

FX TRANSLATION ON AFS SECURITIES

According to the accounting standards, equity instruments are nonmonetary items for the purpose of treatment of foreign exchange differences. Any foreign exchange gains and losses on monetary assets are recognized in the statement of profit and loss except for those items that are designated as hedging instruments. A monetary available-for-sale financial asset is treated as if it were carried at amortized cost in the foreign currency. This applies for debt instruments that are monetary assets. However, for nonmonetary assets such as equity instruments, the gain or loss, including any related foreign exchange component, is recognized directly in the appropriate equity account.

In the balance sheet, a nonmonetary financial asset such as an investment in an equity instrument is translated using the closing rate if it is carried at fair value in the foreign currency, and using a historical rate if it is not carried at fair value when its fair value cannot be reliably measured.

The entire change in the carrying amount of equity instruments held as available-for-sale, including the effect of changes in foreign currency rates, is reported in the equity account.

IMPAIRMENT OF AFS SECURITIES

If an equity instrument measured at fair value with gains and losses recognized in the appropriate equity account becomes impaired, the cumulative net loss recognized in the equity account including any portion attributable to foreign currency changes should be recognized in the statement of profit and loss.

Illustration: AFS—Functional Currency

ABC Fund LLC traded in IBM shares at a U.S. stock exchange through Silver Man & Co. brokers, and the details are as follows:

Trade Details

Date	Product	Quantity	Rate	B/S	Brokerage
5-Jan-X1	IBM	2,000	$48.00	B	$550
15-Jan-X1	IBM	1,000	$50.00	B	$250
5-Feb-X1	IBM	2,600	$52.00	S	$720

Other Details

- Settlement: T + 2.
- Purchases on January 5 are settled on January 9 due to intervening holidays.
- January 28: A dividend at $0.75 per share is declared by IBM, $0.05 being the withholding tax.
- February 4: Dividend is paid by IBM.

Liquidation Method

First in first out (FIFO)

Market Rates

January 31: 51.00
February 28: 55.00
March 31: 58.00

Functional Currency

US$

Prepare

Journal entries, general ledgers, trial balance, income statement, and balance sheet.

Solution

T-1 On Purchase of Shares and Payment of Brokerage

An investment in equity shares here is classified as *available-for-sale*. The brokerage paid is part of the cost of acquisition and hence the investment account is debited to account for the brokerage.

Journal Entry

Date	Particulars	Debit (US$)	Credit (US$)
5-Jan-X1	Investments—Equity Shares—AFS Account	96,000.00	
	To Silver Man Account		96,000.00
	(Being 2,000 IBM shares bought @ $48 per share through the broker, Silver Man)		
5-Jan-X1	Investments—Equity Shares—AFS Account	550.00	
	To Silver Man Account		550.00
	(Being the brokerage payable to Silver Man on purchase of 2,000 IBM shares)		

T-2 On Payment of Contracted Sum

Journal Entry

Date	Particulars	Debit (US$)	Credit (US$)
9-Jan-X1	Silver Man Account	96,550.00	
	To Bank Account		96,550.00
	(Being the payment made to the broker on purchase of IBM shares together with brokerage)		

T-3 On Purchase of Shares and Payment of Brokerage

Journal Entry

Date	Particulars	Debit (US$)	Credit (US$)
15-Jan-X1	Investments—Equity Shares—AFS Account	50,000.00	
	To Silver Man Account		50,000.00
	(Being 1,000 IBM shares bought @ $50 per share through the broker, Silver Man)		
15-Jan-X1	Investments—Equity Shares—AFS Account	250.00	
	To Silver Man Account		250.00
	(Being the brokerage payable to Silver Man on purchase of 1,000 IBM shares)		

T-4 On Payment of Contracted Sum

Journal Entry

Date	Particulars	Debit (US$)	Credit (US$)
17-Jan-X1	Silver Man Account	50,250.00	
	To Bank Account		50,250.00
	(Being the payment made to the broker on purchase of IBM shares together with brokerage)		

T-5 On Declaration of Dividend

Journal Entry

Date	Particulars	Debit (US$)	Credit (US$)
28-Jan-X1	Dividend Receivable Account	2,250.00	
	To Dividend Income Account		2,250.00
	(Being the dividend receivable on 3,000 equity shares of IBM)		

T-6 Mark-to-market at End of Reporting Period

The total long position adds up to 3,000 shares and the market value of the shares is compared with the original cost of acquisition, including brokerage, to arrive at the mark-to-market. The market rate at the end of the reporting period is greater than the cost of acquisition, resulting in mark-to-market gains, which are reflected as an increase in the value of investments. Since the shares are held in the available-for-sale category, the gains are directly taken to the equity and are *not* routed through the profit and loss account.

Mark-to-market at end of reporting period: 31 Jan X1	**US$**
(a) Cost of acquisition of 2,000 shares @ US$48 including brokerage	96,550.00
(b) Cost of acquisition of 1,000 shares @ US$50 including brokerage	50,250.00
(c) Total cost of acquisition	146,800.00
(d) Market value at the end of reporting period	153,000.00
(e) Unrealized gains = (d) − (c)	6,200.00

Journal Entry

Date	Particulars	Debit (US$)	Credit (US$)
31-Jan-X1	Investments—Equity Shares—AFS Account	6,200.00	
	To Unrealized Capital Gains/Loss—Equity Shares—OCI Account		6,200.00
	(Being the unrealized gains on purchase of equity shares)		

T-7 Reversal of Mark-to-market Entry

Journal Entry

Date	Particulars	Debit (US$)	Credit (US$)
1-Feb-X1	Unrealized Capital Gains/Loss—Equity Shares—OCI Account	6,200.00	
	To Investments—Equity Shares—AFS Account		6,200.00
	(Being the reversal of mark-to-market on equity shares)		

T-8 On Receipt of Dividend

Journal Entry

Date	Particulars	Debit (US$)	Credit (US$)
4-Feb-X1	Bank Account	2,100.00	
	To Dividend Receivable Account		2,100.00
	(Being the dividend received on 3,000 equity shares of IBM)		

T-9 Withholding Tax on Dividend

Journal Entry

Date	Particulars	Debit (US$)	Credit (US$)
4-Feb-X1	Withholding tax on dividend receipts Account	150.00	
	To Dividend Receivable Account		150.00
	(Being the dividend received on 3,000 equity shares of IBM)		

T-10 On Sale of Shares and Payment of Brokerage

Journal Entry

Date	Particulars	Debit (US$)	Credit (US$)
5-Feb-X1	Silver Man Account	135,200.00	
	To Investments—Equity Shares—AFS Account		135,200.00
	(Being 2,600 IBM shares sold @ $52 per share through the broker, Silver Man)		
5-Feb-X1	Investments—Equity Shares—AFS Account	720.00	
	To Silver Man Account		720.00
	(Being the brokerage payable to Silver Man on the sale of 2,600 IBM shares)		

T-11 On Recording Profit/Loss on Sale of Shares

The liquidation methodology is first in, first out (FIFO) method. Hence the cost of acquisition of 2,600 shares is first arrived at and compared with the net sales realization to arrive at the realized gains on liquidation.

Calculation of capital gains	US$
(a) Sale value of 2,600 shares @ US$52 less brokerage	134,480.00
(b) Cost of sale of 2,000 shares @ US$48	96,550.00
(c) Cost of sale of 600 shares [(50,250 × 600)/1,000]	30,150.00
(d) Total cost of sales	126,700.00
(e) Realized gains in US$ = (a) − (d)	**7,780.00**

Journal Entry

Date	Particulars	Debit (US$)	Credit (US$)
5-Feb-X1	Investments—Equity Shares—AFS Account	7,780.00	
	To Realized Capital Gains/Loss—Equity Shares Account		7,780.00
	(Being the profit on the sale of 2,600 IBM shares)		

T-12 On Receipt of Contracted Sum

Journal Entry

Date	Particulars	Debit (US$)	Credit (US$)
7-Feb-X1	Bank Account	134,480.00	
	To Silver Man Account		134,480.00
	(Being the net consideration received from Silver Man on sale of 2,600 IBM shares)		

T-13 Mark-to-market at End of Reporting Period

The net long position adds up to 400 shares and the market value of the shares is compared with the original cost of acquisition, including brokerage, to arrive at the mark-to-market. The market rate at the end of the reporting period is greater than the cost of acquisition, resulting in mark-to-market gains, which are reflected as an increase in the value of investments. Since the shares are held in the available-for-sale category, the gains are directly taken to the equity and are *not* routed through the profit and loss account.

Mark-to-market at end of reporting period: 28-Feb-X1	US$
(a) Market value of 400 shares @ US$55	22,000.00
(b) Cost of acquisition [(50,250 × 400)/1,000]	20,100.00
(c) Unrealized gains = (a) – (b)	1,900.00

Journal Entry

Date	Particulars	Debit (US$)	Credit (US$)
28-Feb-X1	Investments—Equity Shares—AFS Account	1,900.00	
	To Unrealized Capital Gains/Loss—Equity Shares—OCI Account		1,900.00
	(Being the unrealized gains on 1,500 equity shares of IBM)		

T-14 Reversal of Mark-to-market Entry

Journal Entry

Date	Particulars	Debit (US$)	Credit (US$)
1-Mar-X1	Unrealized Capital Gains/Loss—Equity Shares—OCI Account	1,900.00	
	To Investments—Equity Shares—AFS Account		1,900.00
	(Being the reversal of mark-to-market on equity shares)		

T-15 Mark-to-market at End of Reporting Period

Mark-to-market at end of reporting period: 31-Mar-X1	**US$**
(a) Market value of 400 shares @ US$58	23,200.00
(b) Cost of acquisition [(50,250 × 400)/1,000]	20,100.00
(c) Unrealized gains = (a) − (b)	3,100.00

Journal Entry

Date	Particulars	Debit (US$)	Credit (US$)
31-Mar-X1	Investments—Equity Shares—AFS Account	3,100.00	
	To Unrealized Capital Gains/Loss—Equity Shares—OCI Account		3,100.00
	(Being the unrealized gains on 400 equity shares of IBM)		

General Ledger Accounts

Investments—Equity Shares—AFS Account

Date	Particulars	Debit (US$)	Date	Particulars	Credit (US$)
5-Jan-X1	To Silver Man Account	96,000.00			
5-Jan-X1	To Silver Man Account	550.00			
15-Jan-X1	To Silver Man Account	50,000.00			
15-Jan-X1	To Silver Man Account	250.00			
31-Jan-X1	To Unrealized Capital Gains/Loss—Equity Shares—OCI Account	6,200.00			
			1-Feb-X1	By Unrealized Capital Gains/Loss—Equity Shares—OCI Account	6,200.00
5-Feb-X1	To Silver Man Account	720.00			
			5-Feb-X1	By Silver Man Account	135,200.00
5-Feb-X1	To Realized Capital Gains/Loss—Equity Shares Account	7,780.00			

Investments—Equity Shares—AFS Account (*Cont'd*)

Date	Particulars	Debit (US$)	Date	Particulars	Credit (US$)
28-Feb-X1	To Unrealized Capital Gains/ Loss—Equity Shares—OCI Account	1,900.00			
			1-Mar-X1	By Unrealized Capital Gains/ Loss—Equity Shares—OCI Account	1,900.00
31-Mar-X1	To Unrealized Capital Gains/ Loss— Equity Shares— OCI Account	3,100.00			
			31-Mar-X1	By Balance	23,200.00
31-Mar-X1	Total	**166,500.00**	31-Mar-X1	Total	**166,500.00**
31-Mar-X1	To Balance	23,200.00			

Dividend Income Account

Date	Particulars	Debit (US$)	Date	Particulars	Credit (US$)
			28-Jan-X1	By Dividend Receivable Account	2,250.00
31-Mar-X1	To Balance	2,250.00			
31-Mar-X1	Total	**2,250.00**	31-Mar-X1	Total	**2,250.00**
			31-Mar-X1	By Balance	2,250.00

Dividend Receivable Account

Date	Particulars	Debit (US$)	Date	Particulars	Credit (US$)
28-Jan-X1	To Dividend Income Account	2,250.00			
			4-Feb-X1	By Bank Account	2,100.00
			4-Feb-X1	By Withholding Tax on Dividend Receipts Account	150.00
31-Mar-X1	Total	**2,250.00**	31-Mar-X1	Total	**2,250.00**

Realized Capital Gains/Loss—Equity Shares-Account

Date	Particulars	Debit (US$)	Date	Particulars	Credit (US$)
			5-Feb-X1	By Investments—Equity Shares—AFS Account	7,780.00
31-Mar-X1	To Balance	7,780.00			
31-Mar-X1	Total	**7,780.00**	31-Mar-X1	Total	**7,780.00**
			31-Mar-X1	By Balance	7,780.00

Unrealized Capital Gains/Loss—Equity Shares—OCI Account

Date	Particulars	Debit (US$)	Date	Particulars	Credit (US$)
			31-Jan-X1	By Investments—Equity Shares—AFS Account	6,200.00
1-Feb-X1	To Investments—Equity Shares—AFS Account	6,200.00			
			28-Feb-X1	By Investments—Equity Shares—AFS Account	1,900.00
1-Mar-X1	To Investments—Equity Shares—AFS Account	1,900.00			
			31-Mar-X1	By Investments—Equity Shares—AFS Account	3,100.00
31-Mar-X1	To Balance	3,100.00			
31-Mar-X1	Total	**11,200.00**	31-Mar-X1	Total	**11,200.00**
			31-Mar-X1	By Balance	3,100.00

Withholding Tax on Dividend Receipts Account

Date	Particulars	Debit (US$)	Date	Particulars	Credit (US$)
4-Feb-X1	To Dividend Receivable Account	150.00			
			31-Mar-X1	By Balance	150.00
31-Mar-X1	Total	**150.00**	31-Mar-X1	Total	**150.00**
31-Mar-X1	To Balance	150.00			

Silver Man Account

Date	Particulars	Debit (US$)	Date	Particulars	Credit (US$)
			5-Jan-X1	By Investments—Equity Shares—AFS Account	96,000.00
			5-Jan-X1	By Investments—Equity Shares—AFS Account	550.00
9-Jan-X1	To Bank Account	96,550.00			
			15-Jan-X1	By Investments—Equity Shares—AFS Account	50,000.00
			15-Jan-X1	By Investments—Equity Shares—AFS Account	250.00
17-Jan-X1	To Bank Account	50,250.00			
			5-Feb-X1	By Investments—Equity Shares—AFS Account	720.00
5-Feb-X1	To Investments—Equity Shares—AFS Account	135,200.00			
			7-Feb-X1	By Bank Account	134,480.00
31-Mar-X1	Total	**282,000.00**	31-Mar-X1	Total	**282,000.00**

Bank Account

Date	Particulars	Debit (US$)	Date	Particulars	Credit (US$)
			9-Jan-X1	By Silver Man Account	96,550.00
			17-Jan-X1	By Silver Man Account	50,250.00
4-Feb-X1	To Dividend Receivable Account	2,100.00			
7-Feb-X1	To Silver Man Account	134,480.00			
31-Mar-X1	To Balance	10,220.00			
31-Mar-X1	Total	**146,800.00**	31-Mar-X1	Total	**146,800.00**
			31-Mar-X1	By Balance	10,220.00

Trial Balance

As on 31-Mar-X1 (US$)

Particulars	Debit	Credit
Current Liabilities		
Bank Account		10,220.00
Investments		
Investments—Equity Shares—AFS Account	23,200.00	
Current Assets		
Withholding Tax on Dividend Receipts Account	150.00	
Direct Income		
Dividend Income Account		2,250.00
Realized Capital Gains/Loss Equity Shares Account		7,780.00
Unrealized Capital Gains/Loss—Equity Shares—OCI Account		3,100.00
Total	**23,350.00**	**23,350.00**

Income Statement

For the period ending 31-Mar-X1

Expenses	US$	Income	US$
		Direct Income	
		Dividend Income Account	2,250.00
		Realized Capital Gains/Loss Equity Shares Account	7,780.00
Net Profit Carryover	10,030.00		
Total	**10,030.00**	Total	**10,030.00**

Balance Sheet

As at 31-Mar-X1

Liabilities	US$	Assets	US$
Capital Account		**Investments**	
Unrealized Capital Gains/Loss Equity—OCI Account	3,100.00	Investments—Equity Shares—AFS Account	23,200.00
Current Liabilities		**Current Assets**	
Bank Account	10,220.00	Withholding Tax on Dividend Receipts Account	150.00
Profit & Loss Account			
Opening Balance	Nil		
Current Period	10,030.00		
Total	**23,350.00**	Total	**23,350.00**

Illustration: AFS Securities—Trade Currency AUD

Sydney Long Term Fund traded in ANZ Bank shares in the Sydney stock exchange through Boon & Co. brokers, and the details are as follows:

Trade Details

Date	Product	Quantity	Rate (AUD)	B/S	Brokerage (AUD)
5-Jan-X1	ANZ Bank	1,000	38.00	B	140
15-Jan-X1	ANZ Bank	1,000	42.00	B	160
5-Feb-X1	ANZ Bank	1,600	48.00	S	230

Other Details

Settlement: T + 2

Liquidation Method

FIFO

Market rate of ANZ Bank Shares in AUD

January 31: 55.00
February 28: 58.00
March 31: 50.00

FX Rate: US$/AUD

January 5: 1.32
January 7: 1.34
January 15: 1.36
January 17: 1.30
January 31: 1.19
February 1: 1.19
February 5: 1.15
February 7: 1.25
February 28: 1.16
March 1: 1.17
March 31: 1.18

Functional Currency

US$

Prepare

Journal entries, general ledgers, trial balance, income statement, and balance sheet.

Solution

T-1 On Purchase of Shares and Payment of Brokerage

Journal Entry

Date	Particulars	Debit (AUD)	Credit (AUD)
5-Jan-X1	Investments—Equity Shares—AFS Account	38,000.00	
	To Boon & Co. Account		38,000.00
	(Being 1,000 ANZ Bank shares bought @ $38 per share through the broker, Boon & Co.)		
5-Jan-X1	Investments—Equity Shares—AFS Account	140.00	
	To Boon & Co. Account		140.00
	(Being the brokerage payable to Boon & Co. on purchase of 1,000 ANZ Bank shares)		

T-2 On Payment of Contracted Sum

Journal Entry

Date	Particulars	Debit (AUD)	Credit (AUD)
7-Jan-X1	Boon & Co. Account	38,140.00	
	To Bank Account		38,140.00
	(Being the amount paid to the broker on purchase of shares together with brokerage)		

T-3 On Purchase of Shares and Payment of Brokerage

Journal Entry

Date	Particulars	Debit (AUD)	Credit (AUD)
15-Jan-X1	Investments—Equity Shares—AFS Account	42,000.00	
	To Boon & Co. Account		42,000.00
	(Being 1,000 ANZ Bank shares bought @ $42 per share through the broker, Boon & Co.)		
15-Jan-X1	Investments—Equity Shares—AFS Account	160.00	
	To Boon & Co. Account		160.00
	(Being the brokerage payable to Boon & Co. on purchase of 1,000 ANZ Bank shares)		

T-4 On Payment of Contracted Sum

Journal Entry

Date	Particulars	Debit (AUD)	Credit (AUD)
17-Jan-X1	Boon & Co. Account	42,160.00	
	To Bank Account		42,160.00
	(Being the amount paid to the broker on purchase of shares together with brokerage)		

T-5 Mark-to-market at End of Reporting Period

Mark-to-market at end of reporting period: 31-Jan-X1	AUD
(a) Cost of acquisition of 1,000 shares @ AUD38	38,140.00
(b) Cost of acquisition of 1,000 shares @ AUD42	42,160.00
(c) Total cost of 2,000 shares = (a) + (b)	80,300.00
(d) Market value	110,000.00
(e) Unrealized gains = (d) − (c)	29,700.00

Journal Entry

Date	Particulars	Debit (AUD)	Credit (AUD)
31-Jan-X1	Investments—Equity Shares—AFS Account	29,700.00	
	To Unrealized Capital Gains/Loss—Equity Shares—OCI Account		29,700.00
	(Being the unrealized gains on purchase of equity shares)		

T-6 Reversal of Mark-to-market Entry

Journal Entry

Date	Particulars	Debit (AUD)	Credit (AUD)
1-Feb-X1	Unrealized Capital Gains/Loss—Equity Shares—OCI Account	29,700.00	
	To Investments—Equity Shares—AFS Account		29,700.00
	(Being the reversal of mark-to-market on equity shares)		

T-7 On Sale of Shares and Payment of Brokerage

Journal Entry

Date	Particulars	Debit (AUD)	Credit (AUD)
5-Feb-X1	Boon & Co. Account	76,800.00	
	To Investments—Equity Shares—AFS Account		76,800.00
	(Being 1,600 ANZ Bank shares sold @ $48 per share through the broker, Boon & Co.)		
5-Feb-X1	Investments—Equity Shares—AFS Account	230.00	
	To Boon & Co. Account		230.00
	(Being brokerage payable to Boon & Co. on sale of 1,600 ANZ Bank shares)		

T-8 Profit/Loss on Sale of Shares

Calculation of capital gains	AUD
(a) Sale value of 1,600 shares @ AUD48 less brokerage	76,570.00
(b) Cost of acquisition of 1,000 shares @ AUD38	38,140.00
(c) Cost of acquisition of 600 shares [(42,160 × 600)/1,000]	25,296.00
(d) Total cost of acquisition = (b) − (c)	63,436.00
(e) Realized capital gains in AUD = (a) − (d)	**13,134.00**

Journal Entry

Date	Particulars	Debit (AUD)	Credit (AUD)
5-Feb-X1	Investments—Equity Shares—AFS Account	13,134.00	
	To Realized Capital Gains/Loss—Equity Shares Account		13,134.00
	(Being the realized loss on the sale of 1,600 ANZ Bank shares)		

T-9 On Receipt of Contracted Sum

Journal Entry

Date	Particulars	Debit (AUD)	Credit (AUD)
7-Feb-X1	Bank Account	76,570.00	
	To Boon & Co. Account		76,570.00
	(Being the receipt of consideration from Boon & Co. on sale of shares)		

T-10 Mark-to-market at End of Reporting Period

Mark-to-market at end of reporting period: 28-Feb-X1	AUD
(a) Market value of 400 shares @ AUD58	23,200.00
(b) Cost of acquisition of 400 shares [(42,160 × 400)/1,000]	16,864.00
(c) Unrealized gains = (a) − (b)	6,336.00

Journal Entry

Date	Particulars	Debit (AUD)	Credit (AUD)
28-Feb-X1	Investments—Equity Shares—AFS Account	6,336.00	
	To Unrealized Capital Gains/Loss—Equity Shares—OCI Account		6,336.00
	(Being the unrealized gains on 400 equity shares of ANZ Bank)		

T-11 Reversal of Mark-to-market

Journal Entry

Date	Particulars	Debit (AUD)	Credit (AUD)
1-Mar-X1	Unrealized Capital Gains/Loss—Equity Shares—OCI Account	6,336.00	
	To Investments—Equity Shares—AFS Account		6,336.00
	(Being the reversal of mark-to-market on equity shares)		

T-12 Mark-to-market at End of Reporting Period

Mark-to-market at end of reporting period: 31-Mar-X1	AUD
(a) Market value of 400 shares @ AUD50	20,000.00
(b) Cost of acquisition of 400 shares	16,864.00
(c) Unrealized gains = (a) − (b)	3,136.00

Journal Entry

Date	Particulars	Debit (AUD)	Credit (AUD)
31-Mar-X1	Investments—Equity Shares—AFS Account	3,136.00	
	To Unrealized Capital Gains/Loss—Equity Shares—OCI Account		3,136.00
	(Being the unrealized gains on 400 equity shares of ANZ Bank)		

General Ledger Accounts

Investments—Equity Shares—AFS Account

Date	Particulars	Debit (AUD)	Date	Particulars	Credit (AUD)
5-Jan-X1	To Boon & Co. Account	138,000.00			
5-Jan-X1	To Boon & Co. Account	140.00			
15-Jan-X1	To Boon & Co. Account	42,000.00			
15-Jan-X1	To Boon & Co. Account	160.00			
31-Jan-X1	To Unrealized Capital Gains/Loss—Equity Shares—OCI Account	29,700.00			
			1-Feb-X1	By Unrealized Capital Gains/Loss Equity Shares OCI Account	29,700.00
			5-Feb-X1	By Boon & Co. Account	76,800.00
5-Feb-X1	To Boon & Co. Account	230.00			
5-Feb-X1	To Realized Capital Gains/Loss—Equity Account	13,134.00			
28-Feb-X1	To Unrealized Capital Gains/Loss—Equity Shares—OCI Account	6,336.00			

Investments—Equity Shares—AFS Account (*Cont'd*)

Date	Particulars	Debit (AUD)	Date	Particulars	Credit (AUD)
			1-Mar-X1	By Unrealized Capital Gains/ Loss—Equity Shares—OCI Account	6,336.00
31-Mar-X1	To Unrealized Capital Gains/ Loss—Equity Shares—OCI Account	3,136			
			31-Mar-X1	By Balance	20,000.00
31-Mar-X1	Total	**132,836.00**	31-Mar-X1	Total	**132,836.00**
31-Mar-X1	To Balance	20,000.00			

Realized Capital Gains/Loss Equity Account

Date	Particulars	Debit (AUD)	Date	Particulars	Credit (AUD)
			5-Feb-X1	By Investments—Equity Shares—AFS Account	13,134.00
31-Mar-X1	To Balance	13,134.00			
31-Mar-X1	Total	**13,134.00**	31-Mar-X1	Total	**13,134.00**
			31-Mar-X1	By Balance	13,134.00

Unrealized Capital Gains/Loss—Equity Shares—OCI Account

Date	Particulars	Debit (AUD)	Date	Particulars	Credit (AUD)
			31-Jan-X1	By Investments—Equity Shares—AFS Account	29,700.00
1-Feb-X1	To Investments—Equity Shares—AFS Account	29,700.00			
			28-Feb-X1	By Investments—Equity Shares—AFS Account	6,336.00
1-Mar-X1	To Investments—Equity Shares—AFS Account	6,336.00			
			31-Mar-X1	By Investments—Equity Shares—AFS Account	3,136.00

Unrealized Capital Gains/Loss—Equity Shares (*Cont'd*)

Date	Particulars	Debit (AUD)	Date	Particulars	Credit (AUD)
31-Mar-X1	To Balance	3,136.00			
31-Mar-X1	Total	**39,172.00**	31-Mar-X1	Total	**39,172.00**
			31-Mar-X1	By Balance	3,136.00

Boon & Co. Account

Date	Particulars	Debit (AUD)	Date	Particulars	Credit (AUD)
			5-Jan-X1	By Investments—Equity Shares—AFS Account	38,000.00
			5-Jan-X1	By Investments—Equity Shares—AFS Account	140.00
7-Jan-X1	To Bank Account	38,140.00			
			15-Jan-X1	By Investments—Equity Shares—AFS Account	42,000.00
			15-Jan-X1	By Investments—Equity Shares—AFS Account	160.00
17-Jan-X1	To Bank Account	42,160.00			
5-Feb-X1	To Investments—Equity Shares—AFS Account	76,800.00			
			5-Feb-X1	By Investments—Equity Shares—AFS Account	230.00
			7-Feb-X1	By Bank Account	76,570.00
31-Mar-X1	Total	**157,100.00**	31-Mar-X1	Total	**157,100.00**

Bank Account

Date	Particulars	Debit (AUD)	Date	Particulars	Credit (AUD)
			7-Jan-X1	By Boon & Co. Account	38,140.00
			17-Jan-X1	By Boon & Co. Account	42,160.00
7-Feb-X1	To Boon & Co. Account	76,570.00			

Bank Account (*Cont'd*)

Date	Particulars	Debit (AUD)	Date	Particulars	Credit (AUD)
31-Mar-X1	To Balance	3,730.00			
31-Mar-X1	Total	**80,300.00**	31-Mar-X1	Total	**80,300.00**
			31-Mar-X1	By Balance	3,730.00

Trial Balance

As of 31-Mar-X1 (AUD)

Particulars	Debit	Credit
Current Liabilities		
Bank Account		3,730.00
Investments		
Investments—Equity Shares—AFS Account	20,000.00	
Direct Income		
Realized Capital Gains/Loss Equity Account		13,134.00
Unrealized Capital Gains/Loss—Equity Shares—OCI Account		3,136.00
Total	**20,000.00**	**20,000.00**

Income Statement

For the period ending 31-Mar-X1

Expenses	AUD	Income	AUD
		Direct Income	
Net Profit Carryover	13,134.00	Realized Capital Gains/Loss Equity Account	13,134.00
Total	**13,134.00**	Total	**13,134.00**

Balance Sheet

As on 31-Mar-X1

Liabilities	AUD	Assets	AUD
Capital Account		**Investments**	
Unrealized Capital Gains/Loss—Equity Shares—OCI Account	3,136.00	Investments—Equity Shares—AFS Account	20,000.00
Current Liabilities			
Bank Account	3,730.00	Current Assets	Nil
Profit & Loss Account			
Opening Balance	Nil		

Balance Sheet (*Cont'd*)

As on 31-Mar-X1

Liabilities	AUD	Assets	AUD
Current Period	13,134.00		
Total	20,000.00	Total	20,000.00

Equity Shares AFS; Functional Currency US$

The following are the FX revaluation entries in the functional currency converted at the respective FX rate which is given within parentheses. FX translation entries are clearly specified, indicating whether each is a consummated FX translation entry or a transient FX translation entry.

F-1 On Purchase of the Shares (T-1 @ FX Rate: 1.32)

Journal Entry

Date	Particulars	Debit (US$)	Credit (US$)
5-Jan-X1	Investments—Equity Shares—AFS Account	28,787.88	
	To Boon & Co. Account		28,787.88
	(Being 1,000 ANZ Bank shares bought @ $38 per share through the Broker—Boon & Co.)		
5-Jan-X1	Investments—Equity Shares—AFS Account	106.06	
	To Boon & Co. Account		106.06
	(Being the brokerage payable to Boon & Co. on purchase of 1,000 ANZ Bank shares)		

F-2 Payment of Contracted Sum (T-2 @ FX Rate: 1.34)

Journal Entry

Date	Particulars	Debit (US$)	Credit (US$)
7-Jan-X1	Boon & Co. Account	28,462.69	
	To Bank Account		28,462.69
	(Being the amount paid to the broker on purchase of 1,000 ANZ Bank shares together with brokerage)		

F-3 Currency Gains/Loss on Settlement (Consummated FX Translation Entry)

The settlement amount when converted into US$ based on the FX rate on the date of settlement results in a different amount than the contracted amount in US$ terms. This represents the currency gains or loss and is taken directly to the profit and loss account. If this FX translation entry is not passed, then the liability account of the broker will continue to have a balance even though the broker is settled in full in the respective local currency.

Calculation of currency gains on settlement	AUD	US$
(a) Purchase price of 1,000 shares @ AUD38	38,000.00	
(b) Add brokerage	140.00	
(c) Total amount payable = (a) + (b)	38,140.00	
(d) January 5—Purchase amount in US$ @ 1.32		28,893.94
(e) January 7—Settlement amount in US$ @ 1.34		28,462.69
(f) Realized currency gains on settlement = (d) − (e)		**431.25**

Journal Entry

Date	Particulars	Debit (US$)	Credit (US$)
7-Jan-X1	Boon & Co. Account	431.25	
	To Realized Currency Gains/Loss Account		431.25
	(Being the realized currency gains on settlement)		

F-4 On Purchase of Equity Shares and Payment of Brokerage (T-3 @ FX Rate: 1.36)

Journal Entry

Date	Particulars	Debit (US$)	Credit (US$)
15-Jan-X1	Investments—Equity Shares—AFS Account	30,882.35	
	To Boon & Co. Account		30,882.35
	(Being 1,000 ANZ Bank shares bought @ $42 per share through the broker, Boon & Co.)		
15-Jan-X1	Investments—Equity Shares—AFS Account	117.65	
	To Boon & Co. Account		117.65
	(Being the brokerage payable to Boon & Co. on purchase of 1,000 ANZ Bank shares)		

F-5 On Payment of Contracted Sum (T-4 @ FX Rate: 1.30)

Journal Entry

Date	Particulars	Debit (US$)	Credit (US$)
17-Jan-X1	Boon & Co. Account	32,430.77	
	To Bank Account		32,430.77
	(Being the amount paid to the broker on purchase of 1,000 ANZ Bank shares together with brokerage)		

F-6 Currency Gains/Loss on Settlement (Consummated FX Translation Entry)

Calculation of currency gains on settlement	AUD	US$
(a) Purchase price of 1,000 shares @ AUD42	42,000.00	
(b) Add brokerage	160.00	
(c) Total amount payable	42,160.00	
(d) January 15—Purchase amount FX Rate US$/AUD = 1.36		31,000.00
(e) January 17—Settlement amount FX Rate US$/AUD = 1.30		32,430.77
(f) Realized currency loss		**(1,430.77)**

Journal Entry

Date	Particulars	Debit (US$)	Credit (US$)
17-Jan-X1	Realized Currency Gains/Loss Account	1,430.77	
	To Boon & Co. Account		1,430.77
	(Being realized currency loss on settlement)		

F-7 Mark-to-market at End of Reporting Period (T-5 @ FX Rate: 1.19)

Mark-to-market at end of reporting period: 31-Jan-X1	AUD	US$
(a) Cost of acquisition of 1,000 shares @ AUD38	38,140.00	
(b) Cost of acquisition of 1,000 shares @ AUD42	42,160.00	
(c) Total cost = (a) + (b)	80,300.00	
(d) Market value of 2,000 shares @ 55 on Jan X1	110,000.00	
(e) Mark-to-market = (d) − (c)	29,700.00	
(f) Unrealized gains in US$ @ 1.19		24,957.98

Journal Entry

Date	Particulars	Debit (US$)	Credit (US$)
31-Jan-X1	Investments—Equity Shares—AFS Account	24,957.98	
	To Unrealized Capital Gains/Loss—Equity Shares—OCI Account		24,957.98
	(Being the unrealized loss on purchase of equity shares)		

F-8 Currency Gains/Loss—Bank FX (Transient FX translation entry)

Date	Particulars	AUD	FX Rate	USD
7-Jan-X1	Purchase price including brokerage as of 5-Jan-X1	(38,140.00)	1.340	(28,462.69)
17-Jan-X1	Purchase price including brokerage as of 5-Jan-X1	(42,160.00)	1.300	(32,430.77)
31-Jan-X1	Net balance	(80,300.00)		(60,893.46)
	Net balance at current FX rate	(80,300.00)	1.190	(67,478.99)
	FX translation on Bank account			**6,585.53**

Journal Entry

Date	Particulars	Debit (US$)	Credit (US$)
31-Jan-X1	Unrealized Currency Gain/Loss – Bank Account	6,585.53	
	To Bank Account		6,585.53
	(Being the unrealized currency Gains/Loss on Bank)		

F-9 Reversal of Mark-to-market Entry (T-6 @ FX Rate: 1.19)

Journal Entry

Date	Particulars	Debit (US$)	Credit (US$)
1-Feb-X1	Unrealized Capital Gains/Loss—Equity Shares—OCI Account	24,957.98	
	To Investments—Equity Shares—AFS Account		24,957.98
	(Being the reversal of mark-to-market on equity shares)		

F-10 Currency Gains/Loss (Transient FX Translation Entry)

Unrealized currency gains on 31-Jan-X1	AUD	US$
(a) January 5 cost of acquisition of 1,000 shares + brokerage	38,140.00	
(b) January 5 value in US$ @ 1.32		28,893.94
(c) January 31 value in US$ @ 1.19		32,050.42
(d) Unrealized currency gains		3,156.48
(e) January 15 cost of acquisition of 1,000 shares + brokerage	42,160.00	
(f) January 15 value in US$ @ 1.36		31,000.00
(g) January 31 value in US$ @ 1.19		35,428.57
(h) Unrealized currency gains		4,428.57
(i) Total unrealized currency gains as of January 31		7,585.05

Journal Entry

Date	Particulars	Debit (US$)	Credit (US$)
31-Jan-X1	Investments—Equity Shares—AFS Account	7,585.05	
	To Unrealized Currency Gains/Loss Equity—OCI Account		7,585.05
	(Being the unrealized currency gains/loss)		

Journal Entry

Date	Particulars	Debit (US$)	Credit (US$)
1-Feb-X1	Unrealized Currency Gains/Loss Equity—OCI Account	7,585.05	
	To Investments—Equity Shares—AFS Account		7,585.05
	(Being the unrealized currency gains/loss)		

F-11 On Sale of Equity Shares and Payment of Brokerage (T-7 @ FX Rate: 1.15)

Journal Entry

Date	Particulars	Debit (US$)	Credit (US$)
5-Feb-X1	Boon & Co. Account	66,782.61	
	To Investments—Equity Shares—AFS Account		66,782.61
	(Being 1,600 ANZ Bank shares sold @ $48 per share through the broker, Boon & Co.)		
5-Feb-X1	Investments—Equity Shares—AFS Account	200.00	
	To Boon & Co. Account		200.00
	(Being the brokerage payable to Boon & Co. on sale of 1,600 ANZ Bank shares)		

F-12 Recording the Profit/Loss on Sale Shares (T-8 @ FX Rate: 1.15)

Journal Entry

Date	Particulars	Debit (US$)	Credit (US$)
5-Feb-X1	Investments—Equity Shares—AFS Account	11,420.87	
	To Realized Capital Gains/Loss—Equity Shares Account		11,420.87
	(Being the gains on the sale of 1,600 ANZ Bank shares)		

F-13 Realized Currency Gains/Loss on Liquidation (Consummated FX Translation Entry)

Calculation of capital gains	AUD	US$
(a) Sale value of 1,600 shares @ AUD48 after brokerage	76,570.00	
(b) Cost of sales of 1,000 shares @ AUD38	38,140.00	
(c) Cost of sale of 600 shares [(42,160 × 600)/1,000]	25,296.00	
(d) Total cost of sales	63,436.00	
(e) Realized gains in AUD = (a) − (d)	13,134.00	
(f) Realized capital gains in US$ @ 1.15	13,134.00	11,420.87
(g) Sale value on February 5 in US$		66,582.61
(h) Cost of sales of 1,000 shares in US$	$ 28,893.94	
(i) Cost of sale of 600 share [(31,000 × 600)/1,000] in US$	$ 18,600.00	
(j) Total cost of sale in US$ = (h) + (i)		47,493.94
(k) Realized gains in US$ = (g) − (j)		19,088.67
(l) Realized currency gain on liquidation = (k) − (f)		**7,667.80**

Journal Entry

Date	Particulars	Debit (US$)	Credit (US$)
5-Feb-X1	Investments—Equity Shares—AFS Account	7,667.80	
	To Realized Currency Gains/Loss Account		7,667.80
	(Being the realized currency gains/loss on liquidation)		

F-14 On Receipt of Contracted Sum (T-9 @ FX Rate: 1.25)

Journal Entry

Date	Particulars	Debit (US$)	Credit (US$)
7-Feb-X1	Bank Account	61,256.00	
	To Boon & Co. Account		61,256.00
	(Being the sale of 1,600 ANZ Bank shares)		

F-15 Currency Gains/Loss on Settlement (Consummated FX Translation Entry)

The settlement amount when converted into US$ based on the FX rate on the date of settlement results in a different amount than the contracted amount in US$ terms. This represents the currency gains or loss and is taken directly to the profit and loss account. If this FX translation entry is not passed, then the liability account of the broker will continue to have a balance even though the broker is settled in full in the respective local currency.

Realized currency gains/loss on settlement	**AUD**	**US$**
(a) Sale value of 1,600 shares @ AUD48	76,800.00	
(b) Less brokerage	230.00	
(c) Total sale value (a) – (b)	76,570.00	
(d) February 5 value in US$ @ 1.15		66,582.61
(e) February 7 settlement amount in US$ @ 1.25		61,256.00
(f) Realized currency loss on settlement = (e) − (d)		**(5,326.61)**

Journal Entry

Date	Particulars	Debit (US$)	Credit (US$)
7-Feb-X1	Realized Currency Gains/Loss Account	5,326.61	
	To Boon & Co. Account		5,326.61
	(Being the realized currency loss on settlement)		

F-16 Mark-to-market at End of Reporting Period (T-10 @ FX Rate: 1.16)

Mark-to-market at end of reporting period: 28-Feb-X1	**AUD**	**US$**
(a) Market value of 400 shares @ AUD58	23,200.00	
(b) Value of 400 shares [(42,160 × 400)/1,000]	16,864.00	
(c) Mark-to-market in AUD = (b) − (a)	6,336.00	
(d) Unrealized gains in US$ @ 1.16		5,462.07

Journal Entry

Date	Particulars	Debit (US$)	Credit (US$)
28-Feb-X1	Investments—Equity Shares—AFS Account	5,462.07	
	To Unrealized Capital Gains/Loss—Equity Shares—OCI Account		5,462.07
	(Being the unrealized gains on 400 equity shares of ANZ Bank)		

F-17 Reversal of Mark-to-market (T-11 @ FX Rate: 1.16)

Journal Entry

Date	Particulars	Debit (US$)	Credit (US$)
1-Mar-X1	Unrealized Capital Gains/Loss—Equity Shares—OCI Account	5,462.07	
	To Investments—Equity Shares—AFS Account		5,462.07
	(Being the reversal of mark-to-market on equity shares)		

F-18 Currency Gains/Loss—FX (Transient FX Translation Entry)

Calculation of unrealized capital gains	**AUD**	**US$**
(a) Market value of 400 shares @ AUD58	23,200.00	
(b) Cost of acquisition of 400 shares [(42,160 × 400/1,000]	16,864.00	
(c) Mark-to-market as of February 28 in AUD = (a) − (b)	6,336.00	
(d) Mark-to-market as of February 28 in US$ @ 1.16		5462.07
Calculation of unrealized currency gains		
(e) Market value of 400 shares @ AUD58/1.16		20,000.00
(f) Cost of acquisition of 400 shares [(31,000 × 400)/1000]		12,400.00
(g) Mark-to-market as of February 28 in US$ = (a) − (b)		7,600.00
(h) Unrealized currency gains = (g) − (d)		2,137.93

Journal Entry

Date	Particulars	Debit (US$)	Credit (US$)
28-Feb-X1	Investments—Equity Shares—AFS Account	2,137.93	
	To Unrealized Currency Gains/Loss Equity—OCI Account		2,137.93
	(Being the unrealized currency gains/loss)		

Journal Entry

Date	Particulars	Debit (US$)	Credit (US$)
1-Mar-X1	Unrealized Currency Gains/Loss Equity—OCI Account	2,137.93	
	To Investments—Equity Shares—AFS Account		2,137.93
	(Being the unrealized currency gains/loss reversed on the next day)		

F-19 Currency Gains/Loss—Bank FX (Transient FX translation entry)

Date	Particulars	AUD	FX Rate	US$
	Opening Balance	(80,300.00)		(67,478.99)
7-Feb-X1	Sell price including brokerage as of 5-Feb-X1	76,570.00	1.250	61,256.00
28-Feb-X1	Net balance	(3,730.00)		(6,222.99)
	Net balance at current FX rate	(3,730.00)	1.160	(3,215.52)
	FX translation on Bank account			3,007.47

Journal Entry

Date	Particulars	Debit (US$)	Credit (US$)
28-Feb-X1	Bank Account	3,007.47	
	To Unrealized Currency Gain/Loss – Bank Account		3,007.47
	(Being the unrealized currency gains/loss on Bank)		

F-20 Mark-to-market at End of Reporting Period (T-12 @ FX Rate: 1.18)

Mark-to-market at end of reporting period: 31-Mar-X1	AUD	US$
(a) Market value of 400 shares @ AUD50	20,000.00	16,949.15
(b) Cost of acquisition of 400 shares	16,864.00	14,291.53
(c) Unrealized gains	3,136.00	2,657.63

Journal Entry

Date	Particulars	Debit (US$)	Credit (US$)
31-Mar-X1	Investments—Equity Shares—AFS Account	2,657.63	
	To Unrealized Capital Gains/Loss—Equity Shares—OCI Account		2,657.63
	(Being the unrealized gains on 400 equity shares of ANZ Bank)		

F-21 Currency Gains/Loss—FX (Transient FX Translation Entry)

Calculation of unrealized capital gains	AUD	US$
(a) Market value of 400 shares @ AUD50	20,000.00	
(b) Cost of acquisition of 400 shares [(42,160 × 400/1,000]	16,864.00	
(c) Mark-to-market as of March 31 in AUD = (a) − (b)	3,136.00	
(d) Mark-to-market as of March 31 in US$		**2,657.63**

Calculation of unrealized currency gains (*Cont'd*)	AUD	US$
(e) Market value of 400 shares @ AUD58/1.18		16,949.15
(f) Cost of acquisition of 400 shares in US$ [(31,000 × 400)/100]		12,400.00
(g) Mark-to-market as of March 31 in US$ = (a) − (b)		4,549.15
(h) Unrealized currency gains as of March 31 = (g) − (d)		1,891.52

Journal Entry

Date	Particulars	Debit (US$)	Credit (US$)
31-Mar-X1	Investments—Equity Shares—AFS Account	1,891.52	
	To Unrealized Currency Gains/Loss Equity—OCI Account		1,891.52
	(Being the unrealized currency gains/loss)		

F-22 Currency Gains/Loss—Bank FX (Transient FX translation entry)

Date	Particulars	AUD	FX Rate	US$
	Opening Balance	(3,730.00)		(3,215.52)
31-Mar-X1	Net balance	(3,730.00)		(3,215.52)
	Net balance at current FX rate	(3,730.00)	1.180	(3,161.02)
	FX translation on Bank account			**54.50**

Journal Entry

Date	Particulars	Debit (US$)	Credit (US$)
31-Mar-X1	Bank Account	54.50	
	To Unrealized Currency Gain/Loss – Bank Account		54.50
	(Being the unrealized currency gains/loss on Bank)		

General Ledger Accounts

Investments—Equity Shares—AFS Account

Date	Particulars	Debit (US$)	Date	Particulars	Credit (US$)
5-Jan-X1	To Boon & Co. Account	28,787.88			
5-Jan-X1	To Boon & Co. Account	106.06			

Investments—Equity Shares—AFS Account (*Cont'd*)

Date	Particulars	Debit (US$)	Date	Particulars	Credit (US$)
15-Jan-X1	To Boon & Co. Account	30,882.35			
15-Jan-X1	To Boon & Co. Account	117.65			
31-Jan-X1	To Unrealized Capital Gains/ Loss—Equity Shares—OCI Account	24,957.98			
			1-Feb-X1	By Unrealized Capital Gains/ Loss—Equity Shares—OCI Account	24,957.98
31-Jan-X1	To Unrealized Currency Gains/ Loss Equity—OCI Account	7,585.05			
			1-Feb-X1	By Unrealized Currency Gains/ Loss Equity—OCI Account	7,585.05
			5-Feb-X1	By Boon & Co. Account	66,782.61
5-Feb-X1	To Boon & Co. Account	200.00			
5-Feb-X1	To Realized Capital Gains/Loss—Equity Account	11,420.87			
5-Feb-X1	To Realized Currency Gains/ Loss Equity Account	7,667.80			
28-Feb-X1	To Unrealized Capital Gains/ Loss—Equity Shares—OCI Account	5,462.07			
			1-Mar-X1	By Unrealized Capital Gains/ Loss—Equity Shares—OCI Account	5,462.07
28-Feb-X1	To Unrealized Currency Gains/ Loss Equity—OCI Account	2,137.93			
			1-Mar-X1	By Unrealized Currency Gains/ Loss Equity—OCI Account	2,137.93

Investments—Equity Shares—AFS Account (*Cont'd*)

Date	Particulars	Debit (US$)	Date	Particulars	Credit (US$)
31-Mar-X1	To Unrealized Currency Gains/ Loss Equity—OCI Account	1,891.52			
31-Mar-X1	To Unrealized Capital Gains/ Loss—Equity Shares—OCI Account	2,657.63			
			31-Mar-X1	By Balance	16,949.15
31-Mar-X1	Total	**123,874.79**	31-Mar-X1	Total	**123,874.79**
31-Mar-X1	To Balance	16,949.15			

Realized Capital Gains/Loss Equity–Account

Date	Particulars	Debit (US$)	Date	Particulars	Credit (US$)
			5-Feb-X1	By Investments—Equity Shares—AFS Account	11,420.87
31-Mar-X1	To Balance	11,420.87			
31-Mar-X1	Total	**11,420.87**	31-Mar-X1	Total	**11,420.87**
			31-Mar-X1	By Balance	11,420.87

Realized Currency Gains/Loss Equity—Account

Date	Particulars	Debit (US$)	Date	Particulars	Credit (US$)
			8-Jan-X1	By Boon & Co.	431.25
17-Jan-X1	To Boon & Co.	1,430.77			
			5-Feb-X1	By Investments—Equity Shares—AFS Account	7,667.80
7-Feb-X1	To Boon & Co. Account	5,326.61			
31-Mar-X1	To Balance	1,341.67			
31-Mar-X1	Total	**8,099.05**	31-Mar-X1	Total	**8,099.05**
			31-Mar-X1	By Balance	1,341.67

Unrealized Capital Gains/Loss—Equity Shares—OCI Account

Date	Particulars	Debit (US$)	Date	Particulars	Credit (US$)
			31-Jan-X1	By Investments—Equity Shares—AFS Account	24,957.98
1-Feb-X1	To Investments—Equity Shares—AFS Account	24,957.98			
			28-Feb-X1	By Investments—Equity Shares—AFS Account	5,462.07
1-Mar-X1	To Investments—Equity Shares—AFS Account	5,462.07			
			31-Mar-X1	By Investments—Equity Shares—AFS Account	2,657.63
31-Mar-X1	To Balance	2,657.63			
31-Mar-X1	Total	**33,077.68**	31-Mar-X1	Total	**33,077.68**
			31-Mar-X1	By Balance	2,657.63

Unrealized Currency Gains/Loss Equity—OCI Account

Date	Particulars	Debit (US$)	Date	Particulars	Credit (US$)
			31-Jan-X1	By Investments—Equity Shares—AFS Account	7,585.05
1-Feb-X1	To Investments—Equity Shares—AFS Account	7,585.05			
			28-Feb-X1	By Investments—Equity Shares—AFS Account	2,137.93
1-Mar-X1	To Investments—Equity Shares—AFS Account	2,137.93			
			31-Mar-X1	By Investments—Equity Shares—AFS Account	1,891.52
31-Mar-X1	To Balance	1,891.52			
31-Mar-X1	Total	**11,614.50**	31-Mar-X1	Total	**11,614.50**
			31-Mar-X1	By Balance	1,891.52

Unrealized Currency Gain/Loss—Bank Account

Date	Particulars	Debit (US$)	Date	Particulars	Credit (US$)
31-Jan-X1	To Bank Account	6,585.53			
			28-Feb-X1	By Bank Account	3,007.47
			31-Mar-X1	By Bank Account	54.50
			31-Mar-X1	By Balance	3,523.56
31-Mar-X1	Total	**6,585.53**	31-Mar-X1	Total	**6,585.53**
31-Mar-X1	To Balance	3,523.56			

Boon & Co. Account

Date	Particulars	Debit (US$)	Date	Particulars	Credit (US$)
			5-Jan-X1	By Investments—Equity Shares—AFS Account	28,787.88
			5-Jan-X1	By Investments—Equity Shares—AFS Account	106.06
7-Jan-X1	To Bank Account	28,462.69			
7-Jan-X1	To Realized Currency Gains/Loss Equity Account	431.25			
			15-Jan-X1	By Investments—Equity Shares—AFS Account	30,882.35
			15-Jan-X1	By Investments—Equity Shares—AFS Account	117.65
			17-Jan-X1	By Realized Currency Gains/Loss Equity Account	1,430.77
17-Jan-X1	To Bank Account	32,430.77			
5-Feb-X1	To Investments—Equity Shares—AFS Account	66,782.61			
			5-Feb-X1	By Investments—Equity Shares—AFS Account	200.00
			7-Feb-X1	By Bank Account	61,256.00
			7-Feb-X1	By Realized Currency Gains/Loss Account	5,326.61
31-Mar-X1	Total	**128,107.32**	31-Mar-X1	Total	**128,107.32**

Bank Account

Date	Particulars	Debit (US$)	Date	Particulars	Credit (US$)
			7-Jan-X1	By Boon & Co. Account	28,462.69
			17-Jan-X1	By Boon & Co. Account	32,430.77
			31-Jan-X1	By Unreal-ized Cur-rency Gain/ Loss – Bank Account	6,585.53
7-Feb-X1	To Boon & Co. Account	61,256.00			
28-Feb-X1	To Unrealized Cur-rency Gain/Loss – Bank Account	3,007.47			
31-Mar-X1	To Unrealized Cur-rency Gain/Loss – Bank Account	54.50			
31-Mar-X1	To Balance	3,161.02			
31-Mar-X1	Total	**67,478.99**	31-Mar-X1	Total	**67,478.99**
			31-Mar-X1	By Balance	3,161.03

Trial Balance

As on 31-Mar-X1 (US$)

Particulars	Debit	Credit
Current Assets		
Bank Account		3,161.02
Investments		
Investments—Equity Shares—AFS Account	16,949.15	
Income		
Realized Capital Gains/Loss Equity Shares Account		11,420.87
Realized Currency Gains/Loss Equity Shares Account		1,341.67
Unrealized Capital Gains/Loss—Equity Shares—OCI Account		2,657.63
Unrealized Currency Gain/Loss – Bank Account	3,523.56	
Unrealized Currency Gains/Loss—Equity Shares—OCI Account		1,891.52
Total	**20,472.71**	**20,472.71**

Income Statement

For the period ending 31-Mar-X1

Expenses	US$	Income	US$
		Direct Income	
		Realized Capital Gains/Loss Equity Shares Account	11,420.87
		Realized Currency Gains/Loss—Equity Shares Account	1,341.67
Unrealized Currency Gain/Loss – Bank Account	3,523.56		
Net Profit Carryover	9,238.98		
Total	**12,762.54**	Total	**12,762.54**

Balance Sheet

As at 31-Mar-X1

Liabilities	US$	Assets	US$
Capital Account		**Investments**	
Unrealized Capital Gains/ Loss—Equity Shares—OCI Account	2,657.63	Investments—Equity Shares—AFS Account	16,949.15
Unrealized Currency Gains/ Loss Equity Shares—OCI Account	1,891.52	**Current Assets**	
Current Liabilities			
Bank Account	3,161.02		
Profit & Loss Account			
Opening Balance	Nil		
Current Period	9,238.98		
Total	**16,949.15**	Total	**16,949.15**

SUMMARY

- According to the accounting standards, available-for-sale (AFS) financial assets are those non-derivative financial assets that are designated as available for sale or are not classified as loans and receivables, held-to-maturity investments, or financial assets at fair value through profit or loss.
- Available-for-sale securities are debt or equity investments that are held for an indefinite period of time without any intention to resell for profit.
- They are not trading assets, as in the case of short-term assets held for speculation, nor are they acquired with an intention to hold till maturity.
- If the market rate is above the purchase rate of AFS securities, then such increase is recorded as part of the other comprehensive income (OCI) and not recognized

as income in the current period. This is shown as part of the shareholders' equity in the balance sheet.

- Any foreign exchange gains and losses on monetary assets are recognized in the statement of profit and loss except for those items that are designated as hedging instruments.
- Equity instruments, being nonmonetary assets, the gain or loss including any related foreign exchange component is recognized directly in the appropriate equity account.
- In the balance sheet, a nonmonetary financial asset such as an investment in equity instrument is translated using the closing rate if it is carried at fair value in the foreign currency, and using the historical rate if it is not carried at fair value when its fair value cannot be reliably measured.
- As per the U.S. GAAP Statement of Position, it is not mandatory to show separately the capital gains/loss due to change in the market rate of the asset, or currency gains/loss due to change in the foreign exchange rate, although the SOP indicates that such separate reporting would provide valuable information to the users of the financial statements.
- If an equity instrument measured at fair value with gains and losses recognized in the appropriate equity account becomes impaired, the cumulative net loss recognized in the equity account, including any portion attributable to foreign currency changes, should be recognized in the statement of profit and loss.
- If the equity securities classified as available-for-sale are sold, then the realized gains/loss on such sale is transferred from the OCI to the income statement and an entry is recorded to that effect.

EXERCISES

Theory Questions

1. When would you classify an investment as *available-for-sale* (AFS)?
2. What are the major differences between trading and available-for-sale securities?
3. What is *other comprehensive income* (OCI) and where is it presented in the final accounts?
4. How is the foreign exchange translation impact on AFS equity securities handled? Is this any different from debt securities? If so, explain why it is so.
5. How is the impairment of AFS securities treated?

Objective Questions

1. AFS securities are debt or equity investments that will be held:
   a. Till maturity
   b. For a predefined period
   c. Only till the current financial year
   d. For an indefinite period of time
   e. None of the above

2. The unrealized gains/losses for AFS securities are:
   a. Recorded as an adjustment to equity on the balance sheet
   b. Not recorded in the balance sheet
   c. Recorded as earnings in P&L for the current period
   d. Both a and c
3. When there is a permanent impairment to the value of the securities held as available-for-sale, such permanent impairment should be recognized as:
   a. Mark-to-market
   b. Current liabilities
   c. Income
   d. Accrued expense
   e. Cost
4. For AFS securities, cost of sales is arrived at by which of the following methods?
   a. Weighted average method
   b. FIFO
   c. LIFO
   d. All of the above methods
   e. None of the above methods

Journal Questions

Available-for-sale, Trade Currency TWD

Taiwan Opportunities Fund traded in Feng Tay Enterprises Co. Ltd., shares in the Taiwan stock exchange through KGI Securities Co. brokers, and the details are as follows:

Trade Details

Date	Product	Quantity	Rate (TWD)	B/S	Brokerage (TWD)
5-Feb-X1	Feng Tay	64,000	27.30	B	5,350
15-Feb-X1	Feng Tay	30,500	26.25	B	2,850
5-Mar-X1	Feng Tay	85,700	25.85	S	4,750

Other Details

Settlement: T + 3

Liquidation Method

FIFO

Market Rate of Feng Tay Shares in TWD

February 28: 26.95
March 31: 27.90
April 30: 30.15

FX Rate: US$/TWD

February 5: 32.67
February 8: 32.63
February 15: 32.76
February 18: 32.79
February 28: 32.98
March 5: 32.83
March 8: 32.87
March 31: 32.90
April 30: 32.77

Functional Currency

US$

Prepare

Journal entries, general ledgers, trial balance, income statement, and balance sheet.

Available-for-sale, Trade Currency SGD

Singapore Fund traded in OCBC Ltd shares in Singapore Exchange through Grayson & Co. brokers, and the details are as follows:

Trade Details

Date	Product	Quantity	Rate (SGD)	B/S	Brokerage (SGD)
8-Feb-X1	OCBC	6,000	9.30	B	558
15-Feb-X1	OCBC	8,000	10.10	B	800
9-Mar-X1	OCBC	11,500	10.30	S	271

Other Details

Settlement: T + 3

Liquidation Method

FIFO

Market Rate of OCBC LTD Shares in SGD

February 28: 10.15
March 31: 9.80
April 30: 10.35

FX Rate: US$/SGD

February 8: 1.54
February 11: 1.52
February 15: 1.51
February 18: 1.53
February 28: 1.52
March 9: 1.55
March 12: 1.53
March 31: 1.50
April 31: 1.54

Functional Currency

US$

Prepare

Journal entries, general ledgers, trial balance, income statement, and balance sheet.

Available-for-sale, Functional Currency CAD

U.S. Fund traded in DSP shares in a Canadian stock exchange through Amazon brokers, and the details are as follows:

Trade Details

Date	Product	Quantity	Rate (CAD)	B/S	Brokerage (CAD)
18-Feb-X1	DSP	5,000	15.15	B	50
25-Feb-X1	DSP	8,000	16.10	B	80
19-Mar-X1	DSP	7,500	16.30	S	75

Other Details

Settlement: T + 3

Liquidation Method

FIFO

Market Rate of DSP LTD Shares in CAD

February 28: 16.15
March 31: 16.80
April 30: 16.35

FX Rate: US$/CAD

February 18: 1.0130
February 21: 1.0140
February 25: 1.0185
February 28: 1.0150
March 19: 1.0220
March 22: 1.0230
March 31: 1.0245
April 31: 1.0190

Functional Currency

US$

Prepare

Journal entries, general ledgers, trial balance, income statement, and balance sheet.

Available-for-Sale, Functional Currency JPY

Dianna Smith buys 10,000 shares of GoldWinner on January 10 for $5.40 per share. Ms. Smith's reporting currency is Japanese yen. The shares are bought without any intention of trading for short-term gains. Record the necessary journal entries for the following events:

1. For the purchase of the 10,000 shares.
2. The US$/JPY rate on January 10 is 109.15. The shares bought on January 10 are settled on January 12. On January 12 the US$/JPY rate is 108.05. Record the FX revaluation entries for these events. Calculate the FX gain/loss and pass relevant entries for FX translation.
3. The shares are sold on January 29 for $6.80 per share and US$/JPY rate on January 29 is 109.00. Calculate the realized gain or loss and pass entry. The US$/JPY rate on January 31(settle date) is 109.24.
4. Prepare relevant ledger accounts to give effect to these transactions.

CHAPTER **4**

Transfer of Categories

LEARNING OBJECTIVES

After studying this chapter, you should have a grasp of the following:

- Transfer of equity investments between trading and available-for-sale categories.
- Presentation in income statement.
- Impairment of securities.
- Deferred tax effects on unrealized gain/loss in trading and available-for-sale securities.
- How to record and report trade transactions of equity investments comprehensively.

Relevant Accounting Standards	
U.S. GAAP	**IFRS**
FAS 52—Foreign Currency Translation	IFRS 7—Financial Instruments: Disclosure
FAS 94—Consolidation of All Majority-owned Subsidiaries	IAS 21—The Effects of Changes in Foreign Exchange Rates
FAS 109—Accounting for Income Taxes	IAS 32—Financial Instruments: Presentation
FAS 115—Accounting for Certain Investments in Debt and Equity Securities	IAS 36—Impairment of Assets
FAS 130—Reporting Comprehensive Income	IAS 39—Financial Instruments: Recognition and Measurement
FAS 157—Fair Value Measurements	
FAS 159—The Fair Value Option for Financial Assets and Financial Liabilities	

TRANSFER BETWEEN CATEGORIES

The classification of securities should be reviewed at each balance sheet date. When the equity securities are transferred from trading securities to the available-for-sale category, then the gain/loss recognized as unrealized should not be reversed and no adjustment should be made to the other comprehensive income (OCI). When the equity securities are transferred from the available-for-sale category to the trading category, then the unrealized gain/loss on such securities based on the fair value of the securities should be transferred from OCI and thus recognized as income immediately on such transfer.

The following table gives the summary of treatment of transfer between the two categories.

Securities Transferred from	Securities Transferred to	Accounting treatment
Available-for-sale	Trading	Unrealized gain/loss is recognized based on fair value
Trading	Available-for-sale	No reversal of gain/loss recognized as unrealized

PRESENTATION IN INCOME STATEMENT

Impairment of Securities

Temporary impairment of the equity securities that are held for trading is automatically tracked by valuing the securities at mark-to-market on every reporting day. Such temporary impairment is not to be recognized and acted upon for available-for-sale securities. However, if the impairment is anything other than temporary, then such impaired security must be written down to fair value. The realized loss on such impairment must be reported in the income statement. Once the impairment is recorded as loss, then even if the security recovers from such impairment, it would not be recognized in the earnings unless it is liquidated through the sale of the security.

Stock Dividend

While the cash dividends received from investments held as trading or as available-for-sale should be reported as income of the current period, the stock dividend should *not* be reported as income. Instead the shares received as stock dividend should be added to the original shares, and when the mark-to-market process is performed, the impact of the stock dividend will be automatically accounted for as unrealized gains and will be reported as income during the period.

Realized and Unrealized Gain/Loss

To summarize, the accounting standards require that investments classified as trading securities, the realized and unrealized gains and losses should be included in the current period's income statement. In the case of investments classified as available-for-sale, however, only realized gains should be taken to the current period's income statement. The unrealized gains on available-for-sale securities should be taken directly to the OCI, which is grouped with the shareholders' equity and is not regarded as income of the current period. However, when the available-for-sale securities are sold, the realized gain/loss should be taken to the income statement and to that extent reversed from the other comprehensive income.

Permanent impairment to the value of the securities held as available-for-sale should be written off as expense in the income statement. This should not be reversed, even if the security recovers from impairment, till such time as the security is liquidated and the actual realized gain/loss is computed.

DEFERRED TAX EFFECTS ON UNREALIZED GAIN/LOSS

The mark-to-market process ensures that the marketable investments held either as trading securities or as available-for-sale securities are to be reported in the balance sheet at fair value and the gain/loss on such investments is to be reported either as income or as other comprehensive income. Such unrealized gain/loss is not recognized for income tax purposes until the same is realized through liquidation. Hence the unrealized gain/loss included in the income or OCI, as the case may be, represents temporary differences as defined by FAS 109.

The tax effects of all temporary differences are to be recognized in the financial statements as deferred tax benefits or deferred tax liabilities. Also, in the case of deferred tax benefits, there is a requirement to provide for an allowance in case it is "more likely than not" going to be unrealized.

Deferred Tax Effect in Trading Securities

For securities classified as trading, the unrealized gain/loss is included in the income and as such represents the temporary differences as defined in the accounting standards. The deferred tax effect of those changes should also be presented in the income statement itself.

Assuming that the fair value of 1,000 Gold Crest shares purchased at $490 is $480 per share, then the unrealized loss on such an investment classified as trading securities would be $10,000. If the effective tax rate of the investor is 35 percent, then $3,500 should be taken to the debit of the deferred tax benefit account.

The accounting entry that is recorded in the books of accounts would be as follows:

Journal Entry

Date	Particulars	Debit (US$)	Credit (US$)
31-Dec-X1	Unrealized Capital Gain/Loss—Equity Account	10,000.00	
	To Investments—Equity Shares—Trading Account		10,000.00
	(Being the unrealized loss on the reporting date on 1,000 Gold Crest shares)		
31-Dec-X1	Deferred tax benefit Account	3,500.00	
	To Provision for Income Taxes Account		3,500.00
	(Being the deferred tax benefit @ 35% on the unrealized loss on the reporting date on 1,000 Gold Crest shares)		

Deferred Tax Effect in Available-for-sale Securities

For securities classified as available-for-sale, the unrealized gain/loss is included in the OCI and as such forms part of the temporary differences as defined in the accounting standards. The deferred tax effect of those changes should also be presented in the OCI itself.

Assuming that the fair value of 1,000 Gold Crest shares purchased at $490 is $480 per share, then the unrealized loss on such investment classified as available-for-sale securities would be $10,000. If the effective tax rate of the investor is 35 percent, then $3,500 should be taken to the debit of the deferred tax benefit account, and the OCI should be reduced to that extent. The accounting entry that is recorded in the books of accounts would be as follows:

Journal Entry

Date	Particulars	Debit (US$)	Credit (US$)
31-Dec-X1	Unrealized Capital Gain/Loss—Equity Account (OCI)	10,000.00	
	To Investments—Equity Account—AFS		10,000.00
	(Being the unrealized loss on the reporting date in respect of 1,000 Gold Crest shares)		
31-Dec-X1	Deferred tax benefit Account	3,500.00	
	To Unrealized Capital Gain/Loss—Equity Account (OCI)		3,500.00
	(Being the deferred tax benefit @ 35% on the unrealized loss on the reporting date on 1,000 Gold Crest shares)		

Illustration—Transfer of Category and Deferred Tax Benefit

Jonathan Swift Inc. traded in Gamut shares that are listed in a U.S. stock exchange through David Brothers Brokers, and the details are as follows:

Trade Details

Date	Product	Quantity	Rate	B/S	Brokerage
5-Jan-X1	Gamut	1,500	$40	B	$150
15-Jan-X1	Gamut	1,200	$42	B	$120
25-Jan-X1	Gamut	1,400	$41	S	$140
25-Mar-X1	Gamut	1,000	$49	S	$100

Other Details

Settlement: T + 2

Liquidation Method

FIFO

Market Rate

January 31: 43
February 28: 45
March 31: 35

The shares were purchased without any intention of trading, nor were they meant to be a long-term investment. However, management changed its mind and decided that

Gamut shares will be classified as trading shares on March 31. Jonathan Swift is charged tax on all its earnings at the rate of 40 percent. Prepare the accounts through March 31.

Prepare

Journal entries, general ledgers, trial balance, income statement, and balance sheet.

Solution

T-1 On Purchase of Equity Shares and Payment of Brokerage

Journal Entry

Date	Particulars	Debit (US$)	Credit (US$)
5-Jan-X1	Investments—Equity Account—AFS Account	60,000.00	
	To David Brothers Account		60,000.00
	(Being the 1,500 Gamut shares bought through the broker, David Brothers)		
5-Jan-X1	Investments—Equity Account—AFS Account	150.00	
	To David Brothers Account		150.00
	(Being the brokerage payable on purchase of 1,500 Gamut shares)		

T-2 On Payment of Contracted Sum

Journal Entry

Date	Particulars	Debit (US$)	Credit (US$)
7-Jan-X1	David Brothers Account	60,150.00	
	To Bank Account		60,150.00
	(Being the payment made to the broker on purchase of 1,500 Gamut shares together with brokerage)		

T-3 On Purchase of Equity Shares and Brokerage

Journal Entry

Date	Particulars	Debit (US$)	Credit (US$)
15-Jan-X1	Investments—Equity Account—AFS Account	50,400.00	
	To David Brothers Account		50,400.00
	(Being 1,200 Gamut shares bought through the broker, David Brothers)		
15-Jan-X1	Investments—Equity Account—AFS Account	120.00	
	To David Brothers Account		120.00
	(Being the brokerage payable on purchase of 1,200 Gamut shares)		

T-4 On Payment of Contracted Sum

Journal Entry

Date	Particulars	Debit (US$)	Credit (US$)
17-Jan-X1	David Brothers Account	50,520.00	
	To Bank Account		50,520.00
	(Being the payment made to the broker on purchase of 1200 Gamut shares together with brokerage)		

T-5 On Sale of Shares and Payment of Brokerage

Journal Entry

Date	Particulars	Debit (US$)	Credit (US$)
25-Jan-X1	David Brothers Account	57,400.00	
	To Investments—Equity Account—AFS Account		57,400.00
	(Being the shares sold through the broker, David Brothers)		
25-Jan-X1	Investments—Equity Account—AFS Account	140.00	
	To David Brothers Account		140.00
	(Being the brokerage payable on sale of 1,400 Gamut shares)		

T-6 On Recording the Profit/Loss on Sale of Shares

Calculation of capital gains	US$
(a) Net sale consideration of 1,400 shares after brokerage	57,260.00
(b) Cost of acquisition of 1,500 shares including brokerage	60,150.00
(c) Proportionate cost of acquisition of 1,400 shares [(60,150 × 1,400)/1,500]	56,140.00
(d) Realized gains = (a) – (c)	**1,120.00**

Journal Entry

Date	Particulars	Debit (US$)	Credit (US$)
25-Jan-X1	Investments—Equity Account—AFS Account	1,120.00	
	To Realized Capital Gains/Loss—Equity Account		1,120.00
	(Being the profit on the sale of 1,400 Gamut shares)		

T-7 On Receipt of Sale Consideration Net of Brokerage

Journal Entry

Date	Particulars	Debit (US$)	Credit (US$)
27-Jan-X1	Bank Account	57,260.00	
	To David Brothers Account		57,260.00
	(Being the net consideration received from David Brothers on sale of 1,400 Gamut shares)		

T-8 Mark-to-market at End of Reporting Period

Mark-to-market at end of reporting period: 31-Jan-X1	**US$**
(a) Cost of acquisition of 100 shares [(60,150/1500) × 100]	4,010.00
(b) Cost of acquisition of 1,200 shares	50,520.00
(c) Total cost of acquisition	54,530.00
(d) Market value at the end of reporting period	55,900.00
(e) Unrealized gains = (d) − (c)	1,370.00

Journal Entry

Date	Particulars	Debit (US$)	Credit (US$)
31-Jan-X1	Investments—Equity Account—AFS Account	1,370.00	
	To Unrealized Capital Gains/Loss—Equity Shares Account—Other Comprehensive Income		1,370.00
	(Being the unrealized gain on 1,300 equity shares of Gamut)		

T-9 Reversal of Mark-to-market on the Next Date

Journal Entry

Date	Particulars	Debit (US$)	Credit (US$)
1-Feb-X1	Unrealized Capital Gains/Loss—Equity Shares Account—Other Comprehensive Income	1,370.00	
	To Investments—Equity Account—AFS Account		1,370.00
	(Being the reversal of mark to market entry)		

T-10 Mark-to-market at End of Reporting Period

Journal Entry

Date	Particulars	Debit (US$)	Credit (US$)
28-Feb-X1	Investments—Equity Account—AFS Account	3,970.00	
	To Unrealized Capital Gains/Loss—Equity Shares Account—Other Comprehensive Income		3,970.00
	(Being the unrealized gain on 1,300 equity shares of Gamut)		

T-11 Reversal of Mark-to-market on the Next Date

Journal Entry

Date	Particulars	Debit (US$)	Credit (US$)
1-Mar-X1	Unrealized Capital Gains/Loss—Equity Shares Account—Other Comprehensive Income	3,970.00	
	To Investments—Equity Account—AFS Account		3,970.00
	(Being the reversal of mark-to-market entry)		

T-12 On Sale of Shares and Payment of Brokerage

Journal Entry

Date	Particulars	Debit (US$)	Credit (US$)
25-Mar-X1	David Brothers Account	49,000.00	
	To Investments—Equity Account—AFS Account		49,000.00
	(Being the Gamut shares sold through the broker, David Brothers)		
25-Mar-X1	Investments—Equity Account—AFS Account	100.00	
	To David Brothers Account		100.00
	(Being the brokerage payable on sale of 1,000 Gamut shares)		

T-13 On Recording the Profit/Loss on Sale of Shares

Calculation of capital gains	**US$**
(a) Net sale consideration of 1,000 shares after brokerage	48,900.00
(b) Cost of acquisition of 100 shares including brokerage	4,010.00
(c) Cost of acquisition of 1,200 shares including brokerage	50,520.00
(d) Proportionate cost of acquisition of 900 shares [(50,520 × 900)/1,200]	37,890.00
(e) Realized gains = (a) − (b) − (d)	**1,120.00**

Journal Entry

Date	Particulars	Debit (US$)	Credit (US$)
25-Mar-X1	Investments—Equity Account—AFS Account	7,000.00	
	To Realized Capital Gains/Loss—Equity Account		7,000.00
	(Being the profit on the sale of 1,000 Gamut shares)		

T-14 On Receipt of Sale Consideration Net of Brokerage

Journal Entry

Date	Particulars	Debit (US$)	Credit (US$)
27-Mar-X1	Bank Account	48,900.00	
	To David Brothers Account		48,900.00
	(Being the net consideration received from David Brothers on sale of 1,000 Gamut shares)		

T-15 Mark-to-market at End of Reporting Period

Mark-to-market at end of reporting period: 31-Mar-X1	**US$**
(a) Cost of acquisition of 300 shares	12,630.00
(b) Market value at the end of reporting period	10,500.00
(c) Unrealized loss (b) − (a)	(2,130.00)

Journal Entry

Date	Particulars	Debit (US$)	Credit (US$)
31-Mar-X1	Unrealized Capital Gains/Loss—Equity Shares Account—Other Comprehensive Income	2,130.00	
	To Investments—Equity Account—AFS Account		2,130.00
	(Being the unrealized loss on 300 equity shares of Gamut shares)		

T-16 Transfer of Unrealized Loss from OCI to P&L Account

Journal Entry

Date	Particulars	Debit (US$)	Credit (US$)
31-Mar-X1	Unrealized Capital Gains/Loss—Equity Shares Account	2,130.00	
	Unrealized Capital Gains/Loss—Equity Shares Account—Other Comprehensive Income		2,130.00
	(Being the unrealized loss on 300 equity shares of Gamut recognized as loss and taken to P&L Account)		

T-17 Transfer of Category from AFS to Trading

Journal Entry

Date	Particulars	Debit (US$)	Credit (US$)
31-Mar-X1	Investments—Equity Account—Trading Account	10,500.00	
	To Investments—Equity Account—AFS Account		10,500.00
	(Being the equity shares of Gamut transferred from AFS to 'trading' category)		

T-18 Deferred Tax Impact on Unrealized Capital Loss

Journal Entry

Date	Particulars	Debit (US$)	Credit (US$)
31-Mar-X1	Deferred Tax Benefit Account	852.00	
	To Provision for Income Taxes Account		852.00
	(Being the tax component on the unrealized loss on 300 equity shares of Gamut treated as deferred tax benefit)		

The provision to be made for taxation is $2,396.

General Ledger Accounts

Investments—Equity Account—AFS Account

Date	Particulars	Debit (US$)	Date	Particulars	Credit (US$)
5-Jan-X1	To David Brothers Account	60,000.00			
5-Jan-X1	To David Brothers Account	150.00			
15-Jan-X1	To David Brothers Account	50,400.00			
15-Jan-X1	To David Brothers Account	120.00			
			25-Jan-X1	By David Brothers Account	57,400.00
25-Jan-X1	To David Brothers Account	140.00			
25-Jan-X1	To Realized Capital Gains/Loss Equity—Trading Account	1,120.00			
31-Jan-X1	To Unrealized Capital Gains/ Loss—Equity Shares Account—Other Comprehensive Income	1,370.00			
			1-Feb-X1	By Unrealized Capital Gains/ Loss—Equity Shares Account—Other Comprehensive Income	1,370.00
28-Feb-X1	To Unrealized Capital Gains/ Loss—Equity Shares Account—Other Comprehensive Income	3,970.00			
			1-Mar-X1	By Unrealized Capital Gains/ Loss—Equity Shares Account—Other Comprehensive Income	3,970.00
			25-Mar-X1	By David Brothers Account	49,000.00
25-Mar-X1	To David Brothers Account	100.00			
25-Mar-X1	To Realized Capital Gains/Loss Equity—Trading Account	7,000.00			

Investments—Equity Account—AFS Account (*Cont'd*)

Date	Particulars	Debit (US$)	Date	Particulars	Credit (US$)
			31-Mar-X1	By Unrealized Capital Gains/ Loss—Equity Shares Account—Other Comprehensive Income	2,130.00
			31-Mar-X1	By Investments—Equity Account—Trading Account	10,500.00
31-Mar-X1	Total	**124,370.00**	31-Mar-X1	Total	**124,370.00**

Investments—Equity Account—Trading Account

Date	Particulars	Debit (US$)	Date	Particulars	Credit (US$)
31-Mar-X1	To Investments Equity Account—AFS Account	10,500.00			
			31-Mar-X1	By Balance	10,500.00
31-Mar-X1	Total	**10,500.00**	31-Mar-X1	Total	**10,500.00**
31-Mar-X1	To Balance	10,500.00			

Deferred Tax Benefit Account

Date	Particulars	Debit (US$)	Date	Particulars	Credit (US$)
31-Mar-X1	To Provision for Income Taxes Account	852.00			
			31-Mar-X1	To Balance	852.00
31-Mar-X1	Total	**852.00**	31-Mar-X1	Total	**852.00**
31-Mar-X1	To Balance	852.00			

Provision for Income Taxes Account

Date	Particulars	Debit (US$)	Date	Particulars	Credit (US$)
			31-Mar-X1	By Deferred Tax benefit Account	852.00
31-Mar-X1	To Balance	852.00			
31-Mar-X1	Total	**852.00**	31-Mar-X1	Total	**852.00**
			31-Mar-X1	By Balance	852.00

Realized Capital Gains/Loss Equity—Trading Account

Date	Particulars	Debit (US$)	Date	Particulars	Credit (US$)
			25-Jan-X1	By Investments—Equity Account—AFS Account	1,120.00
			25-Mar-X1	By Investments—Equity Account—AFS Account	7,000.00
31-Mar-X1	To Balance	8,120.00			
31-Mar-X1	Total	**8,120.00**	31-Mar-X1	Total	**8,120.00**
			31-Mar-X1	By Balance	8,120.00

Unrealized Capital Gains/Loss—Equity Shares Account—Other Comprehensive Income

Date	Particulars	Debit (US$)	Date	Particulars	Credit (US$)
			31-Jan-X1	By Investments—Equity Account—AFS Account	1,370.00
1-Feb-X1	To Investments—Equity Account—AFS Account	1,370.00			
			28-Feb-X1	By Investments—Equity Account—AFS Account	3,970.00
1-Mar-X1	To Investments—Equity Account—AFS Account	3,970.00			
			31-Mar-X1	By Investments—Equity Account—AFS Account	2,130.00
31-Mar-X1	To Unrealized Capital Gain—Equity shares Account	2,130.00			
31-Mar-X1	Total	**7,470.00**	31-Mar-X1	Total	**7,470.00**

Unrealized Capital Gains/Loss—Equity Shares Account

Date	Particulars	Debit (US$)	Date	Particulars	Credit (US$)
31-Mar-X1	To Unrealized Capital Gains/Loss—Equity Shares Account—Other Comprehensive Income	2,130.00			
			31-Mar-X1	By Balance	2,130.00
31-Mar-X1	Total	**2,130.00**	31-Mar-X1	Total	**2,130.00**
31-Mar-X1	To Balance	2,130.00			

David Brothers Account

Date	Particulars	Debit (US$)	Date	Particulars	Credit (US$)
			5-Jan-X1	By Investments—Equity Account—AFS Account	60,000.00
			5-Jan-X1	By Investments—Equity Account—AFS Account	150.00
7-Jan-X1	To Bank Account	60,150.00			
			15-Jan-X1	By Investments—Equity Account—AFS Account	50,400.00
			15-Jan-X1	By Investments—Equity Account—AFS Account	120.00
17-Jan-X1	To Bank Account	50,520.00			
25-Jan-X1	To Investments—Equity Account—AFS Account	57,400.00			
			25-Jan-X1	By Investments—Equity Account—AFS Account	140.00
			27-Jan-X1	By Bank Account	57,260.00
25-Mar-X1	To Investments—Equity Account—AFS Account	49,000.00			
			25-Mar-X1	By Investments—Equity Account—AFS Account	100.00
			27-Mar-X1	By Bank Account	48,900.00
31-Mar-X1	Total	**217,070.00**	31-Mar-X1	Total	**217,070.00**

Bank Account

Date	Particulars	Debit (US$)	Date	Particulars	Credit (US$)
			7-Jan-X1	By David Brothers Account	60,150.00
			17-Jan-X1	By David Brothers Account	50,520.00
27-Jan-X1	To David Brothers Account	57,260.00			
27-Mar-X1	To David Brothers Account	48,900.00			
31-Mar-X1	To Balance	4,510.00			
31-Mar-X1	Total	**110,670.00**	31-Mar-X1	Total	**110,670.00**
			31-Mar-X1	By Balance	4,510.00

Trial Balance

As of 31-Mar-X1 (US$)

Particulars	Debit	Credit
Current Liabilities		
Provision for Income Taxes Account		852.00
Investments		
Investments—Equity Account—Trading Account	10,500.00	
Current Assets		
Bank Account		4,510.00
Deferred Tax Benefit Account	852.00	
Direct Income		
Realized Capital Gains/Loss Equity Shares Account		8,120.00
Unrealized Capital Gains/Loss—Equity shares Account	2,130.00	
Total	**15,948.00**	**15,948.00**

Income Statement

For the period ending 31-Mar-X1

Expenses	US$	Income	US$
		Direct Income	
Unrealized Capital Gain—Equity Shares Account	2,130.00	Realized Capital Gains/Loss Equity Shares Account	8,120.00
Provision for Taxation ($2,396-$852)	1,544.00		
Net Profit	4,446.00		
Total	**8,120.00**	Total	**8,120.00**

Balance Sheet

As of 31-Mar-X1

Liabilities	US$	Assets	US$
Capital Account	Nil	**Investments**	
Current Liabilities		Investments—Equity Shares—Trading Account	10,500.00
Provision for Income Taxes Account	2,396.00		
Bank Account	4,510.00	**Current Assets**	
		Deferred Tax Benefit Account	852.00
Profit & Loss Account			
Opening Balance	Nil		
Current Period	4,446.00		
Total	**11,352.00**	Total	**11,352.00**

SUMMARY

- If the equity securities classified as available-for-sale are sold, then the realized gain/loss on such sale is transferred from the other comprehensive income (OCI) to the income statement and an entry is recorded to that effect.
- When the equity securities are transferred from trading securities to the available-for-sale category, then the unrealized gain/loss should not be reversed and no adjustment should be made to the OCI.
- When the equity securities are transferred from the available-for-sale category to the trading category, then the unrealized gain/loss on such securities based on the fair value of the securities should be transferred from OCI and thus recognized as income immediately on such transfer.
- Temporary impairment with respect to the equity securities that are held for trading is automatically tracked by valuing the securities at mark-to-market on every reporting day. Such temporary impairment is not to be recognized and acted upon for available-for-sale securities. However, if the impairment is anything other than temporary, then such impaired security must be written down to fair value. The realized loss on such impairment must be reported in the income statement. Once the impairment is recorded as loss, then even if the security recovers from such impairment, it would not be recognized in the earnings unless it is liquidated through the sale of the security.
- Unrealized gain/loss is not recognized for income tax purposes until the same is realized through liquidation. Hence the unrealized gain/loss included in the income or OCI represents temporary differences as defined by FAS 109. The tax effects of all temporary differences are to be recognized in the financial statements as deferred tax benefits or deferred tax liabilities.
- For securities classified as trading, the unrealized gain/loss is included in the income and as such represents the temporary differences as defined in the accounting standards. The deferred tax effect of those changes should also be presented in the income statement itself.
- For securities classified as available-for-sale, the unrealized gain/loss is included in the OCI and as such forms part of the temporary differences as defined in the accounting standards. The deferred tax effect of those changes should also be presented in the other comprehensive income itself.
- As per FAS 115, under U.S. GAAP, for securities classified as available-for-sale, all reporting enterprises shall disclose:
  - Aggregate fair value.
  - Gross unrealized holding gains.
  - Gross unrealized holding losses.

  These should be grouped by major security type as of each date for which a statement of financial position is presented.
- IFRS 7 comes into effect for annual periods beginning on or after January 1, 2007. This standard requires that preparers provide quantitative and qualitative disclosures that would enhance a user's understanding of the entity's exposures to financial risks and how the entity manages those risks.

EXERCISES

Theory Questions

1. Can the securities that are classified once be transferred to other category? If so, what precautions should be taken to adjust the unrealized gains or losses?
2. How is the impairment of securities presented in the balance sheet?
3. What is the proper treatment of stock dividends? Can you report this as income?
4. How are the tax effects on unrealized gains/losses treated in the books of accounts in the securities classified as trading and as available-for-sale?

Objective Questions

1. When securities are transferred from trading securities to available-for-sale, then
   a. Gain/Loss recognized as unrealized should be reversed
   b. Gain/Loss recognized as unrealized should not be reversed
   c. Gain/Loss recognized as unrealized will be adjusted with OCI
   d. None of the above
2. When securities are transferred from available-for-sale to trading, then
   a. Unrealized gain/Loss will be transferred from OCI and treated as income
   b. Unrealized gain/Loss should not be reversed
   c. No changes are required at all
   d. None of the above
3. Impairment other than temporary with respect to equity securities should be
   a. Written down to fair value
   b. Treated alike as temporary impairment
   c. Considered a loss to be treated as temporary
   d. None of the above
4. Stock dividend declared should be treated as
   a. Income
   b. Increase in the value of original shares held
   c. Increase to the quantity (position) of shares held
   d. All of the above
5. For securities classified as available-for-sale, which of the following items will be reported in the income statement of the current period?
   a. Both realized and unrealized gains
   b. Realized gain alone
   c. Unrealized gain alone
   d. None of the above

6. For income tax purposes, unrealized gain/loss will be recognized for reporting
   a. Automatically at the end of the financial year
   b. Only if the securities are liquidated and realized
   c. As and when, depending upon the corporate action
   d. None of the above
7. Unrealized gain/loss included in the income/OCI represents
   a. Temporary difference recognized as deferred tax benefits
   b. Permanent difference recognized as deferred tax benefits
   c. No effect
   d. None of the above
8. For available-for-sale securities, the deferred tax effect should be presented in
   a. The income statement itself
   b. Other comprehensive income itself
   c. No need for accounting
   d. None of the above
9. For trading securities, the deferred tax effect should be presented in
   a. The income statement itself
   b. Other comprehensive income itself
   c. No need for accounting
   d. None of the above
10. As per U.S. GAAP, changes in fair value for available-for-sale securities are reported in
    a. The income statement
    b. Other Comprehensive Income
    c. No need to report
    d. None of the above
11. When the equity securities are transferred from AFS to trading securities,
    a. The unrealized gain/loss is recognized on T + 2
    b. The unrealized gain/loss is not recognized at all
    c. The realized gain/loss is recognized immediately
    d. The unrealized gain/loss is recognized immediately
    e. Realized gain/loss of trading securities is treated in the same way as in AFS
12. Shares received as stock dividend should be added to the original shares, and when the mark-to-market process is performed, the impact of the stock dividend
    a. Should be treated as unrealized gains and reported as income for the period
    b. Should be treated as dividend income

c. Should be treated as dividend income but should be shown as a current asset on the asset side of the balance sheet
d. Should be treated as realized gain/income for the period
e. Items b and c

13. According to the definition in FAS 109, the tax effects of all temporary differences arising from unrealized gain/loss are to be recognized in the financial statements as
    a. Non-trading income
    b. Items exempted from taxes
    c. Deferred tax benefits or deferred tax liabilities
    d. They are not recognized for the current period, but are carried forward to the next accounting period
    e. Income or expense for the current period
14. According to FAS 115, under U.S. GAAP, for securities classified as available-for-sale, all reporting enterprises shall disclose
    a. Aggregate fair value
    b. Gross unrealized holding gains
    c. Gross unrealized holding losses
    d. None of the above
    e. All the above

Journal Questions

Transfer the following from AFS to trading category.

Aspen Onshore Fund LLC traded in Epson shares that are listed on the New York Stock Exchange through Remount stockbrokers. The details are as follows:

Trade Details

Date	Product	Quantity	Rate	B/S	Brokerage
11-Jan-X1	Epson	2,000	$97	B	$300
27-Jan-X1	Epson	1,200	$99	S	$180
5-Feb-X1	Epson	1,500	$103	B	$225
25-Mar-X1	Epson	1,000	$100	S	$150

Other Details

Settlement: T + 2

Liquidation Method

FIFO

Market Rate

January 31: 101.00
February 28: 98
March 31: 97.85

The shares were bought without any intention of trading, nor was this meant to be a long-term investment. However, management changed its mind and decided that Epson shares would be classified as trading shares on March 31. Aspen Onshore Fund is charged tax on its earnings at an average rate of 40 percent. Prepare the accounts through March 31.

Prepare

Journal entries, general ledgers, trial balance, income statement, and balance sheet.

CHAPTER 5

Equity Derivatives: Theory

LEARNING OBJECTIVES

After studying this chapter, you will learn the following:

- Accounting standards for equity derivatives.
- Derivatives in a financial security.
- Various types of derivative contracts.
- Definition of derivatives according to accounting standards.
- Differences between U.S. GAAP and IFRS pertaining to derivatives.
- Forward contracts and futures contracts and the difference between futures and forwards.
- Rationale behind hedging, speculation, and arbitrage in a futures contract.
- Limitations of forward market.
- Advantages of a futures contract.
- Components of a futures contract.
- Pricing of a futures contract.
- Stock futures and index futures.

ACCOUNTING STANDARDS FOR EQUITY DERIVATIVES

This chapter covers the accounting requirements for equity futures contracts. An equity future is a form of derivative and, if used for hedging, requires a special hedge accounting treatment.

The accounting treatment under the U.S. GAAP is covered by the accounting standards FAS 115 and FAS 133. Under the International Financial Reporting Standards, IAS 39 deals with this topic.

Relevant Accounting Standards	
U.S. GAAP	**IFRS**
FAS 52—Foreign Currency Translation	IFRS 7—Financial Instruments: Disclosure
FAS 94—Consolidation of All Majority-owned Subsidiaries	IAS 21—The Effects of Changes in Foreign Exchange Rates
FAS 115—Accounting for Certain Investments in Debt and Equity Securities	IAS 32—Financial Instruments: Presentation
FAS 130—Reporting Comprehensive Income	IAS 36—Impairment of Assets
FAS 133—Accounting for Derivative Instruments and Hedging Activities	IAS 39—Financial Instruments: Recognition and Measurement
FAS 157—Fair Value Measurements	
FAS 159—The Fair Value Option for Financial Assets and Financial Liabilities	

DERIVATIVES IN A FINANCIAL SECURITY

A derivative is a financial security, such as an option or futures contract, whose value depends on the performance of an underlying security or asset. Futures contracts, forward contracts, options, and swaps are the most common types of derivatives. Derivatives are generally used by institutional investors to increase overall portfolio return or to hedge portfolio risk. A derivative is a financial instrument that does not constitute ownership, but a promise to convey ownership.

All derivatives are based on some underlying cash product. For example, the underlying cash products could be any of the following:

- *Equity shares.* These include equity shares listed in the stock exchanges, indexes based on the equity market, and so on.
- *Commodities.* These include grain, wheat, pepper, coffee, cotton, crude oil, and so on.
- *Spot foreign exchange.* This is buying and selling of foreign currency at the spot rates that are quoted by the interbanks through the Society for Worldwide Interbank Financial Telecommunication (SWIFT).
- *Bonds.* Bonds come in many varieties, such as Eurobonds, domestic bonds, fixed interest or floating rate notes, and so on. Bonds are medium- to long-term negotiable debt securities issued by governments, government agencies, federal or state bodies, the World Bank, or companies. These bonds may be freely traded without reference to the issuer of the security if they are negotiable.
- *Short-term money market negotiable debt securities.* These instruments include T-bills issued by governments, commercial paper issued by companies, or bankers' acceptances. They are similar to bonds, except that they differ mainly in their maturity. Short-term is usually defined as being up to one year in maturity. Medium-term is commonly taken to mean from one to five years in maturity, and long-term is anything above that.

Various Types of Derivative Contracts

The following table lists various types of contract with the corresponding underlying variable:

Type of Contract	Main Pricing-Settlement Variable
Interest rate swap	Interest rates
Currency swap (foreign exchange swap)	Currency rates
Commodity swap	Commodity prices
Equity swap	Equity prices (equity of another entity)
Credit swap	Credit rating, credit index, or credit price
Total return swap	Total fair value of the reference asset and interest rates
Purchased or written Treasury bond option (call or put)	Interest rates
Purchased or written currency option (call or put)	Currency rates
Purchased or written commodity option (call or put)	Commodity prices
Currency futures	Currency rates
Commodity futures	Commodity prices
Interest rate forward linked to government debt (Treasury forward)	Interest rates
Currency forward	Currency rates
Commodity forward	Commodity prices
Equity forward	Equity prices (equity of another entity)

This chapter covers equity options in particular, even though many of these concepts are applicable to other types of options as well.

DEFINITION OF DERIVATIVES PER ACCOUNTING STANDARDS

The U.S. GAAP accounting standard defines a derivative instrument as a financial instrument or other contract with all three of the following characteristics:

1. It has (a) one or more underlyings and (b) one or more notional amounts or payment provisions, or both. Those terms determine the amount of the settlement or settlements and, in some cases, whether or not a settlement is required.
2. It requires no initial net investment, or an initial net investment that is smaller than would be required for other types of contracts that would be expected to have a similar response to changes in market factors.
3. Its terms require or permit net settlement, it can readily be settled net by a means outside the contract, or it provides for delivery of an asset that puts the recipient in a position not substantially different from net settlement.

According to IAS 39, a derivative is a financial instrument with the following three characteristics:

1. Its value changes in response to a change in price of, or index on, a specified underlying financial or nonfinancial item or other variable.
2. It requires no, or comparatively little, initial investment.
3. It is to be settled at a future date.

A contract can meet this definition of a derivative regardless of whether it is settled net or gross. In this regard, this definition is different from the U.S. GAAP, which excludes contracts that are settled gross. However, an interest rate swap would be a derivative financial instrument whether the parties pay the interest payments to each other on a gross settlement basis or settle the same on a net basis.

Even though the definition of a derivative requires that the instrument is settled at a future date, it is clarified when that this criterion is met even if an option is expected not to be exercised—for example, when it is out of the money. This is so because expiry at maturity is a form of settlement even though there is no additional exchange of consideration.

Differences between U.S. GAAP and IFRS

Derivatives		
Topic	**U.S. GAAP**	**IFRS**
Definition	A derivative is a financial instrument that meets all of the following criteria: • Its value changes in response to a specified variable or underlying rate (for example, interest rate). • It requires no or little net investment. • It is settled at a future date. • It permits net settlement.	The same as U.S. GAAP but with the requirement that the contract should permit net settlement.
Initial Measurement	Measured at fair value on acquisition date and presented in balance sheet.	The same as U.S. GAAP.
Subsequent Measurement	Measured at fair value on subsequent valuation date and presented in balance sheet. This is irrespective of whether the derivative instrument is a hedging instrument or not.	The same as U.S. GAAP except that a derivative settled by delivery of an equity share that is unquoted and whose fair value cannot be reliably measured is carried at cost less impairment until settlement.
Changes in Fair Value of Derivative Instrument	Recognized in the income statement. However, if the instrument qualifies as a hedge, then income is recognized according to the hedge accounting norms.	The same as U.S. GAAP.

FORWARD CONTRACT

A *forward contract* is an agreement between two parties to buy or sell an asset at a predetermined future point in time at a predefined price. The essence of the contract is that the trade date and delivery date are distinctly different, and the delivery date is a future date. One party agrees to sell, the other to buy, at a price agreed upon at the time of entering into the contract. In a forward transaction, no actual cash changes hands. Sometimes there could be an exchange of margin according to some defined rule or convention. But usually no cash is exchanged until the maturity of the contract.

A forward contract, being a derivative, is usually used to effectively hedge risk. However, some use it as a mere tool for taking a leveraged unidirectional position.

Payoff of a Forward Contract

Assume that Mr. Long wants to buy an asset in one year's time, and at the same time, suppose that Mr. Short, who currently owns an asset worth $100,000, wants to sell the same asset in one year's time. Then Mr. Long and Mr. Short would enter into a forward contract with each other. Assume that both agree on a contracted price in one year's time of $105,000. Now that they have entered into a forward contract, Mr. Long, who is buying the underlying, is said to have entered into a long forward contract. Conversely, Mr. Short is said to have entered into a short forward contract.

At the end of one year, suppose that the current market valuation of Mr. Short's asset is $110,000. As Mr. Short is obliged to sell the asset to Mr. Long for $105,000, Mr. Long will make a profit of $5,000 on this contract. In contrast, Mr. Short has incurred a loss of $5,000.

How Forward Prices Are Fixed

Forward price is derived based on the initial price of Mr. Short's asset, which is $100,000. Since Mr. Short knows that he can immediately sell the asset for $100,000 and place the proceeds in the bank, he wants to be compensated for the delayed sale on the basis of at least the risk-free rate of return (the bank rate) for one year, which is 5 percent. Thus, Mr. Short would want at least $105,000 one year from now for the contract to be worthwhile for him—the opportunity cost will thereby be covered.

Mr. Long would seek the lowest price he can for the contract, not lower than the limit of $105,000 below which Mr. Short would not be interested to go. As a result, the contract price would be at least $105,000 or it will not happen at all.

FUTURES CONTRACT

A forward contract that is traded on an exchange is called a *futures contract.*

Exchange-traded futures contracts are not issued like securities, but they are actually created when one party buys a contract from another party.

At any point in time, the number of contracts that are long must equal the number of contracts that are short in the entire market. Futures contracts are routed through the futures exchange, which acts as the counterparty for all trades, thereby almost eliminating the counterparty credit risk by assuming the concept of *novation.* The total number of futures contracts for any particular underlying asset can thus undergo change on a daily basis. This is called the *open interest* in the futures of the underlying concerned.

The futures exchange does not take any positions; in other words, the exchange by itself does not initiate any trade. Furthermore, since the futures exchange is the counterparty for all the trades, the parties to the trade do not know with whom they have ultimately traded.

A future is thus an agreement (obligation) to buy or sell a given quantity of a particular asset, on a specified future date, at a predetermined price. Futures contracts have standard delivery dates, trading units, terms, and conditions. Futures can be based on any number of underlying assets. The investor can contract a futures position by either buying or selling a future just as he can close his futures position by doing the opposite—either selling or buying the same futures. In practice, most futures contract positions are closed out before they expire.

If the investor holds the view that the underlying asset will rise, then the investor would buy futures—known as a long futures position—which commits the buyer to take delivery of the underlying shares, or equivalent cash value, at a prearranged price and by a certain date, known as the expiry date. Conversely, if the investor's view is that the share prices for the underlying asset will fall, then he would sell futures—known as a short futures position—which commits the investor to deliver the underlying shares, or equivalent cash value, at a prearranged price and by a certain date.

FUTURES VERSUS FORWARDS

While both futures and forward contracts are contracts to deliver an underlying asset on a future date, they differ in several respects.

Exchange-Traded

Futures are always traded on an exchange, whereas forwards are always traded over-the-counter, being a simple signed contract between two interested parties.

Standardized versus Customized

Futures are highly standardized and conform to the strict guidelines of the stock exchange where they are traded. This ensures that there is enough liquidity in the market.

The following are some of the key factors that are standardized and form the basis for contract specifications:

- The underlying asset, which could be anything from a stock, a stock index, or a short-term interest rate; in the case of commodities, a bushel of wheat or an ounce of gold.
- The type of settlement, either cash settlement or physical settlement.
- The amount and units of the underlying asset per contract. In the case of equity shares, this could be the number of shares for each contract; in the case of fixed income securities, it could be the notional amount of bonds. In the case of commodities this could be a fixed number of barrels of oil, and so on.
- The currency in which the futures contract is quoted and the currency in which the futures contract is settled.
- The grade of the deliverable. In the case of commodities, this specifies the quality of the underlying goods and the manner and location of delivery.

- The delivery month and the last trading date.
- Certain other details like the percentage of margin to be maintained for the underlying asset of the contract, and the minimum and maximum permissible price fluctuations in any trading day.

Most forward contracts are unique, as they depend upon the conditions laid down by both the parties before they enter into the contract.

Cash versus Physical Settlement

Futures are usually cash settled by calculating the difference between the contracted price and the market price as of the closing of the date of expiry of the futures contract. The percentage of contracts that are settled by physical delivery is very low.

Forward contracts, by contrast, are settled by the delivery of the underlying asset at the specified contract price and terms.

Marked-to-market

A forward contract has no cash flows until the actual delivery takes place. Whereas in futures contracts, the exchange on which the trade takes place would insist on the margin requirements, and on a daily basis both the buyer and the seller's accounts are marked-to-market.

Credit Risk versus Novation

Due to the marked-to-market process, the credit risk in a futures contract is reduced. Also, in an exchange-traded futures contract, the exchange plays the role of novation and as such assumes the credit risk of the contract.

By contrast, the forward contract takes place over-the-counter, which means it is outside the stock exchange. Therefore the credit risk is high, as on the date of delivery any party to the contract may not fulfill its commitment.

Unwinding the Position

Since a forward contract has to be settled by physical delivery, and also because it is done over-the-counter, the party seeking to unwind the position should get into a separate agreement or contract with the other party and do the needful.

A futures contract, however, can be unwound by taking an opposite position on the same exchange where the original position was taken with the same terms of the contract, except that the position is counter to the original position.

Hedging, Speculation, and Arbitrage

An investor can enter into a futures contract with any of three intentions in mind—hedging, speculation, or to get an arbitrage profit. The accounting treatment for hedging is different from the other two, which are classified for the purposes of this book as *non-hedging activities.*

Hedging

One of the key factors in a derivative instrument is that derivatives form an effective medium of transferring risk from a person who wants to avoid risk to a person with a greater tolerance for risk.

Non-hedging

Non-hedging motives could be either speculation or for arbitrage.

Arbitrage is taking advantage of a price differential between two or more markets. Arbitrage refers to the purchase and sale of similar products in two or more different markets in order to take advantage of price discrepancy. A person who engages in arbitrage is called an *arbitrageur*.

When the prices for the futures are greater than the cash prices including the cost of carry, the arbitrageur will purchase the securities from the cash market and will sell in the futures market. This is known as *long arbitrage*. When the prices for the futures including the adjustment for cost of carry are lower than the cash prices, the arbitrageur will sell in the cash market and will purchase in the futures market; this is known as *short arbitrage*.

If the market prices do not allow for profitable arbitrage, the prices are said to constitute an *arbitrage equilibrium* or *arbitrage-free* market. Arbitrage helps with price discovery. Price discovery is the process of determining the spot prices in any market. Prices are dependent upon supply and demand. When the demand for a particular commodity is higher than its supply, the price will typically increase and vice versa.

Speculators in futures markets provide the essential function of assuming risk in the hope of getting a reward. The speculator has no intention of taking actual delivery of the securities purchased.

Limitations of the Forwards Market

Liquidity Issues

The forwards market is customized and hence liquidity is an issue. Lack of liquidity also means there will not be proper price discovery.

Counterparty Risk

The forwards market, being an over-the-counter market, suffers from the greatest drawback of counterparty risk. In the futures market, by contrast, the futures exchange acts as the counterparty, thereby virtually eliminating the counterparty risk.

Lack of Standardization

The forwards market is customized and lacks standardization. The terms are fixed by the parties on an ad hoc basis.

Advantages of Futures Contracts

Risk Management

The futures market enables a market player to reduce risk or to assume risk, depending upon the market player's risk appetite. It provides a convenient mechanism to transfer risk from one market player to another seamlessly. Risks are reduced as the price is predetermined, thereby letting market players know how much they will need to buy or sell.

Low Transaction Cost

The stock exchange members pay much lower transaction costs compared to similar over-the-counter trades.

Performance Guarantee by Clearinghouse

Futures are exchange-traded and the performance of the contract is guaranteed by the clearing house of the exchange concerned. Hence the default risk is virtually nil in futures contracts.

Price Discovery Due to High Liquidity

The futures market provides a prominent place to determine the correct price based on the estimated amount of supply and demand—both present and future. Due to high liquidity and a continuous stream of information from all over the world, several important factors such as weather, war, debt default, and all factors of production that have a major effect on supply and demand are analyzed by the market players continuously, resulting in the determination of the present and future prices of a commodity in a commodity futures exchange. The same is true for price discovery in other futures markets as well, like stock futures, bond futures, and so on. With today's advanced technology of electronic information dissemination, real price discovery is made seamless.

Means of Speculation

The futures market provides an avenue for speculators who hope to make large profits by taking huge risks. Speculation in turn drives liquidity, which in turn ensures price discovery.

Comprehensive Regulation

Exchange-traded futures contracts are highly regulated. Market participants are protected as the exchange ensures that both the buyer and the seller honor their respective commitments by insisting on appropriate margins by the concerned parties.

Arbitrage Opportunities

Futures markets can create arbitrage opportunities. The arbitrageurs purchase the securities via either cash-and-carry or reverse cash-and-carry, depending upon the market conditions. All these arbitrage trades again help enable price discovery and liquidity in the cash market.

COMPONENTS OF A FUTURES CONTRACT

There are some important components that should be specified in a futures contract, including the underlying asset, contract size, expiry, settlement terms, and margin details—both initial margin and variation margin.

Underlying Asset

The underlying asset should be mentioned clearly. The underlying asset could be a single stock or an index computed and published by the exchange on a selected sector or group of stocks. There should not be any ambiguity in identifying the underlying asset, as the settlement takes place in either the underlying asset or the market price of the underlying asset on the date of expiry of the contract.

Contract Size

This is also known as the lot size. Since exchange-traded futures can be squared off by taking an opposite position, the contract size is standardized. An investor can decide to take multiple lots in a single contract. Usually the stock exchange fixes the lot size optimally to help the investors, hedgers, arbitrageurs, speculators, and all other market players to participate in the trade by ensuring that it is neither too small nor too large.

Fixed Expiry

Expiry, or expiration, is the time when the final price of the futures is determined for the purpose of settlement through the exchange. The timing of the expiry depends upon the exchange on which the futures are listed and varies from exchange to exchange.

Initial Margin

The initial margin is the sum of money that should be deposited by a buyer or a seller to the stock exchange. It is typically meant to cover possible future loss in the position.

Hence initial margin is collected by the stock exchange from both the buyer and the seller. Typically the initial margin is calculated based on the value-at-risk, which represents the loss on that contract on any given trading day, taking into account the volatility factor—that is, the historical price changes for a given period of time in the past. To put it simply, this is the likely loss that an investor holding a position in the futures contract would lose with a 99 percent confidence and over a single trading day. Mathematically, several popular methods are being used to compute initial margins. The stock exchanges also provide a mechanism to compute the margins on a daily basis.

The accounts of both the buyer and seller of a futures contract are monitored continuously on a daily basis by the principle of *mark-to-market*. As result of the price fluctuation, if the margin drops below the margin maintenance requirement established by the exchange listing the futures, a margin call will be issued to bring the account back up to the required level.

Margin requirements are reduced or in some cases waived for those hedgers who own the underlying asset or who have offsetting contracts balancing the position.

Variation Margin

The futures exchange also levies mark-to-market margin on a daily basis to cover the difference in the contracted price and the market price. While the unrealized profit is credited to the margin account, the unrealized loss, if any, is collected from the person holding the futures position. At the end of the first day on which the position is taken, the actual contracted price of the futures is taken into account and compared with the market price. Such marked-to-market rate is taken as the cost for the second day, and so on.

Thus, in effect, investors in the futures market hold a margin account with the exchange, and the fluctuation in the value of their positions is added to or deducted from their margin account daily. If the margin account diminishes, they must replenish it. This is one way of ensuring that the investor will be able to fulfill his obligations.

Settlement

The futures contract is closed out by settlement in one of two ways, as specified in the futures contract:

1. *Physical delivery.* The underlying asset specified in the contract is delivered by the seller of the contract to the buyer through the futures exchange. Physical delivery is usually carried out in bonds and commodities, although in practice only a minority of contracts are settled through physical delivery. Most of the contracts are actually liquidated by entering into an opposite position without the contract being consummated through physical delivery. A long contract is squared up by entering into a sell contract with the same terms and expiry date, which actually cancels out the long position. Index futures are settled only in cash.
2. *Cash settlement.* A cash payment is made based on the rate of the underlying asset—for example, the closing value of a stock index or the closing value of the equity stock.

OPEN INTEREST IN DERIVATIVES CONTRACTS

Open interest is the total number of outstanding contracts that are held by market participants at the end of the day. It is also defined as the total number of futures contracts or option contracts that are yet to be exercised, expired, or consummated by delivery.

Open interest applies only to the derivatives market where the contracts are created by the market participants. It is believed that the open interest, or the total number of open derivatives contracts, confirms the trends and trend reversals of the underlying asset.

Open interest measures the flow of money into the derivatives market. If the open interest expands, it means that there are new players in the market or the existing players are expanding their position; consequently, it means there is a greater flow of money into the market.

A seller and a buyer combine to create only one contract. So the total open interest for any given market is computed by adding up the net buyers of the contract *or* the net sellers of the contract, and not both. The open interest position on a day-to-day basis can either expand or contract depending upon how the new contracts are created. The change in open interest reported each day in the financial dailies represents the increase or decrease in the number of contracts for that day, and it is shown as a positive or negative number.

METHOD OF COMPUTING OPEN INTEREST

Each trade concluded on the exchange can have a different impact on the level of open interest at the end of the day. If two parties to the trade initiate a new position—one new buyer and one new seller—then the open interest will increase by one contract. However, if the two parties are closing an existing position—one existing buyer and one existing seller—then the open interest will decline by one contract. When an existing holder of a contract trades his position to a new trader—one existing buyer sells to one new buyer—then the open interest will not undergo any change.

WHAT DOES CHANGE IN OPEN INTEREST INDICATE?

An increase in open interest along with an increase in price is believed to indicate an upward trend. Similarly, an increase in open interest along with a decrease in price indicates a downward trend. An increase or decrease in prices while open interest remains flat or declining may indicate a possible trend reversal.

PRICING OF A FUTURES CONTRACT

The futures price represents the expected future value of the underlying stock discounted at the risk-free rate. When the actual price is different from the theoretical price, it creates an arbitrage opportunity until the actual price converges with the theoretical price.

Cost of Carry

The cost of carry is the cost of holding a position. It is the cost of interest paid on a margin account for long positions and for short positions it is the cost of reimbursing the dividends. Cost of carry refers to the risk-free interest rate that could be earned by investing in a safe investment. Futures prices vary on account of cost of carry apart from transaction costs, differential borrowing, lending rates, and so on.

STOCK FUTURES AND INDEX FUTURES

Stock indexes are constructed to measure the performance of the stock market over a period of time. Separate indexes are developed to measure the overall performance or that of individual sectors of the economy. The primary usefulness of a stock market index is that it provides a benchmark to compare the performance of the stock market with the performance of any other type of asset, be it gold, any commodity, or government debt, historically over a given period of time. A stock market index in fact provides a reliable measure of the performance of the economy as a whole. In a nutshell, the index measures the marketwide movement of the stock market.

The variants that are developed, obviously with different purposes and utility, are as follows:

- Individual stock futures.
- Index futures.
- Options on index futures.

There are several mathematical methods by which the stock market indexes are constructed, but these are beyond the scope of this book.

Indexes are primarily used as information sources. By looking at an index, an investor can find out how the market is performing. Indexes also have another direct application in finance, namely index funds and index derivatives. Index funds are funds that invest in the index passively.

Options on index futures provide a very powerful mechanism of hedging, allowing investors to manage their risk according to their risk appetite. Hedging using futures and options on a market index is now the predominant method of risk management.

A stock market index incidentally serves as a benchmark for measuring the performance of fund managers in any typical fund.

Systematic and Unsystematic Risks

Stock price movements are predominantly caused by two types of factors: (1) news about the company and its performance—for example, product launches, periodical financial results, lawsuits, capability or otherwise of the top management; or (2) news about the country—growth opportunities, public policy, foreign exchange transparency, budget announcements, and so on.

The former factors are defined as *unsystematic risks* that are unique to a company or industry. Factors such as management capability and other similar company- or industry-specific factors contribute to unsystematic risks. Unsystematic risks are controllable and their impact can be considerably minimized by sufficiently diversifying an investor's portfolio.

The latter type of factors in stock price movements are defined as *systematic risks* that are associated with economic, political, sociological, and other country-specific changes. These factors affect the entire market as a whole. Diversification of an investor's portfolio can control or eliminate systematic risk.

An index captures the movements of the stock market as a whole, by the principle of averaging. Each stock contained in the index is a microcosm of two elements: stock news and index news. When the average of returns on several stocks is considered, the individual stock news items tend to cancel each other out. That is, the good stock-specific news for a few companies and bad stock-specific news for others tend to offset each other. In fact, the index is supposed to be effective only if these cancel out, leaving the economy- and country-specific news that is common to all stocks.

SUMMARY

- Equity futures are a form of derivative that, if used for hedging, requires a special hedge accounting treatment.
- A derivative is a financial security, such as an option or futures contract, whose value depends on the performance of an underlying security or asset.
- Futures contracts, forward contracts, options, and swaps are the most common types of derivatives.
- The accounting treatment under the U.S. GAAP is covered by the accounting standards FAS 115 and FAS 133. Under the International Financial Reporting Standards, IAS 39 deals with this topic.
- A *forward contract* is an agreement between two parties to buy or sell an asset at a predetermined future point in time at a predefined price. The essence of the contract is that the trade date and delivery date are distinctly different and the delivery date is a future date.
- A forward contract, being a derivative, is usually used to effectively hedge risk. However, some use it merely as a tool for taking a leveraged unidirectional position.
- A forward contract that is traded on an exchange is called a *futures contract.*
- Exchange-traded futures contracts are not issued like securities; they are actually created when one party buys a contract from another party.
- While both futures and forward contracts entail a promise to deliver an underlying asset on a future date, they differ in several respects.

- An investor can enter into a futures contract with any of three intentions in mind, namely hedging, speculation, or to get an arbitrage profit. The accounting treatment for hedging is different from the other two, which are classified for the purposes of this book as *non-hedging activities*.
- One of the key factors in a derivative instrument is that derivatives form an effective medium of transferring risk to a person with risk appetite from another person who wants to avoid risk.
- *Arbitrage* means taking advantage of a price differential between two or more markets. Arbitrage refers to the purchase and sale of similar products in two or more different markets in order to take advantage of price discrepancy. A person who engages in arbitrage is called an *arbitrageur*.
- Speculators in futures markets provide the essential function of assuming risk in the hope of getting a reward. The speculator has no intention of taking actual delivery of the securities purchased.
- The forward market has serious limitations including liquidity issues, counterparty risk issues, and lack of standardization.
- The futures market has the advantages of risk management, low transaction cost, performance guarantee by the clearinghouse, price discovery due to high liquidity, means of speculation, being well regulated, and providing enormous arbitrage opportunities.
- There are some important components that should be present in a future contract, such as the underlying asset, contract size, expiry, settlement terms, and margin details—both initial margin and variation margin.
- The initial margin is the sum of money that should be deposited by a buyer or a seller to the stock exchange, typically meant to cover possible future loss in the position.
- The primary usefulness of a stock market index is that it provides a benchmark to compare the performance of the stock market with the performance of any other type of asset historically over a given period of time.
- Options on index futures provide a very powerful mechanism of hedging, allowing investors to manage their risk according to their risk appetite.
- Stock price movements are predominantly caused by two types of factors: news about the company and its performance, or news about the country itself. These are categorized as unsystematic and systematic risks, respectively.

EXERCISES

Theory Questions

1. Compare and contrast a forward contract with a futures contract.
2. Discuss the relative merits and disadvantages of hedging, speculation, and arbitrage. Which of these is good for the economy?
3. What are the limitations of forward markets?
4. "A futures contract is more advantageous than a forward contract". Do you agree? If so, why?
5. What are the essential components of a futures contract?
6. What is the fundamental difference between initial margin and a variation margin?
7. How is a futures contract settled?

8. What is meant by open interest? What does the movement of open interest indicate?
9. How is a futures contract priced?
10. What is meant by systematic and unsystematic risk?
11. Do you think that index futures are better than stock futures? If so, why?
12. Why does the margin call occur? What happens if the margin call is not met by the investor?
13. Trading in stock futures versus trading in index futures—which is more risky and why?

Objective Questions

1. Futures contracts are traded

   a. Over the counter
   b. On stock exchanges
   c. Through private placement
   d. All of the above

2. Forward contracts are traded

   a. Over the counter
   b. On stock exchanges
   c. Through private placement
   d. All of the above

3. Which of the following products conform to strict guidelines of the stock exchange?

   a. Futures
   b. Forwards
   c. Both futures and forwards
   d. None of the above

4. Settlement of futures happens through

   a. Cash
   b. Physical delivery of the underlying asset
   c. Either cash or physical delivery
   d. None of the above

5. The marked-to-market process is followed for

   a. Forwards contracts
   b. Futures contracts
   c. Both (a) and (b)
   d. None of the above

6. Settlement of forward contracts happens through

   a. Cash
   b. Physical delivery of the underlying asset

c. Either cash or physical delivery
d. None of the above

7. In a futures contract, the role of novation is played by the
   a. Broker
   b. Stock exchange
   c. Buyer
   d. Seller
8. Unwinding the futures contract takes place through
   a. Entering into a separate agreement
   b. Taking an opposite position
   c. Canceling the agreement
   d. None of the above
9. The intention for entering into the futures contract could be
   a. Hedging
   b. Speculation
   c. Arbitrage profit
   d. All of the above
10. Advantages of futures contracts include
    a. Low transaction cost
    b. Performance guaranteed by the clearinghouse
    c. Comprehensive regulation
    d. All of the above
11. Disadvantages of futures contracts include
    a. Low transaction cost
    b. Comprehensive regulation
    c. Liquidity issues
    d. All of the above
12. The underlying asset in a futures contract could be
    a. A single stock
    b A group of stocks
    c. An index computed and published by the exchange
    d. All of the above
13. The lot size of a futures contract is managed by
    a. The buyer of the contract
    b. The seller of the contract
    c. The stock exchange concerned
    d. Any of the above

14. Initial margin amount is paid by the
    a. Buyer
    b. Seller
    c. Both buyer and seller
    d. Broker
15. Performance of the stock market is measured through
    a. FX rate fluctuations
    b. Stock indexes' movement
    c. A high rate of dividend declared by the investee company
    d. None of the above
16. Purchase and sale of similar products in two or more different markets in order to take advantage of price discrepancy is called
    a. Hedging
    b. Speculation
    c. Parallel positioning
    d. Pyramiding
    e. Arbitrage
17. In the futures market, a margin call will be issued to the person holding the futures position to bring the account back up to the required level, when
    a. Margin drops below the initial margin amount
    b. Margin drops below the fixed margin amount
    c. Margin drops below the variance margin amount
    d. Margin drops below the required margin amount
    e. Margin increases above the initial margin amount
18. Stock price movements are driven partly by unsystematic risks. Which among the following falls in the category of unsystematic risks?
    a. The country's economic growth opportunities
    b. Government policies
    c. Foreign exchange transparency
    d. Budget announcements
    e. All of the above
19. Usually the stock exchange manages to fix the lot size of a futures contract to help the
    a. Exchanges, custodian, and administrators
    b. Buyers and sellers in the physical market
    c. Investors, hedgers, arbitrageurs, speculators
    d. Exchanges, brokers, and traders
    e. Both (a) and (c)

CHAPTER 6

Accounting for Equity Index Futures

LEARNING OBJECTIVES

After studying this chapter, you should have a grasp of the following:

- Trade life cycle of exchange-traded equity index futures.
- Journal entries to be recorded during the different phases of the trade life cycle.
- FX revaluation and FX translation process for these trades.
- Illustration of trades in long index futures with FX translation.
- Preparation of general ledger accounts.
- Preparation of income statement and balance sheet after the equity futures trades are done.
- Illustration of trades in short index futures with FX translation.

THE TRADE LIFE CYCLE FOR EQUITY INDEX FUTURES

- Pay the initial margin on index futures to the exchange.
- Buy the index futures.
- Pay the brokerage/commission on the buy transaction.
- Pay the margin amount for the index futures.
- Ascertain the fair value at the end of the reporting period.
- Pay margin call.
- Sell the index futures and pay brokerage.
- Ascertain the profit/loss on the sale.
- Reversal of margin money.
- Expiry of index futures.
- Receive the consideration.
- FX revaluation entries.
- FX translation entries.

Pay the Initial Margin on Index Futures to the Exchange

Margin is payable to the exchange if the investor either buys or sells a futures contract. For futures, since the stock exchange has the responsibility of ensuring that both the legs of the transaction are complete, the exchange would insist on a deposit of a percentage of the value of the contract as margin money. The margin money would be adjusted against any reduction in the marked-to-market valuation on a daily basis.

Margin is in effect a good faith deposit. Normally a deposit of about 5 to 10 percent of the total value of the contract would signify the investor's willingness to stand good on any price movements against the buyer or seller of an index futures contract. However, for stock futures, the required deposit would be around 25 to 50 percent of the value of the contract. Since it is merely a deposit, the investor would get the margin money back after the contract is liquidated.

The fact that futures operate on margin makes them a highly leveraged investment, meaning a relatively small price move can result in considerable profit/loss swings for the investor. This leverage must be closely monitored and treated with tremendous respect. Leverage can work for or against the investor.

Assume that an investor wants to buy index futures at $540, the contract size is 100, and the stock exchange wants an up-front margin of 10 percent of the value of the contract. Expiry of the contract is December 16 and the broker through whom the trade is executed is Frank Bros.

The margin payable to the exchange through the broker would be 10 percent of $54,000, that is, $5,400.

The accounting entry that is recorded in the books of accounts is shown as follows:

Journal Entry

Date	Particulars	Debit (US$)	Credit (US$)
8-Nov-X1	Index Futures Margin Account	5,400	
	To Frank Bros Account		5,400
	(Being the margin payable to the stock exchange through the broker @ 10% of the value of the contract on purchase of 100 index futures @ $540)		

Buy the Index Futures

If the investor buys a futures contract, then a right to acquire shares at the expiry date is created, along with a liability to the extent of the value of the contract. This is usually recorded off the balance sheet and only a notional entry is passed in the books of accounts to indicate the existence of the asset and a corresponding liability. This entry is called an off-balance-sheet entry.

The accounting entry that is recorded in the books of accounts is shown as follows:

Journal Entry

Date	Particulars	Debit (US$)	Credit (US$)
8-Nov-X1	Equity Index Futures Position Account (Off Balance Sheet)	100.00	
	To Equity Index Futures Contra Account (Off Balance Sheet)		100.00
	(Being the nominal amount of the equity index futures purchased)		

Pay Brokerage/Commission on the Buy Transaction

The broker of the stock exchange charges a commission for the services rendered. This is usually settled by debiting the amount paid to the margin account with the broker, which means it gets paid to the broker on the same day as the trade date. For futures contracts, the brokerage/commission is not treated as part of the cost of the options contract; instead it is debited to the brokerage/commission account. Assuming a brokerage of $120 is payable on the futures contract in this example, the accounting entry that is recorded in the books of accounts is shown as follows:

Journal Entry

Date	Particulars	Debit (US$)	Credit (US$)
8-Nov-X1	Brokerage/commission Account	120.00	
	To Frank Bros Account		120.00
	(Being the brokerage payable on the futures contract)		

Pay the Margin Amount for the Index Futures

The margin is paid to the stock exchange through the broker. This is either paid along with the brokerage or is separately paid. Assuming in this case the margin money is paid along with the brokerage, the accounting entry that is recorded in the books of accounts is shown as follows:

Journal Entry

Date	Particulars	Debit (US$)	Credit (US$)
8-Nov-X1	Frank Bros Account	5,520.00	
	To Bank Account		5,520.00
	(Being the margin money paid to the stock exchange along with the commission/ brokerage payable on the futures contract to the broker)		

Ascertain the Fair Value at the End of the Reporting Period

At the end of every reporting period, the fair value of the futures is ascertained and the futures contracts are marked-to-market. This process is known as *portfolio valuation*, when the market rate at the end of the period is determined from the primary stock exchange where the underlying shares are traded. If the market rate increases above the purchase rate, then such increase is recognized as a gain on the one hand, and the corresponding amount is reflected as increase in the value of such futures.

In the case of futures, it is the market practice to book the mark-to-market entry on an incremental basis. The logic for this is that the unrealized gain or loss is treated more like it is realized as the mark-to-market shortfall, if any, is required to be brought in by the investor by way of additional margin money. Hence, throughout this book the entries for mark-to-market for futures are on incremental basis. The entry for accounting for mark-to-market (MTM) on futures is actually taken to an income/expense account known as MTM—Futures (P&L) Account, and not to the usual Unrealized Gains/Loss Account as in the case of equity shares.

Assume that the fair market value of each share is $525 per share on November 30, the valuation date. The accounting entry that is recorded in the books of accounts is shown as follows:

Journal Entry

Date	Particulars	Debit (US$)	Credit (US$)
30-Nov-X1	MTM—Futures (P&L) Account	1,500.00	
	To Futures Contract MTM Asset Account		1,500.00
	(Being the fair market value recorded on the valuation date and the difference between the cost and fair value taken to current earnings)		

Margin Call

If the margin money gets eroded due to unfavorable price movements then to maintain the percentage of margin fixed for the underlying in question, the exchange would initiate margin call. This is to ensure that the exchange is not caught unawares if there is a wide fluctuation in the value of the underlying causing severe loss to the investor. The stock exchange should ensure that there is sufficient margin money to take care of this.

The investor is always required to keep the margin at a certain level. The percentage is usually lower for an index as opposed to an individual security, and this varies from one underlying stock to another.

In this case, the market value as of the valuation date has decreased to $52,500. The margin requirement on this value would be $5,250 and the margin account itself is reduced from $5,400 to $3,900—that is, $5,400 minus $1,500. Hence there is a requirement to top up the margin account to $5,250. Fresh cash should be brought in by the investor amounting to $5,250 minus $3,900, or $1,350.

The accounting entry that is recorded in the books of accounts is shown as follows:

Journal Entry

Date	Particulars	Debit (US$)	Credit (US$)
30-Nov-X1	Futures Margin Account	1,350.00	
	To Frank Bros Account		1,350.00
	(Being the variation margin payable on account of reduction in the value of the underlying held by the investor)		
30-Nov-X1	Frank Bros Account	1,350.00	
	To Bank Account		1,350.00
	(Being the variation margin paid)		

Sell the Futures and Pay Brokerage

The long position of futures could be liquidated by selling the futures with the same expiry date. Since the sale results in squaring up of the existing position, the margin money paid would be returned back to the investor after adjusting for any profit or loss on account of such trade. The overall open interest could come down upon liquidation of the futures contract if the futures contract is purchased by someone who already has a short position. Otherwise, the sale of the futures contract will not result in a decrease in open interest.

An off-balance-sheet entry is passed to reverse the position account on the date on which the position is liquidated. Brokerage is accounted for on such sale, and again the commission/brokerage is charged to profit and loss directly, as was done on the date of purchase of the futures contract.

Assume that the 100 index futures are sold at $510 on December 12, incurring a brokerage of $75 for the trade. The accounting entry that is recorded in the books of accounts is shown as follows:

Journal Entry

Date	Particulars	Debit (US$)	Credit (US$)
12-Dec-X1	Futures Contra Account (Off Balance Sheet)	100.00	
	To Futures Position Account (Off Balance Sheet)		100.00
	(Being the liquidation of the position and the reversal of the off-balance-sheet entry that was passed on creation of the position)		
12-Dec-X1	Brokerage/commission Account	75.00	
	To Frank Bros Account		75.00
	(Being the brokerage payable on the futures contract)		
12-Dec-X1	Frank Bros Account	75.00	
	To Bank Account		75.00
	(Being the brokerage paid)		

Ascertain the Profit/Loss on the Sale

The profit or loss on sale of the futures contract is determined by comparing the value of the futures contract with the value of the position at the latest mark-to-market. The reason is that the unrealized profit or loss on the position is already recognized in the current earnings and is also adjusted in the margin account. Hence only the latest value of the position would be compared with the sale price to determine the profit. Note the difference in treatment as compared to equity shares, where the mark-to-market entry is reversed and the realized gain entry is passed, comparing the original cost of acquisition with the net sales realization.

In our example, the position is already marked-to-market at $525 for each share. Hence when the position is liquidated for $510, only $15 per share would be treated as loss, even though the original cost of the position was $540. The accounting entry that is recorded in the books of accounts is shown as follows:

Journal Entry

Date	Particulars	Debit (US$)	Credit (US$)
12-Dec-X1	MTM—Futures (P&L) Account	15,000.00	
	To Futures Margin Account		15,000.00
	(Being the loss realized on sale of the futures contract)		

Reversal of Margin Money

The entire amount of money available in the margin account is reversed on the date of liquidation and is returned back to the investor. This account would then have the initial margin money paid, variation margin money paid if any, the daily mark-to-market debit or credit as the case may be, and the profit or loss realized on liquidation of the position.

Assume that in our example, the margin money had a balance of $18,000; this amount would be returned back to the investor on liquidation of the position. The accounting entry that is recorded in the books of accounts is shown as follows:

Journal Entry

Date	Particulars	Debit (US$)	Credit (US$)
12-Dec-X1	Frank Bros Account	18,000.00	
	To Futures Margin Account		18,000.00
	(Being the balance in the futures margin account receivable from the broker)		

Expiry of Index Futures

The futures contract expires on the expiry date of the contract, if it is not liquidated before that. In the case of index futures, no physical delivery happens on the date of expiry. The difference between the value of the position after adjusting for the mark-to-market and the price of the underlying on the expiry date is computed and is settled in cash. The entire process is routed through the exchange. The futures margin account is adjusted with the profit or loss on account of expiry of the futures contract.

Assume, in our example, the closing rate of index futures on the expiry date is $520 and the value of the position as marked-to-market stands at $525. The difference of $5 representing loss is accounted for on the date of expiry. The accounting entry that is recorded in the books of accounts is shown as follows:

Journal Entry

Date	Particulars	Debit (US$)	Credit (US$)
15-Dec-X1	Realized gain—Futures Account	500.00	
	To Futures Margin Account		500.00
	(Being the loss on the futures contract on expiry transferred to the futures margin account)		

Receive the Margin Money Back from Broker

The entire amount of money standing in the margin account is paid back to the investor. The accounting entry that is recorded in the books of accounts is shown as follows:

Journal Entry

Date	Particulars	Debit (US$)	Credit (US$)
15-Dec-X1	Bank Account	18,000.00	
	To Frank Bros Account		18,000.00
	(Being the amount standing to the credit of the margin account received back from the broker on liquidation of the entire position)		

FX Revaluation Entries

All the entries recorded in the preceding example are initially entered in the respective trade currencies. If the functional currency is different from the trade currency, then each and every entry recorded in the trade currency should be entered again in the functional currency by converting the entries at the respective day's FX rates. In other words, for each trade currency that the investor deals with, there will be a complete set of books representing that trade currency. This includes journal entries, general ledger postings, trial balance, income statement, and balance sheet. After revaluing each and every journal entry of all the trade currencies into the functional currency, a separate set of books is prepared again comprising all of these elements—journal entries, general ledger postings, trial balance, income statement, and balance sheet. It should be noted that the ultimate financial reports would be prepared and presented to all the stakeholders based on the financial statements prepared in the functional currency only, as this will encompass all the transactions of the investor in all trade currencies dabbled with.

(For an illustration and detailed explanation, please refer to Chapter 2.)

FX Translation Entries

After revaluing all the entries in the functional currency at the respective FX rates for the day concerned, another entry needs to be passed in the books of the functional currency. This is mainly to adjust the currency gains or losses due to the fluctuations in FX rates between the reporting date and the date of recording the original entries. FX translation entries are recorded only for the asset and liability accounts. For income and expense accounts the amount gets crystallized on the date of passing the FX revaluation entries in the books of the functional currency.

There are fundamentally two types of FX translation entries that are recorded in the books of the functional currency: consummated FX translation entries and transient FX translation entries. (For an illustration and detailed explanation, please refer to Chapter 2.)

ILLUSTRATIONS WITH FX TRANSLATION

Long Futures—Functional Currency US$; Trade Currency INR

Cerebros Fund had the following trades in an index in the futures market. The stock exchange requires that a margin of 10 percent of the value of the contract be maintained throughout the life of the contract. The broker requires the initial margin to be maintained as it is and the investor is required to make good the MTM loss as and when required.

Date	Product Expiry	Quantity	Rate (INR)	B/S	Brokerage
29-Jan-X1	25-Apr-X1	1,000	525	B	530
15-Mar-X1	25-Apr-X1	1,500	510	B	520
10-Apr-X1	25-Apr-X1	1,600	540	S	300
25-Apr-X1	25-Apr-X1	900	530	Expiry	

Date	FX Rate
1-Jan-X1	45.03
29-Jan-X1	44.27
31-Jan-X1	44.17
28-Feb-X1	44.31
15-Mar-X1	44.20
31-Mar-X1	43.59
10-Apr-X1	42.50
25-Apr-X1	41.29

Date	Market Price
31-Jan-X1	520
28-Feb-X1	510
31-Mar-X1	495
25-Apr-X1	530

Solution: Long Index Futures in Trade Currency INR

T-1 Capital Introduced by the Investor into the Fund

Journal Entry

Date	Particulars	Debit (INR)	Credit (INR)
1-Jan-X1	Bank Account	100,000.00	
	To Share Capital Account		100,000.00
	(Being the subscription amount received from the investor into the fund)		

T-2 On Purchasing the Futures

This entry is just an off-balance-sheet entry and thus is not taken into account while preparing the financial statements of the investor. In this illustration, there will not be any postings for this entry:

Journal Entry

Date	Particulars	Debit (INR)	Credit (INR)
29-Jan-X1	Equity Futures Position Account (Off Balance Sheet)	1,000.00	
	To Equity Futures Contra Account (Off Balance Sheet)		1,000.00
	(Being the 1,000 futures contract bought @ INR525)		

T-3 On Payment of Margin

Journal Entry

Date	Particulars	Debit (INR)	Credit (INR)
29-Jan-X1	Futures Margin Account	52,500.00	
	To Bank Account		52,500.00
	(Being the margin amount for purchase of 1,000 Index futures)		

T-4 On Recording the Brokerage/Commission

Brokerage is paid separately, and in derivative instruments, it is not treated as part of the cost of acquisition; hence it is directly charged off to the profit and loss account.

Journal Entry

Date	Particulars	Debit (INR)	Credit (INR)
29-Jan-X1	Brokerage/Commission Account	530.00	
	To Payable to Broker—Futures Account		530.00
	(Being the brokerage amount incurred on the purchase of index futures)		

T-5 On Payment of Brokerage/Commission

Journal Entry

Date	Particulars	Debit (INR)	Credit (INR)
29-Jan-X1	Payable to Broker—Futures Account	530.00	
	To Bank Account		530.00
	(Being the brokerage amount incurred on the purchase of index futures)		

T-6 Mark-to-market at End of Reporting Period

The mark-to-market is computed based on the market rate at the end of every day. However, for this illustration it is assumed that the mark-to-market is computed at the end of the month. If there is a drop in the value of the long position, the same is reduced from the margin account—which eventually is required to be topped up with the erosion in value. Mark-to-market gains are debited to the margin account and credited to the profit and loss account.

Mark-to-market loss at the end of Jan X1	INR
(a) Market value of 1,000 index futures @ 520 on 31-Jan-X1	520,000.00
(b) Purchase value of 1,000 index futures @ 525 on 29-Jan-X1	525,000.00
(c) MTM loss = (a) − (b)	**(5,000.00)**

Journal Entry

Date	Particulars	Debit (INR)	Credit (INR)
31-Jan-X1	MTM—Futures (P&L) Account	5,000.00	
	To Futures Margin Account		5,000.00
	(Being the booking of mark-to-market entry for index futures as of this date)		

T-7 On Payment of Margin to Top Up the Mark-to-market Loss

Since the value of the purchase position is eroded due to a decrease in the market rate of the futures, the investor is required to make good the loss by paying the unrealized loss as margin. The variation margin represents the mark-to-market on the position. This is done on a daily basis. However, for the purpose of this illustration the margin call is invoked at the end of the month.

Journal Entry

Date	Particulars	Debit (INR)	Credit (INR)
31-Jan-X1	Futures Margin Account	5,000.00	
	To Bank Account		5,000.00
	(Being the payment made for the margin call)		

T-8 Mark-to-market at End of Reporting Period

Mark-to-market loss paid at the end of Feb X1	INR
(a) Market value of 1,000 futures @ 510 on 28-Feb-X1	510,000.00
(b) Purchase value of 1,000 futures @ 525 on 29-Jan-X1	525,000.00
(c) Total shortfall as of date = (a) − (b)	(15,000.00)
(d) Less mark-to-market accounted on end of Jan-X1	(5,000.00)
(e) Incremental MTM loss to be accounted on end of Feb-X1 = (c) − (d)	**(10,000.00)**

Journal Entry

Date	Particulars	Debit (INR)	Credit (INR)
28-Feb-X1	MTM—Futures (P&L) Account	10,000.00	
	To Futures Margin Account		10,000.00
	(Being the booking of mark-to-market entry for futures as of date)		

T-9 On Payment of Margin to Top Up the Mark-to-market Loss

Since the value of the purchase position is eroded due to decrease in the market rate of the futures, the investor is required to make good the loss by paying the unrealized loss as margin. The variation margin represents the mark-to-market on the position. This is done on a daily basis; however, for the purpose of this illustration the margin call is invoked at the end of the month.

Journal Entry

Date	Particulars	Debit (INR)	Credit (INR)
28-Feb-X1	Futures Margin Account	10,000.00	
	To Bank Account		10,000.00
	(Being the payment made for the margin call)		

T-10 On Purchasing the Futures

This entry is just an off-balance-sheet entry and thus is not taken into account while preparing the financial statements of the investor. In this illustration, there will not be any postings for this entry.

Journal Entry

Date	Particulars	Debit (INR)	Credit (INR)
15-Mar-X1	Equity Futures Position Account (Off Balance Sheet)	1,500.00	
	To Equity Futures Contra Account (Off Balance Sheet)		1,500.00
	(Being the 1500 futures contract bought @ INR510)		

T-11 On Recording the Brokerage/Commission

Journal Entry

Date	Particulars	Debit (INR)	Credit (INR)
15-Mar-X1	Brokerage/Commission Account	520.00	
	To Payable to Broker—Futures Account		520.00
	(Being the brokerage amount incurred on the purchase of index futures)		

T-12 On Payment of Brokerage/Commission

Journal Entry

Date	Particulars	Debit (INR)	Credit (INR)
15-Mar-X1	Payable to Broker—Futures Account	520.00	
	To Bank Account		520.00
	(Being the brokerage amount incurred on the purchase of index futures)		

T-13 On Payment of Margin on Fresh Purchase

Margin paid on 15-Mar-X1	INR
Margin to be paid for the purchase of 1,500 futures = 10% of (1,500 × 510)	76,500.00

Journal Entry

Date	Particulars	Debit (INR)	Credit (INR)
15-Mar-X1	Futures Margin Account	76,500.00	
	To Bank Account		76,500.00
	(Being the margin paid on purchase of index futures)		

T-14 Mark-to-market at End of Reporting Period

Mark-to-market gains/loss at the end of Mar X1	INR
(a) Market value of 2,500 futures @ 495 on 31-Mar	1,237,500.00
(b) Cost of position of 1,000 futures @ 525 on 29-Jan	525,000.00
(c) Cost of position of 1,500 futures @ 510 on 15-Mar	765,000.00
(d) Mark-to-market loss = (a) − (b) − (c)	(52,500.00)
(e) MTM loss already accounted for	15,000.00
(f) Incremental unrealized loss as of 31-Mar X1 = (d) − (e)	(37,500.00)

Journal Entry

Date	Particulars	Debit (INR)	Credit (INR)
31-Mar-X1	MTM—Futures (P&L) Account	37,500.00	
	To Futures Margin Account		37,500.00
	(Being the mark-to-market loss on futures contract as of this date)		

T-15 On Payment of Margin to Top Up the Mark-to-market Loss

Journal Entry

Date	Particulars	Debit (INR)	Credit (INR)
31-Mar-X1	Futures Margin Account	37,500.00	
	To Bank Account		37,500.00
	(Being the payment made to top up the mark to market loss)		

T-16 On Liquidating the Futures Partially

Journal Entry

Date	Particulars	Debit (INR)	Credit (INR)
10-Apr-X1	Equity Futures Contra Account (Off Balance Sheet)	1,600.00	
	To Equity Futures Position Account (Off Balance Sheet)		1,600.00
	(Being the 1,600 futures contract sold @ INR525)		

T-17 On Recording the Brokerage/Commission

Journal Entry

Date	Particulars	Debit (INR)	Credit (INR)
10-Apr-X1	Brokerage/Commission Account	300.00	
	To Payable to Broker—Futures Account		300.00
	(Being the brokerage incurred on the sale of index futures)		

T-18 On Payment of Brokerage/Commission

Journal Entry

Date	Particulars	Debit (INR)	Credit (INR)
10-Apr-X1	Payable to Broker—Futures Account	300.00	
	To Bank Account		300.00
	(Being the brokerage amount paid)		

T-19 Recording Profit/Loss on the Sale

Profit on liquidation of the futures position is computed by deducting the value of the position on the sale date from the sale consideration. It should be noted that the cost of acquisition of the position is not considered here, as the profit or loss on such position is already recognized through the date of sale by debiting or crediting the futures margin (P&L) account and is already taken as income or expense, as the case may be. It is only the incremental profit or loss on such liquidation that is calculated and taken to the income statement.

Calculation of realized gains on sale of futures	INR
(a) Cost of 1,600 futures position (1600 × 495)	792,000.00
(b) Sale consideration of 1,600 futures @ 540	864,000.00
(c) Realized gains on sale = (b) − (a)	**72,000.00**

Journal Entry

Date	Particulars	Debit (INR)	Credit (INR)
10-Apr-X1	Futures Margin Account	72,000.00	
	To MTM—Futures (P&L) Account		72,000.00
	(Being the realized gains on sale of Index futures)		

T-20 Return of Margin Money

Calculation of Return of Margin Money (Weighted Avg. Method)	INR
(a) Cost of 1,000 futures @ 525	525,000.00
(b) Cost of 1,500 futures @ 510	765,000.00
(c) Average cost of a future contract ((A+B)/2,500)	516.00
Margin on sale of 1,600 futures @ 10% (1,600 * 516* 10%)	**82,560.00**

Journal Entry

Date	Particulars	Debit (INR)	Credit (INR)
10-Apr-X1	Bank Account	82,560.00	
	To Futures Margin Account		82,560.00
	(Refund of margin money on account of sale of shares)		

T-21 On Expiry of Futures

Profit/Loss on expiry of the contract	INR
(a) Cost of open position as on date 900 futures @ 495	445,500.00
(b) Settlement amount for 900 futures @ 530	477,000.00
(c) Realized gains on expiry = (b) − (a)	**31,500.00**

Journal Entry

Date	Particulars	Debit (INR)	Credit (INR)
26-Apr-X1	Futures Margin Account	31,500.00	
	To MTM—Futures (P&L) Account		31,500.00
	(Being the realized gains on sale of Index futures)		

T-22 On Receipt of Margin on Futures

Margin amount received on the date of expiry	INR
(a) Initial margin paid on 29-Jan = 10% of (1,000 × 525)	52,500.00
(b) Mark-to-market loss on 31-Jan X1	(5,000.00)
(c) Margin money paid to top up mark-to-market loss	5,000.00
(d) Mark-to-market loss on 28-Feb X1	(10,000.00)
(e) Margin money paid to top up mark-to-market loss	10,000.00
(f) Initial margin money paid on 15-Mar = 10% of (1,500 × 510)	76,500.00
(g) Mark-to-market loss on 31-Mar X1	(37,500.00)
(h) Margin money paid to top up mark-to-market loss	37,500.00
(i) Profit on sale of 1,600 futures	72,000.00
(j) Return of margin on the date of sake	(82,560.00)
(k) Profit on expiry of futures contract	31,500.00
(l) Margin amount received on the date of expiry = sum of the above	**149,940.00**

Journal Entry

Date	Particulars	Debit (INR)	Credit (INR)
26-Apr-X1	Bank Account	149,940.00	
	To Futures Margin Account		149,940.00
	(Being the margin money received on the date of expiry)		

General Ledger Accounts

Futures Margin Account (for year 20X1)

Date	Particulars	Debit (INR)	Date	Particulars	Credit (INR)
29-Jan	To Bank Account	52,500.00			
31-Jan	To Bank Account	5,000.00			
			31-Jan	By MTM—Futures (P&L) Account	5,000.00
28-Feb	To Bank Account	10,000.00			
			28-Feb	By MTM—Futures (P&L) Account	10,000.00
15-Mar	To Bank Account	76,500.00			
			31-Mar	By MTM—Futures (P&L) Account	37,500.00
31-Mar	To Bank Account	37,500.00			
10-Apr	To MTM—Futures (P&L) Account	72,000.00			
			10-Apr	By Bank Account	82,560.00
26-Apr	To MTM—Futures (P&L) Account	31,500.00			
			26-Apr	By Bank Account	149,940.00
30-Apr	Total	**285,000.00**	30-Apr	Total	**285,000.00**

Brokerage/Commission Account (for year 20X1)

Date	Particulars	Debit (INR)	Date	Particulars	Credit (INR)
29-Jan	To Payable to Broker—Futures Account	530.00			
15-Mar	To Payable to Broker—Futures Account	520.00			
10-Apr	To Payable to Broker—Futures Account	300.00			
			30-Apr	By Balance	1,350.00
30-Apr	Total	**1,350.00**	30-Apr	Total	**1,350.00**
30-Apr	To Balance	1,350.00			

MTM—Futures (P&L) Account (for year 20X1)

Date	Particulars	Debit (INR)	Date	Particulars	Credit (INR)
31-Jan	To Futures Margin Account	5,000.00			
28-Feb	To Futures Margin Account	10,000.00			
31-Mar	To Futures Margin Account	37,500.00			
			10-Apr	By Futures Margin Account	72,000.00
			26-Apr	By Futures Margin Account	31,500.00
30-Apr	To Balance	51,000.00			
30-Apr	Total	**103,500.00**	30-Apr	Total	**103,500.00**
			30-Apr	By Balance	51,00.00

Share Capital Account (for year 20X1)

Date	Particulars	Debit (INR)	Date	Particulars	Credit (INR)
			1-Jan	By Bank Account	100,000.00
30-Apr	To Balance	100,000.00			
30-Apr	Total	**100,000.00**	30-Apr	Total	**100,000.00**
			30-Apr	By Balance	100,000.00

Payable to Broker—Futures Account (for year 20X1)

Date	Particulars	Debit (INR)	Date	Particulars	Credit (INR)
			29-Jan	By Brokerage/ Commission Account	530.00
29-Jan	To Bank Account	530.00			
			15-Mar	By Brokerage/ Commission Account	520.00
15-Mar	To Bank Account	520.00			
			10-Apr	By Brokerage/Commission Account	300.00
10-Apr	To Bank Account	300.00			
30-Apr	Total	**1,350.00**	30-Apr	Total	**1,350.00**

Bank Account (for year 20X1)

Date	Particulars	Debit (INR)	Date	Particulars	Credit (INR)
1-Jan	To Share Capital Account	100,000.00			
			29-Jan	By Futures Margin Account	52,500.00
			29-Jan	By Payable to Broker—Futures Account	530.00
			31-Jan	By Futures Margin Account	5,000.00
			28-Feb	By Futures Margin Account	10,000.00
			15-Mar	By Payable to Broker—Futures Account	520.00
			15-Mar	By Futures Margin Account	76,500.00
			31-Mar	By Futures Margin Account	37,500.00
			10-Apr	By Payable to Broker—Futures Account	300.00
10-Apr	To Futures Margin Account	82,560.00			
26-Apr	To Futures Margin Account	149,940.00			
			30-Apr	By Balance	149,650.00
30-Apr	Total	**332,500.00**	30-Apr	Total	**332,500.00**
30-Apr	To Balance	149,650.00			

Trial Balance

As on 30-Apr-X1 (INR)

Particulars	Debit	Credit
Capital Account		
Share Capital Account		100,000.00
Current Liabilities		
Current Assets		
Bank Account	149,650.00	
Direct Expenses		
MTM—Futures (P&L) Account		51,000.00
Brokerage/Commission Account	1,350.00	
Total	**151,000.00**	**151,000.00**

Income Statement

For the period ending 30-Apr-X1

Expenses	INR	Income	INR
Direct Expenses		**Direct Income**	
Brokerage/Commission Account	1,350.00		
		MTM—Futures (P&L) Account	51,000.00
Net Profit	49,650.00		
Total	**51,000.00**	Total	**51,000.00**

Balance Sheet

As at 30-Apr-X1

Liabilities	INR	Assets	INR
Capital Account		**Investments**	
Share Capital Account	100,000.00	**Current Assets**	
		Bank Account	149,650.00
Profit & Loss Account			
Opening Balance	Nil		
Current Period	49,650.00		
Total	**149,650.00**	Total	**149,650.00**

Long Futures in Functional Currency US$

The following are the FX revaluation entries in the functional currency converted at the respective FX rate, which is given within parenthesis. FX translation entries are clearly specified, indicating whether each is a consummated FX translation entry or a transient FX translation entry.

F-1 Capital Introduced by the Investor into the Fund (T-1 @ FX Rate: 45.03)

Journal Entry

Date	Particulars	Debit (US$)	Credit (US$)
1-Jan-X1	Bank Account	2,220.74	
	To Share Capital Account		2,220.74
	(Being the subscription amount received from the investor into the fund)		

F-2 On Purchasing the Futures (T-2 @ FX Rate: 44.27)

Journal Entry

Date	Particulars	Debit (US$)	Credit (US$)
29-Jan-X1	Equity Futures Position Account (Off Balance Sheet)	1,000.00	
	To Equity Futures Contra Account (Off Balance Sheet)		1,000.00
	(Being the 1,000 futures contract bought @ INR 525)		

F-3 On Payment of Margin (T-3 @ FX Rate: 44.27)

Journal Entry

Date	Particulars	Debit (US$)	Credit (US$)
29-Jan-X1	Futures Margin Account	1,185.90	
	To Bank Account		1,185.90
	(Being the margin amount for purchase of 1,000 index futures)		

F-4 On Recording the Brokerage/Commission (T-4 @ FX Rate: 44.27)

Journal Entry

Date	Particulars	Debit (US$)	Credit (US$)
29-Jan-X1	Brokerage/Commission Account	11.97	
	To Payable to Broker—Futures Account		11.97
	(Being the brokerage amount incurred on the purchase of index futures)		

F-5 On Payment of Brokerage/Commission (T-5 @ FX Rate: 44.27)

Journal Entry

Date	Particulars	Debit (US$)	Credit (US$)
29-Jan-X1	Payable to Broker—Futures Account	11.97	
	To Bank Account		11.97
	(Being the brokerage amount incurred on the purchase of index futures)		

F-6 Mark-to-market at End of Reporting Period (T-6 @ FX Rate: 44.17)

Journal Entry

Date	Particulars	Debit (US$)	Credit (US$)
31-Jan-X1	MTM—Futures (P&L) Account	113.20	
	To Futures Margin Account		113.20
	(Being the mark-to-market for futures as of date)		

F-7 On Payment of Margin (T-7 @ FX Rate: 44.17)

Journal Entry

Date	Particulars	Debit (US$)	Credit (US$)
31-Jan-X1	Futures Margin Account	113.20	
	To Bank Account		113.20
	(Being the payment made towards the margin as of date)		

F-8 FX Translation on Futures Margin Account (Transient FX Translation Entry)

Date	Particulars	INR	FX Rate	US$
29-Jan-X1	Opening balance	52,500.00	44.27	1,185.90
31-Jan-X1	Margin call	(5,000.00)	44.17	(113.20)
31-Jan-X1	Amount paid towards margin call	5,000.00	44.17	113.20
	Net balance	52,500.00		1,185.90
	Net balance at current FX rate	52,500.00	44.17	1,188.59
	FX translation on margin account			2.69

Journal Entry

Date	Particulars	Debit (US$)	Credit (US$)
31-Jan-X1	Futures Margin Account	2.69	
	To Unrealized Currency Gains/Loss Account		2.69
	(Being the FX translation applied on futures margin account)		

F-9 FX Translation on Bank Account (Transient FX Translation Entry)

Date	Particulars	INR	FX Rate	US$
1-Jan-X1	Opening balance	100,000.00	45.03	2,220.74
29-Jan-X1	Transfer out	(52,500.00)	44.27	(1,185.90)
29-Jan-X1	Brokerage	(530.00)	44.27	(11.97)
31-Jan-X1	Margin call	(5,000.00)	44.17	(113.20)
31-Jan-X1	Net balance	41,970.00		909.67
	Net balance at current FX rate	41,970.00	44.17	950.19
	FX translation on bank account			**40.52**

Journal Entry

Date	Particulars	Debit (US$)	Credit (US$)
31-Jan-X1	Bank Account	40.52	
	To Unrealized Currency Gains/Loss Account		40.52
	(Being the FX translation applied on bank account)		

F-10 Mark-to-market at End of Reporting Period (T-8 @ FX Rate: 44.31)

Journal Entry

Date	Particulars	Debit (US$)	Credit (US$)
28-Feb-X1	MTM—Futures (P&L) Account	225.68	
	To Futures Margin Account		225.68
	(Being the mark-to-market on futures on date)		

F-11 On Payment of Margin Call (T-9 @ FX Rate: 44.31)

Journal Entry

Date	Particulars	Debit (US$)	Credit (US$)
28-Feb-X1	Futures Margin Account	225.68	
	To Bank Account		225.68
	(Being the mark-to-market for futures as of date)		

F-12 FX Translation on Futures Margin Account (Transient FX Translation Entry)

Date	Particulars	INR	FX Rate	US$
31-Jan-X1	Opening balance	52,500.00	44.17	1,188.59
28-Feb-X1	Margin call	(10,000.00)	44.31	(225.68)
28-Feb-X1	Amount paid towards margin call	10,000.00	44.31	225.68
	Net balance	52,500.00		1,188.59
	Net balance at current FX rate	52,500.00	44.31	1,184.83
	FX translation on margin account			**(3.76)**

Journal Entry

Date	Particulars	Debit (US$)	Credit (US$)
28-Feb-X1	Unrealized Currency Gains/Loss Account	3.76	
	To Futures Margin Account		3.76
	(Being the FX translation applied on futures margin account)		

F-13 FX Translation on Bank Account (Transient FX Translation Entry)

Date	Particulars	INR	FX Rate	US$
31-Jan-X1	Opening balance	41,970.00	44.17	950.19
28-Feb-X1	Margin call	(10,000.00)	44.31	(225.68)
28-Feb-X1	Net balance	31,970.00		724.51
	Net balance at current FX rate	31,970.00	44.31	721.51
	FX translation on bank account			**(3.00)**

Journal Entry

Date	Particulars	Debit (US$)	Credit (US$)
28-Feb-X1	Unrealized Currency Gains/Loss Account	3.00	
	To Bank Account		3.00
	(Being the FX translation applied on bank account)		

F-14 On Purchasing the Futures

Journal Entry

Date	Particulars	Debit (US$)	Credit (US$)
15-Mar-X1	Equity Futures Position Account (Off Balance Sheet)	1,500.00	
	To Equity Futures Contra Account (Off Balance Sheet)		1,500.00
	(Being the 1,500 futures contract bought @ INR510)		

F-15 On Recording the Brokerage/Commission (T-11 @ FX Rate: 44.20)

Journal Entry

Date	Particulars	Debit (US$)	Credit (US$)
15-Mar-X1	Brokerage/Commission Account	11.76	
	To Payable to Broker—Futures Account		11.76
	(Being the brokerage incurred on purchase of index futures)		

F-16 On Payment of Brokerage/Commission (T-12 @ FX Rate: 44.20)

Journal Entry

Date	Particulars	Debit (US$)	Credit (US$)
15-Mar-X1	Payable to Broker—Futures Account	11.76	
	To Bank Account		11.76
	(Being the brokerage paid for the purchase of index futures)		

F-17 Margin Payment (T-13 @ FX Rate: 44.20)

Journal Entry

Date	Particulars	Debit (US$)	Credit (US$)
15-Mar-X1	Futures Margin Account	1,730.77	
	To Bank Account		1,730.77
	(Being the margin payment towards purchases of 1,500 futures @ 510)		

F-18 Mark-to-market at End of Reporting Period (T-14 @ FX Rate: 43.59)

Mark-to-market loss at the end of Mar X1	INR	US$
(a) Market value of 2,500 futures @ 495 on 31-Mar	1,237,500.00	28,389.54
(b) Cost of bought position 1,000 futures on 29-Jan	525,000.00	12,044.05
(c) Cost of bought position 1,500 futures on 15-Mar	765,000.00	17,549.90
(d) Mark-to-market = (a) − (b) − (c)	52,500.00	(1,204.40)
(e) Incremental MTM for Mar X1 (52,500−1500)	**(37,500.00)**	**(860.29)**

Journal Entry

Date	Particulars	Debit (US$)	Credit (US$)
31-Mar-X1	MTM—Futures (P&L) Account	860.29	
	To Futures Margin Account		860.29
	(Being the mark-to-market on futures contract as on date)		

F-19 On Payment of Margin Call (T-15 @ FX Rate: 43.59)

Journal Entry

Date	Particulars	Debit (US$)	Credit (US$)
31-Mar-X1	Futures Margin Account	860.29	
	To Bank Account		860.29
	(Being the payment made towards margin call)		

F-20 FX Translation on Futures Margin Account (Transient FX Translation Entry)

Date	Particulars	INR	FX Rate	US$
28-Feb-X1	Opening balance	52,500.00	44.31	1,184.83
15-Mar-X1	Margin for purchase of 1,500 futures @ 510	76,500.00	44.20	1,730.77
	Net balance	129,000.00		2,915.60
	Net balance at current FX rate	129,000.00	43.59	2,959.39
	FX translation on margin account			**43.79**

Journal Entry

Date	Particulars	Debit (US$)	Credit (US$)
31-Mar-X1	Futures Margin Account	43.79	
	To Unrealized Currency Gains/Loss Account		43.79
	(Being the FX translation applied on futWures margin account)		

F-21 FX Translation on Bank Account (Transient FX Translation Entry)

Date	Particulars	INR	FX Rate	US$
28-Feb-X1	Opening balance	31,970.00	44.31	721.51
15-Mar-X1	Transfer out	(76,500.00)	44.20	(1,730.77)
15-Mar-X1	Brokerage paid	(520.00)	44.20	(11.76)
31-Mar-X1	Margin call paid	(37,500.00)	43.59	(860.29)
31-Mar-X1	Net balance	(82,550.00)		(1,881.32)
	Net balance at current FX rate	(82,550.00)	43.59	(1,893.78)
	FX translation on bank account			**12.46**

Journal Entry

Date	Particulars	Debit (US$)	Credit (US$)
31-Mar-X1	Unrealized Currency Gains/Loss Account	12.46	
	To Bank Account		12.46
	(Being the FX translation applied on bank account)		

F-22 On Liquidating the Futures Partially (Off Balance Sheet Entry)

Journal Entry

Date	Particulars	Debit (US$)	Credit (US$)
10-Apr-X1	Equity Futures Contra Account (Off Balance Sheet)	1,600.00	
	To Equity Futures Position Account (Off Balance Sheet)		1,600.00
	(Being the 1,600 futures contracts sold @ INR525)		

F-23 On Recording the Brokerage/Commission (T-17 @ FX Rate: 42.50)

Journal Entry

Date	Particulars	Debit (US$)	Credit (US$)
10-Apr-X1	Brokerage/Commission Account	7.06	
	To Payable to Broker—Futures Account		7.06
	(Being the brokerage incurred on purchase of Index futures)		

F-24 On Payment of Brokerage/Commission (T-18 @ FX Rate: 42.50)

Journal Entry

Date	Particulars	Debit (US$)	Credit (US$)
10-Apr-X1	Payable to Broker—Futures Account	7.06	
	To Bank Account		7.06
	(Being the brokerage paid on for the purchase of index futures)		

F-25 Recording Profit/Loss on the Sale (T-19 @ FX Rate: 42.50)

Calculation of realized gains on sale of futures	US$
(a) Cost of sales of 1,600 futures based on weighted average method	18,635.29
(b) Sale value of 1,600 futures	20,329.41
(c) Realized gains on sale = (b) − (a)	**1,694.12**

Journal Entry

Date	Particulars	Debit (US$)	Credit (US$)
10-Apr-X1	Futures Margin Account	1,694.12	
	To MTM—Futures (P&L) Account		1,694.12
	(Being the realized gains on sale of index futures contract)		

F-26 Return of Margin Money (T-20 @ FX Rate: 42.50)

Journal Entry

Date	Particulars	Debit (US$)	Credit (US$)
10-Apr-X1	Bank Account	1,942.59	
	To Futures Margin Account		1,942.59
	(Refund of margin money on account of sale of shares)		

F-27 On Expiry of Futures (T-21 @ FX Rate: 41.29)

Profit/Loss on expiry of the contract	US$
(a) Cost of Sales of 900 futures	10,789.54
(b) Settlement amount of 900 futures	11,552.43
(c) Realized gains on expiry = (b) – (a)	**762.89**

Journal Entry

Date	Particulars	Debit (US$)	Credit (US$)
26-Apr-X1	Futures Margin Account	762.89	
	To MTM—Futures (P&L) Account		762.89
	(Being the realized gain on expiry of Index futures contract)		

F-28 On Receipt of Margin on Futures (T-22 @ FX Rate: 41.29)

Margin amount received on the date of expiry

Particulars	INR	FX Rate	US$
(a) Initial margin paid on 29-Jan = 10% of (1,000 × 525)	52,500.00	41.29	1,271.49
(b) Mark to market loss on 31-Jan X1	(5,000.00)	41.29	(121.09)
(c) Margin money paid to top up mark-to-market loss	5,000.00		121.09
(d) Mark to market loss on 28-Feb X1	(10,000.00)	41.29	(242.19)
(e) Margin money paid to top up mark-to-market loss	10,000.00	41.29	242.19
(f) Initial margin money paid on 15-Mar = 10% of (1,500 × 510)	76,500.00		1,852.75
(g) Mark to market loss on 31-Mar X1	(37,500.00)	41.29	(908.21)
(h) Margin money paid to top up mark-to-market loss	37,500.00		908.21
(i) Profit on sale of 1,600 futures	72,000.00	41.29	1,694.12
(j) Return of margin on the date of sale	82,560.00	42.50	(1,942.59)
(j) Profit on expiry of futures contract	31,500.00		762.89
(k) Margin amount received back = sum of the above	**149,940.00**	41.29	**3,631.39**

Journal Entry

Date	Particulars	Debit (US$)	Credit (US$)
26-Apr-X1	Bank Account	3,631.39	
	To Futures Margin Account		3,631.39
	(Being the balance in margin account received on the date of expiry)		

F-29 FX Translation on Futures Margin Account (Transient FX translation entry)

Date	Particulars	INR	FX Rate	US$
31-Mar-X1	Opening balance	129,000.00	43.59	2,959.39
10-Apr-X1	Profit on sale of 1,600	72,000.00	42.50	1,694.12
10-Apr-X1	Refund of margin on sale	(82,560.00)	42.50	(1,942.59)
26-Apr-X1	Profit on expiry of contract	31,500.00	41.29	762.90
26-Apr-X1	Refund of margin on expiry	(149,940.00)	41.29	(3,631.39)
	FX translation on margin account			**157.57**

Journal Entry

Date	Particulars	Debit (US$)	Credit (US$)
26-Apr-X1	Futures Margin Account	157.57	
	To Unrealized Currency Gains/Loss Account		157.57
	(Being the FX translation applied on futures margin account)		

F-30 FX Translation on Bank Account (Transient FX Translation Entry)

Date	Particulars	INR	FX Rate	US$
31-Mar-X1	Opening balance	(82,550.00)	43.59	(1,893.78)
10-Apr-X1	Transfer out	(300.00)	42.50	(7.06)
10-Apr-X1	Refund of margin on sale	82,560.00	42.50	1,942.59
26-Apr-X1	Refund of margin on expiry	149,940.00	41.29	3,631.39
	Net balance at current FX rate	149,650.00	41.29	3,624.36
	FX translation on bank account			**(48.77)**

Journal Entry

Date	Particulars	Debit (US$)	Credit (US$)
26-Apr-X1	Unrealized Currency Gains/Loss Account	48.77	
	To Bank Account		48.77
	(Being the FX translation applied on bank account)		

General Ledger Accounts

Futures Margin Account (for year 20X1)

Date	Particulars	Debit (US$)	Date	Particulars	Credit (US$)
29-Jan	To Bank Account	1,185.90			
			31-Jan	By MTM—Futures (P&L) Account	113.20
31-Jan	To Bank Account	113.20			
31-Jan	To Unrealized Currency Gains/Loss Account	2.69			
			28-Feb	By MTM—Futures (P&L) Account	225.68
28-Feb	To Bank Account	225.68			
			28-Feb	By Unrealized Currency Gains/Loss Account	3.76
15-Mar	To Bank Account	1,730.77			
			31-Mar	By MTM—Futures (PB&L) Account	860.29
31-Mar	To Bank Account	860.29			
31-Mar	To Unrealized Currency Gains/Loss Account	43.79			
10-Apr	To MTM—Futures (P&L) Account	1,694.12			
			10-Apr	By Bank Account	1,942.59
26-Apr	To MTM—Futures (P&L) Account	762.90			
26-Apr	To Unrealized Currency Gains/Loss Account	157.57			
			26-Apr	By Bank Account	3,631.39
30-Apr	Total	**6,776.91**	30-Apr	Total	**6,776.91**

Brokerage/Commission Account (for year 20X1)

Date	Particulars	Debit (US$)	Date	Particulars	Credit (US$)
29-Jan	To Payable to Broker—Futures Account	11.97			
15-Mar	To Payable to Broker—Futures Account	11.76			
10-Apr	To Payable to Broker—Futures Account	7.06			
			30-Apr	By Balance	30.79
30-Apr	Total	**30.79**	30-Apr	Total	**30.79**
30-Apr	To Balance	30.79			

Unrealized Currency Gains/Loss Account (for year 20X1)

Date	Particulars	Debit (US$)	Date	Particulars	Credit (US$)
			31-Jan	By Futures Margin Account	2.69
			31-Jan	By Bank Account	40.52
28-Feb	To Futures Margin Account	3.76			
28-Feb	To Bank Account	3.00			
			31-Mar	By Futures Margin Account	43.79
31-Mar	To Bank Account	12.46			
			26-Apr	By Futures Margin Account	157.57
26-Apr	To Bank Account	48.77			
30-Apr	To Balance	176.58			
30-Apr	Total	**244.57**	30-Apr	Total	**244.57**
			30-Apr	By Balance	176.58

MTM—Futures (P&L) Account (for year 20X1)

Date	Particulars	Debit (US$)	Date	Particulars	Credit (US$)
31-Jan	To Futures Margin Account	113.20			
28-Feb	To Futures Margin Account	225.68			
31-Mar	To Futures Margin Account	860.29			
			10-Apr	By Futures Margin Account	1,694.12
			26-Apr	By Futures Margin Account	762.90
30-Apr	To Balance	1,257.85			
30-Apr	Total	**2,457.02**	30-Apr	Total	**2,457.02**
			30-Apr	By Balance	1,257.85

Share Capital Account (for year 20X1)

Date	Particulars	Debit (US$)	Date	Particulars	Credit (US$)
			1-Jan	By Bank Account	2,220.74
30-Apr	To Balance	2,220.74			
30-Apr	Total	**2,220.74**	30-Apr	Total	**2,220.74**
			30-Apr	By Balance	2,220.74

Payable to Broker—Futures Account (for year 20X1)

Date	Particulars	Debit (US$)	Date	Particulars	Credit (US$)
			29-Jan	By Brokerage/ Commission Account	11.97
29-Jan	To Bank Account	11.97			
			15-Mar	By Brokerage/ Commission Account	11.76
15-Mar	To Bank Account	11.76			
			10-Apr	By Brokerage/ Commission Account	7.06
10-Apr	To Bank Account	7.06			
30-Apr	Total	**30.79**	30-Apr	Total	**30.79**

Bank Account (for year 20X1)

Date	Particulars	Debit (US$)	Date	Particulars	Credit (US$)
1-Jan	To Share Capital Account	2,220.74			
			29-Jan	By Futures Margin Account	1,185.90
			29-Jan	By Payable to Broker—Futures Account	11.97
31-Jan	To Unrealized Currency Gains/ Loss Account	40.52			
			31-Jan	By Futures Margin Account	113.20
			28-Feb	By Futures Margin Account	225.68
			28-Feb	By Unrealized Currency Gains/Loss Account	3.00
			15-Mar	By Payable to Broker—Futures Account	11.76
			15-Mar	By Futures Margin Account	1,730.77
			31-Mar	By Unrealized Currency Gains/Loss Account	12.46
			31-Mar	By Futures Margin Account	860.29
			10-Apr	By Payable to Broker—Futures Account	7.06

Bank Account (for year 20X1) *(Cont'd)*

Date	Particulars	Debit (US$)	Date	Particulars	Credit (US$)
10-Apr	To Futures Margin Account	1,942.59			
26-Apr	To Futures Margin Account	3,631.39			
			26-Apr	By Unrealized Currency Gains/Loss Account	48.77
			30-Apr	By Balance	3,624.38
30-Apr	Total	**7,834.24**	30-Apr	Total	**7,834.24**
30-Apr	To Balance	3,624.38			

Trial Balance

As on 30-Apr-X1 (US$)

Particulars	Debit	Credit
Capital Account		
Share Capital Account		2,220.74
Current Liabilities		
Current Assets		
Bank Account	3,624.38	
Direct Income		
Unrealized Currency Gains/Loss Account		176.58
MTM—Futures (P&L) Account		1,257.85
Direct Expenses		
Brokerage/Commission Account	30.79	
Total	**3,655.17**	**3,655.17**

Income Statement

For the period ending 30-Apr-X1

Expenses	US$	Income	US$
Direct Expenses		**Direct Income**	
Brokerage/Commission Account	30.79	Unrealized Currency Gains/Loss Account	176.58
		MTM—Futures (P&L) Account	1,257.85
Net Profit	1,403.64		
Total	**1,434.43**	Total	**1,434.43**

Balance Sheet

As at 30-Apr-X1

Liabilities	US$	Assets	US$
Capital Account		**Investments**	Nil
Share Capital Account	2,220.74		
Loans (Liability)		**Current Assets**	
Current Liabilities	Nil	Bank Account	3,624.38
Profit & Loss Account			
Opening Balance	Nil		
Current Period	1,403.64		
Total	**3,624.38**	Total	**3,624.38**

Illustration: Short Futures—Trade Currency INR; Functional Currency US$

Cerebros Fund had the following trades in an index in the futures market. The stock exchange requires that a margin of 20 percent of the value of the contract be maintained throughout the life of the contract.

Date	Product Expiry	Quantity	Rate (INR)	B/S	Brokerage
29-Jan-X1	25-Apr-X1	1,000	320	S	500
15-Mar-X1	25-Apr-X1	1,500	360	S	700
10-Apr-X1	25-Apr-X1	1,600	315	B	450
25-Apr-X1	25-Apr-X1	900	310	Expiry	

Date	FX Rate
1-Jan-X1	45.03
29-Jan-X1	44.27
31-Jan-X1	44.17
28-Feb-X1	44.31
15-Mar-X1	44.20
31-Mar-X1	43.59
10-Apr-X1	42.50
25-Apr-X1	41.29

Date	Market Price
31-Jan-X1	330
28-Feb-X1	345
31-Mar-X1	335
25-Apr-X1	290

Solution: Short Futures, Trade Currency INR

T-1 Capital Introduced by the Fund

Journal Entry

Date	Particulars	Debit (INR)	Credit (INR)
1-Jan-X1	Bank Account	100,000.00	
	To Share Capital Account		100,000.00
	(Being the subscription amount received from the investor into the fund)		

T-2 On Sale of Futures

Journal Entry

Date	Particulars	Debit (INR)	Credit (INR)
29-Jan-X1	Equity Futures Contra Account (Off Balance Sheet)	1,000.00	
	To Equity Futures Position Account (Off Balance Sheet)		1,000.00
	(Being the 1,000 futures contract sold @ INR320)		

T-3 On Payment of Margin

Journal Entry

Date	Particulars	Debit (INR)	Credit (INR)
29-Jan-X1	Futures Margin Account	64,000.00	
	To Bank Account		64,000.00
	(Being the margin amount for sale of 1,000 Index futures)		

T-4 On Recording the Brokerage/Commission

Journal Entry

Date	Particulars	Debit (INR)	Credit (INR)
29-Jan-X1	Brokerage/Commission Account	500.00	
	To Payable to Broker—Futures Account		500.00
	(Being the brokerage incurred on the sale of Index futures)		

T-5 On Payment of Brokerage/Commission

Journal Entry

Date	Particulars	Debit (INR)	Credit (INR)
29-Jan-X1	Payable to Broker—Futures Account	500.00	
	To Bank Account		500.00
	(Being the brokerage paid on the sale of Index futures)		

T-6 Mark-to-market at End of Reporting Period

Mark-to-market loss paid at the end of Jan X1	**INR**
(a) Market value of 1,000 Index futures @ 330 on 31-Jan	(330,000.00)
(b) Sale value of 1,000 Index futures @ 320 on 29-Jan	(320,000.00)
(c) Mark-to-market loss = (a) − (b)	**(10,000.00)**

Journal Entry

Date	Particulars	Debit (INR)	Credit (INR)
31-Jan-X1	MTM—Futures (P&L) Account	10,000.00	
	To Futures Margin Account		10,000.00
	(Being the mark-to-market entry for Index futures as on date)		

T-7 On Payment of Margin to Top Up the Mark-to-market Loss

Since the value of the sales position is eroded due to an increase in the market rate of the futures, the investor is required to make good the loss by paying the unrealized loss as margin. The variation margin represents the mark-to-market on the position. This is normally done on a daily basis, but for the purpose of this illustration the margin call occurs at the end of the month.

Journal Entry

Date	Particulars	Debit (INR)	Credit (INR)
31-Jan-X1	To Futures Margin Account	10,000.00	
	To Bank		10,000.00
	(Being the payment made to top up the margin for the mark-to-market loss incurred)		

T-8 Mark-to-market at End of Reporting Period

Mark-to-market loss paid at the end of Feb X1	**INR**
(a) Market value of 1,000 futures @ 345 on 28-Feb	(345,000.00)
(b) Sale value of 1,000 futures @ 320 on 29-Jan	(320,000.00)
(c) Mark to market = (a) − (b)	(25,000.00)
(d) Incremental mark-to-market for 28-Feb X1 (25,000 − 10,000)	**(15,000.00)**

Journal Entry

Date	Particulars	Debit (INR)	Credit (INR)
28-Feb-X1	MTM—Futures (P&L) Account	15,000.00	
	To Futures Margin Account		15,000.00
	(Being the incremental mark-to-market entry for futures as of date)		

Margin Money Paid at the End of Period Jan X1

Journal Entry

Date	Particulars	Debit (INR)	Credit (INR)
28-Feb-X1	To Futures Margin Account	15,000.00	
	To Bank		15,000.00
	(Being the incremental mark-to-market on futures contract as on date)		

T-9 On Purchasing the Futures

Journal Entry

Date	Particulars	Debit (INR)	Credit (INR)
15-Mar-X1	Equity Futures Contra Account (Off Balance Sheet)	1,500.00	
	To Equity Futures Position Account (Off Balance Sheet)		1,500.00
	(Being the 1,500 futures contract sold @ INR360)		

T-10 On Recording the Brokerage/Commission

Journal Entry

Date	Particulars	Debit (INR)	Credit (INR)
15-Mar-X1	Brokerage/Commission Account	700.00	
	To Payable to Broker—Futures Account		700.00
	(Being the brokerage incurred on purchase of index futures)		

T-11 On Payment of Brokerage/Commission

Journal Entry

Date	Particulars	Debit (INR)	Credit (INR)
15-Mar-X1	Payable to Broker—Futures Account	700.00	
	To Bank Account		700.00
	(Being the brokerage paid on purchase of index futures)		

T-12 On Payment of Margin

Additional margin paid towards the sale of 1,500 futures on 15-Mar	INR
Margin required for the sale of 1,500 futures = 20% of (1500 × 360)	108,000.00
Margin required to be deposited	**108,000.00**

Journal Entry

Date	Particulars	Debit (INR)	Credit (INR)
15-Mar-X1	Futures Margin Account	108,000.00	
	To Bank Account		108,000.00
	(Being the margin amount for sale of 1,500 Index futures)		

T-13 Mark-to-market at End of Reporting Period

Mark-to-market loss paid at the end of Mar X1	INR
(a) Market value of 1,000 futures @ 335 on 31-Mar	(335,000.00)
(b) Sale value of 1,000 futures @ 320 on 29-Jan	320,000.00
(c) Market value of 1,500 futures @ 335 on 31-Mar	(502,500.00)
(d) Sale value of 1,500 futures @ 360 on 15-Mar	540,000.00
(e) Mark-to-market	22,500.00
(f) Incremental MTM for Mar X1 = (22,500−10,000−15,000)	**47,500.00**

Journal Entry

Date	Particulars	Debit (INR)	Credit (INR)
31-Mar-X1	Futures Margin Account	47,500.00	
	To MTM—Futures (P&L) Account		47,500.00
	(Being the incremental mark to market on futures contract as on date)		

T-14 On Liquidating the Futures Partially

Journal Entry

Date	Particulars	Debit (INR)	Credit (INR)
10-Apr-X1	Equity Futures Position Account (Off Balance Sheet)	1,600.00	
	To Equity Futures Contra Account (Off Balance Sheet)		1,600.00
	(Being the 1,600 futures contract bought @ INR315)		

T-15 On Recording the Brokerage/Commission

Journal Entry

Date	Particulars	Debit (INR)	Credit (INR)
10-Apr-X1	Brokerage/Commission Account	450.00	
	To Payable to Broker—Futures Account		450.00
	(Being the brokerage incurred on purchase of Index futures)		

T-16 On Payment of Brokerage/Commission

Journal Entry

Date	Particulars	Debit (INR)	Credit (INR)
10-Apr-X1	Payable to Broker—Futures Account	50.00	
	To Bank Account		450.00
	(Being the brokerage paid on purchase of index futures)		

T-17 Recording Profit/Loss on the Sale

Realized gains on bought to cover	**INR**
(a) Cost of 1,600 futures position as on date @ 335	536,000.00
(b) Sale value of 1,600 futures @ 315	(504,000.00)
Realized gains = (b) – (a)	**32,000.00**

Journal Entry

Date	Particulars	Debit (INR)	Credit (INR)
10-Apr-X1	Futures Margin Account	32,000.00	
	To MTM—Futures (P&L) Account		32,000.00
	(Being the realized gain on bought cover of index futures)		

T-18 Return of Margin Money

Calculation of Return of Margin Money (Weighted Avg. Method)	**INR**
(a) Cost of 1000 futures @ 320	320,000.00
(b) Cost of 1500 futures @ 360	540,000.00
(c) Average cost of a future contract ((A+B)/2500)	344.00
Margin on sale of 1600 futures @ 20% (1600 * 344* 20%)	**110,080.00**

Journal Entry

Date	Particulars	Debit (INR)	Credit (INR)
10-Apr-X1	Bank Account	110,080.00	
	To Futures Margin Account		110,080.00
	(Return of margin money)		

T-19 On Expiry of Futures

Profit/loss on expiry of the contract	INR
Cost of sales of 900 futures (1,000 + 1,500 − 1600)	
(a) Value of short position of 900 futures @ 335	301,500.00
(b) Settlement value of 900 futures @ 310	(279,000.00)
Profit on expiry of the contract = (b) − (a)	**22,500.00**

Journal Entry

Date	Particulars	Debit (INR)	Credit (INR)
25-Apr-X1	Futures Margin Account	22,500.00	
	To MTM—Futures (P&L) Account		22,500.00
	(Being the realized gain on expiry of index futures)		

T-20 On Receipt of Margin on Futures

Margin money received on the date of expiry of contract	INR
(a) Initial margin paid on 29-Jan	64,000.00
(b) Margin call for Jan X1	(10,000.00)
(c) Amount paid towards margin call	10,000.00
(d) Margin call for Feb X1	(15,000.00)
(e) Amount paid towards margin call	15,000.00
(f) Margin call paid on 15-Mar	108,000.00
(g) Mark-to-market gain for Mar X1	47,500.00
(h) Profit on bought to cover of 1600 futures	32,000.00
(i) Refund of margin money	(110,080.00)
(j) Profit on expiry of futures contract	22,500.00
Margin amount received on the date of expiry = sum of the above	**163,920.00**

Journal Entry

Date	Particulars	Debit (INR)	Credit (INR)
25-Apr-X1	Bank Account	163,920.00	
	To Futures Margin Account		163,920.00
	(Being the balance in margin account received on the date of expiry)		

General Ledger Accounts

Futures Margin Account (for year 20X1)

Date	Particulars	Debit (INR)	Date	Particulars	Credit (INR)
29-Jan	To Bank Account	64,000.00			
			31-Jan	By MTM—Futures (P&L) Account	10,000.00
31-Jan	To Bank Account	10,000.00			
			28-Feb	By MTM—Futures (P&L) Account	15,000.00
28-Feb	To Bank Account	15,000.00			
15-Mar	To Bank Account	108,000.00			
31-Mar	To MTM—Futures (P&L) Account	47,500.00			
10-Apr	To MTM—Futures (P&L) Account	32,000.00			
			10-Apr	By Bank Account	110,080.00
25-Apr	To MTM—Futures (P&L) Account	22,500.00			
			25-Apr	By Bank Account	163,920.00
30-Apr	Total	**299.000.00**	30-Apr	Total	**299.000.00**

Brokerage/Commission Account (for year 20X1)

Date	Particulars	Debit (INR)	Date	Particulars	Credit (INR)
29-Jan	To Payable to Broker—Futures Account	500.00			
15-Mar	To Payable to Broker—Futures Account	700.00			
10-Apr	To Payable to Broker—Futures Account	450.00			
			30-Apr	By Balance	1,650.00
30-Apr	Total	**1,650.00**	30-Apr	Total	**1,650.00**
30-Apr	To Balance	1,650.00			

MTM—Futures (P&L) Account (for year 20X1)

Date	Particulars	Debit (INR)	Date	Particulars	Credit (INR)
31-Jan	To Futures Margin Account	10,000.00			
28-Feb	To Futures Margin Account	15,000.00			
			31-Mar	By Futures Margin Account	47,500.00
			10-Apr	By Futures Margin Account	32,000.00
			25-Apr	By Futures Margin Account	22,500.00
30-Apr	To Balance	77,000.00			
30-Apr	Total	**124,500.00**	30-Apr	Total	**102,000.00**
			30-Apr	By Balance	77,000.00

Share Capital Account (for year 20X1)

Date	Particulars	Debit (INR)	Date	Particulars	Credit (INR)
			1-Jan	By Bank Account	100,000.00
30-Apr	To Balance	100,000.00			
30-Apr	Total	**100,000.00**	30-Apr	Total	**100,000.00**
			30-Apr	By Balance	100,000.00

Payable to Broker—Futures Account (for year 20X1)

Date	Particulars	Debit (INR)	Date	Particulars	Credit (INR)
			29-Jan	By Brokerage/ Commission Account	500.00
29-Jan	To Bank Account	500.00			
			15-Mar	By Brokerage/Commission Account	700.00
15-Mar	To Bank Account	700.00			
			10-Apr	By Brokerage/Commission Account	450.00
10-Apr	To Bank Account	450.00			
30-Apr	Total	**1,650.00**	30-Apr	Total	**1,650.00**

Bank Account (for year 20X1)

Date	Particulars	Debit (INR)	Date	Particulars	Credit (INR)
1-Jan	To Share Capital Account	100,000.00			
			29-Jan	By Futures Margin Account	64,000.00
			29-Jan	By Payable to Broker—Futures Account	500.00
			31-Jan	By Futures Margin Account	10,000.00
			28-Feb	By Futures Margin Account	15,000.00
			15-Mar	By Payable to Broker—Futures Account	700.00
			15-Mar	By Futures Margin Account	108,000.00
			10-Apr	By Payable to Broker—Futures Account	450.00
10-Apr	To Futures Margin Account	110,080.00			
25-Apr	To Futures Margin Account	163,920.00			
			30-Apr	By Balance	175,350.00
30-Apr	Total	**374,000.00**	30-Apr	Total	**374,000.00**
30-Apr	To Balance	175,350.00			

Trial Balance

As on 30-Apr-X1 (INR)

Particulars	Debit	Credit
Capital Account		
Share Capital Account		100,000.00
Current Liabilities		Nil
Current Assets		
Bank Account	175,350.00	
Direct Income		
MTM—Futures (P&L) Account		77,000.00
Direct Expenses		
Brokerage/Commission Account	1,650.00	
Total	**177,000.00**	**177,000.00**

Income Statement

For the period ending 30-Apr-X1

Expenses	INR	Income	INR
Direct Expenses		**Direct Income**	
Brokerage/Commission Account	1,650.00	MTM—Futures (P&L) Account	77,000.00
Net Profit	75,350.00		
Total	**77,000.00**	Total	**77,000.00**

Balance Sheet

As at 30-Apr-X1

Liabilities	INR	Assets	INR
Capital Account		**Investments**	Nil
Share Capital Account	100,000.00		
		Current Assets	
Current Liabilities	Nil	Bank Account	175,350.00
Profit & Loss Account			
Opening Balance	Nil		
Current Period	75,350.00		
Total	**175,350.00**	Total	**175,350.00**

Short Futures—Functional Currency US$

The following are the FX revaluation entries in the functional currency converted at the respective FX rate, which is given within parentheses. FX translation entries are clearly specified, indicating whether each is a consummated FX translation entry or a transient FX translation entry.

F-1 Capital Introduced by the Fund (T-1 @ FX Rate: 45.03)

Journal Entry

Date	Particulars	Debit (US$)	Credit (US$)
1-Jan-X1	Bank Account	2,220.74	
	To Share Capital Account		2,220.74
	(Being the subscription received from an investor into the fund)		

F-2 On Sale of Futures

Journal Entry

Date	Particulars	Debit (US$)	Credit (US$)
29-Jan-X1	Equity Futures Contra Account (Off Balance Sheet)	1,000.00	
	To Equity Futures Position Account (Off Balance Sheet)		1,000.00
	(Being the 1,000 futures contract sold @ INR320)		

F-3 On Payment of Margin (T-3 @ FX Rate: 44.27)

Journal Entry

Date	Particulars	Debit (US$)	Credit (US$)
29-Jan-X1	Futures Margin Account	1,445.67	
	To Bank Account		1,445.67
	(Being the margin money paid for sale of 1,000 Index futures)		

F-4 On Recording the Brokerage/Commission (T-4 @ FX Rate: 44.27)

Journal Entry

Date	Particulars	Debit (US$)	Credit (US$)
29-Jan-X1	Brokerage/Commission Account	11.29	
	To Payable to Broker—Futures Account		11.29
	(Being the brokerage incurred on the sale of Index futures)		

F-5 On Payment of Brokerage/Commission (T-5 @ FX Rate: 44.27)

Journal Entry

Date	Particulars	Debit (US$)	Credit (US$)
29-Jan-X1	Payable to Broker—Futures Account	11.29	
	To Bank Account		11.29
	(Being the brokerage paid on the sale of index futures)		

F-6 Mark-to-market at End of Reporting Period (T-6 @ FX Rate: 44.17)

Journal Entry

Date	Particulars	Debit (US$)	Credit (US$)
31-Jan-X1	MTM—Futures (P&L) Account	226.40	
	To Futures Margin Account		226.40
	(Being the mark-to-market on futures contract as on date)		

F-7 On Payment of Margin to Top Up the Mark-to-market Loss (T-7 @ FX Rate: 44.17)

Journal Entry

Date	Particulars	Debit (US$)	Credit (US$)
31-Jan-X1	Futures Margin Account	226.40	
	To Bank Account		226.40
	(Being payment made towards margin call)		

F-8 FX Translation on Futures Margin Account (Transient FX Translation Entry)

Date	Particulars	INR	FX Rate	US$
29-Jan-X1	Opening balance	64,000.00	44.27	1,445.67
31-Jan-X1	Margin call for Jan X1	(10,000.00)	44.17	(226.40)
31-Jan-X1	Margin call paid for Jan X1	10,000.00	44.17	226.40
	Net balance	64,000.00		1,445.67
	Net balance at current FX rate	64,000.00	44.17	1,448.95
	FX translation on margin account			**3.28**

Journal Entry

Date	Particulars	Debit (US$)	Credit (US$)
31-Jan-X1	Futures Margin Account	3.28	
	To Unrealized Currency Gains/Loss Account		3.28
	(Being the FX translation applied on futures margin account)		

F-9 FX Translation on Bank Account (Transient FX Translation Entry)

Date	Particulars	INR	FX Rate	US$
1-Jan-X1	Opening balance	100,000.00	45.03	2,220.74
29-Jan-X1	Transfer out	(64,000.00)	44.27	(1,445.67)
29-Jan-X1	Brokerage paid	(500.00)	44.27	(11.29)
31-Jan-X1	Margin call paid for Jan X1	(10,000.00)	44.17	(226.40)
31-Jan-X1	Net balance	25,500.00		537.38
	Net balance at current FX rate	25,500.00	44.17	577.31
	FX translation on margin account			**39.93**

Journal Entry

Date	Particulars	Debit (US$)	Credit (US$)
31-Jan-X1	Bank Account	39.93	
	To Unrealized Currency Gains/Loss Account		39.93
	(Being the FX translation applied on bank account)		

F-10 Mark-to-market at End of Reporting Period (T-7 @ FX Rate: 44.31)

Journal Entry

Date	Particulars	Debit (US$)	Credit (US$)
28-Feb-X1	MTM—Futures (P&L) Account	338.52	
	To Futures Margin Account		338.52
	(Being the mark-to-market on futures contract as on date)		

Journal Entry

Date	Particulars	Debit (US$)	Credit (US$)
28-Feb-X1	Futures Margin Account	338.52	
	To Bank Account		338.52
	(Being payment made towards margin call)		

F-11 FX Translation on Futures Margin Account (Transient FX Translation Entry)

Date	Particulars	INR	FX Rate	US$
31-Jan-X1	Opening balance	64,000.00	44.17	1,448.95
28-Feb-X1	Margin call for Feb X1	(15,000.00)	44.31	(338.52)
28-Feb-X1	Margin call Paid for Feb X1	15,000.00	44.31	338.52
	Net balance	64,000.00		1,448.95
	Net balance at current FX rate	64,000.00	44.31	1,444.37
	FX translation on margin account			**(4.58)**

Journal Entry

Date	Particulars	Debit (US$)	Credit (US$)
28-Feb-X1	Unrealized Currency Gains/Loss Account	4.58	
	To Futures Margin Account		4.58
	(Being the FX translation applied on futures margin account)		

F-12 FX Translation on Bank Account (Transient FX Translation Entry)

Date	Particulars	INR	FX Rate	US$
31-Jan-X1	Opening balance	25,500.00	44.17	577.31
28-Feb-X1	Margin paid	(15,000.00)	44.31	(338.52)
28-Feb-X1	Net balance	10,500.00		238.79
	Net balance at current FX rate	10,500.00	44.31	236.97
	FX translation on bank account			**(1.82)**

Journal Entry

Date	Particulars	Debit (US$)	Credit (US$)
28-Feb-X1	Unrealized Currency Gains/Loss Account	1.82	
	To Bank Account		1.82
	(Being the FX translation applied on bank account)		

F-13 On Purchasing the Futures

Journal Entry

Date	Particulars	Debit (US$)	Credit (US$)
15-Mar-X1	Equity Futures Contra Account (Off Balance Sheet)	1,500.00	
	To Equity Futures Position Account (Off Balance Sheet)		1,500.00
	(Being the 1,500 futures contract sold @ INR 360)		

F-14 On Recording the Brokerage/Commission (T-10 @ FX Rate: 44.20)

Journal Entry

Date	Particulars	Debit (US$)	Credit (US$)
15-Mar-X1	Brokerage/Commission Account	15.84	
	To Payable to Broker—Futures Account		15.84
	(Being the brokerage incurred on the sale of index futures)		

F-15 On Payment of Brokerage/Commission (T-11 @ FX Rate: 44.20)

Journal Entry

Date	Particulars	Debit (US$)	Credit (US$)
15-Mar-X1	Payable to Broker—Futures Account	15.84	
	To Bank Account		15.84
	(Being the brokerage paid on the sale of index futures)		

F-16 Margin Call (T-12 @ FX Rate: 44.20)

Journal Entry

Date	Particulars	Debit (US$)	Credit (US$)
15-Mar-X1	Futures Margin Account	2,443.44	
	To Bank Account		2,443.44
	(Being the margin call invoked by the broker due to fall in the value of the margin account)		

F-17 Mark-to-market at End of Reporting Period (T-13 @ FX Rate: 43.59)

Journal Entry

Date	Particulars	Debit (US$)	Credit (US$)
31-Mar-X1	Futures Margin Account	1,089.70	
	To MTM—Futures (P&L) Account		1,089.70
	(Being the mark-to-market on futures contract as on date)		

F-18 FX Translation on Futures Margin Account (Transient FX Translation Entry)

Date	Particulars	INR	FX Rate	US$
28-Feb-X1	Opening balance	64,000.00	44.31	1,444.37
15-Mar-X1	Margin paid	108,000.00	44.20	2,443.44
31-Mar-X1	Mark to market	47,500.00	43.59	1,089.70
	Net balance	219,500.00		4,977.51
	Net balance at current FX rate	219,500.00	43.59	5035.56
	FX translation on margin account			**58.05**

Journal Entry

Date	Particulars	Debit (US$)	Credit (US$)
31-Mar-X1	Futures Margin Account	58.05	
	To Unrealized Currency Gains/Loss Account		58.05
	(Being the FX translation applied on futures margin account)		

F-19 FX Translation on Bank Account (Transient FX Translation Entry)

Date	Particulars	INR	FX Rate	US$
28-Feb-X1	Opening balance	10,500.00	44.31	236.97
15-Mar-X1	Transfer out	(108,000.00)	44.20	(2,443.44)
15-Mar-X1	Commission	(700.00)	44.20	(15.84)
31-Mar-X1	Net balance	(98,200.00)		(2,222.31)
	Net balance at current FX rate	(98,200.00)	43.59	(2,252.81)
	FX translation on bank account			**(30.50)**

Journal Entry

Date	Particulars	Debit (US$)	Credit (US$)
31-Mar-X1	Unrealized Currency Gains/Loss Account	30.50	
	To Bank Account		30.50
	(Being the FX translation applied on bank account)		

F-20 On Liquidating the Futures Partially

Journal Entry

Date	Particulars	Debit (US$)	Credit (US$)
10-Apr-X1	Equity Futures Position Account (Off Balance Sheet)	1,600.00	
	To Equity Futures Contra Account (Off Balance Sheet)		1,600.00
	(Being the 1,600 futures contract bought @ INR315)		

F-21 On Recording the Brokerage/Commission (T-15 @ FX Rate: 42.50)

Journal Entry

Date	Particulars	Debit (US$)	Credit (US$)
10-Apr-X1	Brokerage/Commission Account	0.59	
	To Payable to Broker—Futures Account		10.59
	(Being the brokerage incurred on purchase of index futures)		

F-22 On Payment of Brokerage/Commission (T-16 @ FX Rate: 42.50)

Journal Entry

Date	Particulars	Debit (US$)	Credit (US$)
10-Apr-X1	Payable to Broker—Futures Account	10.59	
	To Bank Account		10.59
	(Being the brokerage paid on purchase of index futures)		

F-23 Recording Profit/Loss on the Sale (T-17 @ FX Rate: 42.50)

Journal Entry

Date	Particulars	Debit (US$)	Credit (US$)
10-Apr-X1	Futures Margin Account	752.94	
	To MTM—Futures (P&L) Account		752.94
	(Being the realized gain on bought cover of index futures)		

F-24 Return of Margin Money (T-18 @ FX Rate: 42.50)

Journal Entry

Date	Particulars	Debit (US$)	Credit (US$)
10-Apr-X1	Bank Account	2,590.12	
	To Futures Margin Account		2,590.12
	(Being the realized gain on bought cover of index futures)		

F-25 On Expiry of Futures (T-19 @ FX Rate: 41.29)

Journal Entry

Date	Particulars	Debit (US$)	Credit (US$)
25-Apr-X1	Futures Margin Account	544.93	
	To MTM—Futures (P&L) Account		544.93
	(Being the realized gain on expiry of index futures)		

F-26 On Receipt of Margin on Futures (T-20 @ FX Rate: 41.29)

Journal Entry

Date	Particulars	Debit (US$)	Credit (US$)
25-Apr-X1	Bank Account	3,969.97	
	To Futures Margin Account		3,969.97
	(Being the balance in the margin account received on the date of expiry)		

F-27 FX Translation on Futures Margin Account (Transient FX Translation Entry)

Date	Particulars	INR	FX Rate	US$
31-Mar-X1	Opening balance	219,500.00	43.59	5,035.56
10-Apr-X1	Mark-to-market	32,000.00	42.50	752.94
10-Apr-X1	Refund of margin on sale	(110,080.00)	42.50	(2,590.12)
26-Apr-X1	Mark-to-market	22,500.00	41.29	544.93
26-Apr-X1	Refund on margin money on expiry	(163,920.00)	41.29	(3,969.97)
	FX translation on margin account		41.29	**226.66**

Journal Entry

Date	Particulars	Debit (US$)	Credit (US$)
25-Apr-X1	Futures Margin Account	226.66	
	To Unrealized Currency Gains/Loss Account		226.66
	(Being the FX translation applied on futures margin account)		

F-28 FX Translation on Bank Account (Transient FX Translation Entry)

Date	Particulars	INR	FX Rate	US$
31-Mar-X1	Opening balance	(98,200.00)	43.59	(2,252.81)
10-Apr-X1	Transfer out	(450.00)	42.50	(10.59)
10-Apr-X1	Refund of margin on sale	110,080.00	42.50	2,590.12
26-Apr-X1	Refund on margin money on expiry	163,920.00	41.29	3,969.97
		175,350.00		4,246.79
	FX translation on bank account			**(49.90)**

Journal Entry

Date	Particulars	Debit (US$)	Credit (US$)
25-Apr-X1	Unrealized Currency Gains/Loss Account	49.90	
	To Bank Account		49.90
	(Being the FX translation applied on bank account)		

General Ledger Accounts

Futures Margin Account (for year 20X1)

Date	Particulars	Debit (US$)	Date	Particulars	Credit (US$)
29-Jan	To Bank Account	1,445.67			
			31-Jan	By MTM—Futures (P&L) Account	226.40
31-Jan	To Bank Account	226.40			
31-Jan	To Unrealized Currency Gains/Loss Account	3.28			
			28-Feb	By MTM—Futures (P&L) Account	338.52
28-Feb	To Bank Account	338.52			
			28-Feb	By Unrealized Currency Gains/ Loss Account	4.58
15-Mar	To Bank Account	2,443.44			
31-Mar	To MTM—Futures (P&L) Account	1,089.70			
31-Mar	To Unrealized Currency Gains/Loss Account	58.05			
10-Apr	To MTM—Futures (P&L) Account	752.94			
			10-Apr	By Bank Account	2,590.12
25-Apr	To MTM—Futures (P&L) Account	544.93			
			25-Apr	By Bank Account	3,969.97
25-Apr	To Unrealized Currency Gains/Loss Account	226.66			
30-Apr	Total	**7,129.59**	30-Apr	Total	**7,129.59**

Brokerage/Commission Account (for year 20X1)

Date	Particulars	Debit (US$)	Date	Particulars	Credit (US$)
29-Jan	To Payable to Broker—Futures Account	11.29			
15-Mar	To Payable to Broker—Futures Account	5.84			
10-Apr	To Payable to Broker—Futures Account	0.59			
			30-Apr	By Balance	37.72
30-Apr	Total	**37.72**	30-Apr	Total	**37.72**
30-Apr	To Balance	37.72			

Unrealized Currency Gains/Loss Account (for year 20X1)

Date	Particulars	Debit (US$)	Date	Particulars	Credit (US$)
			31-Jan	By Futures Margin Account	3.28
			31-Jan	By Bank Account	39.93
28-Feb	To Futures Margin Account	4.58			
28-Feb	To Bank Account	1.82			
			31-Mar	By Futures Margin Account	58.05
31-Mar	To Bank Account	30.50			
			25-Apr	By Futures Margin Account	226.66
25-Apr	To Bank Account	49.90			
30-Apr	To Balance	241.12			
30-Apr	Total	**327.92**	30-Apr	Total	**327.92**
			30-Apr	By Balance	241.12

MTM—Futures (P&L) Account (for year 20X1)

Date	Particulars	Debit (US$)	Date	Particulars	Credit (US$)
31-Jan	To Futures Margin Account	226.40			
28-Feb	To Futures Margin Account	338.52			
			31-Mar	By Futures Margin Account	1,089.70
			10-Apr	By Futures Margin Account	752.94
			25-Apr	By Futures Margin Account	544.93
30-Apr	To Balance	1,822.65			
30-Apr	Total	**2,387.57**	30-Apr	Total	**2,387.57**
			30-Apr	By Balance	1,822.65

Share Capital Account (for year 20X1)

Date	Particulars	Debit (US$)	Date	Particulars	Credit (US$)
			1-Jan	By Bank Account	2,220.74
30-Apr	To Balance	2,220.74			
30-Apr	Total	**2,220.74**	30-Apr	Total	**2,220.74**
			30-Apr	By Balance	2,220.74

Payable to Broker—Futures Account (for year 20X1)

Date	Particulars	Debit (US$)	Date	Particulars	Credit (US$)
			29-Jan	By Brokerage/ Commission Account	11.29
29-Jan	To Bank Account	11.29			
			15-Mar	By Brokerage/ Commission Account	15.84
15-Mar	To Bank Account	15.84			
			10-Apr	By Brokerage/Commission Account	10.59
10-Apr	To Bank Account	10.59			
30-Apr	Total	**37.72**	30-Apr	Total	**37.72**

Bank Account (for year 20X1)

Date	Particulars	Debit (US$)	Date	Particulars	Credit (US$)
1-Jan	To Share Capital Account	2,220.74			
			29-Jan-X1	By Futures Margin Account	1,445.67
			29-Jan	By Payable to Broker—Futures Account	11.29
			31-Jan	By Futures Margin Account	226.40
31-Jan	To Unrealized Currency Gains/ Loss Account	39.93			
			28-Feb	By Unrealized Currency Gains/Loss Account	1.82
			28-Feb	By Futures Margin Account	338.52
			15-Mar	By Payable to Broker—Futures Account	15.84
			15-Mar	By Futures Margin Account	2,443.44
			31-Mar	By Unrealized Currency Gains/Loss Account	30.50
			10-Apr	By Payable to Broker—Futures Account	10.59
10-Apr	To Futures Margin Account	2,590.12			
25-Apr	To Futures Margin Account	3,969.97			
			25-Apr	By Unrealized Currency Gains/Loss Account	49.90
			30-Apr	By Balance	4,246.79
30-Apr	Total	**8,820.76**	30-Apr	Total	**8,820.76**
30-Apr	To Balance	4,246.79			

Trial Balance

As on 30-Apr-X1 (US$)

Particulars	Debit	Credit
Capital Account		
Share Capital Account		2,220.74
Current Liabilities		
Current Assets		
Bank Account	4,246.79	
Direct Income		
Unrealized Currency Gains/Loss Account		241.12
MTM—Futures (P&L) Account		1,822.65
Direct Expenses		
Brokerage/Commission Account	37.72	
Total	**4,284.51**	**4,284.51**

Income Statement

For the period ending 30-Apr-X1

Expenses	US$	Income	US$
Direct Expenses		**Direct Income**	
Brokerage/Commission Account	37.72	Unrealized Currency Gains/Loss Account	241.12
		MTM—Futures (P&L) Account	1,822.65
Gross Profit Carryover	2,026.05		
Total	**2,063.77**	Total	**2,063.77**

Balance Sheet

As at 30-Apr-X1

Liabilities	US$	Assets	US$
Capital Account		**Investments**	Nil
Share Capital Account	2,220.74	**Current Assets**	
Current Liabilities	Nil	Bank Account	4,246.79
Profit & Loss Account			
Opening Balance	Nil		
Current Period	2,026.05		
Total	**4,246.79**	Total	**4,246.79**

SUMMARY

- An index future is a form of derivative and if used for hedging requires a special hedge accounting treatment. When used as a mere speculative position, normal accounting entries are recorded.
- When the investor buys the index futures, then the investor has to square off the position by adjusting the difference in cash, as there is no question of settlement through delivery in the case of index futures.

EXERCISES

Theory Questions

1. Enumerate the various events in the trade life cycle of an equity index futures trade and name the journal entries to be passed at each and every event.

Objective Questions

1. The responsibility of ensuring the completeness of both legs of the futures contract vests with
   a. Buyer and seller
   b. Broker
   c. Stock exchange
   d. All of the above
2. Margin money adjustment calculation is based on
   a. Position opening value
   b. Position closing value
   c. Marked-to-market valuation
   d. None of the above
3. An entry for futures contract bought will be recorded and posted
   a. In the income statement
   b. On the balance sheet
   c. Off the balance sheet
   d. None of the above
4. Brokerage/commission paid to the broker for futures contract will be paid on
   a. Trade date
   b. Settlement date
   c. T + 2
   d. None of the above

5. Portfolio valuation process means
   a. Only ascertaining the fair value of the product dealt with
   b. Only marked-to-market process
   c. Both a and b
   d. None of the above

6. Margin call will be initiated by the
   a. Broker
   b. Seller
   c. Stock exchange
   d. None of the above

7. Entry for brokerage on sale of shares will be posted
   a. To the income statement
   b. To the profit and loss account
   c. Off the balance sheet
   d. None of the above

8. Margin money will be reversed on
   a. Expiry date
   b. Date of liquidation
   c. End of accounting period
   d. None of the above

9. Physical delivery of underlying asset will not happen on the expiry date for
   a. Stock futures
   b. Commodity futures
   c. Index futures
   d. All of the above

10. The futures contract will automatically expire on
    a. Settlement date
    b. Expiry date of the contract
    c. End-of-day every day, facilitating the marked-to-market process
    d. None of the above

Journal Questions

Journalize the following scenario:

1. Gregory Williams buys 500 shares of futures contract of ACC for INR950 per share on November 14. Brokerage is 0.3 percent for purchase as well as sales. He then sells the shares on November 21 for INR975 per share. The brokerage settlement is T = 2; the margin requirement is 20 percent.
2. Assume the shares were not sold and physical settlement was effected on November 28, which is the expiry date. On the expiry the price is quoted at INR945 per share. Pass necessary journal entries for purchase, sales, brokerage paid, and physical settlement. Calculate the profit/loss as of November 21 and November 28.
3. What if no physical settlement was effected on November 28? Also pass journal entries to that effect.
4. Prepare the Investments—ACC—Futures Account, treating the shares as physically settled.

Short Futures—Trade Currency AUS$, Functional Currency US$

For the following scenario, prepare journal entries, general ledgers, trial balance, income statement, and balance sheet.

XYZ Fund had the following trades on an index in the futures market. The stock exchange requires that a margin of 20 percent of the value of the contract be maintained throughout the life of the contract.

Date	Product Expiry	Quantity	Rate (AUD)	B/S	Brokerage
22-Feb-X1	25-Apr-X1	–1,700	45	S	320
18-Mar-X1	25-Apr-X1	–1,400	50	S	350
13-Apr-X1	25-Apr-X1	2,000	43	B	400
25-Apr-X1	25-Apr-X1	1,100	42	Expiry	

Date	FX Rate
22-Feb-X1	1.18182
28-Feb-X1	1.17762
15-Mar-X1	1.18322
31-Mar-X1	1.17521
10-Apr-X1	1.18231
25-Apr-X1	1.17425

Date	Market Price
22-Feb-X1	47
28-Feb-X1	55
31-Mar-X1	43
25-Apr-X1	45

Long Futures—Trade Currency SGD, Functional Currency US$

For the following scenario, prepare journal entries, general ledgers, trial balance, income statement, and balance sheet.

AA Fund had the following trades on an index in the futures market. The stock exchange requires that a margin of 10 percent of the value of the contract be maintained throughout the life of the contract.

Date	Product Expiry	Quantity	Rate (SGD)	B/S	Brokerage
25-Aug-X1	25-Nov-X1	10,000	52.5	B	5,300
18-Oct-X1	25-Nov-X1	15,000	51.0	B	5,200
10-Nov-X1	25-Nov-X1	–16,000	54.0	S	3,000
25-Nov-X1	25-Nov-X1	–9,000	53.0	Expiry	

Date	FX Rate
25-Aug-X1	1.5389
31-Aug-X1	1.5432
30-Sep-X1	1.5535
18-Oct-X1	1.5375
31-Oct-X1	1.5296
10-Nov-X1	1.5431
25-Nov-X1	1.5159

Date	Market Price
31-Aug-X1	49
30-Sep-X1	47
31-Oct-X1	53
25-Nov-X1	57

Long Futures—Trade Currency JPY, Functional Currency US$

For the following scenario, prepare journal entries, general ledgers, trial balance, income statement, and balance sheet.

AA Fund had the following trades on an index in the futures market. The stock exchange requires that a margin of 30 percent of the value of the contract be maintained throughout the life of the contract.

Date	Product Expiry	Quantity	Rate (JPY)	B/S	Brokerage
29-Jan-X1	25-Apr-X1	1,000	800	B	530
15-Mar-X1	25-Apr-X1	1,500	820	B	520
10-Apr-X1	25-Apr-X1	–1,600	845	S	300
25-Apr-X1	25-Apr-X1	–900	850	Expiry	

Date	FX Rate
1-Jan-X1	123.805
29-Jan-X1	124.850
31-Jan-X1	125.705
28-Feb-X1	124.805
15-Mar-X1	125.705
31-Mar-X1	125.205
10-Apr-X1	124.235
25-Apr-X1	124.569

Date	Market Price
31-Jan-X1	750
28-Feb-X1	770
31-Mar-X1	855
25-Apr-X1	857

Short Futures—Functional Currency US$

For the following scenario, prepare journal entries, general ledgers, trial balance, income statement, and balance sheet.

ABC Fund had the following trades on an index in the futures market. The stock exchange requires that a margin of 15 percent of the value of the contract be maintained throughout the life of the contract.

Date	Product Expiry	Quantity	Rate (US$)	B/S	Brokerage
22-Feb-X1	25-Apr-X1	−1,500	45	S	320
18-Mar-X1	25-Apr-X1	−1,800	50	S	350
13-Apr-X1	25-Apr-X1	2,000	43	B	400
25-Apr-X1	25-Apr-X1	1,300	42	Expiry	

Date	Market Price
22-Feb-X1	47
28-Feb-X1	55
31-Mar-X1	43
25-Apr-X1	45

CHAPTER 7

Accounting for Equity Stock Futures

LEARNING OBJECTIVES

After studying this chapter, you should have a grasp of the following:

- The trade life cycle of exchange traded equity stock futures.
- Journal entries to be recorded during the different phases of the trade life cycle.
- FX revaluation and FX translation process for these trades.
- Illustration of long stock futures with FX translation.
- Preparation of journal entries and general ledger accounts.
- Preparation of income statement and balance sheet after the equity futures trades are done.
- Illustration of short stock futures with FX translation.

TRADE LIFE CYCLE FOR EQUITY STOCK FUTURES

The sequence of events for trading in equity stock futures is as follows:

1. If you bought futures, then account for the buy trade of equity stock.
2. If you sold futures, then account for the sell trade of equity stock.
3. Transfer the brokerage/commission on the original trade to stock.
4. Perform the FX revaluation entries.
5. Perform the FX translation entries.

Accounting for a Buy Trade

When the investor buys stock futures resulting in physical settlement, then the investor has to pay for the contracted price and take delivery of the stock. The margin money paid will, however, be adjusted against the total money that the investor should pay the exchange. The equity shares will be accounted for as a regular purchase of shares, and the treatment will depend upon whether it is held for trading or as available-for-sale.

Assume that the investor takes delivery of 1,000 shares of Boeing at $93 per share, and assume it is held for trading. The accounting entry that is recorded in the books of accounts is shown as follows:

Journal Entry

Date	Particulars	Debit (US$)	Credit (US$)
15-Dec-X1	Investments—Equity Shares—Trading Account	93,000.00	
	To Broker Payable Account		93,000.00
	(Being the equity shares taken in delivery pursuant to the futures contract)		

Accounting for a Sell Trade

Similarly, when the futures are sold and the trade results in physical settlement, then the physical shares should be delivered by the investor to the exchange, and the transaction is recorded like a regular sale of equity shares held by the investor. The profit or loss on account of the sale is determined and accounted for accordingly depending upon whether the shares are held as trading or available-for-sale. Assuming that 1,000 shares of Intel are sold at $24 per share, the accounting entry that is recorded in the books of accounts is shown as follows:

Journal Entry

Date	Particulars	Debit (US$)	Credit (US$)
15-Dec-X1	Broker Receivable Account	24,000.00	
	To Investments—Equity shares—Trading Account		24,000.00
	(Being the shares delivered pursuant to the futures contract)		

Transferring the Brokerage on the Original Trade to Stock

The brokerage paid on the futures trade would have been directly expensed and not taken as part of the cost of the shares that were to be acquired. Hence, when the futures contract results in physical settlement, then the brokerage originally expensed should be capitalized and taken to the account of the shares concerned. The realized profit or loss will be calculated taking this as part of the cost of shares.

Assume that in the earlier case of purchase of stock futures resulting in physical delivery of shares, the brokerage paid was $400. The accounting entry that is recorded in the books of accounts is shown as follows:

Journal Entry

Date	Particulars	Debit (US$)	Credit (US$)
15-Dec-X1	Investments—Equity Shares—Trading Account	400.00	
	To Brokerage/Commission Account		400.00
	(Being the brokerage charges now treated as part of the cost of acquisition of the shares as the futures contract has resulted in physical delivery of shares)		

FX Revaluation Entries

All the entries recorded to this point are initially entered in the respective trade currencies. If the functional currency is different from the trade currency, then each and every entry recorded in the trade currency should be entered again in the functional currency by converting the entries at the respective day's FX rates. In other words, for each trade currency that the investor deals with, there will be a complete set of books representing that trade currency. This includes journal entries, general ledger postings, trial balance, income statement, and balance sheet.

After revaluing each and every journal entry of all the trade currencies into the functional currency, a separate set of books is prepared comprising all the elements just mentioned: journal entries, general ledger postings, trial balance, income statement, and balance sheet. It should be noted that the ultimate financial reports would be prepared and presented to all the stakeholders based on the financial statements prepared in the functional currency only, as this will encompass all the transactions of the investor in all trade currencies dabbled with. (For illustration and detailed explanation, please refer to Chapter 2.)

FX Revaluation Entries

After revaluing all the entries in the functional currency at the respective FX rates for the day concerned, another entry needs to be passed in the books of the functional currency. This is mainly to adjust the currency gains or losses due to the fluctuations in FX rates between the reporting date and the date of recording the original entries. FX translation entries are recorded only for the asset and liability accounts. For income and expense accounts the amount gets crystallized on the date of passing the FX revaluation entries in the books of the functional currency.

There are fundamentally two types of FX translation entries that are recorded in the books of the functional currency: consummated FX translation entries and transient FX translation entries. (For illustration and detailed explanation, please refer to Chapter 2.)

ILLUSTRATIONS

Consider the following examples.

Stock Futures—Long Stock, JPY

Cerebros Fund had the following trades in ABB in the futures market. The stock exchange requires that a margin of 50 percent of the value of the contract be maintained throughout the life of the contract.

Date	Product	Product Expiry	Quantity	Rate (JPY)	B/S	Brokerage
5-Jan-X1	ABB Futures	15-Feb-X1	1,000,000	50	B	10,0000
25-Feb-X1	ABB Stock		1,000,000	55	S	11,0000

Delivery of the ABB stock was taken on the expiry date of the futures, February 15, when the market rate was JPY 53 per share. Earlier, JPY 100 million was introduced on January 5 as capital into the fund. ABB shares were held with no intention of trading and hence were classified as available-for-sale. Journal entries, general ledgers, trial balance, income statement, and balance sheet must be prepared as follows:

Date	FX Rate
5-Jan-X1	123.805
31-Jan-X1	124.850
15-Feb-X1	124.800
25-Feb-X1	123.560
Date	**ABB Market Price**
31-Jan-X1	52
15-Feb-X1	53

Long Stock Futures—Trade Currency JPY

T-1 Capital Introduced by the Fund

Journal Entry

Date	Particulars	Debit (JPY)	Credit (JPY)
5-Jan-X1	Bank Account	100,000,000	
	To Share Capital Account		100,000,000
	(Being the subscription contributed by an investor into the fund)		

T-2 On Purchasing the Futures

This entry is just an off-balance-sheet entry and thus is not taken into account while preparing the financial statements of the investor. In this illustration, there will not be any postings for this entry.

Journal Entry

Date	Particulars	Debit (JPY)	Credit (JPY)
5-Jan-X1	Equity Futures Position Account (Off Balance Sheet)	1,000,000	
	To Equity Futures Contra Account (Off Balance Sheet)		1,000,000
	(Being 1 million futures contracts of ABB purchased)		

T-3 On Payment of Margin

Journal Entry

Date	Particulars	Debit (JPY)	Credit (JPY)
5-Jan-X1	Futures Margin Account	25,000,000	
	To Bank Account		25,000,000
	(Being the margin amount on purchase of 1,000,000 ABB futures paid)		

T-4 On Recording the Brokerage/Commission

Brokerage is paid separately. In derivative instruments, it is not treated as part of the cost of acquisition, and hence is directly charged off to the profit and loss account.

Journal Entry

Date	Particulars	Debit (JPY)	Credit (JPY)
5-Jan-X1	Brokerage/Commission Account	100,000	
	To Payable to Broker—Futures Account		100,000
	(Being the brokerage incurred on purchase of ABB futures)		

T-5 On Payment of Brokerage/Commission

Journal Entry

Date	Particulars	Debit (JPY)	Credit (JPY)
5-Jan-X1	Payable to Broker—Futures Account	100,000	
	To Bank Account		100,000
	(Being the payment of brokerage incurred on purchase of ABB futures)		

T-6 Mark-to-market at End of Reporting Period

The mark-to-market is computed based on the market rate at the end of each day. However, for this illustration it is assumed that the mark-to-market is computed at the end of the month. If there is a drop in the value of the long position, the same is reduced from the margin account—which eventually is required to be topped up with the erosion in value. Mark-to-market gains are debited to the margin account and the same is credited to the profit and loss account.

Mark-to-market gains at the end of Jan X1	**JPY**
(a) Market value of 1 million ABB stock futures @ 52 on 31-Jan-X1	52,000,000
(b) Purchase value of 1 million ABB stock futures @ 50 on 29-Jan-X1	50,000,000
(c) MTM gains = (a) – (b)	**2,000,000**

Journal Entry

Date	Particulars	Debit (JPY)	Credit (JPY)
31-Jan-X1	Futures Margin Account	2,000,000	
	To MTM—Futures (P&L) Account		2,000,000
	(Being the mark-to-market entry for futures as on date)		

T-7 Reversal of Mark-to-market on the Date of Expiry

The mark-to-market margin is reversed on the date of expiry of the futures contract as delivery of the underlying stock was taken on the expiry of the futures.

Journal Entry

Date	Particulars	Debit (JPY)	Credit (JPY)
15-Feb-X1	MTM—Futures (P&L) Account	2,000,000	
	To Futures Margin Account		2,000,000
	(Being the reversal of mark-to-market on the date of expiry)		

T-8 Margin Payment Returned on the Date of Expiry

Journal Entry

Date	Particulars	Debit (JPY)	Credit (JPY)
15-Feb-X1	Bank Account	25,000,000	
	To Futures Margin Account		25,000,000
	(Being margin payment returned on the date of expiry)		

T-9 On Purchase of Equity Shares on the Date of Expiry

Delivery of the underlying shares is taken on the date of expiry of the futures. The equity shares will be recorded at the rate at which the futures are contracted to be bought, as this is the amount that the investor has to pay to acquire the underlying equity shares, irrespective of the market rate of the shares on the date of expiry. In this case, even though the market rate on the date of expiry is 53, the investments account is debited with only 50 as this is the amount that is to be paid to acquire the shares. In the usual practice, the mark-to-market is done on a daily basis and the investments would be marked up to 53, treating the difference of 3 as unrealized capital gains on such investments.

Journal Entry

Date	Particulars	Debit (JPY)	Credit (JPY)
15-Feb-X1	Investments—Equity Shares—AFS Account	50,000,000	
	To Payable to Broker—Stock Account		50,000,000
	(Being the ABB equity shares purchased on the date of expiry)		

T-10 Commission on Futures Reversed to the Equity Shares

Assuming that the broker does not charge additional commission on taking delivery of the underlying shares on the date of expiry of the futures contract, the commission already paid on the purchase of the futures should be treated as part of the cost of acquisition of the equity shares and hence should be taken to the investments account and the commission account should be reversed.

Journal Entry

Date	Particulars	Debit (JPY)	Credit (JPY)
15-Feb-X1	Investments—Equity Shares—AFS Account	100,000	
	To Brokerage/Commission Account		100,000
	(Being the commission paid on purchase of futures taken as part of cost of the shares)		

T-11 On Payment for Equity Shares Bought on the Date of Expiry

Journal Entry

Date	Particulars	Debit (JPY)	Credit (JPY)
15-Feb-X1	Payable to Broker—Stock Account	50,000,000	
	To Bank Account		50,000,000
	(Being amount paid to bank towards settlement)		

T-12 On Sale of Equity Shares

Journal Entry

Date	Particulars	Debit (JPY)	Credit (JPY)
25-Feb-X1	Receivable from Broker—Stock Account	55,000,000	
	To Investments—Equity Shares—AFS Account		55,000,000
	(Being amount receivable towards sale of equity shares)		

T-13 On Brokerage Paid on Sale of Equity Shares

Journal Entry

Date	Particulars	Debit (JPY)	Credit (JPY)
25-Feb-X1	Investments—Equity Shares—AFS Account	110,000	
	To Receivable from Broker—Stock Account		110,000
	(Being the brokerage paid on sale of equity shares)		

T-14 On Receipt of Money for Sale of Shares

Journal Entry

Date	Particulars	Debit (JPY)	Credit (JPY)
25-Feb-X1	Bank Account	54,890,000	
	To Receivable from Broker—Stock Account		54,890,000
	(Being the amount received on sale of 1 million shares)		

T-15 Recording Profit/Loss on the Sale

Journal Entry

Date	Particulars	Debit (JPY)	Credit (JPY)
25-Feb-X1	Investments—Equity Shares—AFS Account	4,790,000	
	To Realized Gains/Loss—Equity Account		4,790,000
	(Being the realized gain on sale of 1 million shares)		

General Ledger Accounts

Investments—Equity Shares—AFS Account

Date	Particulars	Debit (JPY)	Date	Particulars	Credit (JPY)
15-Feb-X1	To Payable to Broker—Stock Account	50,000,000			
15-Feb-X1	To Brokerage/ Commission Account	100,000			
			25-Feb-X1	By Receivable to Broker—Stock Account	55,000,000
25-Feb-X1	To Receivable to Broker—Stock Account	110,000			
25-Feb-X1	To Realized Gains/ Loss—Equity (P&L) Account	4,790,000			
31-Mar-X1	Total	**55,000,000**	31-Mar-X1	Total	**55,000,000**

Brokerage/Commission Account

Date	Particulars	Debit (JPY)	Date	Particulars	Credit (JPY)
5-Jan-X1	To Payable to Broker—Stock Account	100,000			
			15-Feb-X1	By Investments—Equity Shares—AFS Account	100,000
31-Mar-X1	Total	**100,000**	31-Mar-X1	Total	**100,000**

Futures Margin Account

Date	Particulars	Debit (JPY)	Date	Particulars	Credit (JPY)
5-Jan-X1	To Bank Account	25,000,000			
31-Jan-X1	To MTM—Futures (P&L) Account	2,000,000			
			15-Feb-X1	By MTM—Futures (P&L) Account	2,000,000
			15-Feb-X1	By Bank Account	25,000,000
31-Mar-X1	Total	**27,000,000**	31-Mar-X1	Total	**27,000,000**

MTM—Futures (P&L) Account

Date	Particulars	Debit (JPY)	Date	Particulars	Credit (JPY)
			31-Jan-X1	By Futures Margin Account	2,000,000
15-Feb-X1	To Futures Margin Account	2,000,000			
31-Mar-X1	Total	**2,000,000**	31-Mar-X1	Total	**2,000,000**

Realized Gains/Loss—Equity Account

Date	Particulars	Debit (JPY)	Date	Particulars	Credit (JPY)
			25-Feb-X1	By Investments—Equity Shares—AFS Account	4,790,000
31-Mar-X1	To Balance	4,790,000			
31-Mar-X1	Total	**4,790,000**	31-Mar-X1	Total	**4,790,000**
			31-Mar-X1	By Balance	4,790,000

Receivable from Broker—Stock Account

Date	Particulars	Debit (JPY)	Date	Particulars	Credit (JPY)
25-Feb-X1	To Investments—Equity Shares—AFS Account	55,000,000			
			25-Feb-X1	By Investments—Equity Shares—AFS Account	110,000
			25-Feb-X1	By Bank Account	54,890,000
31-Mar-X1	Total	**55,000,000**	31-Mar-X1	Total	**55,000,000**

Share Capital Account

Date	Particulars	Debit (JPY)	Date	Particulars	Credit (JPY)
			5-Jan-X1	By Bank Account	100,000,000
31-Mar-X1	To Balance	100,000,000			
31-Mar-X1	Total	**100,000,000**	31-Mar-X1	Total	**100,000,000**
			31-Mar-X1	By Balance	100,000,000

Payable to Broker—Stock Account

Date	Particulars	Debit (JPY)	Date	Particulars	Credit (JPY)
			5-Jan-X1	By Brokerage/Commission Account	100,000
5-Jan-X1	To Bank Account	100,000			
			15-Feb-X1	By Investments—Equity Shares—AFS Account	50,000,000
15-Feb-X1	To Bank Account	50,000,000			
31-Mar-X1	Total	**50,100,000**	31-Mar-X1	Total	**50,100,000**

Bank Account

Date	Particulars	Debit (JPY)	Date	Particulars	Credit (JPY)
5-Jan-X1	To Share Capital Account	100,000,000			
			5-Jan-X1	By Futures Margin Account	25,000,000
			5-Jan-X1	By Payable to Broker—Stock Account	100,000
15-Feb-X1	To Futures Margin Account	25,000,000			
			15-Feb-X1	By Payable to Broker—Stock Account	50,000,000
25-Feb-X1	To Investments—Equity Shares—AFS Account	54,890,000			
			31-Mar-X1	By Balance	104,790,000
31-Mar-X1	Total	**179,890,000**	31-Mar-X1	Total	**179,890,000**
31-Mar-X1	To Balance	104,790,000			

Trial Balance

As of 31-Mar-X1 (JPY)

Particulars	Debit	Credit
Capital Account		
Share Capital Account		100,000,000
Current Assets		
Bank Account	104,790,000	
Direct Income		
Realized Gains/Loss—Equity Account		4,790,000
Direct Expenses		
Total	**104,790,000**	**104,790,000**

Income Statement

For the period ending 31-Mar-X1

Expenses	JPY	Income	JPY
Direct Expenses		**Direct Income**	
		Realized Gains/Loss—Equity Account	4,790,000
Net Profit	4,790,000		
Total	**4,790,000**	Total	**4,790,000**

Balance Sheet

As of 31-Mar-X1

Liabilities	JPY	Assets	JPY
Capital Account		**Current Assets**	
Share Capital Account	100,000,000	Bank Account	104,790,000
Current Liabilities	Nil		
Profit & Loss Account			
Opening Balance	Nil		
Current Period	4,790,000		
Total	**104,790,000**	Total	**104,790,000**

Long Stock Futures—Functional Currency US$

The following are the FX revaluation entries in the functional currency converted at the respective FX rate, which is given within parenthesis. FX translation entries are clearly specified, indicating whether each is a consummated FX translation entry or a transient FX translation entry.

F-1 Capital Introduced by the Fund (T-1 @ FX Rate: 123.805)

Journal Entry

Date	Particulars	Debit (US$)	Credit (US$)
5-Jan-X1	Bank Account	807,721.82	
	To Share Capital Account		807,721.82
	(Being subscription received from an investor into the fund)		

F-2 On Purchasing the Futures

This entry is just an off-balance-sheet entry and thus is not taken into account while preparing the financial statements of the investor. In this illustration, there will not be any postings for this entry.

Journal Entry

Date	Particulars	Debit (US$)	Credit (US$)
5-Jan-X1	Equity Futures Position Account (Off Balance Sheet)	1,000,000	
	To Equity Futures Contra Account (Off Balance Sheet)		1,000,000
	(Being the 1 million futures contract purchased)		

F-3 On Payment of Margin (T-3 @ FX Rate: 123.805)

Journal Entry

Date	Particulars	Debit (US$)	Credit (US$)
5-Jan-X1	Futures Margin Account	201,930.46	
	To Bank Account		201,930.46
	(Being the margin amount paid on purchase of 1 million ABB futures)		

F-4 On Recording the Brokerage/Commission (T-4 @ FX Rate: 123.805)

Journal Entry

Date	Particulars	Debit (US$)	Credit (US$)
5-Jan-X1	Brokerage/Commission Account	807.72	
	To Payable to Broker—Futures Account		807.72
	(Being the brokerage incurred on purchase of ABB Futures)		

F-5 On Payment of Brokerage/Commission (T-5 @ FX Rate: 123.805)

Journal Entry

Date	Particulars	Debit (US$)	Credit (US$)
5-Jan-X1	Payable to Broker—Futures Account	807.72	
	To Bank Account		807.72
	(Being the brokerage paid on purchase of ABB futures)		

F-6 Mark-to-market at End of Reporting Period (T-6 @ FX Rate: 124.850)

Journal Entry

Date	Particulars	Debit (US$)	Credit (US$)
31-Jan-X1	Futures Margin Account	16,019.22	
	To MTM—Futures (P&L) Account		16,019.22
	(Being the entry for mark-to-market on futures as on date)		

F-7 FX Translation on Futures Margin Account (Transient FX translation entry)

Date	Particulars	JPY	FX Rate	US$
29-Jan-X1	Opening balance	25,000,000	123.805	201,930.46
31-Jan-X1	Mark-to-market	2,000,000	124.850	16,019.22
	Net balance	27,000,000		217,949.68
	Net balance at current FX rate	27,000,000	124.850	216,259.51
	Unrealized currency loss on margin account			(1,690.17)

Journal Entry

Date	Particulars	Debit (US$)	Credit (US$)
31-Jan-X1	Unrealized Currency Gains/Loss Account	1,690.17	
	To Futures Margin Account		1,690.17
	(Being the FX translation applied on futures margin account)		

F-8 FX Translation on Bank Account (Transient FX translation entry)

Date	Particulars	JPY	FX Rate	US$
1-Jan-X1	Opening balance	100,000,000	123.805	807,721.82
5-Jan-X1	Transfer out	(25,000,000)	123.805	(201,930.46)
5-Jan-X1	Commission	(100,000)	123.805	(807.72)
31-Jan-X1	Net balance	74,900,000		604,983.64
	Net balance at current FX rate	74,900,000	124.85	599,919.90
	Unrealized currency loss on bank account			(5,063.74)

Journal Entry

Date	Particulars	Debit (US$)	Credit (US$)
31-Jan-X1	Unrealized Currency Gains/Loss Account	5,063.74	
	To Bank Account		5,063.74
	(Being the FX translation applied on bank account)		

F-9 Mark-to-market Reversal on the Date of Expiry (T-7 @ FX Rate: 124.850)

Journal Entry

Date	Particulars	Debit (US$)	Credit (US$)
15-Feb-X1	MTM—Futures (P&L) Account	16,019.22	
	To Futures Margin Account		16,019.22
	(Being reversal of mark-to-market entry on the date of expiry of futures contract)		

F-10 Margin Payment Returned on the Date of Expiry (T-8 @ FX Rate: 124.800)

Journal Entry

Date	Particulars	Debit (US$)	Credit (US$)
15-Feb-X1	Bank Account	200,320.51	
	To Futures Margin Account		200,320.51
	(Being margin money returned on the date of expiry)		

F-11 FX Translation on Futures Margin Account (Transient FX Translation Entry)

Date	Particulars	JPY	FX Rate	US$
31-Jan-X1	Opening balance	27,000,000	124.85	216,259.51
15-Feb-X1	Reversal of MTM	(2,000,000)	124.85	(16,019.22)
15-Feb-X1	Refund of margin money on sale	(25,000,000)	124.80	(200,320.51)
	Net balance	—		(80.22)
	Net balance at current FX rate	—		—
	FX translation on margin account			**80.22**

Journal Entry

Date	Particulars	Debit (US$)	Credit (US$)
15-Feb-X1	Futures Margin Account	80.22	
	To Unrealized Currency Gains/Loss Account		80.22
	(Being the FX translation applied on futures margin account)		

F-12 On Purchase of Equity Shares on the Date of Expiry (T-9 @ FX Rate: 124.800)

Journal Entry

Date	Particulars	Debit (US$)	Credit (US$)
15-Feb-X1	Investments—Equity Shares—AFS Account	400,641.03	
	To Payable to Broker—Stock Account		400,641.03
	(Being the equity shares purchased on the date of expiry)		

F-13 Commission on Futures Reversed (T-10 @ FX Rate: 124.800)

Journal Entry

Date	Particulars	Debit (US$)	Credit (US$)
15-Feb-X1	Investments—Equity Shares—AFS Account	807.72	
	To Brokerage/Commission Account		807.72
	(Being the commission paid on purchase of futures transferred as part of cost of equity shares)		

F-14 Equity Shares Bought on the Date of Expiry (T-11 @ FX Rate: 124.800)

Journal Entry

Date	Particulars	Debit (US$)	Credit (US$)
15-Feb-X1	Payable to Broker—Stock Account	400,641.03	
	To Bank Account		400,641.03
	(Being amount paid on purchase of equity shares)		

F-15 Equity Shares Sold (T-12 @ FX Rate: 123.560)

Journal Entry

Date	Particulars	Debit (US$)	Credit (US$)
25-Feb-X1	Receivable from Broker—Stock Account	445,127.87	
	To Investments—Equity Shares—AFS Account		445,127.87
	(Being the receipt of money on sale of equity shares)		

F-16 On Brokerage Paid on Sale of Equity Shares (T-13 @ FX Rate: 123.560)

Journal Entry

Date	Particulars	Debit (US$)	Credit (US$)
25-Feb-X1	Investments—Equity Shares—AFS Account	890.26	
	To Receivable from Broker—Stock Account		890.26
	(Being the brokerage paid on sale of equity shares)		

F-17 On Receipt of Money for Shares Sold (T-14 @ FX Rate: 123.560)

Journal Entry

Date	Particulars	Debit (US$)	Credit (US$)
25-Feb-X1	Bank Account	444,237.62	
	To Receivable from Broker—Stock Account		444,237.62
	(Being the amount received on sale of 1 million shares)		

F-18 On Recording Profit/Loss on Sale (T-15 @ FX Rate: 123.560)

Journal Entry

Date	Particulars	Debit (US$)	Credit (US$)
25-Feb-X1	Investments—Equity Shares—AFS Account	38,766.59	
	To Realized Gains/Loss—Equity Account		38,766.59
	(Being the realized gain on sale of 1 million shares)		

F-19 Realized Currency Gains on Liquidation

Currency gains/loss on liquidation	JPY	US$
(a) Cost of sales in US$ based on FX rate on date of sale @ 123.56	50,100,000	405,471.03
(b) Cost of sales in US$ based on FX rate on date of purchase		401,448.75
(c) Realized currency gains on liquidation = (a) − (b)		**4,022.28**

Journal Entry

Date	Particulars	Debit (US$)	Credit (US$)
25-Feb-X1	Investments—Equity Shares—AFS Account	4,022.28	
	To Realized Currency Gains/Loss Account		4,022.28
	(Being the realized currency gains on liquidation)		

F-20 FX Translation on Bank Account (Transient FX Translation Entry)

Date	Particulars	JPY	FX Rate	US$
31-Jan-X1	Opening balance	74,900,000	124.85	599,919.90
15-Feb-X1	Transfer out	(50,000,000)	124.80	(400,641.03)
15-Feb-X1	Transfer in	25,000,000	124.80	200,320.51
25-Feb-X1	Transfer in	54,890,000	123.56	444,237.62
28-Feb-X1	Net balance	104,790,000		843,837.00
	Net balance at current FX rate	104,790,000	123.56	848,890.99
	Unrealized currency gains on bank account			4,252.99

Journal Entry

Date	Particulars	Debit (US$)	Credit (US$)
25-Feb-X1	Bank Account	4,252.99	
	To Unrealized Currency Gains/Loss Account		4,252.99
	(Being the FX translation applied on bank account)		

General Ledger Accounts

Investments—Equity Shares—AFS Account

Date	Particulars	Debit (US$)	Date	Particulars	Credit (US$)
15-Feb-X1	To Payable to Broker—Stock Account	400,641.03			
15-Feb-X1	To Brokerage/ Commission Account	807.72			
			25-Feb-X1	By Receivable from Broker—Stock Account	445,127.87
25-Feb-X1	To Receivable from Broker—Stock Account	890.26			
25-Feb-X1	To Realized Gains/ Loss—Equity Account	38,766.59			
25-Feb-X1	To Realized Currency Gains/ Loss Account	4,022.28			
31-Mar-X1	Total	**445,127.87**	31-Mar-X1	Total	**445,127.87**

Brokerage/Commission Account

Date	Particulars	Debit (US$)	Date	Particulars	Credit (US$)
5-Jan-X1	To Payable to Broker—Stock Account	807.72			
			15-Feb-X1	By Investments—Equity Shares—AFS Account	807.72
31-Mar-X1	Total	**807.72**	31-Mar-X1	Total	**807.72**

Unrealized Currency Gains/Loss Account

Date	Particulars	Debit (US$)	Date	Particulars	Credit (US$)
31-Jan-X1	To Futures Margin Account	1,690.17			
31-Jan-X1	To Bank Account	5,063.74			
			15-Feb-X1	By Futures Margin Account	80.22
			25-Feb-X1	By Bank Account	4,252.99
			31-Mar-X1	By Balance	2,420.70
31-Mar-X1	Total	**6,753.91**	31-Mar-X1	Total	**6,753.91**
31-Mar-X1	To Balance	2,420.70			

Futures Margin Account

Date	Particulars	Debit (US$)	Date	Particulars	Credit (US$)
5-Jan-X1	To Bank Account	201,930.46			
31-Jan-X1	To MTM—Futures (P&L) Account	16,019.22			
			31-Jan-X1	By Unrealized Currency Gains/Loss Account	1,690.17
			15-Feb-X1	By MTM—Futures (P&L) Account	16,019.22
			15-Feb-X1	By Bank Account	200,320.51
15-Feb-X1	To Unrealized Currency Gains/Loss Account	80.22			
31-Mar-X1	Total	**218,029.90**	31-Mar-X1	Total	**218,029.90**

MTM—Futures (P&L) Account

Date	Particulars	Debit (US$)	Date	Particulars	Credit (US$)
			31-Jan-X1	By Futures Margin Account	16,019.22
15-Feb-X1	To Futures Margin Account	16,019.22			
31-Mar-X1	Total	**16,019.22**	31-Mar-X1	Total	**16,019.22**

Realized Gains/Loss—Equity Account

Date	Particulars	Debit (US$)	Date	Particulars	Credit (US$)
			15-Feb-X1	By Investments—Equity Shares—AFS Account	38,766.59
31-Mar-X1	To Balance	38,766.59			
31-Mar-X1	Total	**38,766.59**	31-Mar-X1	Total	**38,766.59**
			31-Mar-X1	By Balance	38,766.59

Receivable from Broker—Stock Account

Date	Particulars	Debit (US$)	Date	Particulars	Credit (US$)
25-Feb-X1	To Investments—Equity Shares—AFS Account	445,127.87			
			25-Feb-X1	By Investments—Equity Shares—AFS Account	890.26
			25-Feb-X1	By Bank Account	444,237.62
31-Mar-X1	Total	**445,127.87**	31-Mar-X1	Total	**445,127.87**

Share Capital Account

Date	Particulars	Debit (US$)	Date	Particulars	Credit (US$)
			5-Jan-X1	By Bank Account	807,721.82
31-Mar-X1	To Balance	807,721.82			
31-Mar-X1	Total	**807,721.82**	31-Mar-X1	Total	**807,721.82**
			31-Mar-X1	By Balance	807,721.82

Payable to Broker—Stock Account

Date	Particulars	Debit (US$)	Date	Particulars	Credit (US$)
			5-Jan-X1	By Brokerage/Commission Account	807.72
5-Jan-X1	To Bank Account	807.72			
			15-Feb-X1	By Investments—Equity Shares—AFS Account	400,641.03
15-Feb-X1	To Bank Account	400,641.03			
31-Mar-X1	Total	**401,448.75**	31-Mar-X1	Total	**401,448.75**

Realized Currency Gains/Loss Equity—AFS Account

Date	Particulars	Debit (US$)	Date	Particulars	Credit (US$)
			25-Feb-X1	By Investments—Equity Shares—AFS Account	4,022.28
31-Mar-X1	To Balance	4,022.28			
31-Mar-X1	Total	**4,022.28**	31-Mar-X1	Total	**4,022.28**
			31-Mar-X1	By Balance	4,022.28

Bank Account

Date	Particulars	Debit (US$)	Date	Particulars	Credit (US$)
5-Jan-X1	To Share Capital Account	807,721.82			
			5-Jan-X1	By Futures Margin Account	201,930.46
			5-Jan-X1	By Payable to Broker—Stock Account	807.72
			31-Jan-X1	By Unrealized Currency Gains/ Loss Account	5,063.74
15-Feb-X1	To Futures Margin Account	200,320.51			
			15-Feb-X1	By Payable to Broker—Stock Account	400,641.03
25-Feb-X1	To Receivable from Broker—Stock Account	444,237.62			
25-Feb-X1	To Unrealized Currency Gains/ Loss Account	4,252.99			
			31-Mar-X1	By Balance	848,089.99
31-Mar-X1	Total	**1,456,532.94**	31-Mar-X1	Total	**1,456,532.94**
31-Mar-X1	To Balance	848,089.99			

Trial Balance

As of 31-Mar-X1 (US$)

Particulars	Debit	Credit
Capital Account		
Share Capital Account		807,721.82
Current Liabilities		Nil
Current Assets		
Bank Account	848,089.99	
Direct Income		
Unrealized Currency Gains/Loss Account	2,420.70	
Realized Currency Gains/Loss—Equity—AFS Account		4,022.28
Realized Gains/Loss—Futures (P&L) Account		38,766.59
Total	**850,510.69**	**850,510.69**

Income Statement

For the period ending 31-Mar-X1

Expenses	US$	Income	US$
Direct Expenses		**Direct Income**	
Unrealized Currency Gains/ Loss Account	2,420.70		
		Realized Gains/Loss—Futures (P&L) Account	38,766.59
		Realized Currency Gains/Loss Equity—AFS Account	4,022.28
Net Profit	40,368.17		
Total	**42,788.87**	Total	**42,788.87**

Balance Sheet

As of 31-Mar-X1

Liabilities	US$	Assets	US$
Capital Account		**Current Assets**	
Share Capital Account	807,721.82	Bank Account	848,089.99
Current Liabilities			
Profit & Loss Account			
Opening Balance			
Current Period	40,368.17		
Total	**848,089.99**	Total	**848,089.99**

Stock Futures—Short Stock—S$

Cerebros Fund had the following trades in ABB in the futures market. The stock exchange requires that a margin of 50 percent of the value of the contract be maintained throughout the life of the contract.

Date	Product	Product Expiry	Quantity	Rate (S$)	B/S	Brokerage
4-Jan-X1	ABB Stock		1,000	42	B	120
5-Jan-X1	ABB Futures	15-Feb-X1	1,000	45	S	100

ABB stock was delivered on the expiry date of the futures, February 15, when the market rate was S$43 each. Earlier, on January 4, the fund introduced S$100,000 as capital. Journal entries, general ledgers, trial balance, income statement, and balance sheet for Cerebros Fund for the period January 1 to February 28 are prepared as follows:

Date	FX Rate
4-Jan-X1	1.5147
5-Jan-X1	1.5364
31-Jan-X1	1.5478
15-Feb-X1	1.5112

Date	Futures Price
31-Jan-X1	46
15-Feb-X1	43
31-Jan-X1	44

Short Stock Futures—Trade Currency S$

T-1 Capital Introduced by the Fund

Journal Entry

Date	Particulars	Debit (S$)	Credit (S$)
4-Jan-X1	Bank Account	100,000.00	
	To Share Capital Account		100,000.00
	(Being the subscription introduced into the fund as capital)		

T-2 On Purchase of Equity Shares and Brokerage

Journal Entry

Date	Particulars	Debit (S$)	Credit (S$)
4-Jan-X1	Investments—Equity Shares—AFS Account	42,000.00	
	To Payable to Broker Account		42,000.00
	(Being 1,000 shares purchased @ 42)		
4-Jan-X1	Investments—Equity Shares—AFS Account	120.00	
	To Payable to Broker Account		120.00
	(Being the brokerage paid on the purchase of equity shares)		

T-3 On Payment to Broker

Journal Entry

Date	Particulars	Debit (S$)	Credit (S$)
4-Jan-X1	Payable to Broker Account	42,120.00	
	To Bank Account		42,120.00
	(Being amount paid to broker towards purchase of 1,000 equity shares)		

T-4 On Sale of Futures Contract

This entry is just an off-balance-sheet entry and thus is not taken into account while preparing the financial statements of the investor. In this illustration, there will not be any postings for this entry.

Journal Entry

Date	Particulars	Debit (S$)	Credit (S$)
5-Jan-X1	Equity Futures Contra Account (Off Balance Sheet)	1,000.00	
	To Equity Futures Position Account (Off Balance Sheet)		1,000.00
	(Being the 1,000 futures contracts sold)		

T-5 On Payment of Margin

Journal Entry

Date	Particulars	Debit (S$)	Credit (S$)
5-Jan-X1	Futures Margin Account	22,500.00	
	To Bank Account		22,500.00
	(Being the amount transferred to margin account on sale of 1,000 ABB futures)		

T-6 On Recording the Brokerage/Commission

Journal Entry

Date	Particulars	Debit (S$)	Credit (S$)
5-Jan-X1	Brokerage/Commission Account	100.00	
	To Payable to Broker Account		100.00
	(Being the brokerage incurred on sale of ABB futures)		

T-7 On Payment of Brokerage/Commission

Journal Entry

Date	Particulars	Debit (S$)	Credit (S$)
5-Jan-X1	Payable to Broker Account	100.00	
	To Bank Account		100.00
	(Being the brokerage paid to the broker on sale of ABB Futures)		

T-8 Mark-to-market at End of Reporting Period—Futures

The mark-to-market is computed based on the market rate at the end of every day. However, for this illustration it is assumed that the mark-to-market is computed at the end of the month. If there is a drop in the value of the long position, the same is reduced from the margin account—which eventually is required to be topped up with the erosion in value. Mark-to-market gains are debited to the margin account and credited to the profit and loss account.

Journal Entry

Date	Particulars	Debit (S$)	Credit (S$)
31-Jan-X1	MTM—Futures (P&L) Account	1,000.00	
	To Futures Margin Account		1,000.00
	(Being the mark-to-market entry on futures as on date)		

T-9 Mark-to-market at End of Reporting Period—Equity

Journal Entry

Date	Particulars	Debit (S$)	Credit (S$)
31-Jan-X1	Investments—Equity Shares—AFS Account	1,880.00	
	To Unrealized Gain—Equity Shares—OCI Account		1,880.00
	(Being the mark-to-market entry on AFS security at the end of the reporting period)		

T-10 Reversal of Mark-to-market on the Next Date for Equity Shares

Journal Entry

Date	Particulars	Debit (S$)	Credit (S$)
1-Feb-X1	Unrealized Gain—Equity Shares—OCI Account	1,880.00	
	To Investments—Equity Shares—AFS Account		1,880.00
	(Being the mark-to-market reversal on equity)		

T-11 Reversal of Mark-to-market on the Date of Expiry

Journal Entry

Date	Particulars	Debit (S$)	Credit (S$)
15-Feb-X1	Futures Margin Account	1,000.00	
	To MTM—Futures (P&L) Account		1,000.00
	(Being the reversal of mark-to-market on the date of expiry)		

T-12 On Return of Margin Amount on the Date of Expiry

Journal Entry

Date	Particulars	Debit (S$)	Credit (S$)
15-Feb-X1	Bank Account	22,500.00	
	To Futures Margin Account		22,500.00
	(Being the margin money returned on the date of expiry)		

T-13 Equity Shares Sold and Brokerage Paid

Journal Entry

Date	Particulars	Debit (S$)	Credit (S$)
15-Feb-X1	Receivable from Broker Account	45,000.00	
	To Investments—Equity Shares—AFS Account		45,000.00
	(Being the equity shares sold)		
15-Feb-X1	Investments—Equity Shares—AFS Account	100.00	
	To Brokerage/Commission Account		100.00
	(Being the amount of commission paid on short-selling of futures reversed and treated as part of the cost of equity shares)		

T-14 Equity Shares Sold

Journal Entry

Date	Particulars	Debit (S$)	Credit (S$)
15-Feb-X1	Bank Account	45,000.00	
	To Receivable from Broker Account		45,000.00
	(Being the amount received on sale of 1,000 shares)		

T-15 Recording Profit/Loss on the Sale

Journal Entry

Date	Particulars	Debit (S$)	Credit (S$)
15-Feb-X1	Investments—Equity Shares—AFS Account	2,780.00	
	To Realized Gains/Loss—Equity Shares Account		2,780.00
	(Being the realized gain on sale of 1,000 shares)		

General Ledger Accounts

Investments—Equity Shares—AFS Account

Date	Particulars	Debit (S$)	Date	Particulars	Credit (S$)
4-Jan-X1	To Payable to Broker Account	42,000.00			
4-Jan-X1	To Payable to Broker Account	120.00			
31-Jan-X1	To Unrealized Gain—Equity Shares—AFS Account	1,880.00			
			1-Feb-X1	By Unrealized Gain—Equity—AFS Account	1,880.00
			15-Feb-X1	By Receivable from Broker Account	45,000.00
15-Feb-X1	To Brokerage/Commission Account	100.00			

Investments—Equity Shares—AFS Account (*Cont'd*)

Date	Particulars	Debit (S$)	Date	Particulars	Credit (S$)
15-Feb-X1	To Realized Gains/ Loss—Equity Shares Account	2,780.00			
31-Mar-X1	Total	**46,880.00**	31-Mar-X1	Total	**46,880.00**

Brokerage/Commission Account

Date	Particulars	Debit (S$)	Date	Particulars	Credit (S$)
5-Jan-X1	To Payable to Broker Account	100.00			
			1-Feb-X1	By Investments—Equity Shares—AFS Account	100.00
31-Mar-X1	Total	**100.00**	31-Mar-X1	Total	**100.00**

Futures Margin Account

Date	Particulars	Debit (S$)	Date	Particulars	Credit (S$)
5-Jan-X1	To Bank Account	22,500.00			
			31-Jan-X1	By MTM—Futures (P&L) Account	1,000.00
15-Feb-X1	To MTM—Futures (P&L) Account	1,000.00			
			31-Mar-X1	By Bank Account	22,500.00
31-Mar-X1	Total	**23,500.00**	31-Mar-X1	Total	**23,500.00**

MTM—Futures (P&L) Account

Date	Particulars	Debit (S$)	Date	Particulars	Credit (S$)
31-Jan-X1	To Futures Margin Account	1,000.00			
			15-Feb-X1	By Futures Margin Account	1,000.00
31-Mar-X1	Total	**1,000.00**	31-Mar-X1	Total	**1,000.00**

Realized Gains/Loss—Equity Shares Account

Date	Particulars	Debit (S$)	Date	Particulars	Credit (S$)
			15-Feb-X1	By Investments—Equity Shares—AFS Account	2,780.00
31-Mar-X1	To Balance	2,780.00			
31-Mar-X1	Total	**2,780.00**	31-Mar-X1	Total	**2,780.00**
			31-Mar-X1	By Balance	2,780.00

Receivable from Broker Account

Date	Particulars	Debit (S$)	Date	Particulars	Credit (S$)
15-Feb-X1	To Investments—Equity Shares—AFS Account	45,000.00			
			15-Feb-X1	By Bank	45,000.00
31-Mar-X1	Total	**45,000.00**	31-Mar-X1	Total	**45,000.00**

Unrealized Gain—Equity Shares—OCI Account

Date	Particulars	Debit (S$)	Date	Particulars	Credit (S$)
			31-Jan-X1	To Investments—Equity Shares—AFS Account	1,880.00
1-Feb-X1	To Investments—Equity Shares—AFS Account	1,880.00			
31-Mar-X1	Total	**1,880.00**	31-Mar-X1	Total	**1,880.00**

Share Capital Account

Date	Particulars	Debit (S$)	Date	Particulars	Credit (S$)
			4-Jan-X1	By Bank Account	100,000.00
31-Mar-X1	To Balance	100,000.00			
31-Mar-X1	Total	**100,000.00**	31-Mar-X1	Total	**100,000.00**
			31-Mar-X1	By Balance	100,000.00

Payable to Broker Account

Date	Particulars	Debit (S$)	Date	Particulars	Credit (S$)
			4-Jan-X1	By Investments—Equity Shares—AFS Account	42,000.00
			4-Jan-X1	By Investments—Equity Shares—AFS Account	120.00
4-Jan-X1	To Bank Account	42,120.00			
			5-Jan-X1	By Brokerage/Commission	100.00
5-Jan-X1	To Bank Account	100.00			
31-Mar-X1	Total	**42,220.00**	31-Mar-X1	Total	**42,220.00**

Bank Account

Date	Particulars	Debit (S$)	Date	Particulars	Credit (S$)
4-Jan-X1	To Share Capital Account	100,000.00			
			4-Jan-X1	By Payable to Broker Account	42,120.00
			5-Jan-X1	By Futures Margin Account	22,500.00
			5-Jan-X1	By Payable to Broker Account	100.00
15-Feb-X1	To Futures Margin Account	22,500.00			
15-Feb-X1	To Receivable from Broker Account	45,000.00			
			31-Mar-X1	By Balance	102,780.00
31-Mar-X1	Total	**167,500.00**	31-Mar-X1	Total	**167,500.00**
31-Mar-X1	To Balance	102,780.00			

Trial Balance

As of 31-Mar-X1 (S$)

Particulars	Debit	Credit
Capital Account		
Share Capital Account		100,000.00
Current Liabilities		Nil
Current Assets		
Bank Account	102,780.00	
Direct Income		
Realized Gains/Loss—Equity Shares Account		2,780.00
Total	**102,780.00**	**102,780.00**

Income Statement

For the period ending 31-Mar-X1

Expenses	S$	Income	S$
Direct Expenses		**Direct Income**	
		Realized Gains/Loss—Equity Shares Account	2,780.00
Net Profit	2,780.00		
Total	**2,780.00**	Total	**2,780.00**

Balance Sheet

As of 31-Mar-X1

Liabilities	S$	Assets	S$
Capital Account		**Current Assets**	
Share Capital Account	100,000.00	Bank Account	102,780.00
Current Liabilities	Nil		
Profit & Loss Account			
Opening Balance	Nil		
Current Period	2,780.00		
Total	**102,780.00**	Total	**102,780.00**

Short Stock Futures—Functional Currency US$

The following are the FX revaluation entries in the functional currency converted at the respective FX rate, which is given within parenthesis. FX translation entries are clearly specified, indicating whether each is a consummated FX translation entry or a transient FX translation entry.

F-1 Capital Introduced by the Fund (T-1 @ FX Rate: 1.5147)

Journal Entry

Date	Particulars	Debit (US$)	Credit (US$)
4-Jan-X1	Bank Account	66,019.67	
	To Share Capital Account		66,019.67
	(Being the subscription received from an investor deposited into the fund)		

F-2 Equity Shares Purchased and Brokerage Paid (T-2 @ FX Rate: 1.5147)

Journal Entry

Date	Particulars	Debit (US$)	Credit (US$)
4-Jan-X1	Investments—Equity Shares—AFS Account	27,728.26	
	To Payable to Broker Account		27,728.26
	(Being the equity shares purchased)		
4-Jan-X1	Investments—Equity Shares—AFS Account	79.22	
	To Payable to Broker Account		79.22
	(Being the brokerage paid on the purchase of equity shares)		

F-3 On Payment to the Broker on Purchase of Equity Shares (T-3 @ FX Rate: 1.5147)

Journal Entry

Date	Particulars	Debit (US$)	Credit (US$)
4-Jan-X1	Payable to Broker Account	27,807.49	
	To Bank Account		27,807.49
	(Being the amount paid to broker on purchase of equity shares)		

F-4 On Sale of Futures Contract

Journal Entry

Date	Particulars	Debit (US$)	Credit (US$)
5-Jan-X1	Equity Futures Contra Account (Off Balance Sheet)	1,000.00	
	To Equity Futures Position Account (Off Balance Sheet)		1,000.00
	(Being the 1,000 futures contract sold)		

F-5 On Payment of Margin (T-5 @ FX Rate: 1.5364)

Journal Entry

Date	Particulars	Debit (US$)	Credit (US$)
5-Jan-X1	Futures Margin Account	14,644.62	
	To Bank Account		14,644.62
	(Being the amount transferred to margin account on sale of 1,000 ABB futures)		

F-6 On Recording the Brokerage/Commission (T-6 @ FX Rate: 1.5364)

Journal Entry

Date	Particulars	Debit (US$)	Credit (US$)
5-Jan-X1	Brokerage/Commission Account	65.09	
	To Payable to Broker Account		65.09
	(Being the brokerage amount on sale of ABB futures)		

F-7 On Payment of Brokerage/Commission (T-7 @ FX Rate: 1.5364)

Journal Entry

Date	Particulars	Debit (US$)	Credit (US$)
5-Jan-X1	Payable to Broker—Futures Account	65.09	
	To Bank Account		65.09
	(Being the brokerage paid on sale of ABB Futures)		

F-8 Mark-to-market at End of Reporting Period (T-8 @ FX Rate: 1.5478)

Journal Entry

Date	Particulars	Debit (US$)	Credit (US$)
31-Jan-X1	MTM—Futures (P&L) Account	646.08	
	To Futures Margin Account		646.08
	(Being the mark-to-market on futures as on date)		

F-9 Mark-to-market at End of Reporting Period—Equity (T-9 @ FX Rate: 1.5478)

Journal Entry

Date	Particulars	Debit (US$)	Credit (US$)
31-Jan-X1	Investments—Equity Shares—AFS Account	1,214.63	
	To Unrealized Gain—Equity Shares—OCI Account		1,214.63
	(Being the mark to market on equity at the end of the reporting period)		

F-10 Mark-to-market at End of Reporting Period—Equity (T-10 @ FX Rate: 1.5478)

Journal Entry

Date	Particulars	Debit (US$)	Credit (US$)
1-Feb-X1	Unrealized Gain—Equity Shares—OCI Account	1,214.63	
	To Investments—Equity Shares—AFS Account		1,214.63
	(Being reversal of mark-to-market on equity)		

F-11 FX Translation on Futures Margin Account (Transient FX Translation Entry)

Date	Particulars	S$	FX Rate	US$
5-Jan-X1	Opening balance	22,500.00	1.5364	14,644.62
31-Jan-X1	Mark-to-market	(1,000.00)	1.5478	(646.08)
	Net balance	21,500.00		13,998.54
	Net balance at current FX rate	21,500.00	1.5478	13,890.68
	Unrealized currency loss on margin account			(107.86)

Journal Entry

Date	Particulars	Debit (US$)	Credit (US$)
31-Jan-X1	Unrealized Currency Gains/Loss Account	107.86	
	To Futures Margin Account		107.86
	(Being the FX translation applied on margin account)		

F-12 FX Translation on Bank Account (Transient FX Translation Entry)

Date	Particulars	S$	FX Rate	US$
4-Jan-X1	Opening balance	100,000.00	1.5147	66,019.67
5-Jan-X1	Transfer out—Futures	(22,500.00)	1.5364	(14,644.62)
4-Jan-X1	Transfer out	(42,120.00)	1.5147	(27,807.49)
5-Jan-X1	Commission	(100.00)	1.5364	(65.09)
31-Jan-X1	Net balance	35,280.00		23,502.47
	Net balance at current FX rate	35,280.00	1.5478	22,793.64
	Unrealized currency loss on bank account			(708.83)

Journal Entry

Date	Particulars	Debit (US$)	Credit (US$)
31-Jan-X1	Unrealized Currency Gains/Loss Account	708.83	
	To Bank Account		708.83
	(Being the FX translation applied on bank account)		

F-13 Mark-to-market Reversal on the Date of Expiry (T-11 @ FX Rate: 1.5112)

Journal Entry

Date	Particulars	Debit (US$)	Credit (US$)
15-Feb-X1	Futures Margin Account	661.73	
	To MTM—Futures (P&L) Account		661.73
	(Being the reversal of mark-to-market on the date of expiry)		

F-14 Margin Amount Returned on the Date of Expiry (T-12 @ FX Rate: 1.5112)

Journal Entry

Date	Particulars	Debit (US$)	Credit (US$)
15-Feb-X1	Bank Account	14,888.83	
	To Futures Margin Account		14,888.83
	(Being the margin money returned on the date of expiry)		

F-15 FX Translation on Futures Margin Account (Transient FX Translation Entry)

Date	Particulars	S$	FX Rate	US$
31-Jan-X1	Opening balance	21,500.00	1.5478	13,890.68
15-Feb-X1	Return of mark-to-market futures	1,000.00	1.5112	661.73
15-Feb-X1	Return of margin	(22,500.00)	1.5112	(14,888.83)
	Unrealized currency gains on margin account			336.42

Journal Entry

Date	Particulars	Debit (US$)	Credit (US$)
15-Feb-X1	Future Margin Account	336.42	
	To Unrealized Currency Gains/Loss Account		336.42
	(Being the FX translation applied on margin account)		

F-16 Equity Shares Sold and Brokerage Paid (T-13 @ FX Rate: 1.5112)

Journal Entry

Date	Particulars	Debit (US$)	Credit (US$)
15-Feb-X1	Receivable from Broker Account	29,777.66	
	To Investments—Equity Shares—AFS Account		29,777.66
	(Being the equity shares sold)		
15-Feb-X1	Investments—Equity Shares—AFS Account	65.09	
	To Brokerage/Commission Account		65.09
	(Being the brokerage on short sale of futures reversed)		

F-17 Equity Shares Sold (T-14 @ FX Rate: 1.5112)

Journal Entry

Date	Particulars	Debit (US$)	Credit (US$)
15-Feb-X1	Bank Account	29,777.66	
	To Receivable from Broker Account		29,777.66
	(Being the amount received on sale of 1,000 shares)		

F-18 Recording Profit/Loss on the Sale (T-15 @ FX Rate: 1.5112)

Realized gains on sale of equity shares	S$
(a) Net sale of 1,000 shares after brokerage	44,900.00
(b) Cost of acquisition of 1,000 shares	42,120.00
(c) Realized gains = (a) − (b)	2,780.00
(d) Realized gains in US$	**1,839.60**

Journal Entry

Date	Particulars	Debit (US$)	Credit (US$)
15-Feb-X1	Investments—Equity Shares—AFS Account	1,839.60	
	To Realized Gains/Loss—Equity Shares Account		1,839.60
	(Being realized gain booked on sale of 1,000 shares)		

F-19 FX Translation—Sale of Equity

Currency gains/loss on liquidation	S$	US$
(a) Cost of sales in US$ based on FX rate on date of sale @ 1.5112	42,120	27,871.89
(b) Cost of sales in US$ based on FX rate on date of purchase		27,806.40
(c) Realized currency gains on liquidation = (a) − (b)		**65.49**

Journal Entry

Date	Particulars	Debit (US$)	Credit (US$)
15-Feb-X1	Investments—Equity Shares—AFS Account	65.49	
	To Realized Currency Gains/Loss—Equity Account		65.49
	(Being realized currency gain booked on sale of 1,000 shares)		

F-20 FX Translation on Bank Account

Date	Particulars	S$	FX Rate	US$
31-Jan-X1	Opening balance	35,280.00	1.5478	22,793.64
15-Feb-X1	Transfer in	22,500.00	1.5112	14,888.83
15-Feb-X1	Transfer in	45,000.00	1.5112	29,777.66
15-Feb-X1	Net balance	102,780.00		67,460.13
	Net balance at current FX rate	102,780.00	1.5112	68,012.18
	Unrealized currency gains on bank account			552.04

Journal Entry

Date	Particulars	Debit (US$)	Credit (US$)
15-Feb-X1	Bank Account	552.04	
	To Unrealized Currency Gains/Loss Account		552.04
	(Being the FX translation applied on bank account)		

General Ledger Accounts

Investments—Equity Shares—AFS Account

Date	Particulars	Debit (US$)	Date	Particulars	Credit (US$)
4-Jan-X1	To Payable to Broker Account	27,728.26			
4-Jan-X1	To Payable to Broker Account	79.22			
31-Jan-X1	To Unrealized Gain–Equity—OCI Account	1,214.63			
			1-Feb-X1	By Unrealized Gain-Equity—OCI Account	1,214.63
			15-Feb-X1	By Receivable from Broker Account	29,777.66
15-Feb-X1	To Brokerage/ Commission Account	65.09			
15-Feb-X1	To Realized Gains/ Loss—Equity Shares Account	1,839.60			

Investments—Equity Shares—AFS Account (*Cont'd*)

Date	Particulars	Debit (US$)	Date	Particulars	Credit (US$)
15-Feb-X1	To Realized Currency Gains/ Loss—Equity Shares Account	65.49			
31-Mar-X1	Total	**30,992.29**	31-Mar-X1	Total	**30,992.29**

Brokerage/Commission Account

Date	Particulars	Debit (US$)	Date	Particulars	Credit (US$)
5-Jan-X1	To Payable to Broker Account	65.09			
			15-Feb-X1	By Investments—Equity Shares—AFS Account	65.09
31-Mar-X1	Total	**65.09**	31-Mar-X1	Total	**65.09**

Unrealized Currency Gains/Loss Account

Date	Particulars	Debit (US$)	Date	Particulars	Credit (US$)
31-Jan-X1	To Futures Margin Account	107.86			
31-Jan-X1	To Bank Account	708.83			
			15-Feb-X1	By Futures Margin Account	336.42
			15-Feb-X1	By BankAccount	552.04
31-Mar-X1	To Balance	71.77			
31-Mar-X1	Total	**888.46**	31-Mar-X1	Total	**888.46**
			31-Mar-X1	By Balance	71.77

Futures Margin Account

Date	Particulars	Debit (US$)	Date	Particulars	Credit (US$)
5-Jan-X1	To Bank Account	14,644.62			
			31-Jan-X1	By MTM—Futures (P&L) Account	646.08
			31-Jan-X1	By Unrealized Currency Gains/ Loss Account	107.86
15-Feb-X1	To MTM—Futures (P&L) Account	661.73			
			15-Feb-X1	By Bank Account	14,888.83
15-Feb-X1	To Unrealized Currency Gains/ Loss Account	336.42			
31-Mar-X1	Total	**15,642.77**	31-Mar-X1	Total	**15,642.77**

MTM—Futures (P&L) Account

Date	Particulars	Debit (US$)	Date	Particulars	Credit (US$)
31-Jan-X1	To Futures Margin Account	646.08			
			15-Feb-X1	By Future Margin Account	661.73
31-Mar-X1	To Balance	15.65			
31-Mar-X1	Total	**661.73**	31-Mar-X1	Total	**661.73**
			31-Mar-X1	By Balance	15.65

Realized Gains/Loss—Equity Shares Account

Date	Particulars	Debit (US$)	Date	Particulars	Credit (US$)
			15-Feb-X1	By Investments—Equity Shares—AFS Account	1,839.60
31-Mar-X1	To Balance	1,839.60			
31-Mar-X1	Total	**1,839.60**	31-Mar-X1	Total	**1,839.60**
			31-Mar-X1	By Balance	1,839.60

Realized Currency Gains/Loss—Equity Shares Account

Date	Particulars	Debit (US$)	Date	Particulars	Credit (US$)
			15-Feb-X1	By Investments—Equity Shares—AFS Account	65.49
31-Mar-X1	To Balance	65.49			
31-Mar-X1	Total	**65.49**	31-Mar-X1	Total	**65.49**
			31-Mar-X1	By Balance	65.49

Unrealized Currency Gains/Loss—Equity Shares—OCI Account

Date	Particulars	Debit (US$)	Date	Particulars	Credit (US$)
			31-Jan-X1	By Investments—Equity Shares—AFS Account	1,214.63
1-Feb-X1	To Investments—Equity Shares—AFS Account	1,214.63			
31-Mar-X1	Total	**1,214.63**	31-Mar-X1	Total	**1,214.63**

Receivable from Broker Account

Date	Particulars	Debit (US$)	Date	Particulars	Credit (US$)
15-Feb-X1	To Investments—Equity Shares—AFS Account	29,777.66			
			15-Feb-X1	By Bank Account	29,777.66
31-Mar-X1	Total	**29,777.66**	31-Mar-X1	Total	**29,777.66**

Share Capital Account

Date	Particulars	Debit (US$)	Date	Particulars	Credit (US$)
			4-Jan-X1	By Bank Account	66,019.67
31-Mar-X1	To Balance	66,019.67			
31-Mar-X1	Total	**66,019.67**	31-Mar-X1	Total	**66,019.67**
			31-Mar-X1	By Balance	66,019.67

Payable to Broker Account

Date	Particulars	Debit (US$)	Date	Particulars	Credit (US$)
			4-Jan-X1	By Investments—Equity Shares—AFS Account	27,728.26
			4-Jan-X1	ByInvestments—Equity Shares—AFS Account	79.22
4-Jan-X1	To Bank Account	27,807.48			
			5-Jan-X1	ByBrokerage/Commission Account	65.09
5-Jan-X1	To Bank Account	65.09			
31-Mar-X1	Total	**27,872.57**	31-Mar-X1	Total	**27,872.57**

Bank Account

Date	Particulars	Debit (US$)	Date	Particulars	Credit (US$)
4-Jan-X1	To Share Capital Account	66,019.67			
			4-Jan-X1	By Payable to Broker Account	27,807.48
			5-Jan-X1	By Futures Margin Account	14,644.62
			5-Jan-X1	By Payable to Broker Account	65.09
			31-Jan-X1	By Unrealized Currency Gains/Loss Account	708.83
15-Feb-X1	To Futures Margin Account	14,888.83			
15-Feb-X1	To Receivable from Broker Account	29,777.66			
15-Feb-X1	To Unrealized Currency Gains/Loss Account	552.04			
			31-Mar-X1	By Balance	68,012.18
31-Mar-X1	Total	**111,238.20**	31-Mar-X1	Total	**111,238.20**
31-Mar-X1	To Balance	68,012.18			

Trial Balance

As of 31-Mar-X1 (US$)

Particulars	Debit	Credit
Capital Account		
Share Capital Account		66,019.67
Current Assets		
Bank Account	68,012.18	
Direct Income		
Unrealized Currency Gains/Loss Account		71.77
MTM—Futures (P&L) Account		15.65
Realized Gains/Loss—Equity Shares Account		1,839.60
Realized Currency Gains/Loss—Equity Shares Account		65.49
Total	**68,012.18**	**68,012.18**

Income Statement

For the period ending 31-Mar-X1

Expenses	US$	Income	US$
Direct Expenses		**Direct Income**	
		Unrealized Currency Gains/Loss Account	71.77
		MTM—Futures (P&L) Account	15.65
		Realized Gains/Loss—Equity Shares Account	1,839.60
Net Profit	1,992.51	Realized Currency Gains/Loss—Equity Account	65.49
Total	**1,992.51**	Total	**1,992.51**

Balance Sheet

As of 31-Mar-X1

Liabilities	US$	Assets	US$
Capital Account		**Current Assets**	
Share Capital Account	66,019.67	Bank Account	68,012.18
Current Liabilities			
Profit & Loss Account			
Opening Balance	Nil		
Current Period	1,992.51		
Total	**68,012.18**	Total	**68,012.18**

SUMMARY

- When the investor buys the stock futures, and if it results in physical settlement, then the investor has to pay the contracted price and take delivery of the stock. The margin money paid will, however, be adjusted against the total money that the investor should pay the exchange.
- The brokerage paid on the futures trade would have been directly expensed and not taken as part of the cost of the shares that was to be acquired.
- When the futures contract results in physical settlement, then the brokerage originally expensed should be capitalized and taken to the concerned shares account.

EXERCISES

Objective Questions

1. When an investor buys stock futures, and if it results in physical settlement, then
   a. The investor has to pay the margin amount and take delivery of the stock
   b. The investor takes the delivery and pays at an agreed upon future date
   c. The investor can take the delivery on payment of a meager amount
   d. The investor takes the delivery and his broker pays for him
   e. The investor has to pay for the contracted price and take delivery of the stock
2. When the stock futures are sold and it results in physical settlement, then the physical shares should be delivered by the investor to
   a. The broker
   b. The exchange
   c. The buyer
   d. The custodian of the buyer
   e. Any individual who is authorized by the buyer to receive the shares
3. When the futures contract results in physical settlement, then the brokerage originally expensed
   a. Should be capitalized and taken to the concerned shares account
   b. Should be discounted
   c. Should be considered as part of the cost
   d. Should be reversed to the investor account
   e. Both a and d

4. Which among the following is a correct accounting entry on payment of margin?

a.

Date	Particulars	Debit (JPY)	Credit (JPY)
1-Jan-X1	Futures Margin Account	25,000.00	
	To Bank Account		25,000.00
	(Being the margin amount on purchase of futures paid)		

b.

Date	Particulars	Debit (JPY)	Credit (JPY)
1-Jan-X1	Investment Equity Stock Account	25,000.00	
	To Bank Account		25,000.00
	(Being the margin amount on purchase of futures paid)		

c.

Date	Particulars	Debit (JPY)	Credit (JPY)
1-Jan-X1	Bank Account	25,000.00	
	To Futures Margin Account		25,000.00
	(Being the margin amount on purchase of futures paid)		

d.

Date	Particulars	Debit (JPY)	Credit (JPY)
1-Jan-X1	Bank Account	25,000.00	
	To Investment Equity Stock Account		25,000.00
	(Being the margin amount on purchase of futures paid)		

e.

Date	Particulars	Debit (JPY)	Credit (JPY)
1-Jan-X1	Futures Margin Account	25,000.00	
	To Investment Equity Stock Account		25,000.00
	(Being the margin on purchase of futures paid)		

5. Assuming a sale of stock futures being liquidation of long stock futures, which among the following is true?
   a. Receivable from broker amount will be shown as investments on the asset side of balance sheet
   b. Receivable from broker amount will be shown in the P&L account
   c. Receivable from broker will be shown as current assets on the balance sheet
   d. Receivable from broker shown off balance sheet
   e. Receivable from broker will be adjusted to payable to broker

Journal Questions

Short Futures—Trade Currency AUD, Functional Currency US$

6. For the following scenario, prepare journal entries, general ledgers, trial balance, income statement, and balance sheet.
   XYZ Fund had the following trades in ABB in the futures market. The stock exchange requires that a margin of 20 percent of the value of the contract be maintained throughout the life of the contract.

Date	Product Expiry	Quantity	Rate (AUD)	B/S	Brokerage
22-Feb-07	25-Apr-07	–1,700	45	S	320
18-Mar-07	25-Apr-07	–1,400	50	S	350
13-Apr-07	25-Apr-07	2,000	43	B	400
25-Apr-07	25-Apr-07	1,100	42	Expiry	

Date	FX Rate
22-Feb-07	1.18182
28-Feb-07	1.17762
15-Mar-07	1.18322
31-Mar-07	1.17521
10-Apr-07	1.18231
25-Apr-07	1.17425

Date	Market Price
22-Feb-07	47
28-Feb-07	55
31-Mar-07	43
25-Apr-07	45

Long Futures—Trade Currency S$, Functional Currency US$

7. For the following scenario, prepare journal entries, general ledgers, trial balance, income statement, and balance sheet.
   AA Fund had the following trades in ABC in the futures market. The stock exchange requires that a margin of 10 percent of the value of the contract be maintained throughout the life of the contract.

Date	Product Expiry	Quantity	Rate (S$)	B/S	Brokerage
25-Aug-07	25-Nov-07	10,000	52.5	B	5,300
18-Oct-07	25-Nov-07	15,000	51.0	B	5,200
10-Nov-07	25-Nov-07	–16,000	54.0	S	3,000
25-Nov-07	25-Nov-07	–9,000	53.0	Expiry	

Date	FX Rate
25-Aug-07	1.5389
31-Aug-07	1.5432
30-Sep-07	1.5535
18-Oct-07	1.5375
31-Oct-07	1.5296
10-Nov-07	1.5431
25-Nov-07	1.5159

Date	Market Price
31-Aug-07	49
30-Sep-07	47
31-Oct-07	53
25-Nov-07	57

Long Futures—Trade Currency JPY, Functional Currency US$

8. For the following scenario, prepare journal entries, general ledgers, trial balance, income statement, and balance sheet:
AA Fund had the following trades in ABC in the futures market. The stock exchange requires that a margin of 30 percent of the value of the contract be maintained throughout the life of the contract.

Date	Product Expiry	Quantity	Rate (JPY)	B/S	Brokerage
29-Jan-07	25-Apr-07	1,000	800	B	530
15-Mar-07	25-Apr-07	1,500	820	B	520
10-Apr-07	25-Apr-07	–1,600	845	S	300
25-Apr-07	25-Apr-07	–900	850	Expiry	

Date	FX Rrate
1-Jan-07	123.805
29-Jan-07	124.850
31-Jan-07	125.705
28-Feb-07	124.805
15-Mar-07	125.705
31-Mar-07	125.205
10-Apr-07	124.235
25-Apr-07	124.569

Date	Market Price
31-Jan-07	750
28-Feb-07	770
31-Mar-07	855
25-Apr-07	857

Short Futures—Functional Currency US$

9. For the following scenario, prepare journal entries, general ledgers, trial balance, income statement, and balance sheet:
ABC Fund had the following trades in IBM in the futures market. The stock exchange requires that a margin of 15 percent of the value of the contract be maintained throughout the life of the contract.

Date	Product Expiry	Qty	Rate (US$)	B/S	Brokerage
22-Feb-07	25-Apr-07	–1,500	45	S	320
18-Mar-07	25-Apr-07	–1,800	50	S	350
13-Apr-07	25-Apr-07	2,000	43	B	400
25-Apr-07	25-Apr-07	1,300	42	Expiry	

Date	Market Price
22-Feb-07	47
28-Feb-07	55
31-Mar-07	43
25-Apr-07	45

CHAPTER 8

Accounting for Equity Call Options

LEARNING OBJECTIVES

After studying this chapter you should have a grasp of the following:

- Accounting standards for derivative instruments and hedging activities.
- Trade life cycle of exchange-traded options (ETOs) for long call.
- Journal entries to be recorded during the different phases of the trade life cycle.
- FX revaluation and FX translation process for these trades.
- Illustration of long call, non-hedging trades.
- Preparation of journal entries and general ledger accounts.
- Preparation of income statement and balance sheet after the call option trades are made.
- Illustration of long call, non-hedging trades in foreign currency.
- Trade life cycle of exchange-traded options when writing call options.
- Journal entries to be recorded during the different phases of the trade life cycle.
- Illustration of written call options in functional currency.
- Preparation of journal entries and general ledger accounts.
- Preparation of income statement and balance sheet after writing the call options.

ACCOUNTING STANDARDS—DERIVATIVE INSTRUMENTS AND HEDGING ACTIVITIES

The accounting treatment of call options *prima facie* will depend upon the intention with which the call options are purchased, either for hedging or for speculation (non-hedging). If the position is taken as a hedge against some other position, the relevant accounting standards will be applicable and certain conditions must be fulfilled.

Relevant Accounting Standards	
U.S. GAAP	**IFRS**
FAS 52—Foreign Currency Translation	IFRS 7—Financial Instruments: Disclosure
FAS 94—Consolidation of All Majority-owned Subsidiaries	IAS 21—The Effects of Changes in Foreign Exchange Rates

U.S. GAAP	IFRS
FAS 115—Accounting for Certain Investments in Debt and Equity Securities	IAS 32—Financial Instruments: Presentation
FAS 130—Reporting Comprehensive Income	IAS 36—Impairment of Assets
FAS 157—Fair Value Measurements	IAS 39—Financial Instruments: Recognition and Measurement
FAS 159—The Fair Value Option for Financial Assets and Financial Liabilities	

TRADE LIFE CYCLE FOR ETOs—LONG CALL NON-HEDGING

If the call is purchased purely as a speculative trade, then the premium paid towards the purchase of the call option is taken to the expense and the premium received on sale of the options is treated as revenue. However, the value of the option is written back on the valuation date and shown as an asset in the case of purchase of call options.

- Buy the call options.
- Brokerage/commission on the buy transaction.
- Pay for the call options bought.
- Ascertain the fair value at the end of reporting period.
- Reversal of mark-to-market.
- Expiry of options.
- Exercise of options.
- Sell the options.
- Receive the consideration.
- Ascertain the profit/loss on the sale.
- FX revaluation entries.
- FX translation entries.

Buy the Call Options

If the options are purchased other than as a hedge, it is either for speculation or for arbitrage. In this case the income account is debited when the options are purchased. On the valuation date the entire value of the options is written back as income on the one hand and asset on the other. In both cases, the net income and the net value shown on the balance sheet would be the same.

Assume that 10,000 equity call options of Metadata with a strike price of $50 are bought at $5 each through Beckerman & Co. Assume that the market rate of the underlying share is $52 at the time of purchase of these options. The accounting entry that is recorded in the books of accounts is shown as follows:

Journal Entry

Date	Particulars	Debit (US$)	Credit (US$)
23-Jan-X1	Premium paid on Call Options Account	50,000.00	
	To Beckerman & Co. Account		50,000.00
	(Being the purchase of 10,000 equity call options of Metadata @ $5)		

Brokerage/Commission on the Buy Transaction

The broker of the stock exchange charges a commission for the services rendered. This is usually settled along with the purchase value of the options. For option contracts, the brokerage/commission is not treated as part of the cost of the options contract; instead it is debited to the brokerage/commission account.

Assume that the brokerage for this deal is $500. The accounting entry that is recorded in the books of accounts is shown as follows:

Journal Entry

Date	Particulars	Debit (US$)	Credit (US$)
23-Jan-X1	Brokerage/Commission Account	500.00	
	To Beckerman & Co. Account		500.00
	(Being the brokerage payable on purchase of 10,000 equity call options of Metadata)		

Pay for the Options Bought

The next event in the trade life cycle is the payment of the contracted amount for the options bought. Usually this payment happens the same day.

The accounting entry that is recorded in the books of accounts is shown as follows:

Journal Entry

Date	Particulars	Debit (US$)	Credit (US$)
23-Jan-X1	Beckerman & Co. Account	50,500.00	
	To Bank Account		50,500.00
	(Being the payment towards purchase of 10,000 equity call options of Metadata along with brokerage)		

Ascertain the Fair Value at the End of the Reporting Period

The value of the entire position is written back to the profit and loss account and the same amount is shown as an asset in the balance sheet. This is because the entire value of the options at the time of purchase is taken to the expense account.

Assuming that the value of the options at the end of the reporting period is $6 then, the entire amount of $6 per option is recognized as income and is shown as an asset on the balance sheet. The accounting entry that is recorded in the books of accounts is shown as follows:

Journal Entry

Date	Particulars	Debit (US$)	Credit (US$)
31-Jan-X1	Options Contracts—Long Call Account	60,000.00	
	To Options MTM (P&L) Account		60,000.00
	(Being the mark-to-market entry at the end of the reporting period in respect of 10,000 equity call options of Metadata @ $6)		

Reversal of Mark-to-market

The accounting entry for mark-to-market is reversed on the next day or the next valuation date when a fresh entry for the then value is recorded in the books of accounts.

However, if the investor follows this incremental value method then there is no need to reverse the entry for mark-to-market recorded earlier.

The accounting entry that is recorded in the books of accounts is shown next.

Journal Entry

Date	Particulars	Debit (US$)	Credit (US$)
1-Feb-X1	Options MTM (P&L) Account	60,000.00	
	To Options Contracts—Long Call Account		60,000.00
	(Being the reversal of mark-to-market entry on the next date in respect of 10,000 equity call options of Metadata @ $6)		

Expiry of Options

The options expire on the expiry date of the contract. For call options that are bought, the market value of the underlying over and above the strike price of the options represents the profit. In this case, the call option is said to expire in-the-money. By contrast, if the call options expire out-of-the-money—that is, if the market value of the underlying is less than the strike price of the option—then the premium paid by the investor represents the loss. The maximum loss that could be incurred in a long call option can never exceed the premium paid on the purchase of the option.

Case 1: When the options expire worthless, there is no need to record any entry in the books of accounts. The option premium paid is already treated as an expense, and since the options expire worthless there is no need to write back the value of the options on the expiry date.

Case 2: When the options expire in-the-money—that is, where the market rate of the underlying is more than the strike price of the option—the amount of value of the underlying that exceeds the strike price represents the gain accruing to the investor. However, if the price of the underlying is below the strike price and the premium paid to acquire the options, the investor will still lose money. Assuming that the underlying shares close at $53 on the expiry date, the accounting entry that is recorded in the books of accounts is shown as follows:

Journal Entry

Date	Particulars	Debit (US$)	Credit (US$)
15-Feb-X1	Beckerman & Co. Account	30,000.00	
	To Premium paid on Call Options Account		30,000.00
	(Being the value realized on expiry of call options now reversed to premium account)		

In several stock exchanges, exchange traded options (ETOs) which are settled only by cash—usually options on index—that expire in the money are automatically taken care of by the stock exchange. The intrinsic value of the options is credited to the investor without the investor having to liquidate the position. However in cases where the options can be settled by delivery, the investor should either liquidate the position or should take delivery of the underlying in order to profit from an in-the-money option. In the illustrations given in this book it is assumed that either the stock exchange concerned credits the intrinsic value or the investor takes appropriate action that results in his getting the intrinsic value of the options when it expires in the money.

Case 3: The investor makes a profit when the options are exercised in-the-money—that is, when the market rate of the underlying is more than the strike price of the option. Assuming that the underlying shares close at $59 on the excercise date, the accounting entry that is recorded in the books of accounts is shown as follows:

Journal Entry

Date	Particulars	Debit (US$)	Credit (US$)
15-Feb-X1	Beckerman & Co. Account	40,000.00	
	To Profit on Call Options Account		40,000.00
	(Being the profit realized on call options as the options expired more than the original cost of acquisition)		

Exercise of Options

The buyer of the call option has the right but not the obligation to buy the underlying at the strike price. When the call options are exercised, it results in the acquisition of the underlying asset. In such a scenario, the investor has to pay for the underlying at the contracted strike price. The actual cost of carry of the underlying asset would then be the strike price of the contract plus the premium paid on the purchase of the call option. The profit or loss would be arrived at only after the underlying asset is liquidated. Until such time, the asset would be carried in the books at cost. Exercise of options happens only in the case of stock options and not in the case of options on indexes.

Assume that the options are exercised on the date of expiry when the price of the underlying share is $57, and that the equity shares are acquired for trading purposes. The accounting entry that is recorded in the books of accounts is shown as follows:

Journal Entry

Date	Particulars	Debit (US$)	Credit (US$)
15-Feb-X1	Investments—Equity Shares—Trading Account	500,000.00	
	To Beckerman & Co. Account		500,000.00
	(Being the exercise of 10,000 equity call options of Metadata @ $5 resulting in the acquisition of the shares)		
15-Feb-X1	Investments—Equity Shares—Trading Account	50,000.00	
	To Premium paid on Call Options Account		50,000.00
	(Being the premium paid on purchase of call options now taken as part of the cost of the underlying asset on exercise of call options)		
15-Feb-X1	Investments—Equity Shares—Trading Account	500.00	
	To Brokerage/Commission Account		500.00
	(Being the brokerage paid on purchase of 10,000 equity call options of Metadata @ $5 now taken to investment account as part of the cost of acquisition of the underlying shares on exercise of call options)		

Sell the Options

The long position of call options could be liquidated by selling such options. Since the sale results in only squaring up of the existing position, there is no requirement of any margin payment to the exchange on account of this sale of call options.

Assuming that the options are liquidated at $4.20, the accounting entry that is recorded in the books of accounts is shown as follows:

Journal Entry

Date	Particulars	Debit (US$)	Credit (US$)
2-Feb-X1	Beckerman & Co. Account	42,000.00	
	To Premium paid on Call Options Account		42,000.00
	(Being the sale of 10,000 equity call options of Metadata @ $4.20)		

Receive the Consideration

The consideration is received on day T + 2 or according to the requirements of the exchange concerned. The consideration is received net of brokerage. The accounting entry that is recorded in the books of accounts is shown as follows:

Journal Entry

Date	Particulars	Debit (US$)	Credit (US$)
2-Feb-X1	Bank Account	42,000.00	
	To Beckerman & Co. Account		42,000.00
	(Being receipt of funds on account of the sale of 10,000 equity put options of Metadata @ $4.20)		

Ascertain the Profit/Loss on the Sale

Since the expense account is debited while purchasing the options, there is no need to record a separate entry to determine the profit or loss on sale of options in this case.

FX Revaluation Entries

All the entries recorded to this point are initially entered in the respective trade currencies. If the functional currency is different from the trade currency, then each and every entry recorded in the trade currency should be entered again in the functional currency by converting the entries at the respective day's FX rates. In other words, for each trade currency that the investor deals with, there will be a complete set of books representing that trade currency. This includes journal entries, general ledger postings, trial balance, income statement and balance sheet.

After revaluing each and every journal entry of all the trade currencies into the functional currency, a separate set of books is prepared again comprising all the elements just mentioned—that is, journal entries, general ledger postings, trial balance, income statement and balance sheet. It should be noted that the ultimate financial reports would be prepared and presented to all the stakeholders based on the financial statements prepared in the functional currency only as this will encompass all the transactions of the investor in all trade currencies dabbled with. (For illustration and detailed explanation please refer to Chapter 2.)

FX Translation Entries

After revaluing all the entries in the functional currency at the respective FX rates for the day concerned, another entry needs to be passed in the books of the functional currency. This is mainly to adjust the currency gains or losses due to the fluctuations in FX rates between the reporting date and the date of recording the original entries. FX Translation entries are recorded only for the asset and liability accounts. For income and expense accounts the amount gets crystallized on the date of passing the FX revaluation entries in the books of the functional currency.

There are fundamentally two types of FX translation entries that are recorded in the books of the functional currency: consummated FX translation entries and transient FX translation entries. (For illustration and detailed explanation please refer to Chapter 2.)

ILLUSTRATIONS

Consider the following examples.

Long Call, Non-hedging

Victory Fund had the following trades in Metadata in the options market through Silver Man brokers. The stock exchange requires that the writer of the options maintain 10 percent of the value of the contract as margin money throughout the life of the contract. On January 1, $100,000 was introduced as capital into the fund. Journal entries, general ledgers, trial balance, income statement, and balance sheet are as follows:

Date	Product	Strike Price	Expiry	Quantity	Rate	B/S	Brokerage
23-Jan-X1	Call	$50	16-Mar-X1	10,000	$5.00	B	$540
23-Feb-X1	Call	$50	16-Mar-X1	16,000	$4.00	B	$620
10-Mar-X1	Call	$50	16-Mar-X1	16,000	$3.00	S	$320

Liquidation Method
FIFO

Market Rate of Underlying Stock Metadata
31-Jan-X1: 40.00; 28-Feb-X1: 55.00; 16-Mar-X1: $55

Market Rate of Metadata Call Option with Strike Price $50, Expiry March 16
January 31: 2
February 28: 6.00
March 16: 6.00

Long Call Option, Non-hedging—Functional Currency US$

T-1 Capital Brought In

Journal Entry

Date	Particulars	Debit (US$)	Credit (US$)
1-Jan-X1	Bank Account	100,000.00	
	To Share Capital Account		100,000.00
	(Being the capital introduced into the Victory Fund)		

T-2 On Purchase of Call Option

Journal Entry

Date	Particulars	Debit (US$)	Credit (US$)
23-Jan-X1	Options Premium Paid Account	50,000.00	
	To Silver Man Account		50,000.00
	(Being the purchase of equity call options treated as premium expense on date of purchase)		

T-3 Brokerage/Commission

Journal Entry

Date	Particulars	Debit (US$)	Credit (US$)
23-Jan-X1	Brokerage/Commission Account	540.00	
	To Silver Man Account		540.00
	(Being the brokerage incurred on purchase of call options)		

T-4 On Payment of Contracted Sum

Journal Entry

Date	Particulars	Debit (US$)	Credit (US$)
23-Jan-X1	Silver Man Account	50,540.00	
	To Bank Account		50,540.00
	(Being the payment made to the broker on purchase of call options)		

T-5 Market Value at End of Reporting Period

Market value at end of reporting period: 31-Jan-X1	US$
Market value of 10,000 call options @ $2	20,000.00
Market value in US$	20,000.00

Journal Entry

Date	Particulars	Debit (US$)	Credit (US$)
31-Jan-X1	Options Contracts Account	20,000.00	
	To MTM—ETO (P&L)		20,000.00
	(Being the market value of call options at the end of reporting period recognized as an asset)		

T-6 Reversal of Mark-to-market Value

Journal Entry

Date	Particulars	Debit (US$)	Credit (US$)
1-Feb-X1	MTM—ETO (P&L) Account	20,000.00	
	To Options Contracts Account		20,000.00
	(Being the reversal of mark-to-market entry on the next day)		

T-7 On Purchase of Call Option

Journal Entry

Date	Particulars	Debit (US$)	Credit (US$)
23-Feb-X1	Options Premium Paid Account	64,000.00	
	To Silver Man Account		64,000.00
	(Being the purchase of equity call options treated as premium expense on date of purchase)		

T-8 Brokerage/Commission

Journal Entry

Date	Particulars	Debit (US$)	Credit (US$)
23-Feb-X1	Brokerage/Commission Account	620.00	
	To Silver Man Account		620.00
	(Being the brokerage incurred on the purchase of call options)		

T-9 Payment of Contracted Sum

Journal Entry

Date	Particulars	Debit (US$)	Credit (US$)
23-Feb-X1	Silver Man Account	64,620.00	
	To Bank Account		64,620.00
	(Being the amount paid to the broker on the purchase of call options with brokerage)		

T-10 Market Value at End of Reporting Period

Market value at end of reporting period: 28-Feb-X1	US$
Market value for 26,000 options @ $6	156,000.00
Market value in US$	156,000.00

Journal Entry

Date	Particulars	Debit (US$)	Credit (US$)
28-Feb-X1	Options Contracts Account	156,000.00	
	To MTM—ETO (P&L) Account		156,000.00
	(Being the market value of call options at the end of reporting period)		

T-11 Reversal of Mark-to-market on Sale

Journal Entry

Date	Particulars	Debit (US$)	Credit (US$)
1-Mar-X1	MTM—ETO (P&L) Account	156,000.00	
	To Options Contracts Account		156,000.00
	(Being the reversal of mark-to-market value of call options on sale)		

T-12 On Sale of Call Options

Journal Entry

Date	Particulars	Debit (US$)	Credit (US$)
10-Mar-X1	Silver Man Account	48,000.00	
	To Options Premium Received Account		48,000.00
	(Being the sale of call options)		

T-13 Brokerage/Commission on Sale

Journal Entry

Date	Particulars	Debit (US$)	Credit (US$)
10-Mar-X1	Brokerage/Commission Account	320.00	
	To Silver Man Account		320.00
	(Being the brokerage incurred on the sale of call options)		

T-14 Receipt of Sale Proceeds

Journal Entry

Date	Particulars	Debit (US$)	Credit (US$)
10-Mar-X1	Bank Account	47,680.00	
	To Silver Man Account		47,680.00
	(Being net proceeds received from broker on sale of equity call options)		

T-15 Market Value of Net Position after Sale

Journal Entry

Date	Particulars	Debit (US$)	Credit (US$)
10-Mar-X1	Options Contracts Account	30,000.00	
	To MTM—ETO (P&L) Account		30,000.00
	(Being the market value of call options of net position after sale)		

T-16 Reversal of Mark-to-market Value

Journal Entry

Date	Particulars	Debit (US$)	Credit (US$)
11-Mar-X1	MTM—ETO (P&L) Account	30,000.00	
	To Options Contracts Account		30,000.00
	(Being a reversal of mark-to-market value of call options entry on the next day)		

T-17 On Expiry Date of Call Options

Journal Entry

Date	Particulars	Debit (US$)	Credit (US$)
16-Mar-X1	Bank Account	50,000.00	
	To Option Premium Received Account		50,000.00
	(Being the premium received on expiry of call options representing the intrinsic value of the options. It is assumed that the stock exchange automatically credits the intrinsic value of the options on the date of expiry)		

General Ledger Accounts

Option Contracts Account

Date	Particulars	Debit (US$)	Date	Particulars	Credit (US$)
31-Jan-X1	To MTM—ETO (P&L) Account	20,000.00			
			1-Feb-X1	By MTM—ETO (P&L) Account	20,000.00
28-Feb-X1	To MTM—ETO (P&L) Account	156,000.00			
			1-Mar-X1	By MTM—ETO (P&L) Account	156,000.00
10-Mar-X1	To MTM—ETO (P&L) Account	30,000.00			
			11-Mar-X1	By MTM—ETO (P&L) Account	30,000.00
31-Mar-X1	Total	**206,000.00**	31-Mar-X1	Total	**206,000.00**

Brokerage/Commission Account

Date	Particulars	Debit (US$)	Date	Particulars	Credit (US$)
23-Jan-X1	To Silver Man Account	540.00			
23-Feb-X1	To Silver Man Account	620.00			
10-Mar-X1	To Silver Man Account	320.00			
			31-Mar-X1	By Balance	1,480.00
31-Mar-X1	Total	**1,480.00**	31-Mar-X1	Total	**1,480.00**
31-Mar-X1	To Balance	1,480.00			

MTM–ETO (P&L) Account

Date	Particulars	Debit (US$)	Date	Particulars	Credit (US$)
			31-Jan-X1	By Option Contracts Account	20,000.00
1-Feb-X1	To Option Contracts Account	20,000.00			
			28-Feb-X1	By Option Contracts Account	156,000.00
1-Mar-X1	To Option Contracts Account	156,000.00			
			10-Mar-X1	By Option Contracts Account	30,000.00
11-Mar-X1	To Option Contracts Account	30,000.00			
31-Mar-X1	Total	**206,000.00**	31-Mar-X1	Total	**206,000.00**

Option Premium Paid Account

Date	Particulars	Debit (US$)	Date	Particulars	Credit (US$)
23-Jan-X1	To Silver Man Account	50,000.00			
23-Feb-X1	To Silver Man Account	64,000.00			
			31-Mar-X1	By Balance	114,000.00
31-Mar-X1	Total	**114,000.00**	31-Mar-X1	Total	**114,000.00**
31-Mar-X1	To Balance	114,000.00			

Option Premium Received Account

Date	Particulars	Debit (US$)	Date	Particulars	Credit (US$)
			10-Mar-X1	By Silver Man Account	48,000.00
			16-Mar-X1	By Bank Account	50,000.00
31-Mar-X1	To Balance	98,000.00			
31-Mar-X1	Total	**98,000.00**	31-Mar-X1	Total	**98,000.00**
			31-Mar-X1	By Balance	98,000.00

Silver Man Account

Date	Particulars	Debit (US$)	Date	Particulars	Credit (US$)
			23-Jan-X1	By Option Premium Paid Account	50,000.00
			23-Jan-X1	By Brokerage/ Commission Account	540.00
23-Jan-X1	To Bank Account	50,540.00			
			23-Feb-X1	By Option Premium Paid Account	64,000.00
			23-Feb-X1	By Brokerage/ Commission Account	620.00
23-Feb-X1	To Bank Account	64,620.00			
10-Mar-X1	To Option Premium Received Account	48,000.00			
			10-Mar-X1	By Bank Account	47,680.00
			10-Mar-X1	By Brokerage/ Commission Account	320.00
31-Mar-X1	Total	**163,160.00**	31-Mar-X1	Total	**163,160.00**

Share Capital Account

Date	Particulars	Debit (US$)	Date	Particulars	Credit (US$)
			01-Jan-X1	By Bank	100,000.00
.31-Mar-X1	To Balance	100,000.00			
31-Mar-X1	Total	**100,000.00**	31-Mar-X1	Total	**100,000.00**
			31-Mar-X1	By Balance	100,000.00

Bank Account

Date	Particulars	Debit (US$)	Date	Particulars	Credit (US$)
1-Jan-X1	To Share Capital Account	100,000.00			
			23-Jan-X1	By Silver Man Account	50,540.00
			23-Feb-X1	By Silver Man Account	64,620.00
10-Mar-X1	To Silver Man Account	47,680.00			
16-Mar-X1	To Option Premium Received Account	50,000.00			
			31-Mar-X1	By Balance	82,520.00
31-Mar-X1	Total	**197,680.00**	31-Mar-X1	Total	**197,680.00**
31-Mar-X1	To Balance	82,520.00			

Trial Balance

As on 31-Mar-X1 (US$)

Particulars	Debit	Credit
Capital Account		
Share Capital Account		100,000.00
Current Liabilities		Nil
Current Assets		
Bank Account	82,520.00	
Direct Income		
Option Premium Received Account		98,000.00
Direct Expenses		
Brokerage/Commission Account	1,480.00	
Option Premium Paid Account	114,000.00	
Total	**198,000.00**	**198,000.00**

Income Statement

For the period ending 31-Mar-X1

Expenses	US$	Income	US$
Direct Expenses		Direct Income	
Brokerage/Commission Account	1,480.00	Option Premium Received Account	98,000.00
Option Premium Paid Account	114,000.00		
		Net Loss Carryover	17,480.00
Total	**115,480.00**	Total	**115,480.00**

Balance Sheet

As at 31-Mar-X1

Liabilities	US$	Assets	US$
Capital Account		Investments	Nil
Share Capital Account	100,000.00	Current Assets	
		Bank Account	82,520.00
		Profit & Loss Account	
Current Liabilities	Nil	Opening Balance	Nil
		Current Period	17,480.00
Total	**100,000.00**	Total	**100,000.00**

Long Call Options

Victory GBP Fund had the following trades in Beacon shares in the options market on the London stock exchange through Silver Man brokers. The stock exchange requires that the writer of the options maintain 10 percent of the value of the contract as margin money throughout the life of the contract. On January 1, GBP100,000 was introduced into the fund as capital. Journal entries, general ledgers, trial balance, income statement, and balance sheet are as follows:

Date	Product	Strike Price (GBP)	Expiry	Quantity	Rate (GBP)	B/S	Brokerage (GBP)
23-Jan-X1	Call	50	16-Mar-X1	9,000	5.00	B	540
23-Feb-X1	Call	50	16-Mar-X1	12,000	4.00	B	620
10-Mar-X1	Call	50	16-Mar-X1	10,000	3.00	S	320

Liquidation Method
FIFO

Market Rate of Underlying Beacon Shares
January 31: GBP40.00
February 28: GBP55.00
March 16-Mar-X1: GBP55.00

Market Rate of Beacon Call Option with Strike Price £50, Expiry March 16
January 31: GBP2
February 28: GBP6.00

Settle Price
March 16: GBP55.00

FX Rates: US$/GBP

Date	Rate
1-Jan-X1	1.9600
23-Jan-X1	1.9800
31-Jan-X1	1.9600
23-Feb-X1	1.9200
28-Feb-X1	1.9400
10-Mar-X1	1.9300
16-Mar-X1	1.9400
31-Mar-X1	1.9300

Long Call Options—Trade Currency GBP

T-1 Conversion of US$ into GBP

Journal Entry

Date	Particulars	Debit (GBP)	Credit (GBP)
1-Jan-X1	Bank—GBP Account	100,000.00	
	To Share Capital Account		100,000.00
	(Being the capital introduced)		

T-2 On Purchase of Call Option

Journal Entry

Date	Particulars	Debit (GBP)	Credit (GBP)
23-Jan-X1	Options Premium Paid Account	45,000.00	
	To Silver Man Account		45,000.00
	(Being the purchase of 9,000 equity call options @ GBP5)		

T-3 Brokerage/Commission

Journal Entry

Date	Particulars	Debit (GBP)	Credit (GBP)
23-Jan-X1	Brokerage/Commission Account	540.00	
	To Silver Man Account		540.00
	(Being the brokerage incurred on purchase of call options)		

T-4 On Payment of Contracted Sum

Journal Entry

Date	Particulars	Debit (GBP)	Credit (GBP)
23-Jan-X1	Silver Man Account	45,540.00	
	To Bank—GBP Account		45,540.00
	(Being payment to the broker Silver Man on purchase of call options)		

T-5 Market Value at End of Reporting Period

Market value at end of reporting period: 31-Jan-X1	**GBP**
Market value of 9,000 call options @ GBP2	18,000.00
Market value in GBP	**18,000.00**

Journal Entry

Date	Particulars	Debit (GBP)	Credit (GBP)
31-Jan-X1	Options Contracts Account	18,000.00	
	To MTM—ETO (P&L) Account		18,000.00
	(Being the market value of call options now recognized as an asset at the end of the reporting period)		

T-6 Reversal of Mark-to-market Value

Journal Entry

Date	Particulars	Debit (GBP)	Credit (GBP)
1-Feb-X1	MTM—ETO (P&L) Account	18,000.00	
	To Options Contracts Account		18,000.00
	(Being the reversal of mark-to-market entry on call options)		

T-7 On Purchase of Call Option

Journal Entry

Date	Particulars	Debit (GBP)	Credit (GBP)
23-Feb-X1	Options Premium Paid Account	48,000.00	
	To Silver Man Account		48,000.00
	(Being the purchase of equity call options)		

T-8 Brokerage/Commission

Journal Entry

Date	Particulars	Debit (GBP)	Credit (GBP)
23-Feb-X1	Brokerage/Commission Account	620.00	
	To Silver Man Account		620.00
	(Being the brokerage incurred on purchase of call options)		

T-9 Payment of Contracted Sum

Journal Entry

Date	Particulars	Debit (GBP)	Credit (GBP)
23-Feb-X1	Silver Man Account	48,620.00	
	To Bank—GBP Account		48,620.00
	(Being the payment to the broker Silver Man on purchase of call options)		

T-10 Market Value at End of Reporting Period

Market value at end of reporting period: 28-Feb-X1	**GBP**
Market value of 21,000 call options @ GBP6	126,000.00
Market value in GBP	**126,000.00**

Journal Entry

Date	Particulars	Debit (GBP)	Credit (GBP)
28-Feb-X1	Options Contracts Account	126,000.00	
	To MTM—ETO (P&L) Account		126,000.00
	(Being the mark-to-market value of 21,000 call options as of date)		

T-11 Reversal of Mark-to-market

Journal Entry

Date	Particulars	Debit (GBP)	Credit (GBP)
1-Mar-X1	MTM—ETO (P&L) Account	126,000.00	
	To Options Contracts Account		126,000.00
	(Being the reversal of mark-to-market value on 21,000 call options)		

T-12 Sale of the Call Options

Journal Entry

Date	Particulars	Debit (GBP)	Credit (GBP)
10-Mar-X1	Silver Man Account	30,000.00	
	To Options Premium Received Account		30,000.00
	(Being the receivable from broker on sale of 10,000 equity call options)		

T-13 Brokerage/Commission on Sale

Journal Entry

Date	Particulars	Debit (GBP)	Credit (GBP)
10-Mar-X1	Brokerage/Commission Account	320.00	
	To Silver Man Account		320.00
	(Being the brokerage incurred on sale of call options)		

T-14 On Receipt of Sale Proceeds

Journal Entry

Date	Particulars	Debit (GBP)	Credit (GBP)
10-Mar-X1	Bank—GBP Account	29,680.00	
	To Silver Man Account		29,680.00
	(Being the amount received from Silver Man on sale of 10,000 call options)		

T-15 On Expiry of Call Options

Journal Entry

Date	Particulars	Debit (GBP)	Credit (GBP)
16-Mar-X1	Bank—GBP Account	55,000.00	
	To Option Premium Received Account		55,000.00
	(Being the intrinsic value of the call options realized on call options on the date of expiry)		

General Ledger Accounts

Option Contracts Account

Date	Particulars	Debit (GBP)	Date	Particulars	Credit (GBP)
31-Jan-X1	To MTM—ETO (P&L) Account	18,000.00			
			1-Feb-X1	By MTM—ETO (P&L) Account	18,000.00
28-Feb-X1	To MTM—ETO (P&L) Account	126,000.00			
			1-Mar-X1	By MTM—ETO (P&L) Account	126,000.00
31-Mar-X1	Total	**144,000.00**	31-Mar-X1	Total	**144,000.00**

Share Capital Account

Date	Particulars	Debit (GBP)	Date	Particulars	Credit (GBP)
			1-Jan-X1	By Bank—GBP Account	100,000.00
31-Mar-X1	To Balance	100,000.00			
31-Mar-X1	Total	**100,000.00**	31-Mar-X1	Total	**100,000.00**
			31-Mar-X1	By Balance	100,000.00

Brokerage/Commission Account

Date	Particulars	Debit (GBP)	Date	Particulars	Credit (GBP)
23-Jan-X1	To Silver Man Account	540.00			
23-Feb-X1	To Silver Man Account	620.00			
10-Mar-X1	To Silver Man Account	320.00			
			31-Mar-X1	By Balance	1,480.00
31-Mar-X1	Total	**1,480.00**	31-Mar-X1	Total	**1,480.00**
31-Mar-X1	To Balance	1,480.00			

MTM—ETO (P&L) Account

Date	Particulars	Debit (GBP)	Date	Particulars	Credit (GBP)
			31-Jan-X1	By Option Contracts Account	18,000.00
1-Feb-X1	To Option Contracts Account	18,000.00			
			28-Feb-X1	By Option Contracts Account	126,000.00
1-Mar-X1	To Option Contracts Account	126,000.00			
31-Mar-X1	Total	**144,000.00**	31-Mar-X1	Total	**144,000.00**

Option Premium Paid Account

Date	Particulars	Debit (GBP)	Date	Particulars	Credit (GBP)
23-Jan-X1	To Silver Man Account	45,000.00			
23-Feb-X1	To Silver Man Account	48,000.00			
			31-Mar-X1	By Balance	93,000.00
31-Mar-X1	Total	**93,000.00**	31-Mar-X1	Total	**93,000.00**
31-Mar-X1	To Balance	93,000.00			

Option Premium Received Account

Date	Particulars	Debit (GBP)	Date	Particulars	Credit (GBP)
			10-Mar-X1	By Silver Man Awccount	30,000.00
			16-Mar-X1	By Bank—GBP Account	55,000.00
31-Mar-X1	To Balance	85,000.00			
31-Mar-X1	Total	**85,000.00**	31-Mar-X1	Total	**85,000.00**
			31-Mar-X1	By Balance	85,000.00

Silver Man Account

Date	Particulars	Debit (GBP)	Date	Particulars	Credit (GBP)
			23-Jan-X1	By Option Premium Paid Account	45,000.00
			23-Jan-X1	By Brokerage/ Commission Account	540.00
23-Jan-X1	To Bank—GBP Account	45,540.00			
			23-Feb-X1	By Option Premium Paid Account	48,000.00
			23-Feb-X1	By Brokerage/ Commission Account	620.00

Silver Man Account (*Cont'd*)

Date	Particulars	Debit (GBP)	Date	Particulars	Credit (GBP)
23-Feb-X1	To Bank—GBP Account	48,620.00			
10-Mar-X1	To Option Premium Received Account	30,000.00			
			10-Mar-X1	By Brokerage/ Commission Account	320.00
			10-Mar-X1	By Bank—GBP Account	29,680.00
31-Mar-X1	Total	**124,160.00**	31-Mar-X1	Total	**124,160.00**

Bank—GBP Account

Date	Particulars	Debit (GBP)	Date	Particulars	Credit (GBP)
1-Jan-X1	To Share Capital Account	100,000.00			
			23-Jan-X1	By Silver Man Account	45,540.00
			23-Feb-X1	By Silver Man Account	48,620.00
10-Mar-X1	To Silver Man Account	29,680.00			
16-Mar-X1	To Option Premium Received Account	55,000.00			
			31-Mar-X1	To Balance	90,520.00
31-Mar-X1	Total	**184,680.00**	31-Mar-X1	Total	**184,680.00**
31-Mar-X1	To Balance	90,520.00			

Trial Balance

As of 31-Mar-X1 (GBP)

Particulars	Debit	Credit
Capital		
Capital—Share Capital Account		100,000.00
Current Assets		
Bank Account	90,520.00	
Direct Income		
Option Premium Received Account		85,000.00
Direct Expenses		
Brokerage/Commission Account	1,480.00	
Option Premium Paid Account	93,000.00	
Total	**185,000.00**	**185,000.00**

Income Statement

For the period ending 31-Mar-X1

Expenses	GBP	Income	GBP
Direct Expenses		**Direct Income**	
Brokerage/commission Account	1,480.00	Option Premium Received Account	85,000.00
Option Premium Paid Account	93,000.00	Net Loss Carryover	9,480.00
Total	**94,480.00**	Total	**94,480.00**

Balance Sheet

As of 31-Mar-X1

Liabilities	GBP	Assets	GBP
Capital Account	100,000.00	**Investments**	Nil
		Current Assets	
		Bank Account	90,520.00
Current Liabilities	Nil	**Profit & Loss Account**	
		Opening Balance	Nil
		Current Period	9,480.00
Total	**100,000.00**	Total	**100,000.00**

Long Call Options—Functional Currency US$

The following are the FX revaluation entries in the functional currency converted at the respective FX rate, which is given within parenthesis. FX translation entries are clearly specified, indicating whether each is a consummated FX translation entry or a transient FX translation entry.

F-1 Conversion of GBP into US$ (T-1 @ FX Rate: 1.9600)

Journal Entry

Date	Particulars	Debit (US$)	Credit (US$)
1-Jan-X1	Bank—GBP Account	196,000.00	
	To Share Capital Account		196,000.00
	(Being the capital introduced into the fund)		

F-2 On Purchase of Call Options (T-2 @ FX Rate: 1.9800)

Journal Entry

Date	Particulars	Debit (US$)	Credit (US$)
23-Jan-X1	Options Premium Paid Account	89,100.00	
	To Silver Man Account		89,100.00
	(Being the purchase of equity call options)		

F-3 Brokerage/Commission (T-3 @ FX Rate: 1.9800)

Journal Entry

Date	Particulars	Debit (US$)	Credit (US$)
23-Jan-X1	Brokerage/Commission Account	1,069.20	
	To Silver Man Account		1,069.20
	(Being the brokerage incurred on purchase of call options)		

F-4 Payment of Contracted Sum (T-4 @ FX Rate: 1.9800)

Journal Entry

Date	Particulars	Debit (US$)	Credit (US$)
23-Jan-X1	Silver Man Account	90,169.20	
	To Bank—GBP Account		90,169.20
	(Being the payment to Silver Man on purchase of call options)		

F-5 Market Value at End of Reporting Period (T-5 @ FX Rate: 1.9600)

Market value at end of reporting period: 31-Jan-X1	**US$**
Market value of 9,000 call options @ GBP2 * 1.9600	35,280.00
Market value in US$	**35,280.00**

Journal Entry

Date	Particulars	Debit (US$)	Credit (US$)
31-Jan-X1	Options Contracts Account	35,280.00	
	To MTM—ETO (P&L) Account		35,280.00
	(Being the market value of 9,000 call options)		

F-6 Reversal of Mark-to-market Value (T-6 @ FX Rate: 1.9600)

Journal Entry

Date	Particulars	Debit (US$)	Credit (US$)
1-Feb-X1	MTM—ETO (P&L) Account	35,280.00	
	To Options Contracts Account		35,280.00
	(Reversal of mark-to-market value of 9,000 call options)		

F-7 On Purchase of Call Options (T-7 @ FX Rate: 1.9200)

Journal Entry

Date	Particulars	Debit (US$)	Credit (US$)
23-Feb-X1	Options Premium Paid Account	92,160.00	
	To Silver Man Account		92,160.00
	(Being the purchase of equity call options)		

F-8 Brokerage/Commission (T-8 @ FX Rate: 1.9200)

Journal Entry

Date	Particulars	Debit (US$)	Credit (US$)
23-Feb-X1	Brokerage/Commission Account	1,190.40	
	To Silver Man Account		1,190.40
	(Being the brokerage incurred on purchase of equity call options)		

F-9 On Payment of Contracted Sum (T-9 @ FX Rate: 1.9200)

Journal Entry

Date	Particulars	Debit (US$)	Credit (US$)
23-Feb-X1	Silver Man Account	93,350.40	
	To Bank—GBP Account		93,350.40
	(Being payment made to Silver Man on purchase of call options)		

F-10 Market Value at End of Reporting Period (T-10 @ FX Rate: 1.9400)

Market value at end of reporting period: 28-Feb-X1	**US$**
Market value of 21,000 options @ GBP6 * 1.9400	244,440.00
Market value in US$	**244,440.00**

Journal Entry

Date	Particulars	Debit (US$)	Credit (US$)
28-Feb-X1	Options Contracts Account	244,440.00	
	To MTM—ETO (P&L) Account		244,440.00
	(Being the market value of call options as of date)		

F-11 Reversal of Mark-to-market Value (T-11 @ FX Rate: 1.9400)

Journal Entry

Date	Particulars	Debit (US$)	Credit (US$)
1-Mar-X1	MTM—ETO (P&L) Account	244,440.00	
	To Options Contracts Account		244,440.00
	(Being the reversal of mark-to-market value of 21,000 call options)		

F-12 Sale of Call Options (T-12 @ FX Rate: 1.9300)

Journal Entry

Date	Particulars	Debit (US$)	Credit (US$)
10-Mar-X1	Silver Man Account	57,900.00	
	To Options Premium Received Account		57,900.00
	(Being the receivable from broker on sale of 10,000 equity call options)		

F-13 Brokerage/Commission on Sale (T-13 @ FX Rate: 1.9300)

Journal Entry

Date	Particulars	Debit (US$)	Credit (US$)
10-Mar-X1	Brokerage/Commission Account	617.60	
	To Silver Man Account		617.60
	(Being the brokerage incurred on the sale of call options)		

F-14 Receipt of Sale Proceeds (T-14 @ FX Rate: 1.9600)

Journal Entry

Date	Particulars	Debit (US$)	Credit (US$)
10-Mar-X1	Bank—GBP Account	57,282.40	
	To Silver Man Account		57,282.40
	(Being the amount received from Silver Man for the sale of 10,000 call options)		

F-15 On Expiry Date of Call Options (T-15 @ FX Rate: 1.9400)

Journal Entry

Date	Particulars	Debit (US$)	Credit (US$)
16-Mar-X1	Bank—GBP Account	106,700.00	
	To Option Premium Received Account		106,700.00
	(Being the intrinsic value of 11,000 call options on expiry date)		

F-16 FX Translation on Bank Account (Transient FX Translation Entry)

Bank—GBP Account

Date	Description	GBP	FX rate	US$
1-Jan-X1	Opening balance	100,000.00	1.9600	196,000.00
23-Jan- X1	Payment on account of buy call	(45,540.00)	1.9800	(90,169.20)
23-Feb- X1	Payment on account of buy call	(48,620.00)	1.9200	(93,350.40)
10-Mar- X1	Receipt on account of sell call	29,680.00	1.9300	57,282.40
16-Mar- X1	Received on expiry of call	55,000.00	1.9400	106,700.00
				176,462.80
31-Mar- X1	Closing balance	90,520.00	1.9300	174,703.60
	Unrealized currency loss			(1,759.20)

Journal Entry

Date	Particulars	Debit (US$)	Credit (US$)
31-Mar-X1	Unrealized Currency Gains/Loss (P&L) Account	1,759.20	
	To Bank—GBP Account		1,759.20
	(Being the FX translation applied on the bank account)		

General Ledger Accounts

Option Contracts Account

Date	Particulars	Debit (US$)	Date	Particulars	Credit (US$)
31-Jan-X1	To MTM—ETO (P&L) Account	35,280.00			
			1-Feb-X1	By MTM—ETO (P&L) Account	35,280.00
28-Feb-X1	To MTM—ETO (P&L) Account	244,440.00			
			1-Mar-X1	By MTM—ETO (P&L) Account	244,440.00
31-Mar-X1	Total	**279,720.00**	31-Mar-X1	Total	**279,720.00**

Brokerage/Commission Account

Date	Particulars	Debit (US$)	Date	Particulars	Credit (US$)
23-Jan-X1	To Silver Man Account	1,069.20			
23-Feb-X1	To Silver Man Account	1,190.40			
10-Mar-X1	To Silver Man Account	617.60			
			31-Mar-X1	By Balance	2,877.20
31-Mar-X1	Total	**2,877.20**	31-Mar-X1	Total	**2,877.20**
31-Mar-X1	To Balance	2,877.20			

Unrealized Currency Gains/Loss Account

Date	Particulars	Debit (US$)	Date	Particulars	Credit (US$)
31-Mar-X1	To Bank—GBP Account	1,759.20			
			31-Mar-X1	By Balance	1,759.20
31-Mar-X1	Total	**1,759.20**	31-Mar-X1	Total	**1,759.20**
31-Mar-X1	To Balance	1,759.20			

MTM—ETO (P&L) Account

Date	Particulars	Debit (US$)	Date	Particulars	Credit (US$)
			31-Jan-X1	By Option Contracts Account	35,280.00
1-Feb-X1	To Option Contracts Account	35,280.00			
			28-Feb-X1	By Option Contracts Account	244,440.00
1-Mar-X1	To Option Contracts Account	244,440.00			
31-Mar-X1	Total	**279,720.00**	31-Mar-X1	Total	**279,720.00**

Share Capital Account

Date	Particulars	Debit (US$)	Date	Particulars	Credit (US$)
			1-Jan-X1	By Bank GBP Account	196,000.00
31-Mar-X1	To Balance	196,000.00			
31-Mar-X1	Total	**196,000.00**	31-Mar-X1	Total	**196,000.00**
			31-Mar-X1	By Balance	196,000.00

Option Premium Paid Account

Date	Particulars	Debit (US$)	Date	Particulars	Credit (US$)
23-Jan-X1	To Silver Man Account	89,100.00			
23-Feb-X1	To Silver Man Account	92,160.00			
			31-Mar-X1	By Balance	181,260.00
31-Mar-X1	Total	**181,260.00**	31-Mar-X1	Total	**181,260.00**
31-Mar-X1	To Balance	181,260.00			

Option Premium Received Account

Date	Particulars	Debit (US$)	Date	Particulars	Credit (US$)
			10-Mar-X1	By Silver Man Account	57,900.00
			16-Mar-X1	By Bank—GBP Account	106,700.00
31-Mar-X1	To Balance	164,600.00			
31-Mar-X1	Total	**164,600.00**	31-Mar-X1	Total	**164,600.00**
			31-Mar-X1	By Balance	164,600.00

Silver Man Account

Date	Particulars	Debit (US$)	Date	Particulars	Credit (US$)
			23-Jan-X1	By Option Premium Paid Account	89,100.00
			23-Jan-X1	By Brokerage/ Commission Account	1,069.20
23-Jan-X1	To Bank—GBP Account	90,169.20			
			23-Feb-X1	By Option Premium Paid Account	92,160.00
			23-Feb-X1	By Brokerage/ Commission Account	1,190.40
23-Feb-X1	To Bank—GBP Account	93,350.40			
10-Mar-X1	To Option Premium Received Account	57,900.00			
			10-Mar-X1	By Brokerage/ Commission Account	617.60
			10-Mar-X1	By Bank—GBP Account	57,282.40
31-Mar-X1	Total	**241,419.60**	31-Mar-X1	Total	**241,419.60**

Bank—GBP Account

Date	Particulars	Debit (US$)	Date	Particulars	Credit (US$)
1-Jan-X1	To Share Capital Account	196,000.00			
			23-Jan-X1	By Silver Man Account	90,169.20
			23-Feb-X1	By Silver Man Account	93,350.40
10-Mar-X1	To Silver Man Account	57,282.40			
16-Mar-X1	To Option Premium Received Account	106,700.00			
			31-Mar-X1	By Unrealized Currency Gains/ loss Account	1,759.20
			31-Mar-X1	By Balance	178,222.00
31-Mar-X1	Total	**361,741.60**	31-Mar-X1	Total	**361,741.60**
31-Mar-X1	To Balance	174,703.60			

Trial Balance

As on 31-Mar-X1 (US$)

Particulars	Debit	Credit
Capital		
Share Capital Account		196,000.00
Current Assets		
Bank GBP Account	174,703.60	
Direct Income		
Option Premium Received Account		164,600.00
Direct Expenses		
Unrealized Currency Gains/loss Account	1,759.20	
Brokerage/Commission Account	2,877.20	
Option Premium Paid Account	181,260.00	
Total	**360,600.00**	**360,600.00**

Income Statement

For the period ending 31-Mar-X1

Expenses	US$	Income	US$
Direct Expenses		**Direct Income**	
Brokerage/commission Account	2,877.20		
Unrealized Currency Gains/Loss Account	1,759.20	Option Premium Received Account	164,600.00
Option Premium Paid Account	181,260.00	Net Loss Carryover	21,296.40
Total	**185,896.40**	Total	**185,896.40**

Balance Sheet

As at 31-Mar-X1

Liabilities	US$	Assets	US$
Capital Account		**Investments**	Nil
Share Capital Account	196,000.00		
		Current Assets	
Current Liabilities	Nil	Bank GPB Account	174,703.60
		Profit & Loss Account	
		Opening Balance	Nil
		Current Period	21,296.40
Total	**196,000.00**	Total	**196,000.00**

TRADE LIFE CYCLE FOR EXCHANGE-TRADED OPTIONS—ON WRITING A CALL OPTION

- Deposit the margin on options to the exchange.
- Writing the call options.
- Brokerage/commission on the transaction.
- Receive the premium on the call options sold.
- Ascertain the fair value at the end of reporting period.
- Margin call.
- Expiry of options.
- Exercise of options.
- Buy back the call options.
- Ascertain the profit/loss on the sale.
- Get back the deposit of margin money.
- FX revaluation entries.
- FX translation entries.

Deposit the Margin on Options

Margin is payable to the exchange if the investor writes the option. For exchange-traded options (ETOs), since the stock exchange has the responsibility of ensuring that both the legs of the transaction are complete, the exchange would insist that the writer of the option deposit a percentage of the value of the contract as margin money. This is because potentially the writer of an option has unlimited risk. The margin money would be adjusted against any reduction in the marked-to-market valuation on a daily basis.

Margin is in effect a good faith deposit. Normally a deposit of about 5 to 10 percent of the total value of the contract would signify the willingness to stand good on any price movements against the seller of an options contract. The percentage of deposit would be smaller for index options and higher for stock options. Since it is merely a deposit, the investor would get the margin money back after the contract is liquidated.

Assume that an investor wants to sell 1,000 call options on an index at $6, strike price being $70, and the stock exchange insists on an up-front margin of 10 percent of the value of the contract from the option writer. Expiry of the contract is December 16, and the broker through whom the trade is executed is Kingston Bros. The margin payable to the exchange through the broker would be 10 percent of $70,000, or $7,000.

The accounting entry that is recorded in the books of accounts is shown as follows:

Journal Entry

Date	Particulars	Debit (US$)	Credit (US$)
8-Nov-X1	Call Options Margin Account	7,000.00	
	To Kingston Bros Account		7,000.00
	(Being the margin payable to the stock exchange through the broker @ 10% of the value of the contract on sale of 100 call options on Index @ strike price $70)		

Writing the Call Options

If the investor writes a call option, he receives a premium. The premium is normally credited to the margin account already available with the counterparty on the settlement date of the option contract.

The accounting entry that is recorded in the books of accounts is shown as follows:

Journal Entry

Date	Particulars	Debit (US$)	Credit (US$)
8-Nov-X1	Call Options Margin Account	6,000.00	
	To Premium Received on Call Options Account		6,000.00
	(Being the premium received on sale of 10,000 call options on index @ $6)		

Brokerage/Commission on Sale of Options

The broker charges a commission for the services rendered. For option contracts, the brokerage/commission is not treated as a reduction from the sale consideration of the options contract but instead it is debited to the brokerage/commission account.

Assume that the brokerage payable is $300 for this deal. The accounting entry that is recorded in the books of accounts is shown as follows:

Journal Entry

Date	Particulars	Debit (US$)	Credit (US$)
8-Nov-X1	Brokerage/Commission Account	300.00	
	To Kingston Bros. Account		300.00
	(Being the brokerage payable on sale of index call options @ $6)		

Ascertain the Fair Value at the End of the Reporting Period

At the end of every reporting period the fair value of the options is ascertained and the options contracts are marked-to-market. This process is known as portfolio valuation, when the market rate at the end of the period is determined from the primary stock exchange where the underlying shares are traded. If there is a decrease in the market rate below the sale rate, then such decrease is recognized as a gain, on the one hand, and the corresponding amount is reflected as a decrease in the liability on account of such options. This accounting entry is reversed on the next day or the next valuation date when a fresh entry for the then value is recorded in the books of accounts. Alternatively, the accounting entry can be recorded only for the incremental value. If the investor follows this incremental value method, then there is no need to reverse the entry for mark-to-market recorded earlier.

Assuming that the market rate of the call options as of November 30, which is the next valuation date, is $8, then the accounting entry that is recorded in the books of accounts is as follows:

Journal Entry

Date	Particulars	Debit (US$)	Credit (US$)
30-Nov-X1	MTM—Call Options Account	8,000.00	
	To Option Contract Account		8,000.00
	(Being the mark-to-market of sale of 100 call options)		

Margin Call on Options

If the margin money gets eroded due to unfavorable price movement for the investor, then the exchange would initiate a margin call. This is to ensure that the exchange does not get caught unawares if there is a wide fluctuation in the value of the underlying, causing severe loss to the investor. The stock exchange would require that there be sufficient margin money to take care of this.

Assuming that on November 30, the price of the call options shoots up to $20, then the stock exchange would initiate a margin call to compensate the erosion in the margin account of the investor. The margin amount paid initially, amounting to $7,000, would be completely eroded by this unfavorable price movement to the investor. The investor would be required to pay an amount equal to 10 percent of the value of the position after such price movement in addition to the potential loss as of that date.

In this case, assume that the value of the underlying has moved from $65 on the date of sale of the call options to $95, resulting in the price of the call option going up to $20. Even though the potential loss as of this date in this case is 25,000 calculated as (Strike price – Current market price of the underlying share) × quantity ie (70 – 95) × 1000 = 25,000, the broker concerned is likely to make the margin call calculated based on the actual loss incurred as on date which is (Sale price of option – Market price of option) × quantity ie (6 – 20) × 1000 = 14,000 as increased by 10 percent margin based on the value of the position amounting to 9,500 and reduced by the margin money already paid by the investor of 7,000 resulting in a margin call of 16,500.

The accounting entry that is recorded in the books of accounts is shown as follows:

Journal Entry

Date	Particulars	Debit (US$)	Credit (US$)
30-Nov-X1	Call Options Margin Account	16,500.00	
	To Bank Account		16,500.00
	(Being the margin payable on account of the margin call initiated by the stock exchange)		

Expiry of Options

The options expire on the expiry date of the contract. For call options that are written, the excess amount of the market value of the underlying over and above the strike price of the options represents the loss for the investor. In such case, the call option is said to expire in-the-money. Conversely, if the call options expire out-of-the-money—that is, if the market value of the underlying is less than the strike price of the option—then the premium received by the investor represents the profit. The maximum profit that could be earned by the investor shorting or writing in a call option can never exceed the premium received on the sale of the call option.

Case 1: When the options expire worthless, there is no need to record any entry in the books of accounts. The option premium received is already treated as an income, and since the options expire worthless there is no need to record any other entry on the expiry date.

Case 2: When the options expire in-the-money, in other words when the market rate of the underlying is more than the strike price of the option, then the value of the underlying that exceeds the strike price represents the loss accruing to the investor. Assuming that the underlying shares close at $74 on the expiry date, the accounting entry that is recorded in the books of accounts is shown as follows:

Journal Entry

Date	Particulars	Debit (US$)	Credit (US$)
15-Dec-X1	Loss on Call Options Account	4,000.00	
	To Kingston Bros. Account		4,000.00
	(Being the loss on expiry of call options)		

Case 3: The investor incurs a loss when the options expire in-the-money—that is, when the market rate of the underlying is more than the strike price of the option and less than the premium received on the sale of such options. Assuming that the underlying shares close at $79 on the expiry date, the accounting entry that is recorded in the books of accounts is shown as follows:

Journal Entry

Date	Particulars	Debit (US$)	Credit (US$)
15-Dec-X1	Loss on Call Options Account	9,000.00	
	To Kingston Bros. Account		9,000.00
	(Being the loss on expiry of call options)		

Exercise of Options

The seller of the call option has the obligation to deliver the underlying at the strike price, if exercised by the buyer of the option. When the call options are exercised, it results in the delivery of the underlying asset. In such a scenario, the investor has to deliver the underlying at the contracted strike price. The actual realization of the underlying asset would then be the strike price of the contract as increased by the premium received on such sale of the call option.

Exercise of options happens only in the case of stock options and not in the case of options on indexes. Assume that the options are exercised on the date of expiry when the price of the underlying share is $80 and the equity shares are held for trading purposes. The accounting entry that is recorded in the books of accounts is shown as follows:

Journal Entry

Date	Particulars	Debit (US$)	Credit (US$)
15-Dec-X1	Kingston Bros. Account	70,000.00	
	To Investments—Equity Shares—Trading Account		70,000.00
	(Being the exercise of 1,000 equity call options resulting in the sale of the shares)		
15-Dec-X1	Premium received on Call Options Account	6,000.00	
	To Investments—Equity Shares—Trading Account		6,000.00
	(Being the premium received on sale of call options now taken as part of the revenue realized on exercise of call options)		
15-Dec-X1	Investments—Equity Shares—Trading Account	500.00	
	To Brokerage/Commission Account		500.00
	(Being the brokerage paid on sale of 1,000 equity call options now taken to investment account as part of the cost of acquisition of the underlying shares on exercise of call options)		

Buy Back the Call Options

The short position of call options could be covered by buying back such options. The buyback results in squaring up of the existing short position. The overall open interest could come down on liquidation of the call option if it is purchased by someone who already has a short position.

Assuming that the call options are bought back at $9 per option, then the accounting entry that is recorded in the books of accounts is shown as follows:

Journal Entry

Date	Particulars	Debit (US$)	Credit (US$)
10-Dec-X1	Premium paid on Call Options Account	9,000.00	
	To Call Options Margin Account		9,000.00
	(Being the purchase of 1,000 equity call options)		

Ascertain the Profit/Loss on the Buyback

Since the premium received and the premium paid are directly accounted for as income and expense, respectively, there is no need to record any separate entry to ascertain the profit or loss on the buyback of the option contract.

Get Back the Deposit of Margin Money

Once the short positions are squared off, the exchange would automatically release the margin money to the investor concerned. The entire amount lying to the debit of the call options margin account will be returned back to the investor.

The accounting entry that is recorded in the books of accounts is shown as follows:

Journal Entry

Date	Particulars	Debit (US$)	Credit (US$)
15-Dec-X1	Bank Account	24,000.00	
	To Call Options Margin Account		24,000.00
	(Being the Call Options Margin Account balance received from the broker on squaring off the entire position)		

FX Revaluation Entries

All the entries recorded to this point are initially entered in the respective trade currencies. If the functional currency is different from the trade currency, then each and every entry recorded in the trade currency should be entered again in the functional currency by converting the entries at the respective day's FX rates. In other words, for each trade currency that the investor deals with, there will be a complete set of books representing that trade currency. This includes journal entries, general ledger postings, trial balance, income statement, and balance sheet.

After revaluing each and every journal entry of all the trade currencies into the functional currency, a separate set of books is prepared again comprising all the elements just mentioned: journal entries, general ledger postings, trial balance, income statement, and balance sheet. It should be noted that the ultimate financial reports would be prepared and presented to all the stakeholders based on the financial statements prepared in the functional currency only, as this will encompass all the transactions of the investor in all trade currencies dabbled with. (For illustration and detailed explanation please refer to Chapter 2.)

FX Revaluation Entries

After revaluing all the entries in the functional currency at the respective FX rates for the day concerned, another entry needs to be passed in the books of the functional currency. This is mainly to adjust the currency gains or losses due to the fluctuations in FX rates between the reporting date and the date of recording the original entries. FX translation entries are recorded only for the asset and liability accounts. For income and expense accounts the amount gets crystallized on the date of passing the FX revaluation entries in the books of the functional currency.

There are fundamentally two types of FX translation entries that are recorded in the books of the functional currency: consummated FX translation entries and transient FX translation entries. (For illustration and detailed explanation please refer to Chapter 2.)

ILLUSTRATIONS

Writing Call Options

Victory Fund had the following trades in Metadata in the options market through Silver Man brokers. The stock exchange requires that the writer of the options maintain 10 percent of the value of the contract as margin money throughout the life of the contract. Victory Fund introduced $100,000 as capital as of January 23. Journal entries, general ledgers, trial balance, income statement, and balance sheet are as follows:

Date	Product	Strike Price	Expiry	Quantity	Rate	B/S	Brokerage
23-Jan-X1	Call	$50	16-Mar-X1	10,000	$6.25	S	$540
23-Feb-X1	Call	$50	16-Mar-X1	12,000	$7.00	S	$620
10-Mar-X1	Call	$50	16-Mar-X1	18,000	$6.00	B	$320

Liquidation Method
FIFO

Market Rate of Underlying Stock, Metadata
31-Jan-X1: $40.00
28-Feb-X1: $55.00
16-Mar-X1: $55.00

Market Rate of Metadata Call Option with Strike Price $50, Expiry March 16
31-Jan-X1: 2.00
28-Feb-X1: 6.00

Exercise Price
16-Mar-X1: $55

Short Call Option—Functional Currency US$

T-1 Capital Brought In

Journal Entry

Date	Particulars	Debit (US$)	Credit (US$)
23-Jan-X1	Bank Account	100,000.00	
	To Share Capital Account		100,000.00
	(Being the capital brought into the fund)		

T-2 On Payment of Margin Money

Journal Entry

Date	Particulars	Debit (US$)	Credit (US$)
23-Jan-X1	Options Margin Account	50,000.00	
	To Bank Account		50,000.00
	(Being the payment of margin money @ 10% of contract value)		

T-3 Sale of the Call Options

Journal Entry

Date	Particulars	Debit (US$)	Credit (US$)
23-Jan-X1	Options Margin Account	62,500.00	
	To Options Premium Received Account		62,500.00
	(Being the sale of 10,000 equity call options @ $6.25)		

T-4 Brokerage/Commission

Journal Entry

Date	Particulars	Debit (US$)	Credit (US$)
23-Jan-X1	Brokerage/Commission Account	540.00	
	To Silver Man Account		540.00
	(Being the brokerage incurred on the sale of call options)		

T-5 Payment of Brokerage

Journal Entry

Date	Particulars	Debit (US$)	Credit (US$)
23-Jan-X1	Silver Man Account	540.00	
	To Bank Account		540.00
	(Being the brokerage made to the broker Silver Man on sale of 10,000 call options)		

T-6 Market Value at End of Reporting Period

Market value at end of reporting period: 31-Jan-X1	**US$**
Market value of 10,000 call options @ $2	20,000.00
Market value in US$	**20,000.00**

Journal Entry

Date	Particulars	Debit (US$)	Credit (US$)
31-Jan-X1	MTM—ETO (P&L) Account	20,000.00	
	To Option Contracts Account		20,000.00
	(Being the market value of written call options recognized as a liability as of date)		

T-7 Reversal of Mark-to-market Value of Call Options

Journal Entry

Date	Particulars	Debit (US$)	Credit (US$)
1-Feb-X1	Option Contracts Account	20,000.00	
	To MTM—ETO (P&L) Account		20,000.00
	(Being the reversal of mark-to-market value of the call options as of date)		

T-8 On Payment of Margin Money

Journal Entry

Date	Particulars	Debit (US$)	Credit (US$)
23-Feb-X1	Options Margin Account	60,000.00	
	To Bank Account		60,000.00
	(Being the payment of margin money @ 10% of contract value)		

T-9 Sale of the Call Option

Journal Entry

Date	Particulars	Debit (US$)	Credit (US$)
23-Feb-X1	Options Margin Account	84,000.00	
	To Options Premium Received Account		84,000.00
	(Being the sale of equity call options)		

T-10 Brokerage/Commission

Journal Entry

Date	Particulars	Debit (US$)	Credit (US$)
23-Feb-X1	Brokerage/Commission Account	620.00	
	To Silver Man Account		620.00
	(Being the brokerage incurred on the sale of call options)		

T-11 Payment of Brokerage

Journal Entry

Date	Particulars	Debit (US$)	Credit (US$)
23-Feb-X1	Silver Man Account	620.00	
	To Bank Account		620.00
	(Being the payment made to the broker Silver Man on sale of call options)		

T-12 Market Value at End of Reporting Period

Market value at end of reporting period: 28-Feb-X1	**US$**
Market value of 22,000 call options @ $6	132,000.00
Market value in US$	**132,000.00**

Journal Entry

Date	Particulars	Debit (US$)	Credit (US$)
28-Feb-X1	MTM—ETO (P&L) Account	132,000.00	
	To Option Contracts Account		132,000.00
	(Being the market value of written call options recognized as a liability as of date)		

T-13 Reversal of Mark-to-market Value of Options

Journal Entry

Date	Particulars	Debit (US$)	Credit (US$)
1-Mar-X1	Option Contracts Account	132,000.00	
	To MTM—ETO (P&L) Account		132,000.00
	(Being the reversal of mark-to-market value of call options as on date)		

T-14 On Purchase of Call Options

Journal Entry

Date	Particulars	Debit (US$)	Credit (US$)
10-Mar-X1	Options Premium Paid Account	108,000.00	
	To Options Margin Account		108,000.00
	(Being the purchase of 18,000 equity call options).		

T-15 Brokerage/Commission on Purchase

Journal Entry

Date	Particulars	Debit (US$)	Credit (US$)
10-Mar-X1	Brokerage/Commission Account	320.00	
	To Silver Man Account		320.00
	(Being the brokerage incurred on the purchase of call options)		

T-16 Payment of Brokerage

Journal Entry

Date	Particulars	Debit (US$)	Credit (US$)
10-Mar-X1	Silver Man Account	320.00	
	To Bank Account		320.00
	(Being the payment made to the broker Silver Man on sale of 18,000 call options)		

T-17 On Expiry of Call Options

Journal Entry

Date	Particulars	Debit (US$)	Credit (US$)
16-Mar-X1	Options Premium Paid Account	20,000.00	
	To Options Margin Account		20,000.00
	(Being the loss realized based on the intrinsic value of 4,000 call options on the date of expiry—loss for writer of the option)		

T-18 Refund of Margin

Calculation of Margin Account balance

Date	Description	Debit	Credit
23-Jan-X1	10% of margin money of the contract value	50,000.00	
23-Jan-X1	Sell short call	62,500.00	
23-Feb-X1	10% of margin money of the contract value	60,000.00	
23-Feb-X1	Sell short call	84,000.00	
10-Mar-X1	On purchase of call options		108,000.00
16-Mar-X1	On expiry of call options		20,000.00
	Total	**256,500.00**	**128,000.00**
	Outstanding balance in margin account	**128,500.00**	

Journal Entry

Date	Particulars	Debit (US$)	Credit (US$)
16-Mar-X1	Bank Account	128,500.00	
	To Options Margin Account		128,500.00
	(Being the refund of the balance lying in the margin account after the expiry of the contract)		

General Ledger Accounts

Option Contracts Account

Date	Particulars	Debit (US$)	Date	Particulars	Credit (US$)
			31-Jan-X1	By MTM—ETO (P&L) Account	20,000.00
1-Feb-X1	To MTM—ETO (P&L) Account	20,000.00			
			28-Feb-X1	By MTM—ETO (P&L) Account	132,000.00
1-Mar-X1	To MTM—ETO (P&L) Account	132,000.00			
31-Mar-X1	Total	**152,000.00**	31-Mar-X1	Total	**152,000.00**

Brokerage/Commission Account

Date	Particulars	Debit (US$)	Date	Particulars	Credit (US$)
23-Jan-X1	To Silver Man Account	540.00			
23-Feb-X1	To Silver Man Account	620.00			
10-Mar-X1	To Silver Man Account	320.00			
			31-Mar-X1	By Balance	1,480.00
31-Mar-X1	Total	**1,480.00**	31-Mar-X1	Total	**1,480.00**
31-Mar-X1	To Balance	1,480.00			

MTM–ETO (P&L) Account

Date	Particulars	Debit (US$)	Date	Particulars	Credit (US$)
31-Jan-X1	To Option Contracts Account	20,000.00			
			1-Feb-X1	By Option Contracts Account	20,000.00
28-Feb-X1	To Option Contracts Account	132,000.00			
			1-Mar-X1	By Option Contracts Account	132,000.00
31-Mar-X1	Total	**152,000.00**	31-Mar-X1	Total	**152,000.00**

Option Margin Account

Date	Particulars	Debit (US$)	Date	Particulars	Credit (US$)
23-Jan-X1	To Bank Account	50,000.00			
23-Jan-X1	To Option Premium Received Account	62,500.00			
23-Feb-X1	To Bank Account	60,000.00			
23-Feb-X1	To Option Premium Received Account	84,000.00			
			10-Mar-X1	By Option Premium Paid Account	108,000.00
			16-Mar-X1	By Option Premium Paid Account	20,000.00
			16-Mar-X1	By Bank Account	128,500.00
31-Mar-X1	Total	**256,500.00**	31-Mar-X1	Total	**256,500.00**

Option Premium Paid Account

Date	Particulars	Debit (US$)	Date	Particulars	Credit (US$)
10-Mar-X1	To Option Margin Account	108,000.00			
16-Mar-X1	To Option Margin Account	20,000.00			
			31-Mar-X1	By Balance	128,000.00
31-Mar-X1	Total	**128,000.00**	31-Mar-X1	Total	**128,000.00**
31-Mar-X1	To Balance	128,000.00			

Option Premium Received Account

Date	Particulars	Debit (US$)	Date	Particulars	Credit (US$)
			23-Jan-X1	By Option Margin Account	62,500.00
			23-Feb-X1	By Option Margin Account	84,000.00
31-Mar-X1	To Balance	146,500.00			
31-Mar-X1	Total	**146,500.00**	31-Mar-X1	Total	**146,500.00**
			31-Mar-X1	By Balance	146,500.00

Share Capital Account

Date	Particulars	Debit (US$)	Date	Particulars	Credit (US$)
			23-Jan-X1	By Bank Account	100,000.00
31-Mar-X1	To Balance	100,000.00			
31-Mar-X1	Total	**100,000.00**	31-Mar-X1	Total	**100,000.00**
			31-Mar-X1	By Balance	100,000.00

Silver Man Account

Date	Particulars	Debit (US$)	Date	Particulars	Credit (US$)
			23-Jan-X1	By Brokerage/ Commission Account	540.00
23-Jan-X1	To Bank Account	540.00			
			23-Feb-X1	By Brokerage/ Commission Account	620.00
23-Feb-X1	To Bank Account	620.00			
			10-Mar-X1	By Brokerage/ Commission Account	320.00
10-Mar-X1	To Bank Account	320.00			
31-Mar-X1	Total	**1,480.00**	31-Mar-X1	Total	**1,480.00**

Bank Account

Date	Particulars	Debit (US$)	Date	Particulars	Credit (US$)
23-Jan-X1	To Share Capital Account	100,000.00			
			23-Jan-X1	By Option Margin Account	50,000.00
			23-Jan-X1	By Silver Man Account	540.00
			23-Feb-X1	By Silver Man Account	620.00
			23-Feb-X1	By Option Margin Account	60,000.00

Bank Account *(Cont'd)*

Date	Particulars	Debit (US$)	Date	Particulars	Credit (US$)
16-Mar-X1	To Option Margin Account	128,500.00			
			31-Mar-X1	By Balance	117,020.00
31-Mar-X1	Total	**228,500.00**	31-Mar-X1	Total	**228,500.00**
31-Mar-X1	To Balance	117,020.00			

Trial Balance

As of 31-Mar-X1 (US$)

Particulars	Debit	Credit
Capital Account		
Share Capital Account		100,000.00
Current Assets		
Bank Account	117,020.00	
Direct Income		
Option Premium Received Account		146,500.00
Direct Expenses		
Brokerage/Commission Account	1,480.00	
Option Premium Paid Account	128,000.00	
Total	**246,500.00**	**246,500.00**

Income Statement

For the period ending 31-Mar-X1

Expenses	US$	Income	US$
Direct Expenses		**Direct Income**	
Brokerage/Commission Account	1,480.00	Option Premium Received Account	146,500.00
Option Premium Paid Account	128,000.00		
Net Profit Carryover	17,020.00		
Total	**146,500.00**	Total	**146,500.00**

Balance Sheet

As of 31-Mar-X1

Liabilities	US$	Assets	US$
Capital Account		**Investments**	Nil
Share Capital Account	100,000.00		
Current Liabilities	Nil	**Current Assets**	
Profit & Loss Account		Bank Account	117,020.00
Opening Balance	Nil		
Current Period	17,020.00		
Total	**117,020.00**	Total	**117,020.00**

SUMMARY

- The accounting treatment of call options *prima facie* will depend upon the intention with which the call options are purchased—hedging or speculation (non-hedging).
- If the position is taken as a hedge against some other position, then the relevant accounting standards for hedge accounting will be applicable and there are certain conditions that are to be fulfilled for the same.
- If the call is purchased purely as a speculative trade, then the premium paid towards purchase of the call option is taken to the expense and the premium received on sale of the options is treated as revenue.
- However, the value of the option is written back on the valuation date and shown as an asset in the case of purchase of call options. In effect, the net result of this method of accounting and the one shown for hedging activity would be the same.

EXERCISES

Theory Questions

1. Explain the trade life cycle for call options.
2. Is accounting for call options any different if the options were to be held as hedge and not as investment?

Objective Questions

1. Premium paid towards purchase of call options purchased for speculative trade should be treated as
   a. Expense
   b. Revenue
   c. Loss
   d. Gain

2. For an options contract, the commission/brokerage paid is treated as follows:
    a. Part of the cost of options contract
    b. Debited to commission/brokerage account
    c. Adjusted later in the broker account at the time of sale
    d. None of the above
3. For ascertaining fair value at the end of the reporting period, the value of the entire position will be written back to the
    a. Profit and loss account
    b. Expense account
    c. Income account
    d. None of the above
4. Reversal of marked-to-market entry will happen on
    a. Next business day
    b. Next valuation day
    c. Same day itself
    d. None of the above
5. For call options (bought), if the market value of the underlying asset is over the strike price of the contact, then the excess amount denotes
    a. Profit
    b. Loss
    c. Breakeven
    d. None of the above
6. When the options contract is expired, then the option premium paid denotes
    a. Expense
    b. Income
    c. Gain
    d. None of the above
7. Exercising of an options contract means
    a. Creation of underlying asset
    b. Breaking the options contract
    c. Paying the margin amount
    d. None of the above
8. Buyback of the call options results in
    a. Creating a fresh contract
    b. Squaring up of the existing short position
    c. Creating a long position
    d. None of the above

9. Account treatment for a call options contract is decided based on
   a. Position of the contract
   b. Intention of the purchase
   c. Size of the contract
   d. None of the above

10. Assume that a call option with a quantity of 10,000 shares and a premium of $6,000 has a value of $9 at the end of the reporting period. Which of the following amounts is recognized as income which reflects as an asset on the balance sheet?
    a. $9,000
    b. $96,000
    c. $84,000
    d. $90,000
    e. $9,600

11. The accounting entry for mark-to-market reversal of a call option is not required if the valuation is done using the
    a. Reversal method at the end of reporting period
    b. Black-Scholes model
    c. Incremental value method
    d. End of period market price
    e. Beginning of period market price

12. When the call options are exercised, the investor has to pay for the underlying at
    a. The current market price of the stock
    b. The rate at which the exchange decides
    c. The contracted strike price
    d. The previous day's closing price
    e. None of the above

13. If an investor writes a call option, then the investor ______________ on such writing of the call option.
    a. Would pay the premium on the exercise date
    b. Would collect the premium on the exercise date
    c. Would pay the premium on the settlement date
    d. Would collect the premium on the settlement date
    e. Would neither collect nor pay any premium

14. When a call margin is initiated the investor would be required to pay an amount equal to ______ of the value of the position in addition to the potential loss as of that date.
    a. 8 percent
    b. 15 percent

c. 25 percent
d. 12 percent
e. 10 percent

Journal Questions

Journalize the following:

Mr. Berkowitz buys 1,000 equity call options of Normal Electricals for $4 per share for a strike price of $25 on June 12, expiry date being July 16. Brokerage is 0.25 percent and is settled on T + 2 basis. Pass necessary journal entries for the following events:

1. Purchase of the options.
2. Brokerage paid for purchase.
3. At the end of the reporting period, June 30, the shares are quoted at $28 per share and the options were worth $2 per share. Ascertain the fair value at that time and pass entries.
4. Assume the options are exercised on the expiry date and for the price of $27. Pass relevant journal entries on July 16, the expiry date.

Long Call, Non-hedging—Functional Currency US$

Prepare journal entries, general ledgers, trial balance, income statement, and balance sheet for the following scenario.

Freedom Fund had the following trades in GE in the options market through ADC brokers, and on January 1 introduced $100,000 as capital.

Date	Product	Strike Price	Expiry	Quantity	Rate	B/S	Brokerage
25-Jan-X1	Call	$50	16-Mar-X1	10,000	$5.00	B	$540
22-Feb-X1	Call	$50	16-Mar-X1	16,000	$4.00	B	$620
11-Mar-X1	Call	$50	16-Mar-X1	16,000	$3.00	S	$320

Liquidation Method
FIFO

Market Rate of Underlying Stock, GE
January 31: 40.00
February 28: 55.00
March 16: 55.00

Market Rate of GE Call Option with Strike Price $50, Expiry March 16
January 31: 2.00
February 28: 6.00

Functional Currency
US$

Long Call, Non-hedging—Trade Currency AUD

Prepare journal entries, general ledgers, trial balance, income statement, and balance sheet for the following scenario:

AA Fund had the following trades in Metadata in the options market through DDT Man brokers. The stock exchange requires that the writer of the options maintain 10 percent of the value of the contract as margin money throughout the life of the contract. On January 1, AA Fund introduced $100,000 as capital and converted US$50,000 into AUD at the rate of 1.25.

Date	Product	Strike Price	Expiry	Quantity	Rate (AUD)	B/S	Brokerage (AUD)
21-Jan-X1	Call	AUD 40	15-Mar-X1	12,000	4.00	B	$500
20-Feb-X1	Call	AUD 40	15-Mar-X1	13,000	5.00	B	$600
12-Mar-X1	Call	AUD 40	15-Mar-X1	15,000	4.00	S	$300

Liquidation Method
FIFO

Market Rate of Underlying Stock, Metadata (AUD)
January 31: 35.00
February 28: 40.00
March 16: 45.00

Market Rate of Metadata Call Option with Strike Price $40, Expiry March 15
January 31: 3.00
February 28: 5.00

FX Rate AUD/US$
January 21: 1.2178
January 31: 1.28964
February 20: 1.26345
February 28: 1.24789
March 12: 1.23645
March 15: 1.27893

Functional Currency
US$

Short Call, Non-hedging—Trade Currency JPY

Prepare journal entries, general ledgers, trial balance, income statement, and balance sheet for the following scenario:

Stone Fund had the following trades in Gamut in the options market through MML brokers. The stock exchange requires that the writer of the options maintain 15 percent of the value of the contract as margin money throughout the life of the contract. On February 1, Stone Fund introduced $150,000 as capital and converted half of it into JPY at 122.50.

Date	Product	Strike Price	Expiry	Quantity	Rate (JPY)	B/S	Brokerage (JPY)
23-Feb-X1	Call	JPY 55	16-Apr-X1	10,000	6.00	S	520
22-Mar-X1	Call	JPY 55	16-Apr-X1	16,000	5.00	S	600
10-Apr-X1	Call	JPY 55	16-Apr-X1	16,000	4.00	B	300

Liquidation Method
FIFO

Market Rate of Underlying Stock, Gamut
February 28: 59.00
March 31: 58.00
April 16: 61.00

Market Rate of Gamut Call Option with Strike Price $55, Expiry April 16
February 28: 5.00
March 31: 4.00

FX Rate JPY/US$
February 23: 123.589
February 28:122.569
March 22: 124.587
March 31: 124.7891
April 10: 123.1562
April 16: 123.4569

Functional Currency
US$

CHAPTER 9

Accounting for Equity Put Options

LEARNING OBJECTIVES

After studying this chapter you should have a grasp of the following:

- The trade life cycle of exchange-traded options (ETOs) for long put.
- Journal entries to be recorded during the different phases of the trade life cycle.
- FX revaluation and FX translation process.
- Illustration of long put options in both functional and foreign currency, including preparation of journal entries, general ledger accounts, income statement, and balance sheet for long put option.
- The trade life cycle of exchange-traded options on writing a put option, and journal entries to be recorded during the different phases of this trade life cycle.
- Illustration of writing put options in functional currency, including preparation of journal entries, general ledger accounts, income statement, and balance sheet after writing the put options.

TRADE LIFE CYCLE FOR EXCHANGE-TRADED OPTIONS—LONG PUT, NON-HEDGING

If the put is purchased purely as a speculative trade, then the premium paid towards purchase of the put option is taken to the expense and the premium received on sale of the option is treated as revenue. However, the value of the option is written back on the valuation date and shown as an asset in the case of purchase of put options. The trade life cycle events for put options that are not meant as hedging instruments are as follows:

- Buy the put options.
- Brokerage/commission on the buy transaction.
- Pay for the put options bought.
- Ascertain the fair value at the end of the reporting period.
- Reversal of mark-to-market.
- Expiry of options.
- Exercise of options.
- Sell the options.

- Receive the consideration.
- Ascertain the profit/loss on the sale.
- FX revaluation entries.
- FX translation entries.

Buy the Put Options

If the options are purchased other than as a hedge, it is either for speculation or for arbitrage. In this case the income account is debited when the options are purchased. At the valuation date the entire value of the options is written back as income on the one hand and asset on the other. In both cases the net income and the net value shown in the balance sheet would be the same.

Assume that 10,000 equity put options of Siemens with strike price $50 are bought at $5 each through Sharp & Co. Assume that the market rate of the underlying share is $52 at the time of purchase of these options. The accounting entry that is recorded in the books of accounts is shown as follows:

Journal Entry

Date	Particulars	Debit (US$)	Credit (US$)
23-Jan-X1	Premium paid on Put Options Account	50,000.00	
	To Sharp & Co. Account		50,000.00
	(Being the purchase of 10,000 equity put options of Siemens @ $5)		

Brokerage/Commission on the Buy Transaction

The broker charges a commission which is usually settled along with the purchase value of the options. For option contracts, the brokerage/commission is not treated as part of the cost of the options contract; instead it is debited to the brokerage/commission account.

Assume that the brokerage for this deal is $500. The accounting entry that is recorded in the books of accounts is shown as follows:

Journal Entry

Date	Particulars	Debit (US$)	Credit (US$)
23-Jan-X1	Brokerage/Commission Account	500.00	
	To Sharp & Co. Account		500.00
	(Being the brokerage payable on purchase of 10,000 equity put options)		

Pay for the Options Bought

The next event in the trade life cycle is the payment of the contracted amount for the options bought. Usually the payment happens the same day that the purchase contract is created.

The accounting entry that is recorded in the books of accounts is shown as follows:

Journal Entry

Date	Particulars	Debit (US$)	Credit (US$)
23-Jan-X1	Sharp & Co. Account	50,500.00	
	To Bank Account		50,500.00
	(Being the payment towards purchase of 10,000 equity put options along with brokerage)		

Ascertain the Fair Value at the End of the Reporting Period

The value of the entire position is written back to the profit and loss account and the same amount is shown as an asset on the balance sheet. This is because the entire value of the options at the time of purchase is taken to the expense account.

Assuming that the value of the options at the end of the reporting period is $6, then the entire amount of $6 per option is recognized as income and is shown as an asset in the balance sheet. The accounting entry that is recorded in the books of accounts is shown as follows:

Journal Entry

Date	Particulars	Debit (US$)	Credit (US$)
31-Jan-X1	Options Contracts—Long Put Account	60,000.00	
	To Options MTM (P&L) Account		60,000.00
	(Being the mark-to-market at the end of the reporting period in respect of 10,000 equity put options of Siemens @ $6)		

Reversal of Mark-to-market

The accounting entry for mark-to-market is reversed on the next day or the next valuation date when a fresh entry for the then value is recorded in the books of accounts. However, as mentioned earlier, if the investor follows the incremental value method, then there is no need to reverse the entry for mark-to-market recorded earlier.

The accounting entry that is recorded in the books of accounts is shown below:

Journal Entry

Date	Particulars	Debit (US$)	Credit (US$)
1-Feb-X1	Options MTM (P&L) Account	60,000.00	
	To Options Contracts—Long Put Account		60,000.00
	(Being the reversal of mark-to-market at the end of the reporting period in respect of 10,000 equity put options of Siemens @ $6)		

Expiry of Options

The options expire on the expiry date of the contract. For put options that are bought, the excess amount of the strike price of the options below the market price of the underlying represents the profit for the investor. In such case, the put option is said to expire in-the-money. Conversely, if the put options expire out-of-the-money—that is, if the market value of the underlying is more than the strike price of the option—then the premium paid by the investor represents the loss. The maximum loss that could be incurred in a long put option can never exceed the premium paid on the purchase of the put option.

Case 1: When the options expire worthless there is no need to record any entry in the books of accounts. The option premium paid is already treated as an expense, and since the options have no value upon expiration, there is no need to write back the value of the options on the expiry date.

Case 2: When the options expire in-the-money (i.e., when the market rate of the underlying is less than the strike price of the option), then the strike price that exceeds the value of the underlying represents the gain accruing to the investor. However, if the strike price of the option is still below the value of the underlying as increased by the premium paid to acquire the options, the investor will still lose money. Assuming that the underlying shares close at $53 on the expiry date, the accounting entry that is recorded in the books of accounts is shown as follows:

Journal Entry

Date	Particulars	Debit (US$)	Credit (US$)
15-Feb-X1	Sharp & Co. Account	30,000.00	
	To Premium paid on Put Options Account		30,000.00
	(Being the value realized on expiry of put options now reversed to premium account)		

Case 3: The investor makes a profit when the options expire in-the-money, when the market rate of the underlying is more than the strike price of the option by an amount greater than the premium paid for acquiring such options. Assuming that the underlying shares close at $59 on the expiry date, accounting entry that is recorded in the books of accounts is shown as follows:

Journal Entry

Date	Particulars	Debit (US$)	Credit (US$)
15-Feb-X1	Sharp & Co. Account	40,000.00	
	To Profit on Put Options Account		40,000.00
	(Being the profit realized on put options as the options expired more than the original cost of acquisition)		

Exercise of Options

The buyer of the put option has the right but not the obligation to buy the underlying at the strike price. When the put options are exercised, it results in the creation of the underlying asset. In such a scenario, the investor has to pay for the underlying at the contracted strike price. The actual cost of carry of the underlying asset would then be the strike price of the contract and the premium paid on the purchase of the put option. The profit or loss would be arrived at only after the underlying asset is liquidated. Until such time, the asset would be carried in the books at cost. Exercise of options happens only in the case of stock options and not in the case of options on indexes.

Assume that the options are exercised on the date of expiry when the price of the underlying share is $57 and the equity shares are acquired for trading purposes. The accounting entry that is recorded in the books of accounts is shown as follows:

Journal Entry

Date	Particulars	Debit (US$)	Credit (US$)
15-Feb-X1	Investments—Equity Shares—Trading Account	500,000.00	
	To Sharp & Co. Account		500,000.00
	(Being the exercise of 10,000 equity put options of Siemens @ $50 resulting in the acquisition of the shares)		
15-Feb-X1	Investments—Equity Shares—Trading Account	50,000.00	
	To Premium Paid on Put Options Account		50,000.00
	(Being the premium paid on purchase of put options now taken as part of the cost of the underlying asset on exercise of put options)		
15-Feb-X1	Investments—Equity Shares—Trading Account	500.00	
	To Brokerage/Commission Account		500.00
	(Being the brokerage paid on purchase of 10,000 equity put options of Siemens @ $5 now taken to investment account as part of the cost of acquisition of the underlying shares on exercise of put options)		

Sell the Options

The long position of put options could be liquidated by selling the options. Since the sale results in only squaring up of the existing position, there is no requirement for any margin payment to the exchange on account of this sale of put options. The overall open interest could come down on liquidation of the put option if it is purchased by someone who already has a short position. Otherwise the sale of the put option will not result in the shrinkage of open interest.

Assuming that the options are liquidated at $4.20, the accounting entry that is recorded in the books of accounts is shown as follows:

Journal Entry

Date	Particulars	Debit (US$)	Credit (US$)
2-Feb-X1	Sharp & Co. Account	42,000.00	
	To Premium paid on Put Options Account		42,000.00
	(Being the sale of 10,000 equity put options of Siemens @ $4.20)		

Receive the Consideration

The consideration is received on day T + 2 or another date, depending on the exchange concerned. The consideration is received net of brokerage.

The accounting entry that is recorded in the books of accounts is shown as follows:

Journal Entry

Date	Particulars	Debit (US$)	Credit (US$)
2-Feb-X1	Bank Account	42,000.00	
	To Sharp & Co. Account		42,000.00
	(Being receipt of funds on account of the sale of 10,000 equity put options @ $4.20)		

Ascertain the Profit/Loss on the Sale

Since the expense account is debited while purchasing the options, there is no need to record a separate entry to determine the profit or loss on sale of options in this case.

FX Revaluation Entries

All the entries recorded here are initially entered in the respective trade currencies. If the functional currency is different from the trade currency, then each and every entry recorded in the trade currency should be entered again in the functional currency by converting the entries at the respective day's FX rates. In other words, for each trade currency that the investor deals with, there will be a complete set of books representing that trade currency. This includes journal entries, general ledger postings, trial balance, income statement, and balance sheet.

After revaluing each and every journal entry of all the trade currencies into the functional currency, a separate set of books is prepared, again comprising all the elements just mentioned: journal entries, general ledger postings, trial balance, income statement, and balance sheet. It should be noted that the ultimate financial reports would be prepared and presented to all the stakeholders based on the financial statements prepared in the functional currency only, as this will encompass all the transactions of the investor in all trade currencies dabbled with. (For illustration and detailed explanation please refer to Chapter 2.)

FX Revaluation Entries

After revaluing all the entries in the functional currency at the respective FX rates for the day concerned, another entry needs to be passed in the books of the functional currency. This is mainly to adjust the currency gains or losses due to the fluctuations in FX rates between the reporting date and the date of recording the original entries. FX translation entries are recorded only for the asset and liability accounts. For income and expense accounts, the amount gets crystallized on the date of passing the FX revaluation entries in the books of the functional currency.

There are fundamentally two types of FX translation entries that are recorded in the books of the functional currency: consummated FX translation entries and transient FX translation entries. (For illustration and detailed explanation please refer to Chapter 2.)

ILLUSTRATIONS

Long Puts

Konark Fund had the following trades of Lever shares in the options market through Silver Man brokers. The stock exchange requires that the writer of the options maintain 10 percent of the value of the contract as margin money throughout the life of the contract. The fund introduced $100,000 on January 1 as capital. Journal entries, general ledgers, trial balance, income statement, and balance sheet are as follows:

Date	Product	Strike Price	Expiry	Quantity	Rate	B/S	Brokerage
23-Jan-X1	Put	$50	16-Mar-X1	10,000	$5.00	B	$540
23-Feb-X1	Put	$50	16-Mar-X1	8,000	$4.00	B	$440
10-Mar-X1	Put	$50	16-Mar-X1	12,000	$3.00	S	$720

Liquidation Method
FIFO

Market Rate of Underlying Stock, Lloyd
January 31: 40.00
February 28: 55.00
March 16: 55.00

Market Rate of Lloyd Put Option with Strike Price $50, Expiry March 16
January 31: 2.00
February 28: 6.00

Functional Currency
US$

Long Put Options, Non-hedging—Functional Currency

T-1 Introduction of Share Capital into the Fund

Journal Entry

Date	Particulars	Debit (US$)	Credit (US$)
1-Jan-X1	Bank Account	100,000.00	
	To Share Capital Account		100,000.00
	(Being the capital introduced into the fund)		

T-2 On Purchase of Put Options

Journal Entry

Date	Particulars	Debit (US$)	Credit (US$)
23-Jan-X1	Options Premium Paid Account	50,000.00	
	To Silver Man Account		50,000.00
	(Being the purchase of 10,000 equity put options @ $5)		

T-3 Brokerage/Commission

Journal Entry

Date	Particulars	Debit (US$)	Credit (US$)
23-Jan-X1	Brokerage/Commission Account	540.00	
	To Silver Man Account		540.00
	(Being the brokerage incurred on purchase of put options)		

T-4 Payment of Contracted Sum

Journal Entry

Date	Particulars	Debit (US$)	Credit (US$)
23-Jan-X1	Silver Man Account	50,540.00	
	To Bank Account		50,540.00
	(Being the amount paid to the broker on purchase of put options)		

T-5 Market Value at End of Reporting Period

Market value at end of reporting period: 31-Jan-X1	**US$**
Market value of 10,000 share @ $2	20,000.00
Market value in US$	**20,000.00**

Journal Entry

Date	Particulars	Debit (US$)	Credit (US$)
31-Jan-X1	Options Contracts Account	20,000.00	
	To MTM—ETO (P&L) Account		20,000.00
	(Being the mark-to-market value of put options @ $2 each)		

T-6 Reversal of Mark-to-market Value

Journal Entry

Date	Particulars	Debit (US$)	Credit (US$)
1-Feb-X1	MTM—ETO (P&L) Account	20,000.00	
	To Options Contracts Account		20,000.00
	(Being the reversal of mark-to-market value of put options @ $2 each)		

T-7 On Purchase of Put Options

Journal Entry

Date	Particulars	Debit (US$)	Credit (US$)
23-Feb-X1	Options Premium Paid Account	32,000.00	
	To Silver Man Account		32,000.00
	(Being the purchase of 8,000 equity put options @ $4)		

T-8 Brokerage/Commission

Journal Entry

Date	Particulars	Debit (US$)	Credit (US$)
23-Feb-X1	Brokerage/Commission Account	440.00	
	To Silver Man Account		440.00
	(Being the brokerage amount incurred for the purchase of put options)		

T-9 Payment of Contracted Sum

Journal Entry

Date	Particulars	Debit (US$)	Credit (US$)
23-Feb-X1	Silver Man Account	32,440.00	
	To Bank Account		32,440.00
	(Being the amount paid to the broker Silver Man on purchase of put options)		

T-10 Market Value at End of Reporting Period

Market value at end of reporting period: 28-Feb-X1	**US$**
Market value for 18,000 share @ $6	108,000.00
Market value in US$	**108,000.00**

Journal Entry

Date	Particulars	Debit (US$)	Credit (US$)
28-Feb-X1	Options Contracts Account	108,000.00	
	To MTM—ETO (P&L) Account		108,000.00
	(Being the booking of mark-to-market value on 18,000 put options @ $6)		

T-11 Reversal of Mark-to-market Value

Journal Entry

Date	Particulars	Debit (US$)	Credit (US$)
1-Mar-X1	MTM—ETO (P&L) Account	108,000.00	
	To Options Contracts Account		108,000.00
	(Reversal of mark-to-market value of 18,000 put options @ $6)		

T-12 Sale of Put Options

Journal Entry

Date	Particulars	Debit (US$)	Credit (US$)
10-Mar-X1	Silver Man Account	36,000.00	
	To Options Premium Received Account		36,000.00
	(Being the amount receivable from broker on sale of 12,000 equity put options)		

T-13 Brokerage/Commission on Sale

Journal Entry

Date	Particulars	Debit (US$)	Credit (US$)
10-Mar-X1	Brokerage/Commission Account	720.00	
	To Silver Man Account		720.00
	(Being the brokerage incurred on the sale of 12,000 put options)		

T-14 Receipt of Sale Proceeds

Journal Entry

Date	Particulars	Debit (US$)	Credit (US$)
10-Mar-X1	Bank Account	35,280.00	
	To Silver Man Account		35,280.00
	(Being the receipt from broker on sale of put options)		

General Ledger Accounts

Option Contracts Account

Date	Particulars	Debit (US$)	Date	Particulars	Credit (US$)
31-Jan-X1	To MTM—ETO (P&L) Account	20,000.00			
			1-Feb-X1	By MTM—ETO (P&L) Account	20,000.00
28-Feb-X1	To MTM—ETO (P&L) Account	108,000.00			
			1-Mar-X1	By MTM—ETO (P&L) Account	108,000.00
31-Mar-X1	Total	**128,000.00**	31-Mar-X1	Total	**128,000.00**

Brokerage/Commission Account

Date	Particulars	Debit (US$)	Date	Particulars	Credit (US$)
23-Jan-X1	To Silver Man Account	540.00			
23-Feb-X1	To Silver Man Account	440.00			
10-Mar-X1	To Silver Man Account	720.00			
			31-Mar-X1	By Balance	1,700.00
31-Mar-X1	Total	**1,700.00**	31-Mar-X1	Total	**1,700.00**
31-Mar-X1	To Balance	1,700.00			

MTM –ETO (P&L) Account

Date	Particulars	Debit (US$)	Date	Particulars	Credit (US$)
			31-Jan-X1	By Option Contracts Account	20,000.00
1-Feb-X1	To Option Contracts Account	20,000.00			
			28-Feb-X1	By Option Contracts Account	108,000.00
1-Mar-X1	To Option Contracts Account	108,000.00			
31-Mar-X1	Total	**128,000.00**	31-Mar-X1	Total	**128,000.00**

Option Premium Paid Account

Date	Particulars	Debit (US$)	Date	Particulars	Credit (US$)
23-Jan-X1	To Silver Man Account	50,000.00			
23-Feb-X1	To Silver Man Account	32,000.00			
			31-Mar-X1	By Balance	82,000.00
31-Mar-X1	Total	**82,000.00**	31-Mar-X1	Total	**82,000.00**
31-Mar-X1	To Balance	82,000.00			

Option Premium Received Account

Date	Particulars	Debit (US$)	Date	Particulars	Credit (US$)
			10-Mar-X1	By Silver Man Account	36,000.00
31-Mar-X1	To Balance	36,000.00			
31-Mar-X1	Total	**36,000.00**	31-Mar-X1	Total	**36,000.00**
			31-Mar-X1	By Balance	36,000.00

Silver Man Account

Date	Particulars	Debit (US$)	Date	Particulars	Credit (US$)
			23-Jan-X1	By Option Premium Paid Account	50,000.00
			23-Jan-X1	By Brokerage/ Commission Account	540.00
23-Jan-X1	To Bank Account	50,540.00			
			23-Feb-X1	By Option Premium Paid Account	32,000.00
			23-Feb-X1	By Brokerage/ Commission Account	440.00
23-Feb-X1	To Bank Account	32,440.00			
10-Mar-X1	To Option Premium Received Account	36,000.00			
			10-Mar-X1	By Bank Account	35,280.00
			10-Mar-X1	By Brokerage/ Commission Account	720.00
31-Mar-X1	Total	**118,980.00**	31-Mar-X1	Total	**118,980.00**

Equity Share Capital Account

Date	Particulars	Debit (US$)	Date	Particulars	Credit (US$)
			1-Jan-X1	By Bank Account	100,000.00
31-Mar-X1	To Balance	100,000.00			
31-Mar-X1	Total	**100,000.00**	31-Mar-X1	Total	**100,000.00**
			31-Mar-X1	By Balance	100,000.00

Bank Account

Date	Particulars	Debit (US$)	Date	Particulars	Credit (US$)
1-Jan-X1	To Equity Share Capital Account	100,000.00			
			23-Jan-X1	By Silver Man Account	50,540.00
			23-Feb-X1	By Silver Man Account	32,440.00
10-Mar-X1	To Silver Man Account	35,280.00			
			31-Mar-X1	By Balance	52,300.00
31-Mar-X1	Total	**135,280.00**	31-Mar-X1	Total	**135,280.00**
31-Mar-X1	To Balance	52,300.00			

Trial Balance

As of 31-Mar-X1 (US$)

Particulars	Debit	Credit
Capital Account		
Share Capital Account		100,000.00
Current Assets		
Bank Account	52,300.00	
Direct Income		
Option Premium Received Account		36,000.00
Direct Expenses		
Brokerage/Commission Account	1,700.00	
Option Premium Paid Account	82,000.00	
Total	**136,000.00**	**136,000.00**

Income Statement

For the period ending 31-Mar-X1

Expenses	US$	Income	US$
Direct Expenses		**Direct Income**	
Brokerage/Commission Account	1,700.00	Option Premium Received Account	36,000.00
Option Premium Paid Account	82,000.00	Net Loss Carryover	47,700.00
Total	**83,700.00**	Total	**83,700.00**

Balance Sheet

As of 31-Mar-X1

Liabilities	US$	Assets	US$
Capital Account		**Current Assets**	
Share Capital	100,000.00	Bank Account	52,300.00
		Investments	Nil
		Profit & Loss Account	
Current Liabilities	Nil	Opening Balance	Nil
		Current Period	47,700.00
Total	**100,000.00**	Total	**100,000.00**

Long Put Options

Billionaire Fund had the following trades in SingTel shares in the options market through Silver Man brokers. The stock exchange requires that the writer of the options maintain 10 percent of the value of the contract as margin money throughout the life of the contract. On January 1, the fund introduced $200,000 as capital and converted $100,000 into S$ on the same day at a rate of 1.53375. Journal entries, general ledgers, trial balance, income statement, and balance sheet are as follows:

Date	Product	Strike Price	Expiry	Quantity	Rate	B/S	Brokerage
23-Jan-X1	Put	S$50	16-Mar-X1	10,000	S$4.25	B	S$540
23-Feb-X1	Put	S$50	16-Mar-X1	8,000	S$4.00	B	S$440
10-Mar-X1	Put	S$50	16-Mar-X1	15,000	S$4.50	S	S$720

Liquidation Method

FIFO

Market Rate of Underlying Stock, SingTel

January 31: S$40.00
February 28: S$55.00
March 16: S$55.00

Market rate of SingTel Put Option with Strike Price S$50, Expiry 16-Mar-X1

January 31: S$2.00
February 28: S$6.00

Date	FX Rate S$/US$
23-Jan-X1	1.5349
31-Jan-X1	1.5357
23-Feb-X1	1.5307
28-Feb-X1	1.5291
10-Mar-X1	1.5264
31-Mar-X1	1.5171

Long Put, Non-hedging—Trade Currency S$

T-1 On Conversion of US$ into S$

Journal Entry

Date	Particulars	Debit (S$)	Credit (S$)
1-Jan-X1	Bank—S$ Account	153,375.00	
	To Bank Contra Account		153,375.00
	(Being the US$ converted into S$ by FX spot trade @ 1.5337)		

T-2 On Purchase of Put Options

Journal Entry

Date	Particulars	Debit (S$)	Credit (S$)
23-Jan-X1	Options Premium Paid Account	42,500.00	
	To Silver Man Account		42,500.00
	(Being the purchase of 10,000 equity put options @ $4.25)		

T-3 Brokerage/Commission

Journal Entry

Date	Particulars	Debit (S$)	Credit (S$)
23-Jan-X1	Brokerage/Commission Account	540.00	
	To Silver Man Account		540.00
	(Being the brokerage incurred on the purchase of put options)		

T-4 Payment of Contracted Sum

Journal Entry

Date	Particulars	Debit (S$)	Credit (S$)
23-Jan-X1	Silver Man Account	43,040.00	
	To Bank—S$ Account		43,040.00
	(Being the payment made to the broker on purchase of put options)		

T-5 Market Value at End of Reporting Period

Market value at end of reporting period: 31-Jan-X1	**S$**
Market value for 10,000 share @ S$2	20,000.00
Market value in S$	**20,000.00**

Journal Entry

Date	Particulars	Debit (S$)	Credit (S$)
31-Jan-X1	Options Contracts Account	20,000.00	
	To MTM—ETO (P&L)		20,000.00
	(Being the mark-to-market value of 10,000 put options @ $2 each)		

T-6 Reversal of Mark-to-market Value

Journal Entry

Date	Particulars	Debit (S$)	Credit (S$)
1-Feb-X1	MTM—ETO (P&L) Account	20,000.00	
	To Options Contracts Account		20,000.00
	(Reversal of mark-to-market value of 10,000 put options @ $2 each)		

T-7 On Purchase of Put Options

Journal Entry

Date	Particulars	Debit (S$)	Credit (S$)
23-Feb-X1	Options Premium Paid Account	32,000.00	
	To Silver Man Account		32,000.00
	(Being the purchase of 8,000 equity put options @ $4)		

T-8 Brokerage/Commission

Journal Entry

Date	Particulars	Debit (S$)	Credit (S$)
23-Feb-X1	Brokerage/Commission Account	440.00	
	To Silver Man Account		440.00
	(Being the brokerage incurred on purchase of put options)		

T-9 Payment of Contracted Sum

Journal Entry

Date	Particulars	Debit (S$)	Credit (S$)
23-Feb-X1	Silver Man Account	32,440.00	
	To Bank—S$ Account		32,440.00
	(Being the payment made to the broker Silver Man on purchase of put options)		

T-10 Market Value at End of Reporting Period

Market value at end of reporting period: 28-Feb-X1	**S$**
Market value for 18,000 shares @ $6	108,000.00
Market value in S$	**108,000.00**

Journal Entry

Date	Particulars	Debit (S$)	Credit (S$)
28-Feb-X1	Options Contracts Account	108,000.00	
	To MTM—ETO (P&L) Account		108,000.00
	(Being the booking of mark-to-market value of 18,000 put options @ $6)		

T-11 Reversal of Mark-to-market Value

Journal Entry

Date	Particulars	Debit (S$)	Credit (S$)
1-Mar-X1	MTM—ETO (P&L) Account	108,000.00	
	To Options Contracts Account		108,000.00
	(Reversal of mark-to-market value of 18,000 put options @ $6 each)		

T-12 Sale of Put Options

Journal Entry

Date	Particulars	Debit (S$)	Credit (S$)
10-Mar-X1	Silver Man Account	67,500.00	
	To Options Premium Received Account		67,500.00
	(Being the amount receivable from broker on sale of 15,000 put options @ $4.5)		

T-13 Brokerage/Commission on Sale

Journal Entry

Date	Particulars	Debit (S$)	Credit (S$)
10-Mar-X1	Brokerage/Commission Account	720.00	
	To Silver Man Account		720.00
	(Being the brokerage incurred on sale of put options)		

T-14 Receipt of Sale Proceeds

Journal Entry

Date	Particulars	Debit (S$)	Credit (S$)
10-Mar-X1	Bank—S$ Account	66,780.00	
	To Silver Man Account		66,780.00
	(Being the net proceeds received from broker on sale of put options)		

General Ledger Accounts

Option Contracts Account

Date	Particulars	Debit (S$)	Date	Particulars	Credit (S$)
31-Jan-X1	To MTM—ETO (P&L) Account	20,000.00			
			1-Feb-X1	By MTM—ETO (P&L) Account	20,000.00
28-Feb-X1	To MTM—ETO (P&L) Account	108,000.00			
			1-Mar-X1	By MTM—ETO (P&L) Account	108,000.00
31-Mar-X1	Total	**128,000.00**	31-Mar-X1	Total	**128,000.00**

Brokerage/Commission Account

Date	Particulars	Debit (S$)	Date	Particulars	Credit (S$)
23-Jan-X1	To Silver Man Account	540.00			
23-Feb-X1	To Silver Man Account	440.00			
10-Mar-X1	To Silver Man Account	720.00			
			31-Mar-X1	By Balance	1,700.00
31-Mar-X1	Total	**1,700.00**	31-Mar-X1	Total	**1,700.00**
31-Mar-X1	To Balance	1,700.00			

MTM –ETO (P&L) Account

Date	Particulars	Debit (S$)	Date	Particulars	Credit (S$)
			31-Jan-X1	By Option Contracts Account	20,000.00
1-Feb-X1	To Option Contracts Account	20,000.00			
			28-Feb-X1	By Option Contracts Account	108,000.00
1-Mar-X1	To Option Contracts Account	108,000.00			
31-Mar-X1	Total	**128,000.00**	31-Mar-X1	Total	**128,000.00**

Option Premium Paid Account

Date	Particulars	Debit (S$)	Date	Particulars	Credit (S$)
23-Jan-X1	To Silver Man Account	42,500.00			
23-Feb-X1	To Silver Man Account	32,000.00			
			31-Mar-X1	By Balance	74,500.00
31-Mar-X1	Total	**74,500.00**	31-Mar-X1	Total	**74,500.00**
31-Mar-X1	To Balance	74,500.00			

Option Premium Received Account

Date	Particulars	Debit (S$)	Date	Particulars	Credit (S$)
			10-Mar-X1	By Silver Man Account	67,500.00
31-Mar-X1	To Balance	67,500.00			
31-Mar-X1	Total	**67,500.00**	31-Mar-X1	Total	**67,500.00**
			31-Mar-X1	By Balance	67,500.00

Silver Man Account

Date	Particulars	Debit (S$)	Date	Particulars	Credit (S$)
			23-Jan-X1	By Option Premium Paid Account	42,500.00
			23-Jan-X1	By Brokerage/ Commission Account	540.00
23-Jan-X1	To Bank—S$ Account	43,040.00			
			23-Feb-X1	By Option Premium Paid Account	32,000.00

Silver Man Account (*Cont'd*)

Date	Particulars	Debit (S$)	Date	Particulars	Credit (S$)
			23-Feb-X1	By Brokerage/ Commission Account	440.00
23-Feb-X1	To Bank—S$ Account	32,440.00			
10-Mar-X1	To Option Premium Received Account	67,500.00			
			10-Mar-X1	By Brokerage/ Commission Account	720.00
			10-Mar-X1	By Bank—S$ Account	66,780.00
31-Mar-X1	Total	**142,980.00**	31-Mar-X1	Total	**142,980.00**

Bank—S$ Account

Date	Particulars	Debit (S$)	Date	Particulars	Credit (S$)
1-Jan-X1	By Bank Contra Account	153,375.00			
			23-Jan-X1	By Silver Man Account	43,040.00
			23-Feb-X1	By Silver Man Account	32,440.00
10-Mar-X1	To Silver Man Account	66,780.00			
			31-Mar-X1	By Balance	144,675.00
31-Mar-X1	Total	**220,155.00**	31-Mar-X1	Total	**220,155.00**
31-Mar-X1	To Balance	144,675.00			

Bank Contra Account

Date	Particulars	Debit (S$)	Date	Particulars	Credit (S$)
			1-Jan-X1	By Bank—S$ Account	153,375.00
31-Mar-X1	To Balance	153,375.00			
31-Mar-X1	Total	**153,375.00**	31-Mar-X1	Total	**153,375.00**
			31-Mar-X1	By Balance	153,375.00

Trial Balance

As of 31-Mar-X1 (S$)

Particulars	Debit	Credit
Current Assets		
Bank—S$ Account	144,675.00	
Bank Contra Account		153,375.00
Direct Income		
Option Premium Received Account		67,500.00
Direct Expenses		
Brokerage/Commission Account	1,700.00	
Option Premium Paid Account	74,500.00	
Total	**220,875.00**	**220,875.00**

Income Statement

For the period ending 31-Mar-X1

Expenses	S$	Income	S$
Direct Expenses		**Direct Income**	
Brokerage/commission Account	1,700.00	Option Premium Received Account	67,500.00
Option Premium Paid Account	74,500.00	Net Loss Carryover	8,700.00
Total	**76,200.00**	Total	**76,200.00**

Balance Sheet

As of 31-Mar-X1

Liabilities	S$	Assets	S$
Capital Account	Nil	**Current Assets**	
		Bank—S$ Account	144,675.00
Current Liabilities		**Profit & Loss Account**	
Bank Contra Account	153,375.00	Opening Balance	Nil
		Current Period	8,700.00
Total	**153,375.00**	Total	**153,375.00**

Long Put, Non-hedging—Functional Currency US$

The following are the FX revaluation entries in the functional currency converted at the respective FX rate, which is given within parenthesis. FX translation entries are clearly specified, indicating whether each is a consummated FX translation entry or a transient FX translation entry.

F-1 Introducing Capital

Journal Entry

Date	Particulars	Debit (US$)	Credit (US$)
1-Jan-X1	Bank —US$ Account	200,000.00	
	To Share Capital Account		200,000.00
	(Being the capital introduced into the fund)		

F-2 Conversion of US$ into S$

Journal Entry

Date	Particulars	Debit (US$)	Credit (US$)
1-Jan-X1	Bank Contra Account	100,000.00	
	To Bank—US$ Account		100,000.00
	(Being the US$ converted into S$ by FX spot trade @ 1.5337)		

F-3 Conversion of US$ into S$ (T-1 @ FX Rate: 1.5337)

Journal Entry

Date	Particulars	Debit (US$)	Credit (US$)
1-Jan-X1	Bank—S$ Account	100,000.00	
	To Bank Contra Account		100,000.00
	(Being the US$ converted into S$ by FX spot trade @ 1.5337)		

F-4 On Purchase of Put Options (T-2 @ FX Rate: 1.5349)

Journal Entry

Date	Particulars	Debit (US$)	Credit (US$)
23-Jan-X1	Options Premium Paid Account	27,689.10	
	To Silver Man Account		27,689.10
	(Being the purchase of 10,000 put options @ $5)		

F-5 Brokerage/Commission (T-3 @ FX Rate: 1.5349)

Journal Entry

Date	Particulars	Debit (US$)	Credit (US$)
23-Jan-X1	Brokerage/Commission Account	351.81	
	To Silver Man Account		351.81
	(Being the brokerage incurred on purchase of put options)		

F-6 Payment of Contracted Sum (T-4 @ FX Rate: 1.5349)

Journal Entry

Date	Particulars	Debit (US$)	Credit (US$)
23-Jan-X1	Silver Man Account	28,040.91	
	To Bank—S$ Account		28,040.91
	(Being the payment made to the broker Silver Man on purchase of put options)		

F-7 Market Value at End of Reporting Period (T-5 @ FX Rate: 1.5357)

Market value at end of reporting period: 31-Jan-X1	US$
(a) Market value for 10,000 shares @ S$2/1.5357	13,023.38
(b) Market value in US$	**13,023.38**

Journal Entry

Date	Particulars	Debit (US$)	Credit (US$)
31-Jan-X1	Options Contracts Account	13,023.38	
	To MTM—ETO (P&L) Account		13,023.38
	(Being the market value of 10,000 put options @ $2 each)		

F-8 Reversal of Market Value (T-6 @ FX Rate: 1.5357)

Journal Entry

Date	Particulars	Debit (US$)	Credit (US$)
1-Feb-X1	MTM—ETO (P&L) Account	13,023.38	
	To Options Contracts Account		13,023.38
	(Reversal of mark-to-market value of 10,000 put options @ $2 each)		

F-9 On Purchase of Put Options (T-7 @ FX Rate: 1.5307)

Journal Entry

Date	Particulars	Debit (US$)	Credit (US$)
23-Feb-X1	Options Premium Paid Account	20,904.79	
	To Silver Man Account		20,904.79
	(Being the purchase of 8,000 equity put options @ $4)		

F-10 Brokerage/Commission (T-8 @ FX Rate: 1.5307)

Journal Entry

Date	Particulars	Debit (US$)	Credit (US$)
23-Feb-X1	Brokerage/Commission Account	287.44	
	To Silver Man Account		287.44
	Being the brokerage incurred on purchase of put options)		

F-11 Payment of Contracted Sum (T-9 @ FX Rate: 1.5307)

Journal Entry

Date	Particulars	Debit (US$)	Credit (US$)
23-Feb-X1	Silver Man Account	21,192.23	
	To Bank—S$ Account		21,192.23
	(Being the payment made to the broker Silver Man on purchase of put options)		

F-12 Market Value at End of Reporting Period (T-10 @ FX Rate: 1.5291)

Market value at end of reporting period: 28-Feb-X1	**US$**
(a) Market value for 18,000 shares @ S$6/1.5291	70,629.78
(b) Market value in US$	**70,629.78**

Journal Entry

Date	Particulars	Debit (US$)	Credit (US$)
28-Feb-X1	Options Contracts Account	70,629.78	
	To MTM—ETO (P&L) Account		70,629.78
	(Being the booking of market value of 18,000 put options @ $6)		

F-13 Reversal of Mark-to-market Value (T-11 @ FX Rate: 1.5291)

Journal Entry

Date	Particulars	Debit (US$)	Credit (US$)
1-Mar-X1	MTM—ETO (P&L) Account	70,629.78	
	To Options Contracts Account		70,629.78
	(Reversal of mark-to-market value of 18,000 put options @ $6 each)		

F-14 On Sale of Put Options (T-12 @ FX Rate: 1.5264)

Journal Entry

Date	Particulars	Debit (US$)	Credit (US$)
10-Mar-X1	Silver Man Account	44,221.70	
	To Options Premium Received Account		44,221.70
	(Being the amount receivable from broker on sale of put options)		

F-15 Brokerage/Commission on Sale (T-13 @ FX Rate: 1.5264)

Journal Entry

Date	Particulars	Debit (US$)	Credit (US$)
10-Mar-X1	Brokerage/Commission Account	471.70	
	To Silver Man Account		471.70
	(Being the brokerage incurred on sale of put options)		

F-16 Receipt of Sale Proceed (T-14 @ FX Rate: 1.5264)

Journal Entry

Date	Particulars	Debit (US$)	Credit (US$)
10-Mar-X1	Bank—S$ Account	43,750.00	
	To Silver Man Account		43,750.00
	(Being the net proceeds received from broker on sale of 15,000 equity put options)		

F-17 FX Translation on Bank Account (Transient FX translation entry)

S$ Bank Account

Date	Description	S$	FX rate	US$
1-Jan-X1	Opening balance	153,375.00	1.5337	100,000.00
23-Jan- X1	Payment for put	(43,040.00)	1.5349	(28,040.90)
23-Feb- X1	Payment for put	(32,440.00)	1.5307	(21,192.90)
10-Mar- X1	Proceeds from selling put	66,780.00	1.5264	43,750.00
				94,516.17
	FX difference (Gains)			**846.70**
31-Mar- X1	Closing balance	**144,675.00**	**1.5171**	**95,362.86**

Journal Entry

Date	Particulars	Debit (US$)	Credit (US$)
31-Mar-X1	Bank—S$ Account	846.70	
	To Unrealized Currency Gains/Loss Account		846.70
	(Being the FX translation applied on bank account)		

General Ledger Accounts

Option Contracts Account

Date	Particulars	Debit (US$)	Date	Particulars	Credit (US$)
31-Jan-X1	To MTM—ETO (P&L) Account	13,023.38			
			1-Feb-X1	By MTM—ETO (P&L) Account	13,023.38
28-Feb-X1	To MTM—ETO (P&L) Account	70,629.78			
			1-Mar-X1	By MTM—ETO (P&L) Account	70,629.78
31-Mar-X1	Total	**83,653.16**	31-Mar-X1	Total	**83,653.16**

Brokerage/Commission Account

Date	Particulars	Debit (US$)	Date	Particulars	Credit (US$)
23-Jan-X1	To Silver Man Account	351.81			
23-Feb-X1	To Silver Man Account	287.44			
10-Mar-X1	To Silver Man Account	471.70			
			31-Mar-X1	By Balance	1,110.95
31-Mar-X1	Total	**1,110.95**	31-Mar-X1	Total	**1,110.95**
31-Mar-X1	To Balance	1,110.95			

Unrealized Currency Gains/Loss Account

Date	Particulars	Debit (US$)	Date	Particulars	Credit (US$)
			31-Mar-X1	By Bank S$ Account	846.70
31-Mar-X1	To Balance	846.70			
31-Mar-X1	Total	**846.70**	31-Mar-X1	Total	**846.70**
			31-Mar-X1	By Balance	846.70

MTM –ETO (P&L) Account

Date	Particulars	Debit (US$)	Date	Particulars	Credit (US$)
			31-Jan-X1	By Option Contracts Account	13,023.38
1-Feb-X1	To Option Contracts Account	13,023.38			
			28-Feb-X1	By Option Contracts Account	70,629.78
1-Mar-X1	To Option Contracts Account	70,629.78			
31-Mar-X1	Total	**83,653.16**	31-Mar-X1	Total	**83,653.16**

Option Premium Paid Account

Date	Particulars	Debit (US$)	Date	Particulars	Credit (US$)
23-Jan-X1	To Silver Man Account	27,689.10			
23-Feb-X1	To Silver Man Account	20,904.79			
			31-Mar-X1	By Balance	48,593.89
31-Mar-X1	Total	**48,593.89**	31-Mar-X1	Total	**48,593.89**
31-Mar-X1	To Balance	48,593.89			

Option Premium Received Account

Date	Particulars	Debit (US$)	Date	Particulars	Credit (US$)
			10-Mar-X1	By Silver Man Account	44,221.70
31-Mar-X1	To Balance	44,221.70			
31-Mar-X1	Total	**44,221.70**	31-Mar-X1	Total	**44,221.70**
			31-Mar-X1	By Balance	44,221.70

Share Capital Account

Date	Particulars	Debit (US$)	Date	Particulars	Credit (US$)
			1-Jan-X1	By Bank US$ Account	200,000.00
31-Mar-X1	To Balance	200,000.00			
31-Mar-X1	Total	**200,000.00**	31-Mar-X1	Total	**200,000.00**
			31-Mar-X1	By Balance	200,000.00

Silver Man Account

Date	Particulars	Debit (US$)	Date	Particulars	Credit (US$)
			23-Jan-X1	By Option Premium Paid Account	27,689.10
			23-Jan-X1	By Brokerage/ Commission Account	351.81
23-Jan-X1	To Bank—S$ Account	28,040.91			
			23-Feb-X1	By Option Premium Paid Account	20,904.79
			23-Feb-X1	By Brokerage/ Commission Account	287.44
23-Feb-X1	To Bank—S$ Account	21,192.23			
10-Mar-X1	To Option Premium Received Account	44,221.70			
			10-Mar-X1	By Brokerage/ Commission Account	471.70
			10-Mar-X1	By Bank—S$ Account	43,750.00
31-Mar-X1	Total	**93,454.84**	31-Mar-X1	Total	**93,454.84**

Bank US$ Account

Date	Particulars	Debit (US$)	Date	Particulars	Credit (US$)
1-Jan-X1	To Share Capital Account	200,000.00			
			1-Jan-X1	By Bank Contra Account	100,000.00
			31-Mar-X1	By Balance	100,000.00
31-Mar-X1	Total	**200,000.00**	31-Mar-X1	Total	**200,000.00**
31-Mar-X1	To Balance	100,000.00			

Bank Contra Account

Date	Particulars	Debit (US$)	Date	Particulars	Credit (US$)
1-Jan-X1	To Bank US$ Account	100,000.00			
			1-Jan-X1	By Bank S$ Account	100,000.00
31-Mar-X1	Total	**100,000.00**	31-Mar-X1	Total	**100,000.00**

Bank—S$ Account

Date	Particulars	Debit (US$)	Date	Particulars	Credit (US$)
1-Jan-X1	To Bank Contra Account	100,000.00			
			23-Jan-X1	By Silver Man Account	28,040.91
			23-Feb-X1	By Silver Man Account	21,192.23
10-Mar-X1	To Silver Man Account	43,750.00			
31-Mar-X1	To Unrealized Currency Gains/Loss Account	846.70			
			31-Mar-X1	By Balance	95,363.56
31-Mar-X1	Total	**144,596.70**	31-Mar-X1	Total	**144,596.70**
31-Mar-X1	To Balance	95,363.56			

Trial Balance

As of 31-Mar-X1 (US$)

Particulars	Debit	Credit
Capital Account		
Share Capital Account		200,000.00
Current Liabilities		
Current Assets		
Bank—S$ Account	95,363.56	
Bank US$ Account	100,000.00	
Direct Income		
Unrealized Currency Gains/Loss Account		846.70
Option Premium Received Account		44,221.70
Direct Expenses		
Brokerage/Commission Account	1,110.95	
Option Premium Paid Account	48,593.89	
Total	**245,068.40**	**245,068.40**

Income Statement

For the period ending 31-Mar-X1

Expenses	US$	Income	US$
Direct Expenses		**Direct Income**	
Brokerage/commission Account	1,110.95	Unrealized Currency Gains/Loss Account	846.70
Option Premium Paid Account	48,593.89	Option Premium Received Account	44,221.70
		Net Loss Carryover	4,636.44
Total	**49,704.84**	Total	**49,704.84**

Balance Sheet

As of 31-Mar-X1

Liabilities	US$	Assets	US$
Capital Account		**Investments**	Nil
Equity Share Capital	200,000.00	**Current Assets**	
Current Liabilities		Bank US$ Account	100,000.00
		Bank—S$ Account	95,363.56
		Profit & Loss Account	
		Opening Balance	Nil
		Current Period	4,636.44
Total	**200,000.00**	Total	**200,000.00**

TRADE LIFE CYCLE FOR EXCHANGE-TRADED OPTIONS—ON WRITING A PUT OPTION

- Deposit the margin on options to the exchange.
- Writing the put options.
- Brokerage/commission on the transaction.
- Receive the premium on the put options sold.
- Ascertain the fair value at the end of reporting period.
- Margin call.
- Expiry of options.
- Exercise of options.
- Buy back the put options.
- Ascertain the profit/loss on the sale.
- Get back the deposit of margin money.
- FX revaluation entries.
- FX translation entries.

Deposit the Margin on Options

Margin is payable to the exchange if the investor writes the option. For exchange-traded options (ETOs), since the stock exchange has the responsibility of ensuring that both the legs of the transaction are complete, the exchange would insist that the writer of the option deposit a percentage of the value of the contract as margin money. This is because the writer of an option has potentially unlimited risk. The margin money would be adjusted against any reduction in the marked-to-market valuation on a daily basis.

Margin is in effect a good faith deposit. Normally a deposit of about 5 to 10 percent of the total value of the contract would signify the investor's willingness to stand good on any price movements against the seller of an options contract. The percentage of deposit would be smaller for index options and higher for stock options. Since it is merely a deposit, the investor would get the margin money back after the contract is liquidated.

Assume that an investor wants to sell 1,000 put options on an index at $6, strike price being $70, and the stock exchange insists on an up-front margin of 10 percent of the value of the contract from a writer of the options. Expiry of the contract is December 16 and the broker is Kingston Bros. The margin payable to the exchange through the broker would be 10 percent of $70,000, or $7,000. The accounting entry that is recorded in the books of accounts is shown as follows:

Journal Entry

Date	Particulars	Debit (US$)	Credit (US$)
8-Nov-X1	Put Options Margin Account	7,000.00	
	To Kingston Bros Account		7,000.00
	(Being the margin payable to the stock exchange through the broker @ 10% of the value of the contract on sale of 1,000 put options on Index @ $6)		

Writing the Put Options

If the investor writes a put option, then the investor collects the premium. The premium is normally credited to the margin account already available with the counterparty on the settlement date of the option contract.

The accounting entry that is recorded in the books of accounts is shown as follows:

Journal Entry

Date	Particulars	Debit (US$)	Credit (US$)
8-Nov-X1	Put Options Margin Account	6,000.00	
	To Premium Received on Put Options Account		6,000.00
	(Being the premium received on sale of 1,000 put options @ $6)		

Brokerage/Commission on Sale of Options

The broker charges a commission for the services rendered. For option contracts, the brokerage/commission is not treated as a reduction from the sale consideration of the options contract but instead it is debited to the brokerage/commission account.

Assume that the brokerage payable is $300 for this deal. The accounting entry that is recorded in the books of accounts is shown as follows:

Journal Entry

Date	Particulars	Debit (US$)	Credit (US$)
8-Nov-X1	Brokerage/Commission Account	300.00	
	To Kingston Bros. Account		300.00
	(Being the brokerage payable on sale of index put options @ $6)		

Ascertain the Fair Value at the End of the Reporting Period

At the end of every reporting period the fair value of the options is ascertained and the options contracts are marked-to-market. This process is known as portfolio valuation, when the market rate at the end of the period is determined from the primary stock exchange where the underlying shares are traded. If there is a decrease in the market rate, below the sale rate, then such decrease is recognized as a gain on the one hand, and the corresponding amount is reflected as a decrease in the liability on account of such options. This accounting entry is reversed on the next day or the next valuation date when a fresh entry for the then value is recorded in the books of accounts.

Alternatively, the accounting entry can be recorded only for the incremental value. If the investor follows this incremental value method then there is no need to reverse the entry for mark-to-market recorded earlier.

Assuming that the market rate of the put options as of November 30, which is the next valuation date, is $8, then the accounting entry that is recorded in the books of accounts is as follows:

Journal Entry

Date	Particulars	Debit (US$)	Credit (US$)
30-Nov-X1	MTM—Put Options Account	8,000.00	
	To Option Contract Account		8,000.00
	(Being the market value of 1,000 equity put options of Metadata @ $8)		

Margin Call on Options

If the margin money gets eroded due to unfavorable price movement for the investor, then the exchange would initiate margin call. This is to ensure that the exchange does not get caught unawares if there is a wide fluctuation in the value of the underlying, causing severe loss to the investor. The stock exchange would ensure that there is sufficient margin money to take care of this.

Assuming that on November 30, the price of the put options shoots up to $20, then the stock exchange would initiate margin call to compensate the erosion in the margin account of the investor. The margin amount paid initially amounting to $7,000 would be completely eroded by this unfavorable price movement to the investor. The investor would be required to pay an amount equal to 10 percent of the value of the position after such price movement in addition to the potential loss as of that date.

In this case, assume that the value of the underlying has moved from $65 on the date of sale of the put options to $95, resulting in the price of the put option going up to $20. The potential loss as of the date in this case is $14,000 and the 10 percent margin based on the value of the position would be $9,500. The investor should bring in $16,000 on this date to compensate the adverse price movement.

The accounting entry that is recorded in the books of accounts is shown as follows:

Journal Entry

Date	Particulars	Debit (US$)	Credit (US$)
30-Nov-X1	Put Options Margin Account	16,000.00	
	To Bank Account		16,000.00
	(Being the margin payable on account of the margin put initiated by the stock exchange)		

Expiry of Options

The options expire on the expiry date of the contract. For put options that are written, the excess amount of the market value of the underlying over and above the strike price of the options represents the loss for the investor. In such case, the put option is said to expire in-the-money. Conversely, if the put options expire out-of-the-money—that is, if the market value of the underlying is less than the strike price of the option—then the premium received by the investor represents the profit. The maximum profit that could be earned by the investor shorting a put option can never exceed the premium received on the sale of the put option.

Case I: When the options expire worthless there is no need to record any entry in the books of accounts. The option premium paid is already treated as an income, and since the options have no value at expiration there is no need to record any other entry on the expiry date.

Case II: When the options expire in-the-money—that is, when the market rate of the underlying is more than the strike price of the option—then the value of the underlying that exceeds the strike price represents the loss accruing to the investor. Assuming that the underlying shares close at $74 on the expiry date, the accounting entry that is recorded in the books of accounts is shown as follows:

Journal Entry

Date	Particulars	Debit (US$)	Credit (US$)
15-Dec-X1	Loss on Put Options Account	4,000.00	
	To Kingston Bros. Account		4,000.00
	(Being the loss on expiry of put options)		

Case III: The investor takes a loss when the options expire in-the-money by an amount less than the premium received on sale of such options. Assuming that the underlying shares close at $79 on the expiry date, the accounting entry that is recorded in the books of accounts is shown as follows:

Journal Entry

Date	Particulars	Debit (US$)	Credit (US$)
15-Dec-X1	Loss on Put Options Account	9,000.00	
	To Kingston Bros. Account		9,000.00
	(Being the loss on expiry of put options)		

Exercise of Options

The seller of the put option has the obligation to deliver the underlying at the strike price, if exercised by the buyer of the option. Exercising the put options results in the delivery of the underlying asset. In such a scenario, the investor has to deliver the underlying at the contracted strike price. The actual realization of the underlying asset would then be the strike price of the contract as increased by the premium received on the sale of the put option.

Exercise of options happens only in the case of stock options and not in the case of options on indexes. Assume that the options are exercised on the date of expiry when the price of the underlying share is $80 and the equity shares are held for trading purposes. The accounting entry that is recorded in the books of accounts is shown as follows:

Journal Entry

Date	Particulars	Debit (US$)	Credit (US$)
15-Dec-X1	Kingston Bros. Account	70,000.00	
	To Investments—Equity Shares—Trading Account		70,000.00
	(Being the exercise of 1,000 equity put options resulting in the sale of the shares)		
15-Dec-X1	Premium received on Put Options Account	6,000.00	
	To Investments—Equity Shares—Trading Account		6,000.00
	(Being the premium received on sale of put options now taken as part of the revenue realized on exercise of put options)		
15-Dec-X1	Investments—Equity Shares—Trading Account	500.00	
	To Brokerage/Commission Account		500.00
	(Being the brokerage paid on sale of 1,000 equity put options now taken to investment account as part of the cost of acquisition of the underlying shares on exercise of put options)		

Buy Back the Put Options

The short position of put options could be liquidated by buying back such options. The buyback results in squaring up of the existing short position. The overall open interest could come down if the put options are purchased by someone who already has a short position. Assuming that the put options are bought back at $9 per option, then the accounting entry that is recorded in the books of accounts is shown as follows:

Journal Entry

Date	Particulars	Debit (US$)	Credit (US$)
10-Dec-X1	Premium paid on Put Options Account	9,000.00	
	To Put Options Margin Account		9,000.00
	(Being the purchase of 1,000 equity put options)		

Ascertain the Profit/Loss on the Buyback

Since the premium received and the premium paid are directly accounted for as income and expense, respectively, there is no need to record any separate entry to ascertain the profit or loss on the buyback of the option contract.

Get Back the Deposit of Margin Money

Once the short positions are squared off, the exchange would automatically release the margin money to the investor concerned. The entire amount lying to the debit of the put options margin account will be returned to the investor.

The accounting entry that is recorded in the books of accounts is shown as follows:

Journal Entry

Date	Particulars	Debit (US$)	Credit (US$)
15-Dec-X1	Bank Account	24,000.00	
	To Put Options Margin Account		24,000.00
	(Being the Put Options Margin Account balance received from the broker on squaring off the entire position)		

FX Revaluation Entries

All the entries recorded here are initially entered in the respective trade currencies. If the functional currency is different from the trade currency, then each and every entry recorded in the trade currency should be entered again in the functional currency by converting the entries at the respective day's FX rates. In other words, for each trade currency that the investor deals with, there will be a complete set of books representing that trade currency. This includes journal entries, general ledger postings, trial balance, income statement, and balance sheet.

After revaluing each and every journal entry of all the trade currencies into the functional currency, a separate set of books is prepared again comprising all the elements just mentioned: journal entries, general ledger postings, trial balance, income statement, and balance sheet. It should be noted that the ultimate financial reports would be prepared and presented to all the stakeholders based on the financial statements prepared in the functional currency only, as this will encompass all the transactions of the investor in all trade currencies dabbled with. (For illustration and detailed explanation please refer to Chapter 2.)

FX Revaluation Entries

After revaluing all the entries in the functional currency at the respective FX rates for the day concerned, another entry needs to be passed in the books of the functional currency. This is mainly to adjust the currency gains or losses due to the fluctuations in FX rates between the reporting date and the date of recording the original entries. FX translation entries are recorded only for the asset and liability accounts. For income and expense accounts the amount gets crystallized on the date of passing the FX revaluation entries in the books of the functional currency.

There are fundamentally two types of FX translation entries that are recorded in the books of the functional currency: consummated FX translation entries and transient FX translation entries. (For illustration and detailed explanation please refer to Chapter 2.)

ILLUSTRATIONS

Writing Put Options

Konark Fund had the following trades in Lever in the options market through Silver Man brokers. The stock exchange requires that the writer of the options maintain 10 percent of the value of the contract as margin money throughout the life of the contract. On January 23 the fund introduced $100,000 as capital. Journal entries, general ledgers, trial balance, income statement, and balance sheet are as follows:

Date	Product	Strike Price	Expiry	Quantity	Rate	B/S	Brokerage
23-Jan-X1	Put	$50	16-Mar-X1	7,000	$6.00	S	$540
23-Feb-X1	Put	$50	16-Mar-X1	10,000	$5.50	S	$440
10-Mar-X1	Put	$50	16-Mar-X1	12,000	$4.50	B	$720

Liquidation Method

FIFO

Market Rate of Underlying Stock, Lever

January 31: 40.00
February 28: 55.00
March 16: 55.00

Market Rate of Lever Put Option with Strike Price $50, Expiry March 16

January 31: 2.00
February 28: 6.00

Short Put Options—Functional Currency US$

T-1 Capital Brought In

Journal Entry

Date	Particulars	Debit (US$)	Credit (US$)
23-Jan-X1	Bank Account	100,000.00	
	To Share Capital Account		100,000.00
	(Being capital brought into the fund)		

T-2 Margin Payment

Journal Entry

Date	Particulars	Debit (US$)	Credit (US$)
23-Jan-X1	Options Margin Account	35,000.00	
	To Bank Account		35,000.00
	(Being the margin money paid on sale of 7,000 equity put options)		

T-3 Sale of Put Options

Journal Entry

Date	Particulars	Debit (US$)	Credit (US$)
23-Jan-X1	Options Margin Account	42,000.00	
	To Options Premium Received Account		42,000.00
	(Being the options premium received on sale of 7,000 equity put options @ $6)		

T-4 Brokerage/Commission

Journal Entry

Date	Particulars	Debit (US$)	Credit (US$)
23-Jan-X1	Brokerage/Commission Account	540.00	
	To Silver Man Account		540.00
	(Being the brokerage incurred on sale of put options)		

T-5 Payment of Brokerage

Journal Entry

Date	Particulars	Debit (US$)	Credit (US$)
23-Jan-X1	Silver Man Account	540.00	
	To Bank Account		540.00
	(Being the brokerage paid on sale of 10,000 put options)		

T-6 Market Value at End of Reporting Period

Market value at end of reporting period: 31-Jan-X1	US$
(a) Market value for 7,000 share @ $2	14,000.00
(b) Market value in US$	**14,000.00**

Journal Entry

Date	Particulars	Debit (US$)	Credit (US$)
31-Jan-X1	MTM—ETO (P&L) Account	14,000.00	
	To Option Contracts Account		14,000.00
	(Being the mark-to-market value of 7,000 put options @ $2 each)		

T-7 Reversal of Mark-to-market Value of Options

Journal Entry

Date	Particulars	Debit (US$)	Credit (US$)
1-Feb-X1	Option Contracts Account	14,000.00	
	To MTM—ETO (P&L) Account		14,000.00
	(Being the reversal of mark-to-market value on 7,000 put options @ $2)		

T-8 Margin Payment

Journal Entry

Date	Particulars	Debit (US$)	Credit (US$)
23-Feb-X1	Options Margin Account	50,000.00	
	To Bank Account		50,000.00
	(Being the margin money paid on sale of 10,000 equity put options)		

T-9 Sale of Put Options

Journal Entry

Date	Particulars	Debit (US$)	Credit (US$)
23-Feb-X1	Options Margin Account	55,000.00	
	To Options Premium Received Account		55,000.00
	(Being the sale of 10,000 equity put options @ $5.50)		

T-10 Brokerage/Commission

Journal Entry

Date	Particulars	Debit (US$)	Credit (US$)
23-Feb-X1	Brokerage/Commission Account	440.00	
	To Silver Man Account		440.00
	(Being the brokerage incurred on the sale of put options)		

T-11 Payment of Brokerage

Journal Entry

Date	Particulars	Debit (US$)	Credit (US$)
23-Feb-X1	Silver Man Account	440.00	
	To Bank Account		440.00
	(Being the brokerage paid on sale of 7,000 put options)		

T-12 Market Value at End of Reporting Period

Market value at end of reporting period: 28-Feb-X1	**US$**
(a) Market value for 17,000 share @ $6	102,000.00
(b) Market value in US$	**102,000.00**

Journal Entry

Date	Particulars	Debit (US$)	Credit (US$)
28-Feb-X1	MTM—ETO (P&L) Account	102,000.00	
	To Option Contracts Account		102,000.00
	(Being the booking of mark-to-market value for 17,000 put options @ $6)		

T-13 Reversal of Mark-to-market Value of Options

Journal Entry

Date	Particulars	Debit (US$)	Credit (US$)
1-Mar-X1	Option Contracts Account	102,000.00	
	To MTM—ETO (P&L) Account		102,000.00
	(Being for reversal of mark-to-market value)		

T-14 On Purchase of Put Options

Journal Entry

Date	Particulars	Debit (US$)	Credit (US$)
10-Mar-X1	Options Premium Paid Account	54,000.00	
	To Options Margin Account		54,000.00
	(Being the amount paid on account of buy of 12,000 equity put options @ 4.5)		

T-15 Brokerage/Commission on Purchase

Journal Entry

Date	Particulars	Debit (US$)	Credit (US$)
10-Mar-X1	Brokerage/Commission Account	720.00	
	To Silver Man Account		720.00
	(Being the brokerage incurred on purchase of 12,000 put options)		

T-16 Payment of Brokerage

Journal Entry

Date	Particulars	Debit (US$)	Credit (US$)
10-Mar-X1	Silver Man Account	720.00	
	To Bank Account		720.00
	(Being the brokerage paid on purchase of 12,000 put options)		

T-17 Refund of Margin

Journal Entry

Date	Particulars	Debit (US$)	Credit (US$)
16-Mar-X1	Bank Account	128,000.00	
	To Options Margin Account		128,000.00
	(Being the refund of margin on closing short positions)		

General Ledger Accounts

Option Contracts Account

Date	Particulars	Debit (US$)	Date	Particulars	Credit (US$)
			31-Jan-X1	By MTM—ETO (P&L) Account	14,000.00
1-Feb-X1	To MTM—ETO (P&L) Account	14,000.00			
			28-Feb-X1	By MTM—ETO (P&L) Account	102,000.00
1-Mar-X1	To MTM—ETO (P&L) Account	102,000.00			
31-Mar-X1	Total	**116,000.00**	31-Mar-X1	Total	**116,000.00**

Brokerage/Commission Account

Date	Particulars	Debit (US$)	Date	Particulars	Credit (US$)
23-Jan-X1	To Silver Man Account	540.00			
23-Feb-X1	To Silver Man Account	440.00			
10-Mar-X1	To Silver Man Account	720.00			
			31-Mar-X1	By Balance	1,700.00
31-Mar-X1	Total	**1,700.00**	31-Mar-X1	Total	**1,700.00**
31-Mar-X1	To Balance	1,700.00			

MTM–ETO (P&L) Account

Date	Particulars	Debit (US$)	Date	Particulars	Credit (US$)
31-Jan-X1	To Option Contracts Account	14,000.00			
			1-Feb-X1	By Option Contracts Account	14,000.00
28-Feb-X1	To Option Contracts Account	102,000.00			
			1-Mar-X1	By Option Contracts Account	102,000.00
31-Mar-X1	Total	**116,000.00**	31-Mar-X1	Total	**116,000.00**

Option Margin Account

Date	Particulars	Debit (US$)	Date	Particulars	Credit (US$)
23-Jan-X1	To Bank Account	35,000.00			
23-Jan-X1	To Option Premium Received Account	42,000.00			
23-Feb-X1	To Bank Account	50,000.00			
23-Feb-X1	To Option Premium Received Account	55,000.00			
			10-Mar-X1	By Option Premium Paid Account	54,000.00
			16-Mar-X1	By Bank Account	128,000.00
31-Mar-X1	Total	**182,000.00**	31-Mar-X1	Total	**182,000.00**

Option Premium Paid Account

Date	Particulars	Debit (US$)	Date	Particulars	Credit (US$)
10-Mar-X1	To Option Margin Account	54,000.00			
			31-Mar-X1	By Balance	54,000.00
31-Mar-X1	Total	**54,000.00**	31-Mar-X1	Total	**54,000.00**
31-Mar-X1	To Balance	54,000.00			

Option Premium Received Account

Date	Particulars	Debit (US$)	Date	Particulars	Credit (US$)
			23-Jan-X1	By Option Margin Account	42,000.00
			23-Feb-X1	By Option Margin Account	55,000.00
31-Mar-X1	To Balance	97,000.00			
31-Mar-X1	Total	**97,000.00**	31-Mar-X1	Total	**97,000.00**
			31-Mar-X1	By Balance	97,000.00

Share Capital Account

Date	Particulars	Debit (US$)	Date	Particulars	Credit (US$)
			23-Jan-X1	By Bank Account	100,000.00
31-Mar-X1	To Balance	100,000.00			
31-Mar-X1	Total	**100,000.00**	31-Mar-X1	Total	**100,000.00**
			31-Mar-X1	By Balance	100,000.00

Silver Man Account

Date	Particulars	Debit (US$)	Date	Particulars	Credit (US$)
			23-Jan-X1	By Brokerage/ Commission Account	540.00
23-Jan-X1	To Bank Account	540.00			
			23-Feb-X1	By Brokerage/ Commission Account	440.00
23-Feb-X1	To Bank Account	440.00			
			10-Mar-X1	By Brokerage/ Commission Account	720.00
10-Mar-X1	To Bank Account	720.00			
31-Mar-X1	Total	**1,700.00**	31-Mar-X1	Total	**1,700.00**

Bank Account

Date	Particulars	Debit (US$)	Date	Particulars	Credit (US$)
23-Jan-X1	To Share Capital Account	100,000.00			
			23-Jan-X1	By Option Margin Account	35,000.00
			23-Jan-X1	By Silver Man Account	540.00
			23-Feb-X1	By Silver Man Account	440.00
			23-Feb-X1	By Option Margin Account	50,000.00
			10-Mar-X1	By Silver Man Account	720.00
16-Mar-X1	To Option Margin Account	128,000.00			
			31-Mar-X1	To Balance	141,300.00
31-Mar-X1	Total	**228,000.00**	31-Mar-X1	Total	**228,000.00**
31-Mar-X1	To Balance	141,300.00			

Trial Balance

As of 31-Mar-X1 (US$)

Particulars	Debit	Credit
Capital Account		
Share Capital		100,000.00
Current Assets		
Bank Account	141,300.00	
Direct Income		
Option Premium Received Account		97,000.00
Direct Expenses		
Brokerage/Commission Account	1,700.00	
Option Premium Paid Account	54,000.00	
Total	**197,000.00**	**197,000.00**

Income Statement

For the period ending 31-Mar-X1

Expenses	US$	Income	US$
Direct Expenses		**Direct Income**	
Brokerage/Commission Account	1,700.00	MTM—ETO (P&L) Account	
Option Premium Paid Account	54,000.00	Option Premium Received Account	97,000.00
Net Profit Carryover	41,300.00		
Total	**97,000.00**	Total	**97,000.00**

Balance Sheet

As of 31-Mar-X1

Liabilities	US$	Assets	US$
Capital Account		**Investments**	Nil
Share Capital Account	100,000.00		
Current Liabilities	Nil	**Current Assets**	
Profit & Loss Account		Bank Account	141,300.00
Opening Balance	Nil		
Current Period	41,300.00		
Total	**141,300.00**	Total	**141,300.00**

SUMMARY

- The accounting treatment of put options *prima facie* will depend upon the intention with which the put options are purchased—for hedging or speculation (non-hedging).
- If the position is taken as a hedge against some other position, then the relevant accounting standards for hedge accounting will be applicable, and there are certain conditions that are to be fulfilled for the same.
- If the put option is purchased purely as a speculative trade, then the premium paid towards purchase of the put option is taken to the expense and the premium received on sale of the options is treated as revenue.
- However, the value of the option is written back on the valuation date and shown as an asset in the case of purchase of put options. In effect, the net result of this method of accounting and the one shown earlier for hedging activity would be the same.

EXERCISES

Objective Questions

1. If the put option is purchased for speculative trade, then the premium paid towards purchase is treated as

   a. Income
   b. Expense
   c. Gain
   d. None of the above

2. For put options, the premium received towards sale is treated as

   a. Income
   b. Expense
   c. Gain
   d. None of the above

3. If a put option is purchased purely as a speculative trade, then the premium paid towards purchase of the put option is

   a. Treated as revenue
   b. Treated as margin
   c. Treated as an asset
   d. Treated as an expense
   e. Treated as part of the cost

4. For exchange-traded options, since the stock exchange has the responsibility of ensuring that both the legs of the transaction are complete, the exchange would insist that the writer of the option

   a. Deposit the total value of the contract amount as collateral
   b. Pay a percentage value of the contract amount as premium

c. Deposit a percentage value of the contract amount as margin
d. Pay a percentage value of the brokerage amount as premium
e. Receive the margin amount from the counterparty

5. Assuming an investor writes a put option, he need not pay the brokerage because he is actually selling an option. Which of the following statements justifies that the above context is true or false?

   a. True—since the investor receives a premium amount, he should receive the brokerage
   b. False—the investor has to pay the commission to the exchange
   c. True—because there are no brokers in between, no brokerage has to be paid
   d. False—since the trade is exercised through a broker, the investor has to pay the commission
   e. None of the above

Journal Questions

For each of the following scenarios, prepare journal entries, general ledger, trial balance, income statement, and balance sheet.

Long Put, Non-hedging—Functional Currency US$

Cloud Fund had the following trades in Sun in the options market through David Brother Brokers. The stock exchange requires that the writer of the options maintain 10 percent of the value of the contract as margin money throughout the life of the contract. On January 1, Cloud Fund introduced $100,000 as capital.

Date	Product	Strike Price	Expiry	Quantity	Rate	B/S	Brokerage
20-Jan-X1	Put	$50	16-Mar-X1	12,000	$5.00	B	$450
24-Feb-X1	Put	$50	16-Mar-X1	14,000	$4.00	B	$600
12-Mar-X1	Put	$50	16-Mar-X1	15,000	$4.00	S	$400

Liquidation Method
FIFO

Market Rate of Underlying Stock, Sun
January 31: 48.00
February 28: 43.00
March 16: 55.00

Market Rate of Sun Put Option with Strike Price $50, expiry March 16
January 31: 2.00
February 28: 6.00

Long Put, Non-hedging—Trade Currency S$

Cerebros Fund had the following trades in ABB in the options market through James Brothers Brokers. The stock exchange requires that the writer of the options maintain 10 percent of the value of the contract as margin money throughout the life of the contract. On January 1, Cerebros introduced $125,000 as capital.

Date	Product	Strike Price	Expiry	Quantity	Rate (S$)	B/S	Brokerage (S$)
20-Jan-X1	Put	S$ 50	17-Mar-X1	15,000	9.00	B	600
22-Feb-X1	Put	S$ 50	17-Mar-X1	12,000	5.00	B	520
12-Mar-X1	Put	S$ 50	17-Mar-X1	14,000	6.00	S	700

Liquidation Method

FIFO

Market Rate of Underlying Stock, ABB

January 31: 48.00
February 28: 44.00
March 16: 55.00

Market Rate of ABB Put Option with Strike Price $50, Expiry March 17

January 31: 3.00
February 28: 5.00

FX Rate S$/US$

January 20: 1.5210
January 31: 1.532
February 22: 1.4956
February 28: 1.500
March 12: 1.5148
March 17: 1.5463

Short Put, Non-hedging—Trade Currency INR

ABC Fund had the following trades in Andhra Bank in the options market through Silver Man brokers. The stock exchange requires that the writer of the options maintain 10 percent of the value of the contract as margin money throughout the life of the contract. On January 3, ABC Fund introduced $200,000 as capital and converted $100,000 into INR at 42.5 on the same date.

Date	Product	Strike Price	Expiry	Quantity	Rate (INR)	B/S	Brokerage (INR)
23-Jan-X1	Put	INR 50	16-Mar-X1	10,000	5.00	S	540
23-Feb-X1	Put	INR 50	16-Mar-X1	16,000	4.00	S	620
10-Mar-X1	Put	INR 50	16-Mar-X1	16,000	3.00	B	320

Liquidation Method

FIFO

Market Rate of Underlying Stock, Andhra Bank

January 31: 49.00
February 28: 44.00
March 16: 55.00

Market Rate of Andhra Bank Put Option with Strike Price $50, Expiry March 16
January 31: 2.00
February 28: 6.00

FX Rate INR/US$
January 23: 42.56
January 31: 43.56
February 23: 42.86
February 28: 44.00
March 10: 41.56
March 16: 42.00

Short Put, Non-hedging—Trade Currency S$

Billionaire Fund had the following trades in SingTel shares in the options market through ASC Man brokers. The stock exchange requires that the writer of the options maintain 10 percent of the value of the contract as margin money throughout the life of the contract. On September 23 Billionaire Fund introduced $200,000 as capital.

Date	Product	Strike Price	Expiry	Quantity	Rate (S$)	B/S	Brokerage
23-Sep-X1	Put	S$ 50	16-Nov-X1	10,000	5.00	S	540
23-Oct-X1	Put	S$ 50	16-Nov-X1	8,000	4.00	S	440
10-Nov-X1	Put	S$ 50	16-Nov-X1	12,000	3.00	B	720

Liquidation Method
FIFO

Market Rate of Underlying SingTel:
September 30: S$48.00
October 31: S$43.00
November 16: S$55.00

Market Rate of SingTel Put Option with Strike Price S$50, Expiry March 16
September 30: S$2.00
October 31: S$6.00

FX Rate S$/US$
September 23: 1.5210
September 30: 1.532
October 23: 1.4956
October 31: 1.500
November 10: 1.5148
November 16: 1.5463

CHAPTER 10

Equity Options: Hedge Accounting

LEARNING OBJECTIVES

After studying this chapter you will have a grasp of the following:

- Accounting standards for derivative instruments and hedging activities.
- Differences between U.S. GAAP and IFRS pertaining to hedge accounting relative to options.
- Cornerstones of FAS 133; definitions of *underlying, notional amount, payment provision*, and *initial net investment.*
- Contracts that are exempted from FAS 133.
- Recognition and measurement of derivatives and hedged items.
- Accounting for changes in fair value and treatment of gains and losses on derivative instruments.
- Criteria for hedge accounting.
- Eligibility for designation as a hedged item.
- Accounting for gains and losses on a fair value hedge.
- Discontinuation of hedge accounting.
- Features of accounting standards relating to options as hedge, written options, covered call, and the rationale behind the symmetry requirement for hedges.
- Exception to single fair value measure rule.
- Whether hedge accounting is possible for a delta-neutral hedging strategy.
- When hedge accounting is permissible for option contracts.
- The trade life cycle of exchange-traded options (ETOs) for long put held as hedging.
- Journal entries to be recorded during the different phases of the trade life cycle.
- FX revaluation and FX translation relating to this trade life cycle.
- Illustration of long put options as hedge in functional currency.
- Preparation of journal entries and general ledger accounts.
- Preparation of income statement and balance sheet after the call option trades are made.
- Illustration of long put options as hedge in foreign currency.

ACCOUNTING STANDARDS—DERIVATIVE INSTRUMENTS AND HEDGING

The accounting treatment of call or put options *prima facie* will depend upon the intention with which the call or put options are purchased, namely hedging or speculation (nonhedging). If the position is taken as a hedge against some other position, then the accounting standard FAS 133 will be applicable and there are certain conditions that are to be fulfilled for the same.

Under U.S. GAAP, accounting standard FAS 133 prescribes standardized accounting and reporting requirements for all derivative instruments for hedging activities. Under IFRS, accounting standards IAS 39, IAS 32, and IFRS 7 covers the accounting and reporting requirements for all financial instruments including derivative instruments and treatment for hedge accounting.

Relevant Accounting Standards	
U.S. GAAP	**IFRS**
FAS 52—Foreign Currency Translation	IFRS 7—Financial Instruments: Disclosure
FAS 94—Consolidation of All Majority-owned Subsidiaries	IAS 21—The Effects of Changes in Foreign Exchange Rates
FAS 115—Accounting for Certain Investments in Debt and Equity Securities	IAS 32—Financial Instruments: Presentation
FAS 133—Accounting for Derivative Instruments and Hedging Activities	IAS 36—Impairment of Assets
FAS 130—Reporting Comprehensive Income	IAS 39—Financial Instruments: Recognition and Measurement
FAS 157—Fair Value Measurements	
FAS 159—The Fair Value Option for Financial Assets and Financial Liabilities	

Differences between U.S. GAAP and IFRS

Hedge Accounting		
Topic	**U.S. GAAP**	**IFRS**
Hedge accounting—documentation	Requires proper documentation of the entity's risk management objectives and how hedge effectiveness will be assessed both prospectively and retrospectively.	Same as U.S. GAAP.
Hedge accounting—effectiveness	Hedge instruments should be highly effective in offsetting the exposure of the hedged item to changes in the fair value or cash flows, and the effectiveness of the hedge is measured on a continuing basis.	Same as U.S. GAAP.

Hedge Accounting (*Cont'd*)		
Topic	**U.S. GAAP**	**IFRS**
Shortcut method	Allows a shortcut method that assumes perfect effectiveness for certain hedging relationships involving interest-rate swaps, assuming that other stringent conditions are met.	No shortcut method is allowed under IFRS.
Written options as hedge	Written options will not qualify for hedge accounting in most cases.	A written option cannot be designated as a hedging instrument unless it is combined with a purchase option and a net premium is paid.

Salient Features of FAS 133

Cornerstones of FAS 133

- Derivative instruments represent rights or obligations that meet the definitions of assets or liabilities and should be reported in financial statements.
- *Fair value* is the most relevant measure for financial instruments and the only relevant measure for derivative instruments. Derivative instruments should be measured at fair value, and adjustments to the carrying amount of hedged items should reflect changes in their fair value (that is, gains or losses) that are attributable to the risk being hedged and that arise while the hedge is in effect.
- Only items that are assets or liabilities should be reported as such in financial statements.
- Special accounting for items designated as being hedged should be provided only for qualifying items. One aspect of qualification should be an assessment of the expectation of effective offsetting changes in fair values or cash flows during the term of the hedge for the risk being hedged. (*Source*: FAS 133, Paragraph 3.)

Key Definitions

Underlying. An underlying is a specified interest rate, security price, commodity price, foreign exchange rate, index of prices or rates, or other variable. An underlying may be a price or rate of an asset or liability but is not the asset or liability itself.

Notional amount. A notional amount is a number of currency units, shares, bushels, pounds, or other units specified in the contract.

Payment provision. A payment provision specifies a fixed or determinable settlement to be made if the underlying behaves in a specified manner.

Initial net investment. Initial net investment is the amount that is required to initiate a position in a derivative instrument. Some require an initial net investment while many derivative instruments require no initial net investment at all. This can be regarded as compensation for time value, similar to a premium on an option contract.

Contracts That Are Exempted from FAS 133

- *"Regular-way" security trades.* Regular-way security trades are contracts with no net settlement provision and no market mechanism to facilitate net settlement, and which provide for delivery of a security within the time generally established by regulations or conventions in the marketplace or exchange in which the transaction is being executed.
- *Normal purchases and normal sales.* Normal purchases and normal sales are contracts with no net settlement provision and no market mechanism to facilitate net settlement and which provide for the purchase or sale of something other than a financial instrument or derivative instrument that will be delivered in quantities expected to be used or sold by the reporting entity over a reasonable period in the normal course of business.
- Certain *insurance* contracts like traditional life insurance contracts and traditional property and casualty contracts.
- Certain *financial guarantee* contracts.
- *Derivatives* that serve as impediments to sales accounting.

Recognition/Measurement of Derivatives/Hedged Items

- An entity shall recognize all of its derivative instruments in its statement of financial position as either assets or liabilities depending on the rights or obligations under the contracts.
- All derivative instruments shall be measured at fair value.
- If expected future cash flows are used to estimate fair value, those expected cash flows shall be the best estimate based on reasonable and supportable assumptions and projections. (*Source*: FAS 133, Paragraph 17.)

Accounting for Changes in the Fair Value

- This depends on whether it has been designated and qualifies as part of a hedging relationship and, if so, on the reason for holding it.
- Either all or a proportion of a derivative may be designated as the hedging instrument.
- The proportion must be expressed as a percentage of the entire derivative so that the profile of risk exposures in the hedging portion of the derivative is the same as that in the entire derivative. (*Source*: FAS 133, Paragraph 18.)

Gains and Losses on Derivative Instruments

- No hedging designation: The gain or loss on a derivative instrument not designated as a hedging instrument shall be recognized currently in earnings.
- Fair value hedge: The gain or loss on a derivative instrument designated and qualifying as a fair value hedging instrument as well as the offsetting loss or gain on the hedged item attributable to the hedged risk shall be recognized currently in earnings in the same accounting period.
- The gain or loss on the hedging derivative instrument in a hedge of an available-for-sale security and the offsetting loss or gain on the hedged available-for-sale security shall be recognized currently in earnings in the same accounting period. (*Source*: FAS 133, Paragraph 18.)

- Change in the fair value: This refers to the difference between its fair value at the beginning of the period and the end of the period excluding changes in fair value due to the passage of time and changes in fair value related to any payments received or made. (*Source*: FAS 133, Paragraph 19.)

Criteria for Hedge Accounting

- At inception of the hedge, there is formal documentation of the hedging relationship and the entity's risk management objective and strategy for undertaking the hedge, including identification of the hedging instrument, the hedged item, the nature of the risk being hedged, and how the hedging instrument's effectiveness in offsetting the exposure to changes in the hedged item's fair value attributable to the hedged risk will be assessed.
- There must be a reasonable basis for how the entity plans to assess the hedging instrument's effectiveness.
- Formal documentation at the inception of the hedge must include a reasonable method for recognizing in earnings the asset or liability representing the gain or loss on the hedged firm commitment.
- Both at inception of the hedge and on an ongoing basis, the hedging relationship is expected to be highly effective in achieving offsetting changes in fair value attributable to the hedged risk during the period that the hedge is designated.
- An assessment of effectiveness is required whenever financial statements or earnings are reported, and at least every three months.
- All assessments of effectiveness shall be consistent with the risk management strategy documented for that particular hedging relationship. (*Source*: FAS 133, Paragraph 20.)

Eligibility for Designation as a Hedged Item

- The hedged item is specifically identified as either all or a specific portion of a recognized asset or liability or of an unrecognized firm commitment.
- The hedged item is a single asset or liability (or a specific portion thereof) or is a portfolio of similar assets or a portfolio of similar liabilities (or a specific portion thereof).
- The hedged item presents an exposure to changes in fair value attributable to the hedged risk that could affect reported earnings. (*Source*: FAS 133, Paragraph 21.)

Accounting for Gains and Losses on a Fair Value Hedge

- The gain or loss on the hedging instrument shall be recognized currently in earnings.
- The gain or loss on the hedged item attributable to the hedged risk shall adjust the carrying amount of the hedged item and be recognized currently in earnings.
- For effective fair value hedge, the gain or loss on the hedging instrument would exactly offset the loss or gain on the hedged item attributable to the hedged risk.
- Any difference that does arise would be the effect of hedge ineffectiveness, which consequently is recognized currently in earnings.
- The measurement of hedge ineffectiveness for a particular hedging relationship shall be consistent with the entity's risk management strategy and the method of

assessing hedge effectiveness that was documented at the inception of the hedging relationship. (*Source*: FAS 133, Paragraph 22.)

Other Comprehensive Income

- The amount of hedge ineffectiveness recognized in earnings is based on the extent to which exact offset is not achieved.
- Although a hedging relationship must comply with an entity's established policy range of what is considered "highly effective" in order for that relationship to qualify for hedge accounting, that compliance does not assure zero ineffectiveness.
- Hedge ineffectiveness directly affects earnings because there will be no offsetting adjustment of a hedged item's carrying amount for the ineffective aspect of the gain or loss on the related hedging instrument.
- If a hedged item is otherwise measured at fair value with changes in fair value reported in other comprehensive income (such as an available-for-sale security), the adjustment of the hedged item's carrying amount shall be recognized in earnings rather than in other comprehensive income in order to offset the gain or loss on the hedging instrument. (*Source*: FAS 133, Paragraph 23.)

Discontinuation of hedge accounting

An entity shall discontinue prospectively hedge accounting if any one of the following occurs:

- Hedge criteria are not met.
- The derivative expires or is sold, terminated, or exercised.
- The entity removes the designation of the fair value hedge.

Features of Accounting Standards Relating to Options

Options as Hedge

As per the accounting standards, to qualify for hedge accounting, either the upside and downside potential of the net position must be symmetrical or the upside potential must be greater than the downside potential. In other words, the combination of the hedged item and the option on the underlying must result in a position that provides at least as much potential for gains as exposure to losses.

Evaluation of the combined position's relative potential for gains and losses is based on the effect of a favorable or unfavorable change in price of a given percentage. For example, a 25 percent favorable change in the fair value of the hedged item must provide a gain on the combined position that is at least as large as the loss on that combined position that would result from a 25 percent unfavorable change in the fair value of the hedged item.

Written Options

Written options based on symmetry of the gain and loss potential of the combined hedged position qualify for hedge accounting as per the accounting standard.

If a written option is designated as hedging a recognized asset or liability, the combination of the hedged item and the written option provides at least as much potential for gains (as a result of a favorable change in the fair value of the combined instruments) as it does exposure to losses from an unfavorable change in their combined fair value. That test is met if all possible percentage favorable changes in the underlying (from zero percent to 100 percent) would provide at least as much gain as the loss that would be incurred from an unfavorable change in the underlying of the same percentage.

A written option exposes its writer to the possibility of unlimited loss but limits the gain to the amount of premium received. The Financial Accounting Standards Board (FASB) is concerned about permitting written options to be designated as hedging instruments because a written option serves only to reduce the potential for gain in the hedged item or hedged transaction. It leaves the potential for loss on the hedged item or hedged transaction unchanged except for the amount of premium received on the written option. Consequently, on a net basis, an entity may be worse off as a result of trying to hedge with a written option. Because of those concerns, the standard prohibits a written option from being eligible for designation as a hedging instrument.

Covered Call

A covered call is a situation where the investor writes a call on the basis of a long position in an underlying asset. In this case the risk profile of the combined position becomes asymmetrical as there is a limited potential upside and an unlimited downward potential. Hence hedge accounting is not permitted for covered calls. This prohibition is also specifically mentioned in the standard itself.

Rationale behind Symmetry Requirement for Hedges

The symmetry requirement for hedges with written options is intended to preclude a written option that is used to sell a portion of the gain potential on an asset or liability from being eligible for hedge accounting. Hedge accounting should not be available for a transaction that merely sells part of the potential for gain from an existing asset.

Timing of the Written Option

A written option can be entered into at the same time the hedged item is issued or acquired because the combined position is the same regardless of when the position originated (assuming, of course, that the price of the hedged item is the same as the underlying for the option at the time the hedge is entered into.)

Hedge accounting for options is not limited to the items that may be hedged with written options to financial instruments. The FASB decided that hedge accounting provisions as enshrined in FAS 133 for hedging with written options should accommodate similar risk management strategies regardless of the nature of the asset or liability that is the hedged item.

Exception to Single Fair Value Measure Rule

There is normally a single fair value measure for a hedging instrument in its entirety as the factors that cause changes in fair value are codependent. Hence a hedging relationship is designated by an entity for a hedging instrument in its entirety. However, for an option contract an exception is permitted by the accounting standards.

Separating the intrinsic value and time value of an option contract and designating as the hedging instrument only the change in intrinsic value of an option and excluding change in its time value is permitted.

This exception is permitted because the intrinsic value of the option can generally be measured separately. A dynamic hedging strategy that assesses both the intrinsic value and time value of an option contract can qualify for hedge accounting.

Also, a proportion of the entire hedging instrument, such as 50 percent of the notional amount, may be designated as the hedging instrument in a hedging relationship. However, a hedging relationship may not be designated for only a portion of the time period during which a hedging instrument remains outstanding.

Is Hedge Accounting Possible for a Delta-neutral Hedging Strategy?

To the question whether the accounting standards permit an entity to apply hedge accounting for a delta-neutral hedging strategy and other dynamic hedging strategies under which the quantity of the hedging instrument is constantly adjusted in order to maintain a desired hedge ratio—for example, to achieve a delta-neutral position insensitive to changes in the fair value of the hedged item—the answer is yes. According to the accounting standards (IAS 39), "a dynamic hedging strategy that assesses both the intrinsic value and time value of an option contract can qualify for hedge accounting." For example, a portfolio insurance strategy that seeks to ensure that the fair value of the hedged item does not drop below a certain level, while allowing the fair value to increase, may qualify for hedge accounting.

To qualify for hedge accounting, the entity must document how it will monitor and update the hedge and measure hedge effectiveness, be able to track properly all terminations and redesignations of the hedging instrument, and demonstrate that all other criteria for hedge accounting are met. Also, it must be able to demonstrate an expectation that the hedge will be highly effective for a specified short period of time during which the hedge is not expected to be adjusted.

The discussion of a delta-neutral hedging strategy is beyond the scope of this book.

When Is Hedge Accounting Permissible for Options?

Underlying Shares	Options	Is This Hedge?	Hedge Accounting Possible?
Long	Long Call	No	
Long	Long Put	Yes	Yes
Long	Short Call	Yes	No
Long	Short Put	No	
Short	Long Call	Yes	Yes
Short	Long Put	No	
Short	Short Call	No	
Short	Short Put	Yes	No

It will be clear from the table regarding permissible hedge accounting that only long calls and long puts are eligible for hedge accounting. The reason is simple: Written calls or puts limit the profitability while exposing the investor to unlimited risks, whereas the standards require that the potential for gains should be at least equal to the potential for losses. This is known as a *symmetrical risk-reward* situation. For a written option the risk-reward is asymmetrical and hence written options per se do not qualify for hedge accounting. However, a combination of written options and certain other derivative instruments that results in a symmetrical risk-reward may qualify for hedge accounting.

THE TRADE LIFE CYCLE FOR ETOs—LONG PUT AS HEDGING

- Ensure the long position.
- Buy the put options.
- Pay brokerage/commission on the buy transaction.
- Pay for the put options bought.
- Document hedge strategy, the hedge, and the hedged item.
- Ascertain the fair value of the underlying.
- Ascertain the intrinsic value and time value of the option.
- Ascertain the effectiveness of the hedge.
- Reversal of mark-to-market.
- Expiry of options.
- Exercise of options.
- Sell the options.
- Receive the consideration.
- Ascertain the profit/loss on the sale.
- FX revaluation entries.
- FX translation entries.

Ensure the Long Position of the Underlying

Hedging a long position of an underlying is possible by buying puts. For the hedge accounting to be applicable, the accounting standards have very stringent requirements that must be met. First there should be a long position in the underlying shares that needs to be hedged. Assume that the entity owns 10,000 shares of Colgate at a cost of $50. Since it has no immediate intention to resell, the shares are classified as available-for-sale security on the balance sheet.

Buy the Put Options

A put option, as mentioned earlier, is the right, but not an obligation to sell something at a fixed price—the strike price—at any time within the specified time period. If the investor buys the option contract, then no margin is payable; instead the investor would pay for the entire value of the contract on the date of settlement. This is because the maximum loss that could be incurred on purchase of a put option is the premium paid on such purchase. Hence there is no requirement to pay any margin to the exchange.

When the options are bought as a hedge to cover other positions, then the options are treated as an asset when purchased and as a liability when sold. As per FAS 133, the hedge should be shown as an asset or a liability; hence the investments account is debited when the options are purchased. At the valuation date the difference between the market rate and the cost of options is ascertained and taken to the income account on the one hand and recorded as an increase or decrease in the value of the investments on the other.

However, if the options are purchased other than as a hedge, it is either for speculation or for arbitrage. In that case the income account is debited when the options are purchased. At the valuation date the entire value of the options is written back as income on the one hand and as asset on the other. In both cases, the net income and the net value shown in the balance sheet would be the same (see Chapter 8.)

Assume that 10,000 equity put options of Colgate with strike price $50 are bought at $5 each through Laver & Co. The accounting entry that is recorded in the books of accounts is shown as follows:

Journal Entry

Date	Particulars	Debit (US$)	Credit (US$)
23-Jan-X1	Investments—ETO Long Put Account	50,000.00	
	To Laver & Co. Account		50,000.00
	(Being the purchase of 10,000 equity put options of Colgate @ $5)		

Brokerage/Commission on the Buy Transaction

The broker charges a commission for the services rendered. This is usually settled along with the purchase value of the options. For option contracts, the brokerage/commission is not treated as part of the cost of the options contract; instead it is debited to the brokerage/commission account.

Assume that the brokerage for this deal is $500. The accounting entry that is recorded in the books of accounts is shown as follows:

Journal Entry

Date	Particulars	Debit (US$)	Credit (US$)
23-Jan-X1	Brokerage/Commission Account	500.00	
	To Laver & Co. Account		500.00
	(Being the brokerage payable on purchase of 10,000 equity put options of Colgate)		

Pay for the Options Bought

The next event in the trade life cycle is the payment of the contracted amount for the options bought. Usually the payment happens on the day of purchase.

The accounting entry that is recorded in the books of accounts is shown as follows:

Journal Entry

Date	Particulars	Debit (US$)	Credit (US$)
23-Jan-X1	Laver & Co. Account	50,500.00	
	To Bank Account		50,500.00
	(Being the payment towards purchase of 10,000 equity put options of Colgate along with brokerage)		

Document Hedge Strategy, the Hedge, and the Hedged Item

The hedge strategy should be properly documented, clearly specifying the hedge and the hedged item, along with other details as required by the accounting standards governing the hedge. For U.S. GAAP and IFRS, these are clearly laid down, and the investor must follow the requirements to qualify for hedge accounting as prescribed in the standards.

Ascertain the Fair Value of the Underlying

At the end of every reporting period the fair value of the underlying asset is ascertained and the assets are marked-to-market. This process is known as portfolio valuation, when the market rate at the end of the period is determined from the primary stock exchange where the underlying shares are traded. If there is an increase in the market rate over and above the purchase rate, then such increase is recognized as a gain on the one hand, and the corresponding amount is reflected as an increase in the value of the underlying asset. This accounting entry is reversed on the next day or the next valuation date when a fresh entry for the then value is recorded in the books of accounts. Alternatively, the accounting entry can be recorded only for the incremental value. If the investor follows this incremental value method, then there is no need to reverse the entry for mark-to-market recorded earlier.

As mentioned earlier in Chapter 2, for an available-for-sale security, the unrealized gains are treated as other comprehensive income and taken directly to the equity and are not taken to the income statement. But where the underlying asset is hedged, the unrealized gain/loss is taken to the income account. This is so even where the underlying asset is held as an available-for-sale security. The change in the market value should be reported in the current earnings and should not be taken to the other comprehensive income.

Assuming that the value of the underlying share at the end of the reporting period is $39, then the difference between the market rate and the cost, being $11 per share, is recognized as a loss and the same is deducted from the asset account. The income account is designated as the *hedge gain/loss account* and any change in the value of the hedging instrument is also taken to the same account to the extent the hedge is effective. The ineffective portion of the hedge is charged off to expense during the same period.

The accounting entry that is recorded in the books of accounts is shown as follows:

Journal Entry

Date	Particulars	Debit (US$)	Credit (US$)
31-Jan-X1	Hedge Gains/Loss (Effective) Account	11,000.00	
	To Investments—Equity Shares—AFS Account		11,000.00
	(Being the incremental mark-to-market on the underlying hedged equity shares at the end of the reporting period)		

Ascertain the Intrinsic Value of the Option

The portfolio valuation process just described for ascertaining the fair value of the underlying is also followed to ascertain the intrinsic value of the option. Note that where the put options are meant to be a hedge for an underlying share, the difference between the market value and the cost is taken to the revenue.

However, to the extent that the increase in the value of the put represents effective hedge, the gain is treated as part of the hedge gain/loss account. This gain goes towards off-setting the loss, if any, on the underlying asset.

Assuming that the value of the options at the end of the reporting period is $14, then the difference between the market rate and the cost, being $9 per option, is recognized as income and the same is added to the asset account. To the extent of the intrinsic value of the option, it is taken to the hedge gain/loss account and the time value of the option is treated as an expense and written off during the same period.

The accounting entry that is recorded in the books of accounts is shown as follows:

Journal Entry

Date	Particulars	Debit (US$)	Credit (US$)
31-Jan-X1	Investments—ETO Long Put Account	11,000.00	
	To Hedge Gains/Loss (Effective) Account		11,000.00
	(Being the gain in the intrinsic value of the hedging instrument—put options: strike price less the market price times quantity)		

Ascertain the Time Value of the Option

The ineffective potion of the hedge is written off as an expense during the same period. In this case, the actual value of the put option as of the valuation date is $14. The original cost of the put option is $5. Considering the market value of the underlying we know that the intrinsic value of the option is $11. Since the market value is $14 it means that out of the $5 paid for the options, $2 represents the time value of the option that has already been eroded. This is written off as an expense during the same period. The accounting entry that is recorded in the books of accounts is shown as follows:

Journal Entry

Date	Particulars	Debit (US$)	Credit (US$)
31-Jan-X1	Hedge Loss Account (P&L—Ineffective Portion)	2,000.00	
	To Investments—ETO Long Put Account		2,000.00
	(Being the time value loss on hedging instrument—put option: cost of put option less the intrinsic value of put options)		

Reversal of mark-to-market

The accounting entry for mark-to-market is reversed on the next day or the next valuation date when a fresh entry for the then value is recorded in the books of accounts. However, as mentioned earlier, if the investor follows the incremental value method, then there is no need to reverse the entry for mark-to-market recorded earlier.

Expiry of Options

The options expire on the expiry date of the contract. For put options that are bought, the excess amount of strike price over and above the market value of the underlying represents the profit for the investor. In such case, the put option is said to expire in-the-money. Conversely, if the put options expire out of the money—that is, if the strike price of the option is less than the market value of the underlying, then the premium paid by the investor represents the loss. The maximum loss that could be incurred from a long put option can never exceed the premium paid on the purchase of the put option.

Case 1: When the options expire worthless (i.e., the market rate of the underlying is more than the strike price of the option), the accounting entry that is recorded in the books of accounts is shown as follows:

Journal Entry

Date	Particulars	Debit (US$)	Credit (US$)
15-Feb-X1	Loss on Put Options Account	50,000.00	
	To Investments—ETO Long Put Account		50,000.00
	(Being the loss incurred on put options as the options expired worthless)		

Case 2: When the options expire in-the-money (i.e., the market rate of the underlying is less than the strike price of the option), then the difference between the strike price and the value of the underlying represents the gain accruing to the investor. However, if the strike price of the option is still below the market value of the underlying as increased by the premium paid to acquire the options, the investor will still lose money. Assuming that the underlying shares close at $48 on the expiry date, the accounting entry that is recorded in the books of accounts is shown as follows:

Journal Entry

Date	Particulars	Debit (US$)	Credit (US$)
15-Feb-X1	Loss on Put options Account	30,000.00	
	Laver & Co. Account	20,000.00	
	To Investments—ETO Long Put Account		50,000.00
	(Being the loss incurred on put options as the options expired at less than the original cost of acquisition)		

Case 3: The investor makes a profit when the options expire in-the-money, when the market rate of the underlying is less than the strike price of the option as reduced by the premium paid for acquiring such options. Assuming that the underlying shares close at $42 on the expiry date, the accounting entry that is recorded in the books of accounts is shown as follows:

Journal Entry

Date	Particulars	Debit (US$)	Credit (US$)
15-Feb-X1	Laver & Co. Account	80,000.00	
	To Profit on Put Options Account		30,000.00
	To Investments—ETO Long Put Account		50,000.00
	(Being the profit realized on put options as the options expired at more than the original cost of acquisition)		

Exercise of Options

The buyer of the put option has the right but not the obligation to sell the underlying at the strike price. When the put options are exercised, it results in the sale of the underlying asset. In such a scenario, the investor has to deliver the underlying at the contracted strike price. The actual realization of the underlying asset would then be the strike price of the contract as reduced by the premium paid on the purchase of the put option. Exercise of options happens only in the case of stock options and not in the case of options on indexes.

Assume that the options are exercised on the date of expiry when the price of the underlying share is $42 and the underlying equity shares were acquired and held by the investor for trading purposes. The accounting entry that is recorded in the books of accounts is shown as follows:

Journal Entry

Date	Particulars	Debit (US$)	Credit (US$)
15-Feb-X1	Laver & Co. Account	500,000.00	
	To Investments—Equity Shares—AFS Account		500,000.00
	(Being the exercise of 10,000 equity put options of Colgate @ $5 resulting in the liquidation of the underlying shares)		
15-Feb-X1	Investments—Equity Shares—AFS Account	50,000.00	
	To Investments—ETO Long Put Account		50,000.00
	(Being the premium paid on purchase of put options now taken as part of the cost of the underlying asset on exercise of put options)		
15-Feb-X1	Investments—Equity Shares—AFS Account	500.00	
	To Brokerage/Commission Account		500.00
	(Being the brokerage paid on purchase of 10,000 equity put options of Colgate @ $5 now taken as part of the cost of the underlying asset on exercise of options)		

Sell the Options

The long position of put options could be liquidated by selling such options. Since the sale results in only squaring up of the existing position, there is no requirement of any margin payment to the exchange on account of this sale of put options. The overall open interest on put options could come down if the put options are purchased by someone who already has a short position. Otherwise the sale of the put options will not result in the shrinkage of open interest.

Assuming that the options are liquidated at $4.20, the accounting entry that is recorded in the books of accounts is shown as follows:

Journal Entry

Date	Particulars	Debit (US$)	Credit (US$)
2-Feb-X1	Laver & Co. Account	42,000.00	
	To Investments—ETO Long Put Account		42,000.00
	(Being the sale of 10,000 equity put options of Colgate @ $4.20)		

Receive the Consideration

The consideration is received on day T + 2 or another date determined by the exchange concerned. The consideration is received net of brokerage.

The accounting entry that is recorded in the books of accounts is shown as follows:

Journal Entry

Date	Particulars	Debit (US$)	Credit (US$)
2-Feb-X1	Bank Account	42,000.00	
	To Laver & Co. Account		42,000.00
	(Being receipt of funds on account of the sale of 10,000 equity put options of Colgate @ $4.20)		

Ascertain the Profit/Loss on the Sale

The profit or loss on the sale is determined by comparing the premium paid on purchase with the premium received upon sale and accounted for accordingly.

The accounting entry that is recorded in the books of accounts is shown as follows:

Journal Entry

Date	Particulars	Debit (US$)	Credit (US$)
2-Feb-X1	Loss on Put Options Account	8,000.00	
	To Investments—ETO Long Put Account		8,000.00
	(Being the loss booked on sale of 10,000 equity put options of Colgate @ $4.20)		

FX Revaluation Entries

All the entries recorded to this point are initially entered in the respective trade currencies. If the functional currency is different from the trade currency, then each and every entry recorded in the trade currency should be entered again in the functional currency by converting the entries at the respective day's FX rates. In other words, for each trade currency that the investor deals with, there will be a complete set of books representing that trade currency. This includes journal entries, general ledger postings, trial balance, income statement, and balance sheet.

After revaluing each and every journal entry of all the trade currencies into the functional currency, a separate set of books is prepared, again comprising all the elements just mentioned: journal entries, general ledger postings, trial balance, income statement, and balance sheet. It should be noted that the ultimate financial reports would be prepared and presented to all the stakeholders based on the financial statements prepared in the functional currency only, as this will encompass all the transactions of the investor in all trade currencies dabbled with. (For illustration and detailed explanation please refer to Chapter 2.)

FX Revaluation Entries

After revaluing all the entries in the functional currency at the respective FX rates for the day concerned, another entry needs to be passed in the books of the functional currency. This is mainly to adjust the currency gains or losses due to the fluctuations in FX rates between the reporting date and the date of recording the original entries. FX translation entries are recorded only for the asset and liability accounts. For income and expense accounts the amount gets crystallized on the date of passing the FX revaluation entries in the books of the functional currency.

There are fundamentally two types of FX translation entries that are recorded in the books of the functional currency: consummated FX translation entries and transient FX translation entries. (For illustration and detailed explanation please refer to Chapter 2.)

ILLUSTRATIONS

Long Put Options

Davidson Company introduced $100,000 into the fund on May 1. On the same date, Davidson Company purchased 1,000 shares of Lloyd at a cost of $35 per share (inclusive of brokerage.) Davidson had no immediate intention to resell the shares and classified them as available-for-sale. The price shot up to $55 by September 1 and Davidson decided to hedge the investment in Lloyd. Towards this, Davidson purchased put options on Lloyd at $9 with an exercise price of $55, expiry being May 15 of the following year, through the brokers Alex & Co, and brokerage being $550.

- Davidson Company wants to adopt hedge accounting for the put options and must document the hedge strategy, objectives, hedging relationships.
- The intrinsic value of the option would be used to determine the effectiveness of the hedge.
- The time value is to be charged off to income.
- The quarterly accounting period closes on June 30, September 30, December 31, and March 31.

Journal entries, general ledgers, trial balance, income statement, and balance sheet are prepared as follows:

Liquidation Method

FIFO

Market Rate of Underlying Stock, Lloyd ($)

June 30: 49.00
September 1: 55.00
September 30: 50.00
December 31: 46.00
March 31, year 2: 43.00
May 15, year 2: 41.00

Market Rate of Lloyd Put Option with Strike Price $55, Expiry May 15, Year 2

September 1: 9.00
September 30: 13.00
December 31: 12.00
March 31: 13.00
May 15: 14.00

Long Put Options, Hedging—Functional Currency US$

A summary of the market rates of put options, underlying, intrinsic worth of the option contract, and time value of the option contract is given in the following table.

Date	1-Sep-X1	30-Sep-X1	30-Dec-X1	31-Mar-X2	15-May-X2
(a) Market rate—Puts	9	13	12	13	14
(b) Market rate—Equity	55	50	46	43	41
(c) Intrinsic worth	0	5	9	12	14
(d) Incremental increase in (c)		5	4	3	2
(e) Time value = (a) − (c)	9	8	3	1	0
(f) Incremental erosion in time value		1	5	2	1

T-1 On Introducing Share Capital

Journal Entry

Date	Particulars	Debit (US$)	Credit (US$)
1-May-X1	Bank Account	100,000.00	
	To Share Capital Account		100,000.00
	(Being the share capital introduced by the investor)		

T-2 On Purchase of Equity Shares

Journal Entry

Date	Particulars	Debit (US$)	Credit (US$)
1-May-X1	Investments—Equity Shares—AFS Account	35,000.00	
	To Bank Account		35,000.00
	(Being the purchase of 1,000 equity shares of Lloyd)		

T-3 Mark-to-market on the AFS Security

Journal Entry

Date	Particulars	Debit (US$)	Credit (US$)
30-Jun-X1	Investments—Equity Shares—AFS Account	14,000.00	
	To Unrealized Gains/Loss—Other Comprehensive Income Account		14,000.00
	(Being the mark-to-market entry on the AFS security at the end of the reporting period)		

T-4 Mark-to-market on the AFS Security

Journal Entry

Date	Particulars	Debit (US$)	Credit (US$)
1-Sep-X1	Investments—Equity Shares—AFS Account	6,000.00	
	To Unrealized Gains/Loss—Other Comprehensive Income Account		6,000.00
	(Being the mark-to-market entry on the AFS security at the end of the reporting period)		

T-5 On Purchase of Put Options

Journal Entry

Date	Particulars	Debit (US$)	Credit (US$)
1-Sep-X1	Investments—ETO Long Put Account	9,000.00	
	To Alex & Co. Account		9,000.00
	(Being the purchase of 1,000 equity put options of Lloyd)		

T-6 Brokerage/Commission

Journal Entry

Date	Particulars	Debit (US$)	Credit (US$)
1-Sep-X1	Brokerage/Commission Account	550.00	
	To Alex & Co. Account		550.00
	(Being the brokerage incurred on the purchase of put options)		

T-7 On Payment of Contracted Amount

Journal Entry

Date	Particulars	Debit (US$)	Credit (US$)
1-Sep-X1	Alex & Co. Account	9,550.00	
	To Bank Account		9,550.00
	(Being the payment made to Alex & Co. on purchase of put options)		

T-8 Incremental Mark-to-market on the Underlying Hedged Asset

Journal Entry

Date	Particulars	Debit (US$)	Credit (US$)
30-Sep-X1	Hedge Gains/Loss Account (Effective portion)	5,000.00	
	To Investments—Equity Shares—AFS Account		5,000.00
	(Being the incremental mark-to-market on the underlying hedged equity shares at the end of the reporting period)		

T-9 Gain in Intrinsic Value of Hedging Instrument (Put Option)

Journal Entry

Date	Particulars	Debit (US$)	Credit (US$)
30-Sep-X1	Investments—ETO Long Put Account	5,000.00	
	To Hedge Gains/Loss Account (Effective portion)		5,000.00
	(Being the gain in the intrinsic value of the hedging instrument—put options: strike price less the market price times quantity)		

T-10 Time Value Loss on Hedging Instrument (Put Option)

Journal Entry

Date	Particulars	Debit (US$)	Credit (US$)
30-Sep-X1	Hedge Loss Account (P&L—Ineffective portion)	1,000.00	
	To Investments—ETO Long Put Account		1,000.00
	(Being the time value loss on hedging instrument—put option: cost of put option less the intrinsic value of put options)		

T-11 Incremental Mark-to-market on the Underlying Hedged Asset

Journal Entry

Date	Particulars	Debit (US$)	Credit (US$)
31-Dec-X1	Hedge Gains/Loss Account (Effective portion)	4,000.00	
	To Investments—Equity Shares—AFS Account		4,000.00
	(Being the incremental mark-to-market on the underlying hedged equity shares at the end of the reporting period)		

T-12 Gain in Intrinsic Value of Hedging Instrument (Put Option)

Journal Entry

Date	Particulars	Debit (US$)	Credit (US$)
31-Dec-X1	Investments—ETO Long Put Account	4,000.00	
	To Hedge Gains/Loss Account (Effective Portion)		4,000.00
	(Being the gain in the intrinsic value of the hedging instrument—put options: strike price less the market price times quantity)		

T-13 Time Value Loss on Hedging Instrument (Put Option)

Journal Entry

Date	Particulars	Debit (US$)	Credit (US$)
31-Dec-X1	Hedge Loss Account (P&L—Ineffective portion)	5,000.00	
	To Investments—ETO Long Put Account		5,000.00
	(Being the time value loss on hedging instrument—put option: cost of put option less the intrinsic value of put options)		

T-14 Incremental Mark-to-market on the Underlying Hedged Asset

Journal Entry

Date	Particulars	Debit (US$)	Credit (US$)
31-Mar-X2	Hedge Gains/Loss Account (Effective portion)	3,000.00	
	To Investments—Equity Shares—AFS Account		3,000.00
	(Being the incremental mark-to-market on the underlying hedged equity shares at the end of the reporting period)		

T-15 Gain in Intrinsic Value of Hedging Instrument (Put Option)

Journal Entry

Date	Particulars	Debit (US$)	Credit (US$)
31-Mar-X2	Investments—ETO Long Put Account	3,000.00	
	To Hedge Gains/Loss Account (Effective portion)		3,000.00
	(Being the gain in the intrinsic value of the hedging instrument—put options: strike price less the market price times quantity)		

T-16 Time Value Loss on Hedging Instrument (Put Option)

Journal Entry

Date	Particulars	Debit (US$)	Credit (US$)
31-Mar-X2	Hedge Loss Account (P&L—Ineffective portion)	2,000.00	
	To Investments—ETO Long Put Account		2,000.00
	(Being the time value loss on hedging instrument—put option: market rate of put options less the intrinsic value of put options)		

Trial Balance

As of 31-Mar-X2 (US$)

Particulars	Debit	Credit
Capital Account		
Share Capital Account		100,000.00
Unrealized Gains/Loss—Other Comprehensive Income Account		20,000.00
Current Liabilities		
Investments		
Investment—ETO Long Put Account	13,000.00	
Investment—Equity Shares—AFS Account	43,000.00	
Current Assets		
Bank Account	55,450.00	
Direct Expenses		
Brokerage/Commission Account	550.00	
Hedge Loss Account (P&L—Ineffective)	8,000.00	
Total	**120,000.00**	**120,000.00**

Income Statement

For the period ending 31-Mar-X2

Expenses	US$	Income	US$
Direct Expenses		Direct Income	
Brokerage/commission Account	550.00		
Hedge Loss Account (P&L—Ineffective)	8,000.00	Gross Loss Carryover	8,550.00
Total	**11,550.00**	Total	**11,550.00**

Balance Sheet

As of 31-Mar-X2

Liabilities	US$	Assets	US$
Capital Account		**Investments**	
Share Capital Account	100,000.00	Investment—ETO Long Put Account	13,000.00
Unrealized Gains/Loss—Other Comprehensive Income Account	20,000.00	Investment—Equity Shares—AFS Account	43,000.00
		Current Assets	
Current Liabilities	Nil	Bank Account	55,450.00
		Profit & Loss Account	
		Opening Balance	
		Current Period	8,550.00
Total	**120,000.00**	Total	**120,000.00**

Additional entries passed at the time of expiry of the options contract are as follows:

T-17 Incremental Mark-to-market on the Underlying Hedged Asset

Journal Entry

Date	Particulars	Debit (US$)	Credit (US$)
15-May-X2	Hedge Gains/Loss Account (Effective portion)	2,000.00	
	To Investments—Equity Shares—AFS Account		2,000.00
	(Being the incremental mark-to-market on the underlying hedged equity shares at the end of the reporting period)		

T-18 Gain in Intrinsic Value of Hedging Instrument (Put Option)

Journal Entry

Date	Particulars	Debit (US$)	Credit (US$)
15-May-X2	Investments—ETO Long Put Account	2,000.00	
	To Hedge Gains/Loss Account (Effective portion)		2,000.00
	(Being the gain in the intrinsic value of the hedging instrument—put options: strike price less the market price times quantity)		

T-19 Time Value Loss on Hedging Instrument (Put Option)

Journal Entry

Date	Particulars	Debit (US$)	Credit (US$)
15-May-X2	Hedge Loss Account (P&L—Ineffective portion)	1,000.00	
	To Investments—ETO Long Put Account		1,000.00
	(Being the time value loss on hedging instrument—put option: market rate of put options less the intrinsic value of put options)		

T-20 Intrinsic Value of Put Option Realized

Journal Entry

Date	Particulars	Debit (US$)	Credit (US$)
15-May-X2	Bank Account	14,000.00	
	To Investments—ETO Long Put Account		14,000.00
	(Being the intrinsic value of put option realized on expiry of the options)		

Cumulative General Ledger Accounts for the Entire Period

General Ledger Accounts

Alex & Co. Account

Date	Particulars	Debit (US$)	Date	Particulars	Credit (US$)
			1-Sep-X1	By Brokerage/ Commission Account	550.00
			1-Sep-X1	By Investments—ETO Long Put Account	9,000.00
1-Sep-X1	To Bank Account	9,550.00			
31-May-X2	Total	**9,550.00**	31-May-X2	Total	**9,550.00**

Bank Account

Date	Particulars	Debit (US$)	Date	Particulars	Credit (US$)
1-May-X1	To Share Capital Account	100,000.00			
			1-May-X1	By Investments—Equity Shares—AFS Account	35,000.00
			1-Sep-X1	By Alex & Co. Account	9,550.00
15-May-X2	To Investment—ETO Long Put Account	14,000.00			
			31-May-X2	By Balance	69,450.00
31-May-X2	Total	**114,000.00**	31-May-X2	Total	**114,000.00**
31-May-X2	To Balance	69,450.00			

Brokerage/Commission Account

Date	Particulars	Debit (US$)	Date	Particulars	Credit (US$)
1-Sep-X1	To Alex & Co. Account	550.00			
			31-May-X2	By Balance	550.00
31-May-X2	Total	**550.00**	31-May-X2	Total	**550.00**
31-May-X2	To Balance	550.00			

Hedge Gains/Loss Account (Effective)

Date	Particulars	Debit (US$)	Date	Particulars	Credit (US$)
30-Sep-X1	To Investment—Equity Shares—AFS Account	5,000.00			
			30-Sep-X1	By Investment—ETO Long Put Account	5,000.00
31-Dec-X1	To Investment—Equity Shares—AFS Account	4,000.00			
			31-Dec-X1	By Investment—ETO Long Put Account	4,000.00
31-Mar-X2	To Investment—Equity Shares—AFS Account	3,000.00	31-Mar-X2	By Investment—ETO Long Put Account	3,000.00
15-May-X2	To Investment—Equity Shares—AFS Account	2,000.00			
			15-May-X2	By Investment—ETO Long Put Account	2,000.00
31-May-X2	Total	**14,000.00**	31-May-X2	Total	**14,000.00**

Hedge Loss Account (P&L—Ineffective)

Date	Particulars	Debit (US$)	Date	Particulars	Credit (US$)
30-Sep-X1	To Investment—ETO Long Put Account	1,000.00			
31-Dec-X1	To Investment—ETO Long Put Account	5,000.00			
31-Mar-X2	To Investment—ETO Long Put Account	2,000.00			
15-May-X2	To Investment—ETO Long Put Account	1,000.00			
			31-May-X2	By Balance	9,000.00
31-May-X2	Total	**9,000.00**	31-May-X2	Total	**9,000.00**
31-May-X2	To Balance	9,000.00			

Investment—ETO Long Put Account

Date	Particulars	Debit (US$)	Date	Particulars	Credit (US$)
1-Sep-X1	To Alex & Co. Account	9,000.00			
30-Sep-X1	To Hedge Gains/Loss Account (Effective)	5,000.00			
			30-Sep-X1	By Hedge Loss Account (P&L—Ineffective)	1,000.00
31-Dec-X1	To Hedge Gains/Loss Account (Effective)	4,000.00			
			31-Dec-X1	By Hedge Loss Account (P&L—Ineffective)	5,000.00
31-Mar-X2	To Hedge Gains/Loss Account (Effective)	3,000.00			
			31-Mar-X2	By Hedge Loss Account (P&L—Ineffective)	2,000.00
15-May-X2	To Hedge Gains/Loss Account (Effective)	2,000.00			
			15-May-X2	By Hedge Loss Account (P&L—Ineffective)	1,000.00
			15-May-X2	By Bank Account	14,000.00
31-May-X2	Total	**23,000.00**	31-May-X2	Total	**23,000.00**

Investment—Equity Shares—AFS Account

Date	Particulars	Debit (US$)	Date	Particulars	Credit (US$)
1-May-X1	To Bank Account	35,000.00			
30-Jun-X1	To Unrealized Gains/ Loss—Other Comprehensive Income Account	14,000.00			
1-Sep-X1	To Unrealized Gains/ Loss—Other Comprehensive Income Account	6,000.00			
			30-Sep-X1	By Hedge Gains/ Loss Account (Effective)	5,000.00
			31-Dec-X1	By Hedge Gains/ Loss Account (Effective)	4,000.00
			31-Mar-X2	By Hedge Gains/ Loss Account (Effective)	3,000.00
			15-May-X2	By Hedge Gains/ Loss Account (Effective)	2,000.00
			31-May-X2	By Balance	41,000.00
31-May-X2	Total	**55,000.00**	31-May-X2	Total	**55,000.00**
31-May-X2	To Balance	41,000.00			

Share Capital Account

Date	Particulars	Debit (US$)	Date	Particulars	Credit (US$)
			1-May-X1	By Bank Account	100,000.00
31-May-X2	To Balance	100,000.00			
31-May-X2	Total	**100,000.00**	31-May-X2	Total	**100,000.00**
			31-May-X2	By Balance	100,000.00

Unrealized Gains/Loss—Other Comprehensive Income Account

Date	Particulars	Debit (US$)	Date	Particulars	Credit (US$)
			30-Jun-X1	By Investments—Equity Shares—AFS Account	14,000.00
			1-Sep-X1	By Investments—Equity Shares—AFS Account	6,000.00
31-May-X2	To Balance	20,000.00			
31-May-X2	Total	**20,000.00**	31-May-X2	Total	**20,000.00**
			31-May-X2	By Balance	20,000.00

Trial Balance

As of 31-May-X2 (US$)

Particulars	Debit	Credit
Capital Account		
Share Capital Account		100,000.00
Unrealized Gains/Loss—Other Comprehensive Income Account		20,000.00
Current Liabilities		
Investments		
Investment—Equity Shares—AFS Account	41,000.00	
Current Assets		
Bank Account	69,450.00	
Direct Expenses		
Hedge Loss Account (P&L—Ineffective)	1,000.00	
Profit & Loss Account	8,550.00	
Total	**120,000.00**	**120,000.00**

Income Statement

For the period ending 31-May-X2

Expenses	US$	Income	US$
Direct Expenses		**Direct Income**	
Hedge Loss Account (P&L—Ineffective)	1,000.00	Net Loss Carryover	1,000.00
Total	**1,000.00**	Total	**1,000.00**

Balance Sheet

As of 31-May-X2

Liabilities	US$	Assets	US$
Capital Account		**Investments**	
Share Capital Account	100,000.00	Investment—ETO Long Put Account	Nil
Unrealized Gains/Loss—Other Comprehensive Income Account	20,000.00	Investment—Equity Shares—AFS Account	41,000.00
		Current Assets	
Current Liabilities	Nil	Bank Account	69,450.00
		Profit & Loss Account	
		Opening Balance	8,550.00
		Current Period	1,000.00
Total	**120,000.00**	Total	**120,000.00**

Long Put Options—Trade Currency SGD

On May 1, World Trotter Company purchased 1,000 shares of Colgate at a cost of SGD70 per share (inclusive of brokerage.) World Trotter had no immediate intention to resell the shares and classified them as available-for-sale. The price shot up to SGD110 by September 1 and World Trotter decided to hedge the investment in Colgate. Towards this, World Trotter purchased put options on Colgate at SGD18 with an exercise price of SGD110, expiry being May 15 of the following year, through the brokers David & Co, and brokerage being SGD550.

- World Trotter Company wants to adopt hedge accounting for the put options and must document the hedge strategy, objectives, and hedging relationships.
- The intrinsic value of the option would be used to determine the effectiveness of the hedge.
- The time value is to be charged off to income.
- World Trotter Company introduced $100,000 into the fund on May 1 and converted the same into SGD at 1.50 per US$.
- The quarterly accounting period closes on June 30, September 30, December 31, and March 31.

Journal entries, general ledgers, trial balance, income statement, and balance sheet are prepared.

Liquidation Method
FIFO

Market Rate of Underlying Stock, Colgate
30-Jun-X1: SGD98; 1-Sep-X1: SGD110; 30-Sep-X1: SGD100; 31-Dec-X1: SGD92; 31-Mar-X2: SGD86; 15-May-X2: SGD82;

Market Rate of Colgate Put Option with Strike Price $110, Expiry May 15
September 1: SGD18
September 30: SGD26
December 31: SGD24
March 31: SGD26
May 15: SGD28

FX Rates
April 25: 1.500
May 1: 1.525
June 30: 1.535
September 1: 1.515
September 30: 1.520
December 31: 1.57
March 31: 1.495
May 15: 1.515

Long Put Options, Hedging Activity—Trade Currency SGD

A summary of the market rates of put options, underlying, intrinsic worth of the option contract, and time value of the option contract is presented in the following table.

Date	1-Sep-X1	30-Sep-X1	31-Dec-X1	31-Mar-X2	15-May-X2
(a) Market rate—Puts	18	26	24	26	28
(b) Market rate—Equity	110	100	92	86	82
(c) Intrinsic worth	0	10	18	24	28
(d) Incremental increase in (c)		10	8	6	4
(e) Time value = (a) − (c)	18	16	6	2	0
(f) Incremental erosion in time value		2	10	4	2

T-1 Conversion of US$ into SGD

Journal Entry

Date	Particulars	Debit (SGD)	Credit (SGD)
25-Apr-X1	Bank SGD Account	150,000.00	
	To Bank Contra Account		150,000.00
	(Being the US$ converted into SGD by FX spot trade @ 1.5)		

T-2 On Purchase of Put Options

Journal Entry

Date	Particulars	Debit (SGD)	Credit (SGD)
1-May-X1	Investments—Equity Shares—AFS Account	70,000.00	
	To Bank Account		70,000.00
	(Being the purchase of 1,000 equity shares of Lloyd)		

T-3 Mark-to-market on the AFS Security

Journal Entry

Date	Particulars	Debit (SGD)	Credit (SGD)
30-Jun-X1	Investments—Equity Shares—AFS Account	28,000.00	
	To Unrealized Gains/Loss—Other Comprehensive Income Account		28,000.00
	(Being the mark-to-market entry on the AFS security at the end of the reporting period)		

T-4 Mark-to-market on the AFS Security

Journal Entry

Date	Particulars	Debit (SGD)	Credit (SGD)
1-Sep-X1	Investments—Equity shares—AFS Account	12,000.00	
	To Unrealized Gains/Loss—Other Comprehensive Income Account		12,000.00
	(Being the mark-to-market purchase of 1,000 equity put options of Lloyd)		

T-5 On Purchase of Put Options

Journal Entry

Date	Particulars	Debit (SGD)	Credit (SGD)
1-Sep-X1	Investments—ETO Long Put Account	18,000.00	
	To Alex & Co. Account		18,000.00
	(Being the purchase of 1,000 equity put options of Lloyd)		

T-6 Brokerage/Commission

Journal Entry

Date	Particulars	Debit (SGD)	Credit (SGD)
1-Sep-X1	Brokerage/Commission Account	550.00	
	To Alex & Co. Account		550.00
	(Being the brokerage incurred on the purchase of put options)		

T-7 On Payment of Contracted Amount

Journal Entry

Date	Particulars	Debit (SGD)	Credit (SGD)
1-Sep-X1	Alex & Co. Account	18,550.00	
	To Bank Account		18,550.00
	(Being the payment made to Alex & Co. on purchase of put options)		

T-8 Incremental Mark-to-market on the Underlying Hedged Asset

Journal Entry

Date	Particulars	Debit (SGD)	Credit (SGD)
30-Sep-X1	Hedge Gain Account (Effective portion)	10,000.00	
	To Investments—Equity Shares—AFS Account		10,000.00
	(Being the incremental mark-to-market on the underlying hedged equity shares at the end of the reporting period)		

T-9 Gain in Intrinsic Value of Hedging Instrument (Put Option)

Journal Entry

Date	Particulars	Debit (SGD)	Credit (SGD)
30-Sep-X1	Investments—ETO Long Put Account	10,000.00	
	To Hedge Gain Account (Effective portion)		10,000.00
	(Being the gain in the intrinsic value of the hedging instrument—put options: strike price less the market price times quantity)		

T-10 Time Value Loss on Hedging Instrument (Put Option)

Journal Entry

Date	Particulars	Debit (SGD)	Credit (SGD)
30-Sep-X1	Hedge Loss Account (P&L—Ineffective portion)	2,000.00	
	To Investments—ETO Long Put Account		2,000.00
	(Being the time value loss on hedging instrument—put option: cost of put option less the intrinsic value of put options)		

T-11 Incremental Mark-to-market on the Underlying Hedged Asset

Journal Entry

Date	Particulars	Debit (SGD)	Credit (SGD)
31-Dec-X1	Hedge Gains/Loss Account (Effective Portion)	8,000.00	
	To Investments—Equity Shares—AFS Account		8,000.00
	(Being the incremental mark-to-market on the underlying hedged equity shares at the end of the reporting period)		

T-12 Gain in Intrinsic Value of Hedging Instrument (Put Option)

Journal Entry

Date	Particulars	Debit (SGD)	Credit (SGD)
31-Dec-X1	Investments—ETO Long Put Account	8,000.00	
	To Hedge Gains/Loss Account (Effective Portion)		8,000.00
	(Being the gain in the intrinsic value of the hedging instrument—put options: strike price less the market price times quantity)		

T-13 Time Value Loss on Hedging Instrument (Put Option)

Journal Entry

Date	Particulars	Debit (SGD)	Credit (SGD)
31-Dec-X1	Hedge Loss Account (P&L—Ineffective portion)	10,000.00	
	To Investments—ETO Long Put Account		10,000.00
	(Being the time value loss on hedging instrument—put option: cost of put option less the intrinsic value of put options)		

T-14 Incremental Mark-to-market on the Underlying Hedged Asset

Journal Entry

Date	Particulars	Debit (SGD)	Credit (SGD)
31-Mar-X2	Hedge Gains/Loss Account (Effective portion)	6,000.00	
	To Investments—Equity Shares—AFS Account		6,000.00
	(Being the incremental mark-to-market on the underlying hedged equity shares at the end of the reporting period)		

T-15 Gain in Intrinsic Value of Hedging Instrument (Put Option)

Journal Entry

Date	Particulars	Debit (SGD)	Credit (SGD)
31-Mar-X2	Investments—ETO Long Put Account	6,000.00	
	To Hedge Gains/Loss Account (Effective portion)		6,000.00
	(Being the gain in the intrinsic value of the hedging instrument—put options: strike price less the market price times quantity)		

T-16 Time Value Loss on Hedging Instrument (Put Option)

Journal Entry

Date	Particulars	Debit (SGD)	Credit (SGD)
31-Mar-X2	Hedge Loss Account (P&L—Ineffective portion)	4,000.00	
	To Investments—ETO Long Put Account		4,000.00
	(Being the time value loss on hedging instrument—put option: market rate of put options less the intrinsic value of put options)		

General Ledger Accounts

Alex & Co. Account

Date	Particulars	Debit (SGD)	Date	Particulars	Credit (SGD)
			1-Sep-X1	By Investments—ETO Long Put Account	18,000.00
			1-Sep-X1	By Brokerage/Commission Account	550.00
1-Sep-X1	To Bank Account	18,550.00			
31-May-X2	Total	**18,550.00**	31-May-X2	Total	**18,550.00**

Bank Account

Date	Particulars	Debit (SGD)	Date	Particulars	Credit (SGD)
1-May-X1	To Share Capital Account	150,000.00			
			1-May-X1	By Investments—Equity Shares—AFS Account	70,000.00
			1-Sep-X1	By Alex & Co. Account	18,550.00
15-May-X2	To Investment—ETO Long Put Account	28,000.00			
			31-May-X2	By Balance	89,450.00
31-May-X2	Total	**178,000.00**	31-May-X2	Total	**178,000.00**
31-May-X2	To Balance	89,450.00			

Bank Contra Account

Date	Particulars	Debit (SGD)	Date	Particulars	Credit (SGD)
1-May-X1	To Bank Account	150,000.00			
			31-May-X2	By Balance	150,000.00
31-May-X2	Total	**150,000.00**	31-May-X2	Total	**150,000.00**
31-May-X2	To Balance	150,000.00			

Brokerage/Commission Account

Date	Particulars	Debit (SGD)	Date	Particulars	Credit (SGD)
1-Sep-X1	To Alex & Co. Account	550.00			
			31-May-X2	By Balance	550.00
31-May-X2	Total	**550.00**	31-May-X2	Total	**550.00**
31-May-X2	To Balance	550.00			

Hedge Gain Account (Effective)

Date	Particulars	Debit (SGD)	Date	Particulars	Credit (SGD)
30-Sep-X1	To Investment—Equity Shares—AFS Account	10,000.00			
			30-Sep-X1	By Investment—ETO Long Put Account	10,000.00
31-Dec-X1	To Investment—Equity Shares—AFS Account	8,000.00			
			31-Dec-X1	By Investment—ETO Long Put Account	8,000.00
31-Mar-X2	To Investment—Equity Shares—AFS Account	6,000.00			
			31-Mar-X2	By Investment—ETO Long Put Account	6,000.00
15-May-X2	To Investment—Equity Shares—AFS Account	4,000.00			
			15-May-X2	By Investment—ETO Long Put Account	4,000.00
31-May-X2	To Balance	2,000.00			
31-May-X2	Total	**30,000.00**	31-May-X2	Total	**30,000.00**

Hedge Loss Account (P&L—Ineffective)

Date	Particulars	Debit (SGD)	Date	Particulars	Credit (SGD)
30-Sep-X1	To Investment—ETO Long Put Account	2,000.00			
31-Dec-X1	To Investment—ETO Long Put Account	10,000.00			
31-Mar-X2	To Investment—ETO Long Put Account	4,000.00			
15-May-X2	To Investment—ETO Long Put Account	2,000.00			
			31-May-X2	By Balance	18,000.00
31-May-X2	Total	**18,000.00**	31-May-X2	Total	**18,000.00**
31-May-X2	To Balance	18,000.00			

Investment—ETO Long Put Account

Date	Particulars	Debit (SGD)	Date	Particulars	Credit (SGD)
1-Sep-X1	To Alex & Co. Account	18,000.00			
30-Sep-X1	To Hedge Gains/ Loss Account (Effective)	10,000.00			
			30-Sep-X1	By Hedge Loss Account (P&L—Ineffective)	2,000.00
31-Dec-X1	To Hedge Gains/ Loss Account (Effective)	8,000.00			
			31-Dec-X1	By Hedge Loss Account (P&L—Ineffective)	10,000.00
			31-Mar-X2	By Hedge Loss Account (P&L—Ineffective)	4,000.00
31-Mar-X2	To Hedge Gains/ Loss Account (Effective)	6,000.00			
15-May-X2	To Hedge Gains/ Loss Account (Effective)	4,000.00			
			15-May-X2	By Hedge Loss Account (P&L—Ineffective)	2,000.00
			15-May-X2	By Bank Account	28,000.00
31-May-X2	Total	**46,000.00**	31-May-X2	Total	**46,000.00**

Investment—Equity Shares—AFS Account

Date	Particulars	Debit (SGD)	Date	Particulars	Credit (SGD)
1-May-X1	To Bank Account	70,000.00			
30-Jun-X1	To Unrealized Gains/Loss—Other Comprehensive Income Account	28,000.00			
1-Sep-X1	To Unrealized Gains/Loss—Other Comprehensive Income Account	12,000.00			
			30-Sep-X1	By Hedge Gains/ Loss Account (Effective)	10,000.00

Investment—Equity Shares—AFS Account (*Cont'd*)

Date	Particulars	Debit (SGD)	Date	Particulars	Credit (SGD)
			31-Dec-X1	By Hedge Gains/ Loss Account (Effective)	8,000.00
			31-Mar-X2	By Hedge Loss Account (P&L—Ineffective)	6,000.00
			15-May-X2	By Hedge Gains/ Loss Account (Effective)	4,000.00
			31-May-X2	By Balance	82,000.00
31-May-X2	Total	**110,000.00**	31-May-X2	Total	**110,000.00**
31-May-X2	To Balance	82,000.00			

Unrealized Gains/Loss—Other Comprehensive Income Account

Date	Particulars	Debit (SGD)	Date	Particulars	Credit (SGD)
			30-Jun-X1	By Investments—Equity Shares—AFS Account	28,000.00
			1-Sep-X1	By Investments—Equity Shares—AFS Account	12,000.00
31-May-X2	To Balance	40,000.00			
31-May-X2	Total	**40,000.00**	31-May-X2	Total	**40,000.00**
			31-May-X2	By Balance	40,000.00

Trial Balance

As of 31-Mar-X2 (SGD)

Particulars	Debit	Credit
Capital Account		
Unrealized Gains/Loss—Other Comprehensive Income Account		40,000.00
Current Liabilities		Nil
Investments		
Investment—ETO Long Put Account	26,000.00	
Investment—Equity Shares—AFS Account	86,000.00	
Current Assets		
Bank Account	61,450.00	
Bank contra Account		150,000.00
Direct Expenses		
Brokerage/Commission Account	550.00	
Hedge Loss Account (P&L—Ineffective)	16,000.00	
Total	**190,000.00**	**190,000.00**

Income Statement

For the period ending 31-Mar-X2

Expenses	SGD	Income	SGD
Direct Expenses		**Direct Income**	
Brokerage/commission Account	550.00	Net Loss Carryover	16,550.00
Hedge Loss Account (P&L—Ineffective)	16,000.00		
Total	**16,550.00**	Total	**16,550.00**

Balance Sheet

As of 31-Mar-X2

Liabilities	SGD	Assets	SGD
Capital Account		**Investments**	
		Investment—ETO Long Put Account	26,000.00
Unrealized Gains/Loss—Other Comprehensive Income Account	40,000.00	Investment—Equity Shares—AFS Account	86,000.00
		Current Assets	
Current Liabilities	Nil	Bank Account	61,450.00
Bank Contra Account	150,000.00		
		Profit & Loss Account	
		Opening Balance	Nil
		Current Period	16,550.00
Total	**190,000.00**	Total	**190,000.00**

Additional entries passed at the time of expiry of the options contract include the following:

T-17 Incremental Mark-to-market on the Underlying Hedged Asset

Journal Entry

Date	Particulars	Debit (SGD)	Credit (SGD)
15-May-X2	Hedge Gains/Loss Account (Effective portion)	4,000.00	
	To Investments—Equity Shares—AFS Account		4,000.00
	(Being the incremental mark-to-market on the underlying hedged equity shares at the end of the reporting period)		

T-18 Gain in Intrinsic Value of Hedging Instrument (Put Option)

Journal Entry

Date	Particulars	Debit (SGD)	Credit (SGD)
15-May-X2	Investments—ETO Long Put Account	4,000.00	
	To Hedge Gains/Loss Account (Effective portion)		4,000.00
	(Being the gain in the intrinsic value of the hedging instrument—put options: strike price less the market price times quantity)		

T-19 Time Value Loss on Hedging Instrument (Put Option)

Journal Entry

Date	Particulars	Debit (SGD)	Credit (SGD)
15-May-X2	Hedge Loss Account (P&L—Ineffective portion)	2,000.00	
	To Investments—ETO Long Put Account		2,000.00
	(Being the time value loss on hedging instrument—put option: market rate of put options less the intrinsic value of put options)		

T-20 Intrinsic Value of Put Option Realized

Journal Entry

Date	Particulars	Debit (SGD)	Credit (SGD)
15-May-X2	Bank Account	28,000.00	
	To Investments—ETO Long Put Account		28,000.00
	(Being the intrinsic value of put option realized on expiry of the options)		

Trial Balance

As of 31-May-X2 (SGD)

Particulars	Debit	Credit
Capital Account		
Unrealized Gains/Loss—Other Comprehensive Income Account		40,000.00
Current Liabilities		
Investments		
Investment—Equity Shares—AFS Account	82,000.00	
Current Assets		
Bank Account	89,450.00	
Bank Contra Account		150,000.00
Direct Expenses		
Hedge Gains/loss Account (Effective)	2,000.00	
Profit & Loss Account	16,550.00	
Total	190,000.00	190,000.00

Income Statement

For the period ending 31-May-X2

Expenses	SGD	Income	SGD
Direct Expenses		**Direct Income**	
Hedge Loss Account (P&L—Ineffective)	2,000.00	Net Loss Carryover	2,000.00
Total	2,000.00	Total	2,000.00

Balance Sheet

As of 31-May-X2

Liabilities	SGD	Assets	SGD
Capital Account		**Investments**	
		Investment—ETO Long Put Account	Nil
Unrealized Gains/Loss—Other Comprehensive Income Account	40,000.00	Investment—Equity Shares—AFS Account	82,000.00
		Current Assets	
Current Liabilities	Nil	Bank Account	89,450.00
Bank Contra Account	150,000.00		
		Profit & Loss Account	
		Opening Balance	16,550.00
		Current Period	2,000.00
Total	**190,000.00**	Total	**190,000.00**

Long Put Options: Hedging Activity

F-1 On Introducing Share Capital (T-1 @ FX Rate: 1.500)

Journal Entry

Date	Particulars	Debit (US$)	Credit (US$)
25-Apr-X1	Bank US$ Account	100,000.00	
	To Share Capital Account		100,000.00
	(Being the capital introduced by the investor into the company)		

F-2 Conversion of US$ into SGD (T-2 @ FX Rate: 1.500)

Journal Entry

Date	Particulars	Debit (US$)	Credit (US$)
25-Apr-X1	Bank SGD Account	100,000.00	
	To Bank Contra Account		100,000.00
	(Being the US$ converted into SGD by FX spot trade @ 1.5)		

Journal Entry

Date	Particulars	Debit (US$)	Credit (US$)
25-Apr-X1	Bank Contra Account	100,000.00	
	To Bank US$ Account		100,000.00
	(Being the US$ converted into SGD by FX spot trade @ 1.5)		

F-3 On Purchase of Put Options (T-3 @ FX Rate: 1.525)

Journal Entry

Date	Particulars	Debit (US$)	Credit (US$)
1-May-X1	Investments—Equity Shares—AFS Account	45,901.64	
	To Bank SGD Account		45,901.64
	(Being the purchase of 1,000 equity shares of Lloyd)		

F-4 Mark-to-market on the AFS Security (T-4 @ FX Rate: 1.535)

Journal Entry

Date	Particulars	Debit (US$)	Credit (US$)
30-Jun-X1	Investments—Equity Shares—AFS Account	18,241.04	
	To Unrealized Gains/Loss—Other Comprehensive Income Account		18,241.04
	(Being the mark-to-market entry on the AFS security at the end of the reporting period)		

F-5 Mark-to-market on the AFS Security (T-5 @ FX Rate: 1.515)

Journal Entry

Date	Particulars	Debit (US$)	Credit (US$)
1-Sep-X1	Investments—Equity Shares—AFS Account	7,920.79	
	To Unrealized Gains/Loss—Other Comprehensive Income Account		7,920.79
	(Being the mark-to-market purchase of 1,000 equity put options of Lloyd)		

F-6 On Purchase of Put Options (T-6 @ FX Rate: 1.515)

Journal Entry

Date	Particulars	Debit (US$)	Credit (US$)
1-Sep-X1	Investments—ETO Long Put Account	11,881.19	
	To Alex & Co. Account		11,881.19
	(Being the purchase of 1,000 equity put options of Lloyd)		

F-7 Brokerage/Commission (T-7 @ FX Rate: 1.515)

Journal Entry

Date	Particulars	Debit (US$)	Credit (US$)
1-Sep-X1	Brokerage/Commission Account	363.03	
	To Alex & Co. Account		363.03
	(Being the brokerage incurred on the purchase of put options)		

F-8 On Payment of Contracted Amount (T-8 @ FX Rate: 1.515)

Journal Entry

Date	Particulars	Debit (US$)	Credit (US$)
1-Sep-X1	Alex & Co. Account	12,244.22	
	To Bank SGD Account		12,244.22
	(Being the payment made to Alex & Co. on purchase of put options)		

F-9 Incremental Mark-to-market on the Underlying Hedged Asset (T-9 @ FX Rate: 1.5200)

Journal Entry

Date	Particulars	Debit (US$)	Credit (US$)
30-Sep-X1	Hedge Gains/Loss Account (Effective portion)	6,578.95	
	To Investments—Equity Shares—AFS Account		6,578.95
	(Being the incremental mark-to-market on the underlying hedged equity shares at the end of the reporting period)		

F-10 Gain in Intrinsic Value of Hedging Instrument (Put Option) (T-10 @ FX Rate: 1.520)

Journal Entry

Date	Particulars	Debit (US$)	Credit (US$)
30-Sep-X1	Investments—ETO Long Put Account	6,578.95	
	To Hedge Gains/Loss Account (Effective portion)		6,578.95
	(Being the gain in the intrinsic value of the hedging instrument—put options: strike price less the market price times quantity)		

F-11 Time Value Loss on Hedging Instrument (Put Option) (T-11 @ FX Rate: 1.520)

Journal Entry

Date	Particulars	Debit (US$)	Credit (US$)
30-Sep-X1	Hedge Loss Account (P&L—Ineffective portion)	1,315.79	
	To Investments—ETO Long Put Account		1,315.79
	(Being the time value loss on hedging instrument—put option: cost of put option less the intrinsic value of put options)		

F-12 Incremental Mark-to-market on the Underlying Hedged Asset (T-12 @ FX Rate: 1.570)

Journal Entry

Date	Particulars	Debit (US$)	Credit (US$)
31-Dec-X1	Hedge Gains/Loss Account (Effective portion)	5,095.54	
	To Investments—Equity Shares—AFS Account		5,095.54
	(Being the incremental mark-to-market on the underlying hedged equity shares at the end of the reporting period)		

F-13 Gain in Intrinsic Value of Hedging Instrument (Put Option) (T-13 @ FX Rate: 1.570)

Journal Entry

Date	Particulars	Debit (US$)	Credit (US$)
31-Dec-X1	Investments—ETO Long Put Account	5,095.54	
	To Hedge Gains/Loss Account (Effective portion)		5,095.54
	(Being the gain in the intrinsic value of the hedging instrument—put options: strike price less the market price times quantity)		

F-14 Time Value Loss on Hedging Instrument (Put Option) (T-14 @ FX Rate: 1.570)

Journal Entry

Date	Particulars	Debit (US$)	Credit (US$)
31-Dec-X1	Hedge Loss Account (P&L—Ineffective portion)	6,369.43	
	To Investments—ETO Long Put Account		6,369.43
	(Being the time value loss on hedging instrument—put option: cost of put option less the intrinsic value of put options)		

F-15 Incremental Mark-to-market on the Underlying Hedged Asset (T-15 @ FX Rate: 1.495)

Journal Entry

Date	Particulars	Debit (US$)	Credit (US$)
31-Mar-X2	Hedge Gains/Loss Account (Effective portion)	4,013.38	
	To Investments—Equity Shares—AFS Account		4,013.38
	(Being the incremental mark-to-market on the underlying hedged equity shares at the end of the reporting period)		

F-16 Gain in Intrinsic Value of Hedging Instrument (Put Option) (T-16 @ FX Rate: 1.495)

Journal Entry

Date	Particulars	Debit (US$)	Credit (US$)
31-Mar-X2	Investments—ETO Long Put Account	4,013.38	
	To Hedge Gains/Loss Account (Effective portion)		4,013.38
	(Being the gain in the intrinsic value of the hedging instrument—put options: strike price less the market price times quantity)		

F-17 Time Value Loss on Hedging Instrument (Put Option) (T-17 @ FX Rate: 1.495)

Journal Entry

Date	Particulars	Debit (US$)	Credit (US$)
31-Mar-X2	Hedge Loss Account (P&L—Ineffective portion)	2,675.59	
	To Investments—ETO Long Put Account		2,675.59
	(Being the time value loss on hedging instrument—put option: market rate of put options less the intrinsic value of put options)		

F-18 FX Translation on Investments—ETO Puts (Transient FX Translation Entry)

Unrealized Currency Gains/Loss on ETO Put Options

Date	Description	SGD	FX Rate	US$
1-Sep-X1	Purchase of put options	18,000.00	1.515	11,881.19
30-Sep-X1	Gain on put options	10,000.00	1.520	6,578.95
30-Sep-X1	Time vale loss on hedging instrument	(2,000.00)	1.520	(1,315.79)
31-Dec-X1	Gain on put options	8,000.00	1.570	5,095.54

Unrealized Currency Gains/Loss on ETO Put options (*Cont'd*)

Date	Description	SGD	FX Rate	US$
31-Dec-X1	Time value loss on hedging instrument	(10,000.00)	1.570	(6,369.43)
31-Mar-X2	Gain on put options	6,000.00	1.495	4,013.38
31-Mar-X2	Time value loss on hedging instrument	(4,000.00)	1.495	(2,675.59)
	Total			**17,208.25**
31-Mar-X2	Closing balance	26,000.00	1.495	17,391.30
	Unrealized currency gains			183.05

Journal Entry

Date	Particulars	Debit (US$)	Credit (US$)
31-Mar-X2	Investments—ETO Long Put Account	183.05	
	To Unrealized Currency Gains/loss Account		183.05
	(Being the FX translation applied on ETO put options)		

F-19 FX Translation on Equity Shares (Transient FX Translation Entry)

Unrealized Currency Gains/Loss—Equity Shares

Date	Description	SGD	FX rate	US$
1-May-X1	Opening balance	70,000.00	1.525	45,901.64
30-Jun-X1	Incremental mark-to-market	28,000.00	1.535	18,241.04
1-Sep-X1	Incremental mark-to-market	12,000.00	1.515	7,920.79
30-Sep-X1	Incremental mark-to-market	(10,000.00)	1.520	(6,578.95)
31-Dec-X1	Incremental mark-to-market	(8,000.00)	1.570	(5,095.54)
31-Mar-X2	Incremental mark-to-market	(6,000.00)	1.495	(4,013.38)
				56,375.60
31-Mar-X2	Closing balance	86,000.00	1.495	57,525.08
	Unrealized currency gains			1,149.48

Journal Entry

Date	Particulars	Debit (US$)	Credit (US$)
31-Mar-X2	Investments—Equity Shares—AFS Account	1,149.48	
	To Unrealized Currency Gains/loss Account		1,149.48
	(Being the FX translation applied on equity shares account)		

F-20 FX Translation on Bank Account (Transient FX Translation Entry)

Unrealized Currency Gains/Loss Bank Account

Date	Description	SGD	FX rate	US$
1-May-X1	Opening balance	150,000.00	1.525	100,000.00
1-May-X1	Incremental mark-to-market	(70,000.00)	1.525	(45,901.64)
1-Sep-X1	Incremental mark-to-market	(18,550.00)	1.515	(12,244.22)
				41,854.14
31-Mar-X2	Closing balance	61,450.00	1.495	41,103.68
	Unrealized currency loss			(750.46)

Journal Entry

Date	Particulars	Debit (US$)	Credit (US$)
31-Mar-X2	Unrealized Currency Gains/Loss Account	750.46	
	To Bank SGD Account		750.46
	(Being the FX translation applied on bank account)		

Trial Balance

As of 31-Mar-X2 (US$)

Particulars	Debit	Credit
Capital Account		
Share Capital Account		100,000.00
Unrealized Gains/Loss—Other Comprehensive Income Account		26,161.83
Current Liabilities		
Investments		
Investment—ETO Long Put Account	17,391.30	
Investment—Equity Shares—AFS Account	57,525.08	
Current Assets		
Bank SGD Account	41,103.68	
Direct Incomes		
Unrealized Currency Gains/Loss Account		582.07
Direct Expenses		
Brokerage/Commission Account	363.03	
Hedge Loss Account (P&L—Ineffective)	10,360.81	
Total	**126,743.90**	**126,743.90**

Income Statement

For the period ending 31-Mar-X2

Expenses	US$	Income	US$
Direct Expenses		**Direct Income**	
Brokerage/Commission Account	363.03	Unrealized Currency Gains/Loss Account	582.07
Hedge Loss Account (P&L—Ineffective)	10,360.81		
		Net Loss Carryover	10,141.77
Total	**10,723.84**	Total	**10,723.84**

Balance Sheet

As of 31-Mar-X2

Liabilities	US$	Assets	US$
Capital Account		**Investments**	
Share Capital Account	100,000.00	Investment—ETO Long Put Account	17,391.30
Unrealized Gains/Loss—Other Comprehensive Income Account	26,161.83	Investment—Equity Shares—AFS Account	57,525.08
		Current Assets	
Current Liabilities	Nil	Bank Account	41,103.68
		Profit & Loss Account	
		Opening Balance	Nil
		Current Period	10,141.77
Total	**126,161.83**	Total	**126,161.83**

Additional entries passed at the time of expiry of the options are as follows:

F-21 Incremental Mark-to-market on the Underlying Hedged Asset (T-18 @ FX Rate: 1.515)

Journal Entry

Date	Particulars	Debit (US$)	Credit (US$)
15-May-X2	Hedge Gains/Loss Account (Effective portion)	2,640.26	
	To Investments—Equity Shares—AFS Account		2,640.26
	(Being the incremental mark to market on the underlying hedged equity shares at the end of the reporting period)		

F-22 Gain in Intrinsic Value of Hedging Instrument (Put Option) (T-19 @ FX Rate: 1.515)

Journal Entry

Date	Particulars	Debit (US$)	Credit (US$)
15-May-X2	Investments—ETO Long Put Account	2,640.26	
	To Hedge Gains/Loss Account (Effective portion)		2,640.26
	(Being the gain in the intrinsic value of the hedging instrument—put options: strike price less the market price times quantity)		

F-23 Time Value Loss on Hedging Instrument (Put Option) (T-20 @ FX Rate: 1.515)

Journal Entry

Date	Particulars	Debit (US$)	Credit (US$)
15-May-X2	Hedge Loss Account (P&L—Ineffective portion)	1,320.13	
	To Investments—ETO Long Put Account		1,320.13
	(Being the time value loss on hedging instrument—put option: market rate of put options less the intrinsic value of put options)		

F-24 Intrinsic Value of Put Option Realized (T-21 @ FX Rate: 1.515)

Journal Entry

Date	Particulars	Debit (US$)	Credit (US$)
15-May-X2	Bank SGD Account	18,481.85	
	To Investments—ETO Long Put Account		18,481.85
	(Being the intrinsic value of put option realized on expiry of the options)		

F-25 FX Translation on ETO Put Options (Transient FX Translation Entry)

Unrealized Currency Gains/Loss—ETO

Date	Description	SGD	FX rate	US$
31-Mar- X2	Opening balance	26,000.00	1.495	17,391.30
15-May-X2	Gain on put options	4,000.00	1.515	2,640.26
15-May-X2	Time value loss on hedging instrument	(2,000.00)	1.515	(1,320.13)
15-May-X2	Bank	(28,000.00)	1.515	(18,481.85)
	Unrealized currency loss			(229.58)

Journal Entry

Date	Particulars	Debit (US$)	Credit (US$)
15-May-X2	Unrealized Currency Gains/Loss Account	229.58	
	To Investments—ETO Long Put Account		229.58
	(Being the FX translation applied on ETO put options)		

F-26 FX Translation on Equity Account (Transient FX Translation Entry)

Unrealized Currency Gains/Loss Equity Shares

Date	Description	SGD	FX rate	US$
31-Mar-X2	Opening balance	86,000.00	1.525	57,525.08
15-May-X2	Incremental mark-to-market	(4,000.00)	1.515	(2,640.26)
				54,884.82
15-May-X2	Closing balance	82,000.00	1.515	54,125.41
	Unrealized currency loss			(759.41)

Journal Entry

Date	Particulars	Debit (US$)	Credit (US$)
15-May-X2	Unrealized Currency Gains/Loss Account	759.41	
	To Investments—Equity Shares—AFS Account		759.41
	(Being the FX translation applied on equity shares)		

F-27 FX Translation—on Bank Account (Transient FX Translation Entry)

Unrealized Currency Gains/Loss Bank SGD Account

Date	Description	SGD	FX rate	US$
31-Mar-X2	Opening balance	61,450.00	1.495	41,103.68
15-May-X2	Incremental mark-to-market	28,000.00	1.515	18,481.85
				59,585.53
15-May-X2	Closing balance	89,450.00	1.515	59,042.90
	Unrealized currency loss			(542.62)

Journal Entry

Date	Particulars	Debit (US$)	Credit (US$)
15-May-X2	Unrealized Currency Gains/Loss Account	542.62	
	To Bank Account		542.62
	(Being the FX translation applied on bank account)		

General Ledger Accounts

Alex & Co. Account

Date	Particulars	Debit (US$)	Date	Particulars	Credit (US$)
			1-Sep-X1	By Investments—ETO Long Put Account	11,881.19
			1-Sep-X1	By Brokerage/Commission Account	363.03
1-Sep-X1	To Bank Account	12,244.22			
31-May-X2	Total	**12,244.22**	31-May-X2	Total	**12,244.22**

Bank SGD Account

Date	Particulars	Debit (US$)	Date	Particulars	Credit (US$)
1-May-X1	To Bank Contra Account	100,000.00			
			1-May-X1	By Investments—Equity Shares—AFS Account	45,901.64
			1-Sep-X1	By Alex & Co. Account	12,244.22
			31-Mar-X2	By Unrealized Currency Gains/Loss Account	750.46
15-May-X2	To Invest-ment—ETO Long Put Account	18,481.85			
			15-May-X2	By Unrealized Currency Gains/Loss Account	542.62
			31-May-X2	To Balance	59,042.91
31-May-X2	Total	**118,481.85**	31-May-X2	Total	**118,481.85**
31-May-X2	To Balance	59,042.91			

Bank US$ Account

Date	Particulars	Debit (US$)	Date	Particulars	Credit (US$)
1-May-X1	To Share Capital Account	100,000.00			
			1-May-X1	By Bank Contra Account	100,000.00
31-May-X2	Total	**100,000.00**	31-May-X2	Total	**100,000.00**

Bank Contra Account

Date	Particulars	Debit (US$)	Date	Particulars	Credit (US$)
25-Apr-X1	To Bank US$ Account	100,000.00			
			25-Apr-X1	By Bank SGD Account	100,000.00
31-May-X2	Total	**100,000.00**	31-May-X2	Total	**100,000.00**

Brokerage/Commission Account

Date	Particulars	Debit (US$)	Date	Particulars	Credit (US$)
1-Sep-X1	To Alex & Co. Account	363.03			
			31-May-X2	By Balance	363.03
31-May-X2	Total	**363.03**	31-May-X2	Total	**363.03**
31-May-X2	To Balance	363.03			

Unrealized Currency Gains/Loss Account

Date	Particulars	Debit (US$)	Date	Particulars	Credit (US$)
			31-Mar-X2	By Investments—Equity Shares—AFS Account	1,149.48
31-Mar-X2	To Bank Account	750.46			
			31-Mar-X2	By Investment—ETO Long Put Account	183.05
15-May-X2	To Investments—Equity Shares—AFS Account	759.41			
15-May-X2	To Bank Account	542.62			

Unrealized Currency Gains/Loss Account (*Cont'd*)

Date	Particulars	Debit (US$)	Date	Particulars	Credit (US$)
15-May-X2	To Investment—ETO Long Put Account	229.58			
			31-May-X2	By Balance	949.54
31-May-X2	Total	**2,282.07**	31-May-X2	Total	**2,282.07**
31-May-X2	To Balance	949.54			

Hedge Gains/Loss Account (Effective)

Date	Particulars	Debit (US$)	Date	Particulars	Credit (US$)
30-Sep-X1	To Investment—Equity Shares—AFS Account	6,578.95			
			30-Sep-X1	By Investment—ETO Long Put Account	6,578.95
31-Dec-X1	To Investment—Equity Shares—AFS Account	5,095.54			
			31-Dec-X1	By Investment—ETO Long Put Account	5,095.54
31-Mar-X2	To Investment—Equity Shares—AFS Account	4,013.38			
			31-Mar-X2	By Investment—ETO Long Put Account	4,013.38
15-May-X2	To Investment—Equity Shares—AFS Account	2,640.26			
			15-May-X2	By Investment—ETO Long Put Account	2,640.26
31-May-X2	Total	**18,328.13**	31-May-X2	Total	**18,328.13**

Hedge Loss Account (P&L—Ineffective)

Date	Particulars	Debit (US$)	Date	Particulars	Credit (US$)
30-Sep-X1	To Investment—ETO Long Put Account	1,315.79			
31-Dec-X1	To Investment—ETO Long Put Account	6,369.43			

Hedge Loss Account (P&L—Ineffective) (*Cont'd*)

Date	Particulars	Debit (US$)	Date	Particulars	Credit (US$)
31-Mar-X2	To Investment—ETO Long Put Account	2,675.59			
15-May-X2	To Investment—ETO Long Put Account	1,320.13			
			31-May-X2	By Balance	11,680.94
31-May-X2	Total	**11,680.94**	31-May-X2	Total	**11,680.94**
31-May-X2	To Balance	11,680.94			

Investment—ETO Long Put Account

Date	Particulars	Debit (US$)	Date	Particulars	Credit (US$)
1-Sep-X1	To Alex & Co. Account	11,881.19			
30-Sep-X1	To Hedge Gains/Loss Account (Effective)	6,578.95			
			30-Sep-X1	By Hedge Gains/Loss Account (Effective)	1,315.79
31-Dec-X1	To Hedge Gains/Loss Account (Effective)	5,095.54			
			31-Dec-X1	By Hedge Loss Account (P&L—Ineffective)	6,369.43
31-Mar-X2	To Hedge Gains/Loss Account (Effective)	4,013.38			
			31-Mar-X2	By Hedge Loss Account (P&L—Ineffective)	2,675.59
31-Mar-X2	To Unrealized Currency Gains/loss Account	183.05			
15-May-X2	To Hedge Gains/Loss Account (Effective)	2,640.26			
			15-May-X2	By Hedge Loss Account (P&L—Ineffective)	1,320.13
			15-May-X2	By Bank Account	18,481.85
			15-May-X2	By Unrealized Currency Gains/Loss Account	229.58
31-May-X2	Total	**30,392.37**	31-May-X2	Total	**30,392.37**

Investment—Equity Shares—AFS Account

Date	Particulars	Debit (US$)	Date	Particulars	Credit (US$)
1-May-X1	To Bank Account	45,901.64			
30-Jun-X1	To Unrealized Gains/ Loss—Other Comprehensive Income Account	18,241.04			
1-Sep-X1	To Unrealized Gains/ Loss—Other Comprehensive Income Account	7,920.79			
			30-Sep-X1	By Hedge Gains/ Loss Account (Effective)	6,578.95
			31-Dec-X1	By Hedge Gains/ Loss Account (Effective)	5,095.54
			31-Mar-X2	By Hedge Loss Account (P&L—Ineffective)	4,013.38
31-Mar-X2	To Unrealized Currency Gains/ Loss Account	1,149.48			
			15-May-X2	By Hedge Gains/ Loss Account (Effective)	2,640.26
			15-May-X2	By Unrealized Currency Gains/Loss Account	759.41
			31-May-X2	By Balance	54,125.41
31-May-X2	Total	**73,212.95**	31-May-X2	Total	**73,212.95**
31-May-X2	To Balance	54,125.41			

Share Capital Account

Date	Particulars	Debit (US$)	Date	Particulars	Credit (US$)
			1-May-X1	By Bank Account	100,000.00
31-May-X2	To Balance	100,000.00			
31-May-X2	Total	**100,000.00**	31-May-X2	Total	**100,000.00**
			31-May-X2	By Balance	100,000.00

Unrealized Gains/Loss—Other Comprehensive Income Account

Date	Particulars	Debit (US$)	Date	Particulars	Credit (US$)
			30-Jun-X1	By Investments—Equity Shares—AFS Account	18,241.04
			1-Sep-X1	By Investments—Equity Shares—AFS Account	7,920.79
31-May-X2	To Balance	26,161.83			
31-May-X2	Total	**26,161.83**	31-May-X2	Total	**26,161.83**
			31-May-X2	By Balance	26,161.83

Trial Balance

As of 31-May-X2 (US$)

Particulars	Debit	Credit
Capital Account		
Share Capital Account		100,000.00
Unrealized Gains/Loss—Other Comprehensive Income Account		26,161.83
Current Liabilities		
Investments		
Investment—Equity Shares—AFS Account	54,125.41	
Current Assets		
Bank SGD Account	59,042.91	
Direct Income		
Unrealized Currency Gains/Loss Account	1,531.61	
Direct Expenses		
Hedge Loss Account (P&L—Ineffective)	1,320.13	
Profit & Loss Account	10,141.77	
Total	**126,161.83**	**126,161.83**

Income Statement

For the period ending 31-May-X2

Expenses	US$	Income	US$
Direct Expenses		**Direct Income**	
Unrealized Currency Gains/Loss Account	1,531.61		
Brokerage/commission Account			
Hedge Loss Account (P&L—Ineffective)	1,320.13	Net Loss Carryover	2,851.74
Total	**2,851.74**	Total	**2,851.74**

Balance Sheet

As of 31-May-X2

Liabilities	US$	Assets	US$
Capital Account		**Investments**	
Share Capital Account	100,000.00	Investment—Equity Shares—AFS Account	54,125.41
Unrealized Gains/loss—Other Comprehensive Income Account	26,161.83	**Current Assets**	
		Bank Account	59,042.91
		Profit & Loss Account	
		Opening Balance	10,141.77
		Current Period	2,851.74
Total	**126,161.83**	Total	**126,161.83**

SUMMARY

- The accounting treatment of call options *prima facie* will depend upon the intention with which the options are purchased: for hedging or speculation (non-hedging).
- If the position is taken as a hedge against some other position, then the relevant accounting standards will be applicable and there are certain conditions that are to be fulfilled for the same.
- Only long calls and long puts are eligible for hedge accounting, as written calls or puts limit the profitability while exposing the investor to unlimited risks and as such are not eligible for hedge accounting.
- The standards require that the potential for gains should be at least equal to the potential for losses; this is known as a *symmetrical risk-reward* situation. For a written option the risk-reward is asymmetrical; hence, written options per se do not qualify for hedge accounting.
- However, a combination of written options and certain other derivative instruments that results in a symmetrical risk-reward may qualify for hedge accounting.
- To qualify for hedge accounting, either the upside and downside potential of the net position must be symmetrical or the upside potential must be greater than the downside potential.
- Written options based on symmetry of the gain and loss potential of the combined hedged position, qualify for hedge accounting as per the accounting standard.
- If a written option is designated as hedging a recognized asset or liability, the combination of the hedged item and the written option provides at least as much potential for gains (as a result of a favorable change in the fair value of the combined instruments) as it does exposure to losses from an unfavorable change in their combined fair value.
- Hedge accounting is not permitted for covered calls. This prohibition is also specifically mentioned in the standard itself.

- It is permissible to separate the intrinsic value and time value of an option contract, designate as the hedging instrument only the change in intrinsic value of an option, and exclude change in its time value.
- The accounting standards permit an entity to apply hedge accounting for a delta-neutral hedging strategy and other dynamic hedging strategies under which the quantity of the hedging instrument is constantly adjusted in order to maintain a desired hedge ratio.

EXERCISES

Theory Questions

1. Define a derivative instrument as per U.S. GAAP and as per IFRS.
2. What combination of underlying shares and options is permissible in hedge accounting?
3. Can options that are written qualify for hedge accounting?
4. Accounting standards do not permit hedge accounting for covered calls. What are the reasons for this prohibition?
5. What is the rationale behind the symmetry of risk-reward requirements for hedge accounting?
6. What is the exception to the single fair value measure rule?
7. Is hedge accounting permitted for a delta-neutral hedging strategy?
8. Enumerate the trade life cycle for ETOs that are used as a hedge for an underlying position—both long calls and long puts.

Objective Questions

1. FAS 133 prescribes accounting requirements for
   a. Derivative instruments for hedging activities
   b. Debt and equity securities
   c. Fair value measurement
   d. All of the above
2. Characteristics of a financial derivative instrument include which of the following?
   a. Value of the instrument changes in response to underlying
   b. It requires no or comparatively little initial investment
   c. It is to be settled at a future date
   d. All of the above
3. A financial asset definition *does not* include
   a. Cash
   b. Cash equivalent
   c. Equity instrument
   d. All of the above

4. On comparing the definition of derivative financial instrument as per U.S. GAAP and IFRS, the only exception highlighted in IFRS is
   a. Initial net investment requirement
   b. Future date settlement
   c. Permitting net settlement
   d. None of the above
5. Which of the standards allows for a shortcut method that assumes perfect effectiveness for certain hedging relationships?
   a. IFRS
   b. U.S. GAAP
   c. FAS
   d. None of the above
6. In FAS 133, which items will not be reported?
   a. Reserves and provisions
   b. Income and expense
   c. Partner's equity
   d. All of the above
7. Which of the following contracts is *not exempted* from FAS 133?
   a. Derivative instruments
   b. Regular-way security trades
   c. Certain insurance contracts
   d. None of the above
8. Changes in fair value do not include
   a. Changes due to passage of time
   b. Difference in the fair value at the beginning and end of the period
   c. Changes in the accounting period
   d. None of the above
9. Hedge accounting can be discontinued if
   a. The instrument qualifies for speculation
   b. Management wants to change the accounting principles
   c. The derivatives expire
   d. All of the above
10. If the investor writes a call on the basis of a long position in an underlying asset, it is referred to as a
    a. Preferred call
    b. Covered call
    c. Long position call
    d. None of the above

11. A written option cannot be designated as a hedging instrument unless it is combined with a purchase option and a net premium is paid, according to
    a. IFRS
    b. U.S. GAAP
    c. Canadian GAAP
    d. IAS
    e. Not mentioned in any of the above
12. __________ is a number of currency units, shares, bushels, pounds, or other units specified in a contract.
    a. Premium
    b. Margin
    c. Notional amount
    d. Collateral amount
    e. Settlement amount
13. Certain insurance contracts like traditional life insurance contracts and traditional property and casualty contracts are not considered as derivatives, according to
    a. FAS 136
    b. FAS 133
    c. IAS 39
    d. FAS 140
    e. IAS 40
14. A covered call is a situation in which the equity investor writes a call to cover his
    a. Long position in an underlying asset
    b. Short position in an underlying asset
    c. Short position in a different equity
    d. Long position in an underlying commodity
    e. Forward risk exposed in the market
15. Hedging a long position in an underlying is possible by
    a. Selling puts
    b. Buying calls
    c. Selling calls
    d. Squaring of short position
    e. Buying puts

Journal Questions

For the following scenarios, prepare journal entries, general ledgers, trial balance, income statement, and balance sheet.

Put Option as a Hedge—Trade Currency SGD

Konark Fund had the following trades of Lever shares in the options market through Silver Man brokers. The stock exchange requires that the writer of the options maintain 10 percent of the value of the contract as margin money throughout the life of the contract.

Date	Product	Strike Price (SGD)	Expiry	Quantity	Rate (SGD)	B/S	Brokerage (SGD)
23-Jan-X1	Put	50	16-Mar-X1	10,000	5.00	B	540
23-Feb-X1	Put	50	16-Mar-X1	8,000	4.00	B	440
10-Mar-X1	Put	50	16-Mar-X1	12,000	3.00	S	720

Liquidation Method
FIFO

Market Rate of Underlying Stock, Lever
January 31: SGD48.00
February 28: SGD43.00
March 16: SGD55.00

Market Rate of Lever Put Option with Strike Price $50, Expiry March 16
January 31: SGD2.00
February 28: SGD6.00

FX Rate SGD/USGD
January 23: 1.5210
January 31: 1:1.532
February 23: 1.4956
February 28: 1.500
March 10: 1.5148
March 16: 1.5463

Functional Currency
US$

Put Option as a Hedge—Functional Currency US$

Orange Fund had the following trades of Tomco shares in the options market through SMK brokers. The stock exchange requires that the writer of the options maintain 10 percent of the value of the contract as margin money throughout the life of the contract.

Date	Product	Strike Price	Expiry	Quantity	Rate	B/S	Brokerage
20-Jan-X1	Put	$50	16-Mar-X1	10,000	$5.00	B	$450
21-Feb-X1	Put	$50	16-Mar-X1	8,000	$4.00	B	$500
13-Mar-X1	Put	$50	16-Mar-X1	12,000	$3.00	S	$690

Liquidation Method
FIFO

Market Rate of Underlying Stock, Tomco
January 31: 48.00

February 28: 43.00
March 16: 56.00

Market Rate of Tomco Put Option with Strike Price $50, Expiry March 16

January 31: 2.00
February 28: 6.00

Functional Currency

US$

Call Option as a Hedge—Trade Currency AUD

KKR Fund had the following trades in Zenith shares in the options market through Khan Brokers. The stock exchange requires that the writer of the options maintain 10 percent of the value of the contract as margin money throughout the life of the contract. On January 1 KKR Fund introduced US$100,000 as capital and converted US$50,000 into AUD at a rate of 1.24.

Date	Product	Strike Price	Expiry	Quantity	Rate (AUD)	B/S	Brokerage (AUD)
21-Jan-X1	Call	AU$40	15-Mar-X1	12,000	4.00	B	$500
20-Feb-X1	Call	AU$40	15-Mar-X1	13,000	5.00	B	$600
12-Mar-X1	Call	AU$40	15-Mar-X1	15,000	4.00	S	$300

Liquidation Method

FIFO

Market Rate of Underlying Stock, Zenith (AUD)

January 31: 35.00
February 28: 40.00
March 16: 45.00

Market Rate of Zenith Call Option with Strike Price $40, Expiry March 15

January 31: 3.00
February 28: 5.00

FX Rate AUD/US$

January 21: 1.2178
January 31: 1.28964
February 20: 1.26345
February 28: 1.24789
March 12: 1.23645
March 15: 1.27893

Functional Currency

US$

Call Option as a Hedge—Functional Currency US$

Konrad Fund had the following trades in Home Depot in the options market through MMT brokers. On January 1 Konrad Fund introduced $100,000 as capital.

Date	Product	Strike Price	Expiry	Quantity	Rate	B/S	Brokerage
25-Jan-X1	Call	$50	16-Mar-X1	10,000	$5.00	B	$540
22-Feb-X1	Call	$50	16-Mar-X1	16,000	$4.00	B	$620
11-Mar-X1	Call	$50	16-Mar-X1	16,000	$3.00	S	$320

Liquidation Method

FIFO

Market Rate of Underlying Stock, Home Depot

January 31: 40.00
February 28: 55.00
March 16: 55.00

Market Rate of Home Depot Call Option with Strike Price $50, Expiry March 16

January 31: 2.00
February 28: 6.00

Functional Currency

US$

CHAPTER 11

Accounting for Contract for Difference

LEARNING OBJECTIVES

After studying this chapter you should have a grasp of the following:

- Definition of contract for difference (CFD) securities.
- Product features of CFD.
- Short selling and margin requirements.
- Advantages and disadvantages of CFD.
- Terminating a CFD.
- Trade life cycle of equity CFD investments.
- Journal entries to be recorded during the different phases of the trade life cycle.
- FX revaluation and FX translation process.
- Illustration of CFD trades in foreign currency.
- Preparation of journal entries and general ledger accounts.
- Preparation of income statement and balance sheet after the CFD investments are made.

DEFINITION OF CFD

A contract for difference (CFD) is a contract between two parties—buyer and seller—stipulating that the seller will pay to the buyer the difference between the current value of an underlying equity share and its value at expiry date or on date of termination. However, if the difference is negative, then the buyer pays to the seller such difference. A CFD is an equity derivative contract that allows the investor to speculate on share price movements, without the need to own the underlying shares.

In a contract for difference, an investor can take a long or short position. Unlike futures contracts, CFDs have no fixed expiry date or contract size. The parties to the trade determine the expiry date as well as the contract size for the trade. Parties to the trade are required to maintain margins on their positions, typically around 10 to 30 percent of the notional value of the underlying shares.

PRODUCT FEATURES OF CFDs

A CFD contract position can be opened without having to invest the full underlying value up front. In equity stocks the initial deposit is around 20 percent of the value of the contract. The main advantage of CFDs is trading on leverage, which means that any profits made will be larger than with traditional share trading. However, it should be noted that there is a higher risk in that if the position moves against the investor then the losses will also be magnified.

A CFD offers all the benefits of share trading without having to physically own the shares. CFDs are ideal for short-term technical trading and hedging positions in the underlying market. In a CFD contract the investor can simply go long or short and there are no restrictions. The investor can profit from a rising or falling market without owning the stock or borrowing the stock, unlike in traditional share trading.

The CFD market includes equity stocks, indexes, and exchange-traded funds listed in stock exchanges in the United States, Singapore, Hong Kong, Tokyo, and the United Kingdom. Trades placed on U.S., European, or Asian markets are denominated in the currency used by the exchange.

A CFD contract has a preagreed expiry period. However, it can also be structured as an open-ended contract. If the investor does not close the position by the end of the trading day, then the position is automatically rolled over to the next day. Financing is either paid or received depending upon whether the investor is holding a long position or short position. This means that if the investor maintains enough margin, the position can be maintained for any length of time.

Even though the investor does not actually own the share, the investor is entitled to the benefits of corporate actions and in fact would receive dividends declared by the company. In this case, however, the company does not pay the dividend but instead it is recovered from the seller of the CFD and remitted to the investor holding the long position. A dividend adjustment is credited to long positions and debited from short positions held at the close of business on the day before the ex-dividend date. Since the investor does not own the share, the investor is not entitled to any voting rights in the company.

The following instruments are normally traded as CFDs:

- Individual shares.
- Indexes.
- Exchange-traded funds (ETFs).

Short-selling

With CFDs, the investor can short-sell individual stock and index CFDs. Thus, an investor can sell a CFD as an opening position, since a CFD is a contract between the investor and the CFD provider, based upon the price movement of the share. An investor may be able to profit from a falling market using this instrument of CFD. But it should be noted that in some instances, there could be restrictions on shorting particular stocks, due to the nonavailability of shares in the physical market for that particular stock. Thus, it may not be possible to place an opening short CFD on some equities that are not liquid and are of small market capitalization.

While it may be very easy to open a CFD trade, it may not be so easy to close the CFD trade, due to prevailing market conditions, including liquidity issues for that particular stock.

Commission

CFDs are subject to a commission charge that is calculated as a percentage of the value of the contract for each trade. However, if an investor opts to trade with a market maker, the commission can be avoided at the cost of a larger bid/offer spread on the instrument.

Financing

The investor having a long position is required to pay a daily financing charge applied at an agreed interest rate above or below the London Interbank Offered Rate (LIBOR) or some other interest rate benchmark, while an investor holding a short position receives such interest.

If an investor holds a long position in a CFD overnight, the investor must pay interest on the open position at market value. This value is calculated on a daily basis as the quantity of CFDs held multiplied by the closing market price for the underlying share on that day at the prevailing interest rate. The day basis for interest is usually taken as 360 days for most currencies. For UK, Hong Kong, and Singapore CFDs it is calculated as 365 days.

The reference interest rate used could be either the LIBOR or the overnight deposit rate in those markets.

Interest on Clear Margin

Clear margin is the investor margin account adjusted for all positions marked-to-market, less initial margin requirements for all open positions. Interest is normally paid to the investor on such clear margin at a preagreed rate.

Margin Requirements

Investors in CFDs are required to maintain a certain amount of margin as defined by the counterparty or market maker, which could range from 10 to 30 percent.

The amount required to be held in the margin account will be set according to the terms and conditions imposed by the market maker or counterparty. The initial margin required varies depending upon the instrument type. It is higher for individual stocks when compared to the CFDs on indexes.

Thus the initial margin is an amount of money that will be debited to the investor's account at the time the CFD is entered into. The initial margin acts as a security deposit that the investor is required to hold when a CFD position is first opened. The amount of the initial margin represents the assessed risk value of that position.

Maintenance margin is the additional margin required to maintain the open position, especially when that position is moving against the investor. If the maintenance margin as per margin call is not met within a stipulated time limit, the market maker would close out the open position that is resulting in the margin call.

Thus the maintenance margin or variation margin is the unrealized profit or loss on the open position of the investor. This amount is equal to the dollar value movement in all the open positions as compared with the current market price.

Product Length

CFDs are open-ended contracts with no fixed end date. Both the parties to the trade can keep extending the contract by paying the funding cost as appropriate.

Settlement

CFDs are settled in cash and there is no physical settlement of securities. Even by definition, the contract is supposed to be squared off by receiving or remitting the *difference*.

CFDs versus Futures

Conceptually, CFDs and futures are more or less the same in the sense that an investor can take leveraged positions in an underlying equity through both these types of contracts. While CFDs could be exchange-traded or an over-the-counter (OTC) product, futures are an exchange-traded product. The market risk remains the same for both these products. However, the counterparty risk is greater in the case of CFDs than for futures, as exchange-traded futures are properly taken care of by the stock exchange concerned, which tracks the open positions, and collects the mark-to-market margin on a daily basis.

CFDs are convenient for certain investors who want to customize the contract to suit their specific needs, while futures are usually preferred by the traders for indexes and interest rates trading. CFDs avoid stamp duty; increased flexibility and leverage are other advantages of CFD's over more conventional forms of margin trading like futures. Both CFDs and futures, being a form of margin trading, involve financing charges, even though in both these cases the finance charges are already embedded in the price of the instrument. Futures are said to be better regulated. Recently CFD-related hedging is on the rise as CFDs are found to be highly competitive for trading stocks.

Risk

CFDs allow a trader to go short or long on any position with a variable margin, allowing them to trade on margins. While this type of highly leveraged trading can bring in bounties in large numbers, it is a double-edged sword as the potential for losses is equally great. Therefore, while dealing in CFDs, investors should always be aware of what they could lose, instead of merely focusing on what they could gain.

Advantages of CFDs

Transparent Pricing

Pricing of a CFD contract is simple and straightforward as it is arrived at like a futures contract: The underlying market price is adjusted for cost of carry and expected dividends.

Effective Use of Capital

Significantly less capital is required for a CFD contract than for physical shares, as the investor need not physically purchase the stock to take long position, but instead pay only the margin.

Increased Trading Flexibility

Unlike futures, which have a fixed date of expiry, CFDs do not have a fixed maturity date and can be extended by mutual agreement of both the parties to the contract.

Access to International Markets

Trading in shares that are listed elsewhere is restricted. However, through CFDs an investor can trade in virtually any security listed anywhere in the world, provided he finds a counterpart interest in the same security. Thus, CFDs provide unlimited access to any security that is traded in international markets.

Stamp Duty Exemption in Some Markets

Transaction costs are substantially reduced in a CFD trade as the stamp duty is exempted for CFD trades in several markets.

Operational Efficiency—No Physical Settlement

Since the contract itself is for the *difference*, there is no physical settlement, unlike a futures contract which may result in physical delivery.

No Expiry Period

A CFD contract technically is extended for the next day if it is not squared up as there is no fixed expiry period for a CFD contract.

Receive Dividends on Bought Open Positions

Investors with long CFD positions may sometimes have the option of participating in a corporate action such as a rights issue or entitlement. Investors with short CFD positions are obligated to deliver the corporate action if the long holders elect to take up the corporate action.

Receive Interest on Sold Open Positions

For a short position in CFD contract, the seller gets interest by way of financing charges paid by the buyer.

High Leverage

CFDs allows the investor to take leveraged positions, both long and short, without having to take or make delivery of the underlying instrument or security. Instead, the investor only has to provide a cash deposit known as the initial margin as collateral. The high leverage amplifies profits during movements of price that are favorable to the investor.

Disadvantages of CFDs

Geared Trading Risk

The leveraged nature in margin trading means that both profits and losses can be magnified, and unless the investor places a proper stop-loss, the investor could incur huge losses if the position moves against him.

Not Suitable for Long-term Investor

CFDs are not suited to the long-term investor. If the investor holds a CFD position open over a long period of time, then the costs associated with holding the position would increase and it may be more beneficial to invest in the underlying share itself.

No Voting Rights

There are no voting rights granted to investor of long CFD positions, unlike the case for an investor in traditional shares.

Terminating a CFD

CFDs do not have an expiry date. They remain open until they are closed in accordance with the terms of the client agreement. To close a CFD position, the investor should place the order to determine the current market price for the underlying security/instrument, and close the position or even part of it. The total closing value is determined by multiplying the number of CFDs by the price of the underlying instrument or security.

On the day that the CFD is closed, the principal will calculate the remaining payment rights and obligations to reflect movements in the contract value since the previous business close, including interest and other credits/debits.

THE TRADE LIFE CYCLE FOR CFDs

- Buy the CFD.
- Pay brokerage/commission on the buy transaction.
- Pay the margin money for the CFD.
- Pay the funding cost for a long CFD position, or receive the funding cost for a short CFD position.
- Receive interest on margin money over initial margin.
- Ascertain the fair value at the end of the reporting period.
- Margin call.
- Termination of the CFD.
- Expiry of CFD.
- Ascertain the profit/loss on sale.
- Ascertain the profit/loss on termination.
- Ascertain the profit/loss on expiry.
- Receive the consideration and margin money.
- FX revaluation entries.
- FX translation entries.

Buy the CFD

If the investor buys a CFD contract, then the investor is considered to be long in that security and has acquired the right to collect the difference between the current value of the share and the contracted price whenever the investor decides to close out the position. However, if the price of the share drops, then the investor has to pay the difference. Since there is no underlying asset that is acquired, only a notional entry is passed in the books of accounts to indicate the existence of the contract for difference. This entry is called an off-balance-sheet entry.

Assume that an investor is going long in 5,000 ABC shares @ \$45 per share with an expiry period of 60 days expiring on 14th December X1. (ABC is listed on the Singapore stock exchange and traded in SGD in that exchange through the counterparty Mike & Sons.) The accounting entry that is recorded in the books of accounts is shown as follows:

Journal Entry

Date	Particulars	Debit (US$)	Credit (US$)
15-Oct-X1	CFD Long Position Account (Off Balance Sheet)	5,000.00	
	To CFD Long Contra Account (Off Balance Sheet)		5,000.00
	(Being the CFD in respect of 5,000 ABC shares bought @ $45 per share through the counterparty, Mike & Sons)		

Commission on the Buy Transaction

Commission is payable to the counterparty for the services rendered. This is usually settled by transferring the amount to the margin account with the broker, which means it gets paid to the broker on the same day as the trade date. For CFD contracts, the commission is not treated as part of the cost of the CFD contract; instead it is debited to the commission account. Assuming a commission of $250 is payable on this example CFD contract, the accounting entry that is recorded in the books of accounts is shown as follows:

Journal Entry

Date	Particulars	Debit (US$)	Credit (US$)
15-Oct-X1	Commission Account	250.00	
	To Mike & Sons Account		250.00
	(Being the commission payable in respect of 5,000 CFD of ABC shares bought @ $45 per share through the counterparty, Mike & Sons)		

Pay the Margin Money for the CFD

The counterparty collects the margin from the investor for both buying the CFD and selling the CFD. For CFDs, since the counterparty has the responsibility of ensuring that its leg of the transaction is complete, the counterparty would insist that the investor deposit a percentage of the value of the contract as margin money. The margin money would be utilized for any reduction in the mark-to-market valuation on a daily basis.

Margin is a good faith deposit. Normally a deposit of about 10 to 30 percent of the total value of the contract would signify the investor's willingness to stand good on any price movements against the buyer or seller of a CFD contract.

Since it is merely a deposit, the investor would get the margin money back after the contract has either expired or been terminated.

The fact that CFDs operate on margin makes them a highly leveraged investment, meaning a relatively small price move can result in considerable profit/loss swings for the investor. This leverage must be closely monitored and treated with tremendous care. Leverage can work for or against the investor.

Assume that the counterparty demands a deposit of 10 percent of the contract size as margin money up front. Expiry of the contract is December 14 and the counterparty through whom the trade is executed is Mike & Sons.

The margin payable to the counterparty would be 10 percent of $225,000, or $22,500. Assuming that the investor prefers to fund the CFD contract margin account with $30,000, the accounting entry that is recorded in the books of accounts is shown as follows:

Journal Entry

Date	Particulars	Debit (US$)	Credit (US$)
15-Oct-X1	Margin money (CFD) Account	30,000.00	
	To Mike & Sons Account		30,000.00
	(Being the margin money payable in respect of 5,000 CFD of ABC shares bought @ $45 per share to the counterparty, Mike & Sons)		
15-Oct-X1	Mike & Sons Account	30,000.00	
	To Bank Account		30,000.00
	(Being the margin money paid to the counterparty, Mike & Sons)		

Pay the Funding Cost for Long CFD Position

For a long position in CFD contracts, the investor has to pay the funding cost, which is also known as interest on open positions. This value is calculated at an agreed percentage of the closing market value of the underlying asset. Assuming that the closing market value of the share on the date of purchase is $48, let's say the interest is agreed at 9 percent per annum on $240,000 to carry over the position to the next day. This works out to $60 for that day. This is calculated on a daily basis because there would be price fluctuation in the underlying share and the interest should be calculated on the value of the outstanding position.

The accounting entry that is recorded in the books of accounts is shown as follows:

Journal Entry

Date	Particulars	Debit (US$)	Credit (US$)
15-Oct-X1	CFD Funding Cost Account	60.00	
	To CFD Margin Account		60.00
	(Being the funding cost to carry over the long position of CFDs in respect of 5,000 ABC shares bought having a market value of $240,000 @ 9% p.a.)		

Receive the Funding Cost for Short CFD Position

For a short position in CFD contracts, the investor will receive the funding cost from the counterparty, which is also known as interest on open short positions. This value is calculated at an agreed percentage on the closing market value of the underlying asset. This is calculated on a daily basis because there would be price fluctuation in the underlying share and the interest should be calculated on the value of the outstanding position.

Assume in this case that the investor has sold 5,000 shares of ABC, the present market value is $48 per share, and the interest payable by the buyer is 9 percent per annum. The accounting entry that is recorded in the books of accounts is shown as follows:

Journal Entry

Date	Particulars	Debit (US$)	Credit (US$)
15-Oct-X1	CFD Margin Account	60.00	
	To CFD Funding Receipts Account		60.00
	(Being the interest on CFD in respect of 5,000 ABC shares sold per share through the counterparty, Mike & Sons) (5,000 × 48 × 9/100 × 1/365)		

Receive the Interest on Margin Money over Initial Margin

The margin account is adjusted for the fluctuations in the daily market rate, and the funding cost is also adjusted with the margin account. Interest is receivable by the short investor on the balance available in the margin account over and above the initial margin for the CFD position. This is calculated on a daily basis but usually credited only on a monthly basis.

Assume in the present example that there is surplus of $20,000 on average during the 15-day period till October 31, and that the interest accrues at 6 percent per year. The accounting entry that is recorded in the books of accounts is shown as follows:

Journal Entry

Date	Particulars	Debit (US$)	Credit (US$)
31-Oct-X1	CFD Margin Account	50.00	
	To Interest on CFD Margin Account		50.00
	(Being the CFD interest on margin money over initial margin receivable from the counterparty, Mike & Sons) (20,000 × 15/365 × 6/100)		

Ascertain the Fair Value at the End of the Reporting period

At the end of every reporting period, the fair value of the CFD position is ascertained and the CFD contracts are marked-to-market. This process is known as portfolio valuation, when the market rate at the end of the period is determined from the primary stock exchange where the underlying shares are traded. If there is an increase in the market rate over and above the purchase rate, then such increase is recognized as a gain on the one hand, and the corresponding amount is reflected as an increase in the margin account with the counterparty. This accounting entry is reversed on the next day or the next valuation date when a fresh entry for the then value is recorded in the books of accounts.

Alternatively, the accounting entry can be recorded only for the incremental value. If the investor follows this incremental value method, then there is no need to reverse the entry for mark-to-market recorded earlier. It is a usual practice to follow the incremental method for CFD contracts.

Assume that the fair market value of the underlying share is $50 per share on October 31, the valuation date. The accounting entry that is recorded in the books of accounts is shown as follows:

Journal Entry

Date	Particulars	Debit (US$)	Credit (US$)
31-Oct-X1	CFD Margin Account	250,000.00	
	To Unrealized gain—CFD Long Account		250,000.00
	(Being the unrealized gain on CFD position in respect of 5,000 ABC shares @ $50)		

Margin Call

If the margin money gets eroded due to unfavorable price movement for the investor, then to maintain the percentage of margin fixed for the underlying in question, the counterparty would initiate a margin call. This is to ensure that the counterparty is not caught unawares if there is a wide fluctuation in the value of the underlying causing severe loss to the investor.

The investor is always required to keep the margin at a certain level, and this varies from one underlying stock to another. Assuming that there is a decline in the market value as of November 30 and the investor is required to pay $9,000 due to margin call, then the accounting entry would be as follows:

Journal Entry

Date	Particulars	Debit (US$)	Credit (US$)
30-Nov-X1	CFD Margin Account	9,000.00	
	To Bank Account		9,000.00
	(Being the margin call paid to the counterparty due to reduction in the market value of the underlying)		

Termination of the CFD

To liquidate the position, the original position should be terminated. Even partial termination is possible if it is agreed to between the parties. Unlike a futures contract, the position cannot be effectively liquidated by taking an opposite position in a CDF contract. If not terminated, the contract expires automatically on the expiry date as stipulated in the contract. The difference between the value of the position after adjusting for the mark-to-market and the price of the underlying as per the termination contract is computed and is settled in cash.

Assume that the 400 shares in our example CFD contract are terminated on November 5 when the market rate per share is $55, and that the mark-to-market value of the position stands at $56. The accounting entry that is recorded in the books of accounts is shown as follows:

Journal Entry

Date	Particulars	Debit (US$)	Credit (US$)
5-Nov-X1	CFD Long Contra Account	400.00	
	To CFD Long Position Account		400.00
	(Being the 400 shares in the CFD contract of ABC shares terminated with the counterparty @ $55 each)		

Note: This entry is off balance sheet and will not form part of the regular books of accounts. This entry is passed mainly to have a control on the CFD positions. That is the reason why only the nominal amount is taken in consideration and not the actual value of the contract itself.

Expiry of the CFD

The CFD contract expires on the expiry date of the contract, if it is not liquidated before that. The difference between the value of the position after adjusting for the mark-to-market and the price of the underlying on the expiry date is computed and is settled in cash. The entire process is routed through the counterparty. The CFD margin account is adjusted with the profit or loss on account of expiry of the CFD contract.

Assume in our example that the closing rate of the underlying shares on the expiry date is $60 per share and the value of the position as marked-to-market stands at $55. The difference of $5 representing profit is accounted for on the date of expiry. The accounting entry that is recorded in the books of accounts is shown as follows:

Journal Entry

Date	Particulars	Debit (US$)	Credit (US$)
14-Dec-X1	CFD Long Contra Account (Off Balance Sheet)	4,600.00	
	To CFD Long Position Account (Off Balance Sheet)		4,600.00
	(Being the CFD position in respect of 4,600 ABC shares expired on the date of expiry)		

Ascertain the Profit/Loss on the Sale

The profit or loss on termination of a CFD contract or on the date of expiry is determined by comparing the value of the CFD contract with the value of the position after giving effect to the latest mark-to-market. The reason for this is that the unrealized profit or loss on the position is already recognized in the current earnings and is also adjusted in the margin account. Hence, only the latest value of the position would be compared with the sale price to determine the profit. However, the unrealized gain or loss so far accounted in the books gets crystallized and becomes realized gain or loss. Hence the original entry for unrealized gains or loss would be reversed and a fresh entry for realized gains or loss would be recorded. This amount would be the difference between the original contracted price at the time of acquisition and the contracted termination price.

On Termination (400 Shares)

In our example, the position is already marked-to-market at $56 for each share. Hence when the position is partially liquidated for $55, the loss is effectively $1 per share, and the entry is passed accordingly. However, the accounting entry would be passed first to reverse the unrealized gain or loss and then to record the realized gain or loss for this termination.

The cost of acquisition of this position is $45 per share and the mark-to-market valuation of this position is $56. The entry for reversal of unrealized gain is as follows:

Journal Entry

Date	Particulars	Debit (US$)	Credit (US$)
5-Nov-X1	Unrealized Gain/Loss Account	4,400.00	
	To CFD Margin Account		4,400.00
	(Being the unrealized gain reversed to the CFD margin account on termination of 400 CFD in respect of ABC shares bought @ $45 per share through the counterparty Mike & Sons and having a mark-to-market value of $56 as of date)		
5-Nov-X1	CFD Margin Account	4,000.00	
	To Realized Gain/Loss Long CFD Account		4,000.00
	(Being the realized gain accounted on termination of 400 CFD in respect of ABC shares bought @ $45 per share through the counterparty Mike & Sons and terminated @ $55)		

On Expiry (4,600 Shares)

In our example, the position is already marked-to-market at $55 for each share. Hence, when the position expires when the market rate is $60, the profit is effectively $5 per share, and the entry is passed accordingly. However, the accounting entry would first be passed to reverse the unrealized gain or loss and then to record the realized gain or loss on expiry.

The cost of acquisition of this position is $45 per share and the mark-to-market valuation of this position is $55. The entry for reversal of unrealized gain is as follows:

Journal Entry

Date	Particulars	Debit (US$)	Credit (US$)
14-Dec-X1	Unrealized Gain/Loss Account	46,000.00	
	To CFD Margin Account		46,000.00
	(Being the unrealized gain reversed to the CFD margin account on expiry of 4,600 CFD in respect of ABC shares bought @ $45 per share through the counterparty Mike & Sons and having a mark-to-market value of $55 as of date)		
14-Dec-X1	CFD Margin Account	69,000.00	
	To Realized Gain/Loss Long CFD Account		69,000.00
	(Being the realized gain accounted on expiry of 4,600 CFD in respect of ABC shares bought @ $45 per share through the counterparty Mike & Sons and expired @ $60)		

Receive the Consideration

Once the entire CFD position either is liquidated or expires, the entire amount of money standing in the margin account is returned to the investor. This includes the profit or loss on account of the CFD trades as well as the margin money—both initial and variation margin paid on account of the CFD contracts.

Assuming that $108,000 is standing in the margin account after accounting for the profits and the initial margin money paid, the accounting entry that is recorded in the books of accounts is shown as follows:

Journal Entry

Date	Particulars	Debit (US$)	Credit (US$)
14-Dec-X1	Mike & Sons Account	108,000.00	
	To CFD Margin Account		108,000.00
	(Being the balance in the CFD margin account receivable from the counterparty Mike & Sons)		
14-Dec-X1	Bank Account	108,000.00	
	To Mike & Sons Account		108,000.00
	(Being the balance in the CFD margin account received from the counterparty Mike & Sons)		

FX Revaluation Entries

All the entries recorded to this point are initially entered in the respective trade currencies. If the functional currency is different from the trade currency, then each and every entry recorded in the trade currency should be entered again in the functional currency by converting the entries at the respective day's FX rates. In other words, for each trade currency that the investor deals with, there will be a complete set of books representing that trade currency. This includes journal entries, general ledger postings, trial balance, income statement, and balance sheet.

After revaluing each and every journal entry of all the trade currencies into the functional currency, a separate set of books is prepared, again comprising all the elements just mentioned: journal entries, general ledger postings, trial balance, income statement, and balance sheet. It should be noted that the ultimate financial reports would be prepared and presented to all the stakeholders based on the financial statements prepared in the functional currency only, as this will encompass all the transactions of the investor in all trade currencies dabbled with. (For illustration and detailed explanation please refer to Chapter 2.)

FX Revaluation Entries

After revaluing all the entries in the functional currency at the respective FX rates for the day concerned, another entry needs to be passed in the books of the functional currency. This is mainly to adjust the currency gains or losses due to the fluctuations in FX rates between the reporting date and the date of recording the original entries. FX translation entries are recorded only for the asset and liability accounts. For income and expense accounts the amount gets crystallized on the date of passing the FX revaluation entries in the books of the functional currency.

There are fundamentally two types of FX translation entries that are recorded in the books of the functional currency: consummated FX translation entries and transient FX translation entries. (For illustration and detailed explanation please refer to Chapter 2.)

ILLUSTRATIONS

CFD—Functional Currency US$

Gulf Fund had the following trades in Vimta Textiles in the CFD market. The counterparty is Brown & Co. Brown & Co. takes a margin of 10 percent of the value of the contract up front, and the funding cost of the long position is calculated at 2 percent per month for overnight carry of position. Brown & Co. pays interest at 6 percent per annum on the margin money deposited with them. (Actual/365 day convention used for this illustration)

Date	Expiry	Quantity	Rate (US$)	Long/Term	Brokerage
29-Jan-X1	15-Feb-X1	5,000	$35	Long	$500
5-Feb-X1	15-Feb-X1	3,500	$42	Partial Termination	$175

Date	Market Price
29-Jan-X1	37
30-Jan-X1	38
31-Jan-X1	30
1-Feb-X1	32
2-Feb-X1	38
5-Feb-X1	43
6-Feb-X1	48
7-Feb-X1	50
8-Feb-X1	47
9-Feb-X1	45
12-Feb-X1	43
13-Feb-X1	40
14-Feb-X1	43
15-Feb-X1	45

- The fund introduced $100,000 on January 1.
- The market rate of Vimta Textiles fell sharply on January 31, triggering a margin call. The fund decided to make a deposit of $50,000 in the margin account on that date.

- Valuation dates are month ends.
- The CFD contract expired on February 15, when the market rate was $45, and it was not rolled over.

The interest on the margin account is computed as of February 15. Accounts as of March 31 are prepared.

CFD—Functional Currency

T-1 Capital Introduced by the Fund

Journal Entry

Date	Particulars	Debit (US$)	Credit (US$)
1-Jan-X1	Bank Account	100,000.00	
	To Share Capital Account		100,000.00
	(Being share capital received from the investor remitted to bank)		

T-2 On Purchasing the CFD

This entry is just an off-balance-sheet entry and thus is not taken into account while preparing the financial statements of the investor. In this illustration there will not be any postings for this entry.

Journal Entry

Date	Particulars	Debit (US$)	Credit (US$)
29-Jan-X1	CFD Position Account (Off Balance Sheet)	5,000.00	
	To CFD Contra Account (Off Balance Sheet)		5,000.00
	(Being the 5,000 CFDs of Vimta Textiles bought @ $35)		

T-3 Margin Payable to the Counterparty

Journal Entry

Date	Particulars	Debit (US$)	Credit (US$)
29-Jan-X1	CFD Margin Account	17,500.00	
	To Brown & Co. Account		17,500.00
	(Being the margin for purchase of 5,000 CFD of Vimta Textiles @ $35 payable to the counterparty @ 10%)		

T-4 On Recording the Commission

Journal Entry

Date	Particulars	Debit (US$)	Credit (US$)
29-Jan-X1	Commission Account	500.00	
	To Brown & Co. Account		500.00
	(Being the commission incurred on purchase of CFD contract)		

T-5 On payment of commission and margin

Journal Entry

Date	Particulars	Debit (US$)	Credit (US$)
29-Jan-X1	Brown & Co. Account	18,000.00	
	To Bank Account		18,000.00
	(Being the payment made to the counterparty on account of margin and commission)		

T-6 Mark-to-market at End of Reporting Period

Mark-to-market loss at the end of Jan X1	**US$**
(a) Market value of 5,000 CFDs @ $30 on 31-Jan-X1	150,000.00
(b) Purchase value of 5,000 CFDs @ 35	175,000.00
(c) Unrealized loss = (a) – (b)	(25,000.00)

Journal Entry

Date	Particulars	Debit (US$)	Credit (US$)
31-Jan-X1	Unrealized Gains/Loss on CFD Account	25,000.00	
	To CFD Margin Account		25,000.00
	(Being the mark-to-market valuation of CFD contract as of date)		

T-7 Margin Call

To cover the erosion in the value of the investments the fund made a deposit of $50,000 into the margin account. However, the excess of margin, known as *clear margin*, will earn interest at 6 percent per year.

Journal Entry

Date	Particulars	Debit (US$)	Credit (US$)
31-Jan-X1	CFD Margin Account	50,000.00	
	To Bank Account		50,000.00
	(Being the deposit made into the margin account on account of margin call)		

T-8 On Payment of Funding Cost of CFD

Calculation of Interest Payable

Date	Outstanding Position	Market Rate	Market Value	Interest	Total Interest for the period
29-Jan-X1	5,000	37	185,000	121.64	
30-Jan-X1	5,000	38	190,000	124.94	
31-Jan-X1	5,000	30	150,000	98.63	
					345.21

Journal Entry

Date	Particulars	Debit (US$)	Credit (US$)
31-Jan-X1	CFD Long Funding Charges Account	345.21	
	To CFD Margin Account		345.21
	(Being the funding cost of the long position CFD contracts till date)		

T-9 On Receipt of Interest on Clear Margin

Calculation of Interest Receivable

Date	Opening Balance	Realized Gains	Mark-to-market	Interest Payable	Margin Call	Net Margin	6% PA
31-Jan-X1	–		(25,000)	(338.71)	50,000	24,661.29	4.05
	Total interest receivable for the period						**4.05**

Journal Entry

Date	Particulars	Debit (US$)	Credit (US$)
31-Jan-X1	CFD Margin Account	4.05	
	To Interest Received on CFD Margin Account		4.05
	(Being the interest on CFD Margin account as per the calculations given above)		

T-10 On Termination of CFD Partially

Journal Entry

Date	Particulars	Debit (US$)	Credit (US$)
5-Feb-X1	CFD Contra Account (Off Balance Sheet)	3,500.00	
	To CFD Position Account (Off Balance Sheet)		3,500.00
	(Being the partial termination of 3,500 CFD contract)		

T-11 On Recording the Commission

Journal Entry

Date	Particulars	Debit (US$)	Credit (US$)
5-Feb-X1	Commission Account	175.00	
	To Brown & Co. Account		175.00
	(Being the commission incurred on partial termination of CFD contract)		

T-12 On Payment of Commission

Journal Entry

Date	Particulars	Debit (US$)	Credit (US$)
5-Feb-X1	Brown & Co. Account	175.00	
	To Bank Account		175.00
	(Being the commission paid)		

T-13 On Reversal of Unrealized Gains on Partial Termination of CFD

The unrealized gains already recognized in income will be reversed on the date of partial termination as the realized gains will be booked comparing the original cost of the position with the amount realized on liquidation. In this case the mark-to-market loss already realized on the position amounts to $17,500, and this will be reversed on the date of partial termination.

Journal Entry

Date	Particulars	Debit (US$)	Credit (US$)
5-Feb-X1	CFD Margin Account	17,500.00	
	To Unrealized Gains/Loss on CFD Account		17,500.00
	(Being the unrealized gains on the terminated CFD reversed)		

T-14 On Recording Profit/Loss on Partial Termination of CFD

Calculation of realized gains on partial termination of CFDs	US$
(a) Cost of 3,500 CFD position (3,500 × 35)	122,500.00
(b) Sale consideration of 3,500 CFD position @ 42	147,000.00
(c) Realized gains on sale = (b) – (a)	**24,500.00**

Journal Entry

Date	Particulars	Debit (US$)	Credit (US$)
5-Feb-X1	CFD Margin Account	24,500.00	
	To Realized Gains/Loss—CFD Account		24,500.00
	(Being the realized gain on partial termination of CFD contract)		

Journal Entry

Date	Particulars	Debit (US$)	Credit (US$)
5-Feb-X1	CFD Margin Account	24,500.00	
	To Realized Gains/Loss—CFD Account		24,500.00
	(Being the realized gain on partial termination of CFD contract)		

T-15 On Recording Profit/Loss on Expiry of CFD

Calculation of realized gains on expiry of CFDs	US$
(a) Cost of 1,500 CFD position (1,500 × 35)	52,500.00
(b) Value of 1,500 CFD position on expiry @ 45	67,500.00
(c) Realized gains on expiry = (b) – (a)	**15,000.00**

Journal Entry

Date	Particulars	Debit (US$)	Credit (US$)
15-Feb-X1	CFD Margin Account	15,000.00	
	To Realized Gains/Loss—CFD Account		15,000.00
	(Being the realized gain on expiry of CFD contract)		

T-16 On Expiry of CFD Contract

Journal Entry

Date	Particulars	Debit (US$)	Credit (US$)
15-Feb-X1	CFD Contra Account (Off Balance Sheet)	1,500.00	
	To CFD Position Account (Off Balance Sheet)		1,500.00
	(Being the expiry of 1,500 CFD the position and contra account reversed)		

T-17 On Reversal of Unrealized Gains on Expiry of CFD

Journal Entry

Date	Particulars	Debit (US$)	Credit (US$)
15-Feb-X1	CFD Margin Account	7,500.00	
	To Unrealized Gains/Loss on CFD Account		7,500.00
	(Being the unrealized gains on the expiry of CFD contract reversed)		

T-18 On Payment of Funding Cost of CFD

Calculation of Interest Payable

Date	Outstanding Position	Market Rate	Market Value	Interest	Total Interest for the period
01-Feb-X1	5,000	32	160,000	105.21	
02-Feb-X1	5,000	38	190,000	124.93	
03-Feb-X1	5,000	38	190,000	124.93	
04-Feb-X1	5,000	38	190,000	124.93	
05-Feb-X1	1,500	43	64,500	42.41	
06-Feb-X1	1,500	48	72,000	47.34	
07-Feb-X1	1,500	50	75,000	49.32	
08-Feb-X1	1,500	47	70,500	46.36	
09-Feb-X1	1,500	45	67,500	44.38	
10-Feb-X1	1,500	45	67,500	44.38	
11-Feb-X1	1,500	45	67,500	44.39	
12-Feb-X1	1,500	43	64,500	42.41	
13-Feb-X1	1,500	40	60,000	39.45	
14-Feb-X1	1,500	43	64,500	42.41	
15-Feb-X1	0	45	0	0	
					922.85

Journal Entry

Date	Particulars	Debit (US$)	Credit (US$)
15-Feb-X1	CFD Long Funding Charges Account	922.85	
	To CFD Margin Account		922.85
	(Being the funding cost of the long position CFD contracts till date)		

T-19 On Receipt of Interest on Clear Margin

Calculation of Interest Receivable

Date	Opening Balance	Realized Gains	Mark-to-market	Interest Payable	Margin Call	Net Margin	6% PA
01-Feb-X1	24,654.79		10,000	(105.21)	—	34,549.59	2.80
02-Feb-X1	34,549.59		30,000	(124.93)		64,424.66	7.71
03-Feb-X1	64,424.66			(124.93)		64,299.73	7.69
04-Feb-X1	64,299.73			(124.93)		64,174.79	7.67
05-Feb-X1	64,174.79	24,500	(3,000)	(42.41)		85,632.38	11.20
06-Feb-X1	85,632.38		7,500	(47.34)		93,085.04	12.42
07-Feb-X1	93,085.04		3,000	(49.32)		96,035.73	12.91
08-Feb-X1	96,035.73		(4,500)	(46.36)		91,489.37	12.17
09-Feb-X1	91,489.37		(3,000)	(44.38)		88,444.99	11.66
10-Feb-X1	88,444.99			(44.38)		88,400.60	11.65
11-Feb-X1	88,400.60			(44.38)		88,356.22	11.65
12-Feb-X1	88,356.22		(3,000)	(42.41)		85,313.81	11.15
13-Feb-X1	85,313.81		(4,500)	(39.45)		80,774.36	10.40
14-Feb-X1	80,77436		4,500	(42.41)		85,231.95	11.14
15-Feb-X1	85,231.95	15,000	(12,000)	—	—	88,231.95	11.63
Total interest receivable for the period							**153.85**

Journal Entry

Date	Particulars	Debit (US$)	Credit (US$)
15-Feb-X1	CFD Margin Account	153.85	
	To Interest received on CFD Margin Account		153.85
	(Being the interest received on CFD margin account as per the calculations given above)		

T-20 Receivable from Counterparty on Termination of CFD Position

Calculation of CFD Margin Account

Date	Description	Debit	Credit
29-Jan-X1	Margin paid to the counterparty for the purchase of 5,000 shares	17,500.00	
31-Jan-X1	Unrealized gains/loss booked at end of 31-Jan-X1		25,000.00
31-Jan-X1	Deposit made on account of margin call	50,000.00	
31-Jan-X1	Interest payable on long position CFD contract till date		345.21
31-Jan-X1	Interest receivable margin account at the end 31-Jan-X1	4.05	

Calculation of CFD Margin Account (*Cont'd*)

Date	Description	Debit	Credit
5-Feb-X1	Reversal of unrealized gains/loss on partial termination	17,500.00	
5-Feb-X1	On recording profit/loss on partial termination of CFD	24,500.00	
15-Feb-X1	On recording profit/loss on expiry of CFD	15,000.00	
15-Feb-X1	Reversal of unrealized gains/loss on expiry of CFD	7,500.00	
15-Feb-X1	Interest payable on long position CFD contract till date		922.85
15-Feb-X1	Interest receivable on margin account at the end 31-Jan-X1	153.85	
	Total	**132,157.90**	**26,268.06**
	Outstanding balance in margin account	**105,889.84**	

Journal Entry

Date	Particulars	Debit (US$)	Credit (US$)
15-Feb-X1	Brown & Co. Account	105,889.84	
	To CFD Margin Account		105,889.84
	(Being the amount standing in the margin account receivable from the counterparty)		

T-21 On Receipt of Margin Money from the Counterparty

Journal Entry

Date	Particulars	Debit (US$)	Credit (US$)
15-Feb-X1	Bank Account	105,889.84	
	To Brown & Co. Account		105,889.84
	(Being the margin money account balance received from the counterparty)		

General Ledger Accounts
Brown & Co. Account

Date	Particulars	Debit (US$)	Date	Particulars	Credit (US$)
			29-Jan-X1	By CFD Margin Account	17,500.00
			29-Jan-X1	By Commission Account	500.00
29-Jan-X1	To Bank Account	18,000.00			
			5-Feb-X1	By Commission Account	175.00

Brown & Co. Account (*Cont'd*)

Date	Particulars	Debit (US$)	Date	Particulars	Credit (US$)
5-Feb-X1	To Bank Account	175.00			
15-Feb-X1	To CFD Margin Account	105,889.84			
			15-Feb-X1	By Bank Account	105,889.84
31-Mar-X1	Total	**124,064.84**	31-Mar-X1	Total	**124,064.84**

CFD Contra Account

Date	Particulars	Debit (US$)	Date	Particulars	Credit (US$)
			29-Jan-X1	By CFD Position Account	5,000.00
5-Feb-X1	To CFD Position Account	3,500.00			
15-Feb-X1	To CFD Position Account	1,500.00			
31-Mar-X1	Total	**5,000.00**	31-Mar-X1	Total	**5,000.00**

CFD Long Funding Charges Account

Date	Particulars	Debit (US$)	Date	Particulars	Credit (US$)
31-Jan-X1	To CFD Margin Account	345.21			
15-Feb-X1	To CFD Margin Account	922.85			
			31-Mar-X1	By Balance	1,268.06
31-Mar-X1	Total	**1,268.06**	31-Mar-X1	Total	**1,268.06**
31-Mar-X1	To Balance	1,268.06			

CFD Position Account

Date	Particulars	Debit (US$)	Date	Particulars	Credit (US$)
29-Jan-X1	To CFD Contra Account	5,000.00			
			5-Feb-X1	By CFD Contra Account	3,500.00
			15-Feb-X1	By CFD Contra Account	1,500.00
31-Mar-X1	Total	**5,000.00**	31-Mar-X1	Total	**5,000.00**

Commission Account

Date	Particulars	Debit (US$)	Date	Particulars	Credit (US$)
29-Jan-X1	To Brown & Co. Account	500.00			
5-Feb-X1	To Brown & Co. Account	175.00			
			31-Mar-X1	By Balance	675.00
31-Mar-X1	Total	**675.00**	31-Mar-X1	Total	**675.00**
31-Mar-X1	To Balance	675.00			

CFD Margin Account

Date	Particulars	Debit (US$)	Date	Particulars	Credit (US$)
29-Jan-X1	To Brown & Co. Account	17,500.00			
			31-Jan-X1	By Unrealized Gains/Loss on CFD Account	25,000.00
31-Jan-X1	To Bank Account	50,000.00			
			31-Jan-X1	By CFD Long Funding Charges Account	345.21
31-Jan-X1	To Interest Received on CFD Margin Account	4.05			
5-Feb-X1	To Unrealized Gains/Loss on CFD Account	17,500.00			
5-Feb-X1	To Realized Gains/Loss—CFD Account	24,500.00			
15-Feb-X1	To Unrealized Gains/Loss on CFD Account	7,500.00			
15-Feb-X1	To Realized Gains/Loss—CFD Account	15,000.00			
			15-Feb-X1	By Brown & Co. Account	105,889.84
			15-Feb-X1	By CFD Long Funding Charges Account	922.85
15-Feb-X1	To Interest Received on CFD Margin Account	153.85			
31-Mar-X1	Total	**132,157.90**	31-Mar-X1	Total	**132,157.90**

Interest Received on CFD Margin Account

Date	Particulars	Debit (US$)	Date	Particulars	Credit (US$)
			31-Jan-X1	By CFD Margin ccount	4.05
			15-Feb-X1	By CFD Margin Account	153.85
31-Mar-X1	To Balance	157.90			
31-Mar-X1	Total	**157.90**	31-Mar-X1	Total	**157.90**
			31-Mar-X1	By Balance	157.90

Realized Gains/Loss—CFD Account

Date	Particulars	Debit (US$)	Date	Particulars	Credit (US$)
			5-Feb-X1	By CFD Margin Account	24,500.00
			15-Feb-X1	By CFD Margin Account	15,000.00
31-Mar-X1	To Balance	39,500.00			
31-Mar-X1	Total	**39,500.00**	31-Mar-X1	Total	**39,500.00**
			31-Mar-X1	By Balance	39,500.00

Unrealized Gains/Loss on CFD Account

Date	Particulars	Debit (US$)	Date	Particulars	Credit (US$)
31-Jan-X1	To CFD Margin Account	25,000.00			
			5-Feb-X1	By CFD Margin Account	17,500.00
			15-Feb-X1	By CFD Margin Account	7,500.00
31-Mar-X1	Total	**25,000.00**	31-Mar-X1	Total	**25,000.00**

Share Capital Account

Date	Particulars	Debit (US$)	Date	Particulars	Credit (US$)
			1-Jan-X1	By Bank Account	100,000.00
31-Mar-X1	To Balance	100,000.00			
31-Mar-X1	Total	**100,000.00**	31-Mar-X1	Total	**100,000.00**
			31-Mar-X1	By Balance	100,000.00

Bank Account

Date	Particulars	Debit (US$)	Date	Particulars	Credit (US$)
1-Jan-X1	To Share Capital Account	100,000.00			
			29-Jan-X1	By Brown & Co. Account	18,000.00
			31-Jan-X1	By CFD Margin Account	50,000.00
			5-Feb-X1	By Brown & Co. Account	175.00
15-Feb-X1	To Brown & Co. Account	105,889.84			
			31-Mar-X1	By Balance	137,714.84
31-Mar-X1	Total	**205,889.84**	31-Mar-X1	Total	**205,889.84**
31-Mar-X1	To Balance	137,714.84			

Trial Balance

As of 31-Mar-X1 (US$)

Particulars	Debit	Credit
Capital Account		
Share Capital		100,000.00
Investments	Nil	
Current Assets		
Bank Account	137,714.84	
Direct Income		
Interest Received on CFD Margin Account		157.90
Realized Gains/Loss—CFD		39,500.00
Direct Expenses		
CFD Long Funding Charges	1,268.06	
Commission Account	675.00	
Total	**139,657.90**	**139,657.90**

Income Statement

For the period ending 31-Mar-X1

Expenses	US$	Income	US$
Direct Expense		Direct Income	
CFD Long Funding Charges	1,268.06	Interest Received on CFD Margin Account	157.90
Commission Account	675.00	Realized Gain—CFD	39,500.00
Net Profit Carryover	37,714.84		
Total	**39,657.90**	Total	**39,657.90**

Balance Sheet
As of 31-Mar-X1

Liabilities	US$	Assets	US$
Capital Account		Investments	Nil
Share Capital	100,000.00	Current Assets	
Current Liabilities	Nil	Bank Account	137,714.84
Profit & Loss Account			
Opening Balance	Nil		
Current Period	37,714.84		
Total	**137,714.84**	Total	**137,714.84**

Illustration: CFD—Trade Currency AUD

Gulf Fund had the following trades in Boom Textiles in the CFD market. The counterparty, AB & Co., takes a margin of 20 percent of the value of the contract up front, and the funding cost of a long position is calculated at 2 percent per month for overnight carry of position. AB & Co. pays interest at 6 percent per annum on the margin money deposited with them. The fund introduced AUD 1,000,000 on February 1 at 1.2158 to USD.

The market rate of Boom Textiles fell sharply on February 28, triggering a margin call. The fund decided to make a deposit of AUD 500,000 in the margin account on that date. Valuation dates are month ends. Journal entries, general ledgers, trial balance, income statement, and balance sheet as of March 31, when the interest on margin account is also computed are as follows:

Date	Expiry	Quantity	Rate	Long/Term	Brokerage
26-Feb-X1	15-Mar-X1	7,000	AUD 352	Long	AUD 5,000
5-Mar-X1	15-Mar-X1	3,500	AUD 425	Partial Termination	AUD 1,750

Date	Market Price	FX Rate (AUD/USD)
26-Feb-X1	370	1.22182
27-Feb-X1	385	1.22145
28-Feb-X1	300	1.21581
1-Mar-X1	320	1.20766
2-Mar-X1	385	1.20598

Date	Market Price	FX Rate (AUD/USD)
5-Mar-X1	433	1.20964
6-Mar-X1	488	1.21569
7-Mar-X1	502	1.20987
8-Mar-X1	475	1.21655
9-Mar-X1	455	1.20691
12-Mar-X1	434	1.20314
13-Mar-X1	420	1.21596
14-Mar-X1	436	1.21970
15-Mar-X1	450	1.20978

CFD—Local Currency AUD

T-1 Capital Introduced by the Fund

Journal Entry

Date	Particulars	Debit (AUD)	Credit (AUD)
1-Feb-X1	Bank Account	1,000,000.00	
	To Share Capital Account		1,000,000.00
	(Being subscription amount transferred to bank account)		

T-2 On Purchasing the CFD

Journal Entry

Date	Particulars	Debit (AUD)	Credit (AUD)
26-Feb-X1	CFD Position Account (Off Balance Sheet)	7,000.00	
	To CFD Contra Account (Off Balance Sheet)		7,000.00
	(Being the 7,000 CFD of Boom Textiles bought @ $352)		

T-3 Margin Payable to the Counterparty

Journal Entry

Date	Particulars	Debit (AUD)	Credit (AUD)
26-Feb-X1	CFD Margin Account	492,800.00	
	To AB & Co. Account		492,800.00
	(Being the margin amount for purchase of 7,000 CFD of Boom Textiles @ $352 payable to the counterparty)		

T-4 On Recording the Commission

Journal Entry

Date	Particulars	Debit (AUD)	Credit (AUD)
26-Feb-X1	Commission Account	5,000.00	
	To AB & Co. Account		5,000.00
	(Being the commission amount incurred on purchase of CFD contract)		

T-5 On Payment of Commission and Margin

Journal Entry

Date	Particulars	Debit (AUD)	Credit (AUD)
26-Feb-X1	AB & Co. Account	497,800.00	
	To Bank Account		497,800.00
	(Being the payment made to the counterparty on account of margin and commission)		

T-6 Mark-to-market at End of Reporting Period

Mark to market loss at the end of Feb X1	**AUD**
(a) Market value of 7,000 CFDs @ $300 on 28-Feb-X1	2,100,000.00
(b) Purchase value of 7,000 CFDs @ AUD 352	2,464,000.00
(c) Unrealized loss = (a) − (b)	(364,000.00)

Journal Entry

Date	Particulars	Debit (AUD)	Credit (AUD)
28-Feb-X1	Unrealized Gains/Loss on CFD Account	364,000.00	
	To CFD Margin Account		364,000.00
	(Being the mark to market valuation of CFD contract as on date)		

T-7 Margin Call

To cover the erosion in the value of the investments, the fund made a deposit of AUD 500,000 into the margin account. However, the excess of margin, known as clear margin, will earn interest at 6 percent per annum.

Journal Entry

Date	Particulars	Debit (AUD)	Credit (AUD)
28-Feb-X1	CFD Margin Account	500,000.00	
	To Bank Account		500,000.00
	(Being the deposit made into the margin account on account of margin call)		

T-8 On Payment of Funding Cost of CFD

Calculation of Interest Payable

Date	Outstanding Position	Market Rate	Market Value	Interest	Total Interest for the period
26-Feb-X1	7,000	370	2,590,000	1,703.01	
27-Feb-X1	7,000	385	2,695,000	1,772.05	
28-Feb-X1	7,000	300	2,100,000	1,380.82	
					4,855.88

Journal Entry

Date	Particulars	Debit (AUD)	Credit (AUD)
28-Feb-X1	CFD Long Funding Charges Account	4,855.88	
	To CFD Margin Account		4,855.88
	(Being the funding cost of the long position CFD contracts till date)		

Calculation of Interest Receivable

Date	Opening Balance	Realized Gain	Mark-to-market	Interest Payable	MarginCall	Net Margin	6% PA
26-Feb-X1							
27-Feb-X1							
28-Feb-X1	—		(364,000)	(4,855.88)	500,000	131,144.11	**21.56**

T-9 On Receipt of Interest on Clear Margin

Journal Entry

Date	Particulars	Debit (AUD)	Credit (AUD)
28-Feb-X1	CFD Margin Account	21.56	
	To Interest Received on CFD Margin Account		21.56
	(Being the interest received on CFD margin account as per the calculations given below)		

T-10 On Termination of CFD Partially

Journal Entry

Date	Particulars	Debit (AUD)	Credit (AUD)
5-Mar-X1	CFD Contra Account (Off Balance Sheet)	3,500.00	
	To CFD Position Account (Off Balance Sheet)		3,500.00
	(Being the partial termination of 3,500 CFD)		

T-11 On Recording the Commission

Journal Entry

Date	Particulars	Debit (AUD)	Credit (AUD)
5-Mar-X1	Commission Account	1,750.00	
	To AB & Co. Account		1,750.00
	(Being the commission amount incurred on partial termination of CFD contract)		

T-12 On Payment of Commission

Journal Entry

Date	Particulars	Debit (AUD)	Credit (AUD)
5-Mar-X1	AB & Co. Account	1,750.00	
	To Bank Account		1,750.00
	(Being the commission paid transferred to the CFD margin account)		

T-13 On Reversal of Unrealized Gains on Partial Termination of CFD

The unrealized gains/loss already recognized in income will be reversed on the date of partial termination as the realized gains/loss will be booked comparing the original cost of the position with the amount realized on liquidation. In this case the mark-to-market loss already recorded on the position amounts to AUD182,000, and this will be reversed on the date of partial termination.

Journal Entry

Date	Particulars	Debit (AUD)	Credit (AUD)
5-Mar-X1	CFD Margin Account	182,000.00	
	To Unrealized Gains/Loss on CFD Account		182,000.00
	(Being the unrealized gains on the terminated CFD reversed)		

T-14 On Recording Profit/Loss on Partial Termination of CFD

Calculation of realized gains on partial termination of CFDs	AUD
(a) Cost of 3,500 CFD position (3,500 × 352)	1,232,000.00
(b) Sale consideration of 3,500 CFD position @ 425	1,487,500.00
(c) Realized gains on sale = (b) – (a)	**255,500.00**

Journal Entry

Date	Particulars	Debit (AUD)	Credit (AUD)
5-Mar-X1	CFD Margin Account	255,500.00	
	To Realized Gains/Loss—CFD Account		255,500.00
	(Being the realized gain on partial termination of CFD contract)		

T-15 On Recording Profit/Loss on Expiry of CFD

Calculation of realized gains on expiry of CFDs	INR
(a) Cost of 3,500 CFD position (3,500 × 352)	1,232,000.00
(b) Value of 3,500 CFD position on expiry @ 450	1,575,000.00
(c) Realized gains on expiry = (b) − (a)	**343,000.00**

Journal Entry

Date	Particulars	Debit (AUD)	Credit (AUD)
15-Mar-X1	CFD Margin Account	343,000.00	
	To Realized Gains/Loss—CFD Account		343,000.00
	(Being the realized gain on expiry of CFD contract)		

T-16 On Expiry of CFD Contract

Journal Entry

Date	Particulars	Debit (AUD)	Credit (AUD)
15-Mar-X1	CFD Contra Account (Off Balance Sheet)	3,500.00	
	To CFD Position Account (Off Balance Sheet)		3,500.00
	(Being the expiry of 3,500 CFD)		

T-17 On Reversal of Unrealized Gains on Expiry of CFD

Journal Entry

Date	Particulars	Debit (AUD)	Credit (AUD)
15-Mar-X1	CFD Margin Account	182,000.00	
	To Unrealized Gains/Loss on CFD Account		182,000.00
	(Being the unrealized gains on the expiry of CFD contract reversed)		

T-18 On Payment of Funding Cost of CFD

Calculation of Interest Payable

Date	Outstanding Position	Market Rate	Market Value	Interest	Total Interest for the period
1-Mar-X1	7,000	320	2,240,000	1,472.88	
2-Mar-X1	7,000	385	2,695,000	1,772.05	
3-Mar-X1	7,000	385	2,695,000	1,772.05	
4-Mar-X1	7,000	385	2,695,000	1,772.05	
5-Mar-X1	3,500	433	1,515,500	996.49	
6-Mar-X1	3,500	488	1,708,000	1,123.07	
7-Mar-X1	3,500	502	1,757,000	1,155.29	
8-Mar-X1	3,500	475	1,662,500	1,093.15	
9-Mar-X1	3,500	455	1,592,500	1,047.12	
10-Mar-X1	3,500	455	1,592,500	1,047.12	
11-Mar-X1	3,500	455	1,592,500	1,047.12	
12-Mar-X1	3,500	434	1,519,000	998.79	
13-Mar-X1	3,500	420	1,470,000	966.58	
14-Mar-X1	3,500	436	1,526,000	1,003.40	
15-Mar-X1	0	452	0		
					17,267.16

Journal Entry

Date	Particulars	Debit (AUD)	Credit (AUD)
15-Mar-X1	CFD Long Funding Charges Account	17,267.16	
	To CFD Margin Account		17,267.16
	(Being the funding cost of the long position CFD contracts till date)		

Calculation of Interest Receivable

Date	Opening Balance	Realized Gain	Mark-to-market	Interest Payable	Margin Call	Net Margin	6% PA
1-Mar-X1	131,144.11		140,000	(1,472.88)	–	269,671.23	44.33
2-Mar-X1	269671.23		455,000	(1,772.05)		722,899.18	118.83
3-Mar-X1	722,899.18			(1,772.05)		721,127.12	118.54
4-Mar-X1	721,127.12			(1,772.05)		719,355.07	118.25
5-Mar-X1	719,355.07	255,500	52,500	(996.49)		1,026,358.58	168.72
6-Mar-X1	1,026,358.58		192,500	(1,123.07)		1,217,735.51	200.18
7-Mar-X1	1,217,735.51		49,000	(1,155.29)		1,265,580.22	208.04
8-Mar-X1	1,265,580.22		(94,500)	(1,093.15)		1,169,987.07	192.33
9-Mar-X1	1,169,987.07		(70,000)	(1,047.12)		1,098,939.95	180.65

Calculation of Interest Receivable (*Cont'd*)

Date	Opening Balance	Realized Gain	Mark-to-market	Interest Payable	Margin Call	Net Margin	6% PA
10-Mar-X1	1,098,939.95			(1,047.12)		1,097,892.82	180.48
11-Mar-X1	1,097,892.82			(1,047.12)		1,096,845.70	180.30
12-Mar-X1	1,096,845.70		(73,500)	(998.79)		1,022,346.90	168.06
13-Mar-X1	1,022,346.90		(49,000)	(966.58)		972,380.33	159.84
14-Mar-X1	972,380.33		56,000	(1,003.40)		1,027,376.93	168.88
15-Mar-X1	1,027,376.93	343,000	(294,000)	—		1,076,376.93	176.94
Total		**598,500**	—	**(17,267.16)**			**2,384.37**

T-19 On Receipt of Interest on Clear Margin

Journal Entry

Date	Particulars	Debit (AUD)	Credit (AUD)
15-Mar-X1	CFD Margin Account	2,384.37	
	To Interest received on CFD Margin Account		2,384.37
	(Being the interest received on CFD margin account as per the calculations given below)		

T-20 Receivable from Counterparty on Termination of CFD Positions

Calculation of CFD Margin Account—AUD

Date	Description	Debit	Credit
26-Feb-X1	Margin paid for the purchase of 7,000 CFD shares	492,800.00	
28-Feb-X1	Unrealized gains/loss booked at end of 28-Feb-X1		364,000.00
28-Feb-X1	Deposit made on account of margin call	500,000.00	
28-Feb-X1	Interest payable on long position CFD contract till date		4,855.88
28-Feb-X1	Interest receivable on margin at the end of 28-feb-X1	21.56	
5-Mar-X1	Reversal of unrealized gains/loss on partial termination	182,000.00	
5-Mar-X1	On recording profit/loss on partial termination of CFD	255,500.00	
15-Mar-X1	On recording profit/loss on expiry of CFD	343,000.00	
15-Mar-X1	Reversal of unrealized gains/loss on expiry of CFD	182,000.00	
15-Mar-X1	Interest payable on long position CFD contract till date		17,267.16
15-Mar-X1	Interest receivable on margin at the end of 28-feb-X1	2,384.36	
	Total	**1,957,705.93**	**386,123.04**
	Outstanding balance in margin account	**1,571,582.89**	

Journal Entry

Date	Particulars	Debit (AUD)	Credit (AUD)
15-Mar-X1	AB & Co. Account	1,571,582.89	
	To CFD Margin Account		1,571,582.89
	(Being the amount standing in the margin account receivable from the counterparty)		

T-21 On Receipt of Margin Money from the Counterparty

Journal Entry

Date	Particulars	Debit (AUD)	Credit (AUD)
15-Mar-X1	Bank Account	1,571,582.89	
	To AB & Co. Account		1,571,582.89
	(Being the margin money account balance received from the counterparty)		

General Ledger Accounts

AB & Co. Account

Date	Particulars	Debit (AUD)	Date	Particulars	Credit (AUD)
			26-Feb-X1	By CFD Margin Account	492,800.00
			26-Feb-X1	By Commission Account	5,000.00
26-Feb-X1	To Bank Account	497,800.00			
			5-Mar-X1	By Commission Account	1,750.00
5-Mar-X1	To Bank Account	1,750.00			
15-Mar-X1	To CFD Margin Account	1,571,582.89			
			15-Mar-X1	By Bank Account	1,571,582.89
31-Mar-X1	Total	**2,071,132.89**	31-Mar-X1	Total	**2,071,132.89**

CFD Contra Account

Date	Particulars	Debit (AUD)	Date	Particulars	Credit (AUD)
			26-Feb-X1	By CFD Position Account	7,000.00
5-Mar-X1	To CFD Position Account	3.500.00			
15-Mar-X1	To CFD Position Account	3.500.00			
31-Mar-X1	Total	**7,000.00**	31-Mar-X1	Total	**7,000.00**

CFD Long Funding Charges Account

Date	Particulars	Debit (AUD)	Date	Particulars	Credit (AUD)
28-Feb-X1	To CFD Margin Account	4,855.88			
15-Mar-X1	To CFD Margin Account	17,267.16			
			31-Mar-X1	By Balance	22,123.04
31-Mar-X1	Total	**22,123.04**	31-Mar-X1	Total	**22,123.04**
31-Mar-X1	To Balance	**22,123.04**			

CFD Position Account

Date	Particulars	Debit (AUD)	Date	Particulars	Credit (AUD)
26-Feb-X1	To CFD Contra Account	7,000.00			
			5-Mar-X1	By CFD Contra Account	3.500.00
			15-Mar-X1	By CFD Contra Account	3.500.00
31-Mar-X1	Total	**7,000.00**	31-Mar-X1	Total	**7,000.00**

Commission Account

Date	Particulars	Debit (AUD)	Date	Particulars	Credit (AUD)
26-Feb-X1	To AB & Co. Account	5,000.00			
5-Mar-X1	To AB & Co. Account	1,750.00			
			31-Mar-X1	By Balance	6,750.00
31-Mar-X1	Total	**6,750.00**	31-Mar-X1	Total	**6,750.00**
31-Mar-X1	To Balance	6,750.00			

CFD Margin Account

Date	Particulars	Debit (AUD)	Date	Particulars	Credit (AUD)
26-Feb-X1	To AB & Co. Account	492,800.00			
			28-Feb-X1	By Unrealized Gains/Loss on CFD Account	364,000.00
28-Feb-X1	To Bank Account	500,000.00			
			28-Feb-X1	By CFD Long Funding Charges Account	4,855.88

CFD Margin Account (*Cont'd*)

Date	Particulars	Debit (AUD)	Date	Particulars	Credit (AUD)
28-Feb-X1	To Interest Received on CFD Margin Account	21.56			
5-Mar-X1	To Unrealized Gains/ Loss on CFD Account	182,000.00			
5-Mar-X1	To Realized Gains/ Loss—CFD Account	255,500.00			
15-Mar-X1	To Realized Gains/ Loss—CFD Account	343,000.00			
15-Mar-X1	To Unrealized Gains/ Loss on CFD Account	182,000.00			
			15-Mar-X1	By CFD Long Funding Charges Account	17,267.16
15-Mar-X1	To Interest Received on CFD Margin Account	2,384.37			
			15-Mar-X1	To AB & Co. Account	1,571,582.89
31-Mar-X1	Total	**1,957,705.93**	31-Mar-X1	Total	**1,957,705.93**

Interest Received on CFD Margin Account

Date	Particulars	Debit (AUD)	Date	Particulars	Credit (AUD)
			28-Feb-X1	By CFD Margin Account	21.56
			15-Mar-X1	By CFD Margin Account	2,384.37
31-Mar-X1	To Balance	2,405.93			
31-Mar-X1	Total	**2,405.93**	31-Mar-X1	Total	**2,405.93**
			31-Mar-X1	By Balance	2,405.93

Realized Gains/Loss—CFD Account

Date	Particulars	Debit (AUD)	Date	Particulars	Credit (AUD)
			5-Mar-X1	By CFD Margin Account	255,500.00
			15-Mar-X1	By CFD Margin Account	343,000.00
31-Mar-X1	To Balance	598,500.00			
31-Mar-X1	Total	**598,500.00**	31-Mar-X1	Total	**598,500.00**
			31-Mar-X1	By Balance	598,500.00

Unrealized Gains/Loss on CFD Account

Date	Particulars	Debit (AUD)	Date	Particulars	Credit (AUD)
28-Feb-X1	To CFD Margin Account	364,000.00			
			5-Mar-X1	By CFD Margin Account	182,000.00
			15-Mar-X1	By CFD Margin Account	182,000.00
31-Mar-X1	Total	**364,000.00**	31-Mar-X1	Total	**364,000.00**

Share Capital Account

Date	Particulars	Debit (AUD)	Date	Particulars	Credit (AUD)
			1-Feb-X1	By Bank Account	1,000,000.00
31-Mar-X1	To Balance	1,000,000.00			
31-Mar-X1	Total	**1,000,000.00**	31-Mar-X1	Total	**1,000,000.00**
			31-Mar-X1	By Balance	1,000,000.00

Bank Account

Date	Particulars	Debit (AUD)	Date	Particulars	Credit (AUD)
1-Feb-X1	To Share Capital Account	1,000,000.00			
			26-Feb-X1	By AB & Co. Account	497,800.00
			28-Feb-X1	By CFD Margin Account	500,000.00
			5-Mar-X1	By AB & Co. Account	1,750.00
15-Mar-X1	To AB & Co. Account	1,571,582.89			
			31-Mar-X1	By Balance	1,572,032.89
31-Mar-X1	Total	**2,571,582.89**	31-Mar-X1	Total	**2,571,582.89**
31-Mar-X1	To Balance	1,572,032.89			

Trial Balance

As of 31-Mar-X1 (AUD)

Particulars	Debit	Credit
Capital Account		
Share Capital		1,000,000.00
Current Liabilities		Nil
Investments	Nil	
Current Assets		
Bank Account	1,572,032.89	
Direct Income		
Interest Received on CFD Margin Account		2,405.92
Realized Gains/Loss—CFD		598,500.00
Direct Expenses		
CFD Long Funding Charges	22,123.04	
Commission Account	6,750.00	
Total	**1,600,905.93**	**1,600,905.93**

Income Statement

For the period ending 31-Mar-X1

Expenses	AUD	Income	AUD
Direct Expense		**Direct Income**	
CFD Long Funding Charges	22,123.04	Interest Received on CFD Margin Account	2,405.93
Commission Account	6,750.00	Realized Gain—CFD	598,500.00
Net Profit Carryover	572,032.89		
Total	**600,905.93**	Total	**600,905.93**

Balance Sheet

As of 31-Mar-X1

Liabilities	AUD	Assets	AUD
Capital Account		**Investments**	Nil
Share Capital	1,000,000.00	**Current Assets**	
Current Liabilities		Bank Account	1,572,032.89
Profit & Loss Account			
Opening Balance	Nil		
Current Period	572,032.89		
Total	**1,572,032.89**	Total	**1,572,032.89**

CFD—Functional Currency US$

F-1 Capital Introduced by the Fund (T-1 @ FX Rate: 1.21580)

Journal Entry

Date	Particulars	Debit (US$)	Credit (US$)
1-Feb-X1	Bank Account	822,503.70	
	To Share Capital Account		822,503.70
	(Being share capital received from the investor remitted into bank)		

F-2 On Purchasing the CFD: (T-2 @ FX Rate: 1.22182)

Journal Entry

Date	Particulars	Debit (US$)	Credit (US$)
26-Feb-X1	CFD Position Account (Off Balance Sheet)	7,000.00	
	To CFD Contra Account (Off Balance Sheet)		7,000.00
	(Being the 7,000 CFD of Boom Textiles bought @ $352)		

F-3 Margin Payable to the Counterparty (T-3 @ FX Rate: 1.22182)

Journal Entry

Date	Particulars	Debit (US$)	Credit (US$)
26-Feb-X1	CFD Margin Account	403,332.73	
	To AB & Co. Account		403,332.73
	(Being the margin amount for purchase of 7,000 CFD of Boom Textiles @ $352 payable to the counterparty)		

F-4 On Recording the Commission (T-4 @ FX Rate: 1.22182)

Journal Entry

Date	Particulars	Debit (US$)	Credit (US$)
26-Feb-X1	Commission Account	4,092.26	
	To AB & Co. Account		4,092.26
	(Being the commission incurred on purchase of CFD contract)		

F-5 On Payment of Commission and Margin (T-5 @ FX Rate: 1.22182)

Journal Entry

Date	Particulars	Debit (US$)	Credit (US$)
26-Feb-X1	AB & Co. Account	407,424.99	
	To Bank Account		407,424.99
	(Being the payment made to the counterparty on account of margin and commission)		

F-6 Mark-to-market at End of Reporting Period (T-6 @ FX Rate: 1.21581)

Journal Entry

Date	Particulars	Debit (US$)	Credit (US$)
28-Feb-X1	Unrealized Gains/Loss on CFD Account	299,388.88	
	To CFD Margin Account		299,388.88
	(Being the mark-to-market valuation of CFD contract as of date)		

F-7 Margin Call (T-7 @ FX Rate: 1.21581)

Journal Entry

Date	Particulars	Debit (US$)	Credit (US$)
28-Feb-X1	CFD Margin Account	411,248.47	
	To Bank Account		411,248.47
	(Being the deposit made into the margin account due to margin call)		

F-8 On Payment of Funding Cost of CFD (T-8 @ FX Rate: 1.21581)

Journal Entry

Date	Particulars	Debit (US$)	Credit (US$)
28-Feb-X1	CFD Long Funding Charges Account	3,993.95	
	To CFD Margin Account		3,993.95
	(Being the funding cost of the long position CFD contracts till date)		

F-9 On Receipt of Interest on Clear Margin (T-9 @ FX Rate: 1.21581)

Journal Entry

Date	Particulars	Debit (US$)	Credit (US$)
28-Feb-X1	CFD Margin Account	17.73	
	To Interest received on CFD Margin Account		17.73
	(Being the interest received on CFD Margin account)		

F-10 FX Translation on Margin Account (Transient FX Translation Entry)

Date	Particulars	AUD	FX Rate	US$
26-Feb-X1	Opening balance	492,800.00	1.22182	403,332.73
28-Feb-X1	Mark-to-market	(364,000.00)	1.21581	(299,388.88)
28-Feb-X1	Margin call	500,000.00	1.21581	411,248.47
28-Feb-X1	On payment of funding cost CFD	(4,855.88)	1.21581	(3,993.95)
28-Feb-X1	On receipt of interest on clear margin	21.56	1.21581	17.73
28-Feb-X1	Net balance	623,965.67		511,216.10
28-Feb-X1	Net balance at current FX rate	623,965.67	1.21581	513,209.85
	Currency gains on margin account			**1,993.75**

Journal Entry

Date	Particulars	Debit (US$)	Credit (US$)
28-Feb-X1	CFD Margin Account	1,993.75	
	To Unrealized Currency Gains/Loss Account		1,993.75
	(Being the FX translation applied on margin account)		

F-11 FX Translation on Bank Account (Transient FX Translation Entry)

Date	Particulars	AUD	FX Rate	US$
01-Feb-X1	Opening balance	1,000,000	1.21580	822,503.70
26-Feb-X1	Payment of margin amount	(497,800)	1.22182	(407,424.99)
28-Feb-X1	Margin call	(500,000)	1.21581	(411,248.47)
28-Feb-X1	Net balance	2,200		3,830.24
28-Feb-X1	Net balance at current FX rate	2,200	1.21581	1,809.49
28-Feb-X1	FX translation on Bank Account			**(2,020.75)**

Journal Entry

Date	Particulars	Debit (US$)	Credit (US$)
28-Feb-X1	Unrealized Currency Gains/Loss Account	2,020.75	
	To Bank Account		2,020.75
	(Being the FX translation applied on bank account)		

F-12 On Termination of CFD Partially (T-10 @ FX Rate: 1.20964)

Journal Entry

Date	Particulars	Debit (US$)	Credit (US$)
5-Mar-X1	CFD Contra Account (Off Balance Sheet)	3,500.00	
	To CFD Position Account (Off Balance Sheet)		3,500.00
	(Being the partial termination of 3,500 CFD)		

F-13 On Recording the Commission (T-11 @ FX Rate: 1.20964)

Journal Entry

Date	Particulars	Debit (US$)	Credit (US$)
5-Mar-X1	Commission Account	1,446.71	
	To AB & Co. Account		1,446.71
	(Being the commission incurred on partial termination of CFD contract)		

F-14 On Payment of Commission (T-12 @ FX Rate: 1.20964)

Journal Entry

Date	Particulars	Debit (US$)	Credit (US$)
5-Mar-X1	AB & Co. Account	1,446.71	
	To Bank Account		1,446.71
	(Being the commission paid to the counterparty)		

F-15 On Reversal of Unrealized Gains on Partial Termination (T-13 @ FX Rate: 1.20964)

Journal Entry

Date	Particulars	Debit (US$)	Credit (US$)
5-Mar-X1	CFD Margin Account	150,457.99	
	To Unrealized Gains/Loss on CFD Account		150,457.99
	(Being the unrealized gains on partially terminated CFD reversed)		

F-16 On Recording Profit/Loss on Partial Termination (T-14 @ FX Rate: 1.20964)

Journal Entry

Date	Particulars	Debit (US$)	Credit (US$)
5-Mar-X1	CFD Margin Account	211,219.87	
	To Realized Gains/Loss—CFD Account		211,219.87
	(Being the realized gains on termination of CFD contract)		

F-17 On Recording Profit/Loss on Expiry of CFD (T-15 @ FX Rate: 1.20978)

Journal Entry

Date	Particulars	Debit (US$)	Credit (US$)
15-Mar-X1	CFD Margin Account	283,522.62	
	To Realized Gains/Loss—CFD Account		283,522.62
	(Being the realized gains on expiry of CFD contract)		

F-18 On Expiry of CFD Contract (T-16 @ FX Rate: 1.20978)

Journal Entry

Date	Particulars	Debit (US$)	Credit (US$)
15-Mar-X1	CFD Contra Account (Off Balance Sheet)	3,500.00	
	To CFD Position Account (Off Balance Sheet)		3,500.00
	(Being the expiry of 3,500 CFD)		

F-19 On Reversal of Unrealized Gains on Expiry of CFD (T-17 @ FX Rate: 1.20978)

Journal Entry

Date	Particulars	Debit (US$)	Credit (US$)
15-Mar-X1	CFD Margin Account	150,440.58	
	To Unrealized Gains/Loss on CFD Account		150,440.58
	(Being the unrealized gains on the expiry of CFD contract transferred to margin account)		

F-20 On Payment of Funding Cost of CFD (T-18 @ FX Rate: 1.20978)

Journal Entry

Date	Particulars	Debit (US$)	Credit (US$)
15-Mar-X1	CFD Long Funding Charges Account	14,272.98	
	To CFD Margin Account		14,272.98
	(Being the funding cost of the long position CFD contracts till date)		

F-21 On Receipt of Interest on Clear Margin (T-19 @ FX Rate: 1.20978)

Journal Entry

Date	Particulars	Debit (US$)	Credit (US$)
15-Mar-X1	CFD Margin Account	1,970.91	
	To Interest received on CFD Margin Account		1,970.91
	(Being the interest received on CFD margin account)		

F-22 Receivable on Termination of CFD Positions (T-20 @ FX Rate: 1.18)

Calculation of CFD Margin Account—US$

Date	Description	Debit	Credit
26-Feb-X1	Margin paid for the purchase of 7,000 CFDs	403,332.73	
28-Feb-X1	Unrealized gain/loss booked at end of 28-Feb-X1		299,388.88
28-Feb-X1	Deposit made on account of margin call	411,248.47	
28-Feb-X1	Interest payable on long position till date		3,993.95

Calculation of CFD Margin Account—US$ (*Cont'd*)

Date	Description	Debit	Credit
28-Feb-X1	Interest receivable on margin at the end of 28-feb-X1	17.73	
28-Feb-X1	FX gain/loss on margin account at the end of 28-Feb-X1	1,993.76	
5-Mar-X1	Reversal of unrealized gains/loss on partial termination	150,457.98	
5-Mar-X1	On recording profit/loss on partial termination of CFD	211,219.87	
15-Mar-X1	On recording profit/loss on expiry of CFD	283,522.63	
15-Mar-X1	Reversal of unrealized gains/loss on expiry of CFD	150,440.57	
15-Mar-X1	Interest payable on long position CFD contract till date		14,272.98
15-Mar-X1	Interest receivable on margin account at the end of 28-feb-X1	1,970.91	
15-Mar-X1	FX Gains/loss on margin account at the end of 15-Mar-X1	2,516.18	
	Total	**1,616,720.83**	**317,655.81**
	Outstanding balance in margin account	**1,299,065.02**	

Journal Entry

Date	Particulars	Debit (US$)	Credit (US$)
15-Mar-X1	AB & Co. Account	1,299,065.02	
	To CFD Margin Account		1,299,065.02
	(Being the balance amount standing in the margin account receivable from the counterparty)		

F-23 On Receipt of Margin Money from the Counterparty (T-21 @ FX Rate: 1.20978)

Journal Entry

Date	Particulars	Debit (US$)	Credit (US$)
15-Mar-X1	Bank Account	1,299,065.02	
	To AB & Co. Account		1,299,065.02
	(Being the margin money account balance received from the counterparty)		

F-24 FX Translation on CFD Margin Account (Transient FX Translation Entry)

Date	Particulars	AUD	FX Rate	US$
1-Mar-X1	Opening balance	623,965.68	1.21581	513,209.86
5-Mar-X1	Realized gains/loss on partial termination of CFD	255,500.00	1.20964	211,219.87
5-Mar-X1	MTM reversal on termination of CFD	182,000.00	1.20964	150,457.99
15-Mar-X1	Realized gains/loss on expiry of CFD	343,000.00	1.20978	283,522.62
15-Mar-X1	MTM reversal on expiry of CFD	182,000.00	1.20978	150,440.58
15-Mar-X1	Balance in margin account	(1,571,582.89)	1.20978	(1,299,065.03)
15-Mar-X1	On payment of funding cost of CFD	(17,267.16)	1.20978	(14,272.98)
15-Mar-X1	On receipt of interest on clear margin	2,384.37	1.20978	1,970.91
15-Mar-X1	Net balance	0.00		(2,516.18)
15-Mar-X1	Net balance at current FX rate	0.00	1.20978	0.00
	FX translation on margin account			**(2,516.18)**

Journal Entry

Date	Particulars	Debit (US$)	Credit (US$)
15-Mar-X1	CFD Margin Account	2,516.18	
	To Unrealized Currency Gains/Loss Account		2,516.18
	(Being the FX translation applied on margin account)		

F-25 FX Translation on Bank Account (Transient FX Translation Entry)

Date	Particulars	AUD	FX Rate	US$
1-Mar-X1	Opening balance	2,200.00	1.21581	1,809.49
5-Mar-X1	Transferred out	(1,750.00)	1.20964	(1,446.71)
15-Mar-X1	Transferred from margin account	1,566,970.98	1.20978	1,295,252.84
15-Mar-X1	Net balance	1,567,420.98		1,295,615.62
15-Mar-X1	Net balance at current FX rate	1,567,420.98	1.20978	1,295,624.81
15-Mar-X1	FX translation gain on bank account			**9.19**

Journal Entry

Date	Particulars	Debit (US$)	Credit (US$)
15-Mar-X1	Bank Account	9.19	
	To Unrealized Currency Gains/Loss Account		9.19
	(Being the FX translation applied on bank account)		

General Ledger Accounts

AB & Co. Account

Date	Particulars	Debit (US$)	Date	Particulars	Credit (US$)
			26-Feb-X1	By CFD Margin Account	403,332.73
			26-Feb-X1	By Commission Account	4,092.26
26-Feb-X1	To Bank Account	407,424.99			
			5-Mar-X1	By Commission Account	1,446.71
5-Mar-X1	To Bank Account	1,446.71			
15-Mar-X1	To CFD Margin Account	1,299,065.02			
			15-Mar-X1	By Bank Account	1,299,065.02
31-Mar-X1	Total	**1,707,936.72**	31-Mar-X1	Total	**1,707,936.72**

CFD Contra Account

Date	Particulars	Debit (US$)	Date	Particulars	Credit (US$)
			26-Feb-X1	By CFD Position Account	7,000.00
5-Mar-X1	To CFD Position Account	3,500.00			
15-Mar-X1	To CFD Position Account	3,500.00			
31-Mar-X1	Total	**7,000.00**	31-Mar-X1	Total	**7,000.00**

CFD Long Funding Charges Account

Date	Particulars	Debit (US$)	Date	Particulars	Credit (US$)
28-Feb-X1	To CFD Margin Account	3,993.95			
15-Mar-X1	To CFD Margin Account	14,272.98			
			31-Mar-X1	By Balance	18,266.93
31-Mar-X1	Total	**18,266.93**	31-Mar-X1	Total	**18,266.93**
31-Mar-X1	To Balance	18,266.93			

CFD Position Account

Date	Particulars	Debit (US$)	Date	Particulars	Credit (US$)
26-Feb-X1	To CFD Contra Account	7,000.00			
			5-Mar-X1	By CFD Contra Account	3,500.00
			15-Mar-X1	By CFD Contra Account	3,500.00
31-Mar-X1	Total	**7,000.00**	31-Mar-X1	Total	**7,000.00**

Commission Account

Date	Particulars	Debit (US$)	Date	Particulars	Credit (US$)
26-Feb-X1	To AB & co. Account	4,092.26			
5-Mar-X1	To AB & co. Account	1,446.71			
			31-Mar-X1	By Balance	5,538.97
31-Mar-X1	Total	**5,538.97**	31-Mar-X1	Total	**5,538.97**
31-Mar-X1	To Balance	5,538.97			

Unrealized Currency Gains/Loss Account

Date	Particulars	Debit (US$)	Date	Particulars	Credit (US$)
			28-Feb-X1	By CFD Margin Account	1,993.76
28-Feb-X1	To Bank Account	2,020.75			
			15-Mar-X1	By CFD Margin Account	2,514.46
			15-Mar-X1	By Bank Account	9.19
31-Mar-X1	To Balance	2,496.66			
31-Mar-X1	Total	**4,517.41**	31-Mar-X1	Total	**4,517.41**
			31-Mar-X1	By Balance	2,496.66

CFD Margin Account

Date	Particulars	Debit (US$)	Date	Particulars	Credit (US$)
26-Feb-X1	To AB & Co. Account	403,332.73			
			28-Feb-X1	By Unrealized Gains/Loss on CFD Account	299,388.88
28-Feb-X1	To Bank Account	411,248.47			
			28-Feb-X1	By CFD Long Funding Charges Account	3,993.95
28-Feb-X1	To Interest Received on CFD Margin Account	17.73			
28-Feb-X1	To Unrealized Currency Gains/Loss Account	1,993.75			
5-Mar-X1	To Unrealized Gains/Loss on CFD Account	150,457.99			
5-Mar-X1	To Realized Gains/ Loss—CFD Account	211,219.87			
15-Mar-X1	To Realized Gains/ Loss—CFD Account	283,522.62			
15-Mar-X1	To Unrealized Gains/Loss on CFD Account	150,440.58			
			15-Mar-X1	By CFD Long Funding Charges Account	14,272.98
15-Mar-X1	To Interest Received on CFD Margin Account	1,970.91			
			15-Mar-X1	To AB & Co. Account	1,299,065.02
15-Mar-X1	To Unrealized Currency Gains/ Loss (P&L) Account	2,516.18			
31-Mar-X1	Total	**1,616,720.83**	31-Mar-X1	Total	**1,616,720.83**

Interest Received on CFD Margin Account

Date	Particulars	Debit (US$)	Date	Particulars	Credit (US$)
			28-Feb-X1	By CFD Margin Account	17.73
			15-Mar-X1	By CFD Margin Account	1,970.91
31-Mar-X1	To Balance	1,988.64			
31-Mar-X1	Total	**1,988.64**	31-Mar-X1	Total	**1,988.64**
			31-Mar-X1	By Balance	1,988.64

Realized Gains/Loss—CFD Account

Date	Particulars	Debit (US$)	Date	Particulars	Credit (US$)
			5-Mar-X1	By CFD Margin Account	211,219,87
			15-Mar-X1	By CFD Margin Account	283,522.62
31-Mar-X1	To Balance	494,742.49			
31-Mar-X1	Total	**494,742.49**	31-Mar-X1	Total	**494,742.49**
			31-Mar-X1	By Balance	494,742.49

Unrealized Gains/Loss on CFD Account

Date	Particulars	Debit (US$)	Date	Particulars	Credit (US$)
28-Feb-X1	To CFD Margin Account	299,388.88			
			5-Mar-X1	By CFD Margin Account	150,457.99
			15-Mar-X1	By CFD Margin Account	150,440.58
31-Mar-X1	To Balance	1,509.69			
31-Mar-X1	Total	**300,898.57**	31-Mar-X1	Total	**300,898.57**
			31-Mar-X1	By Balance	1,509.69

Share Capital Account

Date	Particulars	Debit (US$)	Date	Particulars	Credit (US$)
			1-Feb-X1	By Bank Account	822,503.70
31-Mar-X1	To Balance	822,503.70			
31-Mar-X1	Total	**822,503.70**	31-Mar-X1	Total	**822,503.70**
			31-Mar-X1	By Balance	822,503.70

Bank Account

Date	Particulars	Debit (US$)	Date	Particulars	Credit (US$)
1-Feb-X1	To Share Capital Account	822,503.70			
			26-Feb-X1	By AB & Co. Account	407,424.99
			28-Feb-X1	By CFD Margin Account	411,248.47
			28-Feb-X1	By Unrealized Currency Gains/Loss Account	2,020.75
			5-Mar-X1	By AB & Co. Account	1,446.71
15-Mar-X1	To AB & Co. Account	1,295,252.84			
15-Mar-X1	To Unrealized Currency Gains/Loss Account	9.19			
			31-Mar-X1	By Balance	1,295,624.81
31-Mar-X1	Total	**2,117,765.73**	31-Mar-X1	Total	**2,117,765.73**
31-Mar-X1	To Balance	1,295,624.81			

Trial Balance

As of 31-Mar-X1 (US$)

Particulars	Debit	Credit
Capital Account		
Share Capital		822,503.70
Current Liabilities		Nil
Investments	Nil	
Current Assets		
Bank Account	1,295,624.81	
Direct Income		
Unrealized Currency Gains/Loss Account		2,496.66
Interest Received on CFD Margin Account		1,490.85
Realized Gains/Loss—CFD		494,742.49
Unrealized Gains/Loss on CFD		1,509.69
Direct Expenses		
CFD Long Funding Charges	21,579.61	
Commission Account	5,538.97	
Total	**1,322,743.39**	**1,322,743.39**

Income Statement

For the Period Ending 31-Mar-X1

Expenses	US$	Income	US$
Direct Expenses		**Direct Income**	
CFD Long Funding Charges	21,579.61	Unrealized Currency Gains/Loss Account	2,496.66
Commission Account	5,538.97	Interest Received on CFD Margin Account	1,490.85
Net Profit C/o	473,121.11	Realized Gain—CFD	494,742.49
		Unrealized Gain on CFD	1,509.69
Total	**500,239.69**	Total	**500,239.69**

Balance Sheet

As of 31-Mar-X1

Liabilities	US$	Assets	US$
Capital Account		**Investments**	Nil
Share Capital	822,503.70	**Current Assets**	
Current Liabilities	Nil	Bank Account	1,295,624.81
Profit & Loss Account			
Opening Balance	Nil		
Current Period	473,121.11		
Total	**1,295,624.81**	Total	**1,295,624.81**

SUMMARY

- A contract for difference is a contract between two parties, buyer and seller, stipulating that the seller will pay to the buyer the difference between the current value of an underlying equity share and its value at contract time.
- However, if the difference is negative, then the buyer pays to the seller such difference. A CFD is an equity derivative contract that allows the investor to speculate on share price movements, without the need to own the underlying shares.
- A contract for difference offers all the benefits of share trading without having to physically own shares. A CFD is ideal for short-term technical trading and hedging positions in the underlying market.
- An investor can sell a CFD as an opening position, since a CFD is a contract between the investor and the CFD provider, based upon the price movement of the share.
- An investor may be able to profit from a falling market using this instrument of CFD.
- The investor having a long position is required to pay a daily financing charge applied at an agreed interest rate above or below LIBOR or some other interest rate benchmark, while an investor holding a short position receives such interest.
- Clear margin is the investor margin account adjusted for all positions marked-to-market, less initial margin requirements for all open positions.

- Interest is normally paid to the investor on such clear margin at a preagreed rate of interest.
- Investors in CFDs are required to maintain a certain amount of margin as defined by the counterparty or market maker, which could range from 10 to 30 percent.
- The amount required to be held in the margin account will be as per the terms and conditions imposed by the market maker or counterparty.
- CFDs offer several advantages, like transparent pricing, effective use of capital, increased trading flexibility, access to international markets, stamp duty exemption in some markets, receipt of dividends on bought open positions, receipt of interest on sold open positions, the ability to go short, high leverage, and so on.
- However, CFDs suffer from increased trading risk due to the high leverage that it inherently offers to the investors. CFDs are not suitable for long-term investment and there are no voting rights for a person who is long in CFDs, unlike an investor holding traditional shares.
- CFDs do not have an expiry date. They remain open until they are closed in accordance with the terms of agreement.

EXERCISES

Theory Questions

1. Define a CFD contract and explain how it is different from a futures contract.
2. What are the salient product features of CFD?
3. Is short-selling possible with CFDs, and if so are there any advantages?
4. How is the funding cost computed for a CFD contract?
5. What are the margin requirements for a CFD contract?
6. Discuss briefly the advantages and disadvantages of a CFD contract.
7. "CFD is highly risky." Do you agree? Give reasons for your answer.
8. How is a CFD contract terminated?
9. Explain the trade life cycle for a CFD contract and what journal entries are passed for each event in the cycle.

Objective Questions

1. The striking difference between CFD and futures is
   a. CFDs have no expiry date
   b. CFDs are derivative contracts
   c. CFDs are of a speculative nature
   d. All of the above
2. With CFDs, the investor can take
   a. A long position
   b. A short position
   c. Either a long or a short position
   d. None of the above

3. The commission on a CFD is calculated as a percentage based on
   a. Performance of the underlying asset
   b. Performance of the market
   c. Value of the contract
   d. All of the above
4. Interest on clear margin is paid to the investor based on
   a. A percentage of the value of trade
   b. A preagreed rate of interest
   c. A percentage against marked-to-market calculated on daily basis
   d. None of the above
5. The initial margin requirement varies upon
   a. The contract between the buyer and seller
   b. The stock market concerned
   c. The underlying asset
   d. All of the above
6. Settlement for CFDs happens through
   a. Physical settlement of securities
   b. Cash
   c. Both cash and physical settlement of securities
   d. None of the above
7. CFDs are traded
   a. Over the counter
   b. On exchanges
   c. Both over the counter and on exchanges
   d. None of the above
8. Funding costs are calculated based on
   a. Average market price of the underlying asset
   b. Agreed percentage on the closing market value
   c. Agreed percentage on the opening market value
   d. None of the above
9. For short positions in CFD contracts, the funding cost will be received by the
   a. Investor
   b. Stock exchange
   c. Seller
   d. None of the above

10. For long positions in CFD contracts, the funding cost will be received by the
    a. Investor
    b. Stock exchange
    c. Seller
    d. None of the above
11. CFDs are open-ended contracts with no fixed end date. So the investor of a long position can keep extending the contract by
    a. Paying a fixed amount at end of every month
    b. Receiving interest based on an interest rate benchmark till he holds the position
    c. Paying interest towards overnight/financing charges based on an interest rate benchmark
    d. Carrying forward the position at no cost
    e. Paying a deposit amount agreed upon with the seller
12. In CFD markets, though an investor does not own a share literally, he is still entitled to
    a. Voting rights
    b. Participate in the annual shareholders meeting
    c. Receive trading recommendations from the exchange
    d. The benefits of corporate actions like dividends
    e. All of the above
13. Which of the following are the advantages of CFDs?
    a. Transparent pricing
    b. No expiry period
    c. Receive dividends on bought open positions
    d. Receive interest on sold open positions
    e. All the above
14. When an investor buys a long CFD with a contract size of 1,000 at $90 per share and the margin deposit required to be paid is 10 percent, then what is the leverage amount that is being financed to the investor?
    a. $90,000
    b. $9,000
    c. $99,000
    d. $81,000
    e. $8,100

15. The following journal entry is passed when

Journal Entry

Date	Particulars	Debit (US$)	Credit (US$)
1-Oct-X1	CFD Funding Cost Account	60.00	
	To CFD Margin Account		60.00
	(Being the funding cost to carry over the long position of CFD in respect to shares bought.)		

a. The buyer of the CFD contract is financed with the leverage amount
b. The interest is paid towards the overnight open position
c. The seller of the CFD contract is financed with the leverage amount
d. The interest for the overnight position is received
e. The buyer of the CFD contract pays the margin amount

Journal Questions

CFD—Functional Currency US$

Stamford Fund had the following trades in Alcoa in the CFD market. The counterparty is Robinson & Co., which takes a margin of 10 percent of the value of the contract upfront. The funding cost of a long position is calculated at 2 percent per month for overnight carry of position. Brown & Co. pays interest at 6 percent per annum on the margin money deposited with them.

Stamford Fund introduced $1 million on January 1. The market rate of Alcoa fluctuated widely, triggering a margin call. Stamford Fund decided to make a deposit of $200,000 in the margin account on that date. Valuation dates are month ends. Prepare journal entries, general ledgers, trial balance, income statement, and balance sheet as of February 15, when the interest on margin account is also computed.

Date	Expiry	Quantity	Rate (US$)	Long/Short	Brokerage
29-Jan-X1	15-Feb-X1	10,000	$65	Long	$700
5-Feb-X1	15-Feb-X1	3,500	$72	Partial Termination	$200

Date	Market Price
29-Jan-X1	67
30-Jan-X1	68
31-Jan-X1	70
1-Feb-X1	72
2-Feb-X1	78
5-Feb-X1	73
6-Feb-X1	78
7-Feb-X1	80

Date	Market Price
8-Feb-X1	77
9-Feb-X1	75
12-Feb-X1	83
13-Feb-X1	80
14-Feb-X1	83
15-Feb-X1	75

CFD—Trade Currency SGD

Asian Fund had the following trades in SingTel in the CFD market. The counterparty is Jing Jang & Co., which collects a margin of 10 percent of the value of the contract up front. The funding cost of a long position is calculated at 2 percent per month for overnight carry of position. Jing Jang & Co. pays interest at 6 percent per annum on the margin money deposited with them. The fund introduced US$1 million on February 1. On the same day, Asian Fund converted $500,000 into SGD at 1.45.

There was a margin call on March 4 and Asian Fund decided to make a deposit of SGD500,000 in the margin account on that date. Valuation dates are month ends. Prepare journal entries, general ledgers, trial balance, income statement, and balance sheet as of March 15, when the interest on margin account is also computed.

Date	Expiry	Quantity	Rate	Long/Term	Brokerage (SGD)
26-Feb-X1	15-Mar-X1	12,000	SGD 55	Long	1,200
5-Mar-X1	15-Mar-X1	4,500	SGD 48	Partial Termination	450

Date	Market Price	FX Rate
26-Feb-X1	55	1.47
27-Feb-X1	54	1.46
28-Feb-X1	55	1.45
1-Mar-X1	52	1.46
2-Mar-X1	50	1.47
5-Mar-X1	49	1.49
6-Mar-X1	50	1.50
7-Mar-X1	51	1.54
8-Mar-X1	52	1.57
9-Mar-X1	53	1.52
12-Mar-X1	55	1.51
13-Mar-X1	57	1.55
14-Mar-X1	59	1.57
15-Mar-X1	58	1.54

CFD—Trade Currency JPY

Kyoto Fund had the following trades in PQR shares in the CFD market. The counterparty is Yamashita & Co., which collects a margin of 15 percent of the value of the contract upfront and the funding cost of long position is calculated at 1 percent per month for overnight carry of position. Jing Jang & Co. pays interest at 3 percent per annum on the margin money deposited with them. The fund introduced US$1 million on February 1. On the same day, Kyoto Fund converted $500,000 into JPY at 117.

There was a margin call on March 7, and Kyoto Fund decided to make a deposit of JPY5 million in the margin account on that date. Valuation dates are month ends. Prepare journal entries, general ledgers, trial balance, income statement, and balance sheet as of March 15, when the interest on margin account is also computed.

Date	Expiry	Quantity	Rate	Long/Term	Brokerage
26-Feb-X1	15-Mar-X1	3,000	JPY 2,250	Long	JPY 5,600
5-Mar-X1	15-Mar-X1	1,250	JPY 2,600	Partial Termination	JPY 2,600

Date	Market Price	FX Rate
26-Feb-X1	2,250	117
27-Feb-X1	2,350	116
28-Feb-X1	2,450	115
1-Mar-X1	2,550	116
2-Mar-X1	2,450	114
5-Mar-X1	2,350	116
6-Mar-X1	2,450	117
7-Mar-X1	2,550	118
8-Mar-X1	2,650	119
9-Mar-X1	2,750	121
12-Mar-X1	2,850	122
13-Mar-X1	2,750	121
14-Mar-X1	2,650	120
15-Mar-X1	2,550	118

CHAPTER 12

Accounting for Short Equity Investments

LEARNING OBJECTIVES

After studying this chapter you should have a grasp of the following:

- Definition of short equity securities.
- Types of short sales.
- Process of short-selling.
- Risks of short-selling.
- Box position and short-selling.
- Rationale of short-selling.
- Regulatory requirements of short sales.
- Meaning of stock lending and an illustration.
- Participants in securities lending.
- Regulation of securities lending market.
- Trade life cycle of short equity investments for trading purposes.
- Journal entries to be recorded during the different phases of the trade life cycle.
- Illustration of short equity shares trading.
- Preparation of journal entries and general ledger accounts.
- Preparation of income statement and balance sheet after short equity investments are made.
- Illustration of short equity shares with box position in functional currency.
- Illustration of short equity shares with box position in foreign currency.

DEFINITION OF SHORT EQUITY SECURITIES

Short-selling

Short-selling or *shorting* is the practice of selling securities the seller does not own, in the hope of repurchasing them later at a lower price. This is done with the intention to profit from an expected decline in the price of a *security*, as opposed to the ordinary investment practice, where an investor buys or *goes long* in a security in the hope that the price will rise subsequently.

The term *short-selling* or *being short* also represents strategies that allow an investor to gain from the decline in price of a security. Such strategies include buying put *options*.

A put option grants the right but not an obligation to sell an asset at a given price before a specified time. Thus, the buyer of put options benefits when the market price of the asset falls. Similarly, a short position in a *futures contract* means the holder of the position has the obligation to *sell* the underlying asset at a specified future date.

Short-selling is the opposite of *going long*. The short-seller takes a fundamentally bearish view of the market, with the expectation that the price of the stock will fall, which will ultimately enable him to buy the same stock at a lower price, thereby making a profit. The process of buying back the shares that are sold short is called *buying to cover*. Day traders and hedge funds use investment strategies that include selling short in stocks that are overvalued. Later they buy to cover the short, and make a handsome gain on the transaction.

In order to profit from the stock price going down, investors can borrow a security and sell it, with the expectation that the price will decrease in value so that they can buy it back at a lower price and keep the difference. The short-seller is obliged to deliver the shares to his broker, who usually in turn would have borrowed the shares from some other investor who is in actual possession of the said shares.

In most countries the regulatory requirements are such that if an investor goes short in a cash market, the investor should arrange to borrow the security and deliver the same as if he has sold a security that was in his possession.

TYPES OF SHORT SALES

Regular Short Sale

Short sales as just described are also known as regular short sales, where the short sale is followed up with proper delivery of the shares after borrowing the same. In most countries regulatory requirements enforce the practice that the short sales are of regular short sales type.

Naked Short Sale

When the seller does not borrow or arrange to borrow the securities in time to make delivery to the buyer within the standard three-day settlement period, then such short sale is known as a *naked* short sale. The buyer of such shares seldom receives the shares and is technically described as *failing to deliver*. Failure to deliver occurs routinely on regular long sales as well, due to several genuine reasons. It should be noted that naked short-selling is not necessarily a violation of securities laws so long as the broker-dealers who are market makers of the security are ready to buy and sell the security on a continuous basis at a publicly quoted price, irrespective of the existence of any buyer or seller.

PROCESS OF SHORT-SELLING

Short-selling stock consists of the following activities:

- An investor borrows shares in which he needs to go short.
- For borrowing, the investor should first ensure that cash, equity, or government securities equivalent in value are on deposit with his brokerage firm as collateral for the *initial short margin requirement*.
- The investor sells them and the proceeds are credited to his account with the brokerage firm.

- The investor must close out the position by buying back the share, called *buy to cover*.
- If the price drops, he makes a profit. Otherwise he takes a loss.
- The investor pays a *stock lending fee* to the broker who has arranged for the securities.
- The investor also surrenders all the benefits received from the stock while he was the temporary owner of the shares to the original owner of the stock.
- The investor finally returns the shares to the lender.

RISKS OF SHORT-SELLING

Buying shares has a very different risk profile from selling short. When an investor buys shares, losses are limited as the price can only go down to zero. While going long, gains are theoretically unlimited as there is no limit on how high the price can go. However, in short-selling it is exactly the opposite. The possible gains are limited as the stock can only go down to a price of zero. But the potential loss can be more than the original value of the share, with virtually no upper limit. For this reason, short-selling is best resorted to only as part of a hedge rather than as an investment strategy by itself.

Other risks include the following:

- In short-selling there is no potential for dividend income or interest income, and the return is exclusively from capital gains. In fact, any dividends declared by the company during the short-selling period should be surrendered back by the investor to the lender of the stock.
- There is a potential for the price of the share sold short to rise abnormally due to *short squeeze*. When the price of a stock rises significantly, the short-sellers will cover their positions, thereby increasing the demand for the stock, which leads to further increase in the price of the shares.
- Sometimes the short-sellers are forced by the broker to close their position to meet a margin call.
- If the person who lent the stock wants to have his shares back, the short-seller may be forced to buy the shares from the market, creating a short squeeze. The short squeeze causes an ever further rise in the price of the stock, which in turn may trigger additional covering.
- Sometimes a short squeeze is also deliberately planned by certain group of players in the market when they notice that there is a significant number of short positions in the market.

BOX POSITION AND SHORT-SELLING

Typically hedge funds resort to selling short to profit from the long position. Selling short *against the box* means holding a long position on which one enters a short-sell order. The term *box* refers to the days when a safe deposit box was used to store the physical shares that are long positions. The psychology behind this technique is to lock in paper profits on the long position without having to sell that position. Whether prices increase or decrease, the short position balances the long position and the profits are locked in.

It should be noted that a transaction involving shorting against the box would be deemed by the tax authorities as a constructive sale of the long position, and as such the profits on it are taxable. The exception to this rule is the requirement that the short position be closed out within 30 days of the end of the year, and that the investor must hold his long position, without entering into any hedging strategies, for a minimum of 60 days after the short position has been closed.

RATIONALE OF SHORT-SELLING

Short-sellers are generally treated with animosity as, in the views of many people, they are profiting from the misfortune of others.

However, advocates of short-sellers argue that the practice is a key ingredient of the price discovery mechanism. Noted investors have said that short-sellers actually help the market, as short-sellers are a useful counterweight to the widespread bullishness of the markets. Some believe that short-sellers are useful in uncovering fraudulent accounting and other problems at companies.

REGULATORY REQUIREMENTS OF SHORT SALES

There are several regulatory requirements of short sales in different countries depending upon the current status of the economy. By and large there exists certain fundamental regulation regarding the requirements for short sales which should be adhered to by the market players.

The requirements for the U.S. markets are given here briefly. Note that this is not an exhaustive treatment of the regulatory requirements governing short sales in different countries, but just enough to give the readers an overview of such regulatory requirements.

- Prior to initiating a short sale, the broker-dealers responsible for it must have reasonable grounds to believe that the security can be borrowed so that it can be delivered on the settlement date. This effectively ensures the prevention of failure to deliver.
- Where there is substantial number of extended delivery failures, the broker–dealer must close out the position immediately by making delivery. Typically, these failures to deliver refer to broker–dealers that have open failures for 13 consecutive days in a threshold security.
- Where the broker–dealer has an open fail for 13 consecutive settlement days in a threshold security, no other short sales are allowed until the position is closed out by the broker–dealer.
- Threshold securities are equity securities that have an aggregate fail-to-deliver position for five consecutive settlement days totaling 10,000 shares or more, equal to at least 0.5 percent of the issuer's total shares outstanding.

SECURITIES LENDING

Securities lending or *stock lending* refers to the lending of securities by one party to another. The terms of the loan are governed by a *securities lending agreement*, which normally requires that the borrower provide the lender with collateral, which could be in the form of either cash or government securities of value equal to or greater than the loaned securities.

Towards the charges for the loan, both the parties negotiate a fee, quoted as an annualized percentage of the value of the loaned securities.

If the collateral provided by the borrower is cash, then the fee is quoted as a *rebate.* This means that the lender will earn interest on the cash collateral provided by him, and will adjust this as a rebate from the agreed rate of interest to the borrower.

To sum up, securities lending is the temporary transfer of a security by its owner to a short-seller. The title and voting rights are transferred to the borrower, who can use the same towards settling the short position during the life of the loan. Towards this the borrower agrees to return the loaned securities; secure the loan with collateral of not less value than the loaned securities; pay stock loan fees; and remit to the lender any dividends, coupon interest, or other corporate actions that occur during the time the securities are loaned to the borrower. The borrower also collects from the lender an agreed rate of interest on the cash collateral provided to the lender.

As securities lending is an over-the-counter market, it is difficult to estimate precisely the size of this industry. According to the International Securities Lending Association (ISLA), currently the balance of securities on loan exceeds $2 trillion globally. (See www.isla.co.uk.)

Large Security Lenders
ABN AMRO (New York, London, Hong Kong)
Bank of America (New York)
Bank of New York (New York)
Barclays Global Investors (San Francisco, London, Tokyo)
Charles Schwab Corporation (San Francisco)
Citibank (New York)
Credit Suisse (New York, London)
Deutsche Bank (New York)
Dresdner Bank (Frankfurt)
Fortis Bank (New York, Amsterdam, London, Hong Kong)
Goldman Sachs (New York, London, UK)
JPMorgan Chase (New York)
Mellon Bank (Pittsburgh)
Morgan Stanley (New York)
Penson Financial Services (New York, Dallas)
RBC Dexia (London, Luxembourg, Toronto)
Robeco (Rotterdam, the Netherlands)
State Street Corporation (Boston, London)
The Northern Trust Company (Chicago)
UBS (Zürich, Switzerland, London)

An Illustration of Securities Lending

Assume that a large stock lending firm having a significant position in a particular stock agrees to transfer a particular amount of stock to a hedge fund that has gone short in that security. In exchange for the stock loan, the hedge fund should transfer at least 100 percent of the stock value in cash or government securities as collateral. The cash value of the collateral would be marked-to-market on a daily basis to maintain 100 percent of the market value of the stock shorted.

For example, assume that shares in ABC Company trades at $50 per share. An investor going short in ABC would borrow 100 shares of ABC Company, and then immediately sell those shares in the market for a total of $5,000. If the price of ABC shares subsequently falls to $45 per share, the investor would then buy 100 shares back for $4,500, return the shares to their original owner, and make a $500 profit.

Note that this short-selling has unlimited potential losses as well. If the shares of ABC after selling short went up to $75, the short-seller would have to buy back all the shares at $7,500, thereby losing $2,500.

Regulation of Securities Lending Market

Securities lending is regulated in most of the world's major securities markets and is perfectly legal. Most markets require that the borrowing of securities be conducted only for specifically permitted purposes that include the following:

- To facilitate settlement of a trade.
- To facilitate delivery of a short sale.
- To finance the security.
- To facilitate a loan to another borrower for one of the permitted purposes listed above.

When a security is loaned, the title of the security is transferred to the borrower. Thus the borrower is entitled to receive all coupon and/or dividend payments, and any other rights such as voting rights. However, these dividends or coupons must be passed back to the lender.

Stock lending was originally resorted to as a means to cover settlement failures. When a seller failed, for whatever reason, to deliver the shares he had sold, he would incur additional costs and penalties due to settlement failure. In those circumstances, the seller would borrow the stock at a fee and deliver it to the buyer. When the seller was able to procure the shares, he would return the same to the lender and pay a fee for the stock borrowed.

However, nowadays the principal reason for borrowing a stock is to take a short position. As the seller is obliged to deliver the shares, the seller should borrow the same by incurring a fee for the same. At the end of the deal, the seller would return an *equivalent* security to the lender.

Participants in Securities Lending

- *Borrowers* are typically investment banks, broker/dealers, intermediaries, or hedge funds.
- *Lenders* with assets in the form of equities and fixed income securities will most commonly participate in the market in one of two ways—either directly or indirectly through an agent.
- *Direct lenders* tend to be large institutional investors such as pension plans and insurance companies.

The International Securities Lending Association (ISLA) is a trade association established in 1989 to represent the common interests of participants in the securities lending industry. ISLA works closely with European regulators and in the United Kingdom has representation on the Securities Lending and Repo Committee, a committee of market practitioners chaired by the Bank of England. The Association has contributed to a number of major market initiatives, including the development of the UK Stock Borrowing and Lending Code of Guidance and the industry standard lending agreement, the Global Master Securities Lending Agreement (GMSLA). ISLA's priorities for 2007 and 2008 include:

- Working with regulators to provide a safe and efficient framework for securities lending.
- Providing information to members about securities lending market developments.
- Opening up new markets for securities lending.
- Developing good industry practices.
- Reviewing the GMSLA.
- Enhancing the public profile of the securities lending industry.

ISLA has more than 90 members comprising insurance companies, pension funds, asset managers, banks, and securities dealers representing more than 4,000 clients. While based in London, ISLA represents members from more than 20 countries in Europe and North America.

(*Source:* ISLA website, www.isla.co.uk)

- *Agent lenders* will act for any beneficial owner regardless of size, where the beneficial owner does not wish to, for reasons of cost or size, participate directly. Agent lenders tend to be global custodians or asset managers participating on behalf of a large number of clients.

THE TRADE LIFE CYCLE FOR EQUITY SHORT SALES

- Short-sell the share.
- Pay brokerage/commission on the sell transaction.
- Deposit the collateral for the value of short sales.
- Receive the contracted amount for the share.
- Pay the stock lending fees.
- Ascertain the fair value at the end of the reporting period.
- Reverse the mark-to-market.
- Dividend declaration by the company.
- Convey the dividend to the original owner of the shares.
- Receive the interest on cash collateral pledged with the broker.
- Buy to cover the share.
- Pay the brokerage/commission on the buy transaction.
- Pay the consideration.

- Ascertain the profit/loss on the sale.
- Get back the cash collateral from the broker.
- FX revaluation entries.
- FX translation entries.

Short-sell the Share

The investor should first ensure that he has made arrangements for delivering the shares that he intends to short. Even though the onus is on the broker-dealer, it is better to ensure this beforehand to avoid any hassles later.

When the net holding of any share is negative—that is, where the shares sold are greater than the shares bought of the same security—it is referred to as *short position.*

Alan Kimberly Inc. short-sells 1,000 equity shares of Gold Crest at $490 per share through the broker Silver Man on October 3. The accounting entry that is recorded in the books of accounts is as follows:

Journal Entry

Date	Particulars	Debit (US$)	Credit (US$)
3-Oct-X1	Receivable from broker—Silver Man Account	490,000.00	
	To Equity Shares—Gold Crest Account—Short sales		490,000.00
	(Being the Gold Crest shares sold short @ $490 per share through the Broker—Silver Man)		

Brokerage/Commission on the Transaction

The broker of the stock exchange charges commission for the services rendered. This is usually settled along with the sale value of the shares. Accounting standards require that this is treated as part of the cost of the shares procured/sold. Hence this is usually built into the cost of purchase/sale of the shares.

On the 1,000 Gold Crest shares purchased through Silver Man, the brokerage payable per share is $3. The accounting entry that is recorded in the books of accounts is as follows:

Journal Entry

Date	Particulars	Debit (US$)	Credit (US$)
3-Oct-X1	Equity Shares—Gold Crest Account—Short Sales	3,000.00	
	To Silver Man Account		3,000.00
	(Being the brokerage payable to Silver Man @ $3 per share on 1,000 Gold Crest shares bought through them)		

Deposit Cash Collateral with the Broker

The next event in the trade life cycle of short sales is the deposit of collateral with the broker through whom the short sale is effected. It is assumed that the collateral in this case is cash, even though the collateral can be in any acceptable form to the broker, such as government securities. Based on the collateral deposited by the investor, the broker will arrange for procuring the stock loan and deliver the same to the stock exchange on the settlement date.

Assuming that the broker is paid on day T + 2, then the accounting entry that is recorded in the books of accounts is as follows:

Journal Entry

Date	Particulars	Debit (US$)	Credit (US$)
5-Oct-X1	Cash collateral paid to Broker Account	490,000.00	
	To Bank Account		490,000.00
	(Being the amount paid to Silver Man on short sale of 1,000 Gold Crest shares as cash collateral)		

Receive the Contracted Amount for the Share

The next event in the trade life cycle of short sales is the receipt of the contracted amount for the shares sold. Usually the delivery of the shares and the receipt for the same happens two days after the date of the trade; this is referred to as T + 2. However, this varies from exchange to exchange.

The shares are usually delivered electronically by the seller and the payment is made by the buyer on the same date. During this stage the actual asset comes into the physical possession of the buyer and the liability created earlier is settled. For exchange-traded securities, the settlement automatically takes place on the settlement date through the clearing system of the exchange concerned. For over-the-counter (OTC) trades, both the parties resort to their own accepted method of settlement to ensure that they effectively avoid each other's counterparty risk.

Assuming that the broker is paid on T + 2, then the accounting entry that is recorded in the books of accounts is as follows:

Journal Entry

Date	Particulars	Debit (US$)	Credit (US$)
5-Oct-X1	Bank	487,000.00	
	To Receivable from Broker Account		487,000.00
	(Being the amount received from Silver Man on short sale of 1,000 Gold Crest shares after adjusting for the brokerage)		

Ascertain the Fair Value at the End of the Reporting Period

At the end of every reporting period the fair value of the shares is ascertained and the shares are marked-to-market. This process is known as portfolio valuation, when the market rate at the end of the period is determined from the primary stock exchange where the shares are traded.

If there is a decrease in the market rate over and above the sale rate, then such decrease is recognized as a gain on the one hand, and the corresponding amount is reflected as a decrease in the value of short-sold shares. Conversely, if there is an increase in the market rate over and above the sale rate, then such increase is recognized as a loss on the one hand, and the corresponding amount is reflected as an increase in the value of short-sold shares. Note that any increase in the market rate over and above the sale rate can result in additional collateral being deposited by the investor with the broker concerned.

This accounting entry is reversed on the next day or the next valuation date when a fresh entry for the then value is recorded in the books of accounts. Alternatively, the accounting entry can also be recorded only for the incremental value. If the investor follows this incremental value method then there is no need to reverse the entry for mark-to-market recorded earlier.

Assuming that the market rate of Gold Crest as of October 31, which is the next valuation date, is $483, then the accounting entry that is recorded in the books of accounts is as follows:

Journal Entry

Date	Particulars	Debit (US$)	Credit (US$)
31-Oct-X1	Equity Shares—Gold Crest Account—Short Sales Account	4,000.00	
	To Unrealized Capital Gains—Equity Shares Account		4,000.00
	(Being the mark-to-market entry for 1,000 short position in Gold Crest Shares)		

Reversal of Mark-to-market Entry

The accounting entry for mark-to-market is reversed on the next day or the next valuation date when a fresh entry for the then value is recorded in the books of accounts. However, as mentioned earlier, if the investor follows this incremental value method then there is no need to reverse the entry for mark-to-market recorded earlier.

The accounting entry that is recorded in the books of accounts is shown below:

Journal Entry

Date	Particulars	Debit (US$)	Credit (US$)
1-Nov-X1	Unrealized Capital Gains/Loss—Equity Shares Account	4,000.00	
	To Equity Shares—Gold Crest Account—Short Sales Account		4,000.00
	(Being the reversal of mark-to-market entry for 1,000 short position in Gold Crest Shares)		

Corporate Action—Dividend Declaration by the Company

In a short sale, the corporate actions by the issuing company should be surrendered to the original owner of the shares. For example, if a dividend is declared by the company during the time when the short sale is effective, then such dividend must be compensated to the original owner of the shares. Since the shares are not currently held by the investor, the investor will not receive any dividend from the company. Nevertheless, the original owner of the shares is deprived of the dividend declared by the company and hence needs to be compensated by the investor.

It should be noted that technically, the investor will not be at any disadvantage on account of the dividend declared by the company even though the investor is required to compensate the dividend to the original owner without having received anything from the company—the reason being that after such dividend declaration, the market rate of the security effectively stands reduced by the dollar amount of dividend per share, thereby reducing the short sale liability of the investor.

No accounting entry would be recorded in the books of accounts of the investor on account of Gold Crest announcing a dividend of $7 per share, the ex-dividend date being October 17.

Compensate the Dividend to the Original Owner of the Shares

The original owner should be compensated for the dividend forgone by him due to lending the stock to the investor.

Assuming that the actual cash dividend announced by the company amounts to $7 per share, the ex-dividend date being October 17, the accounting entry that is recorded in the books of accounts is as follows:

Journal Entry

Date	Particulars	Debit (US$)	Credit (US$)
17-Oct-X1	Dividend Expense on Short Sales Account	7,000.00	
	To Bank Account		7,000.00
	(Being the dividend on the 1,000 shares of short position in Gold Crest, amounting to $7,000 being compensated to the original owner of the shares through the broker)		

Buy to Cover the Shares

Ultimately the short-sold shares should be covered through a broker of the exchange. An accounting entry is recorded for the contracted amount to be paid on such purchase. Note that this entry will be posted to the account called Equity Shares—Gold Crest Account—Short Sales, just as Long Account and Sell Long Account are posted to the same account.

Assuming that the entire quantity of 1,000 shares of Gold Crest is covered on November 6 for a consideration of $460 each, and assuming the brokerage per share amounts to $4, then the accounting entry that is recorded in the books of accounts is shown as follows:

Journal Entry

Date	Particulars	Debit (US$)	Credit (US$)
6-Nov-X1	Equity Shares—Gold Crest Account—Buy to Cover	460,000.00	
	To Silver Man Account		460,000.00
	(Being the 1,000 Gold Crest shares bought to cover @ $460 per share through the broker—Silver Man)		

Brokerage/Commission on the Sell Transaction

Brokerage is paid when the shares are sold and only the net proceeds are taken into account. The accounting entry that is recorded in the books of accounts is shown as follows:

Journal Entry

Date	Particulars	Debit (US$)	Credit (US$)
6-Nov-X1	Equity Shares—Gold Crest Account—Buy to Cover	4,000.00	
	To Silver Man Account		4,000.00
	(Being the brokerage payable to Silver Man @ $4 per share on 1,000 Gold Crest shares bought through them)		

Pay the Consideration

The consideration is paid on day T + 2 or another day based on the exchange concerned. The consideration is paid including brokerage. The accounting entry that is recorded in the books of accounts is shown as follows:

Journal Entry

Date	Particulars	Debit (US$)	Credit (US$)
8-Nov-X1	Silver Man Account	464,000.00	
	To Bank Account		464,000.00
	(Being the net consideration of $464 paid to the broker Silver Man on bought-to-cover 1,000 Gold Crest shares)		

Pay the Stock Lending Fees

The stock lending fees should be paid to the broker, who in turn has to pay the same to the original owner of the shares. The stock lending fees are arrived at as a percentage per annum on the value of the shares.

Assuming that $700 is paid towards the stock lending fees, the accounting entry that is recorded in the books of accounts is shown as follows:

Journal Entry

Date	Particulars	Debit (US$)	Credit (US$)
8-Nov-X1	Stock Lending Fees Account	700.00	
	To Bank Account		700.00
	(Being the stock lending fees paid to the broker Silver Man on procuring 1,000 Gold Crest shares)		

Receive the Interest on Cash Collateral with the Broker

The cash collateral deposited with the broker earns interest at an agreed-on rate. Assuming in this case the interest on the cash collateral with the broker amounted to $500, the accounting entry that is recorded in the books of accounts is shown as follows:

Journal Entry

Date	Particulars	Debit (US$)	Credit (US$)
8-Nov-X1	Bank Account	500.00	
	To Interest Received on Cash Collateral Account		500.00
	(Being the interest received on the cash collateral with the broker)		

Ascertain the Profit/Loss on the Sale

The profit or loss on liquidation of the shares is ascertained by deducting the cost of sales from the net sale consideration. Cost of sales is arrived at by following first in first out (FIFO), last in first out (LIFO), or weighted average method.

In this case 1,000 shares of Gold Crest were first sold at the rate of $490 and $3 was paid per share towards brokerage, resulting in the net sale realization of Gold Crest shares at $487 per share. This was subsequently bought to cover for a net cost of $464 including brokerage. Hence the profit on each share is $23 and the total profit for the entire lot amounts to $23,000. The profit or loss realized is always recognized on the date of liquidation and not on the date on which the net proceeds are received from the broker.

The accounting entry that is recorded in the books of accounts is shown as follows:

Journal Entry

Date	Particulars	Debit (US$)	Credit (US$)
6-Nov-X1	Equity Shares—Gold Crest Account—Short Sales	23,000.00	
	To Realized Capital Gains/Loss—Equity Account		23,000.00
	(Being the realized gains on 1,000 Gold Crest shares)		

Get Back the Cash Collateral from the Broker

The cash collateral deposited with the broker would be returned by the broker on squaring up of the short position as the shares bought from such short covering would be returned to the original owner of the shares.

The accounting entry that is recorded in the books of accounts is shown as follows:

Journal Entry

Date	Particulars	Debit (US$)	Credit (US$)
8-Nov-X1	Bank Account	490,000.00	
	To Cash Collateral with the Broker Account		490,000.00
	(Being the cash collateral with the broker received back from the broker)		

FX Revaluation Entries

All the entries recorded to this point are initially entered in the respective trade currencies. If the functional currency is different from the trade currency, then each and every entry recorded in the trade currency should be entered again in the functional currency by converting the entries at the respective day's FX rates. In other words, for each trade currency that the investor deals with, there will be a complete set of books representing that trade currency. This includes journal entries, general ledger postings, trial balance, income statement, and balance sheet.

After revaluing each and every journal entry of all the trade currencies into the functional currency, a separate set of books is prepared again comprising all the elements just mentioned: journal entries, general ledger postings, trial balance, income statement, and balance sheet. It should be noted that the ultimate financial reports would be prepared and presented to all the stakeholders based on the financial statements prepared in the functional currency only, as this will encompass all the transactions of the investor in all trade currencies dabbled with. (For illustration and detailed explanation please refer to Chapter 2.)

FX Revaluation Entries

After revaluing all the entries in the functional currency at the respective FX rates for the day concerned, another entry needs to be passed in the books of the functional currency. This is mainly to adjust the currency gains or losses due to the fluctuations in FX rates between the reporting date and the date of recording the original entries. FX translation entries are recorded only for the asset and liability accounts. For income and expense accounts, the amount gets crystallized on the date of passing the FX revaluation entries in the books of the functional currency.

There are fundamentally two types of FX translation entries that are recorded in the books of the functional currency: consummated FX translation entries and transient FX translation entries. (For illustration and detailed explanation please refer to Chapter 2.)

ILLUSTRATIONS

Short Equity Shares—Trading

Crystal Inc. traded in Delta shares in a U.S. stock exchange through Baron Brokers, and the details are as follows:

Trade Details

Date	Product	Quantity	Rate	B/S	Brokerage
6-Jan-X1	Delta	1,500	$45.00	Short sales	$300
14-Jan-X1	Delta	2,200	$48.00	Short sales	$600
5-Mar-X1	Delta	1,800	$46.00	Buy to cover	$400

Other Details

- On February 28 a dividend of $1.25/share is declared by Delta.
- Stock loan fees paid by Crystal on short sales:
  - January 31: $750
  - February 28: $1,300
  - March 31: $450
- Settlement: T + 3
- Crystal Inc. makes a deposit of $68,000 with the broker on January 6 and $107,000 on January 14.
- Broker returns the deposit amounting to $87,000 along with interest of $1,100 to Crystal on March 5. Interest accrued on the deposit with broker as of March 31 is $250.

Liquidation Method

FIFO

Market Rate

January 31: 49.00
February 28: 47.00
March 31: 41.00

Journal entries, general ledgers, trial balance, income statement, and balance sheet for Crystal Inc. for the period January 1 to March 31 are as follows:

Solution

T-1 On Deposit of Cash Collateral with the Broker

Journal Entry

Date	Particulars	Debit (US$)	Credit (US$)
6-Jan-X1	Cash collateral paid to Broker Account	68,000.00	
	To Bank Account		68,000.00
	(Being the amount paid to Baron on short sale of 1,500 Delta shares as cash collateral)		

T-2 On Short Sale of Equity Shares and Brokerage

Journal Entry

Date	Particulars	Debit (US$)	Credit (US$)
6-Jan-X1	Broker—Baron Account	67,500.00	
	To Investments—Equity Shares—Short Sales Account		67,500.00
	(Being the 1,500 equity shares sold short @ $45 per share through the broker—Baron Brokers)		
6-Jan-X1	Investments—Equity Shares—Short sales Account	300.00	
	To Broker—Baron Account		300.00
	(Being brokerage payable to the broker on sale of equity shares)		

T-3 On Receipt of Share Sale Amount from the Broker

Journal Entry

Date	Particulars	Debit (US$)	Credit (US$)
9-Jan-X1	Bank Account	67,200.00	
	To Broker—Baron Account		67,200.00
	(Being the amount received for the sale of 1,500 Delta shares)		

T-4 On Deposit of Cash Collateral with the Broker

Journal Entry

Date	Particulars	Debit (US$)	Credit (US$)
14-Jan-X1	Cash collateral paid to Broker Account	107,000.00	
	To Bank Account		107,000.00
	(Being the amount paid to Baron on short sale of 2,200 Delta shares as cash collateral)		

T-5 On Sale of Equity Shares and Brokerage

Journal Entry

Date	Particulars	Debit (US$)	Credit (US$)
14-Jan-X1	Broker—Baron Account	105,600.00	
	To Investments—Equity Shares—Short Sales Account		105,600.00
	(Being the 2,200 equity shares sold short @ $48 per share through the broker—Baron Brokers)		
14-Jan-X1	Investments—Equity Shares—Short Sales Account	600.00	
	To Broker—Baron Account		600.00
	(Being brokerage payable to the broker on sale of equity shares)		

T-6 On Receipt of Share Sale Amount from the Broker

Journal Entry

Date	Particulars	Debit (US$)	Credit (US$)
17-Jan-X1	Bank Account	105,000.00	
	To Broker—Baron Account		105,000.00
	(Being the amount received for the sale of 1,500 Delta shares)		

T-7 On Payment of Stock Lending Fees

Journal Entry

Date	Particulars	Debit (US$)	Credit (US$)
31-Jan-X1	Stock Lending Fees Account	750.00	
	To Bank Account		750.00
	(Being the stock lending fees paid to the broker Baron on sale of Delta shares)		

T-8 Mark-to-market at End of Reporting Period Jan X1

Mark-to-market at end of reporting period: 31-Jan-X1	US$
(a) Market value for 3,700 shares @ US$49	(181,300.00)
(b) Sale value of the short position (67,200 + 105,000)	(172,200.00)
(c) Unrealized loss in US$ (a) – (b)	(9,100.00)

Journal Entry

Date	Particulars	Debit (US$)	Credit (US$)
31-Jan-X1	Unrealized Capital Gains/Loss—Equity Shares Account	9,100.00	
	To Investments—Equity Shares—Short Sales Account		9,100.00
	(Being the mark-to-market entry for 1,000 short position in Gold Crest Shares)		

T-9 Reversal of Mark-to-market Entry

Journal Entry

Date	Particulars	Debit (US$)	Credit (US$)
1-Feb-X1	Investments—Equity Shares—Short Sales Account	9,100.00	
	To Unrealized Capital Gains/Loss—Equity Shares Account		9,100.00
	(Being the reversal of mark-to-market entry for 1,000 short position in Gold Crest Shares)		

T-10 On Payment of Stock Lending Fees

Journal Entry

Date	Particulars	Debit (US$)	Credit (US$)
28-Feb-X1	Stock Lending Fees Account	1,300.00	
	To Bank Account		1,300.00
	(Being the stock lending fees paid to the broker Baron on sale of Delta shares)		

T-11 On Compensation of Dividend to the Original Owner of the Shares

Journal Entry

Date	Particulars	Debit (US$)	Credit (US$)
28-Feb-X1	Dividend Expense on Short Sales Account	4,625.00	
	To Bank Account		4,625.00
	(Being the dividend on the 3,700 shares of short position in Delta amounting to $4,625 being compensated to the original owner of the shares through the broker)		

T-12 Mark-to-market at End of Reporting Period Feb-X1

Mark-to-market at end of reporting period: 28-Feb-X1	US$
(a) Market value of 3700 shares @ US$47	(173,900.00)
(b) Sale value of the short position (67,500 + 105,600)	(172,200.00)
(c) Unrealized loss in US$ (a) − (b)	(1,700.00)

Journal Entry

Date	Particulars	Debit (US$)	Credit (US$)
28-Feb-X1	Unrealized Capital Gains/Loss—Equity Shares Account	1,700.00	
	To Investments—Equity Shares—Short Sales Account		1,700.00
	(Being the mark-to-market entry for 1,000 short position in Gold Crest shares)		

T-13 Reversal of Mark-to-market Entry

Journal Entry

Date	Particulars	Debit (US$)	Credit (US$)
1-Mar-X1	Investments—Equity Shares—Short Sales Account	1,700.00	
	To Unrealized Capital Gains/Loss—Equity Shares Account		1,700.00
	(Being the reversal of mark-to-market entry for 1,000 short position in Gold Crest shares)		

T-14 On Purchase of Shares—Buy to Cover

Equity shares bought to cover will be posted to the short sales account as this is the liquidation entry for the short sales.

Journal Entry

Date	Particulars	Debit (US$)	Credit (US$)
5-Mar-X1	Investments—Equity Shares—Buy to Cover Account	82,800.00	
	To Broker—Baron Account		82,800.00
	(Being the 1,800 Delta shares bought to cover @ $46 per share through the broker—Baron)		

T-15 Brokerage on the Bought-to-Cover Transaction

Journal Entry

Date	Particulars	Debit (US$)	Credit (US$)
5-Mar-X1	Investments—Equity Shares—Buy to Cover Account	400.00	
	To Broker—Baron Account		400.00
	(Being the brokerage payable to Baron on 1,800 Delta shares bought through them)		

T-16 Being the Amount Paid on Purchase of Shares

Journal Entry

Date	Particulars	Debit (US$)	Credit (US$)
8-Mar-X1	Broker—Baron Account	83,200.00	
	To Bank Account		83,200.00
	(Being the amount paid to the broker for 1,800 Delta shares bought through them)		

T-17 On Receipt of the Contracted Amount for the Shares

Journal Entry

Date	Particulars	Debit (US$)	Credit (US$)
5-Mar-X1	Bank Account	87,000.00	
	To Cash Collateral Paid to Broker Account		87,000.00
	(Being the cash collateral amount received from the broker on squaring up the short position partially)		

T-18 On Receipt of the Interest on Cash Collateral with the Broker

Journal Entry

Date	Particulars	Debit (US$)	Credit (US$)
8-Mar-X1	Ba nk Account	1,100.00	
	To Interest Receipts on Cash Collateral Account		1,100.00
	(Being the interest received on the cash collateral with the broker)		

T-19 On Realizing the Profit/Loss on Liquidation

Calculation of capital gains		US$	US$
(a)	Bought value of 1,800 shares @ US$46 less brokerage		83,200.00
	Sale value:		
	1,500 shares @ US$ 45 after brokerage	67,200.00	
	2,200 shares @ US$ 48 after brokerage	105,000.00	
	Proportional value of 300 shares [105,000 × 300)/2,200]	14,318.18	
b)	Total sale value of 1,800 shares		81,518.18
	Realized loss in US$ = (b) − (a)		**(1,681.82)**

Journal Entry

Date	Particulars	Debit (US$)	Credit (US$)
5-Mar-X1	Realized Capital Gains/Loss—Equity Account	1,681.82	
	To Investments—Equity Shares—Short Sales Account		1,681.82
	(Being the realized loss on 1,800 Delta shares)		

T-20 Interest Receivable on Cash Collateral with the Broker Booked as Accrual at End of the Reporting Period

Journal Entry

Date	Particulars	Debit (US$)	Credit (US$)
31-Mar-X1	Interest Receivable on Cash Collateral Account	250.00	
	To Interest Receipts on Cash Collateral Account		250.00
	(Being the interest receivable on the cash collateral with the broker)		

T-21 On Payment of Stock Lending Fees

Journal Entry

Date	Particulars	Debit (US$)	Credit (US$)
31-Mar-X1	Stock Lending Fees Account	450.00	
	To Bank Account		450.00
	(Being the stock lending fees paid to the broker Baron on sale of Delta shares)		

T-22 Mark-to-market at End of Reporting Period Mar-X1

Mark-to-market at end of reporting period: 31-Mar-X1	US$	US$
(a) Market value of 1,900 shares @ US$41		77,900.00
(b) Net sale value of the short position 2,200 shares	105,000.00	
(c) Proportionate sale value of 1,900 shares		90,681.82
(d) Unrealized gains in US$ (a) − (c)		12,781.82

Journal Entry

Date	Particulars	Debit (US$)	Credit (US$)
31-Mar-X1	Investments—Equity Shares—Short Sales Account	12,781.82	
	To Unrealized Capital Gains/Loss—Equity Shares Account		12,781.82
	(Being the mark-to-market entry for 1,900 short position in Delta shares)		

General Ledger Accounts

Investments—Equity Shares—Short Sales Account/Buy to Cover

Date	Particulars	Debit (US$)	Date	Particulars	Credit (US$)
			6-Jan-X1	By Receivable from broker—Baron Account	67,500.00
6-Jan-X1	To Baron Account	300.00			
			14-Jan-X1	By Receivable from broker—Baron Account	105,600.00
14-Jan-X1	To Baron Account	600.00			
			31-Jan-X1	By Unrealized Capital Gains/Loss—Equity Shares Account	9,100.00
1-Feb-X1	To Unrealized Capital Gains/Loss—Equity Shares Account	9,100.00			
			28-Feb-X1	By Unrealized Capital Gains/Loss—Equity Shares Account	1,700.00
1-Mar-X1	To Unrealized Capital Gains/Loss—Equity Shares Account	1,700.00			
			5-Mar-X1	By Realized Capital Gains/Loss—Equity Account	1,681.82
5-Mar-X1	To Broker—Baron Account	82,800.00			
5-Mar-X1	To Broker—Baron Account	400.00			
31-Mar-X1	To Unrealized Capital Gains/Loss—Equity Shares Account	12,781.82			
31-Mar-X1	To Balance	77,900.00			
31-Mar-X1	Total	**185,581.82**	31-Mar-X1	Total	**185,581.82**
			31-Mar-X1	By Balance	77,900.00

Broker—Baron Account

Date	Particulars	Debit (US$)	Date	Particulars	Credit (US$)
6-Jan-X1	To Investments—Equity Shares—Short Sales Account	67,500.00			
			6-Jan-X1	By Investments—Equity Shares—Short Sales Account	300.00
			9-Jan-X1	By Bank Account	67,200.00
			14-Jan-X1	By Investments—Equity Shares—Short Sales Account	600.00
14-Jan-X1	To Investments—Equity Shares—Short Sales Account	105,600.00			
			17-Jan-X1	By Bank Account	105,000.00
			5-Mar-X1	By Investments—Equity Shares—Buy to Cover Account	82,800.00
			5-Mar-X1	By Investments—Equity Shares—Buy to Cover Account	400.00
8-Mar-X1	To Bank Account	83,200.00			
31-Mar-X1	Total	**256,300.00**	31-Mar-X1	Total	**256,300.00**

Cash Collateral Paid to Broker Account

Date	Particulars	Debit (US$)	Date	Particulars	Credit (US$)
6-Jan-X1	To Bank Account	68,000.00			
14-Jan-X1	To Bank Account	107,000.00			
			5-Mar-X1	By Bank Account	87,000.00
			31-Mar-X1	By Balance	88,000.00
31-Mar-X1	Total	**175,000.00**	31-Mar-X1	Total	**175,000.00**
31-Mar-X1	To Balance	88,000.00			

Interest Receipts on Cash Collateral Account

Date	Particulars	Debit (US$)	Date	Particulars	Credit (US$)
			8-Mar-X1	By Bank Account	1,100.00
			31-Mar-X1	By Interest Receivable on Cash Collateral Account	250.00
31-Mar-X1	To Balance	1,350.00			
31-Mar-X1	Total	**1,350.00**	31-Mar-X1	Total	**1,350.00**
			31-Mar-X1	By Balance	1,350.00

Interest Receivable on Cash Collateral Account

Date	Particulars	Debit (US$)	Date	Particulars	Credit (US$)
31-Mar-X1	To Interest Receipts on Cash Collateral Account	250.00			
			31-Mar-X1	By Balance	250.00
31-Mar-X1	Total	**250.00**	31-Mar-X1	Total	**250.00**
31-Mar-X1	To Balance	250.00			

Stock Lending Fees Account

Date	Particulars	Debit (US$)	Date	Particulars	Credit (US$)
31-Jan-X1	To Bank Account	750.00			
28-Feb-X1	To Bank Account	1,300.00			
31-Mar-X1	To Bank Account	450.00			
			31-Mar-X1	By Balance	2,500.00
31-Mar-X1	Total	**2,500.00**	31-Mar-X1	Total	**2,500.00**
31-Mar-X1	To Balance	2,500.00			

Unrealized Capital Gains/Loss—Equity Shares Account

Date	Particulars	Debit (US$)	Date	Particulars	Credit (US$)
31-Jan-X1	To Investments—Equity Shares—Short Sales Account	9,100.00			
			1-Feb-X1	By Investments—Equity Shares—Short Sales Account	9,100.00
28-Feb-X1	To Investments—Equity Shares—Short Sales Account	1,700.00			
			1-Mar-X1	By Investments—Equity Shares—Short Sales Account	1,700.00
			31-Mar-X1	By Investments—Equity Shares—Short Sales Account	12,781.82
31-Mar-X1	To Balance	12,781.82			
31-Mar-X1	Total	**23,581.82**	31-Mar-X1	Total	**23,581.82**
			31-Mar-X1	By Balance	12,781.82

Realized Capital Gains/Loss—Equity Account

Date	Particulars	Debit (US$)	Date	Particulars	Credit (US$)
5-Mar-X1	To Investments—Equity Shares—Short Sales Account	1,681.82			
			31-Mar-X1	By Balance	1,681.82
31-Mar-X1	Total	**1,681.82**	31-Mar-X1	Total	**1,681.82**
31-Mar-X1	To Balance	1,681.82			

Dividend Expense on Short Sales Account

Date	Particulars	Debit (US$)	Date	Particulars	Credit (US$)
28-Feb-X1	To Bank Account	4,625.00			
			31-Mar-X1	By Balance	4,625.00
31-Mar-X1	Total	**4,625.00**	31-Mar-X1	Total	**4,625.00**
31-Mar-X1	To Balance	4,625.00			

Bank Account

Date	Particulars	Debit (US$)	Date	Particulars	Credit (US$)
			6-Jan-X1	By Cash Collateral Paid to Broker Account	68,000.00
9-Jan-X1	To Baron Account	67,200.00			
			14-Jan-X1	By Cash Collateral Paid to Broker Account	107,000.00
17-Jan-X1	To Baron Account	105,000.00			
			31-Jan-X1	By Stock Lending Fees Account	750.00
			28-Feb-X1	By Stock Lending Fees Account	1,300.00
			28-Feb-X1	By Dividend Expense on Short Sales Account	4,625.00
			8-Mar-X1	By Baron Account	83,200.00
5-Mar-X1	To Cash Collateral Paid to Broker Account	87,000.00			
8-Mar-X1	To Interest Received on Cash Collateral Account	1,100.00			
			31-Mar-X1	By Stock Lending Fees Account	450.00
31-Mar-X1	To Balance	5,025.00			
31-Mar-X1	Total	**265,325.00**	31-Mar-X1	Total	**265,325.00**
			31-Mar-X1	By Balance	5,025.00

Trial Balance

As of 31-Mar-X1

Particulars	Debit	Credit
Current Liabilities		
Investments		
Investments—Equity Shares Account—Short Sales/Buy to Cover		77,900.00
Current Assets		
Cash Collateral Paid to Broker Account	88,000.00	
Bank Account		5,025.00
Income		
Interest Receipts on Cash Collateral Account		1,350.00
Interest Receivable on Cash Collateral Account	250.00	
Unrealized Capital Gains/Loss—Equity Shares Account		12,781.82
Realized Capital Gains/Loss—Equity Account	1,681.82	
Expense		
Stock Lending Fees Account	2,500.00	
Dividend Expense on Short Sales Account	4,625.00	
Total	**97,056.82**	**97,056.82**

Income Statement

For the period ending 31-Mar-X1

Expenses	US$	Income	US$
Direct Expenses		**Direct Income**	
Dividend Expense on Short Sales Account	4,625.00	Unrealized Capital Gains/Loss—Equity Shares Account	12,781.82
Realized Capital Gains/Loss—Equity Account	1,681.82	Interest Received on Cash Collateral Account	1,350.00
Stock Lending Fees Account	2,500.00		
Net Profit Carryover	5,325.00		
Total	**14,131.82**	Total	**14,131.82**

Balance Sheet

As of 31-Mar-X1

Liabilities	US$	Assets	US$
Capital Account	Nil	**Investments**	
Current Liabilities			
Investments—Equity Shares Account—Short Sales/Buy to Cover	77,900.00	**Current Assets**	
		Cash Collateral Paid to Broker Account	88,000.00
Bank Account	5,025.00	Interest Receivable on Cash Collateral Account	250.00
Profit & Loss Account			
Current Period	5,325.00		
Total	**88,250.00**	Total	**88,250.00**

Short Equity Shares—Box Position—US$

Band Bros Inc. traded in ID Auto shares in a U.S. stock exchange through Astron brokers and the details are as follows:

Trade Details

Date	Product	Quantity	Rate	B/S	Brokerage
11-Jan-X1	ID Auto	70,000	$4.32	Short sales	$2,500
25-Jan-X1	ID Auto	30,000	$3.92	Short sales	$1,200
5-Feb-X1	ID Auto	85,000	$4.00	Bought long	$3,800

Other Details

- A dividend declared by ID Auto amounts to $0.25 per share on January 28.
- Stock loan fee by Band Bros on short sales:
  - January 31: $850
  - February 28: $300
- Settlement: T + 3
- Band Bros Inc. makes a deposit of $302,000 with the broker on January 11 and $118,000 on January 25.
- Broker pays interest of $970 on cash collateral to Band Bros Inc. on February 5. Interest accrued on the cash collateral with broker as of February 28 is $200.
- The bought-long position is not liquidated against the short position and is held as box position.

Market Rate

January 31: 4.00
February 28: 4.25

Journal entries, general ledgers, trial balance, income statement, and balance sheet for Band Brothers Inc. for the period January 1 to February 28 are as follows:

Solution

T-1 On Deposit of Cash Collateral with the Broker

Journal Entry

Date	Particulars	Debit (US$)	Credit (US$)
11-Jan-X1	Cash Collateral Paid to Broker Account	302,000.00	
	To Bank Account		302,000.00
	(Being the amount paid to Astron on short sale of 70,000 ID Auto shares as cash collateral)		

T-2 On Sale of Equity Shares and Brokerage

Journal Entry

Date	Particulars	Debit (US$)	Credit (US$)
11-Jan-X1	Broker—Astron Account	302,400.00	
	To Investments—Equity Shares—Short Sales Account		302,400.00
	(Being the 70,000 equity shares sold short @ $4.32 per share through the broker—Baron Brokers)		
11-Jan-X1	Investments—Equity Shares—Short Sales Account	2,500.00	
	To Broker—Astron Account		2,500.00
	(Being brokerage payable to the broker on sale of equity shares)		

T-3 On Receipt of Share Sale Amount from the Broker

Journal Entry

Date	Particulars	Debit (US$)	Credit (US$)
14-Jan-X1	Bank Account	299,900.00	
	To Broker—Astron Account		299,900.00
	(Being the amount received for the sale of 70,000 Delta shares)		

T-4 On Deposit of Cash Collateral with the Broker

Journal Entry

Date	Particulars	Debit (US$)	Credit (US$)
25-Jan-X1	Cash Collateral Paid to Broker Account	118,000.00	
	To Bank Account		118,000.00
	(Being the amount paid to Astron on short sale of 30,000 ID Auto shares as cash collateral)		

T-5 On Sale of Equity Shares and Brokerage

Journal Entry

Date	Particulars	Debit (US$)	Credit (US$)
25-Jan-X1	Broker—Astron Account	117,600.00	
	To Investments—Equity Shares—Short Sales Account		117,600.00
	(Being the 30,000 equity shares sold short @ $3.92 per share through the broker—Baron Brokers)		
25-Jan-X1	Investments—Equity Shares—Short Sales Account	1,200.00	
	To Broker—Astron Account		1,200.00
	(Being brokerage payable to the broker on sale of equity shares)		

T-6 On Receipt of Share Sale Amount from the Broker

Journal Entry

Date	Particulars	Debit (US$)	Credit (US$)
28-Jan-X1	Bank Account	116,400.00	
	To Broker—Astron Account		116,400.00
	(Being the amount received for the sale of 30,000 Delta shares)		

T-7 On Payment of Stock Loan Fees

Journal Entry

Date	Particulars	Debit (US$)	Credit (US$)
31-Jan-X1	Stock Loan Fees Account	850.00	
	To Bank Account		850.00
	(Being the stock lending fees paid to the broker Astron on sale of ID Auto shares)		

T-8 On Payment of Dividend

Journal Entry

Date	Particulars	Debit (US$)	Credit (US$)
28-Jan-X1	Dividend Expense on Short Sales Account	25,000.00	
	To Bank Account		25,000.00
	(Being the dividend on the 100,000 shares of short position in Delta amounting to $25,000 being compensated to the original owner of the shares through the broker)		

T-9 Mark-to-market at End of Reporting Period Jan X1

Mark-to-market at end of reporting period: 31-Jan-X1—Short position	US$
(a) Market value of 100,000 shares @ US$4	400,000.00
(b) Sale value of the short position (299,900 + 116,400)	416,300.00
(c) Unrealized gains in US$ (b) − (a)	16,300.00

Journal Entry

Date	Particulars	Debit (US$)	Credit (US$)
31-Jan-X1	Investments—Equity Shares—Short Sales Account	16,300.00	
	To Unrealized Capital Gains/Loss—Equity Shares Account		16,300.00
	(Being the mark-to-market entry for 100,000 short position in ID Auto Shares)		

T-10 Reversal of Mark-to-market Entry

Journal Entry

Date	Particulars	Debit (US$)	Credit (US$)
1-Feb-X1	Unrealized Capital Gains/Loss—Equity Shares Account	16,300.00	
	To Investments—Equity Shares—Short Sales Account		16,300.00
	(Being the reversal of mark-to-market entry for 100,000 short position in ID Auto Shares)		

T-11 On Purchase of Shares

Journal Entry

Date	Particulars	Debit (US$)	Credit (US$)
5-Feb-X1	Investments—Equity Shares—Buy Long Account	340,000.00	
	To Broker—Astron Account		340,000.00
	(Being the 85,000 Delta shares bought @ $4 per share through the broker—Astron)		

T-12 Brokerage on the Bought Shares

Journal Entry

Date	Particulars	Debit (US$)	Credit (US$)
5-Feb-X1	Investments—Equity Shares—Buy Long Account	3,800.00	
	To Broker—Astron Account		3,800.00
	(Being the brokerage payable to Astron on 85,000 ID Auto shares bought through them)		

T-13 Being the Amount Paid on Purchase of Shares

Journal Entry

Date	Particulars	Debit (US$)	Credit (US$)
8-Feb-X1	Broker—Astron Account	343,800.00	
	To Bank Account		343,800.00
	(Being the brokerage payable to Astron on 85,000 ID Auto shares bought through them)		

T-14 On Receipt of the Interest on Cash Collateral with the Broker

Journal Entry

Date	Particulars	Debit (US$)	Credit (US$)
5-Feb-X1	Bank Account	970.00	
	To Interest Receipts on Cash Collateral Account		970.00
	(Being the interest received on the cash collateral with the broker)		

T-15 Interest Receivable on Accrued Interest from Cash Collateral with the Broker

Journal Entry

Date	Particulars	Debit (US$)	Credit (US$)
28-Feb-X1	Interest Receivable on Cash Collateral Account	200.00	
	To Interest Receipts on Cash Collateral Account		200.00
	(Being the interest receivable on the cash collateral with the broker)		

T-16 On Payment of Stock Loan Fees

Journal Entry

Date	Particulars	Debit (US$)	Credit (US$)
28-Feb-X1	Stock Loan Fees Account	300.00	
	To Bank Account		300.00
	(Being the stock lending fees paid to the broker Astron on sale of ID Auto shares)		

T-17 Mark-to-market at End of Reporting Period Feb X1

Mark-to-market at end of reporting period: 28-Feb-X1—Short position	US$
(a) Market value of 100,000 shares @ $4.25	425,000.00
(b) Sale value for the short position (299,900 + 116,400)	416,300.00
(c) Unrealized loss in US$ (b) − (a)	(8,700.00)

Journal Entry

Date	Particulars	Debit (US$)	Credit (US$)
28-Feb-X1	Unrealized Capital Gains/Loss—Equity Shares Account	8,700.00	
	To Investments—Equity Shares—Short sales Account		8,700.00
	(Being the mark-to-market entry for 100,000 short position in ID Auto Shares)		

T-18 Mark-to-market at End of Reporting Period Feb-X1

Mark-to-market at end of reporting period: 28-Feb-X1—Long Position	US$
(a) Market value of 85,000 shares	361,250.00
(b) Cost of long position	343,800.00
(c) Unrealized gains in US$ (a) − (b)	17,450.00

Journal Entry

Date	Particulars	Debit (US$)	Credit (US$)
28-Feb-X1	Investments—Equity Shares—Buy Long Account	17,450.00	
	To Unrealized Capital Gains/Loss—Equity Shares Account		17,450.00
	(Being the mark-to-market entry for 85,000 buy-long position in ID Auto Shares)		

General Ledger Accounts

Investments—Equity Shares—Short Sales Account

Date	Particulars	Debit (US$)	Date	Particulars	Credit (US$)
			11-Jan-X1	By Broker—Astron Account	302,400.00
11-Jan-X1	To Broker—Astron Account	2,500.00			
			25-Jan-X1	By Broker—Astron Account	117,600.00
25-Jan-X1	To Broker—Astron Account	1,200.00			
31-Jan-X1	To Unrealized Capital Gains/ Loss—Equity Shares Account	16,300.00			
			1-Feb-X1	By Unrealized Capital Gains/ Loss—Equity Shares Account	16,300.00
			28-Feb-X1	By Unrealized Capital Gains/ Loss—Equity Shares Account	8,700.00
28-Feb-X1	To Balance	425,000.00			
28-Feb-X1	Total	**445,000.00**	28-Feb-X1	Total	**445,000.00**
			28-Feb-X1	By Balance	425,000.00

Investments—Equity Shares—Buy Long Account

Date	Particulars	Debit (US$)	Date	Particulars	Credit (US$)
5-Feb-X1	To Broker—Astron Account	340,000.00			
5-Feb-X1	To Broker—Astron Account	3,800.00			
28-Feb-X1	To Unrealized Capital Gains/ Loss—Equity Shares Account	17,450.00			
			28-Feb-X1	By Balance	361,250.00
28-Feb-X1	Total	**361,250.00**	28-Feb-X1	Total	**361,250.00**
28-Feb-X1	To Balance	361,250.00			

Broker—Astron Account

Date	Particulars	Debit (US$)	Date	Particulars	Credit (US$)
11-Jan-X1	To Investments—Equity Shares—Short Sales Account	302,400.00			
			11-Jan-X1	By Investments—Equity Shares—Short Sales Account	2,500.00
			14-Jan-X1	By Bank Account	299,900.00
25-Jan-X1	To Investments—Equity Shares—Short Sales Account	117,600.00			
			25-Jan-X1	By Investments—Equity Shares—Short Sales Account	1,200.00
			28-Jan-X1	By Bank Account	116,400.00
			5-Feb-X1	By Investments—Equity Shares—Buy Long Account	340,000.00
			5-Feb-X1	By Investments—Equity Shares—Buy Long Account	3,800.00
8-Feb-X1	To Bank Account	343,800.00			
28-Feb-X1	Total	**763,800.00**	28-Feb-X1	Total	**763,800.00**

Cash Collateral Paid to Broker Account

Date	Particulars	Debit (US$)	Date	Particulars	Credit (US$)
11-Jan-X1	To Bank Account	302,000.00			
25-Jan-X1	To Bank Account	118,000.00			
			28-Feb-X1	By Balance	420,000.00
28-Feb-X1	Total	**420,000.00**	28-Feb-X1	Total	**420,000.00**
28-Feb-X1	To Balance	420,000.00			

Interest Receipts on Cash Collateral Account

Date	Particulars	Debit (US$)	Date	Particulars	Credit (US$)
			5-Feb-X1	By Bank Account	970.00
			28-Feb-X1	By Interest Receivable on Cash Collateral Account	200.00
28-Feb-X1	To Balance	1,170.00			
28-Feb-X1	Total	**1,170.00**	28-Feb-X1	Total	**1,170.00**
			28-Feb-X1	By Balance	1,170.00

Interest Receivable on Cash Collateral Account

Date	Particulars	Debit (US$)	Date	Particulars	Credit (US$)
28-Feb-X1	To Interest Receipts on Cash Collateral Account	200.00			
			28-Feb-X1	By Balance	200.00
28-Feb-X1	Total	**200.00**	28-Feb-X1	Total	**200.00**
28-Feb-X1	To Balance	200.00			

Stock Loan Fees Account

Date	Particulars	Debit (US$)	Date	Particulars	Credit (US$)
31-Jan-X1	To Bank Account	850.00			
28-Feb-X1	To Bank Account	300.00			
			28-Feb-X1	By Balance	1,150.00
28-Feb-X1	Total	**1,150.00**	28-Feb-X1	Total	**1,150.00**
28-Feb-X1	To Balance	1,150.00			

Unrealized Capital Gains/Loss—Equity Shares Account

Date	Particulars	Debit (US$)	Date	Particulars	Credit (US$)
			31-Jan-X1	By Investments—Equity Shares—Short Sales Account	16,300.00
1-Feb-X1	By Investments—Equity Shares—Short Sales Account	16,300.00			
28-Feb-X1	By Investments—Equity Shares—Short Sales Account	8,700.00			
			28-Feb-X1	By Investments—Equity Shares—Buy Long Account	17,450.00
28-Feb-X1	To Balance	8,750.00			
28-Feb-X1	Total	**33,750.00**	28-Feb-X1	Total	**33,750.00**
			28-Feb-X1	By Balance	8,750.00

Dividend Expense on Short Sales Account

Date	Particulars	Debit (US$)	Date	Particulars	Credit (US$)
28-Jan-X1	To Bank Account	25,000.00			
			28-Feb-X1	By Balance	25,000.00
28-Feb-X1	Total	**25,000.00**	28-Feb-X1	Total	**25,000.00**
28-Feb-X1	To Balance	25,000.00			

Bank Account

Date	Particulars	Debit (US$)	Date	Particulars	Credit (US$)
			11-Jan-X1	By Cash Collateral Paid to Broker Account	302,000.00
14-Jan-X1	To Broker—Astron Account	299,900.00			
			25-Jan-X1	By Cash Collateral Paid to Broker Account	118,000.00
28-Jan-X1	To Broker—Astron Account	116,400.00			
			28-Jan-X1	By Dividend Expense on Short Sales Account	25,000.00
			31-Jan-X1	By Stock Loan Fees Account	850.00
			8-Feb-X1	By Broker—Astron Account	343,800.00
5-Feb-X1	To Interest Receipts on Cash Collateral Account	970.00			
			28-Feb-X1	By Stock Loan Fees Account	300.00
28-Feb-X1	To Balance	372,680.00			
28-Feb-X1	Total	**789,950.00**	28-Feb-X1	Total	**789,950.00**
			28-Feb-X1	By Balance	372,680.00

Trial Balance

As of 28-Feb-X1

Particulars	Debit	Credit
Current Liabilities		
Investments		
Investments—Equity Shares—Short Sales Account		425,000.00
Investments—Equity Shares—Buy Long Account	361,250.00	
Current Assets		
Bank Account		372,680.00
Interest Receivable on Cash Collateral Account	200.00	
Cash Collateral Paid to Broker Account	420,000.00	
Income		
Interest Receipts on Cash Collateral Account		1,170.00
Unrealized Capital Gains/Loss—Equity Shares Account		8,750.00
Expense		
Stock Lending Fees Account	1,150.00	
Dividend Expense on Short Sales Account	25,000.00	
Total	**807,600.00**	**807,600.00**

Income Statement

For the period ending 28-Feb-X1

Expenses	US$	Income	US$
Direct Expenses		**Direct Income**	
Dividend Expense on Short Sales Account	25,000.00	Unrealized Capital Gains/ Loss—Equity Shares Account	8,750.00
		Interest Received on Cash Collateral Account	1,170.00
Stock Loan Fees Account	1,150.00		
		Net Loss Carryover	16,230.00
Total	**26,150.00**	Total	**26,150.00**

Balance Sheet

As of 28-Feb-X1

Liabilities	US$	Assets	US$
Capital Account	Nil	**Investments**	
		Investments—Equity Shares—Buy Long Account	361,250.00
		Interest Receivable on Cash Collateral Account	200.00
Current Liabilities		**Current Assets**	
Investments—Equity Shares—Short Sales Account	425,000.00	Cash Collateral Paid to Broker Account	420,000.00
Bank Account	372,680.00	**Profit & Loss Account**	
		Current Period	16,230.00
Total	**797,680.00**	Total	**797,680.00**

Short Equity Shares—Box Position—BRL

Rosario Inc. traded in Petro Gold shares in a Brazilian stock exchange through Astron brokers and the details are as follows:

Trade Details

Date	Product	Quantity	Rate (BRL)	B/S	Brokerage
11-Jan-X1	Petro Gold	7,000	341.00	Bought Long	BRL 12,500
25-Jan-X1	Petro Gold	4,000	391.00	Bought Long	BRL 7,800
5-Feb-X1	Petro Gold	13,000	395.00	Short sales	BRL 25,600

Other Details

- The stock loan fee paid by Rosario Inc. on short sales on February 28 was BRL1500.
- An investor has introduced an amount of BRL 10 million as share capital on January 1 in the Rosario Inc. fund.

- Settlement: T + 2
- Rosario Inc. makes a deposit of BRL 5.150 million with the broker on February 5 as collateral.
- Interest accrued on cash collateral amounts to BRL 9,500 due from the broker as of February 28.

FX Rates

Date	FX Rate
1-Jan-X	1.6540
11-Jan-X1	1.6505
13-Jan-X1	1.6525
25-Jan-X1	1.6484
27-Jan-X1	1.6444
31-Jan-X1	1.6311
5-Feb-X1	1.6255
7-Feb-X1	1.6201
28-Feb-X1	1.6150

Market Rate

January 31: 405.00
February 28: 390.00

Journal entries, general ledgers, trial balance, income statement, and balance sheet for Rosario Inc., for the period January 1 to March 31 are as follows:

Solution

T-1 Capital Introduced by the Fund

Journal Entry

Date	Particulars	Debit (BRL)	Credit (BRL)
1-Jan-X1	Bank Account	10,000,000.00	
	To Share Capital Account		10,000,000.00
	(Being the subscription contributed by investor into the fund)		

T-2 On Purchase of Shares

Journal Entry

Date	Particulars	Debit (BRL)	Credit (BRL)
11-Jan-X1	Investments—Equity Shares—Buy Long Account	2,387,000.00	
	To Broker—Astron Account		2,387,000.00
	(Being the 7,000 Petro Gold shares bought @ BRL 341.00 per share through the broker—Astron)		

T-3 Brokerage on the Bought Shares

Journal Entry

Date	Particulars	Debit (BRL)	Credit (BRL)
11-Jan-X1	Investments—Equity Shares—Buy Long Account	12,500.00	
	To Broker—Astron Account		12,500.00
	(Being the brokerage payable to Astron on 7,000 Petro Gold shares bought through them)		

T-4 Being the Amount Paid on Purchase of Shares

Journal Entry

Date	Particulars	Debit (BRL)	Credit (BRL)
3-Jan-X1	Broker—Astron Account	2,399,500.00	
	To Bank Account		2,399,500.00
	(Being the brokerage payable to Astron on 7,000 Petro Gold shares bought through them)		

T-5 On Purchase of Shares

Journal Entry

Date	Particulars	Debit (BRL)	Credit (BRL)
25-Jan-X1	Investments—Equity Shares—Buy Long Account	1,564,000.00	
	To Broker—Astron Account		1,564,000.00
	(Being the 4,000 Petro Gold shares bought @ BRL 391.00 per share through the broker—Astron)		

T-6 Brokerage on the Bought Shares

Journal Entry

Date	Particulars	Debit (BRL)	Credit (BRL)
25-Jan-X1	Investments—Equity Shares—Buy Long Account	7,800.00	
	To Broker—Astron Account		7,800.00
	(Being the brokerage payable to Astron on 4,000 Petro Gold shares bought through them)		

T-7 Being the Amount Paid on Purchase of Shares

Journal Entry

Date	Particulars	Debit (BRL)	Credit (BRL)
7-Jan-X1	Broker—Astron Account	1,571,800.00	
	To Bank Account		1,571,800.00
	(Being the brokerage payable to Astron on 4,000 Petro Gold shares bought through them)		

T-8 Mark-to-market at End of Reporting Period Jan X1

Mark-to-market at end of reporting period: 31-Jan-X1	**BRL**
(a) Market value of 11,000 shares @ BRL 405	4,455,000.00
(b) Cost of acquisition (2,399,500.00 + 1,571,800.00)	3,971,300.00
(c) Unrealized gains in BRL (a) − (b)	483,700.00

Journal Entry

Date	Particulars	Debit (BRL)	Credit (BRL)
31-Jan-X1	Investments—Equity Shares—Buy Long Account	483,700.00	
	To Unrealized Capital Gains/Loss—Equity Shares Account		483,700.00
	(Being the mark-to-market entry for 11,000 buy long position in Petro Gold Shares)		

T-9 Reversal of Mark-to-market Entry

Journal Entry

Date	Particulars	Debit (BRL)	Credit (BRL)
1-Feb-X1	Unrealized Capital Gains/Loss—Equity Shares Account	483,700.00	
	To Investments—Equity Shares—Buy Long Account		483,700.00
	(Being the reversal of mark-to-market entry for 11,000 long position in Petro Gold shares)		

T-10 On Deposit of Cash Collateral with the Broker

Journal Entry

Date	Particulars	Debit (BRL)	Credit (BRL)
5-Feb-X1	Cash Collateral Paid to Broker Account	5,150,000.00	
	To Bank Account		5,150,000.00
	(Being the amount paid to Astron on short sale of 13,000 Petro Gold shares as cash collateral)		

T-11 On Sale of Equity Shares and Brokerage

Journal Entry

Date	Particulars	Debit (BRL)	Credit (BRL)
5-Feb-X1	Broker—Astron Account	5,135,000.00	
	To Investments—Equity Shares—Short Sales Account		5,135,000.00
	(Being the 13,000 equity shares sold short @ BRL 395 per share through the broker—Astron Brokers)		
5-Feb-X1	Investments—Equity Shares—Short Sales Account	25,600.00	
	To Broker—Astron Account		25,600.00
	(Being brokerage payable to the broker on sale of equity shares)		

T-12 On Receipt of Share Sale Amount from the Broker

Journal Entry

Date	Particulars	Debit (BRL)	Credit (BRL)
7-Feb-X1	Bank Account	5,109,400.00	
	To Broker—Astron Account		5,109,400.00
	(Being the amount received for the sale of 13,000 Petro Gold shares)		

T-13 On Payment of Stock Loan Fees

Journal Entry

Date	Particulars	Debit (BRL)	Credit (BRL)
28-Feb-X1	Stock Loan Fees Account	1,500.00	
	To Bank Account		1,500.00
	(Being the stock loan fees paid to the broker Astron on sale of Petro Gold shares)		

T-14 Mark-to-market at End of Reporting Period Feb X1

Mark-to-market of long position at end of reporting period: 28-Feb-X1	BRL
(a) Market value of 11,000 shares @ BRL 390	4,290,000.00
(b) Cost of acquisition (2,399,500.00 + 1,571,800.00)	3,971,300.00
(c) Unrealized gains in BRL (a) − (b)	318,700.00

Journal Entry

Date	Particulars	Debit (BRL)	Credit (BRL)
28-Feb-X1	Investments—Equity Shares—Buy Long Account	318,700.00	
	To Unrealized Capital Gains/Loss—Equity Shares Account		318,700.00
	(Being the mark-to-market entry for 11,000 buy long position in Petro Gold Shares)		

T-15 Mark-to-market at End of Reporting Period Feb X1

Mark-to-market of short position at end of reporting period: 28-Feb-X1	BRL
(a) Market value of 13,000 shares @ BRL 390	5,070,000.00
(b) Sale value of the short position (13,000 × 395) + 25,600	5,109,400.00
(c) Unrealized gains in BRL = (b) − (a)	39,400.00

Journal Entry

Date	Particulars	Debit (BRL)	Credit (BRL)
28-Feb-X1	Investments—Equity Shares—Short Sales Account	39,400.00	
	To Unrealized Capital Gains/Loss—Equity Shares Account		39,400.00
	(Being the mark-to-market entry for 13,000 short position in Petro Gold shares)		

T-16 Interest Receivable on Accrued Interest from Cash Collateral with the Broker

Journal Entry

Date	Particulars	Debit (BRL)	Credit (BRL)
28-Feb-X1	Interest Receivable on Cash Collateral Account	9,500.00	
	To Interest Receipts on Cash Collateral Account		9,500.00
	(Being the interest receivable on the cash collateral with the broker)		

General Ledger Accounts

Investments—Equity Shares—Buy Long Account

Date	Particulars	Debit (BRL)	Date	Particulars	Credit (BRL)
11-Jan-X1	To Broker—Astron Account	2,387,000.00			
11-Jan-X1	To Broker—Astron Account	12,500.00			
25-Jan-X1	To Broker—Astron Account	1,564,000.00			
25-Jan-X1	To Broker—Astron Account	7,800.00			
31-Jan-X1	To Unrealized Capital Gains/Loss—Equity Shares Account	483,700.00			
			1-Feb-X1	By Unrealized Capital Gains/Loss—Equity Shares Account	483,700.00
28-Feb-X1	To Unrealized Capital Gains/Loss—Equity Shares Account	318,700.00			
			28-Feb-X1	By Balance	4,290,000.00
28-Feb-X1	Total	**4,773,700.00**	28-Feb-X1	Total	**4,773,700.00**
28-Feb-X1	To Balance	4,290,000.00			

Investments—Equity Shares—Short Sales Account

Date	Particulars	Debit (BRL)	Date	Particulars	Credit (BRL)
			5-Feb-X1	By Broker—Astron Account	5,135,000.00
5-Feb-X1	To Broker—Astron Account	25,600.00			
28-Feb-X1	To Unrealized Capital Gains/Loss—Equity Shares Account	39,400.00			
28-Feb-X1	To Balance	5,070,000.00			
28-Feb-X1	Total	**5,135,000.00**	28-Feb-X1	Total	**5,135,000.00**
			28-Feb-X1	By Balance	5,070,000.00

Unrealized Capital Gains/Loss—Equity Shares Account

Date	Particulars	Debit (BRL)	Date	Particulars	Credit (BRL)
			31-Jan-X1	By Investments—Equity Shares—Buy Long Account	483,700.00
1-Feb-X1	To Investments—Equity Shares—Buy Long Account	483,700.00			
			28-Feb-X1	By Investments—Equity Shares—Buy Long Account	318,700.00
			28-Feb-X1	By Investments—Equity Shares—Short Sales Account	39,400.00
28-Feb-X1	To Balance	358,100.00			
28-Feb-X1	Total	**841,800.00**	28-Feb-X1	Total	**841,800.00**
			28-Feb-X1	By Balance	358,100.00

Cash Collateral Paid to Broker Account

Date	Particulars	Debit (BRL)	Date	Particulars	Credit (BRL)
5-Feb-X1	To Bank Account	5,150,000.00			
			28-Feb-X1	By Balance	5,150,000.00
28-Feb-X1	Total	**5,150,000.00**	28-Feb-X1	Total	**5,150,000.00**
28-Feb-X1	To Balance	5,150,000.00			

Interest Receivable on Cash Collateral Account

Date	Particulars	Debit (BRL)	Date	Particulars	Credit (BRL)
28-Feb-X1	To Interest receipts on cash collateral Account	9,500.00			
			28-Feb-X1	By Balance	9,500.00
28-Feb-X1	Total	**9,500.00**	28-Feb-X1	Total	**9,500.00**
28-Feb-X1	To Balance	9,500.00			

Interest Receipts on Cash Collateral Account

Date	Particulars	Debit (BRL)	Date	Particulars	Credit (BRL)
			28-Feb-X1	By Interest Receivable on Cash Collateral Account	9,500.00
28-Feb-X1	To Balance	9,500.00			
28-Feb-X1	Total	**9,500.00**	28-Feb-X1	Total	**9,500.00**
			28-Feb-X1	By Balance	9,500.00

Stock Loan Fees Account

Date	Particulars	Debit (BRL)	Date	Particulars	Credit (BRL)
28-Feb-X1	To Bank Account	1,500.00			
			28-Feb-X1	By Balance	1,500.00
28-Feb-X1	Total	**1,500.00**	28-Feb-X1	Total	**1,500.00**
28-Feb-X1	To Balance	1,500.00			

Share Capital Account

Date	Particulars	Debit (BRL)	Date	Particulars	Credit (BRL)
			1-Jan-X1	By Bank Account	10,000,000.00
28-Feb-X1	To Balance	10,000,000.00			
28-Feb-X1	Total	**10,000,000.00**	28-Feb-X1	Total	**10,000,000.00**
			28-Feb-X1	By Balance	10,000,000.00

Broker—Astron Account

Date	Particulars	Debit (BRL)	Date	Particulars	Credit (BRL)
			11-Jan-X1	By Investments—Equity Shares—Buy Long Account	2,387,000.00
			11-Jan-X1	By Investments—Equity Shares—Buy Long Account	12,500.00
3-Jan-X1	To Bank Account	2,399,500.00			
			25-Jan-X1	By Investments—Equity Shares—Buy Long Account	1,564,000.00
			25-Jan-X1	By Investments—Equity Shares—Buy Long Account	7,800.00
7-Jan-X1	To Bank Account	1,571,800.00			
			5-Feb-X1	By Investments—Equity Shares—Short Sales Account	25,600.00
5-Feb-X1	To Investments—Equity Shares—Short Sales Account	5,135,000.00			
			7-Feb-X1	By Bank Account	5,109,400.00
28-Feb-X1	Total	**9,106,300.00**	28-Feb-X1	Total	**9,106,300.00**

Bank Account

Date	Particulars	Debit (BRL)	Date	Particulars	Credit (BRL)
1-Jan-X1	To Share Capital Account	10,000,000.00			
			3-Jan-X1	By Broker—Astron Account	2,399,500.00
			7-Jan-X1	By Broker—Astron Account	1,571,800.00
			5-Feb-X1	By Cash Collateral Paid to Broker Account	5,150,000.00
7-Feb-X1	To Broker—Astron Account	5,109,400.00			
			28-Feb-X1	By Stock Loan Fees Account	1,500.00
			28-Feb-X1	By Balance	5,986,600.00
28-Feb-X1	Total	**15,109,400.00**	28-Feb-X1	Total	**15,109,400.00**
28-Feb-X1	To Balance	5,986,600.00			

Trial Balance

As of 28-Feb-X1 (BRL)

Particulars	Debit	Credit
Capital		
Share Capital Account		10,000,000.00
Current Liabilities		
Investments—Equity Shares—Buy Long Account	4,290,000.00	
Investments—Equity Shares—Short Sales Account		5,070,000.00
Current Assets		
Bank Account	5,986,600.00	
Interest Receivable on Cash Collateral Account	9,500.00	
Cash Collateral Paid to Broker Account	5,150,000.00	
Income		
Unrealized Capital Gains/Loss—Equity Shares Account		358,100.00
Interest Receipts on Cash Collateral Account		9,500.00
Expense		
Stock Loan Fees Account	1,500.00	
Total	**15,437,600.00**	**15,437,600.00**

Income Statement

For the Period Ending 28-Feb-X1

Expenses	BRL	Income	BRL
Direct Expenses		**Direct Income**	
Stock Loan Fees Account	1,500.00	Unrealized Capital Gains/Loss—Equity Shares Account	358,100.00
		Interest Receipts on Cash Collateral Account	9,500.00
Net Profit Carryover	366,100.00		
Total	**367,600.00**	Total	**367,600.00**

Balance Sheet

As of 28-Feb-X1

Liabilities	BRL	Assets	BRL
Capital Account		**Investments**	
Share Capital Account	10,000,000.00	Investments—Equity Shares—Buy Long Account	4,290,000.00
Current Liabilities			
Investments—Equity Shares—Short Sales Account	5,070,000.00	Cash Collateral Paid to Broker Account	5,150,000.00
		Current Assets	
Profit & Loss Account		Bank Account	5,986,600.00
Opening Balance	Nil	Interest Receivable on Cash Collateral Account	9,500.00
Current Period	366,100.00		
Total	**15,436,100.00**	Total	**15,436,100.00**

Short Equity Shares—Box Position—BRL to US$

F-1 Capital Introduced by the Fund (T-1 @ FX Rate: 1.6540)

Journal Entry

Date	Particulars	Debit (US$)	Credit (US$)
1-Jan-X1	Bank Account	6,045,949.21	
	To Share Capital Account		6,045,949.21
	(Being the subscription contributed by investor into the fund)		

F-2 On Purchase of Shares (T-2 @ FX Rate: 1.6505)

Journal Entry

Date	Particulars	Debit (US$)	Credit (US$)
11-Jan-X1	Investments—Equity Shares—Buy Long Account	1,446,228.42	
	To Broker—Astron Account		1,446,228.42
	(Being the 7,000 Petro Gold shares bought @ US$ 341.00 per share through the broker—Astron)		

F-3 Brokerage on the Bought Shares (T-3 @ FX Rate: 1.6505)

Journal Entry

Date	Particulars	Debit (US$)	Credit (US$)
11-Jan-X1	Investments—Equity Shares—Buy Long Account	7,573.46	
	To Broker—Astron Account		7,573.46
	(Being the brokerage payable to Astron on 7,000 Petro Gold shares bought through them)		

F-4 Being the Amount Paid on Purchase of Shares (T-4 @ FX Rate: 1.6525)

Journal Entry

Date	Particulars	Debit (US$)	Credit (US$)
3-Jan-X1	Broker—Astron Account	1,452,042.36	
	To Bank Account		1,452,042.36
	(Being the brokerage payable to Astron on 7,000 Petro Gold shares bought through them)		

F-5 FX Translation (Consummated FX Translation Entry)

Date	Particulars	BRL	FX Rate	US$
11-Jan-X1	Cost of acquisition of 7,000 shares	2,387,000.00	1.6505	1,446,228.42
11-Jan-X1	Brokerage	12,500.00	1.6505	7,573.46
		2,399,500.00		1,453,801.88
13-Jan-X1	Settlement value on settle date	2,399,500.00	1.6525	1,452,042.36
	Realized currency gains			**1,759.52**

Journal Entry

Date	Particulars	Debit (US$)	Credit (US$)
13-Jan-X1	Broker—Astron Account	1,759.52	
	To Realized Currency Gains/Loss (P/L) Account		1,759.52
	(Being the realized currency gains on purchase of equity shares)		

F-6 On Purchase of Shares (T-5 @ FX Rate: 1.6484)

Journal Entry

Date	Particulars	Debit (US$)	Credit (US$)
25-Jan-X1	Investments—Equity Shares—Buy Long Account	948,798.84	
	To Broker—Astron Account		948,798.84
	(Being the 4,000 Petro Gold shares bought @ US$ 391.00 per share through the broker—Astron)		

F-7 Brokerage on the Bought Shares (T-6 @ FX Rate: 1.6484)

Journal Entry

Date	Particulars	Debit (US$)	Credit (US$)
25-Jan-X1	Investments—Equity Shares—Buy Long Account	4,731.86	
	To Broker—Astron Account		4,731.86
	(Being the brokerage payable to Astron on 4,000 Petro Gold shares bought through them)		

F-8 Being the Amount Paid on Purchase of Shares (T-7 @ FX Rate: 1.6444)

Journal Entry

Date	Particulars	Debit (US$)	Credit (US$)
27-Jan-X1	Broker—Astron Account	955,850.16	
	To Bank Account		955,850.16
	(Being the brokerage payable to Astron on 4,000 Petro Gold shares bought through them)		

F-9 FX Translation (Consummated FX Translation Entry)

Date	Particulars	BRL	FX Rate	US$
25-Jan-X1	Cost of acquisition of 4,000 shares	1.564,000.00	1.6484	948,798.84
25-Jan-X1	Brokerage	7,800.00	1.6484	4,731.86
		1,571,800.00		953,530.70
27-Jan-X1	Settlement value on settle date	1,571,800.00	1.6444	955,850.16
	Realized currency loss			**(2,319.46)**

Journal Entry

Date	Particulars	Debit (US$)	Credit (US$)
27-Jan-X1	Realized Currency Gains/Loss (P/L) Account	2,319.46	
	To Broker—Astron Account		2,319.46
	(Being the realized currency loss on payment to the broker)		

F-10 Mark-to-market at End of Reporting Period Jan X1: (T-8 @ FX Rate: 1.6311)

Mark-to-market at end of reporting period: 31-Jan-X1	**BRL**	**US$**
(a) Market value of 11,000 shares @ BRL 405	4,455,000.00	2,731,285.63
(b) Cost of acquisition (2,399,500.00 + 1,571,800.00)	3,971,300.00	2,434,737.29
(c) Unrealized gains in BRL (a) − (b)	483,700.00	296,548.34

Journal Entry

Date	Particulars	Debit (US$)	Credit (US$)
31-Jan-X1	Investments—Equity Shares—Buy Long Account	296,548.34	
	To Unrealized Capital Gains/Loss—Equity Shares Account		296,548.34
	(Being the mark-to-market entry for 11,000 buy long position in Petro Gold Shares)		

F-11 Reversal of Mark-to-market Entry (T-9 @ FX Rate: 1.6311)

Journal Entry

Date	Particulars	Debit (US$)	Credit (US$)
1-Feb-X1	Unrealized Capital Gains/Loss—Equity Shares Account	296,548.34	
	To Investments—Equity Shares—Buy Long Account		296,548.34
	(Being the reversal of mark-to-market entry for 11,000 long position in Petro Gold Shares)		

F-12 FX Translation (Transient FX Translation Entry)

Particulars	BLR	FX Rate	US$
(a) Market value of 11,000 shares @ US$ 405	4,455,000.00	1.6311	2,731,285.64
(b) Cost of bought long position (2,399,500 + 1,571,800)	3,971,300.00	1.6505	2,407,332.57
(c) Total unrealized gains = (a) − (b)	483,700.00		323,953.07
(d) Unrealized capital gains	483,700.00	1.6201	296,548.34
(e) Unrealized currency gains = (c) − (d)			27,404.73

Journal Entry

Date	Particulars	Debit (US$)	Credit (US$)
31-Jan-X1	Investments—Equity Shares—Buy Long Account	27,404.73	
	To Unrealized Currency Gains/Loss Account		27,404.73
	(Being the FX translation applied on end of period valuation)		

F-13 Reversal of FX Gains/Loss

Journal Entry

Date	Particulars	Debit (US$)	Credit (US$)
1-Feb-X1	Unrealized Currency Gains/Loss Account	27,404.73	
	To Investments—Equity Shares—Buy Long Account		27,404.73
	(Being the FX translation applied on end of period valuation)		

F-14 Currency Gains/Loss—Bank FX (Transient FX translation entry)

Date	Particulars	BRL	FX Rate	US$
01-Jan-X1	Share capital	10,000,000.00	1.654	6,045,949.21
13-Jan-X1	Purchase price including brokerage as of 11-Jan-X1	(2,399,500.00)	1.653	(1,452,042.36)
27-Jan-X1	Purchase price including brokerage as of 25-Jan-X1	(1,571,800.00)	1.644	(955,850.16)
31-Jan-X1	Net balance	6,028,700.00		3,638,056.69
	Net balance at current FX rate	6,028,700.00	1.631	3,696,094.66
	FX translation on Bank account			**58,037.97**

Journal Entry

Date	Particulars	Debit (US$)	Credit (US$)
31-Jan-X1	Bank Account	58,037.97	
	To Unrealized Currency Gain/Loss – Bank Account		58,037.97
	(Being the unrealized currency gains/loss on Bank)		

F-15 On Deposit of Cash Collateral with the Broker (T-10 @ FX Rate: 1.6255)

Journal Entry

Date	Particulars	Debit (US$)	Credit (US$)
5-Feb-X1	Cash Collateral Paid to Broker Account	3,168,255.92	
	To Bank Account		3,168,255.92
	(Being the amount paid to Astron on short sale of 13,000 Petro Gold shares as cash collateral)		

F-16 On Short Sale of Equity Shares and Payment of Brokerage (T-11 @ FX Rate: 1.6255)

Journal Entry

Date	Particulars	Debit (US$)	Credit (US$)
5-Feb-X1	Receivable from Broker—Astron Account	3,159,027.99	
	To Investments—Equity Shares—Short Sales Account		3,159,027.99
	(Being the 13,000 equity shares sold short @ US$395 per share through the broker—Astron Brokers)		
5-Feb-X1	Investments—Equity Shares—Short Sales Account	15,749.00	
	To Astron Account		15,749.00
	(Being brokerage payable to the broker on sale of equity shares)		

F-17 On Receipt of Share Sale Amount from the Broker (T-12 @ FX Rate: 1.6201)

Journal Entry

Date	Particulars	Debit (US$)	Credit (US$)
7-Feb-X1	Bank Account	3,153,755.94	
	To Broker—Astron Account		3,153,755.94
	(Being the amount received for the sale of 13,000 Petro Gold shares)		

F-18 FX Translation (Consummated FX Translation Entry)

Date	Particulars	BLR	FX Rate	US$
5-Feb-X1	Sale value of 13,000 equity shares	5,135,000.00	1.6255	3,159,027.99
	Less brokerage	25,600.00	1.6201	15,749.00
	Net consideration receivable	5,109,400.00		3,143,278.99
7-Feb-X1	Settlement value on settle date	5,109,400.00	1.6201	3,153,755.94
	Realized currency gains			**10,476.95**

Journal Entry

Date	Particulars	Debit (US$)	Credit (US$)
7-Feb-X1	Broker—Astron Account	10,476.95	
	To Realized Currency Gains/Loss Account		10,476.95
	(Being the FX translation on purchase of equity shares)		

F-19 On Payment of Stock Loan Fees (T-13 @ FX Rate: 1.6150)

Journal Entry

Date	Particulars	Debit (US$)	Credit (US$)
28-Feb-X1	Stock Loan Fees Account	928.79	
	To Bank Account		928.79
	(Being the stock loan fees paid to the broker Astron on sale of Petro Gold shares)		

F-20 Mark-to-market at End of Reporting Period Feb X1 (T-14 @ FX Rate: 1.6150)

Mark-to-market of long position at end of reporting period: 28-Feb-X1	BRL	US$
(a) Market value of 11,000 shares @ BRL390	4,290,000.00	2,656,346.75
(b) Cost of acquisition (2,399,500.00 + 1,571,800.00)	3,971,300.00	2,459,009.29
(c) Unrealized gains in BRL (a) − (b)	318,700.00	197,337.46

Journal Entry

Date	Particulars	Debit (US$)	Credit (US$)
28-Feb-X1	Investments—Equity Shares—Buy Long Account	197,337.46	
	To Unrealized Capital Gains/Loss—Equity Shares Account		197,337.46
	(Being the mark-to-market entry for 11,000 buy long position in Petro Gold Shares)		

F-21 FX Translation (Transient FX Translation Entry)

Calculation of unrealized currency gains/loss	BLR	FX Rate	US$
(a) Market value for 11,000 shares @ US$390	4,290,000.00	1.6150	2,656,346.75
(b) Cost of bought long position (2,399,500 + 1,571,800)	3,971,300.00	1.6505	2,407,332.57
(c) Mark-to-market in US$ = (a) − (b)	**318,700.00**		**249,014.17**
(d) Unrealized capital gains	318,700.00	1.6150	197,337.46
(e) Unrealized currency gains			51,676.71

Journal Entry

Date	Particulars	Debit (US$)	Credit (US$)
28-Feb-X1	Investments—Equity Shares—Buy Long Account	51,676.71	
	To Unrealized Currency Gains/Loss Account		51,676.71
	(Being the FX translation on valuation of equity shares)		

F-22 Mark-to-market at End of Reporting Period Feb X1 (T-15 @ FX Rate: 1.6150)

Mark-to-market of short position at end of 28-Feb-X1	BRL	US$
(a) Market value of 13,000 shares @ BRL390	5,070,000.00	3,139,318.89
(b) Sale value of the short position (13,000 × 395) − 25,600	5,109,400.00	3,163,715.17
(c) Unrealized gains in BRL = (b) − (a)	39,400.00	24,396.28

Journal Entry

Date	Particulars	Debit (US$)	Credit (US$)
28-Feb-X1	Investments—Equity Shares—Short Sales Account	24,396.28	
	To Unrealized Capital Gains/Loss—Equity Shares Account		24,396.28
	(Being the mark-to-market entry for 13,000 short position in Petro Gold Shares)		

F-23 FX Translation (Transient FX Translation Entry)

Calculation of unrealized currency gains/loss	BRL	FX Rate	US$
(a) Market value of 13,000 shares @ US$390	5,070,000.00	1.6150	3,139,318.89
(b) Sale value of the short position 13,000 × 395 − 25,600	5,109,400.00	1.6255	3,143,278.99
(c) Mark-to-market in US$ = (b) − (a)	**39,400.00**		**3,690.11**
	39,400.00	1.6150	24,396.28
(d) Unrealized currency loss			(20,436.18)

Journal Entry

Date	Particulars	Debit (US$)	Credit (US$)
28-Feb-X1	Unrealized Currency Gains/Loss Account	20,436.18	
	To Equity Shares—Petro Gold Account—Short Sale		20,436.18
	(Being the FX translation on sale of equity shares)		

F-24 Interest Receivable on Accrued Interest from Cash Collateral with the Broker (T-16 @ FX Rate: 1.6150)

Journal Entry

Date	Particulars	Debit (US$)	Credit (US$)
28-Feb-X1	Interest Receivable on Cash Collateral Account	5,882.35	
	To Interest Receipts on Cash Collateral Account		5,882.35
	(Being the interest receivable on the cash collateral with the broker)		

F-25 Currency Gains/Loss—Bank FX (Transient FX translation entry)

Date	Particulars	BRL	FX Rate	US$
	Opening balance	6,028,700.00		3,696,094.66
5-Feb-X1	Cash Collateral	(5,150,000.00)	1.626	(3,168,255.92)
7-Feb-X1	Sell price including brokerage as of 5-Feb-X1	5,109,400.00	1.620	3,153,755.94
28-Feb-X1	Stock loan fees	(1,500.00)	1.615	(928.79)
28-Feb-X1	Net balance	5,986,600.00		3,680,665.89
	Net balance at current FX rate	5,986,600.00	1.615	3,706,873.07
	FX translation on Bank account			**26,207.18**

Journal Entry

Date	Particulars	Debit (US$)	Credit (US$)
28-Feb-X1	Bank Account	26,207.18	
	To Unrealized Currency Gain/Loss – Bank Account		26,207.18
	(Being the unrealized currency gains/ loss on Bank)		

General Ledger Accounts

Investments—Equity Shares—Buy Long Account

Date	Particulars	Debit (US$)	Date	Particulars	Credit (US$)
11-Jan-X1	To Broker—Astron Account	1,446,228.42			
11-Jan-X1	To Broker—Astron Account	7,573.46			
25-Jan-X1	To Broker—Astron Account	948,798.84			
25-Jan-X1	To Broker—Astron Account	4,731.86			
31-Jan-X1	To Unrealized Capital Gains/ Loss—Equity Shares Account	296,548.34			
31-Jan-X1	To Unrealized currency Gains/ Loss Account	27,404.73			
			1-Feb-X1	By Unrealized Capital Gains/ Loss—Equity Shares Account	296,548.34
			1-Feb-X1	By Unrealized currency Gains/ Loss Account	27,404.73
28-Feb-X1	To Unrealized Capital Gains/ Loss—Equity Shares Account	197,337.46			
28-Feb-X1	To Unrealized currency Gains/ Loss Account	51,676.71			
			28-Feb-X1	By Balance	2,656,346.75
28-Feb-X1	Total	**2,980,299.82**	28-Feb-X1	Total	**2,980,299.82**
28-Feb-X1	To Balance	2,656,346.75			

Investments—Equity Shares—Short Sales Account

Date	Particulars	Debit (US$)	Date	Particulars	Credit (US$)
			5-Feb-X1	By Broker—Astron Account	3,159,027.99
5-Feb-X1	To Broker—Astron Account	15,749.00			
28-Feb-X1	To Unrealized Capital Gains/Loss—Equity Shares Account	24,396.28			
			28-Feb-X1	By Unrealized currency Gains/Loss Account	20,436.18
28-Feb-X1	To Balance	3,139,318.89			
28-Feb-X1	Total	**3,179,464.17**	28-Feb-X1	Total	**3,179,464.17**
			28-Feb-X1	By Balance	3,139,318.89

Interest Receivable on Cash Collateral Account

Date	Particulars	Debit (US$)	Date	Particulars	Credit (US$)
28-Feb-X1	To Interest Receipts on Cash Collateral Account	5,882.35			
			28-Feb-X1	By Balance	5,882.35
28-Feb-X1	Total	**5,882.35**	28-Feb-X1	Total	**5,882.35**
28-Feb-X1	To Balance	5,882.35			

Interest Receipts on Cash Collateral Account

Date	Particulars	Debit (US$)	Date	Particulars	Credit (US$)
			28-Feb-X1	By Interest Receivable on Cash Collateral Account	5,882.35
28-Feb-X1	To Balance	5,882.35			
28-Feb-X1	Total	**5,882.35**	28-Feb-X1	Total	**5,882.35**
			28-Feb-X1	By Balance	5,882.35

Unrealized Capital Gains/Loss—Equity Shares Account

Date	Particulars	Debit (US$)	Date	Particulars	Credit (US$)
			31-Jan-X1	By Investments—Equity Shares—Buy Long Account	296,548.34
1-Feb-X1	To Investments—Equity Shares—Buy Long Account	296,548.34			
			28-Feb-X1	By Investments—Equity Shares—Buy Long Account	197,337.46
			28-Feb-X1	By Investments—Equity Shares—Short Sales Account	24,396.28
28-Feb-X1	To Balance	221,733.74			
28-Feb-X1	Total	**518,282.08**	28-Feb-X1	Total	**518,282.08**
			28-Feb-X1	By Balance	221,733.74

Unrealized Currency Gains/Loss—Equity Shares Account

Date	Particulars	Debit (US$)	Date	Particulars	Credit (US$)
			31-Jan-X1	By Investments—Equity Shares—Buy Long Account	27,404.73
1-Feb-X1	To Investments—Equity Shares—Buy Long Account	27,404.73			
			28-Feb-X1	By Investments—Equity Shares—Buy Long Account	51,676.71
28-Feb-X1	To Equity Shares—Petro Gold Account—Short Sale	20,436.18			
28-Feb-X1	To Balance	31,240.53			
28-Feb-X1	Total	**79,081.44**	28-Feb-X1	Total	**79,081.44**
			28-Feb-X1	By Balance	31,240.53

Unrealized Currency Gain/Loss—Bank Account

Date	Particulars	Debit (US$)	Date	Particulars	Credit (US$)
			31-Jan-X1	By Bank Account	58,037.97
			28-Feb-X1	By Bank Account	26,207.18
31-Mar-X1	To Balance	84,245.15			
31-Mar-X1	Total	**84,245.15**	31-Mar-X1	Total	**84,245.15**
			31-Mar-X1	By Balance	84,245.15

Realized Currency Gains/Loss Account

Date	Particulars	Debit (US$)	Date	Particulars	Credit (US$)
			13-Jan-X1	By Broker—Astron Account	1,759.52
27-Jan-X1	To Broker—Astron Account	2,319.46			
			7-Feb-X1	By Broker—Astron Account	10,476.95
28-Feb-X1	To Balance	9,917.01			
28-Feb-X1	Total	**12,236.47**	28-Feb-X1	Total	**12,236.47**
			28-Feb-X1	By Balance	9,917.01

Cash Collateral Paid to Broker Account

Date	Particulars	Debit (US$)	Date	Particulars	Credit (US$)
5-Feb-X1	To Bank Account	3,168,255.92			
			28-Feb-X1	By Balance	3,168,255.92
28-Feb-X1	Total	**3,168,255.92**	28-Feb-X1	Total	**3,168,255.92**
28-Feb-X1	To Balance	3,168,255.92			

Stock Loan Fees Account

Date	Particulars	Debit (US$)	Date	Particulars	Credit (US$)
28-Feb-X1	To Bank Account	928.79			
			28-Feb-X1	By Balance	928.79
28-Feb-X1	Total	**928.79**	28-Feb-X1	Total	**928.79**
28-Feb-X1	To Balance	928.79			

Share Capital Account

Date	Particulars	Debit (US$)	Date	Particulars	Credit (US$)
			1Jan-X1	By Bank Account	6,045,949.21
28-Feb-X1	To Balance	6,045,949.21			
28-Feb-X1	Total	**6,045,949.21**	28-Feb-X1	Total	**6,045,949.21**
			28-Feb-X1	By Balance	6,045,949.21

Astron Account

Date	Particulars	Debit (US$)	Date	Particulars	Credit (US$)
			11-Jan-X1	By Investments—Equity Shares—Buy Long Account	1,446,228.42
			11-Jan-X1	By Investments—Equity Shares—Buy Long Account	7,573.46
3-Jan-X1	To Bank Account	1,452,042.36			
13-Jan-X1	To Realized Currency Gains/Loss (P/L) Account	1,759.52			
			25-Jan-X1	By Investments—Equity Shares—Buy Long Account	948,798.84
			25-Jan-X1	By Investments—Equity Shares—Buy Long Account	4,731.86
27-Jan-X1	To Bank Account	955,850.16			
			27-Jan-X1	Realized Currency Gains/Loss (P/L) Account	2,319.46
			5-Feb-X1	By Investments—Equity Shares—Short Sales Account	15,749.00
5-Feb-X1	To Investments—Equity Shares—Short Sales Account	3,159,027.99			
			7-Feb-X1	By Bank Account	3,153,755.94
7-Feb-X1	To Realized Currency Gains/Loss Account	10,476.95			
28-Feb-X1	Total	**5,579,156.98**	28-Feb-X1	Total	**5,579,156.98**

Bank Account

Date	Particulars	Debit (US$)	Date	Particulars	Credit (US$)
1-Jan-X1	To Share Capital Account	6,045,949.21			
			11-Jan-X1	By Broker—Astron Account	1,452,042.36
			27-Jan-X1	By Broker—Astron Account	955,850.16
31-Jan-X1	To Unrealized Currency Gain/Loss—Bank Account	58,037.97			
			5-Feb-X1	By Cash Collateral Paid to Broker Account	3,168,255.92
7-Feb-X1	To Broker—Astron Account	3,153,755.94			
			28-Feb-X1	By Stock Loan Fees Account	928.79
28-Feb-X1	To Unrealized Currency Gain/Loss—Bank Account	26,207.18			
			28-Feb-X1	By Balance	3,706,873.07
28-Feb-X1	Total	**9,283,950.30**	28-Feb-X1	Total	**9,283,950.30**
28-Feb-X1	To Balance	3,706,873.07			

Trial Balance

As of 28-Feb-X1 (US$)

Particulars	Debit	Credit
Capital		
Share Capital Account		6,045,949.21
Current Liabilities		
Investments—Equity Shares—Short Sales Account		3,139,318.89
Investments		
Investments—Equity Shares—Buy Long Account	2,656,346.75	
Current Assets		
Bank Account	3,706,873.07	
Cash Collateral Paid to Broker Account	3,168,255.92	
Interest Receivable on Cash Collateral Account	5,882.35	
Income		
Unrealized Capital Gains/Loss—Equity Shares Account		221,733.74
Unrealized Currency Gains/Loss—Equity Shares Account		31,240.53
Unrealized Currency Gain/Loss - Bank Account		84,245.15
Realized Currency Gains/Loss Account		9,917.01
Interest Receipts on Cash Collateral Account		5,882.35
Expense		
Stock Loan Fees Account	928.79	
Total	**9,538,286.88**	**9,538,286.88**

Income Statement

For the period ending 28-Feb-X1

Expenses	US$	Income	US$
Direct Expenses		**Direct Income**	
Stock Loan Fees Account	928.79	Unrealized Capital Gains/ Loss—Equity Shares Account	221,733.74
		Unrealized Currency Gains/ Loss—Equity Shares Account	31,240.53
		Unrealized Currency Gain/ Loss—Bank Account	84,245.15
Net Profit Carryover	352,089.99	Realized Currency Gains/ Loss Account	9,917.01
		Interest Receipts on Cash Collateral Account	5,882.35
Total	**353,018.78**	Total	**353,018.78**

Balance Sheet

As of 28-Feb-X1

Liabilities	US$	Assets	US$
Capital		**Investments**	
Share Capital Account	6,045,949.21	Investments—Equity Shares—Buy Long Account	2,656,346.75
Current Liabilities		**Current Assets**	
Investments—Equity Shares—Short Sales Account	3,139,318.89	Bank Account	3,706,873.07
		Interest Receivable on Cash Collateral Account	5,882.35
Profit & Loss Account		Cash Collateral Paid to Broker Account	3,168,255.92
Opening Balance	Nil		
Current Period	352,089.99		
Total	**9,537,358.09**	Total	**9,537,358.09**

SUMMARY

- Short-selling is the practice of selling securities the seller does not own, in the hope of repurchasing them later at a lower price.
- This is done with the intention to profit from an expected decline in the price of a *security*, as opposed to the ordinary investment practice in which an investor buys or *goes long* in a security in the hope that the price will rise subsequently.

- In order to profit from the stock price going down, investors can borrow a security and sell it, with the expectation that the price will decrease so that they can buy it back at a lower price and keep the difference.
- The short-seller is obliged to deliver the shares to his broker, who usually in turn would have borrowed the shares from some other investor who is in actual possession of the said shares.
- In most countries, the regulatory requirements are such that if an investor goes short in a cash market, the investor should arrange to borrow the security and deliver the same as if he has sold a security that was in his possession.
- When the seller does not borrow or arrange to borrow the securities in time to make delivery to the buyer with the standard three-day settlement period, the short sale is known as *naked* short sale. The buyer of such shares seldom receives the shares, and the situation is technically described as *failure to deliver.*
- The short-selling process involves several steps, starting with borrowing the shares, selling short, buying to cover, and thus closing out the position.
- Short-selling is fraught with several risks and is quite dangerous as an investment strategy, as the investor can get into a short squeeze caused either by market forces or deliberately by any group of market players to corner the investor.
- Hedge funds often resort to short-selling shares in which they already hold long positions, which is also known as a *box* position. Strictly, box positions do not alter the profits or profitability for the investor except that the accounting for the same gets a little complicated. However, for tax purposes, box position short sales are treated as if the original long position is liquidated.
- In spite of the severe criticism of short-selling, it is not without merits, especially as it is an essential part of the price discovery mechanism. Several leading investors have hailed short-selling as a useful counterweight to the widespread bullishness in the market, and some believe that short-sellers are useful in uncovering fraudulent accounting and other problems at companies.
- There are several regulatory requirements regarding short sales in different countries, depending upon the current status of the economy. By and large there exist certain fundamental regulations regarding the requirements for short sales, which should be adhered to by the market players.
- Securities lending or stock lending refers to the lending of securities by one party to another. The terms of the loan are governed by a securities lending agreement, which normally requires that the borrower provide the lender with collateral, which could be in the form of either cash or government securities of value equal to or greater than the loaned securities.
- Towards the charges for the loan, both the parties negotiate a fee, quoted as an annualized percentage of the value of the loaned securities.
- If the collateral provided by the borrower is cash, then the fee is quoted as a rebate. This means that the lender will earn interest on the cash collateral provided by him, and will adjust this as a rebate from the agreed rate of interest to the borrower.
- Securities lending is legal and regulated in most of the world's major securities markets. Most markets mandate that the borrowing of securities be conducted only for specifically permitted purposes.

EXERCISES

Theory Questions

1. What is short-selling and is it legal?
2. What are the different types of short sales?
3. Outline the process of short-selling.
4. Can an investor short a share without first arranging for the delivery of the shares?
5. What are the potential risks of short-selling? How does it compare with going long on a security?
6. Can an investor simultaneously hold both long and short positions in the same security? If so, will it result in any realized gain from the accounting perspective as well as from the tax authorities' perspective?
7. Is short-selling good for the stock markets?
8. Describe the rationale behind short-selling.
9. Are there any regulatory requirements of short selling in the U.S. stock markets?
10. What do you understand by securities lending?
11. How are the securities lending market regulated?
12. Who are the participants in securities lending?

Objective Questions

1. Short-selling is preferred by traders based on the expectation that the
   a. Price of the security will go up
   b. Price of the security will go down
   c. Price of the security will remain stable
   d. None of the above
2. The strategy allowing the investor to gain from the declining price of security includes
   a. Buying call options
   b. Selling call options
   c. Buying put options
   d. None of the above
3. The process of buying back the shares that are sold short is called
   a. Buy to square off
   b. Buy to cover
   c. Buy back to cover
   d. None of the above

4. A short sale followed up with proper delivery of shares after borrowing is referred to as a
   a. Regular short sale
   b. Naked short sale
   c. Sale on delivery
   d. None of the above
5. A short sale not followed up with proper delivery of shares within the standard three-day settlement period is referred to as a
   a. Regular short sale
   b. Naked short sale
   c. Sale on delivery
   d. None of the above
6. In short-selling there is no potential for
   a. Dividend income
   b. Return from capital gains
   c. Profit on sale
   d. All of the above
7. The action of lending the security of one person to another is referred to as a
   a. Security transfer
   b. Corporate action
   c. Security lending
   d. None of the above
8. When the collateral provided by the buyer to the lender is in the form of cash, the fee is referred to as
   a. Brokerage
   b. Rebate
   c. Lending fee
   d. None of the above
9. The permitted purposes of stock borrowing include
   a. To facilitate settlement of trade
   b. To facilitate delivery of short sale
   c. To finance the security
   d. All of the above

10. Which of the following is not a participant in security lending?
    a. Borrowers
    b. Agent lenders
    c. Brokers
    d. All of the above

Journal Questions

For the following scenario, prepare journal entries, general ledgers, trial balance, income statement, and balance sheet for Abdul Razack Inc. for the period January 1 through February 28.

Box Position—Trade Currency BRL

Abdul Razack Inc. traded in Coca-Cola shares in a Brazilian stock exchange through Pompoodle brokers and the details are as follows:

Trade Details

Date	Product	Quantity	Rate (BRL)	B/S	Brokerage
11-Jan-X1	Coco Cola	17,000	34.00	Bought Long	BRL 12,500
25-Jan-X1	Coco Cola	14,000	39.00	Bought Long	BRL 7,800
5-Feb-X1	Coco Cola	23,000	45.00	Short Sale	BRL 25,600

Other Details

- The stock loan fee paid by Abdul Razack Inc. on short sales on February 28 is BRL4,800.
- An investor has introduced an amount of BRL10 million as share capital on January 1 into the Abdul Razack Inc. fund.
- Settlement: T + 2
- Abdul Razack Inc. makes a deposit of BRL1.05 million with the broker on February 5 as collateral.
- Interest accrued on cash collateral amounts to BRL7,800 due from the broker as of February 28.

FX Rates

Date	FX Rate
1-Jan-X	1.6540
11-Jan-X1	1.6505
13-Jan-X1	1.6525
25-Jan-X1	1.6484
27-Jan-X1	1.6444
31-Jan-X1	1.6311
5-Feb-X1	1.6255
7-Feb-X1	1.6201
28-Feb-X1	1.6150

Market Rate

January 31: 42.00
February 28: 39.00

CHAPTER 13

Accounting for ADR/GDR Investments

LEARNING OBJECTIVES

After studying this chapter you should have a grasp of the following:

- Definition of a depositary receipt (DR).
- Issuance and cancellation of DRs.
- DR ratio and pricing.
- Benefits of DRs to issuers.
- Advantages of DRs to investors.
- Definition of American depositary receipt (ADR) and global depositary receipt (GDR).
- Different types of ADR issues.
- Risks associated with investment in depositary receipts.
- Trade life cycle of equity investments in ADR.
- Journal entries to be recorded during the different phases of the trade life cycle.
- FX revaluation and FX translation process.
- Illustration of investments in ADRs converted to equity shares in foreign currency.
- Preparation of journal entries and general ledger accounts.
- Preparation of income statement and balance sheet after the investments in ADRs are made.

DEFINITION OF A DEPOSITARY RECEIPT

A depositary receipt (DR) represents an ownership interest in securities of a foreign issuer typically trading outside its home market. A DR is a tradable instrument.

The depositary receipts that are trading in the United States are known as American depositary receipts (ADRs). Depositary receipts that are traded in an international market outside the United States are known as global depositary receipts (GDRs). Most depositary receipts are quoted and traded in US$ terms. There are some DRs that are traded in euros and pounds sterling.

The DRs are traded just like equity shares, being traded in recognized stock exchanges and settled according to procedures governing the relevant clearing system in which they are held. The main benefit of DRs is that they allow investors to invest in securities without having to deal with complex cross-border transactions. Additionally, DRs offer almost the same economic, corporate, and voting rights enjoyed by shareholders of the underlying shares.

ISSUANCE AND CANCELLATION OF DRs

Typically a bank issues depositary receipts and also functions as a depository and issuing agent for the same. The depositary receipt is issued against the deposit of domestic ordinary shares in the bank's custody account in the home market. These shares continue to remain on deposit with the bank's custodian until the depositary receipts are cancelled.

When the depositary receipt is returned for cancellation to the bank that acts as the depository, the depositary bank instructs its custodian to deliver the underlying local share as per the instructions received from the party delivering the depositary receipt.

Depositary receipts are issued or canceled to meet supply and demand in the different markets in which they trade. Generally, depositary receipts are issued as investor demand increases in the international market and are canceled as demand is greater in the home market, even though there are some limitations to the same due to legal constraints.

DR RATIO AND PRICING

Each depositary receipt is backed by a specified number of the issuer's local shares, known as the depositary receipt ratio. The ratio is manipulated in such a way that the price of each DR falls in a competitive price range that is considered attractive compared to the issuer's international peer group. The ratio of depositary receipts to underlying shares can be in whole numbers or fractions, depending upon the local share price.

It is usual to price DRs in the range between \$6 and \$20. The ratio of DRs to ordinary shares is tweaked when the depositary receipt price goes well over \$20 or if it falls substantially below \$6. Changing the DR ratio allows the company to keep its DR price in line with its peers and maintain investor interest.

BENEFITS OF DRs TO ISSUERS

The issuers are immensely benefited by depositary receipts due to the following reasons:

- Among institutional investors, DRs enhance the company's visibility and profile internationally among institutional investors.
- They make the company's presence felt in new markets, thus increasing the visibility of the company for its products and services.
- Depositary receipts broaden and diversify the investor base of the company, attracting new investors globally.
- They enable the company to get better valuation, as the company will be valued alongside its international peer group.
- They enable the issuers to migrate into better internationally accepted corporate governance standards.
- They establish a new avenue for raising equity capital beyond the home market.

BENEFITS TO INVESTORS

- Investors can trade conveniently in US\$ and settle through established clearing-houses.
- Depositary receipts are easier to purchase in dollar terms than the issuer's underlying ordinary shares in the respective local currency.

- Investors get excellent international exposure for institutional investors and hedge funds.
- There is greater ease of custodial services for dollar-denominated securities.
- Investors get dividends in US$.
- Investors can get good diversification into securities originating from different geographical locations.

WHAT ARE ADR AND GDR?

American Depositary Receipt

An American depositary receipt (ADR) is a stock that trades in the United States but represents a specified number of shares in a foreign corporation. ADRs are bought and sold on American markets just like regular stocks. They were first introduced to the financial markets in 1927.

The sponsor bank purchases a bulk lot of shares from a foreign company and then bundles the shares into groups for the purpose of reissuing the same in any of the American stock exchanges. The issuing company is required to provide detailed financial information to the sponsor bank.

The depositary bank determines the ratio of ADRs per local share. This ratio is manipulated to price an ADR high enough to show substantial value, yet low enough to make it affordable for individual investors.

Global Depositary Receipt

Global depositary receipts (GDRs) are depositary receipts in Europe or other non-U.S. markets pursuant to Regulation S promulgated under the U.S. Securities Act of 1933. GDRs are listed on European stock exchanges such as London or Luxembourg and are cleared through the Euromarkets clearing systems, namely Euroclear and Clearstream. GDRs may also be listed on other exchanges, such as Dubai and Singapore.

A company can choose to combine its GDR offering with an ADR offering into the U.S. markets. Then the ADRs may be publicly listed on a U.S. exchange and offered to retail investors, or may be privately placed with qualified institutional buyers (QIBs) pursuant to Rule 144A. Only QIBs can own 144A ADRs, and retail investors cannot participate in such ADRs.

It appears of late that there is a clear shift towards GDRs as global corporations are increasingly seeking to raise capital in the international markets. Perhaps amendments to the U.S. regulations could be playing a major role as the initial and annual reporting requirements for companies listed in the United States are more stringent and new requirements have been imposed relating to financial reporting controls.

DIFFERENT TYPES OF ADR ISSUES

There are three levels of ADRs available, each having its own merits and demerits. The issuing company will choose the level that fits best when considering the other requirements.

Level 1. This is the most basic type of ADR where the foreign company does not wish its ADRs listed on an exchange. Level 1 ADRs are found in the over-the-counter (OTC) market and are resorted to as an inexpensive way to measure the interest for the company's securities in North America. Level 1 ADRs also have the least stringent requirements from the Securities and Exchange Commission (SEC).

Level 2. This type of ADR is listed on an American exchange. Level 2 ADRs have slightly more requirements from the SEC, but they also get higher visibility and better trading volumes.

Level 3. This type of ADR is the most prestigious of the three. When an issuer floats a public offering of ADRs on a U.S. exchange, Level 3 ADRs are issued. Through this type of ADR, companies are able to raise capital and gain substantial visibility in the U.S. financial markets.

RISKS ASSOCIATED WITH INVESTING IN DRs

Analyzing foreign companies involves further scrutiny than merely looking at the fundamentals. In fact, there are innumerable risk factors that determine the value of the depositary receipts in addition to the performance of the company. Risks that investors should be aware of are as follows:

- *Political risk.* Stability of the government in the home country of the ADR is a vital risk factor. If the government is unstable the performance of the issuer becomes vulnerable, contributing to the risk.
- *Exchange rate risk.* Stability of the currency of the home country of the ADR is another important factor. Since ADR shares track the shares in the home country, if the country's currency is devalued, it will impact the price of the ADR, which can potentially result in a big loss, despite the company performing well.
- *Inflationary risk.* This goes hand in hand with the exchange rate risk. Inflation is the rate at which the general price level is rising, while the purchasing power is falling. Inflation can be catastrophic to business because the currency of a country with high inflation becomes less and less valuable each day.
- *Special risks.* In addition to currency exchange rates, the investor should be aware that some countries may impose foreign currency controls that restrict or delay the investor from moving currency out of a country.
- *Lower volumes and lack of liquidity.* Foreign markets may have lower trading volumes and may only be open a few hours a day. Some countries restrict the amount or type of stocks that foreign investors may purchase. The investor may sometimes have to pay premium prices to buy a foreign security and may have difficulty finding a buyer when the investor wants to sell.
- *Lack of proper information about the company.* Certain foreign companies do not provide investors with the same type of information as U.S. public companies. Lack of proper information about the company released in a timely manner may be a serious risk, and it could arrive too late to exit the position. One way to reduce the impact of price changes due to release of information is to invest for the long term and try to ride out sharp upswings and downturns in the market.
- *Lack of legal remedies.* Suing the company in the United States is not possible if the investor has a problem with the investment. Even assuming the investor is able to sue successfully in a U.S. court, it might be difficult to recover on a U.S. judgment against a foreign company. The only recourse for the investor would be to rely on the legal remedies that are available in the company's home country, which might prove very expensive.

- *Unexpected taxes including withholding taxes.* Due to unexpected taxes, such as withholding taxes on dividends, international investing might become more expensive than investing in U.S. companies, thereby making it quite unattractive. Additionally, international transaction costs such as fees, broker's commissions, and taxes often prove to be on the higher side than in the U.S. markets.

RESTRICTED PROGRAMS

Restricted programs are those that are meant to be traded by only certain individuals. In the United States, the SEC allows these types of issuance of shares as per Rule 144-A and Regulation S.

Rule 144-A Issuance

Certain foreign companies set up an ADR issuance under SEC Rule 144-A. This provision makes the issuance of shares a private placement. Shares issued under this rule are restricted stock and may only be issued to or traded by qualified institutional buyers.

Regular shareholders will have nothing to do with these shares. Most are held exclusively through the Clearing Corporation, and the public often has very little information on the valuation of these securities.

Regulation S

The other restriction in the trading of ADR shares is to issue them under the terms of SEC Regulation S. This regulation states that the shares are not and will not be registered with any U.S. securities regulation authority.

Regulation S shares cannot be held or traded by any "U.S. person," as defined by SEC Regulation S rules. The shares are registered and issued to offshore, non-U.S. residents only.

THE TRADE LIFE CYCLE FOR EQUITY ADR SECURITIES

- Buy ADRs.
- Brokerage/commission on the buy transaction.
- Pay the contracted amount for the ADRs.
- Ascertain the fair value at the end of the reporting period.
- Reversal of mark-to-market.
- Sell the equity shares against ADRs.
- Pay brokerage/commission on the sell transaction.
- Receive the consideration.
- Conversion of ADRs into local equity shares.
- Pay charges for converting ADRs into local equity shares.
- Ascertain the profit/loss on the sale.
- FX revaluation entries.
- FX translation entries.

Buy ADRs

For ADRs, the buy order is placed with the broker registered with the stock exchange in the United States. The stock exchange usually takes the responsibility for specific performance of the contract, ensuring that both the legs of the contract are fulfilled by the respective parties. When the investor places the buy order and when the broker executes the same, it becomes a binding contract between the investor and the stock exchange.

Usually the trade date is referred to as T + 0 or simply "trade date." At this stage, the asset, being the equity shares, and the liability, being the amount payable to the broker, are recognized in the books of accounts.

Note that all the entries are passed in the trade currency and then revalued in the functional currency. In the present case let us assume that the functional currency is US$.

Alan Kimberly Inc., acquires 1,000 ADRs of Gold Crest at $490 per share from the Stock Exchange through the broker Silver Man on October 3. The ADR represents two equity shares of Gold Crest, which is listed in the stock exchanges of Australia. The accounting entry that is recorded in the books of accounts is as follows:

Journal Entry

Date	Particulars	Debit (US$)	Credit (US$)
3-Oct-X1	Investments—ADR Account	490,000.00	
	To Silver Man Account		490,000.00
	(Being the Gold Crest ADRs bought @ $490 per share through the Broker—Silver Man)		

Brokerage/Commission on the Buy Transaction

The broker of the stock exchange charges a commission for the services rendered. This is usually settled along with the purchase value of the shares. Accounting standards require that this be treated as part of the cost of the shares procured. Hence this is usually built into the cost of purchase of the shares.

On the 1,000 Gold Crest ADRs purchased through Silver Man, the brokerage payable per share is $3. The accounting entry that is recorded in the books of accounts is as follows:

Journal Entry

Date	Particulars	Debit (US$)	Credit (US$)
3-Oct-X1	Investments—ADR Account	3,000.00	
	To Silver Man Account		3,000.00
	(Being the brokerage payable to Silver Man @ $3 per share on 1,000 Gold Crest ADRs bought through them)		

Pay the Contracted Amount for the ADRs

The next event in the trade life cycle is the payment of the contracted amount for the ADRs bought. Usually the receipt of the ADRs and the payment for the same happens two days after the date of the trade, referred to as T + 2. However, this varies from exchange to exchange. The shares are usually delivered electronically by the seller and the payment is made by the buyer on the same date. During this stage the actual asset comes into the physical possession of the buyer and the liability created earlier is settled. For exchange-traded securities, the settlement automatically takes place on the settlement date through the clearing system of the exchange concerned.

Assuming that the broker is paid on T + 2, then the accounting entry that is recorded in the books of accounts is as follows:

Journal Entry

Date	Particulars	Debit (US$)	Credit (US$)
5-Oct-X1	Silver Man Account	493,000.00	
	To Bank Account		493,000.00
	(Being the amount paid to Silver Man on purchase of 1,000 Gold Crest ADRs together with the brokerage)		

Ascertain the Fair Value at the End of Reporting Period

At the end of every reporting period the fair value of the ADRs is ascertained and the ADRs are marked-to-market. This process is known as portfolio valuation, when the market rate at the end of the period is determined from the primary stock exchange where the shares are traded. If there is an increase in the market rate over and above the purchase rate, then such increase is recorded as a gain on the one hand, and the corresponding amount is reflected as an increase in the value of such shares. This accounting entry is reversed on the next day or the next valuation date when a fresh entry for the then value is recorded in the books of accounts. Alternatively, the accounting entry can be recorded only for the incremental value. If the investor follows this incremental value method then there is no need to reverse the entry for mark-to-market recorded earlier.

Assume that the market rate of Gold Crest as of October 31, which is the next valuation date, is $497. The accounting entry that is recorded in the books of accounts is as follows:

Journal Entry

Date	Particulars	Debit (US$)	Credit (US$)
31-Oct-X1	Investments—ADR Account	4,000.00	
	To Unrealized Capital Gains/Loss—ADR Account		4,000.00
	(Being the mark-to-market entry for 1,000 long position in Gold Crest ADRs @ $497 less the cost of acquisition viz., $490 plus $3 per ADR amounting to $4,000)		

Reversal of Mark-to-market Entry

The accounting entry for mark-to-market is reversed on the next day or the next valuation date when a fresh entry for the then value is recorded in the books of accounts. However, as mentioned earlier, if the investor follows the incremental value method, there is no need to reverse the entry for mark-to-market recorded earlier.

The accounting entry that is recorded in the books of accounts is shown as follows:

Journal Entry

Date	Particulars	Debit (US$)	Credit (US$)
1-Nov-X1	Unrealized Capital Gains/Loss—ADR Account	4,000.00	
	To Investments—ADR Account		4,000.00
	(Being the reversal of mark-to-market entry for 1,000 long position in Gold Crest ADRs)		

Sell the Equity Shares against ADRs

Ultimately, when the shares are sold through a broker of the exchange, an accounting entry is recorded for the contracted amount to be received on such sale. The ADRs bought can be sold in the market. The treatment of sale of ADRs is exactly the same as that of long equity, considered in earlier chapters, and hence is not dealt with here.

Alternatively, the local shares of Gold Crest can be sold in the stock exchange of the home country—in this case, Australia. If the equity shares of Gold Crest are sold in the local stock exchange against the long position of ADR, then the ADRs should be converted into local equity shares denominated in the local trade currency.

Assume that 2,000 shares of Gold Crest is sold on November 6 for a consideration of AUD 310 each, and assume that the brokerage per share amounts to AUD4. The accounting entry that is recorded in the books of accounts is shown as follows:

Journal Entry

Date	Particulars	Debit (AUD)	Credit (AUD)
6-Nov-X1	Silver Man Account	620,000.00	
	To Investments—Equity Shares Account—Trading		620,000.00
	(Being the 2,000 Gold Crest shares sold @ AUD310 per share through the broker—Silver Man)		

Brokerage/Commission on the Sell Transaction

Brokerage is paid when the shares are sold and only the net proceeds are taken into account. The accounting entry that is recorded in the books of accounts is shown as follows:

Journal Entry

Date	Particulars	Debit (AUD)	Credit (AUD)
6-Nov-X1	Investments—Equity Shares Account—Trading	8,000.00	
	To Silver Man Account		8,000.00
	(Being the brokerage payable to Silver Man @ AUD4 per share on 2,000 Gold Crest shares sold through them)		

Receive the Consideration

The consideration is received on T+2 or on another date, based on the exchange concerned. The consideration is received net of brokerage. The accounting entry that is recorded in the books of accounts is shown as follows:

Journal Entry

Date	Particulars	Debit (AUD)	Credit (AUD)
8-Nov-X1	Bank Account	6,12,000.00	
	To Silver Man Account		6,12,000.00
	(Being the net consideration received from the broker Silver Man on sale of 2,000 Gold Crest shares)		

Conversion of ADRs into Local Equity Shares

The ADRs should be converted into local shares as the shares are sold in the local stock exchange. The net purchase consideration of the shares bought in ADR in US$ terms should be converted into AUD terms at the current FX rate, and thus the cost of acquisition of the shares sold will be arrived at. Assuming that the FX rate of US$/ADR is 1.2, the accounting entry that is recorded in the books of accounts is as follows:

Journal Entry

Date	Particulars	Debit (AUD)	Credit (AUD)
6-Nov-X1	Investments—Equity Shares Account—Trading	591,600.00	
	To Investments—ADR Account		591,600.00
	(Being the conversion of 1,000 ADRS into 2,000 Gold Crest equity shares. The AUD value is arrived at by converting the US$ cost of acquisition at the current FX rate.)		

Pay Charges for Converting ADRs into Local Equity Shares

Each ADR converts to two local shares, and usually the cost of conversion hovers around 0.5 percent of the shares. Conversion charges are paid in US$ terms and appropriate journal entries are passed for conversion in the functional currency to represent properly such conversion.

Assume that the conversion charges to be paid to the broker amount to $2,450. The accounting entry that is recorded in the books of accounts is shown as follows:

Journal Entry

Date	Particulars	Debit (US$)	Credit (US$)
6-Nov-X1	Conversion Charges Paid Account	2,450.00	
	To Bank Account		2,450.00
	(Being the conversion charges paid to the broker on conversion of 1,000 ADRs into 2,000 Gold Crest equity shares)		

Ascertain the Profit/Loss on the Sale

The profit or loss on liquidation of the shares is ascertained by deducting the cost of sales from the net sale consideration. Cost of sales is arrived at by following first in first out (FIFO), last in first out (LIFO), or weighted average method.

In this case 1,000 shares of Gold Crest were bought at a total cost of acquisition of AUD591,600. This is arrived at by converting the US$ terms of acquiring 1,000 ADRs at $493,000 into AUD terms by applying the FX rate of 1.2. These are sold for a net consideration of AUD612,000 after accounting for the brokerage. Hence, the realized gain on the deal is AUD20,400. The profit or loss realized is always recognized on the date of liquidation and not on the date on which the net proceeds are received from the broker.

The accounting entry that is recorded in the books of accounts is shown as follows:

Journal Entry

Date	Particulars	Debit (AUD)	Credit (AUD)
6-Nov-X1	Investments—Equity Shares Account—Trading	20,400.00	
	To Realized Capital Gains/Loss—ADR Account		20,400.00
	(Being the realized gains on the sale of 2,000 Gold Crest equity shares)		

FX Revaluation Entries

All the entries recorded to this point are initially entered in the respective trade currencies. If the functional currency is different from the trade currency, then each and every entry recorded in the trade currency should be entered again in the functional currency by converting the entries at the respective day's FX rates. In other words, for each trade currency that the investor deals with, there will be a complete set of books representing that trade currency. This includes journal entries, general ledger postings, trial balance, income statement, and balance sheet.

After revaluing each and every journal entry of all the trade currencies into the functional currency, a separate set of books is prepared again comprising all the elements just mentioned: journal entries, general ledger postings, trial balance, income statement, and balance sheet. It should be noted that the ultimate financial reports would be prepared and presented to all the stakeholders based on the financial statements prepared in the functional currency only, as this will encompass all the transactions of the investor in all trade currencies dabbled with. (For illustration and detailed explanation please refer to Chapter 2.)

FX Revaluation Entries

After revaluing all the entries in the functional currency at the respective FX rates for the day concerned, another entry needs to be passed in the books of the functional currency. This is mainly to adjust the currency gains or losses due to the fluctuations in FX rates between the reporting date and the date of recording the original entries.

FX translation entries are recorded only for the asset and liability accounts. For income and expense accounts, the amount gets crystallized on the date of passing the FX revaluation entries in the books of the functional currency.

There are fundamentally two types of FX translation entries that are recorded in the books of the functional currency: consummated FX translation entries and transient FX translation entries. (For illustration and detailed explanation please refer to Chapter 2.)

ILLUSTRATIONS

ADRs Converted to Equity Shares

Rosario Inc. traded in PetroGold shares in a Brazilian stock exchange through Silver Man brokers and the details are as follows. Journal entries, general ledger, trial balance, income statement, and balance sheet for Rosario Inc. for the period January 1 through February 28 are prepared.

Trade Details

Date	Product	CCY	Quantity	Rate	B/S	Brokerage
11-Jan-X1	PetroGold—ADR	US$	7,000	35.00	B	US$735
25-Jan-X1	PetroGold—ADR	US$	4,000	37.00	B	US$444
5-Feb-X1	PetroGold—Local	BRL	14,000	29.50	S	BRL1,240

Other Details

- One ADR converts to two local shares in BRL currency.
- Settlement: T + 2.
- Conversion fees levied by broker to convert ADR shares into local shares for 7,000 ADR amount to $1,250.
- Functional currency is US$.

Liquidation Methodology

Weighted average

FX Rates

Date	FX Rate
11-Jan-X1	1.6505
13-Jan-X1	1.6525
25-Jan-X1	1.6484
27-Jan-X1	1.6444
31-Jan-X1	1.6311
5-Feb-X1	1.6255
7-Feb-X1	1.6201
28-Feb-X1	1.6201

Market Rate

PetroGold ADR

January 31: $36.00

February 28: $40.00

PetroGold local
January 31: BRL 27.00
February 28: BRL 30.50

Trade Currency BRL

T-1 On Sale of Equity Shares and Brokerage

Journal Entry

Date	Particulars	Debit (BRL)	Credit (BRL)
5-Feb-X1	Silver Man Account	413,000.00	
	To Investments—Equity Shares—Trading Account		413,000.00
	(Being the shares sold @ BRL 29.50 per share through the broker—Silver Man)		
5-Feb-X1	Investments—Equity Shares—Trading Account	1,240.00	
	To Silver Man Account		1,240.00
	(Being the brokerage payable to the broker—Silver Man on sale of equity shares)		

T-2 On Conversion of ADRs into Local Equity Shares

The cost of the equity shares sold is arrived at by first valuing the ADRs and computing the cost of acquisition based on the liquidation methodology, and then converting such ADR cost into local equity shares at the FX rate prevailing on the date of conversion. Hence, there will be not be any realized gains in ADRs, as upon conversion the ADRs are converted at cost into the local equity shares. There will be realized gains in the trade currency—BRL in this example.

Also, it is pertinent to note that the books of accounts in BRL will show a credit balance in the Investments ADR account. Ultimately when this is revalued in the base currency, this gets squared up with the debit balance in the Investments ADR account.

Calculation of ADRs converted into equity shares (BRL)	US$	BRL
(a) Cost of acquisition of 7,000 ADRs	245,735.00	
(b) Cost of acquisition of 4,000 ADRs	148,444.00	
(c) Weighted average cost of 7,000 ADRs	250,841.18	
(d) Converted into local equity shares @ 1.6255 (in BRL)		**407,742.34**

Journal Entry

Date	Particulars	Debit (BRL)	Credit (BRL)
5-Feb-X1	Investments—Equity Shares—Trading Account	407,742.34	
	To Investments—ADR Account		407,742.34
	(Being the ADRs converted into local equity shares)		

T-3 On Recording Profit/Loss on Sale of Shares

Calculation of capital gains	BRL
(a) Net sale consideration of 7,000 shares after brokerage	411,760.00
(b) Weighted average cost of acquisition of 7,000 shares	407,742.34
(c) Realized capital gains = (a) − (b)	**4,017.66**

Journal Entry

Date	Particulars	Debit (BRL)	Credit (BRL)
5-Feb-X1	Investments—Equity Shares—Trading Account	4,017.66	
	To Realized Capital Gains/Loss Equity—Trading Account		4,017.66
	(Being the realized gain on sale of equity shares)		

T-4 On Receipt of Contracted Sum

Journal Entry

Date	Particulars	Debit (BRL)	Credit (BRL)
7-Feb-X1	Bank–BRL Account	411,760.00	
	To Silver Man Account		411,760.00
	(Being the receipt of sale consideration from the broker on sale of shares after adjusting for the brokerage)		

General Ledger Accounts

Investments—Equity Shares—Trading Account

Date	Particulars	Debit (BRL)	Date	Particulars	Credit (BRL)
5-Feb-X1	To Investments—ADR Account	407,742.34			
			5-Feb-X1	By Silver Man Account	413,000.00
5-Feb-X1	To Silver Man Account	1,240.00			
5-Feb-X1	To Realized Capital Gains/Loss Equity—Trading Account	4,017.66			
28-Feb-X1	Total	**413,000.00**	28-Feb-X1	Total	**413,000.00**

Investments—ADR Account

Date	Particulars	Debit (BRL)	Date	Particulars	Credit (BRL)
			5-Feb-X1	By Investments—Equity Shares—Trading Account	407,742.34
28-Feb-X1	To Balance	407,742.34			
28-Feb-X1	Total	**407,742.34**	28-Feb-X1	Total	**407,742.34**
			28-Feb-X1	By Balance	407,742.34

Silver Man Account

Date	Particulars	Debit (BRL)	Date	Particulars	Credit (BRL)
5-Feb-X1	To Investments—Equity Shares—Trading Account	413,000.00			
			5-Feb-X1	By Investments—Equity Shares—Trading Account	1,240.00
			7-Feb-X1	By Bank–BRL Account	411,760.00
28-Feb-X1	Total	**413,000.00**	28-Feb-X1	Total	**413,000.00**

Realized Capital Gains/Loss Equity—Trading Account

Date	Particulars	Debit (BRL)	Date	Particulars	Credit (BRL)
			5-Feb-X1	By Investments—Equity Shares—Trading Account	4,017.66
28-Feb-X1	To Balance	4,017.66			
28-Feb-X1	Total	**4,017.66**	28-Feb-X1	Total	**4,017.66**
			28-Feb-X1	By Balance	4,017.66

Bank—BRL Account

Date	Particulars	Debit (BRL)	Date	Particulars	Credit (BRL)
7-Feb-X1	To Silver Man Account	411,760.00			
			28-Feb-X1	By Balance	411,760.00
28-Feb-X1	Total	**411,760.00**	28-Feb-X1	Total	**411,760.00**
28-Feb-X1	To Balance	411,760.00			

Trial Balance

As of 28-Feb-X1 (BRL)

Particulars	Debit	Credit
Current Assets		
Bank–BRL Account	411,760.00	
Investments		
Investments—ADR Account		407,742.34
Income		
Realized Capital Gains/Loss Equity—Trading Account		4,017.66
Total	**411,760.00**	**411,760.00**

Income Statement

For the period ending 28-Feb-X1

Expenses	BRL	Income	BRL
Direct Expenses		**Direct Income**	
Net Profit Carryover	4,017.66	Realized Capital Gains/Loss Equity—Trading Account	4,017.66
Total	**4,017.66**	Total	**4,017.66**

Balance Sheet

As of 28-Feb-X1

Liabilities	BRL	Assets	BRL
Capital Account	Nil	**Investments**	Nil
Current Liabilities			
Investments—ADR Account	407,742.34	**Current Assets**	
Profit & Loss Account		Bank–BRL Account	411,760.00
Opening Balance	Nil		
Current Period	4,017.66		
Total	**411,760.00**	Total	**411,760.00**

Functional Currency US$

F-1 On Purchase of ADR and Assessment of Brokerage

Journal Entry

Date	Particulars	Debit (US$)	Credit (US$)
11-Jan-X1	Investments—ADR Account	245,000.00	
	To Silver Man Account		245,000.00
	(Being the ADR bought through the broker—Silver Man)		
11-Jan-X1	Investments—ADR Account	735.00	
	To Silver Man Account		735.00
	(Being brokerage payable to the broker on purchase of equity shares)		

F-2 On Payment of Contracted Sum

Journal Entry

Date	Particulars	Debit (US$)	Credit (US$)
13-Jan-X1	Silver Man Account	245,735.00	
	To Bank–US$ Account		245,735.00
	(Being the payment made to the broker on purchase of shares together with the brokerage)		

F-3 On Purchase of ADR and Assessment of Brokerage

Journal Entry

Date	Particulars	Debit (US$)	Credit (US$)
25-Jan-X1	Investments—ADR Account	148,000.00	
	To Silver Man Account		148,000.00
	(Being the ADR bought through the broker—Silver Man)		
25-Jan-X1	Investments—ADR Account	444.00	
	To Silver Man Account		444.00
	(Being brokerage payable to the broker on purchase of equity shares)		

F-4 On Payment of Contracted Sum

Journal Entry

Date	Particulars	Debit (US$)	Credit (US$)
27-Jan-X1	Silver Man Account	148,444.00	
	To Bank–US$ Account		148,444.00
	(Being the payment made to the broker on purchase of shares together with the brokerage)		

F-5 Mark-to-market at End of Reporting Period

Mark-to-market at end of reporting period: 31 Jan X1	US$
(a) Cost of acquisition of 7,000 ADRs including brokerage	245,735.00
(b) Cost of acquisition of 4,000 ADRs including brokerage	148,444.00
(c) Total cost of acquisition	394,179.00
(d) Market value at the end of reporting period	396,000.00
(e) Unrealized gain (d) − (c)	1,821.00

Journal Entry

Date	Particulars	Debit (US$)	Credit (US$)
31-Jan-X1	Investments—ADR Account	1,821.00	
	To Unrealized Capital Gains/Loss—ADR Account		1,821.00
	(Being the unrealized gains on ADRs)		

F-6 Reversal of Mark-to-market Entry

Journal Entry

Date	Particulars	Debit (US$)	Credit (US$)
1-Feb-X1	Unrealized Capital Gains/Loss—ADR Account	1,821.00	
	To Investments—ADR Account		1,821.00
	(Being the reversal of mark-to-market on ADRs)		

F-7 On Sale of Equity Shares and Assessment of Brokerage (T-1 @ FX Rate: 1.6255)

Journal Entry

Date	Particulars	Debit (US$)	Credit (US$)
5-Feb-X1	Silver Man Account	254,075.67	
	To Investments—Equity Shares—Trading Account		254,075.67
	(Being the shares sold through the broker—Silver Man)		
5-Feb-X1	Investments—Equity Shares—Trading Account	762.84	
	To Silver Man Account		762.84
	(Being the brokerage payable to the broker—Silver Man on sale of shares)		

F-8 Conversion Fees

Journal Entry

Date	Particulars	Debit (US$)	Credit (US$)
5-Feb-X1	ADR Conversion Charges Account	1,250.00	
	To Bank–US$ Account		1,250.00
	(Being the conversion charges paid for converting the ADRs into local equity shares in BRL)		

F-9 On Conversion of ADRs into Local Equity Shares (T-2 @ FX Rate: 1.6255)

Calculation of ADRs conversion into local equity shares (BRL)	US$
(a) Cost of acquisition of 7,000 ADRs	245,735.00
(b) Cost of acquisition of 4,000 ADRs	148,444.00
(c) Weighted average cost of 7,000 ADRs	**250,841.18**

Journal Entry

Date	Particulars	Debit (US$)	Credit (US$)
5-Feb-X1	Investments—Equity Shares—Trading Account	250,841.18	
	To Investments—ADR Account		250,841.18
	(Being the ADRs converted into local equity shares)		

F-10 On Recording Profit/Loss on Sale of Shares (T-3 @ FX Rate: 1.6255)

Calculation of capital gains	BRL	US$
(a) Net sale consideration of 7,000 shares after brokerage	411,760.00	253,312.83
(b) Weighted average cost of acquisition of 7,000 shares	407,742.34	250,841.18
(c) Realized capital gains = (a) – (b)	**4,017.66**	**2,471.65**

Journal Entry

Date	Particulars	Debit (US$)	Credit (US$)
5-Feb-X1	Investments—Equity Shares—Trading Account	2,471.65	
	To Realized Capital Gains/Loss Equity—Trading Account		2,471.65
	(Being the profit realized on sale of equity shares)		

F-11 On Receipt of Contracted Sum (T-4 @ FX Rate: 1.6201)

Journal Entry

Date	Particulars	Debit (US$)	Credit (US$)
7-Feb-X1	Bank–BRL Account	254,157.15	
	To Silver Man Account		254,157.15
	(Being the amount received from the broker on sale of shares together after brokerage)		

F-12 Recording Currency Gains/Loss on Settlement to Broker (Consummated FX Translation Entry)

Realized currency gains/loss on settlement date: 7-Feb-X1	US$
(a) Net realization amount after brokerage as of 5-Feb-X1	253,312.83
(b) Settlement amount received as on 7-Feb-X1	254,156.15
(c) Realized currency gains on settlement = (b) – (a)	**844.32**

Journal Entry

Date	Particulars	Debit (US$)	Credit (US$)
7-Feb-X1	Silver Man Account	844.32	
	To Realized Currency Gains/Loss Account		844.32
	(Being the realized currency gains on settlement)		

F-13 Mark-to-market at End of Reporting Period (Transient FX Translation Entry)

Mark-to-market at end of reporting period: 28 Feb X1	**US$**
(a) Cost of acquisition of 4,000 ADRs including brokerage	143,337.82
(b) Market value at the end of reporting period	160,000.00
(c) Unrealized gain (b) − (a)	16,662.18

Journal Entry

Date	Particulars	Debit (US$)	Credit (US$)
28-Feb-X1	Investments—ADR Account	16,662.18	
	To Unrealized Capital Gains/Loss—ADR Account		16,662.18
	(Being the unrealized capital gains on 4,000 ADRs)		

General Ledger Accounts

Investments—ADR Account

Date	Particulars	Debit (US$)	Date	Particulars	Credit (US$)
11-Jan-X1	To Silver Man Account	245,000.00			
11-Jan-X1	To Silver Man Account	735.00			
25-Jan-X1	To Silver Man Account	148,000.00			
25-Jan-X1	To Silver Man Account	444.00			
31-Jan-X1	To Unrealized Capital Gains/Loss—ADR Account	1,821.00			
			1-Feb-X1	By Unrealized Capital Gains/Loss—ADR Account	1,821.00
			5-Feb-X1	By Investments—Equity Shares—Trading Account	250,841.18
28-Feb-X1	To Unrealized Capital Gains/Loss—ADR Account	16,662.18			
			28-Feb-X1	By Balance	160,000.00
28-Feb-X1	Total	**412,662.18**	28-Feb-X1	Total	**412,662.18**
28-Feb-X1	To Balance	160,000.00			

Investments—Equity Shares—Trading Account

Date	Particulars	Debit (US$)	Date	Particulars	Credit (US$)
5-Feb-X1	To Investments —ADR Account	250,841.18			
			5-Feb-X1	By Silver Man Account	254,075.67
5-Feb-X1	To Silver Man Account	762.84			
5-Feb-X1	To Realized Capital Gains/ Loss Equity— Trading Account	2,471.65			
28-Feb-X1	Total	**254,075.67**	28-Feb-X1	Total	**254,075.67**

ADR Conversion Charges Account

Date	Particulars	Debit (US$)	Date	Particulars	Credit (US$)
5-Feb-X1	To Bank–US$ Account	1,250.00			
			28-Feb-X1	By Balance	1,250.00
28-Feb-X1	Total	**1,250.00**	28-Feb-X1	Total	**1,250.00**
28-Feb-X1	To Balance	1,250.00			

Realized Currency Gains/Loss Account

Date	Particulars	Debit (US$)	Date	Particulars	Credit (US$)
			7-Feb-X1	By Silver Man Account	844.32
28-Feb-X1	To Balance	844.32			
28-Feb-X1	Total	**844.32**	28-Feb-X1	Total	**844.32**
			28-Feb-X1	By Balance	844.32

Realized Capital Gains/Loss Equity—Trading Account

Date	Particulars	Debit (US$)	Date	Particulars	Credit (US$)
			5-Feb-X1	By Investments— Equity Shares— Trading Account	2,471.65
28-Feb-X1	To Balance	2,471.65			
28-Feb-X1	Total	**2,471.65**	28-Feb-X1	Total	**2,471.65**
			28-Feb-X1	By Balance	2,471.65

Unrealized Capital Gains/Loss—ADR Account

Date	Particulars	Debit (US$)	Date	Particulars	Credit (US$)
			31-Jan-X1	By Investments—ADR Account	1,821.00
1-Feb-X1	To Investments—ADR Account	1,821.00			
			28-Feb-X1	By Investments—ADR Account	16,662.18
28-Feb-X1	To Balance	16,662.18			
28-Feb-X1	Total	**18,483.18**	28-Feb-X1	Total	**18,483.18**
			28-Feb-X1	By Balance	16,662.18

Silver Man Account

Date	Particulars	Debit (US$)	Date	Particulars	Credit (US$)
			11-Jan-X1	By Investments—ADR Account	245,000.00
			11-Jan-X1	By Investments—ADR Account	735.00
13-Jan-X1	To Bank–US$ Account	245,735.00			
			25-Jan-X1	By Investments—ADR Account	148,000.00
			25-Jan-X1	By Investments—ADR Account	444.00
27-Jan-X1	To Bank–US$ Account	148,444.00			
5-Feb-X1	To Investments—Equity Shares—Trading Account	254,075.67			
			5-Feb-X1	By Investments—Equity Shares—Trading Account	762.84
			7-Feb-X1	By Bank–BRL Account	254,157.15
7-Feb-X1	To Realized Currency Gains/Loss Account	844.32			
28-Feb-X1	Total	**649,098.99**	28-Feb-X1	Total	**649,098.99**

Bank–US$ Account

Date	Particulars	Debit (US$)	Date	Particulars	Credit (US$)
			13-Jan-X1	By Silver Man Account	245,735.00
			27-Jan-X1	By Silver Man Account	148,444.00
			5-Feb-X1	By ADR Conversion Charges Account	1,250.00
28-Feb-X1	To Balance	395,429.00			
28-Feb-X1	Total	**395,429.00**	28-Feb-X1	Total	**395,429.00**
			28-Feb-X1	By Balance	395,429.00

Bank–BRL Account

Date	Particulars	Debit (US$)	Date	Particulars	Credit (US$)
7-Feb-X1	To Silver Man Account	254,157.15			
			28-Feb-X1	By Balance	254,157.15
28-Feb-X1	Total	**254,157.15**	28-Feb-X1	Total	**254,157.15**
28-Feb-X1	To Balance	254,157.15			

Trial Balance

As of 28-Feb-X1 (US$)

Particulars	Debit	Credit
Current Liabilities		
Bank–US$ Account		395,429.00
Investments		
Investments—ADR Account	160,000.00	
Current Assets		
Bank–BRL Account	254,157.15	
Income		
Realized Capital Gains/Loss—Equity Trading Account		2,471.65
Realized Currency Gains/Loss Account		844.32
Unrealized Capital Gains/Loss—Equity Shares—Trading Account		16,662.18
Direct Expenses		
ADR Conversion Charges Account	1,250.00	
Total	**415,407.15**	**415,407.15**

Income Statement

For the period ending 28-Feb-X1

Expenses	US$	Income	US$
Direct Expenses		**Direct Income**	
ADR Conversion Charges Account	1,250.00	Realized Capital Gains/Loss Equity—Trading Account	2,471.65
		Realized Currency Gains/Loss Account	844.32
		Unrealized Capital Gains/Loss Equity—Trading Account	16,662.18
Net Profit Carryover	18,728.15		
Total	**19,978.15**	Total	**19,978.15**

Balance Sheet

As of 28-Feb-X1

Liabilities	US$	Assets	US$
Capital Account	Nil	**Investments**	
Current Liabilities		Investments—ADR Account	160,000.00
Bank–US$ Account	395,429.00	**Current Assets**	
		Bank–BRL Account	254,157.15
Profit & Loss Account			
Opening Balance	Nil		
Current Period	18,728.15		
Total	**414,157.15**	Total	**414,157.15**

ADR Shares in MXN

Alberto Ltd. traded in Coco Cola shares in a Mexican stock exchange through Goldman Sachs and the details are as follows. Journal entries, general ledger, trial balance, income statement, and balance sheet for Alberto Ltd. for the period January 1 through February 28 are prepared.

Trade Details

Date	Product	CCY	Quantity	Rate	B/S	Brokerage
11-Jan-X1	Coco Cola—ADR	US$	2,500	53.50	B	US$ 400
25-Jan-X1	Coco Cola—ADR	US$	5,500	54.50	B	US$ 900
28-Jan-X1	Coco Cola—ADR	US$	2,800	55.50	S	US$ 460
5-Feb-X1	Coco Cola—Local	MXN	30,000	59.50	S	MXN 5,175

Other Details

- One ADR converts to 10 local shares in MXN currency.
- Settlement: T + 2.
- Conversion fees levied by broker to convert ADR shares into local shares amount to $810.
- Functional currency is US$.

Liquidation Methodology

FIFO

FX Rates

Date	FX Rate
11-Jan-X1	10.6505
13-Jan-X1	10.6525
25-Jan-X1	10.6484
28-Jan-X1	10.6444
31-Jan-X1	10.6311
5-Feb-X1	10.6255
7-Feb-X1	10.6201
28-Feb-X1	10.6201

Market Rate

Coco-Cola ADR

January 31: $56.00

February 28: $52.00

Coco-Cola local

January 31: MXN 55.00

February 28: MXN 51.00

Trade Currency MXN

T-1 On Sale of Equity Shares and Brokerage

Journal Entry

Date	Particulars	Debit (MXN)	Credit (MXN)
5-Feb-X1	Goldman Sachs Account	1,785,000.00	
	To Investments—Equity Shares—Trading Account		1,785,000.00
	(Being the shares sold @ MXN59.50 per share through the broker—Silver Man)		
5-Feb-X1	Investments—Equity Shares—Trading Account	5,175.00	
	To Goldman Sachs Account		5,175.00
	(Being the brokerage payable to the broker—Goldman Sachs on sale of equity shares)		

T-2 On Conversion of ADRs into Local Equity Shares

The cost of the equity shares sold is arrived at by first valuing the ADRs and computing the cost of acquisition based on the liquidation methodology and then converting such ADR cost into local equity shares at the FX rate prevailing on the date of conversion. Hence, there will not be any realized gains in ADRs, as the ADRs are converted at cost into the local equity shares. There will be realized gains in the trade currency—MXN in this example.

Also it is pertinent to note that the books of accounts in MXN will show a credit balance in the Investments ADR account. Ultimately when this is revalued in the base currency it gets squared up with the debit balance in the Investments ADR account.

Calculation of cost of ADRs converted into MXN	Amount
(a) Cost of 3,000 ADRs (US$)	163,990.91
(b) Cost of 30,000 shares (163,990.91 × 10.6255) (MXN)	**1,742,485.40**

Journal Entry

Date	Particulars	Debit (MXN)	Credit (MXN)
5-Feb-X1	Investments—Equity Shares—Trading Account	1,742,485.40	
	To Investments—ADR Account		1,742,485.40
	(Being the ADRs converted into local equity shares)		

T-3 On Recording Profit/Loss on Sale of Shares

Calculation of capital gains	MXN
(a) Net sale consideration of 30,000 shares after brokerage	1,779,825.00
(b) FIFO cost of acquisition of 30,000 shares	1,742,485.40
(c) Realized capital gains = (a) – (b)	**37,339.60**

Journal Entry

Date	Particulars	Debit (MXN)	Credit (MXN)
5-Feb-X1	Investments—Equity Shares—Trading Account	37,339.60	
	To Realized Capital Gains/Loss Equity—Trading Account		37,339.60
	(Being the realized gain on sale of equity shares)		

T-4 On Receipt of Contracted Sum

Journal Entry

Date	Particulars	Debit (MXN)	Credit (MXN)
7-Feb-X1	Bank–MXN Account	1,779,825.00	
	To Goldman Sachs Account		1,779,825.00
	(Being the receipt of sale consideration from the broker on sale of shares after adjusting for the brokerage)		

General Ledger Accounts

Investments—Equity Shares—Trading Account

Date	Particulars	Debit (MXN)	Date	Particulars	Credit (MXN)
5-Feb-X1	To Investments—ADR Account	1,742,485.40			
			5-Feb-X1	By Goldman Sachs Account	1,785,000.00
5-Feb-X1	To Goldman Sachs Account	5,175.00			
5-Feb-X1	To Realized Capital Gains/Loss Equity—Trading Account	37,339.60			
28-Feb-X1	Total	**1,785,000.00**	28-Feb-X1	Total	**1,785,000.00**

Investments—ADR Account

Date	Particulars	Debit (MXN)	Date	Particulars	Credit (MXN)
			5-Feb-X1	By Investments—Equity Shares—Trading Account	1,742,485.40
28-Feb-X1	To Balance	1,742,485.40			
28-Feb-X1	Total	**1,742,485.40**	28-Feb-X1	Total	**1,742,485.40**
			28-Feb-X1	By Balance	1,742,485.40

Goldman Sachs Account

Date	Particulars	Debit (MXN)	Date	Particulars	Credit (MXN)
5-Feb-X1	To Investments—Equity Shares—Trading Account	1,785,000.00			
			5-Feb-X1	By Investments—Equity Shares—Trading Account	5,175.00
			7-Feb-X1	By Bank-MXN Account	1,779,825.00
28-Feb-X1	Total	**1,785,000.00**	28-Feb-X1	Total	**1,785,000.00**

Realized Capital Gains/Loss Equity—Trading Account

Date	Particulars	Debit (MXN)	Date	Particulars	Credit (MXN)
			5-Feb-X1	By Investments—Equity Shares—Trading Account	37,339.60
28-Feb-X1	To Balance	37,339.60			
28-Feb-X1	Total	**37,339.60**	28-Feb-X1	Total	**37,339.60**
			28-Feb-X1	By Balance	37,339.60

Bank—MXN Account

Date	Particulars	Debit (MXN)	Date	Particulars	Credit (MXN)
7-Feb-X1	To Goldman Sachs Account	1,779,825.00			
			28-Feb-X1	By Balance	1,779,825.00
28-Feb-X1	Total	**1,779,825.00**	28-Feb-X1	Total	**1,779,825.00**
28-Feb-X1	To Balance	1,779,825.00			

Trial Balance
As of 28-Feb-X1 (MXN)

Particulars	Debit	Credit
Current Assets		
Bank–MXN Account	1,779,825.00	
Investments		
Investments—ADR Account		1,742,485.40
Income		
Realized Capital Gains/Loss Equity—Trading Account		37,339.60
Total	**1,779,825.00**	**1,779,825.00**

Income Statement
For the period ending 28-Feb-X1

Expenses	MXN	Income	MXN
Direct Expenses		**Direct Income**	
Gross Profit Carryover	37,339.60	Realized Capital Gains/Loss —Equity Trading Account	37,339.60
Total	**37,339.60**	Total	**37,339.60**

Balance Sheet
As of 28-Feb-X1

Liabilities	MXN	Assets	MXN
Capital Account	Nil	**Investments**	Nil
Current Liabilities			
Investments—ADR Account	1,742,485.40	**Current Assets**	
Profit & Loss Account		Bank–MXN Account	1,779,825.00
Opening Balance	Nil		
Current Period	37,339.60		
Total	**1,779,825.00**	Total	**1,779,825.00**

Functional Currency US$

F-1 On Purchase of ADR and Assessment of Brokerage

Journal Entry

Date	Particulars	Debit (US$)	Credit (US$)
11-Jan-X1	Investments—ADR Account	133,750.00	
	To Goldman Sachs Account		133,750.00
	(Being the ADR bought through the broker—Silver Man)		
11-Jan-X1	Investments—ADR Account	400.00	
	To Goldman Sachs Account		400.00
	(Being brokerage payable to the broker on purchase of 2,500 equity shares)		

F-2 On Payment of Contracted Sum

Journal Entry

Date	Particulars	Debit (US$)	Credit (US$)
13-Jan-X1	Goldman Sachs Account	134,150.00	
	To Bank–US$ Account		134,150.00
	(Being the payment made to the broker on purchase of 2,500 shares together with the brokerage)		

F-3 On Purchase of ADR and Assessment of Brokerage

Journal Entry

Date	Particulars	Debit (US$)	Credit (US$)
25-Jan-X1	Investments—ADR Account	299,750.00	
	To Goldman Sachs Account		299,750.00
	(Being the ADR bought through the broker—Goldman Sachs)		
25-Jan-X1	Investments—ADR Account	900.00	
	To Goldman Sachs Account		900.00
	(Being brokerage payable to the broker on purchase of 5,500 equity shares)		

F-4 On Payment of Contracted Sum

Journal Entry

Date	Particulars	Debit (US$)	Credit (US$)
27-Jan-X1	Goldman Sachs Account	300,650.00	
	To Bank–US$ Account		300,650.00
	(Being the payment made to the broker on purchase of 5,500 shares together with the brokerage)		

F-5 On Sale of ADR and Assessment of Brokerage

Journal Entry

Date	Particulars	Debit (US$)	Credit (US$)
28-Jan-X1	Goldman Sachs Account	155,400.00	
	To Investments—ADR Account		155,400.00
	(Being the shares sold through the broker—Goldman Sachs)		
28-Jan-X1	Investments—ADR Account	460.00	
	To Goldman Sachs Account		460.00
	(Being the brokerage payable to the broker—Goldman Sachs on sale of 2,800 shares)		

F-6 On Recording Profit/Loss on Sale of Shares

Calculation of capital gains	**US$**
(a) Net sale consideration of 2,800 shares after brokerage	154,940.00
(b) Cost of acquisition of 2,500 shares including brokerage	134,150.00
(c) Proportionate cost of acquisition of 300 shares [(300,650.00 × 300) / 5500]	16,399.09
(d) Total cost of acquisition of 1,700 shares	150,549.09
(e) Realized gains = (a) – (d)	**4,390.91**

Journal Entry

Date	Particulars	Debit (US$)	Credit (US$)
28-Jan-X1	Investments—ADR Account	4,390.91	
	To Realized Capital Gains/Loss —ADR Account		4,390.91
	(Being the profit realized on sale of ADR shares)		

F-7 On Receipt of Contracted Sum

Journal Entry

Date	Particulars	Debit (US$)	Credit (US$)
30-Jan-X1	Bank–MXN Account	154,940.00	
	To Goldman Sachs Account		154,940.00
	(Being the amount received from the broker on sale of shares after brokerage)		

F-8 Mark-to-market at End of Reporting Period

Mark-to-market at end of reporting period: 31 Jan X1	**US$**
(a) Cost of acquisition of 5,200 ADRs including brokerage	284,250.91
(b) Market value at the end of reporting period (5200 × 56)	291,200.00
(c) Unrealized gains (b)–(a)	6,949.09

Journal Entry

Date	Particulars	Debit (US$)	Credit (US$)
31-Jan-X1	Investments—ADR Account	6,949.09	
	To Unrealized Capital Gains/Loss—ADR Account		6,949.09
	(Being the unrealized gains on ADRs)		

F-9 Reversal of Mark-to-market Entry

Journal Entry

Date	Particulars	Debit (US$)	Credit (US$)
1-Feb-X1	Unrealized Capital Gains/Loss—ADR Account	6,949.09	
	To Investments—ADR Account		6,949.09
	(Being the reversal of mark-to-market on ADRs)		

F-10 On Sale of Equity Shares and Brokerage (T-1 @ FX Rate: 10.6255)

Journal Entry

Date	Particulars	Debit (US$)	Credit (US$)
5-Feb-X1	Goldman Sachs Account	167,992.10	
	To Investments—Equity Shares—Trading Account		167,992.10
	(Being the shares sold through the broker—Goldman Sachs)		
5-Feb-X1	Investments—Equity Shares—Trading Account	487.04	
	To Goldman Sachs Account		487.04
	(Being the brokerage payable to the broker—Goldman Sachs on sale of shares)		

F-11 On Conversion of ADRs into Local Equity Shares (T-2 @ FX Rate: 10.6255)

Calculation of cost of ADRs converted into local equity shares	**US$**
(a) Cost of acquisition of 5,500 ADRs	300,650.00
(b) Proportionate cost of 3,000 ADRs [300,650 × 3,000) / 5,500]	**163,990.91**

Journal Entry

Date	Particulars	Debit (US$)	Credit (US$)
5-Feb-X1	Investments—Equity Shares—Trading Account	163,990.91	
	To Investments—ADR Account		163,990.91
	(Being the ADRs converted into local equity shares)		

F -12 On Recording Profit/Loss on Sale of Shares (T-3 @ FX Rate: 10.6255)

Calculation of capital gains	**MXN**	**US$**
(a) Net sale consideration of 30,000 shares after brokerage	1,779,825.00	167,505.06
(b) FIFO cost of acquisition of 30,000 shares	1,742,485.40	163,990.91
(c) Realized capital gains = (a) – (b)	**37,339.60**	**3,514.15**

Journal Entry

Date	Particulars	Debit (US$)	Credit (US$)
5-Feb-X1	Investments—Equity Shares—Trading Account	3,514.15	
	To Realized Capital Gains/Loss Equity—Trading Account		3,514.15
	(Being the profit realized on sale of equity shares)		

F-13 Conversion Fees

Journal Entry

Date	Particulars	Debit (US$)	Credit (US$)
5-Feb-X1	ADR Conversion Charges Account	810.00	
	To Bank–US$ Account		810.00
	(ADR conversion charges paid)		

F-14 On Receipt of Contracted Sum (T-4 @ FX Rate: 10.6201)

Journal Entry

Date	Particulars	Debit (US$)	Credit (US$)
7-Feb-X1	Bank–US$ Account	167,590.23	
	To Goldman Sachs Account		167,590.23
	(Being the amount received from the broker on sale of shares after brokerage)		

F-15 Recording Currency Gains/Loss on Settlement to Broker (Consummated FX Translation Entry)

Currency gains/loss on settlement date: 7-Feb-X1	US$
(a) Net sale consideration after brokerage as of 5-Feb-X1	167,505.06
(b) Settlement amount received on 7-Feb-X1	167,590.23
(c) Realized currency gains on settlement = (a) – (b)	**85.17**

Journal Entry

Date	Particulars	Debit (US$)	Credit (US$)
7-Feb-X1	Goldman Sachs Account	85.17	
	To Realized Currency Gains/Loss Account		85.17
	(Being the realized currency gains on settlement)		

F-16 Mark-to-market at End of Reporting Period (Transient FX Translation Entry)

Journal Entry

Date	Particulars	Debit (US$)	Credit (US$)
28-Feb-X1	Unrealized Capital Gains/Loss—ADR Account	5,860.00	
	To Investments—ADR Account		5,860.00
	(Being the unrealized capital loss on 2,200 ADRs)		

General Ledger Accounts

Investments—ADR Account

Date	Particulars	Debit (US$)	Date	Particulars	Credit (US$)
11-Jan-X1	To Goldman Sachs Account	133,750.00			
11-Jan-X1	To Goldman Sachs Account	400.00			
25-Jan-X1	To Goldman Sachs Account	299,750.00			
25-Jan-X1	To Goldman Sachs Account	900.00			
			28-Jan-X1	By Goldman Sachs Account	155,400.00
28-Jan-X1	To Goldman Sachs Account	460.00			
28-Jan-X1	To Realized Capital Gains/Loss — ADR Account	4,390.91			
31-Jan-X1	To Unrealized Capital Gains/Loss—ADR Account	6,949.09			
			1-Feb-X1	By Unrealized Capital Gains/Loss—ADR Account	6,949.09
			5-Feb-X1	By Investments—Equity Shares—Trading Account	163,990.91
			28-Feb-X1	By Unrealized Capital Gains/Loss—ADR Account	5,860.00
			28-Feb-X1	By Balance	114,400.00
28-Feb-X1	Total	**446,600.00**	28-Feb-X1	Total	**446,600.00**
28-Feb-X1	To Balance	114,400.00			

Investments—Equity Shares—Trading Account

Date	Particulars	Debit (US$)	Date	Particulars	Credit (US$)
5-Feb-X1	To Investments—ADR Account	163,990.91			
			5-Feb-X1	By Goldman Sachs Account	167,992.10
5-Feb-X1	To Goldman Sachs Account	487.04			
5-Feb-X1	To Realized Capital Gains/Loss Equity—Trading Account	3,514.15			
28-Feb-X1	Total	**167,992.10**	28-Feb-X1	Total	**167,992.10**

ADR Conversion Charges Account

Date	Particulars	Debit (US$)	Date	Particulars	Credit (US$)
5-Feb-X1	To Bank–US$ Account	810.00			
			28-Feb-X1	By Balance	810.00
28-Feb-X1	Total	**810.00**	28-Feb-X1	Total	**810.00**
28-Feb-X1	To Balance	810.00			

Realized Currency Gains/Loss Account

Date	Particulars	Debit (US$)	Date	Particulars	Credit (US$)
			7-Feb-X1	By Goldman Sachs Account	85.17
28-Feb-X1	To Balance	85.17			
28-Feb-X1	Total	**85.17**	28-Feb-X1	Total	**85.17**
			28-Feb-X1	By Balance	85.17

Realized Capital Gains/Loss—ADR Account

Date	Particulars	Debit (US$)	Date	Particulars	Credit (US$)
			28-Jan-X1	By Investments—ADR Account	4,390.91
28-Feb-X1	To Balance	4,390.91			
28-Feb-X1	Total	**4,390.91**	28-Feb-X1	Total	**4,390.91**
			28-Feb-X1	By Balance	4,390.91

Realized Capital Gains/Loss—Equity Trading Account

Date	Particulars	Debit (US$)	Date	Particulars	Credit (US$)
			5-Feb-X1	By Investments—Equity Shares—Trading Account	3,514.15
28-Feb-X1	To Balance	3,514.15			
28-Feb-X1	Total	**3,514.15**	28-Feb-X1	Total	**3,514.15**
			28-Feb-X1	By Balance	3,514.15

Unrealized Capital Gains/Loss—ADR Account

Date	Particulars	Debit (US$)	Date	Particulars	Credit (US$)
			31-Jan-X1	By Investments—ADR Account	6,949.09
1-Feb-X1	To Investments—ADR Account	6,949.09			
28-Feb-X1	To Investments—ADR Account	5,860.00			
			28-Feb-X1	By Balance	5,860.00

Unrealized Capital Gains/Loss—ADR Account (*Cont'd*)

Date	Particulars	Debit (US$)	Date	Particulars	Credit (US$)
28-Feb-X1	Total	**12,809.09**	28-Feb-X1	Total	**12,809.09**
28-Feb-X1	To Balance	5,860.00			

Goldman Sachs Account

Date	Particulars	Debit (US$)	Date	Particulars	Credit (US$)
			11-Jan-X1	By Investments—ADR Account	133,750.00
			11-Jan-X1	By Investments—ADR Account	400.00
13-Jan-X1	To Bank–US$ Account	134,150.00			
			25-Jan-X1	By Investments—ADR Account	299,750.00
			25-Jan-X1	By Investments—ADR Account	900.00
27-Jan-X1	To Bank–US$ Account	300,650.00			
28-Jan-X1	To Investments—ADR Account	155,400.00			
			28-Jan-X1	By Investments—ADR Account	460.00
			30-Jan-X1	By Bank US$ Account	154,940.00
5-Feb-X1	To Investments—Equity Shares—Trading Account	167,992.10			
			5-Feb-X1	By Investments—Equity Shares—Trading Account	487.04
			7-Feb-X1	By Bank–MXN Account	167,590.23
7-Feb-X1	To Realized Currency Gains/Loss Account	85.17			
28-Feb-X1	Total	**758,277.27**	28-Feb-X1	Total	**758,277.27**

Bank–US$ Account

Date	Particulars	Debit (US$)	Date	Particulars	Credit (US$)
			13-Jan-X1	By Goldman Sachs Account	134,150.00
			27-Jan-X1	By Goldman Sachs Account	300,650.00
30-Jan-X1	To Goldman Sachs Account	154,940.00			
			5-Feb-X1	By ADR Conversion Charges Account	810.00

Bank–US$ Account (*Cont'd*)

Date	Particulars	Debit (US$)	Date	Particulars	Credit (US$)
28-Feb-X1	To Balance	280,670.00			
28-Feb-X1	Total	**435,610.00**	28-Feb-X1	Total	**435,610.00**
			28-Feb-X1	By Balance	280,670.00

Bank – MXN Account

Date	Particulars	Debit (US$)	Date	Particulars	Credit (US$)
7-Feb-X1	By Goldman Sachs Account	167,590.23			
			28-Feb-X1	By Balance	167,590.23
28-Feb-X1	Total	**167,590.23**	28-Feb-X1	Total	**167,590.23**
28-Feb-X1	To Balance	167,590.23			

Trial Balance

As of 28-Feb-X1 (US$)

Particulars	Debit	Credit
Current Liabilities		
Bank–US$ Account		280,670.00
Investments		
Investments—ADR Account	114,400.00	
Current Assets		
Bank–MXN Account	167,590.23	
Income		
Realized Capital Gains/Loss—Equity Trading Account		3,514.15
Realized Capital Gains/Loss—ADR Account		4,390.91
Realized Currency Gains/Loss Account		85.17
Unrealized Capital Gains/Loss—Equity Shares—Trading Account	5,860.00	
Direct Expenses		
ADR Conversion Charges Account	810.00	
Total	**288,660.23**	**288,660.23**

Income Statement

For the period ending 28-Feb-X1

Expenses	US$	Income	US$
Direct Expenses		**Direct Income**	
ADR Conversion Charges Account	810.00	Realized Capital Gains/Loss Equity—Trading Account	3,514.15
Unrealized Capital Gains/Loss Equity—Trading Account	5,860.00	Realized Currency Gains/Loss Account	85.17
		Realized Capital Gains/Loss —ADR Account	4,390.91
Net Profit Carryover	1,320.23		
Total	**7,990.23**	Total	**7,990.23**

Balance Sheet

As of 28-Feb-X1

Liabilities	US$	Assets	US$
Capital Account	Nil	**Investments**	
Current Liabilities		Investments—ADR Account	114,400.00
Bank–US$ Account	280,670.00	**Current Assets**	
Profit & Loss Account		Bank–MXN Account	167,590.23
Opening Balance	Nil		
Current Period	1,320.23		
Total	**281,990.23**	Total	**281,990.23**

SUMMARY

A depositary receipt (DR) represents an ownership interest in securities of a foreign issuer typically trading outside its home market. A DR is a tradable instrument, and the depositary receipts that are trading in the United States are known as American depositary receipts, or ADRs.

- Depositary receipts that are traded in an international market outside the United States are known as global depositary receipts, or GDRs. Most depositary receipts are quoted and traded in US$ terms. There are some DRs that are traded in euros and pounds sterling.
- Typically, a bank issues depositary receipts and also functions as a depository and issuing agent for the same.
- The depositary receipt is issued against the deposit of domestic ordinary shares in the bank's custody account in the home market.
- These shares continue to remain on deposit with the bank's custodian until the depositary receipts are cancelled.

- When the depositary receipt is returned to the bank that acts as the depository for cancellation, the depositary bank instructs its custodian to deliver the underlying local share as per the instructions received from the party delivering the depositary receipt.
- Each depositary receipt is backed by a specified number of the issuer's local shares, known as the depositary receipt ratio. The ratio is manipulated in such a way that the price of each DR falls in a competitive price range that is considered attractive to the issuer's international peer group. The ratio of depositary receipt to underlying shares can be in whole numbers or fractions, depending upon the local share price.
- There are several benefits of DRs to the issuers as well as the investors.
- An American depositary receipt (ADR) is a stock that trades in the United States but represents a specified number of shares in a foreign corporation. ADRs are bought and sold on American markets just like regular stocks. They were first introduced to the financial markets in 1927.
- The sponsor bank purchases a bulk lot of shares from a foreign company and then bundles the shares into groups for the purpose of reissuing the same in any of the American stock exchanges. The issuing company is required to provide detailed financial information to the sponsor bank.
- Global depositary receipts are depositary receipts in Europe or other non-U.S. markets pursuant to Regulation S promulgated under the U.S. Securities Act of 1933. GDRs are listed on European stock exchanges such as London or Luxembourg.
- A company can choose to combine its GDR offering with an ADR offering into the U.S. markets. Then the ADRs may be publicly listed on a U.S. exchange and offered to retail investors, or may be privately placed with qualified institutional buyers pursuant to Rule 144A.
- There are basically three levels of ADRs available, each having its own merits and disadvantages. The issuing company will choose the level that fits best considering the other requirements.
- Analyzing foreign companies involves further scrutiny than merely looking at the fundamentals. In fact there are innumerable risk factors that determine the value of the depositary receipts in addition to the performance of the company. Investors should be aware of those risks.
- Restricted programs are those that are meant to be traded by only certain individuals. In the United States, the Securities Exchange Commission allows these types of issuance of shares as per Rule 144-A and Regulation S.

EXERCISES

Theory Questions

1. What is a depositary receipt?
2. What are the different forms of depositary receipt?
3. How is a depositary receipt issued and how does it get cancelled?
4. What is the raison-d'être behind pricing of a depositary receipt?
5. Enumerate the benefits of depositary receipts to the issuers.
6. List the benefits of depositary receipts to the investors.
7. What is an American depositary receipt and how is it different from a global depositary receipt?

8. What are the different types of ADR issues that a company can resort to?
9. Are there any risks associated with investments in depositary receipts? If so, list the risks.
10. What are restricted programs under the U.S. security laws in the context of depositary receipts issuance?
11. What is the journal entry that is recorded in the books of the investor when the equity shares against ADRs are sold in the local stock exchange?
12. Further to question 11, will there be any realized gain or loss recorded on the conversion of ADRs into local shares?

Objective Questions

1. An instrument representing ownership interest in securities of a foreign issuer is referred to as
   a. An ownership certificate
   b. A depositary receipt
   c. An ownership receipt
   d. None of the above
2. Depositary receipts that are traded in an international market other than the United States are referred to as
   a. Global depositary receipts
   b. International depositary receipts
   c. Open market depositary receipts
   d. None of the above
3. Issuance of DRs is based on the increase of demand in the
   a. Local market
   b. International market
   c. Existing shareholders
   d. All of the above
4. Each DR is backed by a specific number of an issuer's local shares. This is referred to as the
   a. DR ratio
   b. Issuer's holding ratio
   c. Market holding ratio
   d. None of the above
5. Which of the following does not constitute a benefit of DRs for the issuer?
   a. Offer a new avenue for raising equity capital
   b. Broaden and diversify a company's investor base
   c. Enhance a company's visibility and status
   d. None of the above

6. Which of the following does not constitute a benefit of DRs for investors?
   a. Facilitate diversification into securities of foreign issuers
   b. Eliminate unfamiliar custody safekeeping arrangements
   c. Broaden and diversify the investment base
   d. None of the above
7. ADRs that do not qualify or are not intended to be listed on stock exchanges are referred to as
   a. Level 1 ADRs
   b. Level 2 ADRs
   c. Level 3 ADRs
   d. None of the above
8. ADRs listed on stock exchanges are referred to as
   a. Level 1 ADRs
   b. Level 2 ADRs
   c. Level 3 ADRs
   d. None of the above
9. Which of the following is not an advantage of ADRs?
   a. Cost-effectiveness
   b. Diversification of investment
   c. Reduction in administration cost
   d. None of the above
10. Which of the following is not associated with the risk involved in ADRs?
    a. Political risk
    b. Exchange rate risk
    c. Inflationary risk
    d. None of the above
11. Level 1 is the most basic type of ADR where the foreign company
    a. Wishes its ADR to be listed on the U.S. exchanges alone
    b. Does not wish its ADR to be listed on an exchange
    c. Does not wish its ADR to be listed on a U.S. exchange
    d. Wishes its ADR to be listed on any exchange around the world
    e. Wishes its ADR to be listed on any exchange other than U.S. exchanges
12. Regulation S shares cannot be held or traded by any ______________, as defined by SEC Regulation S rules.
    a. Non-U.S. person
    b. U.S. person
    c. European person

   d. U.S. investment firm
   e. Non-U.S. investment firm

13. In ADR trading, when the investor places the buy order and when the broker executes the same, it becomes a binding contract between the investor and the
   a. Foreign company
   b. Broker
   c. Securities Exchange Commission
   d. Stock exchange
   e. All of the above

14. The process of valuing ADRs is known as portfolio valuation, when the market rate at the end of the period is determined from the
   a. Primary stock exchange where the shares are traded
   b. Secondary market
   c. Prime broker
   d. Broker
   e. Credit rating companies

Journal Questions

Prepare journal entries, general ledger, trial balance, income statement, and balance sheet for the following scenarios:

ADR Conversion to Local Equity Shares—BRL

Mark Antony Inc. traded in Bovespa shares in a Brazilian Stock Exchange through Henry Frank Brothers brokers and the details are as follows:

Trade Details

Date	Product	CCY	Quantity	Rate	B/S	Brokerage
15-Jan-X1	Bovespa—ADR	US$	9,000	32.00	B	US$ 900
28-Jan-X1	Bovespa—ADR	US$	5,000	35.00	B	US$ 525
5-Feb-X1	Bovespa—Local	BRL	15,000	28.50	S	BRL 1,280

Other Details

- One ADR converts to two local shares in BRL currency.
- Settlement: T+2.
- Conversion fees levied by broker to convert ADR shares into local shares for 7,500 ADRs amounts to $1,300.
- Functional currency is US$.

Liquidation Methodology

FIFO

FX Rates

Date	FX Rate
11-Jan-X1	1.6505
13-Jan-X1	1.6525
25-Jan-X1	1.6484
27-Jan-X1	1.6444
31-Jan-X1	1.6311
5-Feb-X1	1.6255
7-Feb-X1	1.6201
28-Feb-X1	1.6150

Market Rate
Bovespa ADR
January 31: $33.50
February 28: $38.00
Bovespa Local
January 31: BRL 26.25
February 28: BRL 32.50

ADR Conversion to Local Equity Shares—MXN

Mexico Opportunities Fund traded in America Movil shares in a Mexican Stock Exchange through Goldman Sachs and the details are as follows:

Trade Details

Date	Product	CCY	Quantity	Rate	B/S	Brokerage
12-Jan-X1	America Movil—ADR	US$	1,500	51.50	B	US$ 200
22-Jan-X1	America Movil—ADR	US$	3,500	52.50	B	US$ 700
24-Jan-X1	America Movil—ADR	US$	1,800	53.50	S	US$ 260
5-Feb-X1	America Movil—Local	MXN	30,000	57.50	S	MXN 5,200

Other Details

- One ADR converts to 10 local shares in MXN currency.
- Settlement: T + 2.
- Conversion fees levied by broker to convert ADR shares into local shares amount to $810.
- Functional currency is US$.

Liquidation Methodology
Weighted average

FX Rates

Date	FX Rate
11-Jan-X1	10.6505

Date	FX Rate
13-Jan-X1	10.6525
25-Jan-X1	10.6484
28-Jan-X1	10.6444
31-Jan-X1	10.6311
5-Feb-X1	10.6255
7-Feb-X1	10.6201
28-Feb-X1	10.6150

Market Rate

- America Movil ADR
  - January 31: $54.50
  - February 28: $53.00
- America Movil Local
  - January 31: MXN 58.00
  - February 28: MXN 55.00

CHAPTER 14

Presentation and Disclosures

LEARNING OBJECTIVES

After studying this chapter, you will have a grasp of the following:

- How to record and report trade transactions of equity investments comprehensively.
- Similarities and differences between U.S. GAAP and IFRS in accounting for equity investments.
- Disclosure requirements for equity investments under U.S. GAAP.
- Disclosure requirements for equity investments under IFRS.

ACCOUNTING STANDARDS FOR PRESENTATION AND DISCLOSURE

Relevant Accounting Standards	
U.S. GAAP	**IFRS**
FAS 52—Foreign Currency Translation	IFRS 7—Financial Instruments: Disclosure
FAS 94—Consolidation of All Majority-owned Subsidiaries	IAS 21—The Effects of Changes in Foreign Exchange Rates
FAS 109—Accounting for Income Taxes	IAS 32—Financial Instruments: Presentation
FAS 115—Accounting for Certain Investments in Debt and Equity Securities	IAS 36—Impairment of Assets
FAS 130—Reporting Comprehensive Income	IAS 39—Financial Instruments: Recognition and Measurement
FAS 157—Fair Value Measurements	
FAS 159—The Fair Value Option for Financial Assets and Financial Liabilities	

PRESENTATION IN INCOME STATEMENT

Impairment of Securities

Temporary impairment of the equity securities that are held for trading is automatically tracked by valuing the securities at mark-to-market on every reporting day. Such temporary impairment is not to be recognized and acted upon for available-for-sale securities. However, if the impairment is anything other than temporary, then such impaired security must be written down to fair value. The realized loss on such impairment must be reported in the income statement. Once the impairment is recorded as a loss, then even if the security recovers from such impairment, it would not be recognized in the earnings unless it is liquidated.

Stock Dividend

While the cash dividends received from investments held as trading or as available-for-sale should be reported as income of the current period, the stock dividend should *not* be reported as income. Instead, the shares received as stock dividend should be added to the original shares and when the mark-to-market process is performed, the impact of the stock dividend will be automatically accounted for as unrealized gains and will be reported as income during the period.

Realized and Unrealized Gain/Loss

When investments are classified as trading securities, the realized and unrealized gains and losses should be included in the current period's income statement. In the case of investments classified as available-for-sale, however, only realized gains should be taken to the current period's income statement. The unrealized gains on available-for-sale securities should be taken directly to the other comprehensive income, which is grouped with the shareholders' equity and not regarded as income of the current period. However, when the available-for-sale securities are sold, the realized gain/loss should be taken to the income statement and to that extent reversed from the other comprehensive income.

Permanent impairment to the value of the securities held as available-for-sale should be written off as expense in the income statement. This should not be reversed even if the security recovers from impairment until the security is liquidated and the actual realized gain/loss is computed.

DIFFERENCES BETWEEN U.S. GAAP AND IFRS

Accounting for Equity Investments		
Topic	**U.S. GAAP**	**IFRS**
Definition	Equity security is defined in FAS 115 as any security representing an ownership interest in an enterprise like common, preferred, or other capital stock or the right to acquire warrants, rights, and call options or to dispose of an ownership interest in an enterprise at fixed or determinable prices.	Same as U.S. GAAP
Recognition	U.S. GAAP requires an entity to recognize a financial asset when and only when the entity becomes a party to the contractual provisions of a financial instrument.	Same as U.S. GAAP

Topic	U.S. GAAP	IFRS
Accounting date	While FAS 115 is silent on the date on which the transaction should be recorded, the other levels of U.S. GAAP literature requires trade date accounting to be followed for regular-way contracts.	For regular-way contracts, the IASB gives the option to follow either trade date accounting or settle date accounting, provided it is followed consistently for purchases and sales of financial assets in the same category.
Initial measurement	A financial asset is recognized initially at its fair value (which is normally the transaction price) plus, in the case of a financial asset that is not recognized at fair value with changes in fair value recognized in the income statement, transaction costs that are directly attributable to the acquisition of that asset.	Same as U.S. GAAP.
Financial asset at fair value concept	An entity has an option to designate financial assets at fair value with changes in fair value recognized in the income statement. This is possible only if the financial asset is a hybrid financial instrument that contains an embedded derivative which otherwise requires separation.	An entity can decide to classify a financial asset at fair value, with changes in fair value recognized in the income statement, provided it results in more relevant information. This decision is irrevocable by the entity.
Subsequent changes in fair value	Changes in fair value are recognized in the income statement.	Same as U.S. GAAP.
Trading securities	Frequent buying and selling usually indicates a trading instrument.	The intention should be to hold the financial asset for a relatively short period, or as part of a portfolio with the intention of making profit on a short-term basis.
Available-for-sale securities	Unlisted equity securities are carried at cost. Changes in fair value are reported in other comprehensive income.	Changes in fair value are recognized net of tax effects in shareholders' equity and shown in the income statement when liquidated or impaired.
Reclassification	Where the asset is reclassified as held-for-trading, the asset is remeasured to fair value with the difference taken to the income statement.	Reclassifications between categories are not usual under IFRS. They are prohibited into and out of the fair value through profit or loss category.
Impairment	Impairment is when an entity considers a decline in fair value to be "other than temporary." Indicators of impairment include the financial health of the counterparty, intention of the investor to hold the asset for a reasonable length of time to permit recovery in value, the duration and extent that the market value has been below cost, and the prospects of a market price recovery.	In the case of an investment in an equity instrument, impairment means a significant or prolonged decline in the fair value of that investment below its cost.

Topic	U.S. GAAP	IFRS
Cost basis after impairment	A new cost basis is established after a security is impaired.	An impairment of a security does not establish a new cost basis.
Reversal of impairment	U.S. GAAP prohibits the reversal of an impairment charge on available-for-sale debt and equity securities.	IFRS, similar to U.S. GAAP, prohibits reversals of impairment on available-for-sale equity securities.

DISCLOSURE REQUIREMENTS UNDER U.S. GAAP

Available-for-sale Securities—Unrealized Gains

For securities classified as available-for-sale, all reporting enterprises shall disclose:

- Aggregate fair value.
- Gross unrealized holding gains.
- Gross unrealized holding losses.

These should be grouped by major security type as of each date for which a statement of financial position is presented.

Available-for-sale Securities—Realized Gains and OCI

For each period for which the results of operations are presented, an enterprise shall disclose:

- The sale proceeds of available-for-sale securities and the gross realized gains and gross realized losses on those sales.
- The basis on which cost was determined in computing realized gain or loss (that is, specific identification, average cost, or other method used).
- The gross gains and gross losses included in earnings from transfers of securities from the available-for-sale category into the trading category.
- The change in net unrealized holding gain or loss on available-for-sale securities that has been included in the separate component of shareholders' equity during the period.
- The change in net unrealized holding gain or loss on trading securities that has been included in earnings during the period.

Transfer from Held-to-maturity Securities

For any sales of or transfers from securities classified as held-to-maturity, the amortized cost amount of the sold or transferred security, the related realized or unrealized gain or loss, and the circumstances leading to the decision to sell or transfer the security shall be disclosed in the notes to the financial statements for each period for which the results of operations are presented, even though such sales or transfers should be rare, except for sales and transfers due to the changes in circumstances mentioned in the standard. (*Source*: Paragraphs 19, 21, and 22 of FAS 115.)

Disclosure Pursuant to FASB Staff Position (FSP) FAS 115-1 and FAS 124-1

The following should be disclosed in annual financial statements for all investments in an unrealized loss position for which other-than-temporary impairments have not been recognized:

1. At each presentation date, quantitative information, aggregated by category of investment—each category of investment that the investor discloses and cost-method investments—is prepared in tabular form:

   - The aggregate related fair value of investments with unrealized losses.
   - The aggregate amount of unrealized losses (that is, the amount by which cost exceeds fair value).

   The disclosures above shall be segregated by those investments that have been in a continuous unrealized loss position for less than 12 months and those that have been in a continuous unrealized loss position for 12 months or longer. The reference point for determining how long an investment has been in a continuous unrealized loss position is the balance sheet date of the reporting period in which the impairment is identified. For entities that do not prepare interim financial information, the reference point would be the annual balance sheet date of the period during which the impairment was identified.

   The continuous unrealized loss position ceases upon either (1) the recognition of an "other-than temporary" impairment or (2) the investor becoming aware of a recovery of fair value up to (or beyond) the cost of the investment during the period.

2. In the most recent statement of financial position, additional information (in narrative form) that sufficiently explains the quantitative disclosures and the information that the investor considered (both positive and negative) in reaching the conclusion that the impairment(s) are not other than temporary, so as to provide insight into the investor's rationale for concluding that unrealized losses are not other-than-temporary impairments. The disclosures required may be aggregated by investment categories, but individually significant unrealized losses generally shall not be aggregated. This disclosure could include:

   - The nature of the investment(s).
   - The cause(s) of the impairment(s).
   - The number of investment positions that are in an unrealized loss position.
   - The severity and duration of the impairment(s).
   - Other evidence considered by the investor in reaching its conclusion that the investment is not other-than-temporarily impaired, including, for example, industry analyst reports, sector credit ratings, volatility of the security's fair value, and/or any other information that the investor considers relevant.

Disclosures for Cost-method Investments

For cost-method investments, an investor shall disclose the following additional information, if applicable, as of each date for which a statement of financial position is presented in its annual financial statements:

- The aggregate carrying amount of all cost-method investments.
- The aggregate carrying amount of cost-method investments that the investor did not evaluate for impairment.
- The fact that the fair value of a cost-method investment is not estimated if there are no identified events or changes in circumstances that may have a significant adverse effect on the fair value of the investment.

The guidance in this FSP shall be applied to reporting periods beginning after December 15, 2005.

DISCLOSURE REQUIREMENTS UNDER IFRS

Quantitative and Qualitative Disclosures

For financial instruments that create a potentially significant exposure to risks, the terms and conditions disclosed might include:

- The principal, stated, face, or other similar amount.
- The date of maturity, expiry, or execution.
- Early settlement and conversion options, including details of their exercise.
- The amount and timing of scheduled future cash flows in respect of the instrument's principal amount.
- Interest, dividends, or other periodic returns on principal and their timing.
- Collateral held or pledged.
- Where appropriate, the currency in which receipts or payments are denominated.

Terms, Conditions, and Accounting Policies

An entity must disclose the extent and nature of financial instruments, including significant terms and conditions that may affect future cash flows; and the accounting policies and methods adopted, including the criteria for recognition and the basis of measurement applied.

Fair Value

The fair value of each class of financial assets should be disclosed.

In the rare case where the fair value of investments in unquoted equity instruments cannot be measured reliably and they are carried at cost, disclosure may take the form of a statement of that fact together with a description of the assets; their carrying amount; an explanation of why their fair value cannot be measured reliably; if possible, the range of estimates within which fair value is highly likely to lie; and any gains/losses arising on sale of such assets.

Additionally, it should include:

- The methods and significant assumptions applied in determining fair values.
- The extent to which fair values are determined by market prices/transactions or estimates using a valuation technique.
- The valuation techniques used to determine fair value.
- The extent to which fair values are based on assumptions not supported by observable market prices.

- Where applicable, the sensitivity of valuation assumptions used.
- The change in fair value recognized in profit or loss for the period.

Other Disclosures

Significant items of income, expense, and gains and losses resulting from financial assets and financial liabilities, whether included in profit or loss or as a separate component of equity, must be disclosed, including:

- For financial assets not designated as at fair value through profit or loss: total interest income and expense.
- For available-for-sale financial assets: gains/losses recognized in equity and amounts released from equity into profit or loss for the period.
- The amount of interest income accrued on impaired financial assets.

Other Specific Disclosures

- The reason or reasons for reclassification of a financial asset as one required to be reported at cost/amortized cost rather than at fair value.
- Impairment losses for each significant class of financial asset.
- Extensive disclosures in respect of any accepted and pledged collateral.
- The carrying amounts of financial assets and financial liabilities that (1) are classified as held for trading, and (2) were designated as at fair value through profit or loss.

REQUIREMENTS BY IFRS 7

Objective

The objective of this accounting standard is to require entities to provide disclosures in their financial statements that enable users to evaluate:

- The significance of financial instruments for the entity's financial position and performance.
- The nature and extent of risks arising from financial instruments to which the entity is exposed during the period and at the reporting date, and how the entity manages those risks.

Classes of Financial Instruments and Level of Disclosure

An entity should group financial instruments into classes that are appropriate to the nature of the information disclosed and that take into account the characteristics of those financial instruments. An entity should provide sufficient information to permit reconciliation to the line items presented in the balance sheet.

Significance for Financial Position and Performance

An entity should disclose information that enables users of its financial statements to evaluate the significance of financial instruments for its financial position and performance.

Balance Sheet

The carrying amounts of each of the following four categories should be disclosed either on the face of the balance sheet or in the notes:

1. Financial assets at fair value through profit or loss, showing separately
   - Those designated as such upon initial recognition.
   - Those classified as held for trading.
2. Held-to-maturity investments.
3. Loans and receivables.
4. Available-for-sale financial assets.

Reclassification

If the entity has reclassified a financial asset as one measured (1) at cost or amortized cost, rather than at fair value, or (2) at fair value, rather than at cost or amortized cost, it should disclose the amount reclassified into and out of each category and the reason for that reclassification.

Derecognition

An entity may have transferred financial assets in such a way that part or all of the financial assets do not qualify for derecognition. In such cases, the entity should disclose for each class of such financial assets:

- The nature of the assets.
- The nature of the risks and rewards of ownership to which the entity remains exposed.
- When the entity continues to recognize all of the assets, the carrying amounts of the assets and of the associated liabilities.
- When the entity continues to recognize the assets to the extent of its continuing involvement, the total carrying amount of the original assets, the amount of the assets that the entity continues to recognize, and the carrying amount of the associated liabilities.

Collateral

An entity should disclose:

- The carrying amount of financial assets it has pledged as collateral for liabilities or contingent liabilities, including amounts that have been reclassified.
- The terms and conditions relating to its pledge.

When an entity holds collateral (of financial or nonfinancial assets) and is permitted to sell or repledge the collateral in the absence of default by the owner of the collateral, it should disclose:

- The fair value of the collateral held.
- The fair value of any such collateral sold or repledged, and whether the entity has an obligation to return it.
- The terms and conditions associated with its use of the collateral.

Allowance Account for Credit Losses

When financial assets are impaired by credit losses and the entity records the impairment in a separate account (e.g., an allowance account used to record individual impairments or a similar account used to record a collective impairment of assets) rather than directly reducing the carrying amount of the asset, it should disclose a reconciliation of changes in that account during the period for each class of financial assets.

STATEMENT OF PROFIT AND LOSS AND EQUITY

Items of Income, Expense, Gains, or Losses

An entity should disclose the following items of income, expense, gains, or losses either on the face of the financial statements or in the notes.

1. Net gains or net losses on:
   - Financial assets or financial liabilities at fair value through profit or loss, showing separately those net gains or net losses on financial assets or financial liabilities designated as such upon initial recognition, and those on financial assets or financial liabilities that are classified as held for trading.
   - Available-for-sale financial assets, showing separately the amount of gain or loss recognized directly in equity during the period and the amount removed from equity and recognized in the statement of profit and loss for the period.
   - Held-to-maturity investments.
2. Total interest income and total interest expense (calculated using the effective interest method) for financial assets or financial liabilities that are not at fair value through profit or loss.
3. Fee income and expense (other than amounts included in determining the effective interest rate) arising from:
   - Financial assets or financial liabilities that are not at fair value through profit or loss.
   - Trust and other fiduciary activities that result in the holding or investing of assets on behalf of individuals, trusts, retirement benefit plans, and other institutions.
4. Interest income on impaired financial assets accrued.
5. The amount of any impairment loss for each class of financial asset.

OTHER DISCLOSURES

Accounting Policies

In accordance with standards regarding presentation of financial statements, an entity discloses, in the summary of significant accounting policies, the measurement basis (or bases) used in preparing the financial statements and the other accounting policies used that are relevant to an understanding of the financial statements.

Hedge Accounting

An entity should disclose the following separately for each type of hedge—fair value hedges, cash flow hedges, and hedges of net investments in foreign operations:

- A description of each type of hedge.
- A description of the financial instruments designated as hedging instruments and their fair values at the reporting date.
- The nature of the risks being hedged.

For *cash flow hedges*, an entity should disclose:

- The periods when the cash flows are expected to occur and when they are expected to affect profit or loss.
- A description of any forecast transaction for which hedge accounting had previously been used, but which is no longer expected to occur.
- The amount that was recognized in the appropriate equity account (Hedging Reserve Account) during the period.
- The amount that was removed from the appropriate equity account (Hedging Reserve Account) and included in the statement of profit and loss for the period, showing the amount included in each line item in the statement.
- The amount that was removed from the appropriate equity account (Hedging Reserve Account) during the period and included in the initial cost or other carrying amount of a nonfinancial asset or nonfinancial liability whose acquisition or incurrence was a hedged, highly probable forecast transaction.

An entity should disclose separately:

- In fair value hedges, gains or losses:
  - Details on the hedging instrument.
  - Details on the hedged item attributable to the hedged risk.
- The ineffectiveness recognized in the statement of profit and loss that arises from cash flow hedges.
- The ineffectiveness recognized in the statement of profit and loss that arises from hedges of net investments in foreign operations.

Fair Value

For each class of financial assets and financial liabilities, the fair value of that class should be disclosed in a way that permits it to be compared with its carrying amount.

In disclosing fair values, an entity should group financial assets and financial liabilities into classes, but should offset them only to the extent that their carrying amounts are offset in the balance sheet.

An entity should disclose:

1. The methods and, when a valuation technique is used, the assumptions applied in determining fair values of each class of financial assets or financial liabilities. For example, if applicable, an entity discloses information about the assumptions relating to prepayment rates, rates of estimated credit losses, and interest rates or discount rates.

2. Whether fair values are determined, in whole or in part, directly by reference to published price quotations in an active market or are estimated using a valuation technique.
3. Whether the fair values recognized or disclosed in the financial statements are determined in whole or in part using a valuation technique based on assumptions that are not supported by prices from observable current market transactions in the same instrument (i.e., without modification or repackaging) and not based on available observable market data. For fair values that are recognized in the financial statements, if changing one or more of those assumptions to reasonably possible alternative assumptions would change fair value significantly, the entity should state this fact and disclose the effect of those changes. For this purpose, significance should be judged with respect to profit or loss, and total assets or total liabilities, or, when changes in fair value are recognized in equity, total equity.
4. If (3) applies, the total amount of the change in fair value estimated using such a valuation technique that was recognized in the statement of profit and loss during the period.

If the market for a financial instrument is not active, an entity establishes its fair value using a valuation technique. Nevertheless, the best evidence of fair value at initial recognition is the transaction price. It follows that there could be a difference between the fair value at initial recognition and the value on the date of using the valuation technique. If such a difference exists, an entity should disclose, by class of financial instrument:

- Its accounting policy for recognizing that difference in the statement of profit and loss to reflect a change in factors (including time) that market participants would consider in setting a price.
- The aggregate difference yet to be recognized in the statement of profit and loss at the beginning and end of the period and a reconciliation of changes in the balance of this difference.

Disclosures of fair value are not required:

- When the carrying amount is a reasonable approximation of fair value—for example, for financial instruments such as short-term trade receivables and payables.
- For an investment in equity instruments that do not have a quoted market price in an active market, or derivatives linked to such equity instruments that are measured at cost in accordance with the accounting standard because its fair value cannot be measured reliably.
- For a contract containing a discretionary participation feature (as described in the accounting standard on insurance contracts) if the fair value of that feature cannot be measured reliably.

An entity should disclose information to help users of the financial statements make their own judgments about the extent of possible differences between the carrying amount of those financial assets or financial liabilities and their fair value, including:

- The fact that fair value information has not been disclosed for these instruments because their fair value cannot be measured reliably.

- A description of the financial instruments, their carrying amount, and an explanation of why fair value cannot be measured reliably.
- Information about the market for the instruments.
- Information about whether and how the entity intends to dispose of the financial instruments.
- If financial instruments whose fair value previously could not be reliably measured are derecognized, that fact, their carrying amount at the time of derecognition, and the amount of gain or loss recognized.

Nature and Extent of Risks Arising from Financial Instruments

An entity should disclose information that enables users of its financial statements to evaluate the nature and extent of risks arising from financial instruments to which the entity is exposed at the reporting date.

The disclosures focus on the risks that arise from financial instruments and how they have been managed. These risks typically include, but are not limited to, credit risk, liquidity risk, and market risk.

Qualitative Disclosures

For each type of risk arising from financial instruments, an entity should disclose:

1. The exposures to risk and how they arise.
2. Its objectives, policies, and processes for managing the risk and the methods used to measure the risk.
3. Any changes in (1) or (2) from the previous period.

Quantitative Disclosures

For each type of risk arising from financial instruments, an entity should disclose:

1. Summary quantitative data about its exposure to that risk at the reporting date. This disclosure should be based on the information provided internally to key management personnel of the entity—for example, the entity's board of directors or chief executive officer.
2. The disclosures to the extent not provided in (1), unless the risk is not material.
3. Concentrations of risk if not apparent from (1) and (2).

If the quantitative data disclosed as of the reporting date are unrepresentative of an entity's exposure to risk during the period, an entity should provide further information that is representative.

Credit Risk

An entity should disclose by class of financial instrument:

1. The amount that best represents its maximum exposure to credit risk at the reporting date without taking account of any collateral held or other credit enhancements.
2. In respect of the amount disclosed in (1), a description of collateral held as security and other credit enhancement.

3. Information about the credit quality of financial assets that are neither past due nor impaired.
4. The carrying amount of financial assets that would otherwise be past due or impaired whose terms have been renegotiated.

Financial Assets That Are Either Past Due or Impaired

An entity should disclose by class of financial asset:

1. An analysis of the age of financial assets that are past due as of the reporting date but not impaired.
2. An analysis of financial assets that are individually determined to be impaired as of the reporting date, including the factors considered in determining that they are impaired.
3. For the amounts disclosed in (1) and (2), a description of collateral held by the entity as security and other credit enhancements and, unless impracticable, an estimate of their fair value.

Collateral and Other Credit Enhancements Obtained

When an entity obtains financial or nonfinancial assets during the period by taking possession of collateral it holds as security or calling on other credit enhancements (e.g., guarantees), and such assets meet the recognition criteria in other standards, an entity should disclose:

1. The nature and carrying amount of the assets obtained.
2. When the assets are not readily convertible into cash, its policies for disposing of such assets or for using them in its operations.

Liquidity Risk

An entity should disclose:

1. A maturity analysis for financial liabilities that shows the remaining contractual maturities.
2. A description of how it manages the liquidity risk inherent in (1).

MARKET RISK

Sensitivity Analysis

1. Unless an entity complies with (2) above it should disclose:
    - A sensitivity analysis for each type of market risk to which the entity is exposed at the reporting date, showing how profit or loss and equity would have been affected by changes in the relevant risk variable that were reasonably possible at that date.
    - The methods and assumptions used in preparing the sensitivity analysis.
    - Changes from the previous period in the methods and assumptions used, and the reasons for such changes.

2. If an entity prepares a sensitivity analysis, such as value-at-risk, that reflects interdependencies between risk variables (e.g., interest rates and exchange rates) and uses it to manage financial risks, it may use that sensitivity analysis in place of the analysis specified in (1). The entity should also disclose:
   - An explanation of the method used in preparing such a sensitivity analysis, and of the main parameters and assumptions underlying the data provided.
   - An explanation of the objective of the method used and of limitations that may result in the information not fully reflecting the fair value of the assets and liabilities involved.

Other Market Risk Disclosures

When the sensitivity analyses disclosed in accordance with paragraph 40 or 41 are unrepresentative of a risk inherent in a financial instrument (for example, because the year-end exposure does not reflect the exposure during the year), the entity should disclose that fact and the reason it believes the sensitivity analyses are unrepresentative.

The main objective of IFRS 7 is that the preparers should provide quantitative and qualitative disclosures that would enhance a user's understanding of the entity's exposures to financial risks and how the entity manages those risks. IFRS 7 deals with the disclosure requirements in relation to all risks arising from financial instruments.

This standard applies to any entity that holds financial instruments. The level of disclosure required depends on the extent of the entity's use of financial instruments and its exposure to financial risk.

More specifically, IFRS 7 requires an entity to disclose:

- Information on the significance of financial instruments to the entity's financial position and performance.
- The nature and extent of risk exposures arising from financial instruments (quantitative disclosures).
- The approach taken in managing those risks (qualitative disclosures).

The entity should disclose the carrying amounts of financial assets and financial liabilities under each of the classifications in IAS 39—Financial Instruments: Recognition and Measurement, namely, financial assets designated as at fair value through profit or loss (FVTPL) and available-for-sale financial assets.

Where there is a difference between the fair value of a financial instrument at initial recognition and the amount that would be determined at that date using a valuation technique, IFRS 7 requires disclosure of the entity's accounting policy for recognizing that difference in profit or loss, the aggregate difference yet to be recognized in profit or loss at the beginning and end of the period, and a reconciliation of changes in the balance of this difference.

Where an entity records an impairment on a financial asset or a group of financial assets through an allowance account instead of a direct reduction to the carrying amount of the financial asset, it shall disclose, for each class of financial asset, a reconciliation of changes in carrying amounts in that account during the period.

SUMMARY

- If the equity securities classified as available-for-sale are sold, then the realized gain/loss on such sale is transferred from the other comprehensive income (OCI) in the income statement and an entry is recorded to that effect.
- When the equity securities are transferred from trading securities to available-for-sale category, then the unrealized gain/loss should not be reversed and no adjustment should be made to the OCI.
- When the equity securities are transferred from available-for-sale category to trading category, then the unrealized gain/loss on such securities based on the fair value of the securities should be transferred from OCI and thus recognized as income immediately upon transfer.
- Temporary impairment of the equity securities that are held for trading is automatically tracked by valuing the securities at mark-to-market on every reporting day. Such temporary impairment is not to be recognized and acted upon for available-for-sale securities. However, if the impairment is anything other than temporary, then such impaired security must be written down to fair value. The realized loss on such impairment must be reported in the income statement. Once the impairment is recorded as loss, then even if the security recovers from such impairment, it would not be recognized in the earnings unless it is liquidated through the sale of the security.
- Unrealized gain/loss is not recognized for income tax purposes until gain/loss is realized through liquidation. Hence the unrealized gain/loss included in the income or other comprehensive income represents temporary differences as defined by FAS 109. The tax effects of all temporary differences are to be recognized in the financial statements as deferred tax benefits or deferred tax liabilities.
- For securities classified as trading, the unrealized gain/loss is included in the income and as such represents the temporary differences as defined in the accounting standard. The deferred tax effect of those changes should also be presented in the income statement itself.
- For securities classified as available-for-sale, the unrealized gain/loss is included in the other comprehensive income and as such forms part of the temporary differences as defined in the accounting standard. The deferred tax effect of those changes should also be presented in the other comprehensive income itself.
- As per FAS 115, under U.S. GAAP, for securities classified as available-for-sale, all reporting enterprises shall disclose:
  - Aggregate fair value.
  - Gross unrealized holding gains.
  - Gross unrealized holding losses.

These should be grouped by major security type as of each date for which a statement of financial position is presented.

- IFRS 7 comes into effect for annual periods beginning on or after January 1, 2007. This standard requires preparers to provide quantitative and qualitative disclosures that would enhance a user's understanding of the entity's exposures to financial risks and how the entity manages those risks.

EXERCISES

Theory Questions

1. Can securities be transferred from one classification to another category? If so, what precautions should be taken to adjust the unrealized gains or losses?
2. How is the impairment of securities presented in the balance sheet?
3. What is the treatment of stock dividend? Can you report this as income?
4. How are the tax effects on unrealized gains/losses treated in the books of accounts in the securities classified as trading and as available-for-sale?
5. What are the similarities in U.S. GAAP and IFRS as far as accounting for equity shares is concerned?
6. What are the differences in U.S. GAAP and IFRS as far as accounting for equity shares is concerned?
7. Critically examine the disclosure requirements under U.S. GAAP vis-à-vis IFRS.
8. What are the recent developments in the disclosure requirements under IFRS pursuant to IFRS 7, becoming effective from January 1, 2007?
9. What is disclosure of cost method investment?

Objective Questions

1. When securities are transferred from trading securities to available-for-sale, then
   a. Gain/loss recognized as unrealized should be reversed
   b. Gain/loss recognized as unrealized should not be reversed
   c. Gain/loss recognized as unrealized will be adjusted with other comprehensive income
   d. None of the above
2. When securities are transferred from available-for-sale to trading, then
   a. Unrealized gain/loss will be transferred from other comprehensive income and treated as income
   b. Unrealized gain/loss should not be reversed
   c. No changes are required at all
   d. None of the above
3. Impairment other than temporary in respect of equity securities should be
   a. Written down to fair value
   b. Treated alike as temporary impairment
   c. Written as a loss to be treated as temporary
   d. None of the above

4. A stock dividend declared should be treated as
   a. Income
   b. Increase in the value of original shares held
   c. Increase to the quantity (position) of shares held
   d. All of the above
5. For securities classified as available-for-sale, which of the following items will be reported in the income statement of current period?
   a. Both realized and unrealized gains
   b. Realized gain alone
   c. Unrealized gain alone
   d. None of the above
6. For income tax purposes, unrealized gain/loss will be recognized for reporting
   a. Automatically at the end of financial year
   b. Only if the securities are liquidated and realized
   c. As and when depending upon the corporate action
   d. None of the above
7. Unrealized gain/loss included in the income/other comprehensive income represents
   a. Temporary difference recognized as deferred tax benefits
   b. Permanent difference recognized as deferred tax benefits
   c. No effect
   d. None of the above
8. For available-for-sale securities, the deferred tax effect should be presented in
   a. The income statement
   b. Other comprehensive income
   c. No need for accounting
   d. None of the above
9. For trading securities, the deferred tax effect should be presented in
   a. The income statement
   b. Other comprehensive income
   c. No need for accounting
   d. None of the above
10. As per U.S. GAAP, changes in fair value for available-for-sale securities are reported in
    a. The income statement
    b. Other comprehensive income

   c. No need to report
   d. None of the above

11. When the equity securities are transferred from available-for-sale (AFS) to trading securities,
    a. The unrealized gain/loss is recognized on T + 2
    b. The unrealized gain/loss is not recognized at all
    c. The realized gain/loss is recognized immediately
    d. The unrealized gain/loss is recognized immediately
    e. Realized gain/loss of trading securities is treated in the same way as in AFS
12. Shares received as stock dividend should be added to the original shares and when the mark-to-market process is performed, the impact of the stock dividend
    a. Should be treated as unrealized gains and reported as income for the period
    b. Should be treated as dividend income
    c. Should be treated as dividend income but should be shown as current asset on asset side of balance sheet
    d. Should be treated as realized gain/income for the period
    e. Both b and c
13. As per the definition in FAS 109, the tax effects of all temporary differences arising from unrealized gain/loss are to be recognized in the financial statements as
    a. Non-trading income
    b. Items exempted from taxes
    c. Deferred tax benefits or deferred tax liabilities
    d. Not recognized for current period, but carried forward to the next accounting period
    e. Income or expense for current period
14. As per FAS 115, under U.S. GAAP, for securities classified as available-for-sale, all reporting enterprises shall disclose
    a. Aggregate fair value
    b. Gross unrealized holding gains
    c. Gross unrealized holding losses
    d. All of the above
    e. None of the above

15. For regular-way contracts, the IASB gives the option to follow either trade date accounting or settlement date accounting, provided it is followed consistently for purchases and sales of financial assets in the same category. This accounting standard is as per
    a. U.S. GAAP (generally accepted accounting principles)
    b. FASB (Financial Accounting Standards Board)
    c. IFRS (International Financial Reporting Standards)
    d. GASB (Governmental Accounting Standards Board)
    e. IASC (International Accounting Standards Committee)

APPENDIX A

Basics of Accounting Theory

BASIC ASSUMPTIONS

Basic assumptions define the basic objectives of accounting practice. They provide ground rules, which are essential characteristics of a traditional accounting model.

Accounting Entity Assumption

According to this assumption, the business is considered to be separate from its individual owners. This is to ensure that the proprietor does not include any of his personal or family financial activities in the results of the business. The business transactions are identified, measured, and communicated as accounting data that is separate from the owner.

Money Measurement Assumption

This assumption states that not all activities of the business are recorded in the accounting books. Only those transactions that are measured in monetary terms are recorded. For example, wages paid can be measured in terms of money and hence it is recorded. But employee compatibility with each other cannot be measured in terms of money and is not recorded in the accounting records.

Accounting Period Assumption

The periodicity assumption refers to the qualitative characteristic of timeliness. The users require periodic information to make decisions. A natural business year is the 12-month period or 52 weeks or 365 days, where the business activities end for the year and a new accounting year begins. If the annual time period ends on December 31, it is known as calendar year. But some companies have a fiscal year that corresponds to their nature of business.

Going Concern Assumption

The going concern assumption is necessary as it is an anticipation that a business entity will continue to operate indefinitely. A company is begun with the hope of a long life and continuing its existence into the foreseeable future. The corollary of this assumption is that the expenses are classified as capital expenditure and revenue expenditure: capital expenditures are long standing while revenue expenditure is supposed to be utilized within the accounting period.

BASIC CONCEPTS

Basic concepts indicate which events will be accounted for and in what manner. They form the underlying principles of financial accounting practices.

Dual Aspect Concept

The dual aspect refers to the double-entry system, which reflects that each transaction has two sides to it. Both the increases and decreases of each transaction that forms an element of a company's financial position are recorded.

Revenue Realization Concept

Revenues are inflows of assets resulting from providing a service or product to a customer. This concept states that the revenue is recognized in the period it is earned, regardless of when cash actually is received. The two criteria that must be satisfied for revenue to be recognized are:

1. The earning process is complete or at least virtually complete.
2. There is reasonable certainty that the asset to be received is collectable.

In satisfying the first criterion, the seller has done something; satisfying the second criterion demonstrates that the buyer has done something.

Historical Cost Concept

The historical cost concept refers to the measurement of assets and liabilities based on their original transaction value on the day on which they were acquired. For example, an asset that cost $200,000 at the time of purchase may have a present market value of $600,000. For the purpose of recording in books, the asset will be valued at $200,000, which is the money actually given at the time of purchase.

Matching Concept

This concept states that expenses are recognized in the same period as their related revenues. While revenue is recognized according to the realization concept, the matching concept requires that all expenses incurred in generating the same revenue be recognized at the same time.

Objectivity Concept

According to this concept, each business transaction requires proper evidence to support it. For example, the historical cost of a land is highly verifiable. The cost of the land can be traced back to the time when it was purchased.

Full Disclosure Concept

The full disclosure concept means that the financial statements must include all relevant information that can influence the decision-making process of their users. This supplemental information gives more insight to the information that is available in the financial statements. The supplemental information is disclosed in a number of ways:

- Parenthetical comments.
- Disclosure notes.
- Supplemental financial statements.

BASIC PRINCIPLES OF ACCOUNTING

Cost Benefit Principle

The information gathering process is done to assess both costs and benefits of a proposed accounting principle. This principle states that in order to apply a principle in practice, the cost of doing it should not exceed its benefit. If the cost exceeds the benefit, the principle is modified to achieve more benefit from it.

Materiality Principle

Any information that will have an effect on its decision makers is known as material information. Materiality is mainly dependent on the relative amount of money involved in the transaction. It also depends on the nature of the item. The context of materiality is left to the judgment of the company that prepares the financial statement.

Consistency Principle

The financial statements provided by the company should be consistent year after year. Each rule, concept, and principle that is used by the company must be observed and applied every year. Comparison of financial statement between different accounting periods will be significant only if the practices followed by the company are consistent.

Prudence Principle

The principle of conservatism or principle of prudence requires that the company make prudent accounting choices and estimates for the future. It is always better to understate assets and overstate liabilities. For example, a part of the accounts receivable may not be collected, and this is known as bad debts. So the accountant would have to make provisions for such a situation.

ACCOUNTING MODEL

Financial Position

The balance sheet or statement of financial position shows the assets, liabilities, and shareholders' equity at a specific point in time. It gives a snapshot of the company's financial position in a particular time period. This provides a wealth of information to external decision makers.

One of the important features of a balance sheet is that it helps the decision makers to assess what resources are available to generate future cash flows. It also provides information about liquidity and long-term solvency.

Assets are the resources of a company. The company's obligations are known as *liabilities. Owners' equity* refers to the assets that are available after all obligations have been satisfied.

Results of Operation

The record of the amount of net income earned by a company during a period of time is known as the *income statement* or *results of operation.* It represents the measurement of economic performance of a company. It is in effect a summarization of revenues generated and the costs incurred to generate the revenues. Net income or net loss is derived from the difference between revenues and expenses. Net income is used to evaluate the health and performance of a business.

Revenues refer to the inflow of resources when goods are sold or services are performed. It represents an increase in total assets. The outflow of resources to generate such revenue is referred to as *expenses.*

Statement of Cash Flows

The statement of cash flows captures the cash inflows and cash outflows of a company for a specified period of time. In other words, it is the summarization of transactions that caused cash amounts to change for a reporting period. The cash flows are classified into three main categories: operating activities, investing activities, and financing activities.

1. Cash flows that appear in day-to-day operations are known as *operating* activities—for example, paying wages, paying taxes, interest, dividends, and so on.
2. Cash flows related to the acquisition and disposition of land, buildings, and equipment, are known as *investing* activities. They entail the buying and selling of long-term assets.
3. The external financing of a company is known as *financing* activities—for example, cash invested by owners, cash paid back to creditors, and so on.

ELEMENTS OF BASIC REPORTING

Assets

Assets of a company include cash, accounts receivable, inventory, land, building, machinery, and intangible items. In other words, assets represent everything that a business owns. Each asset must be assigned a monetary value.

Assets are classified into two categories:

1. Tangible assets.
2. Intangible assets.

Tangible assets are those that have some physical existence—in other words, something that can be touched and felt, for example, buildings, plants, machinery, and so on. Tangible assets are further classified into two types:

1. Fixed assets—those that have a permanent life and cannot be converted into cash immediately (e.g., equipment).
2. Current assets—those that can be converted into cash within a year (e.g., accounts receivable).

Intangible assets are those that do not have a physical existence and cannot be touched or felt. They include such things as goodwill, patents, copyrights, and so on.

Liabilities

Liabilities are amounts that the company owes, such as accounts payable, loans, and so on. Liabilities are also classified into three categories:

1. Long-term.
2. Current.
3. Contingent.

Debt or other obligations that will not be paid off within one year are known as *long-term* liabilities. Liabilities that are repayable within one year are known as *current* liabilities. A liability that can be anticipated to arise in the future is known as *contingent* liability.

FASB Concepts Statement 6, *Elements of Financial Statements,* describes the characteristics of assets and liabilities as follows:

An asset has three essential characteristics:

(a) it embodies a probable future benefit that involves a capacity, singly or in combination with other assets, to contribute directly or indirectly to future net cash inflows,
(b) a particular entity can obtain the benefit and control others' access to it; and
(c) the transaction or other event giving rise to the entity's right to or control of the benefit has already occurred.

A liability has three essential characteristics:

(a) it embodies a present duty or responsibility to one or more other entities that entails settlement by probable future transfer or use of assets at a specified or determinable date, on occurrence of a specified event, or on demand,
(b) the duty or responsibility obligates a particular entity, leaving it little or no discretion to avoid the future sacrifice; and
(c) the transaction or other event obligating the entity has already happened.

Owners' Equity

Owners' equity equals total assets minus total liabilities. To start a business, investors put in the money initially in return for part ownership. Ownership restricted to a single person is known as sole proprietorship; ownership by a small group is a partnership; and ownership that is represented by transferable shares is known as a corporation.

Equity increases through investments made by owners. Such investment involves a transfer of resources by the investor to the company in exchange for ownership rights. For example, a person becomes a shareholder of a company by the exchange of resources for the issuance of stock by the company. Owners' equity increases also when profits are generated by the business and retained for the business's use. The amount of profit that is not distributed to the investors is known as *retained earnings.*

A decrease in equity is a result of distributions to owners. In other words, owners' equity decreases when investors take back part of their investment. In the case of a corporation, distribution to owners is in the form of dividends. Owners' equity is also decreased when the company generates a loss instead of a profit.

Income

Revenue or *income* refers to the inflow of resources when goods are sold or services are performed. It represents an increase in total assets. Assets are increased by borrowing or through money invested by people. Similarly, assets also increase when the company provides a product or service for which customers pay. But these assets are not tied to any liability obligation; hence the assets belong to the company and result in an increase in owners' equity. Companies also earn revenue by charging interest or by collecting rent. For the good sold or services performed, income is in the form of cash or accounts receivable.

Expenses

The outflow of resources to generate revenue is referred to as *expenses*. This means the amount of assets used to conduct business operations—for example, payment of salary to employees.

One important feature of expenses is that they represent outflows of resources incurred in the process of generating revenues. Expenses are paid for by cash or as a credit, wherein cash payment is to be made at a later date.

Other Comprehensive Income

Items incurred or earned outside of normal operations are known as other comprehensive income. Examples of other comprehensive income include unrealized gains and losses on available-for-sale securities, gains and losses resulting from converting foreign currency subsidiaries to parent currency, gains and losses on derivatives held as cash flow hedges, and so on.

Off-balance-sheet Items

These are items that are not reported as part of the balance sheet, but are reported in the footnotes to the financial statements. There must be certain legitimate reasons to report an item as off-balance-sheet. The items most commonly reported are lease agreements, pension assets and liabilities, investment in joint ventures, and securitization of assets.

In the case of lease agreements, if the contract does not have a buyout option at the end of the lease, then it cannot become a personal asset. So at the end of the lease the item must be returned and hence it cannot become an asset of your own.

The assets of pensions are put into a trust or invested in a financial vehicle. These assets belong to the employees, so it is not right for the companies to claim them as their own.

APPENDIX B

Accounting Standards for Financial Instruments

The main ingredients of IAS 39 on Financial Instruments: Measurement and Recognition are as follows.

FINANCIAL INSTRUMENTS

A financial instrument is any contract that gives rise to a financial asset of one entity and a financial liability or equity instrument of another entity.

Financial Asset

Examples of financial assets include the following:

- Cash.
- Equity instrument of another entity.
- A contractual right
  - To receive cash or another financial asset from another entity.
  - To exchange financial assets or financial liabilities with another entity under conditions that are, potentially favorable to the entity.
- A contract that will or may be settled in the entity's own equity instruments and is
  - A non-derivative resulting in receiving a variable number of the entity's own equity instruments.
  - A derivative that will or may be settled other than by the exchange of a fixed amount of cash or another financial asset for a fixed number of the entity's own equity instruments.

Financial Liability

A financial liability can be described in one of two ways:

1. A contractual obligation
   - To deliver cash or another financial asset to another entity.
   - To exchange financial assets or financial liabilities with another entity under conditions that are, potentially unfavorable to the entity.
2. A contract that will or may be settled in the entity's own equity instruments and is
   - A non-derivative resulting in delivering a variable number of the entity's own equity instruments.

- A derivative that will or may be settled other than by the exchange of a fixed amount of cash or another financial asset for a fixed number of the entity's own equity instruments.

Equity Instrument

An equity instrument is any contract that evidences a residual interest in the assets of an entity after deducting all of its liabilities.

Derivative

A derivative is a financial instrument or other contract with all three of the following characteristics:

1. Its value changes in response to the change in an underlying.
2. It requires no initial net investment or an initial net investment that is smaller than would be required for other types of contracts.
3. It is settled at a future date.

Scope of IAS 39

IAS 39 is concerned with contracts to buy or sell a nonfinancial item that can be settled in cash or another financial instrument. Exception: Contracts that are entered into for the purpose of receipt or delivery of a nonfinancial item followed by the entity usually are outside the scope of IAS 39.

Four Ways of Settlement of a Contract:

1. Terms permit either party to settle in net in cash.
2. Terms are not explicit but net settlement is the practice.
3. Practice is to take delivery but item is sold within a short period with profit motive.
4. Contract is readily convertible to cash.

All the four types of contracts are within the scope of IAS 39, with the following exceptions:

- Types 2 and 3, if usually meant to take delivery.
- Types 1 and 4, even if it results in taking delivery is within the scope. In other words, written options of types 1 and 4 are also included.

Four Categories of Financial Instruments

1. Fair value through profit and loss (FVPL).
2. Held-to-maturity (HTM).
3. Loans and receivables (LAR).
4. Available-for-sale (AFS).

Fair Value through Profit and Loss (FVPL)

A financial asset or financial liability at fair value through profit or loss is one that meets any of the following conditions:

- It is classified as held for trading.
- It is acquired or incurred principally for the purpose of selling or repurchasing it in the near term.

- It is part of a portfolio of identified financial instruments that are managed together and for which there is evidence of a recent actual pattern of short-term profit-taking.
- It is a derivative other than a financial guarantee contract or for hedging purposes.
- Upon initial recognition it is designated by the entity as at fair value through profit or loss.

Note: Investments in equity instruments that do not have a quoted market price in an active market, and whose fair value cannot be reliably measured, should not be designated as at fair value through profit or loss.

Held-to-maturity (HTM)

Held-to-maturity investments are financial assets with fixed or determinable payments and fixed maturity. The entity has the positive intention and ability to hold the asset to maturity. The following are not HTM investments:

- Those that the entity upon initial recognition designates as FVPL.
- Those that meet the definition of loans and receivables.
- Those that the entity designates as available-for-sale.

HTM classification is not possible if the entity has, during the current financial year or during the two preceding financial years, sold or reclassified more than an insignificant number of HTM investments before maturity.

Exceptions are sales or reclassifications on account of the following:

- Close to maturity or call date (for example, less than three months before maturity).
- Occurring after the entity has substantially collected the financial asset's original principal.
- Being attributable to an isolated event beyond the entity's control, nonrecurring, and not something that could have been reasonably anticipated by the entity.

Loans and Receivables (LAR)

Loans and receivables are financial assets with fixed or determinable payments that are not quoted in an active market, other than:

- Those that the entity intends to sell immediately or in the near term, classified as held for trading.
- Those that the entity designates as FVPL.
- Those that the entity designates as available-for-sale.
- Those for which the holder may not recover substantially all of its initial investment, other than because of credit deterioration, which should be classified as available-for-sale.

Available-for-sale (AFS)

Available-for-sale financial assets are those non-derivative financial assets that are designated as available-for-sale or are not classified as loans and receivables, held-to-maturity investments, or financial assets at fair value through profit or loss.

FAIR VALUE AND FAIR VALUE DETERMINATION

The fair value of a financial asset or liability is the amount for which the financial asset could be exchanged, or the financial liability settled, between knowledgeable, willing parties in an arm's-length transaction. The presumption is that an entity is a going concern without any intention or need to liquidate or curtail materially the scale of its operations or to undertake a transaction on adverse terms.

When determining the fair value of a financial instrument, IFRS sets out a hierarchy to be applied to the valuation. If quoted prices or rates exist in an active market for the instrument, they must be used to determine the fair value. Under IFRS, the appropriate quoted market price for an asset held is the bid price, and for a liability that is held, the offer price. Where there is no active market available from which to draw quoted prices, a valuation technique should be used. Valuation techniques include:

- Recent market prices or rates, where available, adjusted for relevant subsequent events.
- Reference to the current fair value of another instrument that is substantially the same.
- Discounted cash flow analysis.
- Option pricing models.
- A standard industry valuation technique that has been demonstrated to provide reliable estimates of prices obtained in actual market transactions.

Fair value should reflect the credit quality of the instrument. For those items traded in an open market, this is likely to be incorporated in the price. For over-the-counter derivatives, the standard approach is to value the derivative using the AA-rated curve in the valuation model. For others, the market quoted rates used in the valuation model should be adjusted for credit risk. Any changes in the credit quality will need to be considered when remeasuring fair value.

RECOGNITION AND DERECOGNITION OF FINANCIAL INSTRUMENTS

Derecognition of a financial asset or a portion of a financial asset occurs under the current standards when, and only when, the entity loses control of the contractual rights that comprise the financial asset. An entity loses control if it realizes the rights to benefits specified in the contract, if those rights expire, or if the entity surrenders those rights.

Components of a Financial Asset

Financial assets have two distinct components: cash flows from principal repayment and cash flows from interest coupons. In several financial assets, these cash flows can be segregated and potentially transferred to other parties. The accounting standard lays down the implications of transferring each component separately without transferring the other.

Control over a Financial Asset

Control over a financial asset is determined based on identifying the risks and rewards of the asset and evaluating which party has exposure to the risks and which party has benefits from the financial asset. The accounting standard analyzes the transfer of risks and rewards while transferring a financial asset.

There are several situations where a transferor has not lost control of a transferred financial asset but retains the risks and rewards related to such asset.

Examples of Transfer of Asset without Transfer of Risk/Reward

The transferor has the right to reacquire the asset unless either (1) the reacquisition price is fair value, or (2) the assets are readily obtainable in the market. Also note the following cases:

- The transferor is both entitled and obliged to repurchase or redeem the transferred asset on terms that effectively provide the transferee with a rate of return similar to that on a loan secured by the transferred asset.
- The transferor has retained substantially all of the risks and returns of ownership through a total return swap with the transferee.
- The transferor has retained substantially all of the risks of ownership through an unconditional put option on a transferred asset held by the transferee.

Application of Derecognition

Derecognition is permitted to be considered for a component of a financial asset as against the asset in its entirety in the following situations:

- Specifically identified contractual cash flows, such as a stream of interest-only or principal-only cash flows.
- A fully proportionate share of the cash flows from the asset—for example, 40 percent of all the interest and principal payments received on a loan.
- A fully proportionate share of specifically identified contractual cash flows—for example, 50 percent of the interest cash flows received on a bond.

Rights to the Cash Flows Expired

When a debt instrument has been repaid or a purchased option expires unexercised, then the asset is derecognized.

Rights to the Cash Flows Transferred

Where there is a legal sale of the asset, or where there is a legal assignment of the rights to its cash flows, then the rights to the cash flows from the asset gets transferred.

Where Rights to Cash Flows is not Transferred

If the entity has not transferred the rights to cash flows from the asset, then the entity should have assumed an obligation to *pass through* the cash flows from the asset to another party. The following situations are pass-through arrangements:

- The entity has no obligation to pay amounts to the other party unless it collects equivalent amounts from the original asset.
- The entity is prohibited by the terms of the transfer contract from selling or pledging the original asset other than as security to the other party for the obligation to pay that party cash flows.

- The entity has an obligation to remit any cash flows it collects on behalf of the other party without material delay. In addition, during any short period between collection by the entity and payment to the other party, the funds may not be reinvested other than in cash and cash equivalents and any interest earned must be passed to the other party.

Transfer of Risks and Rewards

If the asset has been transferred, either through a legal sale or a qualifying pass through arrangement, then all the risks and rewards should be transferred. For example, where there is a clean sale or where there is a qualifying arrangement to pass through all cash flows with no further interest by the entity in any of the future economic outcomes from the asset, then the asset is derecognized. The transfer of risks and rewards is evaluated by comparing the entity's exposure, before and after the transfer, to the variability in the amounts and timing of the net cash flows of the assets.

Retaining All the Risks and Rewards

If there is neither a legal sale nor a qualifying pass-through arrangement, no derecognition is permitted and the transaction is treated as a secured borrowing. For example, in a sale with a fixed price repurchase agreement or a sale with a total return swap, no derecognition is permitted and the transaction is treated as a secured borrowing.

Transfer of Control of the Asset

If the asset is transferred, but all its risks and rewards are neither transferred nor retained—in other words, where some risks and rewards are retained and some are transferred—then the entity retains control of the asset and the financial asset is not derecognized.

An example would be a sale with a retained call option or a sale with a written put option. Control in this context means the practical ability to sell the asset. If the buyer has an unfettered and practical ability to sell the asset, for example, because the asset is listed and therefore the buyer could sell it and subsequently repurchase it if required, then control has been transferred and the asset is derecognized.

Recognition to the Extent of Continuing Involvement

If control has not been transferred, then the entity continues to recognize the asset to the extent of its continuing involvement. This covers those circumstances where an entity has neither transferred nor retained substantially all the risks and rewards relating to the transferred asset, but has retained control.

Here the asset is derecognized to the extent the entity has no continuing exposure to the asset. The asset remains on the balance sheet to the extent of the maximum potential exposure and a corresponding liability is recognized.

TREATMENT FOR DIFFERENT CATEGORIES OF FINANCIAL INSTRUMENTS

Category	Measured at	Changes in carrying amount (other than a designated hedge)	Impairment test required?
Financial assets and liabilities at fair value through profit or loss	Fair value	Income statement	No
Loans and receivables	Amortized cost	Income statement	Yes
Held-to-maturity investments	Amortized cost	Income statement	Yes
Available-for-sale	Fair value	Equity	Yes
Other financial liabilities	Amortized cost	Income statement	N/A

Effect of Changes in Fair Value

FVPL—Gain or Loss on Fair Value Changes

Activity	Action
Gain/Loss	Gain or loss on changes in fair value is recognized in the statement of profit and loss.
Interest	Shown in statement of profit and loss.
Dividend	Recognized in statement of profit and loss.

AFS—Gain or Loss on Fair Value Changes

Activity	Action
Gain/Loss	Gain or loss on changes in fair value is recognized in appropriate equity account: Investment Revaluation Account.
Till when?	Till the financial asset is derecognized.
After that?	On derecognition the cumulative gain/loss previously recognized in equity is recognized in the statement of profit and loss.
Interest	Shown in statement of profit and loss using effective rate method, if applicable.
Dividend	Recognized in statement of profit and loss.

HTM/LAR—Gain or Loss on Fair Value Changes

Activity	Action
Gain/Loss	Gain or loss on changes in fair value is recognized in the statement of profit and loss when the financial asset/liability is derecognized or impaired through amortization process.
Interest	Shown in statement of profit and loss using effective rate method.

Reclassification and Its Impact

Reclassification—HTM to AFS

Reclassification	Reason
HTM to AFS	Change in intention or ability.
	No longer appropriate to classify as HTM.
	Due to reclassification, the remaining HTM investments should also be reclassified as AFS.

HTM to AFS—Effects

Activity	Action
Remeasurement	Remeasured at fair value.
Gain/Loss	Gain or loss on such remeasurement is recognized in appropriate equity account: Investment Revaluation Account.
Till when?	Till the financial asset is derecognized.
After that?	On derecognition, the cumulative gain/loss previously recognized in equity is recognized in the statement of profit and loss.
Interest	Continue to show in statement of profit and loss using effective rate method.
Dividend	Recognized in statement of profit and loss.

HTM or AFS to AFS

Reclassification	Reason
HTM or AFS to AFS	Reliable measure becomes available for a financial asset or financial liability for which such a measure was previously not available.

HTM or AFS to AFS—Effects

Activity	Action
Remeasurement	Remeasured at fair value.
Gain/Loss	Gain or loss on such remeasurement is recognized in appropriate equity account: Investment Revaluation Account.
Till when?	Till the financial asset is derecognized.
After that?	On derecognition the cumulative gain/loss previously recognized in equity is recognized in the statement of profit and loss.
Interest	Continue to show in statement of profit and loss using effective rate method, if applicable.
Dividend	Recognized in statement of profit and loss.

Reclassification—AFS to HTM

Reclassification	Reason
AFS to HTM	Change in intention or ability to sell.
	Reliable measure of fair value is no longer available.
	"Two preceding financial years" for HTM classification time limit has elapsed.

AFS to HTM—Effects

Activity	Action
Remeasurement	Remeasured at fair value and that becomes amortized cost.
Amortization	Gain or loss on such remeasurement is amortized to the statement of profit and loss over the remaining life of the HTM using effective interest method.
Difference between new amortized cost and maturity amount	Amortized to the statement of profit and loss over the remaining life of the HTM using effective interest method.
Subsequent impairment	Gain or loss that has been recognized directly in equity is recognized in the statement of profit and loss.

AFS to LAR—Effects

Activity	Action
Remeasurement	Remeasured at fair value and that becomes cost.
Amortization	Gain or loss on such remeasurement should remain in the equity account until it is sold or otherwise disposed of.
When sold or otherwise disposed of	Gain or loss on remeasurement should be recognized in the statement of profit and loss.
Subsequent impairment	Gain or loss that has been recognized directly in equity is recognized in the statement of profit and loss.

Impairment and Its Treatment for Different Categories

HTM/LAR—Impairment Requirements

Activity	Action
Amount of loss	Difference between asset's carrying amount and the present value of estimated cash flows discounted at original effective interest rate.
Method of write-off	Reduced directly from the carrying amount or through an allowance account.
Where to take the loss?	Recognized in statement of profit and loss.
Subsequent decrease in impairment loss	Reversed and added to carrying amount or through an allowance account.
Maximum amount of reversal	Reversal should not result in carrying amount exceeding the amortized cost before impairment.
Where to take the profit?	Recognized in statement of profit and loss.

Short-term Receivables—Impairment Requirements

Activity	Action
Amount of loss	Difference between receivables' carrying amount and the undiscounted amount of estimated future cash flows.
Method of write-off	Reduced directly from the carrying amount or through an allowance account.
Where to take the loss?	Recognized in statement of profit and loss.
Subsequent decrease in impairment loss	Reversed and added to carrying amount or through an allowance account.
Maximum amount of reversal	Reversal should not result in carrying amount exceeding the short-term receivables before impairment.
Where to take the profit?	Recognized in statement of profit and loss.

Assets Carried at Cost—Impairment requirements

Activity	Action
Amount of loss	Difference between asset's carrying amount and the present value of estimated cash flows discounted at the current market rate of return for a similar financial asset.
Where to take the loss?	Recognized in statement of profit and loss.
Subsequent decrease in impairment loss	Impairment losses should not be reversed.

AFS Assets—Impairment requirements

Activity	Action
Amount of loss	Cumulative loss that had been recognized directly in the equity account should be removed from the equity account.
Method of write-off	The cumulative loss is recognized in the statement of profit and loss.
What is the quantum of write-off?	The quantum of write-off should be the difference between the acquisition cost and the current fair value of the asset.
Subsequent decrease in impairment loss—equity instrument	Impairment losses recognized in the profit and loss account for an equity investment should not be reversed.
Subsequent decrease in impairment loss—debt instrument	Impairment losses recognized in the profit and loss account for a debt investment should be reversed to statement of profit and loss.

AMENDMENTS TO IAS 39 & IFRS 7—OCTOBER 2008

Reclassification of Financial Assets

Certain non-derivative financial assets recognized are permitted to be reclassified with effect from November 1, 2008, prospectively. If the decision to reclassify is taken before November 1, then the entity has the option of giving effect to the reclassification retrospectively from any date starting July 1, 2008, until October 31, 2008.

Reclassification out of FVPL and AFS Categories

If a financial asset would have met the definition of loans and receivables (LAR) had it not been classified as FVPL or AFS at initial recognition, then such a financial asset can be reclassified out of FVPL or AFS. Note that the reclassification option is not applicable for financial liabilities, derivatives, and financial assets that are designated as at FVPL on initial recognition under the fair value option.

A debt instrument that would have met the definition of LAR may be reclassified out of FVPL if the entity has the intention and ability to hold the asset for the foreseeable future or until maturity.

A debt instrument classified as AFS that would have met the definition of LAR may be reclassified to the LAR category if the entity has the intention and ability to hold the financial asset for the foreseeable future or until maturity.

Any other debt instrument or any equity instrument may be reclassified from FVPL to AFS or from FVPL to HTM (in the case of debt instruments), if the financial asset is no longer held for the purpose of selling in the near term—but only in rare circumstances. The IASB has already announced that the market conditions in the third quarter of 2008 are an example of rare circumstances.

Measurement at the Reclassification Date

All reclassifications are required to be made at the fair value of the financial asset and any previously recognized gains or losses cannot be reversed. The fair value at the date of reclassification becomes the new cost or amortized cost of the financial asset as applicable.

Measurement after the Reclassification Date

For financial assets measured at amortized cost, a new effective interest rate will be determined at the date of reclassification. In the case of reclassifications of a fixed rate debt instrument to LAR and HTM this effective interest rate will be used as the discount rate for future impairment calculations.

Disclosures under Amended IFRS 7

The following additional disclosures are required for reclassifications just described:

- The amount reclassified into and out of each category.
- For each reporting period until derecognition, the carrying amounts and fair values of all financial assets reclassified in the current or previous reporting periods.
- If the financial asset has been reclassified based on the "rare circumstances" exception, the details of those circumstances—including the factors that indicated that the situation was rare.
- The fair value gain or loss recognized in profit or loss or OCI for the reporting period in which reclassification occurs and in the previous period.
- In the period of reclassification and in subsequent periods until the financial asset is derecognized, the gain or loss that would have been recognized in profit or loss or other comprehensive income had the financial asset not been reclassified, and the actual gain, loss, income, and expense recognized in profit or loss.
- The effective interest rate and estimated cash flows the entity expects to recover as of the date of reclassification of the financial asset.

APPENDIX C

Financial Statements of Sample Fund

(Prepared in accordance with the IFRS requirements)

BALANCE SHEET AS OF DECEMBER, 20X2 AND 20X1

(€ thousands—Note A)	20X2	20X1
Assets		
Due from Banks	1,139,580	432,720
Investments (Note C)	34,262,280	34,516,800
Accounts Receivable		
Accrued income and receivables on loans	3,007,440	1,743,300
Accrued income on investments	93,600	172,800
Other receivables	31,860	16,020
	3,132,900	1,932,120
Loans (Note B)		
Disbursed and outstanding	11,586,940	11,569,320
	11,588,940	11,569,320
Total Assets	**50,123,700**	**48,450,960**
Liabilities and Equity	**20X2**	**20X1**
Accounts Payable	899,820	189,180
Equity (Note D)		
Fund capital	23,145,480	23,145,480
Reserves		
Retained earnings	48,538,260	45,216,180
Cumulative Currency Translation Adjustment (Note A)	(22,459,860)	(20,099,880)
Total reserves	26,078,400	25,116,300
Total equity	49,223,880	48,261,780
Total Liabilities and Equity	**50,123,700**	**48,450,960**

The accompanying notes to the financial statements form part of this statement.

INCOME STATEMENT

For the years ended December 31, 20X2 and 20X1

(€ thousands—Note A)	**20X2**	**20X1**
Income (Note G)		
Interest and charges on loans	466,920	605,160
Income from investments	1,861,740	2,163,780
Other income	7,020	239,220
Total income	2,335,680	3,008,160
Expenses		
Administrative expenses (Note F)	465,660	525,600
Bank charges	9,540	16,920
Total expenses	475,200	542,520
Provision for impairment on loan interest and charges	(1,231,920)	41,580
Total expenses and provision for impairment	(1,234,800)	524,340
Income before transfers approved by the Board	3,570,480	2,483,820
Transfers of income approved by the Board	(248,400)	(193,140)
Net Income	**3,322,080**	**2,290,680**

The accompanying notes to the financial statements form part of this statement.

STATEMENT OF CHANGES IN EQUITY

For the years ended December 31, 20X2 and 20X1
(€ thousands—Note A)

	Fund Capital	**Retained Earnings**	**Cumulative Currency Translation Adjustment**	**Total Equity**
Balance at January 1, 20X1	23,145,480	67,352,940	(16,864,740)	73,633,680
Net income for the year	0	2,290,680	0	2,290,680
Withdrawal of funds by the investors	0	(24,427,440)	0	(24,427,440)
Currency translation adjustment	0	0	(3,235,140)	(3,235,140)
Balance at December 31, 20X1 and January 1, 20X2	**23,145,480**	**45,216,180**	**(20,099,880)**	**48,261,780**
Net income for the current year	0	3,322,080	0	3,322,080
Currency translation adjustment	0	0	(2,359,980)	(2,359,980)
Balance at December 31, 20X2	**23,145,480**	**48,538,260**	**(22,459,860)**	**49,223,880**

The accompanying notes to the financial statements form part of this statement.

STATEMENT OF CASH FLOWS

For the years ended December 31, 20X2 and 20X1

(€ thousands—Note A)	20X2	20X1
Cash Flows from:		
Operating Activities:		
Net income	3,322,080	2,290,680
Adjustments to reconcile net income to net cash provided by operating activities:		
Amortization of held-to-maturity investments	0	155,700
Provision for impairment on loan principal and charges	(1,710,000)	(18,180)
Unrealized gains (losses) on investments	21,960	(7,020)
Changes in accrued income and receivables on loans	(490,140)	614,880
Changes in net current assets	1,142,820	71,460
Net cash provided by operating activities	2,286,720	3,107,520
Investing and Lending Activities:		
Disbursements on loans	(1,068,840)	(976,860)
Repayment of loans	984,960	1,645,560
Investments maturing after 3 months of acquisition:		
Held-to-maturity portfolio	0	40,280,400
Trading portfolio	21,434,580	(18,117,540)
Withdrawal of funds by the investors	0	(24,427,440)
Net cash provided by (used in) investing and lending activities	21,350,700	(1,595,880)
Effect of exchange rate changes on cash and liquid investments	(1,234,620)	(330,120)
Net increase in cash and liquid investments	22,402,800	1,181,520
Cash and cash equivalents at the beginning of the year	1,697,580	516,060
Cash and cash equivalents at the end of the year	24,100,380	1,697,580
Composed of:		
Investments maturing within 3 months of acquisition	22,960,800	1,264,860
Cash	1,139,580	432,720
Cash and cash equivalents at the end of the year	24,100,380	1,697,580
Supplementary disclosure:		
Movement resulting from exchange rate fluctuation on loans	440,280	498,960

NOTES TO THE FINANCIAL STATEMENTS

For the years ended December 31, 20X2 and 20X1

Note A: Summary of Significant Accounting Policies

The financial statements of the Fund are prepared in accordance with International Financial Reporting Standards (IFRS) promulgated by the International Accounting Standards Board (IASB). The financial statements have been prepared under the historical cost convention except for certain financial assets that are carried at fair value. The significant accounting policies of the Fund are summarized below.

Revenue Recognition

Interest income is accrued on a time basis and recognized based on the effective interest method during the time an investment or loan is outstanding and held by the Fund. The effective interest rate is the rate that discounts the estimated future cash flows through the expected life of the financial asset to the asset's net carrying amount. Commitment fees are accrued in arrears for unutilized loan facilities.

Income from investments includes realized and unrealized gains and losses on held-for-trading investments.

Functional and Presentation Currencies

The Fund conducts its operations in U.S. dollars, and has determined that its functional currency is the U.S. dollar. In accordance with Article of the Agreement of the Fund, the financial statements are presented in euros (€).

The value of €1 at December 31, 20X2, was equivalent to US$1.58025 (20X1: US$1.50440).

Currency Translation

Income and expenses are translated to € at the rates prevailing on the date of the transaction. Monetary assets and liabilities are translated from US$ to € at rates prevailing on the balance sheet date. Translation differences are included in reserves under cumulative currency translation adjustment (CCTA). Changes in CCTA are reported in the statement of changes in equity. Capital replenishments are recorded in € at the exchange rates prevailing at the time of receipt. Translation gains and losses on conversion of currencies into € are included in the determination of net income.

Financial Instruments

Financial assets and financial liabilities are recognized when the Fund assumes related contractual rights or obligations.

1. Financial Assets

The Fund classifies its financial assets in the following categories: held-for-trading financial assets, loans and receivables, and held-to-maturity investments. Management determines the classification of its investments upon initial recognition.

a. Held-for-Trading Financial Assets
All held-for-trading assets are carried at fair value through the income statement. Investments in the held-for-trading portfolio are acquired principally for the purpose of selling in the short term. Held-for-trading financial assets are measured at fair value, with gains and losses arising from changes in fair value included in the income statement in the period in which they arise.

b. Loans and Receivables
Loans include outstanding balances receivable from borrowers in respect of amounts disbursed. The Fund has also classified accrued income and receivables from loans and

investments and other sundry amounts as receivables. Loans and receivables are non-derivative financial assets with fixed or determinable payments that are not quoted in an active market. They arise when the Fund provides money, goods, or services directly to a borrower with no intention of trading the receivable. Loans and receivables are subsequently measured at amortized cost using the effective interest method.

c. Held-to-Maturity Investments

The Fund has classified its investments in certain debt securities as held-to-maturity. Held-to-maturity investments are non-derivative financial assets with fixed or determinable payments and fixed maturities that the Fund's management has the positive intention and ability to hold to maturity. Held-to-maturity investments are subsequently measured at amortized cost using the effective interest method.

Purchases and sales of held-for-trading and held-to-maturity investments are recognized on a trade-date basis, which is the date the Fund commits to purchase or sell the asset. Loans are recognized when cash is advanced to the borrowers.

Cash and cash equivalents include amounts due from banks, demand deposits, and other short-term, highly liquid investments that are readily convertible to a known amount of cash, are subject to an insignificant risk of changes in value, and have a time to maturity upon acquisition of three months or less.

Financial assets are derecognized when the rights to receive cash flows from the financial assets have expired or where the Fund has transferred substantially all risks and rewards of ownership.

2. Financial Liabilities

Financial liabilities include accounts payable and are subsequently measured at amortized cost. Financial liabilities are derecognized upon discharge, cancellation or expiration.

Impairment of Financial Assets

The Fund assesses at each balance sheet date whether there is objective evidence that a financial asset or group of financial assets is impaired. A financial asset or a group of financial assets is impaired and impairment losses are incurred if, and only if, there is objective evidence of impairment as a result of one or more events that occurred after the initial recognition of the asset (a "loss event") and that loss event (or events) has an impact on the estimated future cash flows of the financial asset or group of financial assets that can be reliably estimated.

If the Fund determines that there is objective evidence that an impairment loss has been incurred on a loan, receivable, or held-to-maturity investment carried at amortized cost, the amount of the loss is measured as the difference between the asset's carrying amount and the present value of its estimated future cash flows (excluding future credit losses that have not been incurred), discounted at the financial asset's original effective interest rate. The estimated impairment loss may arise from delays that may be experienced in receiving amounts due, and the impairment calculations reflect management's best estimate of the effect of such delays.

The impairment loss is reported as a reduction to the carrying amount of the asset through the use of an allowance account and recognized in the income statement. If a loan or held-to-maturity investment has a variable interest rate, the discount rate for measuring any impairment loss is the current effective interest rate determined under the contract. Interest and charges are accrued on all loans, including those in arrears.

Fair Value Disclosure

The fair values of investments that are quoted in active markets are based on current bid prices. Fair values of financial assets listed in inactive markets or unlisted securities are determined by using valuation techniques that incorporate the maximum use of market data inputs. These valuation techniques include the use of recent arm's-length transactions, discounted cash flow analysis, option pricing models, and other valuation techniques commonly used by market participants.

Fair values for financial instruments for which market quotations are not readily available have been determined using methodologies and assumptions that necessarily require the use of subjective judgments. Accordingly, the actual value at which such financial instruments could be exchanged in a current transaction, or whether they are exchangeable at all, is not readily determinable. Management believes that these methodologies and assumptions are reasonable; however, the values actually realizable in a sale might differ from the fair values disclosed.

The methods and assumptions used by the Fund in estimating the fair values of financial instruments are as follows:

Cash and cash equivalents: The carrying amount is the fair value.

Investments: Fair values for investment securities are based on quoted market prices, where available. If quoted market prices are not available, fair values are based on quoted market prices of comparable instruments.

Loans: The Fund does not sell its loans, nor does it believe there is a comparable market for its loans. The fair value of loans reported in these financial statements represents management's best estimates of the present value of the loans' expected cash flows. Fair values are estimated using a discounted cash flow model based on the year-end market equivalent lending rate in that currency, adjusted for estimated credit risk.

Retained Earnings

Retained earnings of the Fund consist of amounts allocated to reserves from prior years' income and unallocated current year net income.

Critical Accounting Judgments and Key Sources of Estimation Uncertainty

The preparation of financial statements in conformity with IFRS requires management to make certain estimates, assumptions, and judgments that affect the reported amounts of assets, liabilities, revenue, and expenses as well as the disclosure of contingent liabilities. Actual results could differ from such estimates. Estimates and judgments are continually evaluated and are based on historical experience and other factors, including expectations of future events that are believed to be reasonable under the circumstances. The most significant judgments and estimates are summarized below:

1. Impairment Losses on Assets Carried at Amortized Cost

The Fund first assesses whether objective evidence of impairment exists individually for financial assets. If the Fund determines that no objective evidence of impairment exists for an individually assessed financial asset, that asset is included in a group of financial assets with similar credit characteristics and collectively assessed for impairment. Assets that are individually assessed for impairment and for which an impairment loss is or continues to be recognized are not included in a collective assessment of impairment. A financial asset or a group of financial assets is impaired and impairment losses are incurred if, and only if, there is objective evidence of impairment as a result of one or more events that occurred after the initial recognition of the asset (a "loss event") and that loss event (or events) has an impact on the estimated future cash flows of the financial asset or group of financial assets and can be reliably estimated.

If the Fund determines that there is objective evidence that an impairment loss on loans and receivables or held-to-maturity investments carried at amortized cost has been incurred, the amount of the loss is measured as the difference between the asset's carrying amount and the present value of its estimated future cash flows (excluding future credit losses that have not been incurred) discounted at the financial asset's original effective interest rate.

The carrying amount of the asset is reduced through the use of an allowance account and the amount of the loss is recognized in the income statement.

2. Fair Values of Financial Instruments

The fair values of financial instruments that are not quoted in active markets are determined by using valuation techniques. Valuation techniques, for example, models that are used to determine fair values, are validated and periodically reviewed by qualified personnel independent of the area that created them. All models are periodically calibrated to ensure that outputs reflect actual data and comparative market prices. To a practical extent, models use only observable data; however, areas such as credit risk (both own and counterparty), volatilities, and correlations require management to make estimates. Changes in assumptions about these factors could affect the reported fair value of financial instruments.

3. Held-to-Maturity Investments

The Fund follows the guidance of IAS 39 on classifying certain financial assets as held-to-maturity. This classification requires significant judgment. In making the judgment to designate an asset as held-to-maturity, the Fund makes a positive determination as to its intention and ability to hold such investments to maturity.

Note B: Risk Management Policies and Procedures

In the course of exercising its fiduciary duties, the Fund applies specific risk management policies designed to protect the resources of the Fund through the Fund's General Authority on Asset and Liability Management (the ALM Authority). The ALM Authority sets out the guiding principles for managing the Fund's risks, including interest rate risk, currency risk, liquidity risk, counterparty credit risk, and operational risk.

Under the ALM Authority, the President of the Fund is authorized to approve and amend more detailed operational guidelines as necessary, upon the recommendations of the Asset and Liability Management Committee (ALCO).

Day-to-day operational responsibility for implementing the Fund's risk management policies and guidelines is delegated to the appropriate business units, and the Financial Management Department is responsible for monitoring the day-to-day compliance with those policies and guidelines.

Note C: Investments

As part of its portfolio management strategy, the Fund invests in government and other obligations, time deposits, and asset-backed securities.

For government and other obligations with final maturities longer than one year, the Fund may only invest in obligations with counterparties having a minimum credit rating of AA–issued or unconditionally guaranteed by governments of member countries or other official entities. For asset-backed securities, the Fund may only invest in securities with AAA credit rating. Investments in money market instruments are restricted to instruments having maturities of not more than one year and a minimum rating of A.

As at December 31, 20X2 and 20X1, all the Fund's investments are held-for-trading and are summarized below:

(€ thousands)	**20X2**	**20X1**
Time deposits	21,834,000	1,264,860
Asset-backed securities	891,000	12,172,140
Government and other obligations	7,375,680	0
Corporate bonds	4,161,600	21,079,800
Total	**34,262,280**	**34,516,800**

The contractual maturity structure of held-for-trading investments as of December 31, 20X2 and 20X1, was as follows:

(€ thousands)	**20X2**	**20X1**
One year or less	31,111,200	1,744,200
More than one year but less than two years	0	1,495,800
More than two years but less than three years	113,400	14,086,800
More than three years but less than four years	0	601,200
More than four years but less than five years	0	3,589,200
More than five years	3,037,680	12,999,600
Total	**34,262,280**	**34,516,800**

The notional balance of investments as of December 31, 20X2, was € 190.46 million (20X1: € 191.61 million), while the average yield was 5.81% (20X1: 5.55%).

Note D: Equity

Equity is composed of Fund capital, retained earnings, and cumulative currency translation adjustments. These are further detailed as follows:

Retained Earnings

Retained earnings as of December 31, 20X2 and 20X1, were as follows:
(**€ thousands**)

Balance as of January 1, 20X1	67,352,940
Net income for the year	2,290,680
Withdrawal of funds by the Investors	(24,427,440)

Balance as of December 31, 20X1, and January 1, 20X2	**45,216,180**
Net income for the current year	3,322,080
Balance as of December 31, 20X2	**48,538,260**

Cumulative Currency Translation Adjustments (CCTA)

Cumulative currency translation adjustments as of December 31, 20X2 and 20X1, were as follows:

(€ thousands)	**20X2**	**20X1**
Balance at January 1	20,099,880	16,864,740
Movements during the year	2,359,980	3,235,140
Balance at December 31	**22,459,860**	**20,099,880**

Note E: Income

Interest and Charges on Loans

Interest and charges on loans for the years ended December 31, 20X2 and 20X1, were as follows:

(€ thousands)	**20X2**	**20X1**
Interest income on loans not impaired	255,780	327,600
Interest income on impaired loans	163,440	218,160
Commitment charges	47,700	59,400
Total	**466,920**	**605,160**

Income from Investments

Income from investments for the years ended December 31, 20X2 and 20X1, was as follows:

(€ thousands)	**20X2**	**20X1**
Interest income	1,756,800	2,109,420
Realized and unrealized fair value gains	104,940	54,360
Total	**1,861,740**	**2,163,780**

Note F: Administrative Expenses

According to the Agreement, the Fund shall pay to the Bank the expenses incurred in the management of the Fund as follows:

1. Separately identifiable costs incurred by the Bank for the Fund.
2. Indirect costs incurred by the Bank in the management of the Fund.

However, the annual payment for the aforementioned expenses incurred by the Bank shall not exceed 20 percent of the Fund's gross income during the course of each year.

APPENDIX D

Glossary of Technical Terms

American Depositary Receipts (ADRs) Certificates issued by a U.S. depository bank, representing foreign shares held by the bank in the country of issue. Each ADR can represent a fraction of a share, a single share, or multiple shares of foreign stock. If the ADRs are *sponsored*, the corporation provides financial information and other assistance to the bank and may subsidize the administration of the ADRs. *Unsponsored* ADRs do not receive such assistance.

American-style option An option contract that can be exercised at any time between the date of purchase and the expiration date.

amortized cost The amount at which a financial asset or liability is measured at initial recognition less principal repayments, plus or minus the cumulative amortization of any premium or discount, and minus any write-down for impairment.

arbitrage The simultaneous buying and selling of a security at two different prices in two different markets, resulting in profits without risk.

arm's-length price The price at which two unrelated and non-desperate parties would agree to a transaction.

Asian option Option based on the average price of the asset during the life of the option.

ask price The quoted offer, or the lowest price an investor will accept to sell a stock to a buyer; also called the offer price.

asset-backed security A security that is collateralized by loans, leases, receivables, or installment contracts on personal property, not real estate.

at-the-money An option is at-the-money if the strike price of the option is equal to the market price of the underlying security. For example, if ABC stock is trading at 50, then the ABC option of strike price 50 is at-the-money.

bear An investor who believes a stock or the overall market will decline. A bear market is a prolonged period of falling stock prices.

bid price The quoted bid, or the highest price an investor is willing to pay to buy a security from a seller.

bid-ask spread The difference between the bid and asked prices.

binomial option pricing model An option pricing model in which the underlying asset can take on only two possible, discrete values in the next time period for each value that it can take on in the preceding time period.

Black-Scholes option-pricing model A model for pricing call options based on the stock price, the exercise price, the risk-free interest rate, the time to expiration, and the standard deviation of the stock return.

broker An individual who is paid a commission or brokerage for executing customer orders of buying and selling financial instruments.

call option An option contract that gives its holder the right (but not the obligation) to purchase a specified number of shares of the underlying stock at the given strike price, on or before the expiry date of the contract.

capital gain When a stock is sold for a profit, the difference between the net sales price of securities and their net cost, or original basis, is the capital gain. If a stock is sold below cost, the difference is a capital loss.

cash dividend A dividend paid in cash to the shareholders of the company. A cash distribution may include capital gains and return of capital in addition to the dividend.

commission The fee paid to a broker to execute a trade, based on number of shares, bonds, options, and/or their value.

common stock Securities that represent equity ownership in a company. Common shares carry voting rights. They also give the holder a share in a company's profits via dividend payments or the capital appreciation of the security.

contract An agreement between two or more parties, having commercial consequences that the parties have little discretion to avoid as the agreement is usually enforceable by law. Contracts may take a variety of forms and need not be in writing.

counterparty risk Counterparty is the other party in a non-exchange-traded contract. The risk that the other party to an agreement will default is *counterparty risk.*

covered call A written call option position in which the writer owns the number of shares of the underlying stock represented by the option contracts. Covered calls limit the risk the writer takes, as the writer owns the underlying shares.

cumulative preferred stock Preferred stock whose dividends accrue, should the issuer not make timely dividend payments.

custodial fees Fees charged by an institution that holds securities in safekeeping for an investor.

day-trading Refers to establishing and liquidating the same position or positions within the same trading day.

debt securities Any debt instrument that can be bought or sold between two parties and has basic terms defined, such as notional amount, interest rate, and maturity/renewal date. Debt securities include government bonds, corporate bonds, municipal bonds, preferred stock, collateralized securities, and zero-coupon securities.

deferred taxes Amount allocated during the period to cover tax liabilities that have not yet been paid.

delivery versus payment A transaction in which the buyer's payment for securities is due at the time of delivery (usually to a bank acting as agent for the buyer) upon receipt of the securities. The payment may be made by bank wire, check, or direct credit to an account.

derecognition The removal of a previously recognized financial asset or financial liability from an entity's balance sheet.

derivative instrument A financial security, such as an option or a future, whose value is derived in part from the value and characteristics of another security, the underlying security.

detachable warrant A warrant entitles the holder to buy a given number of shares of stock at a stipulated price. A detachable warrant is one that may be sold separately from the package with which it may have originally been issued.

discount rate The interest rate that the Federal Reserve charges a bank to borrow funds when a bank is temporarily short of funds.

dividend payout ratio Percentage of earnings paid out as dividends.

dividend policy An established guide for the firm to determine the amount of money it will pay as dividends.

dividend rights A shareholder's rights to receive per-share dividends identical to those other shareholders receive.

embedded derivative Implicit or explicit terms in a contract that affect some or all of the cash flows of a contract in a manner similar to a freestanding derivative instrument.

embedded option An option that is part of the structure of a bond that provides either the bondholder or issuer the right to take some action against the other party, as opposed to a *bare option*, which trades separately from any underlying security.

equity Represents ownership interest in a firm. Also the residual dollar value of a futures trading account, assuming it is liquidated at the going market price.

equity instrument Any contract that evidences a residual interest in the assets of an entity after deducting all of its liabilities.

equity options Securities that give the holder the right to buy or sell a specified number of shares of stock, at a specified price for a certain limited time period.

equity swap A swap in which the cash flows that are exchanged are based on the total return on some stock market index and an interest rate—either a fixed rate or a floating rate.

exchange The marketplace in which shares, options, and futures on stocks, bonds, commodities, and indexes are traded. Principal U.S. stock exchanges are the New York Stock Exchange (NYSE), the American Stock Exchange (AMEX), and the National Association of Securities Dealers Automated Quotation System (NASDAQ).

exchange rate risk Also called *currency risk*, the risk of an investment's value changing because of currency exchange rates.

ex-dividend This means the price does not include dividend. The buyer of shares when they are quoted ex-dividend is not entitled to receive a declared dividend.

ex-dividend date The first day of trading when the seller, rather than the buyer, of a stock will be entitled to the most recently announced dividend payment. A stock that has gone ex-dividend is marked with an "x" in listings on that date.

exercise price The price at which an underlying instrument may be bought, sold, or settled upon exercise of an option.

ex-rights In connection with a rights offering, shares of stock that are trading without the rights attached.

ex-rights date The date on which a share of common stock begins trading without the rights.

fair market price Amount at which an asset would change hands between two parties, both having knowledge of the relevant facts. Also referred to as *fair value.*

FASB Since 1973, the Financial Accounting Standards Board (FASB) has been the designated organization in the private sector for establishing standards of financial accounting and reporting (U.S. GAAP). These standards govern the preparation of financial reports. They are officially recognized as authoritative by the Securities and Exchange Commission (SEC) and the American Institute of Certified Public Accountants (AICPA). Such standards are essential to the efficient functioning of the economy since investors, creditors, auditors, and others rely on credible, transparent, and comparable financial information.

FIFO (first-in-first-out) A valuation method that assumes the assets produced or acquired first are sold or used first, meaning that the assets that are remaining in inventory are matched to the assets that are most recently purchased or produced.

financial asset Any asset that is (1) cash; (2) an equity instrument of another entity; (3) a contractual right to receive cash or another financial asset from another entity or to exchange financial assets/financial liabilities with another entity under conditions that are potentially favorable to the entity; or (4) a contract that will or may be settled in the entity's own equity instruments, and is either a non-derivative for which the entity is or may be obliged to receive a variable number of the entity's own equity instruments, or a derivative that will or may be settled other than by the exchange of a fixed amount of cash or another financial asset for a fixed number of the entity's own equity instruments.

financial instrument Any contract that gives rise to both a financial asset of an entity and a financial liability or equity instrument of another entity.

financial liability A liability that is a contractual obligation to deliver cash or another financial asset to another entity; or to exchange financial instruments with another entity under conditions that are potentially unfavorable to the entity; or a contract that will or may be settled in the entity's own equity instruments, and is either a non-derivative for which the entity is or may be obliged to deliver a variable number of the entity's own equity instruments, or a derivative that will or may be settled other than by the exchange of a fixed amount of cash or another financial asset for a fixed number of entity's own equity instruments.

forward contract A cash market transaction in which delivery of the commodity is deferred until after the contract has been made. It is not standardized and is not traded on organized exchanges. Although the delivery is made in the future, the price is determined at the initial trade date.

forward rate The foreign exchange rate used in an agreement to exchange, at a specified future date, a specified amount of a commodity, currency, or other asset.

functional currency The currency of the primary economic environment in which an entity operates.

futures contract A contractual agreement, generally made on the trading floor of a futures exchange, to buy or sell a particular commodity or financial instrument at a predetermined price in the future.

hedge fund A fund that may employ a variety of techniques to enhance returns, such as both buying and shorting stocks and a host of other innovative financial instruments.

hedging A strategy designed to reduce investment risk using derivative products. A hedge can help lock in existing profits. The purpose of hedging is to reduce the volatility of a portfolio by reducing the risk of loss.

hedging instrument A strategy used in risk management whereby an entity seeks to reduce or eliminate financial risks by entering into transactions that offset the risks. To deploy hedge accounting, special accounting rules may be used if specific hedge effectiveness and other criteria are met.

hedged item An asset, liability, firm commitment, highly probable forecast transaction, or net investment in a foreign operation that (1) exposes the entity to risk of changes in fair value or future cash flows and (2) is designated as being hedged.

hedge effectiveness The degree to which changes in the fair value or cash flows of the hedged item that are attributable to a hedged risk are offset by changes in fair value or cash flows of the hedging instrument.

held-to-maturity asset Financial assets that have fixed or determinable payments and a fixed maturity and that an entity has the positive intent and ability to hold until maturity.

IASB International Accounting Standards Board; standard-setting body responsible for the development of International Financial Reporting Standards (IFRSs), permitted or required by over 100 countries across the world.

IFRS International Financial Reporting Standards, the body of accounting standards and interpretations issued or endorsed by the IASB. IFRS is a summation of generally accepted accounting principles (GAAP) in many countries and on many stock exchanges around the world.

impairment A situation where the estimated recoverable amount of a financial asset has declined below its carrying amount.

income statement A statement showing the revenues, expenses, and income being the difference between revenues and expenses of an entity during a defined period of time.

initial margin requirement When buying securities on margin, the proportion of the total market value of the securities that the investor must pay for in cash. The regulatory authorities set initial margin requirements, but individual brokerage firms are free to set higher requirements. In futures contracts, initial margin requirements are set by the exchange.

initial public offering (IPO) A company's first sale of stock to the public. Securities offered in an IPO are often those of small companies seeking outside equity capital and a public market for their stock.

interest The cost of borrowing money, expressed as a percentage rate over a period of time.

in-the-money Used to describe a put option that has a strike price higher than the underlying spot price, or a call option with a strike price lower than the underlying spot price. For example, if the March ABC spot contract is trading at $7, a March call with a strike price of $6 would be considered in-the-money by $1.

intrinsic value The positive difference between the current price of the underlying and the exercise price in those situations when an option is in-the-money.

LIBOR The London Interbank Offered Rate; the rate of interest that major international banks in London charge each other for borrowings. Most of the variable interest rates are based on spreads off of LIBOR.

LIFO (last in, first out) The last in, first out inventory valuation methodology; a method of valuing inventory that uses the cost of the most recent item in inventory first.

liquidity A market is liquid when it has a high level of trading activity, allowing buying and selling with minimum price disturbance.

liquidity risk The risk that an entity will encounter difficulty in meeting obligations associated with financial liabilities.

management fee An investment advisory fee charged by the financial advisor to a fund based on the fund's assets under management, but sometimes determined on a sliding basis that declines as the assets under management of the fund increases.

margin The difference between the market value of a stock and the loan a broker makes. Margin allows investors to buy securities by borrowing money from a broker.

margin account An account in which stocks are purchased for a combination of cash and a loan. The loan in the margin account is collateralized by the stock and, if the value of the stock drops significantly, the owner will be asked to bring in additional margin; otherwise a portion of the stock will be liquidated.

margin call A demand for additional funds because of adverse price movement.

marked-to-market An arrangement whereby the unrealized profits or losses on a futures contract are recorded each day.

market capitalization The total dollar value of all outstanding shares, computed as shares multiplied by current market price. It is a measure of the corporation's size.

monetary item Money held and assets to be received or liabilities to be paid in fixed or determinable amounts of money.

mutual fund A pool of money that is managed by an investment company.

NASDAQ National Association of Securities Dealers Automatic Quotation System is an electronic quotation system that provides price quotations to market participants about the more actively traded common stock issues in the over-the-counter (OTC) market.

net asset value (NAV) The value of a fund's investments. For a mutual fund or hedge fund, the net asset value per share represents the fund's market value, subject to a possible sales or redemption charge.

net assets The difference between total assets on the one hand and current liabilities and non-capitalized long-term liabilities on the other hand.

net income A company's total earnings, reflecting revenues adjusted for costs of doing business, depreciation, interest, taxes, and other expenses.

net present value (NPV) The present value of the expected future cash flows less the cost.

notional amount An amount of currency, number of shares, a number of units of weight or volume, or other units specified in a derivative contract.

option The right, but not the obligation, to buy or sell an asset at a set price on or before a given date.

options contract A contract that, in exchange for the option price, gives the option buyer the right, but not the obligation, to buy (or sell) a financial asset at the exercise price from (or to) the option seller within a specified time period, or on a specified date (expiration date).

out-of-the-money option A put option is out-of-the-money if the strike price is less than the market price of the underlying security. A call option is out-of-the-money if the strike price is greater than the market price of the underlying security.

P/E ratio A valuation ratio of a company's current share price compared to its per-share earnings. For example, if a company is currently trading at $5 a share and earnings over the past 12 months were $1 per share, the P/E ratio for the stock would be 5 ($5/$1).

preferred shares Preferred shares give investors a fixed dividend from the company's earnings and preferred shareholders get paid before common shareholders.

premium The price of an option contract; in futures trading, the amount by which the futures price exceeds the price of the spot commodity.

put option An option contract that gives its holder the right (but not the obligation) to sell a fixed number of shares at a fixed price within a given time frame.

quotation The bid and offered prices at which a dealer is willing to buy or sell.

record date Date by which a shareholder must officially own shares in order to be entitled to a dividend.

redeemable Eligible for redemption under the terms of the contract.

regular-way purchase or sale A purchase or sale of a financial asset under a contract whose terms require delivery of the asset within the time frame established generally by regulation or convention in the marketplace concerned.

secondary market The market where securities are traded after they are initially offered in the primary market. Most trading is done in the secondary market.

settlement date The date on which payment is effected to settle a trade. For stocks traded on U.S. exchanges, settlement is currently three business days after the trade. For over-the-counter trades, this will vary for different products.

settlement price The price determined by the exchange, usually the closing rate on any given date, which is used to calculate gains and losses in derivatives markets. Settlement prices are used to determine gains, losses, margin calls, and invoice prices for deliveries.

shareholders' equity A company's total assets minus total liabilities; also known as a company's *net worth.*

short position When a person sells stocks he does not yet own, a short position is created. Shares must be borrowed before the sale to make good delivery to the buyer. Eventually, the shares must be bought to close out the transaction.

spread The gap between bid and ask prices of a stock or other security.

stock Ownership of a corporation, conveyed in shares which represent a piece of the corporation's assets and earnings.

stock dividend When the payment of a corporate dividend is in the form of stock rather than cash, it is known as a stock dividend. The stock dividend may be additional shares in the company, or it may be shares in a subsidiary being spun off to shareholders. Stock dividends, unlike a cash dividend, are not taxed until sold.

stock split This occurs when a firm issues new shares of stock but in turn lowers the current market price of its stock to a level that is proportionate to presplit prices. For example, if ABC trades at $400 before a two-for-one split, after the split it will trade at $200 and holders of the stock will have twice as many shares as they had before the split.

time value The difference between the total market value of an option and its intrinsic value.

trade date The date on which a trade occurs. Trades generally settle two to 15 business days after a trade date depending upon the security traded. With stocks, settlement is generally three business days after the trade.

transactions costs The time, effort, and money necessary to complete a transaction, including such things as commission fees and the cost of physically moving the asset from seller to buyer.

underlying The "something" that the parties agree to exchange in a derivative contract. In the case of an options contract, for example, the underlying is the security subject to being purchased or sold upon exercise of an option contract. For example, Microsoft stock is the underlying security to Microsoft options.

withholding tax A tax, levied by a country of source, on income paid, usually on dividends remitted to the home country of the firm operating in a foreign country; tax levied on dividends paid abroad.

writer The seller of an option, who issues the option and consequently has the obligation to sell the asset (if a call) or to buy the asset (if a put) on which the option is written if the option buyer exercises the option.

written option An option contract for which a net premium is received.

Bibliography

Accounting Standards

Epstein, Barry. *Interpretation and Application of Generally Accepted Accounting Principles.* 2005 edition. New Jersey: John Wiley & Sons, 2004.

Epstein, Barry. *Interpretation and Application of International Financial Reporting Standards.* 2007 edition. New Jersey: John Wiley & Sons, 2007.

Financial Instruments

Sangiuolo, Rosemarie, and Leslie Seidman. *Financial Instruments: A Comprehensive Guide to Accounting and Reporting.* 2007 edition. Chicago: CCH, 2007.

Futures and Options

Dubofsky, David. *Options and Financial Futures Valuation and Uses.* International edition. Singapore: McGraw-Hill, 1992.

Hull, John. *Fundamentals of Futures and Options Markets.* Fourth edition. India: Pearson Education, Inc., 2002.

Williams, Michael, and Amy Hoffman. *Fundamentals of the Options Market.* New York: McGraw-Hill, 2001.

Parameswaran, Sunil. *Futures Markets: Theory and Practice.* New Delhi: Tata McGraw-Hill, 2003.

Gupta, S. L. *Financial Derivatives: Theory, Concepts and Problems.* New Delhi: Prentice-Hall, 2006.

Index